VAT &
SALES TAXES
WORLDWIDE

VAT &
SALES TAXES
WORLDWIDE

A guide to practice and procedures
in 61 countries

 ERNST & YOUNG

John Wiley & Sons
Chicester • New York • Brisbane • Toronto • Singapore

First published in 1995

John Wiley & Sons Ltd
Baffins Lane, Chichester, West Sussex PO19 1UD, England
Tel: 01243 779777

© Ernst & Young International 1995

Printed in Great Britain by Bookcraft Ltd, Midsomer Norton

This book has been compiled and edited by:

Jim Somers
Partner in Charge, VAT and Customs Services
Ernst & Young, Dublin, Ireland
Co-Chairman, Ernst & Young European VAT Group

The country chapters were written by partners and senior executives in Ernst & Young offices. The name, address, telephone and fax numbers of each author are shown in the appropriate chapter.

Ernst & Young is a leading firm of international business and financial advisers, committed to providing the best possible management advice to its clients worldwide. Ernst & Young has more than 680 offices in over 125 countries, with 66,000 partners and staff worldwide.

As one of the world's largest tax practices, Ernst & Young has experience in all aspects of corporate, personal and indirect taxation, both on a domestic and international scale. With our extensive network of offices worldwide, Ernst & Young can offer a comprehensive range of services to meet the needs of the global investor.

Our VAT and Customs practice consists of specialist consulting groups in every EU Member State as well as in the other major trading nations of the world.

If you would like to discuss any aspect of our services or would like to talk informally about your particular concerns and the ways in which we may be able to help you, please contact any of the individuals listed inside the back cover, or your local Ernst & Young office.

PREFACE

This book has been prepared as a general guide to the value added tax and sales tax implications of commercial activities in the major trading nations of the world. As far as possible, the same headings have been used in the same order for each country, to enable the reader to be able to find and compare more easily the rules applicable in a particular situation in any country.

This book is not exhaustive and is not intended to cover in detail all the VAT and sales tax laws and practices in every country. It does, however, give the basic principles and it outlines potential problems. For these reasons the book is not designed to answer every question which arises in practice and it is recommended that specific advice be sought on any particular matter before action is taken.

My thanks are extended to all of the Ernst & Young VAT and sales tax specialists who contributed to this book. My thanks also go to my secretary Emer Gavin for her help in typing the manuscript.

Jim Somers
Partner in Charge of VAT and Customs Services
Ernst & Young
Dublin, Ireland
May 1995

FOREWORD

This is the third edition of Ernst & Young's guide to VAT and sales taxes which gives to both taxable persons and business people a useful and necessary overview of value added and other sales tax regimes in the major trading nations of the world. This publication has been expanded to 61 countries.

VAT is one of the biggest revenue earners for governments worldwide and its popularity has grown enormously in the last number of years. There are, for example, almost 90 countries which now have some form of federal VAT or sales tax system. Mindful of the need for the book to be user-friendly, the framework for each chapter has been co-ordinated to ensure consistency and accessibility for the reader.

For the first time this guide is being released in the United States and we feel that this is opportune in that the introduction of a value added tax or sales tax regime is currently under review here. This volume should add to informed discussion about the problems to be resolved before such a law is enacted.

I offer my thanks to the Ernst & Young partners and executives who were involved in the production of this book.

I am particularly grateful to Jim Somers, Partner in Charge of VAT and Customs Services in our Dublin, Ireland office, for initiating and co-ordinating all the contributions and for editing this book.

Mike Henning
Chairman
Ernst & Young International
New York
May 1995

CONTENTS

HOW TO USE THIS BOOK

This book contains chapters describing the legislation and practice for VAT and sales taxes in 61 countries.

The country chapters have been arranged in geographical sections as follows:

- Europe
  - European Union
  - Other countries

- America
  - North, Central and South

- Asia and Australasia

- Africa

The section on the European Union is preceded by an outline of the institutions and workings of the European Union, its value added tax legislative basis and in particular the very special and detailed rules it has adopted for the 'transitional' period which started on 1 January 1993 and will continue at least until 31 December 1996 but probably until the end of the century.

Each chapter contains a step by step guide which identifies who is taxable, what is taxable, where is it taxable, at what rate should tax be paid and what are the compliance obligations. These issues are dealt with in each chapter using the same numbering system for ease of access, eg:

1   *General Background*
2   *Who is Taxable?*
3   *What is Taxable?*
4   *Place of Supply*
5   *Basis of Taxation*
6   *Tax Rates*
7   *Exemptions*
8   *Credit/Refund for Input Tax*
9   *Administrative Obligations*
10 *Special VAT Regimes*
11 *Further Reading*

Direct comparison of issues in different countries is easily achieved on this basis, eg if one wanted to compare the rates of VAT in Ireland and Belgium this information is immediately available at paragraph 6 in the respective chapters.

Starting on page 749, there is a glossary which explains the various terms used in VAT and sales tax legislation.

EUROPE –
EUROPEAN UNION

INTRODUCTION TO THE EUROPEAN UNION [1]

1   THE BEGINNING

The project of a united Europe goes back to the year 1945 when western European governments felt the need for closer co-operation after the devastation of the second world war.

In 1951 a treaty signed by Belgium, The Netherlands, Luxembourg, Germany, Italy and France established the European Coal and Steel Community (ECSC). This was the start of a gradual process of European integration. While limited to one sector, this co-operation soon evolved towards the idea of a European entity with common institutions and integrated national economies.

In 1955 a conference in Brussels started work on a proposal which was submitted to the Ministers of Foreign Affairs in 1956 and which was used as the basis of negotiations for two treaties. Finally, in Rome in 1957 the two treaties establishing the European Economic Community (EEC) and the European Atomic Energy Community (EURATOM) were signed by Belgium, France, The Netherlands, Luxembourg, Italy and the Federal Republic of Germany. After ratification by the six Member States, the Community came into being on 1 January 1958.

The European Community was enlarged to nine members on 1 January 1973 with the accession of Denmark, Ireland and the United Kingdom.

On 1 January 1981 Greece became a member of the Community, and Portugal and Spain followed on 1 January 1986.

The name of the Community was changed to the European Union following the Maastricht Treaty in November 1993.

On 1 January 1995 Austria, Finland and Sweden became members of the Union, bringing to 15 the total number of Member States.

The 15 Member States of the present European Union have a total population of around 380 million, which makes it the largest single free market in the world. It already accounts for over 30% of world trade.

---

1 Whilst the formal title of the group of countries in Europe which have come together to form a single market has, over the years, changed from the European Economic Community to the European Community and finally to the European Union, the title (and attendant abbreviations) used in legislation has not been amended. New legislation passed since the change of title refers to the European Community, the EC, etc. In this section of the book I have used 'Community' in connection with legislation, institutions, etc and 'Union' in all other circumstances.

2   THE TREATY OF ROME

The Treaty of Rome, which established the European Economic Community in 1957, provides the constitution of the Community. It contains the principles and objectives which have been agreed by the Member States. The Community is, in essence, a union of European states formed mainly for economic purposes, although in recent years there have been strong moves towards a more political form of union. The provisions of the Treaty aim at the progressive removal of economic barriers between the Member States and a correlative integration of the economies of the signatories into a single common market. As such, the Treaty identified specific objectives to sustain the realisation of a true common market.

The first of these is the free movement of goods. The Treaty's essential goal is the creation of a customs union within which no duties, tariffs, restrictions or quotas will exist. This union was partly achieved in July 1968 when customs duties were abolished on the movement of goods between Member States and when a common customs tariff was adopted for trading with non-Community countries. The reduction and final elimination of national quotas is still to be achieved.

The removal of fiscal frontiers was achieved on 1 January 1993 but, for VAT and the movement of goods within the Union, a transitional system was introduced which will run at least until 31 December 1996. Full details of the system are given in section 7 of this Introduction.

Another objective is the establishment of a common agricultural policy with common rules concerning competition, co-ordination of the national market organisations and control of imports into the Union in circumstances where foreign goods might affect the position of similar products in one of the Member States.

It is essential not only that goods should be allowed to move freely within the European Union but that workers, businesses, services and capital should also have that right. Over the years Directives have been issued and Regulations have been adopted gradually to provide for the freedom of establishment of nationals in any of the Member States, and the freedom to supply services within the Community. The Member States have also agreed to remove restrictions on the movement of capital by residents of the Community and to eliminate discrimination based on the nationality or on the place of investment of capital.

The European Treaty also contains provisions for the setting up of a common transport policy with agreed rules for international transport in, out and through the territory of the Community.

3   THE UNION'S INSTITUTIONS

The three treaties which created the European Coal and Steel Union, the European Economic Union and EURATOM provided for specific institutions to control each of these communities. On 1 July 1967 the executive bodies of the three organisations were merged and the institutions which exist at present were established. The main executive bodies include a Parliament, a Council of Ministers, a Commission, a Court of Justice and a Court of First Instance.

3.1 The European Parliament

The Parliament of the European Community is composed of 519 delegates elected directly by the nationals of the 15 Member States. Its role is of a consultative nature and it has general advisory and supervisory powers.

Since 1979, when the Parliament was first directly elected, its role within the Community has increased. In 1986 a new co-operation procedure was introduced whereby the Parliament would have to be consulted not only once but twice where certain provisions of the Treaty, or measures relating to the completion of the single market, were concerned.

3.2 The Council of Ministers

The essential function of the Council of Ministers is the realisation of the Treaty of Rome's objectives. For this purpose, it has been given the power to make Decisions, to adopt Directives, to issue Regulations and to make Recommendations (see section 3.3).

As a general rule, it is the Commission which has the right of initiative in Community activities. However the Council of Ministers may ask the Commission (see section 3.3) to make proposals or to undertake any specific studies it feels are necessary for the achievement of a single market. The Treaty has conferred on the Council the special task of setting the rules under which the committees (European Community, Steel and Coal and EURATOM) should function and of deciding on the salaries and allowances of the members of the Commission and the Court of Justice.

The Council of Ministers is composed of ministers from the various Member States. Each State takes it in turn to have the presidency of the Council for six months. The work of the Council of Ministers is carried out at two types of Council meeting:

- the General Affairs Council, usually attended by the Ministers of Foreign Affairs from the 15 Member States, which co-ordinates the activities of the Council
- specialised Councils which deal with specific subjects such as education, finance, justice, and commercial policy with non-European Union countries.

Commission proposals are submitted to the Council of Ministers where they are discussed, reviewed and altered by the Council itself or by the Committee of Permanent Representatives of the Member States, assisted by various expert working groups.

Decisions of the Council, such as the adoption of Regulations or Directives, are taken usually by qualified majority vote. However, a unanimous vote is still required in all matters relating to taxation or when the Council wishes to amend a proposal of the Commission.

3.3 The Commission

The Commission is the executive body of the Community institutions. It ensures that the Treaty of Rome and the Decisions taken to implement it are carried out by the Member States. It also prepares Recommendations or gives opinions on matters covered by the Treaty. Like the Council, the Commission issues Directives and Regulations, takes Decisions and makes Recommendations. It is important to recognise the status of these declarations:

- Regulations both from the Council and the Commission, are binding in all their terms and are directly applicable in all the Member States.
- Directives are binding as to the result to be achieved by the Member State to which they are addressed. National authorities must initiate the appropriate legislation to

give legal effect to European Community Directives.

■ Decisions of the Commission are binding on those to whom they are addressed.

■ Recommendations and Opinions are not binding.

The Commission consists of 20 members, each Member State being represented by at least one and not more than two people. Members are appointed by mutual agreement between the governments of the Member States.

3.4 The Court of Justice of the European Community

The general function of the Court of Justice (ECJ) is to ensure the application of laws according to the interpretation and implementation of the Treaty of Rome.

The Court of Justice can adjudicate in disputes between Member States and institutions of the Community or between one Member State and another or between private individuals and corporations and various Member States or institutions of the Union.

It has the power to decide on the legality of acts (or omissions) of the Council or the Commission. Member States, the Council and the Commission may ask the Court of Justice to condemn the actions of the Commission or the Council on the grounds of lack of jurisdiction or violation of the Treaty or misuse of powers. When the Court confirms that an action or a provision is not legal, that action or legislation becomes null and void.

A very important power which the Court has is the power to rule on questions referred from a court of a Member State. These rulings, which are usually given as preliminary rulings, can only be made concerning the interpretation of the Treaty and the legality of the actions of the European Community institutions.

Preliminary rulings are very important because they are the means whereby the Court ensures the uniform interpretation and application of Community law throughout the Member States.

Finally, the Court has jurisdiction in disputes arising between the Community and its employees.

The Court comprises fifteen judges, nine advocates general and one registrar.

The advocate general is an officer unknown in common law systems but he plays a very important role in many other jurisdictions. He is not a judge but has the same status as one. He is consulted by the Court about most procedural difficulties as the case unfolds and at the end of the case, when the parties have concluded their submissions, the advocate general sums up the arguments on both sides and gives his own independent reasoned opinion as to what the Decision of the Court should be. His opinion is frequently, but not always, adopted by the Court.

3.5 The Court of First Instance

Over the years the workload of the Court of Justice has increased greatly.

In an effort to ease the burden on the Court by reducing the types of cases which had direct access, article 168A of the Treaty of Rome was amended by the Single European Act in 1987 with the result that a Court of First Access, with the right of appeal to the Court of Justice, was established with jurisdiction in certain types of cases, particularly in the areas of employment and competition and cases arising under the European Coal and Steel Treaty.

The Court comprises 15 judges – one from each Member State, and often sits in Chambers of five or three judges to hear less important cases. It has no advocates general though any of the judges may be called upon to act as advocate general in certain cases.

4   THE FINANCIAL MEANS OF THE EUROPEAN UNION – OWN RESOURCES

At its start, the Union was financed by contributions from the Member States but, in 1970, following a Decision of the Council, a new system of self-financing was implemented. It is now financed by a portion of the customs duties collected by the Member States on goods imported from non-European Union countries, by agricultural levies and by financial contributions from the Member States. Since 1977, the financial contributions from the Member States have been replaced by a percentage of the value added tax (VAT) collected by each Member State, calculated on a uniform basis. The level of that contribution was increased to 1.4% in 1986.

5   VAT IN THE EUROPEAN UNION

VAT in its present form was first introduced in a very limited form in France in 1954 and, since the Treaty of Rome, it has been adopted as the method of collection of a Community-wide indirect tax. The tax was introduced at different times in Member States and, with the exception of Denmark and the United Kingdom, is administered by the local tax inspectors.

While VAT is levied on the supply of certain goods and services in the territory of each Member State there are some important exceptions. These are:

DENMARK: VAT is not applicable in the Faroe Islands, Greenland or the Free Port of Copenhagen

FRANCE: VAT is applicable in the French overseas departments of Martinique, Guadeloupe and Reunion but there are special rules and, in particular, transactions between France and these departments are treated as exports or imports. French VAT is also applicable in Corsica and Monaco

GERMANY: VAT is not applicable in customs and duty free zones (Zollanschlusse, Zollfreigebiete)

GREECE: VAT is not applicable in the area of Mount Athos

ITALY: VAT is not applicable in the municipalities of Campione d'Italia and Livigno

NETHERLANDS: VAT is not applicable in the overseas territories of the Netherlands Antilles

PORTUGAL: VAT is applicable in Madeira and the Azores Islands.

SPAIN: VAT is applicable to the Balearic Islands but not in the Canary Islands or in Ceuta or Melilla (North African areas under Spanish sovereignty).

UNITED KINGDOM: VAT is applicable in the Isle of Man and Gibraltar but not in the Channel Islands which are not only outside the United Kingdom but also outside the European Union.

6   HARMONISATION OF VAT WITHIN THE EUROPEAN UNION

6.1   *General*

The idea of creating a single European market is exactly as old as the Treaty of Rome which clearly envisaged that the Community's prosperity and, in turn, its political and economic unity, would depend on a single, integrated market. Article 2 of the Treaty declares that:

> 'The Community shall have as its task, by establishing a common market and progressively approximating the economic policies of Member States, to promote throughout the Community a harmonious development of economic activity, a continuous and balanced expansion, an increase in stability, an accelerated raising of the standards of living and closer relations between the states belonging to it'.

> (Article 2 Treaty of Rome, 1957.)

Article 99 of the Treaty deals with taxation in particular. It reads as follows:

> 'The Commission shall consider how the legislation of the various Member States concerning turnover taxes, excise duties and other forms of indirect taxation, including countervailing measures applicable to trade between Member States, can be harmonised in the interest of the common market.'

> The Commission shall submit proposals to the Council, which shall act unanimously without prejudice to the provisions of Articles 100 and 101.'

> (Article 99 Treaty of Rome 1957.)

Article 100 of the Treaty authorises the Council of Ministers to issue Directives, based on proposals of the European Commission, aimed at further harmonisation of domestic, legal and administrative provisions which have a direct impact on the formation and functioning of the single market. It states:

> 'The Council shall, acting unanimously on a proposal from the Commission, issue Directives for the approximation of such provisions laid down by law, Regulation or administrative action in Member States as directly affect the establishment or functioning of the common market.

> The Assembly and the Economic and Social Committee shall be consulted in the case of Directives whose implementation would, in one or more Member States, involve the amendment of legislation.'

> (Article 100 Treaty of Rome 1957.)

6.2   *Council Directives*

Directives issued by the Council of Ministers are the primary vehicle for harmonisation of national legislation. These Directives do not attempt to dictate uniform national rules for the whole Community, but try to harmonise national legislation to achieve Community goals.

Unlike Regulations (which are binding and have a direct effect in all Member States), Directives are binding only as to the result to be achieved (Article 189 of the Treaty). Thus, Directives leave the choice of form and method of implementation to national authorities. Directives therefore require national legislation to implement their policies.

The Court of Justice of the European Community in Luxembourg has ruled that a Directive may have direct effect, provided that the period granted to Member States to implement it has lapsed. The Court has also ruled that the concept of direct effect means that a provision of Community law can be relied upon by individuals before national courts, whether or not such provisions have been adopted as national law. This applies even where national law is in conflict with the European Community provision. However, European Community law does not prevent a citizen from applying a more favourable national law.

Under these circumstances, taxpayers may be entitled to rely on the provisions of a Directive as against opposing national law. It is assumed generally that the Sixth VAT Directive (see below) has direct effect where its provisions are explicit or do not give Member States the freedom to derogate.

The right to invoke European Community law has in practice only been granted to persons (individuals and legal entities). Until now, no Court of Justice cases have arisen regarding use of European Community law by governmental administrations. Article 189 of the Treaty does not indicate whether a national tax administration may rely on a Directive when a provision of national law, pleaded by a taxpayer, is contrary to that Directive. However, if a national administration were allowed to use European Community law against its subjects where the Directive (whether intentional or not) had not been implemented in national law, it would seem that the intent of European Community law would be contradicted.

In 1967, ten years after the Treaty of Rome, the Council of Ministers adopted two Directives which resulted in the implementation of VAT by all Member States (the First and Second Council Directives on Value Added Tax). Although these laid the foundation for a standardised system, they still left the Member States considerable scope for derogations and special arrangements.

The First Directive provided that all Member States replace existing cumulative tax systems with a non-cumulative value-added tax system. The Second Directive introduced some basic concepts (for example, definition of taxable person, supply of goods and services, basis of taxation, etc). However, many other important points were left to the Member States.

Further harmonisation was required to provide the European Union with its own financial means, as well as to eliminate fiscal frontiers in the future and promote greater freedom of movement of people, goods, services and capital. This led to the Sixth Council Directive on VAT, effective as of 17 May 1977, which provided for a uniform basis of taxation.

The Sixth VAT Directive, nevertheless, allowed Member States to continue certain incompatible arrangements for an agreed period of time. Moreover, it did not require harmonisation of VAT rates and did not eliminate fiscal frontiers.

The process of harmonisation is helped by the existence and work of the VAT Committee established under Article 29 of the Sixth Directive. This provides for an Advisory Committee on VAT which consists of representatives of the VAT authorities of the European Union Member States. It reviews measures proposed by Member States for which the Sixth Directive stipulates consultation. The Committee also considers specific questions concerning application of the Directive upon request by either the chairman or a representative of the Member States. Unfortunately while the deliberations of the Committee are disseminated to revenue officials of the Member States, they are somewhat hidden from the citizens of the Union in that the work of the committee has only been discussed in two reports – the last one being in 1988.

Another effective tool in the process of harmonisation is the power of the Court of Justice to rule on interpretation of Directives. Article 177 of the Treaty allows all national courts of the Member States to refer questions of interpretation of European Union law to the Court of Justice in Luxembourg.

However, the highest national courts (whose decisions are final and are normally followed by the lower courts), are obliged to refer questions on interpretation of European Community law to the European Court of Justice for a preliminary ruling whenever such a question arises in cases put before them. Thus Article 177 guarantees uniform interpretation of European Community law throughout the Community.

6.3   The Single Market

The Single Market was created on 1 January 1993. Under the rules of the Single Market goods, capital and people can move freely between Member States without hindrance. In effect, the political borders between States are ignored for all trade purposes with the exception of some special controls in the area of terrorism, the movement of contraband goods such as drugs, arms, etc and the concept of border controls for tax purposes has been abolished.

However, the main thrust of the European Commission's proposals for VAT in the single market could not be implemented. This involved the introduction of the 'origin principle' which would govern the taxation of all goods and services supplied within the new single market. Under the origin principle a supplier would charge VAT in the Member State in which the goods or services were supplied or performed and at the rate appropriate to that supply in the country where the supply was made. For example, a manufacturer of computers in Ireland who sold goods to a distributor in Austria would charge Irish VAT at the rate appropriate to computers, ie 21% even though the goods were 'exported' out of Ireland.

The purchaser in a second Member State would be entitled to recover from his own VAT authorities any VAT correctly charged and invoiced by a supplier in the first Member State. Thus the Austrian distributor in the example above would be entitled to recover the Irish VAT by including the amount of the Irish VAT as input tax on his Austrian VAT return.

This system was resisted by politicians and officials for many reasons, the most important amongst them being that such a system would create distortions of trade because of a lack of harmonisation of VAT rates. It would also involve some clearing house type of mechanism to compensate repayment countries for VAT collected in other Member States and would involve very detailed Revenue Audit procedures to avoid fraud, etc.

While the origin system is still the ideal set by the European Commission, a transitional regime (see section 7 below) has been introduced until a definitive system for VAT taxation in the single market is adopted.

The position with regard to imports and exports from third countries has not been altered by the introduction of the single market.

7 THE TRANSITIONAL PROVISIONS

7.1 Introduction
A transitional regime was put in place to run from 1 January 1993 to at least 31 December 1996 and thereafter until Member States decide otherwise. This transitional regime was introduced by way of Directives, the principal one being Directive No. 91/680/EEC which amended the Sixth VAT Directive.

The rules for the transitional regime are contained in Title XVIA – Articles 28a to Article 28o inclusive of the Sixth VAT Directive. The format for these rules follows the format of the rules under the Sixth VAT Directive, ie what is subject to VAT, the place of supply, exemptions, chargeable event and chargeability to tax, right of deduction, etc.

The general rule is that private individuals will pay VAT in the country in which they purchase goods at the rate applicable there. Such goods can then be removed to any other Member State without the payment of any further VAT. However, new means of transport and goods sold to final customers by distance sellers (eg mail order goods) are treated differently (see sections 7.2.6 and 7.4). Supplies of goods between taxable persons and supplies to exempt persons, public bodies, etc also have special treatment applied.

It should be remembered that these are special rules which only apply to the taxation of trade between Member States during the transitional period and they may be substantially amended when the transitional period ends.

7.2 Who is Taxable?

7.2.1 Acquisitions and Supplies by Taxable Persons
An intra-Community acquisition of goods is defined as:

> 'acquisition of the right to dispose as owner of movable tangible property dispatched or transported to the person acquiring the goods by or on behalf of the vendor or the person acquiring the goods to a Member State other than that from which the goods are dispatched or transported'.

As a general rule, supplies of goods by taxable persons to taxable persons in another Member State are treated as exempt with refund of input tax/zero-rated. A condition of exemption is that the acquirer's VAT registration number must be quoted on the supplier's invoice. As the direct counterpart of supplies of goods, the corresponding intra-Community acquisition of these goods by a taxable person is taxable in the country of destination at the rate of VAT applicable there. (The VAT due on the acquisition is deductible in so far as the goods are used for activities for which a right to deduction exists – see section 7.3 below for the rules governing accounting for an acquisition.)

7.2.2 'Fictitious acquisitions' – intra-branch transfers

The transfer by a taxable person of goods from his undertaking in one Member State to his undertaking in another Member State (ie intra-branch) is deemed to be an exempt (zero-rated) intra-Community supply followed by an acquisition of the goods in the other Member State. Therefore, the person transferring the goods must be registered for VAT in both Member States. Certain transfers are excluded from this provision (see section 7.2.3) either because the rules regarding the place of supply already provide for taxation (eg in cases when goods are assembled or installed or in cases of distance sales), or because the resulting acquisition would have been exempt or zero-rated anyway.

7.2.3 Transfers Deemed not to be Acquisitions

Not all intra-Community movements of goods qualify as acquisitions and the following are excluded from that treatment:

- goods to be installed or assembled for a customer in the other Member State
- goods transported to another Member State under the distance selling rules
- goods transported to another Member State for supply on board transport
- goods which will be exported to a destination outside the European Union from another Member State
- goods moved to another Member State for processing and to be returned
- goods sent to another Member State for work on those goods, eg repair work
- goods temporarily used in another Member State in order to provide a supply of services there, eg taking a lap-top computer or tools to use whilst in another Member State, or the hire of goods to a lessee in another Member State
- goods temporarily (in this case for a period not exceeding two years) used in another Member State where, if those goods were imported into the European Union, customs duty relief would be available
- acquisitions from a person not registered for VAT except where the goods acquired from the non-registered person are a new means of transport or are subject to excise duty.

As these items are not acquisitions they do not need to be reported for VIES purposes (see section 7.9.2) or to be declared on the VAT return in the country of departure.

7.2.4 Acquisitions by Flat-Rate Farmers, Public Bodies and Exempt Persons

When a farmer who is eligible for the flat-rate scheme, a person who is exempt from VAT or a public body purchases goods (excluding new means of transport and excise products – see sections 7.2.6 and 7.2.7 below) in another Member State the seller will charge VAT in the country from which the goods are supplied.

However, if such persons purchase goods in other Member States for a value in excess of ECU10,000 (Member States may determine a higher threshold), then they are obliged to register for VAT and pay tax in their own country. Once they are registered for VAT the supplier can quote the purchaser's registration number on his invoice and zero-rate the supply of the goods. The purchaser will then treat the acquisition as a supply to himself on which he is obliged to pay VAT in his own country. As he is not entitled to a deduction for input VAT he must pay over the VAT due to his own VAT authorities.

Such persons may elect to be treated as taxable persons even if their acquisitions do not exceed the statutory registration limits.

7.2.5 Contract Work

When a person sends his goods to another Member State for a person there to carry out a process on those goods, (eg a shirt retailer sending a roll of material to a third party in another Member State in order for that third party to manufacture the material into shirts for him), no VAT need be accounted for on the movement of those goods into that Member State. However, when the goods are returned in their manufactured state, the owner will have to account for VAT on their return.

Note that if the goods are not returned after process, the owner will have to account for VAT upon their removal into the other Member State since they will then be treated as a fictitious acquisition (see section 7.2.2) into that Member State.

7.2.6 New Means of Transport

As mentioned above, the general rule is that all supplies of goods to another Member State are exempted/zero-rated provided that the acquirer is registered for VAT. This rule is expanded in cases of intra-Community supplies of new private vehicles and other new means of transport. All such supplies are exempt/zero-rated regardless of the status of the acquirer or the vendor. Thus, when the purchaser or vendor is a private person or a public body or a totally exempt person the supply from another Member State of a new means of transport is also exempted/zero-rated followed by an acquisition.

The following are considered to be a 'means of transport':

■ boats with a length exceeding 7.5 metres, aircraft with a take-off weight exceeding 1,550 kilograms, motorised land vehicles with a capacity exceeding 48 cubic centimetres or with a power exceeding 7.2 kilowatts, intended to transport persons or goods.

In order not to be considered as 'new' means of transport, both of the following conditions must be fulfilled:

■ in the case of boats and aircraft they must be supplied more than three months after the date of first entry into service and in the case of motorised land vehicles they must be supplied more than six months after the date of first entry into service
■ they must have travelled more than 6,000 kilometres in the case of land vehicles, sailed more than 100 hours in the case of boats, or flown more than 40 hours in the case of aircraft.

Anyone who purchases a new means of transport in one Member State and transfers it to another Member State must treat the purchase as an acquisition in the second Member State and account for VAT at the time of acquisition. For those already registered for VAT, accounting for VAT will be in the same manner as for any other acquisition. For those not already registered for VAT they must account for VAT in respect of this transaction(s) as if they themselves had supplied the new means of transport and since they are not taxable persons, they will not be entitled to any input VAT credit.

If the means of transport does not qualify as 'new' as set out above it will be treated as the supply of 'second-hand' goods (see section 7.10.2).

7.2.7 Excise Products

The Sixth VAT Directive transitional measures provide that a taxable person or non-taxable legal persons shall not be subject to VAT in respect of intra-Community acquisitions of goods where the total value of their intra-Community acquisitions in a calendar year does not exceed a specified threshold. The threshold must not be less than ECU10,000. However, there is a special provision with regard to new means of transport and goods subject to excise duty whereby the above threshold does not apply and in all cases the acquirer must register for VAT in respect of the intra-Community acquisition. The purpose of this provision is to ensure that the intra-Community acquisitions are recorded so that excise duty is paid on the goods coming into the respective Member States.

7.3   What is Taxable?

An intra-Community supply of goods which is followed by an acquisition is zero-rated/exempt with credit so long as the supplier quotes the VAT registration number, complete with the European Union Member State national identification number (see below).

The European Union national identification numbers are as follows:

Austria	AT
Belgium	BE
Denmark	DK
Finland	FI
France	FR
Germany	DE
Greece	EL
Ireland	IE
Italy	IT
Luxembourg	LU
Netherlands	NL
Portugal	PT
Spain	ES
Sweden	SE
United Kingdom	GB

An acquisition is taxable in the hands of the acquirer and VAT must be accounted for by him at the appropriate rate as output tax on the statutory VAT return. The acquirer will be entitled to recover as input tax the full amount of tax accounted for as output tax if he is entitled to full input credit under the normal rules.

7.4   Place of Supply

The Directive changes the place of the supply of goods, sets out new rules with respect to the place of supply of intra-Community acquisitions of goods, and provides derogations from the Sixth VAT Directive with respect to the place of supply of services.

7.4.1 ABC Contracts and Chain Transactions

An intra-Community acquisition is deemed to take the place where the goods are at the time when dispatch or transport to the person acquiring them ends. This is known as the main rule and is to be found in Article 28b(A)(1) of the Sixth VAT Directive. However, the final place of destination is not always known in the so-called ABC contracts (sales by connected contract) where the same goods may be sold through a series of parties but delivered by the first party directly to the last party in the chain. Under such circumstances the place of acquisition is deemed to be within the territory of the Member State which issued the VAT identification number under which the goods are acquired without prejudice to the main rule.

Thus, for example, when goods are sold by a manufacturer in Ireland to a distributor in France, the intra-Community acquisition is deemed to take place in France. When the French distributor sells the goods to a retailer established in Germany, the intra-Community acquisition of the goods by the retailer is deemed to take place in Germany. However, if the manufacturer delivers the goods directly to the retailer in Germany, based on the main rule (Article 28b(A)(1)), the wholesaler is also deemed to have made an intra-Community acquisition in Germany and must register and account for VAT there. The wholesaler will also be required to charge VAT on an internal German supply to the retailer.

However, on 14 December 1992, the European Council of Ministers adopted a new Directive (Directive 92/111/EEC), to simplify, inter alia, the provisions on ABC contracts. It should be noted that the rules mentioned below are applicable when only three taxable persons registered in three different Member States are involved, ie A, B or C must not have a presence in any of the two other Member States.

The simplification rule basically has the effect that the distributor in the above mentioned example does not have to register in Germany if:

- the acquirer (ie the distributor) establishes that he has effected this intra-Community acquisition for the needs of a subsequent supply effected in Germany and for which the retailer has been designated as the person liable for the tax
- the distributor has satisfied the VIES listing requirements
- the distributor states in his invoice to the retailer that the simplified triangulation rules apply.

Note that the application of the simplification rules is not mandatory; the distributor in the above example may opt for the application of the normal VAT rules and register as a non-resident company for German VAT purposes and account for German VAT on the intra-Community acquisition and on the subsequent domestic supply. Simplification rules do not apply to similar transactions involving four or more parties.

7.4.2 Distance Sales/Mail Order

The place of supply of goods dispatched or transported by or on behalf of the supplier from one Member State to another to a customer which is not registered for VAT is the place where the goods are at the time when the dispatch or transports ends (in other words, the country of destination) if the total value of the supplies by the distance seller to the same Member State of arrival exceeds ECU100,000 (or has exceeded this threshold in the previous calendar year). This rule is further complicated by a provision that the Member States where the goods arrive may limit the annual threshold to ECU35,000 per vendor.

15

The Member States which have limited the threshold to ECU35,000 are:

Belgium	Greece	Portugal
Denmark	Ireland	Spain
Finland	Italy	Sweden

Distance sellers may also opt to be taxed in the Member State of destination of the goods, even if their sales do not exceed the threshold mentioned above. In that case the distance seller must register for VAT and in most cases appoint a fiscal representative.

Where the sales do not exceed the limits set by the Member State of destination, the supplier must charge the VAT applicable in the Member State from which the goods are dispatched.

This rule affects supplies to non-taxable legal persons, public bodies, flat-rate farmers, exempt taxable persons and to any other non-taxable (ie private) persons. For example, where a department store or mail order company sends goods to a private customer in another Member State this is a 'distance sale'.

7.4.3 Goods Placed on Board Ships, Aircraft or Trains During Transport
When goods are supplied for consumption on board ships, aircraft or trains during transport, and the places of departure and destination are within the territory of the European Union, the place of supply is the place where the goods are at the time of departure of the transport.

7.4.4 Transportation Services – Goods
The general rule provides that the place where transport services are supplied is the place where the transport takes place, having regard to the distances covered.

The place of supply of intra-Community goods transportation services to private persons is the place where the transportation starts, ie VAT is charged by the supplier in the Member State in which the transportation started.

However, when transport services are rendered to a customer registered for VAT in a Member State other than that of departure of the transport, the place of supply of the transport services is deemed to be within the territory of the Member State which issued the VAT identification number to the customer and the customer is liable for payment of the VAT by way of the reverse charge mechanism (provided the transporter is not located in the Member State which issued the VAT identification number to the customer). The supplier does not charge any VAT.

Under the general rule, the national leg of an intra-Community transportation of goods is taxed in the country in which it is performed. This means that a VAT-registered person who does not perform taxable activities in the Member State where the transportation takes place will have to claim a refund of the VAT charged to him. To simplify matters, all the Member States except Greece have asked for a derogation from the general rule. The effect is that supplies to VAT-registered persons in other Member States are zero-rated by the suppliers, ie no refund claims are required. The rule is also applicable to traders from third countries who are registered for VAT in a Member State of the European Union.

7.4.5 Services Ancillary to Intra-Community Goods Transport Services
The place of supply of services ancillary to intra-Community goods transport services

provided to a customer registered for VAT in another Member State is also deemed to be within the territory of the Member State which issued the VAT identification number to the customer. Again, the customer must account for VAT in his Member State provided the service supplier is not located in the same Member State as the customer.

The zero-rating mentioned in section 7.4.4 for supplies of domestic transportation services involving intra-Community transportation of goods is also applicable to services ancillary to intra-Community goods transportation services.

7.4.6 Services Provided by Brokers or Other Intermediaries

The place of supply of services which form part of an intra-Community transport of goods by intermediaries and brokers is the place of departure of the transportation. The place of intermediaries' ancillary transport services is the place where the ancillary services are physically carried out.

However, in both cases the place of supply of the intermediaries' services is deemed to be within the territory of the Member State which issued the VAT identification number to the customer, and he must account for VAT in his Member State provided that the service supplier is not located in the same Member State as the customer.

For example, transport services by a transporter or the intermediary services by broker A established in Ireland rendered to customer B in France under B's VAT identification number, even though the transport of the goods may commence in Germany, are taxable in France (B's Member State).

7.4.7 Other Services Rendered by Brokers or Other Intermediaries

Finally, with regard to all other services rendered by brokers or other intermediaries, except those mentioned above and those relating to supplies of intangible services (eg advice, transfers of patent rights, etc (Article 9.2 (e) of the Sixth VAT Directive), the place of supply is where the services are carried out unless the services are rendered to a customer registered for VAT in a Member State other than that of the intermediary. Those services are deemed to take place in the Member State which issued the customer's VAT identification number.

7.4.8 Supplies of Services on Movable Goods

The place of supply of services on movable goods (eg repair and valuation) is where the services are actually performed. This means that a foreign trader who has goods repaired in another Member State and who does not himself perform taxable activities in that other Member State will have to claim a refund of the VAT charged to him.

To simplify matters, all the Member States except Greece have asked for a derogation from the normal rules. The effect is that supplies to the above mentioned traders are zero-rated by the suppliers, ie no Eighth VAT Directive refund claims are necessary. The rule is also applicable to traders from third countries who are registered (but not established) for VAT in a Member State of the European Community.

7.5   Basis of Taxation

7.5.1 Acquisitions

The value of an acquisition is the contract price, including commission, packing, transport charges and any other charges.

If the acquisition is fictitious, then there is no change in ownership and the VAT value is deemed to be the purchase price, cost price or value of similar goods. The VAT rate to be applied to a supply of acquisitions is zero or exempt with credit – provided the purchaser's VAT registration identification number in the other Member State is shown on the invoice. The VAT rate applicable to an acquisition made in the country of the acquirer is the rate of VAT applicable to similar goods supplied within the acquirer's Member State.

7.5.2 Chargeable Event
The chargeable event occurs when an intra-Community acquisition of goods is effected. An intra-Community acquisition of goods takes place when a supply of similar goods is regarded as being effected within the territory of the country of the acquirer.

Tax chargeable in respect of intra-Community acquisition of goods becomes due at the earlier of:

■ the fifteenth day of the month following that in which the removal to or from another Member State occurred; or
■ the date of issue of a tax invoice.

The rules for chargeable event in regard to services supplied during the transitional period have not been amended.

7.5.3 Persons Liable for Payment of the Tax
Where an acquisition is effected by a person established in another Member State, the Member State may apply arrangements whereby another person, such as a tax representative, becomes liable to pay VAT.

As can be seen below this provision is applied to triangular transactions, intra-Community transport services of goods and various intermediary services when effected by a taxable person established in another Member State.

7.6 Rates of Tax
The transitional provisions imposed guidelines for any alterations in the level or number of rates imposed by Member States as at 1 January 1991. Under these provisions Member States are permitted to apply a standard rate of at least 15% and either one or two reduced rates. These reduced rates may not be less than 5% and shall only apply to a certain specified category of goods and services which is set out in Annex H to the Sixth VAT Directive. An exception to the reduced rate rule is that Member States may continue to provide a reduced rate to goods not included in Annex H or a reduced rate of less than 5% provided that such rates were in force on 1 January 1991.

The rate of tax to be applied to a supply of an acquisition is either zero or exempt with credit depending on the legislation in each Member State.

The rate of VAT to be applied to an acquisition in the acquirer's Member State is the rate of VAT which would be charged on similar goods supplied within the acquirer's Member State.

7.7   Exemptions

7.7.1   Exempt with Credit
Provided the acquirer's VAT registration number in another Member State is shown on an invoice then the supply may be zero-rated or exempt with input credit as appropriate.

7.7.2   Exempt Importation
With regard to importation of goods from a third country into a Member State, the Directive provides for exempt importation under the following conditions:

- the final destination of the goods must be in a Member State other than that of importation
- the importer must supply the goods from the Member State of importation to another Member State.

This means that, in cases where a person imports goods into Member State A, the importation is zero-rated or exempt with credit if the importer, at the time of importation, can show that the goods have been further supplied to a person in Member State B or that he has made a fictitious supply (see section 7.2.2). This rule is only applicable to persons who are taxable persons in the Member States into which the goods are first imported.

7.8   Credit/Refund for Input Tax

7.8.1   Acquisition
A person who supplies intra-Community acquisitions of goods (including fictitious acquisitions of goods) is entitled to recover input VAT incurred in connection with such supplies. The same right exists for the acquirer of goods subject to the usual rules with regard to full entitlement, partial recovery entitlement, etc.

7.9   Compliance/Administrative Obligations

7.9.1   VAT Identification Numbers
Intra-Community traders must show their individual VAT identification or registration number (including the prefix by which the Member State of issue is identified) on all invoices when making zero-rated or exempt intra-Community supplies, issuing invoices for intra-Community transportation services to other taxable persons, etc.

The numbers must also be mentioned in the sales listing (recapitulative statements, see section 7.9.2). It should be noted that some Member States require, during the transitional period, additional information on periodic VAT returns concerning intra-Community goods movement.

7.9.2   VIES (Sales Listings, Recapitulative Statements)
VIES statements must be submitted by entrepreneurs/taxable persons on a quarterly basis.

Intra-Community supplies of the prior calendar quarter must be specified in the VIES statement. Note that intra-Community supplies treated under the simplification rules must be mentioned separately. Corrections (eg mistakes or (partly) non-payment of the consideration by the customer) of prior VIES statements should be made by filling in separate boxes.

It should be indicated separately when the supplies relate to intra-Community contract work. Statements must be submitted on the last day of the month following the calendar quarter to which the supplies relate.

In certain circumstances, a written request may be made to file VIES statements with the competent VAT authorities annually.

The information obtained from the VIES statements is verified with the information indicated on the VAT returns. Substantial differences between the VIES statements and VAT returns may result in an examination of an entrepreneur's records. The VIES data is sent for verification purposes to the VAT authorities in other Member States. VIES statements can be submitted on disc, cartridge, (magnetic) tape or via EDI.

7.9.3 INTRASTAT
In order to collect statistical information on intra-Community trade from 1 January 1993, a system known as INTRASTAT was introduced. Intra-Community acquirers and suppliers must submit information on a periodic basis to the tax authorities when movements of goods exceed a certain value per year.

7.9.4 Registers
Taxable persons must keep a register of certain goods which have been transported or dispatched to another Member State, eg materials dispatched for contract work.

7.9.5 Penalties
There are penalties for not completing, not submitting or incorrectly completing sales listings and INTRASTAT documents.

7.10 Special Regimes

7.10.1 Tax-Free Shops
Until 30 June 1999 Member States may exempt supplies by tax-free shops of goods to be taken in the personal luggage of travellers taking intra-Community flights or sea-crossings and to supplies of goods effected by tax-free shops in either of the two (English) Channel Tunnel terminals, for passengers holding valid tickets for the journey between those two terminals. There are various restrictions on the value and number of goods which may be purchased tax free under these provisions.

7.10.2 Antiques and Second-Hand Goods
The Seventh VAT Directive, which took almost 17 years to negotiate, was adopted in 1994 and came into effect on 1 January 1995 in all Member States. This Directive, known as 'the second-hand goods Directive' makes special provision for the taxation of certain sales of second-hand goods, on the basis of the margin earned by the seller (as opposed to the total sales price). It also makes special provisions for taxation of the import and certain supplies of works of art, collectors items and antiques. It also makes very special rules with regard to the supply of goods by way of public auction.

Jim Somers
May 1995

AUSTRIA

1   INTRODUCTION

The referendum on Austria's accession to the European Union held on 12 June 1994 resulted in an overwhelming two-thirds vote in favour of accession. Consequently, the work to harmonise the Austrian tax law, in particular the value added tax (VAT), started immediately after the voters' declaration.

Although a system of VAT was introduced in Austria on 1 January 1973 (Umsatzsteuergesetz 1972 – UStG 1972) it was not harmonised with the Sixth VAT Directive. Therefore, at the end of August 1994, the VAT Law was adapted to take account of the Sixth VAT Directive and the Act of Accession through the Umsatzsteuergesetz 1994 (UStG 1994). This Law came into force on 1 January 1995, the date of accession. However, many of its provisions have now been clarified and simplified by the Amendment Law, published in January 1995, with the aim of reducing the likelihood of distortion of competition.

Those transitional internal market provisions of UStG 1994 which are to be replaced by final provisions are separated out from the main text and summarised in Articles to the Law; a clear system of cross-referencing to the main text is also included.

On 12 February 1995 a first decree relating to the interpretation and practical application of the most urgent aspects of UStG was published. However, it will be some time before a general decree concerning the whole of UStG 1994 will be published.

Austrian VAT applies within the territory of the Federal Republic of Austria (Bundesgebiet).

VAT is levied on the supply of goods and services performed by an entrepreneur in Austria and on intra-Community acquisition or importation of goods.

VAT is administered by the tax office responsible for the tax affairs of the enterprise, ie normally in the place where the enterprise is located. VAT matters of foreign enterprises without a branch or fixed establishment in Austria are handled by the tax office, Graz-Stadt.

VAT on imports is dealt with by the Customs Duty Office.

Noticeable or significant deviations from the Sixth VAT Directive and options or derogations allowed by that Directive and used by Austria are mentioned in the following comments. Unless otherwise stated, articles and subsequent subparts cited without a defined source are those of the Sixth VAT Directive.

1.1   The Single Market – Intra-Community Acquisitions
As a Member State of the European Union, Austria applies the rules for VAT applicable to the Single Market and in particular the transitional arrangements which apply in respect of intra-Community supplies during the transition period which commenced on 1 January 1993.

This chapter reflects the law on VAT in Austria on 31 January 1995.

For ease of reference the transitional arrangements are set out in detail in section 7 of the Introduction to the European Union which precedes this section of the book.

This chapter should be read in conjunction with the transitional arrangements.

2   TAXABLE PERSONS

2.1   *General*

The definition of taxable persons in general, with the exception of the following, is in accordance with the Sixth VAT Directive.

VAT is levied on taxable transactions carried out in Austria by an entrepreneur (taxable person), regardless of whether the entrepreneur is a citizen or resident of Austria or has a place of business in Austria.

An entrepreneur is any person who independently carries on a commercial or professional activity. Any activity for the purpose of obtaining income on a continuing basis is commercial or professional even in the absence of an intention to make profits (for example, an association acting only vis-à-vis its members).

Private persons who engage in an occasional transaction are not deemed to be entrepreneurs within the meaning of the VAT law.

Since the legal status of a person is irrelevant, VAT will apply indifferently to an individual, an association of individuals or a legal person.

Activities which are not expected eventually to generate profits are not deemed to be an enterprise (Liebhaberei – hobby activity) as the Austrian authorities argue that these are not an economic activity in the sense of the Sixth VAT Directive. But in the author's opinion this definition is too broad and extensive and is contradictory to the Sixth VAT Directive, which defines a taxable person as a person who carries out any economic activity whatever the purpose or results of the economic activity and lists specific activities which constitute economic activities. In practice, however, the principles of the Sixth VAT Directive are applied on the basis of prescripts and decrees.

Transportation of goods by post is not considered to be an economic activity as Austria has opted, within the rules of the Sixth VAT Directive, to consider this as a supply engaged in by a public authority. This has the same result as if it were exempt.

2.2   *Transactions with Branch/Subsidiary*

Services supplied between branches of the same legal entity are not subject to VAT. Thus services supplied between a branch and its head office or another branch are not taxable even if the head office or branch is situated outside Austria. However, the importation of goods (see section 2.9), and the intra-Community acquisition of goods (see section 2.11) by a branch are taxable events. Subsidiaries of foreign firms which supply taxable goods and services in Austria are treated in the same manner as other taxable persons, even where the goods and services are supplied to the subsidiary by the parent company situated outside Austria (unless fiscal/group registration applies – see section 2.4).

2.3   Government Bodies

Juridical persons under public law are not subject to VAT as long as they fulfil governmental functions only; however, if, within the scope of their operations, they are engaged in commercial or professional activities of a commercial kind or in agricultural or forestry operations, they will qualify as entrepreneurs (see section 7.2.4 of the Introduction to the European Union).

2.4   Fiscal Unity/Group Registration

Austria applies the option (subject to consultation with the EC VAT Committee) of treating those juridical persons established in its territory who, while legally independent, are closely bound to one another by financial, economic and organisational links (Organschaft, VAT group), as a single taxable person restricted to internal supplies within Austria. In the case of a parent company outside Austria the most economically important part of the enterprise within Austria is deemed to be the Austrian entrepreneur.

Consequently the fiscal unity concept is also applicable where the parent and its controlled subsidiary are resident in different countries but restricted to the Austrian part of group.

Transactions between the parent company and the controlled subsidiary company or the parts of group within Austria are considered to be internal transactions and therefore are not taxable.

The application of the fiscal unity concept for VAT purposes is determined by the circumstances and no special application to the tax authorities is necessary.

2.5   Foreign Entrepreneurs

Foreign entrepreneurs who have neither their registered office, their place of abode, nor a permanent establishment in Austria are in principle liable to VAT if they acquire and/or deliver goods in Austria or supply services which are taxable in Austria (unless reverse charge, VAT deduction or invoicing without VAT applies).

Such foreign entrepreneurs have to register with the tax office (Graz-Stadt) which is in charge of the tax matters of non-resident entrepreneurs (see section 10.2 'Registration').

2.6   Representative Offices

Representative and information offices of foreign entrepreneurs which only perform activities of a preparatory or similar nature, qualify as a fixed establishment for VAT purposes.

2.7   VAT Representatives

See the following section 2.8 'Reverse charge mechanism and other procedures applied to foreign entrepreneurs'.

2.8   Reverse Charge Mechanism and Other Procedures Applied to Foreign Entrepreneurs

The provisions relating to persons liable for payment of the tax conform, in general, to the Sixth VAT Directive.

A foreign taxable person who is not established in Austria and who performs taxable supplies or intra-Community services from Austria or intra-Community acquisitions in Austria must appoint a fiscal representative. This representative is fully and severally liable for the transactions of the foreign taxable person (possibly causing indefinite risks and trouble in practice). A fiscal representative is not necessary in the cases where the recipient of a supply is liable for the tax (see section below).

Accountants, tax advisers, lawyers and public notaries established in Austria and forwarding agents who are members of the respective section of the Chamber of Commerce are approved as fiscal representatives. Furthermore, any entrepreneur established in Austria may be licensed, on application, if he is accepted by the tax authorities as being solvent and in a position to meet tax obligations, but the approval may be revoked at any time.

In general, a taxable person or a public body established in Austria who receives a supply made by a foreign entrepreneur not established in Austria must withhold and pay the VAT to the tax authorities in the name and for the account of the foreign entrepreneur. If the recipient of the supply does not observe the obligation, he will be liable for the (possible) loss of tax.

If a foreign entrepreneur who is not established in Austria performs:

- the services as mentioned in Article 9.2(e) (intangible services)
- intra-Community services of agents, in name and for account of another, excluding services connected with immovable property or if the services referred to in Article 9.2(e) are procured
- transport services and ancillary transport services connected with intra-Community transportation of goods

to a taxable person established in Austria, a kind of reverse charge applies and, therefore, the tax liability shifts to the Austrian recipient of the services, but the foreign entrepreneur who rendered the services also remains liable.

According to prescript no. 800 (issued in 1974), an exemption without deduction of input tax continues to be optional for foreign entrepreneurs not established in Austria. This applies only if no VAT is shown on the invoice, provided that the supply of goods or services is provided to an Austrian entrepreneur who is entitled to deduction of the VAT in connection with the supply in question.

2.9   Importers
Persons who import goods into Austria are subject to VAT at the same rates as those applying to the sale of similar goods within Austria. The VAT must be paid by the importer when the goods cross the Austrian border.

2.10   Supplier of New Means of Transport
Any person who undertakes on an occasional basis intra-Community supplies of new means of transport that are dispatched or transported from Austria to another Member State is regarded as a taxable person (see section 7.2.6 of the Introduction to the European Union).

2.11   Acquirers of Goods from Other European Union Member States
The movement of goods from one Member State to another is an acquisition. If there is an acquisition by an Austrian business, the business in the other European Union Member State is not obliged to register. If there is a 'fictitious acquisition' (because, for example, there is no change in title) VAT registration in Austria will be required (see section 7.2 of the Introduction to the European Union).

2.12 Acquisitions by Non-Taxable Legal Persons – Taxable Persons with no Right to Recover VAT and Farmers Benefiting from Notional Refunds

Such persons are considered to be outside the scope of VAT when, during the civil year and the preceding one, their yearly intra-Community acquisitions are below a threshold of ATS150,000. As soon as an acquisition puts them above this threshold they are subject to common intra-Community rules and must pay VAT on their acquisitions. They must then obtain an identification number and submit VAT returns.

The same persons may opt to be subject to the common rules even for acquisitions below the threshold. The exercise of this option must be reported to the tax authorities with the first monthly/quarterly VAT return of a calendar year and it expires on 31 December of the second year following its commencement.

3   TAXABLE TRANSACTIONS

3.1   Supply of Goods
The provisions in the Austrian VAT Law on the supply of goods are in accordance with the Sixth VAT Directive. The Austrian VAT Law also applies the provisions regarding self-supplies.

3.2   Importation
The definition of 'importation of goods' into Austrian territory is based on Article 7 of the Sixth VAT Directive, but does not cover the arrangements or procedures of Article 7.3.

3.3   Intra-Community Acquisition of Goods
The definition of an intra-Community acquisition of goods is in accordance with the Sixth VAT Directive.

The threshold for acquisition by non-taxable legal persons, exempt taxable persons and flat-rate farmers is fixed at the amount of ATS150,000 – which is equivalent to ECU10,700.

VAT is levied on the intra-Community acquisition of vehicles, whether they are new or second-hand. Consequently, VAT is levied on the acquisition of used cars acquired by enterprises, but for certain vehicles the input tax is not deductible by the enterprises.

3.4   Distance Sellers
Persons who supply goods from another Member State to private persons, certain exempted entrepreneurs, farmers taxed under a margin scheme, and juridical persons outside the entrepreneurial sphere may be taxable in respect of such supplies (see section 7.4.2 of the Introduction to the European Union).

3.5   New Means of Transport
All supplies of new means of transport made in Austria are considered to be supplies of goods (see section 7.2.6 of the Introduction to the European Union).

3.6   Contract Work
If a VAT registered person in another Member State transfers goods to be processed in Austria and the processed goods are not returned to the other Member State, then the owner

of the goods will have to register and account for VAT in Austria (see section 7.2.5 of the Introduction to the European Union).

3.7 Excise Products

In certain circumstances a non-registered acquirer of excise products may have to register and account for VAT on acquisitions of products which are subject to excise duty (see section 7.2.7 of the Introduction to the European Union).

3.8 Assembly/Installation

According to the Austrian VAT Act in the case of assembly/installation contracts two different facts have to be distinguished as follows:

- if the essential parts/goods are procured by the installer, the total supply is treated as 'delivery' (Werklieferung), ie a supply of goods
- in all other cases (ie, essential parts/goods not procured or essential parts/goods not processed by the installer) the total supply is treated as supply of a service (Werkleistung).

In regard to foreign entrepreneurs see section 2.8 'Reverse charge mechanism and other procedures applied to foreign entrepreneurs'.

3.9 Supply of Services

'Supply of services' is defined as any taxable transaction which does not constitute a supply of goods in the sense of the Code.

3.10 Self-Supply of Goods/Services

Generally, if a taxable person supplies himself or his employees with goods from his business or uses them for private use, this is considered to be a taxable self-supply.

A new provision, aimed at the use of cars or representation costs, has been added by the Amendment Law which provides additional guidance on those events which are to be taxed as a self-supply.

A self-supply is subject to VAT at the standard rate of 20%. Where an entrepreneur has expenses in connection with services performed outside Austria which would not have entitled him to an input VAT refund if they had been carried out in Austria, the supply is considered to be a self-supply. This rule applies in so far as the Austrian entrepreneur can reclaim the foreign input VAT.

This new taxable event is mainly based on the fact that the input VAT on cars and the operation costs for cars are not deductible in Austria, combined with the fiction that cars are not part of the sphere of the enterprise; however, it is also targeted at representation expenses spent abroad.

If cars are leased in other Member States where it is possible to deduct input tax (such as Germany, Luxembourg and The Netherlands), and the place of supply is considered to be in that other Member State (under the general rule of Article 9), taxation could be avoided if the above provision had not been implemented into the Austrian VAT Law.

The provision in the Austrian VAT Law can be derived from Article 5.1, Article 5.4(b), as applied to financial leasing contracts, in connection with Article 5.7(b) of the Sixth VAT Directive.

4   PLACE OF TAXABLE TRANSACTIONS

4.1   Place of Supply of Goods
The provisions in the Austrian VAT Law are in accordance with the Sixth VAT Directive. The threshold for distance sales to Austrian consumers amounts to ATS1,400,000 (equivalent to ECU100,000).

4.2   Place of Intra-Community Acquisition of Goods
The provisions in the Austrian VAT Law on the place of an intra-Community acquisition of goods are in accordance with the Sixth VAT Directive (see section 7.4.1 of the Introduction to the European Union).

If the person acquiring the goods uses a VAT identification number issued by another Member State and the place of the intra-Community acquisition is Austria, the Austrian authorities will tax the acquisition in conformity with the main rule of the Sixth VAT Directive, since Austria is the Member State of arrival, except in the cases where the provisions on simplified triangulation measures are applicable.

The simplification measures regarding triangulation (ie no more than three parties in three different European Union countries may be involved) have been adopted in their entirety. In the case of chain transactions involving intra-Community acquisition, the interpretation of the Austrian rules follows the movement of the goods (ie the provisions are in accordance with the Commission's point of view) and not the German derogation which identifies the place of acquisition on the basis of the invoicing and the VAT identification numbers given. However, the German method of determining the place of acquisition by VAT registration number (ie avoidance of double taxation is achieved according to the general German definition of the place of acquisition) makes it possible to find a solution for long chain transactions compatible with the simplification measures for triangulation.

4.2.1 Chain Transactions
If the goods are not acquired in another Member State within the chain, each entrepreneur is deemed to have carried out a taxable transaction in the form of a simultaneous supply of goods at the place of supply by the first entrepreneur to the last recipient. This simplification measure is not applicable in the case of chain transactions within the European Union.

4.2.2 Goods Placed on Board Ships, Aircraft or Trains During Transport
When goods are supplied for consumption on board ships, aircraft or trains during transport and the place of departure and destination are within the territory of the European Union, the place of supply is the place where the goods are at the time of departure of the transport.

4.3   Place of Supply of Services
Austrian provisions on the place of supply of services in special cases are designed mainly as a protection against distortion of competition.

4.3.1 General Rule

As a general rule the place where a service is supplied is the place where the supplier has established his business, has a fixed establishment from which the service is supplied, or has his domicile.

4.3.2 Exceptions

Services carried out for any work connected with real estate and certain other services such as teaching, sports, transport or ancillary transport activities (loading, unloading, handling), are exceptions to the above and are taxable at the place where the real estate is located or where the services are rendered materially.

In accordance with Article 9.2(e) of the Sixth VAT Directive the place of supply of the following services, is the place where the recipient is located:

- transfers and assignments of copyrights, patents, licences, trademarks and similar rights
- transfers and assignments of goodwill and obligations to refrain from engaging in a particular business activity or from exploiting a right referred to above
- advertising services
- intellectual services performed within the ordinary course of their professional activity by consultants, accountants, engineers and those engaged in the supply of similar services
- main professional transactions engaged in by banks and other financial institutions with the exception of the renting of safes
- the supply of staff
- the activities of agents in relation to the above services
- the leasing of movable tangible property other than means of transport.

4.3.2.1 Intra-Community goods transportation

Intra-Community goods transport means the transportation of goods from one Member State to another. The basic rule is that the place of supply is the place of departure (Article 28bC Sixth VAT Directive). However, if the customer uses a VAT identification number of a different Member State (to that of the supplier) the place of supply is deemed to be in the Member State which issued the VAT identification number used by the customer, and he must account for VAT on the reverse charge basis (see section 7.4.4 of the Introduction to the European Union).

4.3.2.2 Services ancillary to intra-Community goods transport

The place of supply of ancillary services to intra-Community transport services of goods is treated in the same manner as the supply of the transportation service.

4.3.2.3 Intermediaries/brokers

The place of supply of services rendered by intermediaries acting in the name and for the account of other persons, when such services form part of transactions other than those for which the place of supply is deemed to be where the recipient of the service is located and to the extent that those transactions take place within the European Union, is the place where the main transactions for which the intermediary services are performed are deemed to take place.

By derogation from this rule, where the customer is identified for VAT purposes in a Member State other than that within the territory of which the main transactions are deemed to take place, the place of supply of services rendered by the intermediaries is deemed to be within the territory of the Member State which issued the VAT number under which the service was rendered to him by the intermediary (see section 7.4.7 of the Introduction to the European Union). Certain kinds of service are excluded from this allocation by VAT identification number, for instance in connection with real estate and services connected with reverse charge mechanism.

4.3.2.4 Work on movable goods
The place of supply of services on movable goods (such as repairs and valuations) is moved to the Member State of the customer if the customer is identified for VAT in a different Member State.

4.4 Place of Importation
There is no separate provision, since the place of importation is in accordance with Article 7.1(b) and (2) of the Sixth VAT Directive, but it does not refer to the fact that the place of importation is within the territory of the Member State where, according to Article 7.3, goods cease to be covered by certain arrangements and procedures (see section 3.2 'Importation').

5 CHARGEABLE EVENT AND TAXABLE AMOUNT

5.1 Taxable Amount
VAT applies to the total amount of the purchase price and other consideration payable for the goods or services, including, for example, insurance and transport costs.

The following items are excluded from the taxable base:

- amounts deductible from the price as a discount for early payment and price reduction given by the supplier to which the purchaser is entitled at the time the tax becomes due
- the VAT itself
- amounts advanced by the supplier for expenses he incurred in the name and for the account of the other contracting party.

When the consideration does not (wholly) consist of a sum of money, it is to be estimated at the normal value, which can be defined as the price which can be obtained in Austria for the same goods on an arm's length basis.

As a transitional measure until 31 December 2000, Austria may continue to tax international passenger transport by motor vehicles not registered in Austria and carried out by taxable persons not established in Austria, under the following conditions:

- the distance covered in Austria shall be taxed on the basis of an average taxable amount per person and per kilometre (ATS0.60)
- the system may not involve fiscal controls at frontiers between Member States
- such a measure, intended to simplify the procedure for charging the tax, may not affect (except to a negligible extent) the amount of tax due at the final consumption stage.

5.2 Self-Supplies
The taxable base for self-supplied goods is the cost price of the goods self-supplied or of comparable goods.

5.3 Imports
VAT is payable on the value of the goods on which customs duties are levied plus such duties. The VAT itself does not form part of the taxable basis.

5.4 Acquisitions
The value used is the contract price, which may include commission, packing, transport and excise duties. If the acquisition is fictitious in that no change in ownership has occurred the VAT value is the purchase price, cost price or value of similar goods. The value of acquisitions must be shown separately on the VAT return (see section 7.5.1 of the Introduction to the European Union).

5.5 Chargeable Event and Chargeability of the Tax/Time of Payment
A chargeable event occurs when a supply of goods or services is performed and an invoice is issued.

The law makes no provision as to when an invoice must be issued but in all cases a chargeable event must be reported no later than the month following that in which the supply took place.

The chargeable event occurs for goods acquisition when a supply of those goods is regarded as effected within the territory of Austria (see section 7.5.2 of the Introduction to the European Union). Tax becomes chargeable on the fifteenth day of the month following that during which the chargeable event occurs.

Certain entrepreneurs are entitled to opt to account for VAT on a cash basis. In such cases, VAT is payable at the time the consideration for the supply is actually received. The options, relating to certain persons, which allow that tax becomes chargeable no later than the receipt of the price (cash receipts basis) or, in the case of the invoice being issued late, the tax becomes chargeable at the end of the month following the month when the invoice should have been issued and the fact that the tax does not become due until the end of the month following the month of supply, are implemented into the Austrian VAT Law.

In case of payments on account the tax always becomes chargeable without applying a minimum amount (see section 11 'National transitional provisions').

When goods are imported, the tax is payable to the Customs authorities. The delay of the chargeable event and of the chargeability until the arrangements cease to be applied, referred to in Article 7.3 of the Sixth VAT Directive, has not been implemented into the Law (see section 3.2 'Importation').

An optional flat rate scheme for payment on the basis of a decree by the Minister of Finance for certain groups of entrepreneurs has been introduced from 1994.

5.6 Credit Notes/Bad Debts
Where a price reduction is agreed after an invoice has been issued, a partial recovery of the VAT paid can be effected by issuing a credit note.

When a taxable person believes a debt will not be paid, he can recover the VAT paid on the supply when the bad debt is entered as such in the books. The related VAT will be refunded.

6   RATES

The current rates are:

10%: – letting of immovable property for residential use and meals
 – hospital activities in the field of public health care and welfare and to the transport of sick or injured persons in vehicles specially designed for the purpose by duly authorised bodies (from 1997 these services will be exempt without credit for input tax)
 – collectors' items of coins and medals made of precious metals, if the consideration exceeds 250% of the fine metal value (VAT excluded)
 – wine from farm production carried out by the producing farmer (12% from 1996)

12%: – supplies of electrically driven vehicles

20%: – (16% in the regions of Jungholz and Mittelberg)
 – medical care by physicians in the field of public health and social welfare (exempted without credit for input tax from 1997)
 – all other supplies of goods or services which are not exempt or not taxable at either the 10% or 12% rate.

7   EXEMPTIONS

7.1   Exemptions with Credit for Input Tax

Generally, input tax relating to goods and services used for export operations (to non-European Union countries) and for intra-Community supplies of goods dispatched or transported from Austria to other Member States is recoverable (see section 7.7.1 of the Introduction to the European Union). This does not apply to entrepreneurs personally exempted, for instance, through the small enterprises scheme (see section 10.1 'Small and medium-sized enterprises').

Imports of goods from third territories are exempt from VAT to the extent that the imported goods are destined by the addressee on import for exempt intra-Community supplies from Austria to other Member States.

The following exemptions apply until 31 December 1996:

- exemption, with refund of tax paid at the preceding stage, of supplies carried out by social security and social welfare institutions
- with refund of tax paid at the preceding stage, all parts of international passenger transport by air, sea or inland waterways from Austria to a Member State or to a third country and vice versa, other than passenger transport on Lake Constance, so long as the same exemption applies to any of the present Member States.

7.2   Exemptions without Credit for Input Tax

The list of exemptions is essentially in accordance with the Sixth VAT Directive. There are, however, some temporary exemptions provided for in the Accession Act.

Exemptions applicable until the end of the following individual transitional periods include:

■   telecommunications services supplied by public postal services, until such a time as the Council has adopted a common scheme for taxation of such services, or until the date on which all the present Member States currently applying full exemption cease to apply it, whichever comes first, but in any event until 31 December 1995

■   the transactions listed in points 7 and 16 of Annex F (supplies by the blind and supplies of buildings and building land as described in Article 4 (3)), so long as the same exemptions are applied to any of the present Member States.

On the other hand, Austria may continue to subject to tax (on the basis of the Act of Accession) the following:

■   until 31 December 1996 services supplied by dental technicians in their professional capacity and dental prostheses supplied by dentists and dental technicians to Austrian social security institutions; and

■   the transactions listed in point 7 of Annex E of the Sixth VAT Directive (activities of public radio and television bodies).

Services in the field of public health care and welfare are taxed at the reduced rate of 10% (see section 6 'Rates').

A right to opt for taxation at the standard rate of 20% may be exercised for the letting and leasing of immovable property, but not in relation to residential use – which is taxed at the reduced rate of 10% (see section 6 'Rates').

7.3   Non-Taxable Transactions

7.3.1 Transactions within the Same Legal Entity

Transactions within a fiscal unity (see section 2.4 'Fiscal unity/group registration') and transactions between Austrian head office and Austrian branches are treated as internal transactions and therefore not liable to VAT.

7.3.2 Subsidies/Penalty Payments/Compensation

Certain transactions are deemed to be outside the scope of VAT because the payments received are not treated as a consideration for a supply. This applies to the payment of damage claims, the receipt of actual subsidies, inheritance, etc.

7.4   Option to Tax

In the case of entrepreneurs being exempt without credit, any related input VAT paid with respect to the output transaction becomes a cost factor. There is a limited number of circumstances in which the entrepreneur who is generally exempt has the right to waive the tax exemption and opt for VAT in order to qualify for input VAT credit. The option is also available to distance sellers (see section 3.4) and non-taxable legal persons, government bodies and farmers taxed under the margin scheme (see section 7.2.4 of the Introduction to the European Union).

8   DEDUCTIONS AND REFUNDS

8.1   General

In computing the amount of tax payable, a taxable person may deduct the tax relating to goods and services purchased, imported or acquired from another Member State by him which are used for the purposes of his taxable business (see section 7.8.1 of the Introduction to the European Union).

A credit is not allowed for VAT paid on:

■   goods and services used for non-business purposes
■   goods and services used for certain exempt transactions.

If, at the end of a tax period, VAT paid to suppliers exceeds the VAT billed to customers, the balance will be refunded.

Generally input VAT incurred on the acquisition and maintenance of certain vehicles is not deductible (see section 3.3 'Intra-Community acquisition of goods').

The following supplies and services are deemed as not being performed for business purposes and accordingly the input tax is not deductible:

■   expenses which are not deductible according to the income tax law (for example, expenses for representation)
■   expenses in connection with the purchase, the rent or the use of certain vehicles.

Excluded from input tax deductions is the VAT paid on supplies of goods and services and imports which the entrepreneur uses for the execution of the following supplies:

■   certain tax-exempt transactions
■   transactions carried out abroad which would be tax-exempt if executed within Austria.

VAT on food and beverages generally is not recoverable. Such meals are regarded as expenses for representation which do not belong to the business sphere.

An exemption from this general rule may be accepted in the individual cases of business-related meals for predominantly public relations purposes, such as meals in connection with defined business transactions. The VAT on such meals is recoverable if the entrepreneur provides adequate documentation.

Where the expenditure is on meals for employees during travel in Austria, VAT is recoverable only up to an amount computed on the basis of a lump-sum according to the regulations of the Austrian Income Tax Law (ie ATS360 per day. If the journey time exceeds three hours the lump-sum is 1/12 of ATS360 for each hour. For a journey under three hours the lump-sum is nil). The entrepreneur is only entitled to deduct 9.0909% of these amounts as input VAT. Breakfast is not included in the lump-sum. The breakfast and the hotel expenses are chargeable according to the actual amount invoiced; the invoices have to meet the general formal requirements for VAT recovery, and a voucher concerning the business travel containing the following information has to be issued:

■   name of the person who has made the journey
■   start, destination and purpose of the journey
■   the amounts of the invoices which are the basis for the VAT recovery.

Optional flat rate schemes for recovery on the basis of provision in the law itself for certain entrepreneurs, and on the basis of a decree by the Minister for Finance for certain groups of entrepreneurs, were introduced in 1994.

8.2   Adjustment of Entitlement to Credit

During a certain period (four years for fixed assets, nine years for real estate, an unlimited period for current assets and services) the entitlement to input tax credit at the time of purchase will be adjusted on a pro rata time basis, minimum amount being ATS3,000 per item. This will lead to additional credits or additional tax liabilities, depending on whether the use of the goods changes from exempt to taxable transactions and vice versa.

8.3   Partial Exemption

Entrepreneurs making both taxable and exempt supplies are entitled to recover only the input VAT related to their taxable supplies.

If the goods or services purchased can be attributed to being used for taxable supplies the credit for input VAT will be fully allowed.

If the goods or services purchased are used both for taxable and exempt supplies, the creditable input tax is calculated based on the ratio of the turnover of supplies entitled to credit to the total turnover.

8.4   Time of Recovery

Input credit can be claimed for the month/calendar quarter in which the supply was made if the entrepreneur is in possession of the appropriate invoice. In cases where an entrepreneur accounts for VAT on a cash basis (see section 5.5 'Chargeable Event and Chargeability of the Tax/Time of Payment') the VAT can be claimed for the month in which the payment for the supply was actually made.

The VAT on imports can be claimed for the month during which the import VAT was paid.

If the input VAT exceeds the output VAT the balance will be refunded upon application.

8.5   Refund for Foreign Entrepreneurs

The Federal Minister for Finance is authorised to issue prescripts concerning minimum amounts and procedures for repayments to foreign entrepreneurs. He has already issued such a decree for entrepreneurs who perform cross-border transportation services. A further prescript on this matter is not expected before 1996.

Furthermore, the Minister for Finance may determine special rules for VAT refunds to entrepreneurs established outside of the European Union, and may restrict by decree the VAT refund to such entrepreneurs on the basis of reciprocity.

Invoices relating to travel expenses (especially hotel invoices) have to be addressed to the non-resident entrepreneur himself to entitle him to recover. It would not be sufficient to address the invoice to the person who has performed the business travel.

9   ADMINISTRATIVE OBLIGATIONS

9.1   Registration

All taxable entrepreneurs have to register with the regional tax office. There is no minimum registration threshold. Registration is compulsory if an entrepreneur performs VAT-able transactions in Austria, is liable under the reverse charge mechanism, or invoicing without VAT does not apply (see section 2.8 'Reverse Charge Mechanism and Other Procedures applied to Foreign Entrepreneurs'). Generally, there is no voluntary registration, however, please see section 7.4 'Option to Tax'.

The compliance obligations regarding registration with the Austrian tax authorities are determined by the Bundesabgabenordnung (BAO) (federal tax administration rules).

An entrepreneur establishing an enterprise in Austria has to register with the regional tax office, generally the tax office where the head office of the enterprise is located. This registration requirement applies to foreign entrepreneurs having a registered office or a permanent establishment in Austria.

There is no specially prescribed form for registration only an informal application for a fiscal code and a short description of the date of start and kind of business activities is required. Subsequently the competent tax office will send a questionnaire and allocate a fiscal code.

The system of VAT identification numbers was introduced in Austria on 1 January 1995.

An entrepreneur who has ceased to be a taxable person must cancel his registration by informing the competent tax office within one month.

Failure to register makes the entrepreneur liable to a penalty up to ATS50,000.

9.2   Books and Records

The entrepreneur or fiscal representative must keep accounts in sufficient detail to permit the proper application of the Value Added Tax Law and inspection by the tax authorities. The records must be kept for a period of seven years.

9.3   Invoices

Invoices must contain the following information:

■   the name and the address of the supplying entrepreneur
■   the name and the address of the recipient of the supply
■   the quantity and the description of the supplied goods or the type and volume of services
■   the date of the supply of goods or services
■   the consideration for the supply of goods or services
■   the tax amount relating to the consideration.

Where the total value of the supplies is less than ATS2,000, the amount of VAT need not be shown separately (the percentage of VAT must still be added) nor the name given of the recipient of the supply or service. However, failure to comply with only one of these formal requirements may prevent the recovery of input VAT unless a correction has been made by the issuer or a new invoice meeting these formalities has been submitted.

9.4   VAT Returns and Payment

The date for filing the monthly return and payment of the tax is on the fifteenth of the second following month. The date for filing the yearly return is 31 March of the following year, but may be extended, in practice, for one year if an accountant or tax adviser is involved. A thirteenth (or a fifth) prepayment must be paid with the prepayment for the month of October based on the average VAT due in the preceding twelve months (or four quarters), which can be credited against the VAT due in the next VAT return.

The filing of VAT monthly (as opposed to quarterly) returns is restricted to the following cases:

- if the VAT balance payable is not remitted in due course
- where there is a VAT credit balance (to enable credit entry)
- where proper records are not maintained and the tax authorities request the filing of a return.

In all cases a breakdown of VAT figures according to the content of a monthly (quarterly) VAT return has to be prepared and kept on file.

9.5   VIES Statements/Sales Listings

Recapitulative statements of intra-Community supplies (Zusammenfassende Meldung – FM') must be submitted on a quarterly basis by entrepreneurs/taxable persons to the individual tax office (Finanzamt) which deals with their VAT affairs (see section 7.9.2 of the Introduction to the European Union).

9.6   INTRASTAT

Traders who supply goods to other Member States or who acquire goods from other Member States must provide monthly details of the goods movement if their sales exceed ATS1,500,000 or their acquisitions exceed ATS1,500,000 per year. INTRASTAT has to be reported to Statistisches Zentralamt in Vienna (see section 7.9.3 of the Introduction to the European Union).

9.7   Registers

Certain registers of goods movements must also be kept (see 7.9.4 of the Introduction to the European Union.)

9.8   Power of the Authorities

9.8.1 Estimate of Tax Paid (Estimated Assessment)

If the VAT returns are not filed by the due date, the tax authorities will issue an assessment for an estimated amount.

9.8.2 Statute of Limitation

The period of limitation for assessment of taxes is five years from the end of the calendar year during which tax authorities have performed their latest external activities (such as assessment) concerning the VAT.

9.9   Correction of Returns

The monthly returns are preliminary as long as a tax assessment notice was not issued by the tax authorities. It is possible to correct errors that may have been made in a monthly return which has already been submitted. Additionally the tax authorities may declare a tax assessment notice to be preliminary.

9.10 Penalties for Late Filing/Late Payment

A penalty of 2% of the tax liability for late payment and between 0% and 10% of the tax liability for late filing of tax returns can be assessed.

9.11 Objections/Appeals

The taxpayer has the right to file an appeal with the tax authorities against a VAT assessment notice. The time limit for appeals is one month from the date the assessment notice is received. Further appeals are possible to the District Tax Court or to the Supreme Court if the tax authorities do not amend the tax assessment notice as requested.

10   SPECIAL REGIMES

10.1 Small and Medium-Sized Enterprises

According to the Act of Accession, a threshold of less than ECU35,000 (approximately ATS490,000) may be applied.

Consequently, small entrepreneurs, whose annual turnover does not exceed ATS300,000 – approximately ECU21,400, are exempt from VAT but not entitled to deduction. Nevertheless small entrepreneurs have to register if their turnover exceeds ATS100,000 per annum. Foreign entrepreneurs cannot avoid registering if their turnover is below these limits. However, the small entrepreneurs may opt to account for VAT according to the general rules. This decision is binding for five years.

Small entrepreneurs whose turnover did not exceed ATS300,000 during the previous year have to file quarterly VAT returns if they do not opt for monthly returns.

Upon application, entrepreneurs whose turnover did not exceed ATS1,500,000 during the previous year or the year before may account for VAT on a cash basis.

Furthermore, the Federal Minister of Finance may, by prescript, establish flat-rate schemes for certain categories of entrepreneurs. These simplified procedures are based on the Sixth VAT Directive.

10.2 Farmers

A flat-rate scheme for farmers is applied in accordance with the Sixth VAT Directive.

A reduced flat rate of 10% is fixed for both payment and recovery on supplies of wine from farm production carried out by the producing farmer. From 1996, a reduced rate of 12% (based on the Act of Accession, see section 6 'Rates'), is levied on beverages not annexed to the Act of Accession and the standard rate of 20% is levied on supplies of liquor not meeting the specified requirements. In these cases no deduction is allowed. For 1995, the recovery of the flat rate computed on the basis of the special reduced rate of 12% is only applicable to wine.

10.3 Travel Agents and Second-Hand Goods

The margin schemes stipulated in the Sixth VAT Directive applicable to travel agents and second-hand goods have been adopted.

11 NATIONAL TRANSITIONAL PROVISIONS

The VAT Act of 1994 (UStG 1994) came into force on the date of the accession of Austria to the European Union, ie on 1 January 1995. Several conventions, laws and prescripts continue to apply as follows.

Tax on payments on account becomes chargeable on receipt of the payment if the agreement is based on a contract signed after 1 January 1995.

Double or non-taxation due to the changes to the VAT Law in relation to movements of goods around 1 January 1995 is avoided by transitional provisions based on Article 28n.

Provisions being limited in time, especially by virtue of the Act of Accession, are summarised.

The transitional arrangements for the taxation of transactions between Member States according to Title XVIa, condensed in Articles annexed to the Law and corresponding to the relevant sections, have been integrated (see section 1 'Introduction').

Long term contracts or assurances to grant public subsidies regulating supplies since 1 January 1995, but having been signed before that date, may be adapted regarding the compensation on request of the party which would suffer a disadvantage from a varied VAT burden caused by any changes in law. This is not effective if the parties have concluded other agreements expressly or by means of conclusion, or if the compensation having been contracted would not be adjusted even if the changes would have been known by the parties. This applies unless an invoice showing VAT has been issued.

12 FURTHER READING

Doralt-Ruppe, *Grundriß des österreichischen*, Steuerrechtes I, 5. Aulage, Vienna 1994

Gaedke-Ziegler-Eitler, *Absatz Praxisleitfaden*, Die Umsatzsteuer in Beispielen, Graz 1994

Khun, *VAT in the enlarged European Union, Austria, VAT Monitor*, Vol 6, No A, January/February 1995 pp. 8 -13

Kolacny-Mayer, *Umsatzsteuergesetz*, Vienna 1992

Kolacny-Scheiner, *Fallbeispiele zur Mehrwertsteuer*, Vienna 1985

Kranich, *Mehrwertsteuer, Weinsteuer und Normverbrauchsabgabe*, Vienna 1993

Kranich-Siegl-Waba, *Mehrwertsteuer-Handbuch, 5. Auflage*, Vienna 1988

Kranich-Siegl-Waba, *Kommentar zur Mehrwertsteuer, Loseblattausgabe, 30. Lieferung*, Vienna 1993

Scheiner/Kolacny/Caganek/Zehetner, *Umsatzsteuergesetz 1994, mit Novelle BGBL Nr.*

21/1995, Gesetzestext (einschließlich Binnen-marktregelung) Erläuterungen zur Regierungsvorlage, Bericht des Finanz-ausschusses, 2. Auflage, Vienna 1995

Wirtschaftskammer/Kammer *Der Wirtschaftstreu-Händer, Das neue Umsatzsteuergesetz 1994*, EU-Binnenmarkt, Vienna 1994

Contributor: Wolfgang Khun
Ernst & Young
SOT Sud-Ost Treuhand AG
Praterstrassa 23
1021 Vienna, Austria
Tel: +43 1 21170 0
Fax: +43 1 216 20 77

BELGIUM

1   GENERAL BACKGROUND

Value added tax (VAT) was introduced on 1 January 1971 to replace the so-called 'taxe de transmission'. The Sixth EU Directive was introduced into the Belgian tax system in December 1977 and became effective on 1 January 1978.

A department of the Ministry of Finance, the 'Administration de la TVA/BTW Administratie' supervises all operations of taxable persons in Belgium. VAT due on importation is dealt with by the Department of Customs and Excise.

1.1   The Single Market – Intra-Community Acquisitions

As a Member State of the European Union, Belgium applies the rules for VAT applicable to the Single Market and in particular the transitional arrangements which apply in respect of intra-Community supplies during the transition period which commenced on 1 January 1993.

For ease of reference, and to avoid repetition, the transitional arrangements are set out in detail in section 7 of the Introduction to the European Union which precedes this section of the book. This chapter should therefore be read in conjunction with the transitional arrangements.

2   WHO IS TAXABLE?

2.1   General

A taxable person is any person who independently and regularly supplies, within the scope of his economic activity, goods or services as defined by Belgian VAT law (section 3.1 below). The sale of goods or the rendering of services may occur as a principal or auxiliary purpose, with or without a profit motive.

The definition of a taxable person in Belgian law is generally consistent with the definition used in the Sixth VAT Directive.

Taxable persons who carry out general operations within the meaning of the law by non-equivocal deeds, (ie by setting up an organisation for delivery of goods or services which will be made regularly) are subject to tax as soon as those deeds are performed. Consequently, all deliveries of goods and rendering of services carried out by this taxable person are subject to VAT. A company will be subject to VAT only if it carries on a taxable activity.

2.2   Transactions with Branch/Subsidiary

Subsidiaries of foreign firms supplying taxable goods and services in Belgium are treated in the same manner as other taxable persons.

This chapter reflects the law on VAT in Belgium as at 31 December 1994.

Services supplied between branches of the same legal entity are not subject to VAT. Thus services supplied between a branch and its head office or another branch are not taxable even if one of the parties is situated outside Belgium. However, the importation of goods (see section 2.9) and the intra-Community acquisition of goods (see section 2.11) by a branch are taxable events..

2.3   Government Bodies

Government bodies are generally not considered to be taxable persons. However, when they are making supplies on a regular basis, they may qualify as entrepreneurs and become subject to VAT in order to prevent distortion of competition (see section 7.2.4 of the Introduction to the European Union.)

2.4   Fiscal Unity/Group Registration

A 'group' or 'fiscal unity' concept is foreseen in the Belgian VAT Code, but not yet implemented via Royal Decree and is thus not yet applicable in practice.

2.5   Foreign Entrepreneurs

Taxable person status applies to all individuals and companies even if they have no domicile or office in Belgium. The tax treatment of taxable persons operating from outside Belgium depends on whether or not they have a permanent establishment in Belgium. Those who have such a permanent establishment are treated as a normal Belgian taxable person and pay VAT when supplying goods and services or acquiring or importing goods into Belgium.

2.6   Representative Office

A representative office of a foreign entrepreneur dealing with activities of a preparatory or auxiliary nature cannot register as a domestic entrepreneur and thus cannot recover the input VAT. The tax authorities will refuse the registration on the basis that there is no output. The foreign entrepreneur may however claim back the input VAT by filing a special claim for VAT refund (section 8.5 below).

2.7   VAT Representative

Foreign taxable persons who have no permanent establishment must, as a rule, appoint an approved responsible agent in Belgium before supplying goods or rendering services subject to VAT.

Appointment of a responsible agent is compulsory when the taxable person established abroad:

- imports goods and enters them for home use on payment of tax in his name
- takes delivery in Belgium of goods which are intended either for sale in Belgium or for export
- carries out construction work, assembly operations, maintenance or repair work in Belgium.

Non-resident entrepreneurs who fail to appoint a responsible representative, will not receive a credit for input VAT.

Foreign taxable persons do not require an approved, responsible agent in respect of:

- services of a material character occasionally rendered in Belgium
- transactions of an occasional character consisting of reselling, in their own country, goods which have been bought in Belgium or imported therein
- delivery of goods and the rendering of services in Belgium which are exempt from tax under the Code (for example, international transport of goods)
- the payment of tax on behalf of a customer established in Belgium when the goods are imported for home use
- when goods are imported for warehousing, transit or temporary importation
- transfers and assignment of copyrights, patents, licences, trademarks and similar rights
- transfers and assignments of goodwill and obligations to refrain from engaging in a particular business activity or from exploiting a right referred to above
- advertising services
- intellectual services performed within the ordinary course of their professional activity by consultants, accountants, engineers and those engaged in the supply of similar services
- professional transactions engaged in by banks and other financial institutions, with the exception of the renting of safes
- the provision of staff/personnel
- the activities of agents in relation to the above-mentioned services
- the leasing of agents in relation to the above-mentioned services
- intermediary services rendered as a disclosed agent to Belgian taxable persons
- the leasing of movable tangible property other than means of transport
- intra-Community transport services and ancillary services rendered to Belgian taxable persons.

2.8   *Reverse Charge Mechanism*
Sometimes the person receiving services for business use from abroad is obliged to account for VAT on the value of the services. The recipient of such services is regarded as supplying the services to himself.

2.9   *Importers*
Persons who import goods into Belgium are subject to VAT at the same rates as apply to the sale of similar goods within Belgium. The VAT must be paid by the importer when the goods cross the Belgian border. However, where authorised, payment is generally deferred for entrepreneurs until the first tax return following importation (postponed accounting system, see section 5.4 below).

2.10   *Supplier of New Means of Transport*
Any person who undertakes on an occasional basis intra-Community supplies of new means of transport that are dispatched or transported from Belgium to another Member State, is regarded as a taxable person (see section 7.2.6 of the Introduction to the European Union).

2.11   *Acquirers of Goods from other EU Member States*
The movement of goods from one Member State to another is an acquisition. If there is an acquisition by a Belgian business, the business in the other EU Member State is not obliged to register. If there is a 'fictitious acquisition' (because, for example, there is no change in title) VAT registration in Belgium will be required for the business in the other EU Member State (see section 7.2 of the Introduction to the European Union).

2.12 Non-Taxable Legal Persons – Taxable Persons with No Right to Recover VAT and Farmers Benefiting from Notional Refunds

Such persons are considered as outside the scope of VAT when, during the current year and the preceding year their yearly intra-Community acquisitions are below a threshold of BEF450,000. As soon as an acquisition puts them above this threshold they are subject to common intra-Community rules and must pay VAT on their acquisitions. When this happens they must obtain an identification number and begin to submit VAT returns.

The same persons may opt to be subject to common rules even for acquisitions below the threshold. The option takes effect on the first day of the month in which it is exercised and expires on 31 December of the second year following the option.

3 WHAT IS TAXABLE?

As a rule, the supply of goods and services and the intra-Community acquisition of goods (see section 7.2.4 of the Introduction to the European Union) is taxable only if it takes place in Belgium or when goods are imported from a third country into Belgian territory.

3.1 Supply of Goods

Goods are 'supplied' when the right to dispose of tangible property as owner is transferred from one person to another, for example:

- the transfer of ownership of goods by agreement
- the handing over by a contractor of goods made up from materials supplied in whole or part by his customer.

The term 'goods' includes all immovable, movable and tangible property. Supplies of fuel, refrigeration and energy, etc are also considered goods.

3.2 Imports of Goods

'Importation of goods' is the entry into the Community of goods which do not fulfil the conditions laid down in Articles 9 and 10 of the Treaty establishing the European Economic Community or, where the goods are covered by the Treaty establishing the European Coal and Steel Community, are not in free circulation. Importation of goods is also the entry into the Community of goods from a third territory, other than the goods mentioned above.

However, goods may cross the border without VAT, using the transit regime. Goods may also stay in a bonded warehouse without VAT becoming due. They may also sometimes be imported free of VAT if they are to be re-exported after processing.

3.3 Intra-Community Acquisition of Goods

'Intra-Community acquisition' means the acquisition of the right to dispose as owner of movable tangible property dispatched or transported to the person acquiring the goods by or on behalf of the vendor or the person acquiring the goods to a Member State other than that from which the goods are dispatched or transported (see section 7.3 of the Introduction to the European Union).

Intra-Community acquisitions of goods for consideration are subject to VAT when:

- they are performed by a taxable person acting as such
- by a non-taxable legal person where the vendor is a taxable person acting as such who is not eligible for the tax exemption as a small undertaking
- where the goods are not installed by or on behalf of the vendor
- where the vendor is not involved in distance selling (see section 4.1 below and sections 7.2 and 7.3.4 of the Introduction to the European Union).

3.4 Distance Sellers
Persons who supply goods from another Member State to non-VAT registered persons in Belgium may be taxable in respect of such supplies (see section 7.4.2 of the Introduction to the European Union).

3.5 New Means of Transport
All supplies of new means of transport made in Belgium are considered to be supplies of goods (see section 7.2.6 of the Introduction to the European Union).

3.6 Contract Work
If a VAT registered person in another Member State sends goods to Belgium to be processed there and the processed goods are not returned to the Member State from which the goods for process originated, then the owner of the goods will have to register and account for VAT in Belgium (see section 7.2.5 of the Introduction to the European Union).

3.7 Excise Products
In certain circumstances a non-registered acquirer of excise products may have to register and account for VAT on acquisitions of products which are subject to excise duty (see section 7.2.7 of the Introduction to the European Union).

3.8 Assembly/Installation
A 'supply of goods' takes place in Belgium if the specific goods to be supplied are located in Belgium. This applies even if an overseas entrepreneur has no place of business in Belgium. However, the liability of supply of assembled or installed goods may be passed to a Belgian customer under the reverse charge mechanism (section 4.4 below).

3.9 Supply of Services
'Supply of services' means any transaction which does not constitute a supply of goods in the sense of the Code. Such services are only subject to VAT if there is a contract with remuneration for goods, hire of workmen or intellectual work performed in an independent way, etc.

3.10 Self-Supply of Goods/Services
If a taxable person supplies himself or his employees with goods for his business for private use, this operation is considered to be a supply of goods and VAT is applicable thereon.

Another case of self-supply is the situation where the entrepreneur uses as capital goods movable goods which he produced or which he acquired or imported as non-capital goods.

4 PLACE OF SUPPLY

The supply of goods and services is subject to VAT only if it takes place in Belgium.

4.1 Supply of Goods

A supply of goods takes place in Belgium when at the time of transfer the goods are in Belgium with the following exceptions:

- When the goods sold are installed or assembled by or on behalf of the supplier, the supply is deemed to take place where the goods are installed.
- When transport of the goods is necessary for delivery, the supply is deemed to take place where the transport begins.
- Where goods are supplied on board ships, aircraft or trains during the part of a transport of passengers effected in the Union, the supply is deemed to take place at the point of departure of the transport – (see section 7.4.3 of the Introduction to the European Union).
- Special rules also apply to the distance selling regime (see section 7.4.2 of the Introduction to the European Union).

4.2 Place of Intra-Community Acquisitions of Goods

Intra-Community acquisitions of goods are deemed to occur at the place where the goods are at the time the dispatch or where the transportation to the person acquiring the goods ends.

Without prejudice to the above rule, the intra-Community acquisitions of goods are deemed to take place within the territory of the Member State which issued the VAT number under which the person acquiring the goods made the acquisition, to the extent that the person acquiring the goods does not establish that the acquisitions have been subject to VAT in accordance with the first rule.

Special rules for taxation apply to 'triangular operations', ie sale-resale operations involving three parties in which the goods are dispatched or transported directly from the Member State of the first seller to the Member State of the third buyer (see section 7.4.1 of the Introduction to the European Union).

4.2.1 Chain Transactions

Triangulation is the situation where three parties in three different countries are involved in selling and purchasing the same goods. For example, A in France sells goods to B in The Netherlands who sells the goods to C in Belgium and the goods are sent directly from A to C (see section 7.4.1 of the Introduction to the European Union).

4.2.2 Goods Placed on Board Ships, Aircraft or Trains During Transport

When goods are supplied for consumption on board ships, aircraft or trains during transport and the places of departure and destination are within the territory of the European Union, the place of supply is the place where the goods are at the time of departure of the transport.

4.3 Supply of Services

4.3.1 General Rule

As a general rule the place where a service is supplied is the place where the supplier has established his business, has a fixed establishment from which the service is supplied, or has his domicile.

4.3.2 Exceptions

Services carried out in connection with real estate and certain other services, such as teaching, sports, transport, ancillary transport activities (loading, unloading, handling, etc), are exceptions to the above and are taxable at the place where the real estate is located or where the services are rendered materially.

Provided the recipient is located outside the Union or is a taxable person who is established in another Member State of the Union, the place where the recipient of the service is located is the place where the service is rendered for services such as:

■   transfers and assignments of copyrights, patents, licences, trademarks and similar rights
■   transfers and assignments of goodwill and obligations to refrain from engaging in a particular business activity or from exploiting a right referred to above
■   advertising services
■   intellectual services performed within the ordinary course of their professional activity by consultants, accountants, engineers and those engaged in the supply of similar services
■   professional transactions engaged in by banks and other financial institutions with the exception of the renting of safes
■   the supply of staff
■   the activities of agents in relation to the above services
■   the leasing of movable tangible property other than means of transport.

4.3.2.1 Intra-Community goods transportation

Intra-Community goods transport means the transportation of goods from one Member State to another. The basic rule is that the place of supply is the place of departure (Article 28bC Sixth VAT Directive). However, if the customer is registered for VAT in a different Member State to the supplier the place of supply is deemed to be the Member State of the customer, who must account for VAT on the reverse charge basis (see section 7.4.4 of the Introduction to the European Union).

4.3.2.2 Services ancillary to Intra-Community goods transport

Where the customer is VAT-registered in another Member State, the place of supply of services ancillary to intra-Community transport services of goods is not taxable in the country where the services are materially rendered. In these circumstances the supply is within the territory of the Member State which issued the customer with the VAT registration number and under the reverse charge mechanism the customer must account for the VAT (see section 7.4.5 of the Introduction to the European Union).

4.3.2.3 Intermediaries/brokers

The place of supply of services rendered by intermediaries acting in the name and for the account of other persons, when such services form part of transactions other than those for which the place of supply is deemed to be where the recipient of the service is located, and to the extent that those transactions take place within the Union, is the place where the main transactions, for which the intermediary services are performed, are deemed to take place.

By derogation from this rule, where the customer is identified for VAT purposes in a Member State other than that within the territory of which the main transactions are deemed to take place, the place of supply of services rendered by the intermediaries is deemed to be within the territory of the Member State which issued the customer with the VAT number under which the service was rendered to him by the intermediary (see section 7.4.7 of the Introduction to the European Union).

4.3.2.4 Work on movable goods

The place of supply of services on movable goods (such as repairs and valuations) is where those services are physically carried out.

However, such services are exempt from Belgian VAT where the customer is registered for VAT in a Member State other than Belgium, and to the extent the customer could get a Belgian VAT refund based on the Eighth or Thirteenth EC VAT Directive.

4.4 Reverse Charge Mechanism

Sometimes the VAT is collected from the Belgian customer of the foreign entrepreneur. This happens when the foreign entrepreneur has no permanent establishment or VAT representative in Belgium. In such circumstances, the tax liability for the supply of both goods and services shifts from the foreign entrepreneur to the Belgian taxpayer. Generally, this situation would arise in the case of services of an 'intellectual' nature and, under certain conditions, in the case of intra-Community transport services, services ancillary to intra-Community transport and intermediary services.

The reverse charge system is also generally applicable to intra-Community acquisitions of goods and to construction where supplied to taxable persons who are subject to file periodic VAT returns.

5 BASIS OF TAXATION

5.1 Supplies within Belgium

VAT applies to the total amount of the purchase price and other consideration payable for the goods or services including, for example, insurance and transport costs.

The following items are excluded from the taxable base:

- amounts deductible from the price as a discount for early payment, and price reduction given by the supplier to which the purchaser is entitled at the time the tax becomes due

- the VAT itself

- interest charges for late payment

- costs for ordinary and usual packaging materials for which the supplier agrees to reimburse the purchaser if the materials are returned

- amounts advanced by the supplier for expenses he incurred in the name and for the account of the other contracting party.

When the consideration does not consist wholly of a sum of money, it is to be estimated at the normal value, which can be defined as the price which can be obtained in Belgium for the same goods on an arm's length basis.

5.2   Self-Supplies
The taxable base for self-supplied goods is the purchase price of comparable goods. If, however, there is no comparable price, the taxable base is the cost of supplying such goods, ie the cost price.

5.3   Imports
VAT is payable on the value of the goods upon which Customs duties are levied increased by the amount of the duty levied. The VAT itself does not form part of the taxable basis.

5.4   Acquisitions
The value used is the contract price, which may include commission, packing and transport. If the acquisition is fictitious, then there is no change in ownership and the VAT value is the purchase price, cost price or value of similar goods. The value of acquisitions must be shown separately on the VAT return (see section 7.5.1 of the Introduction to the European Union).

5.5   Chargeable Event/Time of Payment
An invoice relating to the goods or services supplied must be issued by the fifth working day of the month following that in which the goods or services were supplied. The VAT is to be paid to the State at the time of the monthly or quarterly returns. The same rules apply with regard to the issuing of invoices and payment of tax in respect of self-supplies.

When goods are imported, the tax is paid to the Customs authorities. However, provided they have obtained the required authorisation, resident entrepreneurs or foreign taxable persons who are registered for Belgian VAT can defer payment until they file their periodic VAT return and they can then claim a credit for the tax. By doing so, the disadvantage of pre-financing the VAT on import is avoided.

The chargeable event occurs for an acquisition when a supply of similar goods is regarded as effected within the territory of Belgium (see section 7.5.2 of the Introduction to the European Union).

VAT due is normally accounted for on the basis of the value of the invoices issued in an appropriate VAT period. Sometimes entrepreneurs can account for VAT on a cash basis when they do not issue invoices. However, these are generally very small retailers who can opt for a regime exempting them from most formalities, such as issuing invoices and filing returns.

5.6   Credit Notes/Bad Debts
Where a price reduction is agreed after an invoice has been issued, a partial recovery of the VAT paid can be effected through the issue of a credit note.

When a taxable person believes a debt will not be paid, he can recover the VAT paid on the supply when the bad debt is entered as such in the books. The related VAT will then be refunded.

6 TAX RATES

The present rates are as follows:

0%:   newspapers and periodicals, manufactured tobacco and waste materials

1%:   gold transactions

6%:   goods of basic necessity and to services of a social nature

12%:   goods of current consumption and services which are particularly important from an economic, social or cultural viewpoint

20.5%: all supplies of goods and services not exempt or covered by other rates.

7 EXEMPTIONS

7.1 *Exemption with Credit for Input Tax*
The export of goods from the Union is exempt with entitlement to input credit. Input tax relating to goods and services used for export operations and for exempt intra-Community supplies of goods dispatched or transported from Belgium to other Member States is recoverable (see section 7.7.1 of the Introduction to the European Union).

Import of goods from third territories are exempt from VAT to the extent that the imported goods are destined by the addressee on import for exempt intra-Community supplies from Belgium to other Member States.

The supplies of goods in a VAT warehouse (a particular type of warehouse in Belgium in which goods can be entered under clearance for customs duties but under a temporary suspension of import for VAT until their final destination is known) are exempt from VAT.

While supplies of banking, financial and insurance services are exempt from VAT if the recipient of these services is resident or established outside the European Union, input credit attributable to such supplies is recoverable.

7.2 *Exemptions without Credit for Input Tax*
Recovery of input tax incurred in respect of certain exempt activities which are listed in the tax code is not permitted. These activities include financial transactions carried on by banks, insurance companies, lawyers, notaries, doctors, et, in addition to certain educational, cultural and sports activities.

Certain imports, such as the personal effects of travellers, personal goods imported on permanent transfer of private residence, goods imported by diplomats, packing containers and means of transport which will be re-exported, are exempt from VAT.

7.3 *Exempt Importation*
The importation of goods which is followed by an intra-Community supply may be exempt (see section 7.7.2 of the Introduction to the European Union).

7.4   Non-Taxable Transactions

7.4.1 Transactions within the Same Legal Entity
Supplies within the same VAT entity are not subject to VAT because they are considered to be outside the scope of VAT.

7.4.2 Transfer of Business
The transfer of an entire business or an independent part thereof as a sale or a consideration of assets is not considered to be a delivery of goods or a rendering of services when the recipient is subject to VAT.

7.4.3 Subsidies/Penalty Payments/Compensation
Subsidies (ie the intervention of a third party in a supply) are subject to VAT. Penalty payments are not subject to VAT when they are the consequence of damage to the supplies. Compensation does not normally fall within the scope of VAT.

7.5   Election to be Subject to VAT
In some cases, entrepreneurs may elect to be subject to VAT, for example, the sale of a new building or operations such as deposits and withdrawals. The option is also available to distance sellers (see section 3.4 above) and to non-taxable legal persons and government bodies (see section 7.2.4 of the Introduction to the European Union).

8   CREDIT/REFUND FOR INPUT TAX

8.1   General Rule
In computing the amount of tax payable, a taxable person may deduct the tax relating to goods and services purchased, imported or acquired by him from another Member State and which are used for the purposes of his taxable business (see section 7.8.1 of the Introduction to the European Union).

A credit is not allowed for VAT paid on:

- goods and services used for non-business purposes
- goods and services used for exempt transactions
- tobacco, alcohol, hotels and meals, entertainment expenses and 50% of the expenses relating to cars.

If, at the end of a three-month tax period, the VAT paid to suppliers exceeds the VAT billed to customers by at least BEF60,000 (for VAT returns made monthly) or BEF25,000 (for VAT returns made quarterly), the balance will be refunded.

In either case, at the end of the calendar year, any excess of BEF10,000 or more is refunded.

8.2   Adjustment of Entitlement to Credit
For a certain period (four book years for movable depreciable goods and nine book years for immovable goods following the year of purchase) the entitlement to a credit for input tax at the time of purchase may be adjusted on a pro rata basis, depending on whether or not the goods continue to be considered as fixed assets.

8.3 Partial Exemption

Persons who make both taxable and exempt supplies as well as supplies outside the scope of VAT are only entitled to recover VAT incurred in making the taxable supplies. A preliminary ratio per calendar year is computed, but the exact ratio, taking into consideration the actual figures, must be calculated (at the latest) by 20 April of the year following that in which a revision is due.

Such persons may also opt (or may be obliged by the VAT authorities) to apply a real use calculation in order to determine the part of VAT that is recoverable as input tax. This means that the VAT is:

- entirely recoverable to the extent that it relates to costs destined for the taxable outgoing operations
- not at all recoverable to the extent that it relates to costs destined for the outgoing operations outside the scope of VAT.

8.4 Time of Recovery

A credit for input tax may be claimed on the VAT returns for the tax period in which the supplier made his supply, although such sum is only refunded if the VAT liability is less than the VAT credit. The question of whether or not the invoice has been paid is irrelevant for the purposes of obtaining a VAT credit.

8.5 Refund for Foreign Entrepreneurs

A refund is also available to any taxable person who, although not located in Belgium, is within the European Community in respect of the VAT suffered on goods or services purchased in or imported into Belgium. Such a taxable person must:

- file a special claim form in triplicate to the following authorities:

French language applications:	Dutch language applications:
Bureau Central de TVA. pour Assujettis	Centraal BTW Mantoor Voor
Etrangers	Buitenlandse
Service des remboursements	Belastingplichtlge
Avenue Bisschofsheims	Dienst Teruggeve
1000 Bruxelles	Bisschofsheimlaan 38
Belgium	1000 Bruxelles
	Belgium

- indicate the nature of the activities for which he requests a VAT refund
- attach a certificate issued by the taxpayer's own VAT authorities indicating that he is subject to VAT, and
- attach the original invoices or import documents.

Depending on the precise circumstances, the VAT authorities may require some additional information.

The claim must relate to a period of between three months and one year, and must be made within a period of five years from the date the VAT became due (normally the date of the invoice or import document). The refund should generally be made within six months.

A taxable person located outside the European Union must file a form 803 in triplicate with the authorities mentioned above and provide proof that he has an economic activity by submitting:

- a certificate from his resident country translated into French, Dutch or German
- a copy of the applicant's company bye-laws and balance sheet relating to the last fiscal year. This document must be certified as an exact copy and the signature must be legalised.

Depending on the precise circumstances, the VAT authorities may require some additional information.

Only one request may be introduced per calendar quarter. Each refund request may include only invoices not more than five years old.

As a general rule, a refund is only granted in accordance with Belgian law. Consequently, VAT is not refundable for the items referred to in section 8.1 above.

9   ADMINISTRATIVE OBLIGATIONS

9.1   Registration

Registration is required when an activity which is considered subject to VAT is effectively performed. However, an intention to perform such activity is sufficient provided that the intention is sustained by an organisation created for the purposes of performing the activity.

9.2   Books and Records

Any person who is subject to the VAT laws and regulations is required to observe certain requirements regarding invoices, books, accounts, monthly or quarterly returns and other documents.

According to the Code of Commerce, a trader (including a company or branch) must keep the following books:

- a journal for the entry of the day-to-day transactions
- a record ('livre des inventaires'/'inventarisboek') for the annual registration of the inventory of assets and liabilities (ie balance sheet and support details such as an income statement).

The VAT inspector must be informed of the commencement, change in location or nature, and cessation of activities to which the VAT law applies.

Incoming invoices and credit notes, documents supporting the import of goods and documents related to the transfer of fixed assets should be recorded daily in a register of incoming invoices.

The outgoing invoices and internal documents relating to transfers out of inventory for private use and transfers out of inventory to fixed assets should be recorded in a register of outgoing invoices.

Collections related to transactions which are subject to VAT but for which no invoices are issued should be recorded daily in a collection register. There should be separate columns or registers for collections by cash, postal cheque and banks, although such a register need not be kept where appropriate financial ledgers are maintained.

Except in cases where a dispensation is granted, incoming and outgoing invoices and documents should be kept for a period of ten years beginning on 1 January following the date of the document.

9.3 Invoices

An invoice must be issued for each transaction. This requirement applies also to partial payment for goods or services. The minimum information required on the invoice (a copy of which must be kept by the supplier) is as follows:

- date of invoice – this must not be later than the fifth working day following the month in which goods were delivered or services performed
- sequential number in register of outgoing invoices
- name and address of the supplier
- VAT registration number of the supplier
- registration number of the supplier in the Register of Commerce
- name and address of the purchaser/recipient. In the event that the purchaser/recipient is also subject to VAT law and regulations, his registration number should also be shown
- the date of delivery of the goods or completion of the services rendered
- the usual description (including the quantity) of the goods supplied or the nature of the service rendered, inclusive of all the data required to determine the applicable tax rate
- the selling price and other data required to determine the basis of VAT
- the applicable VAT rate(s)
- the amount of VAT
- the reason of exemption in the case of transactions not subject to VAT
- for some operations on which no Belgian VAT is charged, the VAT number under which the foreign customer is identified in a Member State other than Belgium should appear on the invoice (eg exempt intra-Community supplies of goods, intra-Community transport of goods and services ancillary to those transports, intermediary services). See section 7.9.1 of the Introduction to the European Union
- in particular cases, some additional information should appear on the invoices (eg supplies of new means of transport and construction work for which the VAT is shifted towards the customer).

Invoices do not need to be issued to individuals for goods supplied or services rendered to them unless the goods or services rendered are used by the individual for business or professional purposes. However, the rendering of an invoice to an individual is compulsory for the following transactions:

- sale of motor cars and other items (such as yachts, etc) which are considered to be luxury goods
- new buildings
- work carried out on real property
- sales by instalment payments and rents
- the supplies with regard to goods which, given their nature, the way they are offered,

the sold quantities or used prices apparently are destined for his business, as well as the supplies of goods of the kind in which the recipient is doing business or which he usually destines for his business

■ the supplies effected in establishments or places which are in general not accessible by private persons

■ the supplies effected by producing or wholesale companies

■ the supply of parts, spare parts and equipment, cars, yachts, etc together with other maintenance (washing excluded) and repair work effected on these goods, including the supply of goods which are being consumed for carrying out the repair works when the price, including VAT, exceeds BEF2,500

■ the transactions of moving and furniture storage and performance auxiliary to these transactions

■ distance selling transactions.

9.4   VAT Returns
Monthly returns should be submitted to the appropriate VAT 'Office de Controle' within 20 days following each calendar month.

Quarterly returns may apply to enterprises, the yearly turnover of which (exclusive of VAT) does not exceed BEF20 million.

Additional returns are required in respect of intra-Community goods movements – a register, a sales listing (VIES) and Intrastat (see section 7.6 of the Introduction to the European Union).

9.5   VIES Statements
VIES statements ('Kwartamopgave van de Vrigestelde intra-Communautaire Leveringen'/'Releve Trimestriel des Livraisons intra-Communautaires') must be submitted by entrepreneurs/taxable persons to their local VAT office on a quarterly basis (see 7.9.2 of the Introduction to the European Union).

9.6   INTRASTAT
Traders who supply goods to other Member States or who acquire goods from other Member States must provide monthly details of the goods movement if their sales and acquisitions each exceed BEF4,200,000 (see section 7.9.3 of the Introduction to the European Union).

9.7   Registers
Certain registers of goods movements must also be kept (see 7.9.4 of the Introduction to the European Union).

9.8   Powers of Authorities
If a return is lodged with the tax authorities later than the required date, the taxpayer fails to pay the VAT or makes non-authorised deductions, the tax authorities can impose assessments for additional tax and/or administrative penalties of between 10% and 200% of the non-authorised deductions together with interest amounting to 0.8% per month.

The statutory time limit for additional assessment is five years from the day the VAT liability arose.

9.9 Objection/Appeal

Where a person is dissatisfied with a formal determination of the amount to be paid to the tax authorities, he may lodge a claim with a court.

10 SPECIAL VAT REGIMES

10.1 Agricultural and Forestry Enterprises

Farmers have a special regime. Farmers are not required to apply VAT formalities when they supply services or goods. However, a taxable person who supplies farmers must refund to the farmer the VAT amount included in the invoice price.

10.2 Financial Institutions

Banking and financial activities are generally exempt.

10.3 Free Port/Bonded Warehouse/VAT Warehouse

Free port facilities are not available in Belgium. However, a bonded warehousing system exists where goods can be stored without being subject to import duties and VAT. A particular type of VAT warehouse exists in Belgium in which goods can be entered under clearance for customs duties but under a temporary suspension of import for VAT until their final destination is known. As long as the goods remain in the VAT warehouse system, no VAT on import is due since the import is not yet considered to have taken place for VAT purposes. Furthermore, the supply of goods in a VAT warehouse is exempt from VAT.

10.4 Small Entrepreneurs

Small entrepreneurs who are normally located in retail businesses are taxed on a fixed amount in order to simplify the formalities.

Small undertakings with a yearly turnover of less than BEF225,000 are exempt from most of the VAT formalities and should not charge VAT on their outgoing operations. They have no right to recover VAT as input tax. They may, however, opt for the normal VAT system if they wish.

10.5 Travel Agencies

Travel agencies qualify for a special regime. Where a travel agent acts as an agent for someone else who organises the travel he is only liable to VAT on his margin (commission). Where travel agents directly organise the travel themselves they are subject to the normal VAT rules.

10.6 Transfer and Leasing of Real Property

Buildings (but not the ground on which they are erected) are subject to VAT, provided they are transferred before 31 December of the year following that in which a fixed assessment of withholding tax on these buildings has been levied. Use of the VAT regime is optional. After this date, the buildings are subject to registration duties of about 12.5%.

Under certain conditions, the lease of buildings through a finance lease is subject to VAT.

11 FURTHER READING

Gecoördineerde BTW-aanschrijvingen, Kluwer Rechtswetenschappen, Antwerp (loose leaf publication)

Import-export; gunstregelingen en procedures in de douane, en BTW-reglementering, Kluwer Rechtswetenschappen, Antwerp (loose leaf publication)

H Vandebergh, *BTW-vraagstukken*, Kluwer Rechtswetenschappen, Antwerp

H Vandebergh, *Fiscale praktijkstudies; Taxatie en verweer inzake BTW*, Kluwer Rechtswetenschappen, Antwerp

G. Peeters, Ph. Baervoets, I. Lejeune and P. Wille, *BTW-praktijkboek '93*, Kluwer Rechtswetenschappen, Antwerp

H. Vandebergh, *BTW-handboek*, Mys & Breesch uitgevers, Gent

Contributor: Rudi Hanssens
Ernst & Young Tax Consultants
Avenue Marcel Thiry 204
B-1200 Brussels
Belgium
Tel: + 32 2 774 91 11
Fax: + 32 2 774 90 90

DENMARK

1   GENERAL BACKGROUND

Value added tax (VAT – in Danish: MOMS) came into force on 3 July 1967. Most of the subsequent changes were introduced in 1978 due to the harmonisation process of the European Community. In particular, a number of new services became taxable under the VAT Act of 1967.

An updated VAT Act, passed on 18 May 1994, took effect from 1 July 1994 but contained very few major changes.

The VAT Act covers the Kingdom of Denmark but it excludes the Faroe Islands and Greenland.

VAT is administered by the customs and tax authorities, who are also responsible for releasing information about new VAT regulations. The day-to-day administration is handled by their 30 regional branch offices.

1.1   The Single Market – Intra-Community Acquisitions
As a Member State of the European Union, Denmark applies the rules for VAT applicable to the single market and in particular the transitional arrangements which apply in respect of intra-Community supplies during the transition period which commenced on 1 January 1993.

For ease of reference and to reduce repetition the transitional arrangements are set out in detail in section 7 of the Introduction to the European Union which precedes this section of the book. It is recommended that it is read in conjunction with the transitional arrangements.

2   WHO IS TAXABLE?

2.1   General
VAT must be paid by a taxable person who is defined as anyone who independently operates a business supplying goods or taxable services.

The obligation to pay VAT also applies to co-operatives and other societies.

A taxable person has to register with the customs and tax authorities when its annual taxable turnover exceeds DKK20,000 (ECU2,548). This rule also applies to seasonal activities.

Artists and their successors are VAT liable on their first sale of their own art when exceeding a threshold of DKK300,000.

Non-taxable entrepreneurs and government bodies are taxable when they make intra-Community acquisitions for more than DKK80,000.

This chapter reflects the law on VAT in Denmark as at 1 January 1995.

Anyone who purchases new means of transport from another Member State of the European Union also has to pay Danish VAT (see section 7.2.6 of the Introduction to the European Union).

2.2 Transactions with Branch/Subsidiary

Transactions between a parent company and its subsidiary are treated as transactions between independent parties.

Transactions between a head office and its branch are VAT-exempt, unless the parties are registered separately or the branch or the head office is located in a foreign country. In the latter case, goods transactions are treated as either exports or imports. Within the European Union, goods transactions between the different Member States are treated as intra-Community acquisitions. Services are disregarded for VAT purposes.

2.3 Government Bodies

For the central government, counties, municipal institutions and other bodies governed by public law (for example, water supplies and electricity), the obligation to pay VAT is limited to sales of goods or services which may distort competition with commercial enterprises. For example, there is no VAT on public certificates or the issue of passports. They are also to be treated as taxable persons if they make intra-Community acquisitions (see section 7.2.4 of the Introduction to the European Union).

2.4 Fiscal Unity/Group Registration

If an enterprise consists of more than one unit, division or branch, taxation as one single enterprise is required. If separate accounts are kept for the individual units, divisions or branches, they may be registered and taxed separately on request.

A company with one or more subsidiaries is not automatically regarded as one entity, but may be registered as one enterprise on request provided that all the companies involved carry out taxable businesses. Thus, normally it is impossible to group register both taxable and non-taxable enterprises as one enterprise. However, a group registration with a pure holding company and its 100% (taxable) subsidiaries is possible.

If enterprises have been registered as one enterprise, they are jointly and severally liable for the VAT in respect of the enterprises covered by the joint registration.

2.5 Foreign Entrepreneurs

Foreign undertakings are liable to Danish VAT when making taxable supplies of goods and services within Denmark, when importing goods into Denmark, or when making intra-Community acquisitions in Denmark as described earlier in the Introduction to the European Union.

Foreign undertakings with a fixed establishment in Denmark, including branches or agencies, carrying out taxable activities in Denmark are liable to Danish VAT.

Foreign entrepreneurs situated in another European Union Member State involved in distance selling to Danish customers have to register in Denmark when exceeding a threshold of DKK280,000 (see section 7.4.2 of the Introduction to the European Union).

On application, a foreign enterprise having no registered office, residence or the like in Denmark may obtain reimbursement of VAT paid on goods and services purchased or imported for the commercial purpose of such enterprise in Denmark (see section 8.4 'Refund for Foreign Entrepreneurs').

2.6 Representative Offices

A representative office of a foreign enterprise providing services of a supporting and auxiliary nature (for example, taking orders) may apply for voluntary registration even if no supplies are made in Denmark. This enables the enterprise to obtain a refund of VAT on local purchases of goods or services without having to go through the mutual recovery procedure referred to in section 8.4 'Refund for Foreign Entrepreneurs'. This facility, however, is not available for representative offices of enterprises carrying out activities which are VAT-exempt in Denmark (for example, banks).

2.7 VAT Representative

If the foreign entrepreneur carrying out taxable activities (for example, supplies, intra-Community acquisitions or imports) in Denmark has no branch, office or the like in Denmark, he has to be registered by a person (or a company) who has a permanent address in the country. The person or company will act as a local representative for the enterprise, and he will be severally and jointly liable for the VAT attributable to the foreign entrepreneur.

2.8 Reverse Charge Mechanism

For certain services supplied by an entrepreneur not established in Denmark, the resident recipient of the services will be liable to VAT, rather than the non-resident supplier.

This special rule applies, for example, to services of consultants, lawyers and accountants, copyrights, patents, advertising and the hiring out of movable property (see section 4.4 'Reverse Charge Mechanism').

2.9 Importers

The rules on imported goods concern goods from non-European Union countries only.

Enterprises importing goods for business purposes have to register separately in accordance with the provisions of the Tariff Act 1993. These rules also apply for VAT purposes. Likewise, a private individual is liable to pay VAT on importation of goods and on intra-Community acquisitions of new means of transport. However, no registration is required.

Imported goods are taxed at the same rate as if the goods were supplied from within Denmark.

2.10 Acquisitions of Goods – European Union Trade

Cross-border transactions between enterprises in the 15 European Union Member States are not treated as imported goods, but as intra-Community acquisitions. These rules are described in greater detail in section 7.2 of the Introduction to the European Union.

2.11 Non-Taxable Legal Persons – Taxable Persons with No Right to Recover VAT

Such persons are considered as outside the scope of VAT when, during the civil year and the preceding one, their yearly intra-Community acquisitions are below DKK80,000. As soon as an acquisition puts them above that threshold they are subject to common intra-

Community rules and must pay VAT on their acquisitions. They must therefore obtain an identification number and submit VAT returns.

The same persons may opt to be subject to common rules even for acquisitions below the threshold. The option takes effect on the first day of the month in which it is exercised and expires on 31 December of the second year following the option; the option is renewable for periods of two years except if renounced two months before the end of the two-year period.

2.12 Supplier of New Means of Transport

Any person who undertakes on an occasional basis intra-Community supplies of new means of transport that are dispatched or transported from Denmark to another Member State, is regarded as a taxable person (see section 7.2.6 of the Introduction to the European Union).

3 WHAT IS TAXABLE?

Danish VAT is levied on the supply of goods and services in Denmark and the import of goods. Occasional transactions are also taxable.

3.1 Supply of Goods

On the basis of the 1994 Act and case law, VAT is levied on all goods, both new and second-hand (unless treated under the second-hand margin scheme, see section 10 below), when the right to dispose of these goods is transferred by the owner. For example, a hire purchase contract qualifies as a supply of goods which takes place at the actual time of delivery. The assembly of, for example, a building, machine or installation is also regarded as a supply of goods.

The term 'goods' is not defined in the Act. Gas, water, electricity, heating and livestock are, however, regarded as goods. The following items are not regarded as goods and are not subject to VAT:

- bonds, shares, and other securities
- real property; however, the owner of the real property may register voluntarily in certain situations (see section 7.5 'Election to be Subject to VAT').

3.2 Importation of Goods

The taxability of imported goods is based on the act of importation itself. The liability to pay VAT is usually settled with the customs authorities at the time of importation, regardless of whether the person importing the goods is a taxable person. Exemptions may apply in specific situations. For example, household equipment imported by a person who is moving to Denmark to take up residence is VAT-exempt.

A registered enterprise can postpone the VAT payment by paying on a monthly basis on receipt of a statement from the customs and tax authorities.

Goods stored in bonded warehouses or tax warehouses are not subject to VAT before the end of the storage arrangement.

3.3 Intra-Community Acquisitions

From 1 January 1993 VAT is charged, levied and in some cases paid on the intra-Community acquisition of goods, other than new means of transport, effected within Denmark for consideration by a taxable person, and on the intra-Community acquisition of new means of transport effected by anyone within Denmark for consideration (see section 7 of the Introduction to the European Union).

3.4   Distance Sellers
Persons who supply goods from another Member State to non-VAT-registered persons in Denmark may be taxable in respect of such supplies (see section 7.4.2 of the Introduction to the European Union).

3.5   New Means of Transport
The transfer to Denmark from another Member State of new means of transport is always taxable as an intra-Community acquisition regardless of the status of the supplier or the purchaser (see section 7.2.6 of the Introduction to the European Union).

3.6   Contract Work
If a VAT registered person in another Member State sends goods to Denmark to be processed there and the processed goods are not returned to the Member State from which the goods for process originated, then the owner of the goods will have to register and account for VAT in Denmark (see section 7.2.5 of the Introduction to the European Union).

3.7   Excise Products
In certain circumstances a non-registered acquirer of excise products may have to register and account for VAT on acquisitions of products which are subject to excise duty (see section 7.2.7 of the Introduction to the European Union).

3.8   Assembly/Installation
A supply of goods takes place in Denmark if the specific goods to be supplied are located in Denmark. This applies even if an overseas entrepreneur has no place of business in Denmark. However, the liability of supply of assembled or installed goods may be passed to the Danish customer under the reverse charge mechanism (see section 2.8 'Reverse Charge Mechanism').

3.9   Supply of Services
From 1 October 1978, VAT was levied on all services apart from those specifically exempt (see section 7.4 'Non-taxable Transactions'). The term 'services' is not defined in the Act. Services include, for example:

- leasing of movable and immovable tangible property
- transfer of patents, copyrights, licences, etc
- supply of staff
- advertising
- services of consultants, engineers, lawyers, etc.

3.10   Self-Supply of Goods/Services
Self-supply is the transfer of goods or services within the enterprise. In general, such transactions are not subject to VAT.

However, the authorities may decide that an enterprise is liable to VAT on goods and services used by the enterprise itself. For example, the construction of buildings on the constructor's own land for sale or letting purposes has been deemed to be subject to VAT.

If goods or services are purchased by the enterprise, but partly used for private purposes, a special provision applies. At the time of the purchase, credit for input VAT is given, but the input VAT is adjusted for the part relating to the private use, normally an estimated value. For the private use of certain items (for example, the telephone of the enterprise), a fixed rate applies.

If goods or services are purchased by the enterprise, but wholly used for private purposes, no input VAT is creditable.

If goods are purchased for business purposes but are removed from the enterprise for private purposes later on, such a removal will be treated as a taxable turnover of the goods. VAT will then be levied on the purchase price of the goods.

4   PLACE OF SUPPLY

VAT applies to taxable supplies made within Denmark, imports of goods and certain services and acquisitions.

4.1   Supply of Goods
Goods located abroad and sold by a Danish enterprise will be considered outside the scope of Danish VAT, even if the Danish or foreign enterprise is registered in Denmark for VAT purposes. However, if such goods are imported into Denmark, VAT will be levied on importation. If the goods are transferred into Denmark from another European Union Member State, they will be treated as intra-Community acquisitions. For a description of the transitional VAT system see section 7.2 of the Introduction to the European Union.

Goods being exported from Denmark are VAT-exempt. As a result, no VAT is actually levied whereas the right to credit is still maintained.

4.2   Intra-Community Acquisitions
As a general rule, the place where an intra-Community acquisition of goods takes place is deemed to be the place where the goods are when transportation to the person acquiring the goods ends.

To make a zero-rated intra-Community supply followed by a taxed intra-Community acquisition on which the VAT may be deducted by the acquirer, the VAT identification numbers of the parties involved must be stated on the invoice.

If, for any reason, the goods arrive finally in a Member State other than that which issued the VAT number to the acquirer, the person purchasing the goods acquires the goods in the Member State of arrival of the goods. In this case double taxation could occur, since the purchaser must account for VAT both in the Member State which issued the VAT number to him and in the Member State of arrival of the goods.

The presumption is that the place of acquisition is the country which issued the VAT number to the acquirer. However, if the acquirer can show that he has paid VAT in the Member State of arrival of the goods he will not be liable for payment of acquisition VAT in his own Member State.

4.2.1 Chain Transactions

'Triangulation' involves the situation where three parties in three different countries are involved in selling and purchasing the same goods. For example, *A* in France sells goods to *B* in Belgium who sells the goods to *C* in Denmark and the goods are sent directly from *A* to *C* (see section 7.4.1 of the Introduction to the European Union).

4.2.2 Goods Placed on Board Ships, Aircraft or Trains During Transport

When goods are supplied for consumption on board ships, aircraft or trains during transport, and the place of departure and destination are within the territory of the European Union, the place of supply is the place where the goods are at the time of departure of the transport.

4.3 Supply of Services

4.3.1 General Rule

The Act does not define the rendering of services. The legislation is, however, based on the guidelines contained in the Sixth VAT Directive as to the place where the services are rendered. In general, services are rendered where the entrepreneur rendering the service is resident or has a fixed establishment from where the service is rendered.

4.3.2 Exceptions

The general rule does not apply to the following services, despite the supplier's place of business or residence:

■   Services connected with immovable property are deemed to take place where the real property is situated. For example, services performed by a real property agent, project planning, etc.

■   Transport of goods and passengers is deemed to take place where it actually occurs. However, transport of goods directly to a foreign country is taxable in the country where the transport starts. Transport of passengers is usually exempt without credit (see section 7.1 'Exemptions'). With regard to intra-Community transportation of goods see section 7.4.4 of the Introduction to the European Union.

■   Services of a scientific, cultural or entertainment nature are deemed to be supplied where the arrangements are actually and physically performed

■   *Work on movable goods:* valuation of or work in respect of movable tangible property is deemed to take place where the property is situated

■   *Services ancillary to transport services:* when supplied in connection with intra-Community goods transport such services may be zero-rated (see section 7.4.5 of the Introduction to the European Union)

■   *Brokers/intermediaries:* the place of supply of services provided by brokers or other intermediaries which form part of an intra-Community transport of goods is the European Union Member State which issued the VAT identification number of the customer (see section 7.4.6 of the Introduction to the European Union)

■   *Other brokers/intermediaries:* the place of supply of certain services provided by brokers or other intermediaries (which do not come within the scope of Article 9.2(e) of the Sixth VAT Directive) is the Member State of the customer which issued his VAT registration number to them (see section 7.4.7 of the Introduction to the European Union).

4.4   Reverse Charge Mechanism

For certain services supplied by an entrepreneur not established in Denmark, the resident recipient of the services will be liable to VAT, rather than the non-resident supplier. This special rule applies to the following services:

- transfers and assignments of copyrights, patents, licences, trademarks and similar rights
- advertising services
- services of consultants and engineers, project planning, services of lawyers, accountants and similar services, data processing and information services
- taxable and financial services, except for hiring out of bank deposit boxes (see section 7.1 'Exemptions without Credit for Input Tax')
- supply of staff
- hiring out of movable tangible property, except for all forms of transportation
- services consisting of a commitment to refrain from any professional activity or right referred to above
- services of agents who act in the name and for the account of a principal when they procure the services of this group for their principal.

The reverse charge mechanism applies to services rendered by a supplier resident outside the European Union territory to a Danish recipient, or by a taxable supplier resident within the European Union territory to a Danish taxable person.

The liability to account for Danish VAT arises for the Danish recipient of the services listed above and, if he is a registered entrepreneur but entitled to only partial or no credit, the VAT has to be paid when calculated on the VAT return. Persons not registered as entrepreneurs have to account for and pay the VAT directly to the authorities.

If the supplier resident outside the European Union is rendering services to private persons in Denmark, the supplier must register for VAT in Denmark.

5   BASIS OF TAXATION

5.1   Supplies within Denmark

VAT is charged on the total amount of consideration paid by the buyer. This can, for example, include:

- other duties or taxes which have been levied on the goods at previous stages of distribution or by import
- packing, transport or distribution expenses
- agent's commission
- cash discounts and other discounts which are subject to requirements that have not been met at the time of delivery.

If there is a common interest between the supplier and the buyer of goods and taxable services (for example, one party holding a financial interest in the other enterprise), the customs and tax authorities may determine a taxable base other than the one agreed between the parties and levy VAT accordingly.

5.2 Self-Supplies
The taxable base for self-supplied goods and services is the value of the transaction to a third party, ie at arm's length value. If goods or services are used for private purposes by the owner, shareholders or employees, etc, the taxable value is determined at the purchase or production price.

5.3 Imports
The taxable value for imported goods will be the same as the taxable value for customs duty purposes (see the definition in the Tariff Act). The taxable value has to include freight charges, insurance premiums, etc incurred before the goods reach their first destination in Denmark, plus customs duties and other taxes levied.

5.4 Acquisitions
The value used for acquisitions is the contract price, which may include commission, packing and transport.

If the acquisition is fictitious, then there is no change in ownership and the VAT value is the purchase price, cost price or value of similar goods. The value of acquisitions is also separately shown on the VAT return.

5.5 Chargeable Event/Time of Payment
The general rule is that a taxable transaction occurs when the goods are actually supplied. However, where invoices are made out with respect to supplies, the time of invoicing is to be regarded as the time of supply, provided that the invoice is made out before or directly after completion of the supply, or before the fifteenth day of the month following that in which the supply has occurred.

A taxable entrepreneur has to submit periodical accounts to the authorities, usually based on a calendar quarter. Settlement has to be made not later than one month and ten days after the end of each period.

With every supply of goods or services, it is common practice to issue an invoice connected to the taxable transaction. The invoice normally has to be made directly after the supply.

However, no invoice is required for sales to private customers. Retailers and other entrepreneurs who mainly sell to private customers may account for VAT on a cash basis and may also omit to issue an invoice to registered enterprises unless the recipient requests an invoice.

VAT chargeable on the intra-Community acquisition of goods is due on the fifteenth day of the month following the month during which the intra-Community acquisition occurred (see section 7.5.2 of the Introduction to the European Union). If an invoice is issued prior to the fifteenth day by the supplier, the tax shall be due when the invoice is issued.

A taxable person/entrepreneur accounts for VAT on an intra-Community acquisition by reporting the acquisition VAT on his periodic VAT return. If he is entitled to full deduction of VAT he deducts the acquisition VAT as input tax on the same return. However, if the taxable person/entrepreneur is not entitled to full or partial deduction he must pay to the tax authorities the difference between the VAT on the acquisition and the amount he is entitled to deduct.

VAT in respect of fictitious intra-Community acquisitions becomes due at the time the acquisition of the goods was made.

5.6   Credit Notes/Bad Debts

An enterprise may deduct from its taxable turnover the value shown on credit notes for returned goods, cash discounts and other discounts which are subject to requirements which have not been met at the time of delivery, provided that:

- the discounts were given to a registered enterprise which is entitled to a full credit of input tax; and
- a credit note is made, indicating the VAT relating to the discount allowed.

A refund of VAT on bad debts is normally available when the loss has been realised. A loss is realised under the following circumstances:

- bankruptcy
- compulsory set-off of debts
- set-off of debts with creditors
- failed enforcement proceedings
- compulsory sales
- a proper valuation of facts and the amount involved.

6   TAX RATES

The present rates are as follows:

0%:   newspapers

5%:   artists' and their successors' sale of their own art

25%:   all goods and services which are not exempted or liable at the 5% rate.

7   EXEMPTIONS

7.1   Exemptions with Credit for Input Tax

The following exemptions are with credit for input tax:

- goods sold or transferred to another taxable enterprise in a European Union Member State, except for second-hand goods sold under the Second-hand Goods Scheme (see section 10 'Special Schemes')
- goods exported by an enterprise and services performed in a foreign country
- work performed on goods for a foreign account (non-European Union country), provided that the enterprise exports the goods after the treatment; and technical design and style of goods for foreign accounts, provided that the goods are to be manufactured abroad

- project planning, design, and other taxable services concerning buildings and other real properties located outside Denmark
- necessary equipment delivered for aircraft and ships in international traffic (other than sports aircraft and pleasure craft) and services performed on such aircraft and ships
- the sale and hire of ships of not less than five gross register tons and of aircraft other than sports aircraft and pleasure craft
- repairs, maintenance, and installation work performed on the aircraft and ships referred to above and on their permanent equipment and materials supplied by the enterprise in question
- the sale of newspapers which are normally published in not less than one monthly issue
- supply of new means of transportation to other European Union countries
- transport services and related services to customers outside the European Union
- supply of goods for storage in the free port of Copenhagen or other customs warehouse arrangements.

While supplies of banking, financial and insurance services are exempt from VAT if the recipient is resident or established outside the European Union, input credit attributable to such supplies is recoverable.

The Minister of Taxation or the customs and tax authorities may decide whether and to which extent supplies delivered to ships or aircraft for the use on board or for sales to passengers, etc may be excluded from taxable sales.

7.2   Exemptions without Credit for Input Tax
The following exemptions are without credit for input tax:

- hospital treatment, medical practice, dentistry and other dental services. This means that nearly the whole health care sector is exempted, unless not approved by the authorities, for example, homeopathy
- social services and aid
- school and university education, language training, excluding some educational programmes; for example, driving lessons, and educational programmes sold by a taxable person for business purposes to other enterprises
- cultural activities, including libraries, museums and zoological gardens, etc excluding radio and television transmissions, theatre and cinema performances, concerts, etc
- sporting activities and arrangements, including arrangements to which betting, etc is attached; but excluding motor racing and arrangements in which professional sportsmen and athletes participate. Football matches are only included when professionals participate on both teams
- passenger transport; but excluding commercial passenger bus transport other than regular services
- postal services, parcel post services included, but excluding telecommunications services
- letting, leasing and administration of real property, but excluding the letting of rooms in hotels, inns, motels, etc, letting out for periods less than one month, and letting out of camping, parking and advertising space
- insurance activities
- bank, savings bank, and financial activities, but excluding the hiring out of bank

deposit boxes. Also excluded from exemption is the management of credit and credit guarantees offered by a person or a body other than the one who granted the credit, the safekeeping and management of shares, interests in companies and associations and other securities or negotiable instruments

- lotteries and the like, gambling for money
- literary, musical and other artistic activities
- travel agencies, information activities and tourist offices, etc
- services performed by undertakers, etc in direct connection with funerals
- certain arrangements connected to charities, ie sale of goods where the profit is only used for charity
- works of authors, composers, etc.

7.3   Exempt Importation

The importation of goods which is followed by an intra-Community supply may be exempt (see section 7.7.2 of the Introduction to the European Union).

7.4   Non-Taxable Transactions

7.4.1 Transactions within the Same Legal Entity

Transactions between a head office and its branch are not subject to VAT unless the branch or head office is situated in a foreign country. If so, the transactions are treated as either exports or imports.

However, a VAT liability may arise under the place of supply of services rules and the reverse charge mechanism (see section 2.8 'Reverse Charge Mechanism').

Transactions between a parent company and its subsidiary are subject to VAT unless jointly registered (see section 2.4 'Fiscal Unity/Group Registration').

7.4.2 Transfer of Business

Taxable sales do not include sales of stock, machinery and other assets, provided they are sold in connection with the sale of all or part of an enterprise, and the new owner operates a registered enterprise.

Within eight days of the sale, the seller must notify the customs and tax authorities of the new owner's name and address, and the sales price for the stocks, machinery, and other assets sold. With regard to a potential adjustment, see section 8.2 'Adjustment of Entitlement to Credit'.

The rule does not apply when an arrangement of sale and leaseback is established. In such cases, VAT is charged at the normal rate.

7.4.3 Subsidies/Penalty Payments/Compensation

Subsidies given to an enterprise are only VAT-exempt if given as a gift or when no services are performed.

There is no VAT on penalty payments (for example, for premature termination of a lease), unless it is also a payment for a supply.

Usually, there is no VAT on damage claims, payments from an insurance company, or on payments for unfulfilled contracts.

7.5   Election to be Subject to VAT

A voluntary registration applies for a very limited number of exempted activities but it is also available for distance sellers (see section 3.4 (and) for non-taxable legal bodies and government departments (see section 7.2.4 of the Introduction to the European Union). It is mainly the areas of letting or leasing of real property which are accepted. In Denmark VAT is always payable on the letting of premises and car parks.

8   CREDIT/REFUND FOR INPUT VAT

8.1   General Rule

VAT owed to the Treasury by taxable persons is calculated as the difference between the output VAT and the input VAT, import VAT included.

VAT on intra-Community acquisitions is accounted for on the VAT return.

In principle, all input VAT on purchases, including VAT on investments made during a VAT period and intra-Community acquisitions, is recoverable.

However, there is no recovery for input VAT related to a non- taxable turnover.

Moreover, input VAT is not recoverable for:

■   meals for the owner and employees of the enterprise
■   acquisition and use of housing accommodation for the owner and employees of the enterprise
■   remuneration in kind of the employees of the enterprise
■   acquisition and operation of crèches, kindergartens, recreation centres, holiday homes, summer cottages, etc for the employees of the enterprise
■   entertainment expenses and gifts
■   hotel accommodation
■   acquisition and operation of passenger motor vehicles adapted for transport of not more than ten persons
■   expenses for hotel accommodation and meals incurred by employees of enterprises which supply taxable education programmes.

8.2   Adjustment of Entitlement to Credit

Special provisions apply in relation to input VAT on certain investment goods:

■   machinery, inventory, and working plant, provided that the cost exceeds DKK50,000, (ECU6,280)
■   immovable property.

On the sale of an enterprise, no adjustment may be made by the seller if the purchaser is a taxable person who is willing to undertake the obligation of recomputing the allowable credit.

Adjustments need only be made during a five-year period (ten years for immovable property) and will be calculated on the basis of one-fifth (one-tenth for immovable property), including the year of delivery, of the VAT paid at the time of acquisition for the year when a change occurs.

8.3   Partial Exemption

Input VAT on purchases in connection with exempt transactions may not be reclaimed. However, where VAT is incurred on purchases which are attributable to both taxable (exemption with credit included) and non-taxable supplies, the input VAT incurred must be apportioned pro rata between taxable and non-taxable supplies for the period of turnover.

It is not possible to divide one enterprise into profit centres to obtain a better position for a VAT refund instead of the pro rata refund by, for example, using floor space, number of employees, etc. However, the enterprise may reorganise and form two entities, for example, as a parent company and a subsidiary.

If an estimated ratio is used, an adjustment to the actual amount must be made by the end of the accounting year.

No special provisions are available to allow a partly exempt enterprise to be treated as fully taxable.

8.4   Refund for Foreign Entrepreneurs

A foreign entrepreneur making taxable supplies in Denmark may register for VAT if he has an office or another business establishment in Denmark. He is then treated in the same way as a Danish enterprise. If no such establishment exists in Denmark, a VAT representative should be appointed. A credit or refund is then claimed when filing the normal periodic VAT return.

A special refund procedure applies for VAT paid on goods and taxable services purchased or imported in Denmark for commercial purposes for a non-registered entrepreneur such as, for example, advertising expenses and exhibition costs. A refund of this Danish input VAT can be obtained on application on the following conditions:

- the business must not have an office or registered address in Denmark
- the business must be subject to VAT according to the rules applied in Denmark if the activity was carried out there; this means that for banking activities, insurance businesses, and travel agencies, it is not possible to obtain VAT refunds
- the foreign business must not supply goods or services in Denmark
- the foreign business can only obtain a refund on the same conditions as a Danish business subject to VAT.

This means that there is no refund of VAT on purchases relating to the specific items for which a credit for input tax is disallowed (see section 8.1 'General Rule').

To obtain the refund, it is necessary to fill in a standard form in Danish and send it in to the customs and tax authorities at:

> Told-og Skatteregion
> Soenderborg
> Hilmar Finsensgade 18
> 6400 Soenderborg
> Denmark

The application must be filed together with the original VAT invoices and a statement indicating the purpose of the expenses. A statement from the relevant competent authority to prove that the enterprise is subject to VAT in its country of domicile must also be enclosed. Such statement is only valid for a period of one year from the date of issue. The enterprise must also provide a statement that it has not exercised any activities subject to VAT in Denmark during the reimbursement period.

The application must relate to purchases of goods or taxable services for periods of between three months and one calendar year. It must concern a VAT amount of not less than DKK1,500. When the application covers a calendar year or the rest of a calendar year, the amount may, however, not be less than DKK200.

9   ADMINISTRATIVE OBLIGATIONS

9.1   *Registration*
Any entrepreneur who is taxable (see section 2.1 'General') must apply to the customs and tax authorities for registration. Upon completion of the registration, a certificate of registration will be issued to the enterprise. Enterprises whose taxable sales of goods and services do not exceed DKK20,000 per annum are not taxable.

For enterprises selling non-taxable services, a voluntary registration is possible. This may be beneficial to, for example, an entrepreneur who rents out real property in order to obtain a refund of the input VAT. A voluntary registration covers a minimum period of two years during which de-registration cannot take place.

It is possible for registered enterprises carrying out export business to apply for and obtain a VAT refund after one month or even one week.

9.2   *Books and Records*
The purchases and sales of taxable goods and taxable services of registered enterprises must be recorded in accounts which can serve as a basis for the calculation and control of the VAT amounts for each taxation period.

Such records must contain separate accounts for VAT receivables, VAT calculated on intra-Community acquisitions, and VAT payable. VAT accounts may be kept by periodical entries, provided that VAT can be directly calculated on the basis of the records of purchases and taxable sales of goods and services of the enterprise.

With respect to purchases and sales of taxable goods and services, taxable persons and enterprises exempted from VAT must retain books and records, including invoices, invoice copies, cash register tapes, etc, for five years after the end of the accounting year.

Taxable persons must take stock at least once a year. Accounting records must be kept for five years after the end of the accounting year.

9.3   *Invoices*
Invoices must be issued to consignees for all taxable goods or services supplied by taxable persons. If payment is required for partial deliveries before the entire delivery has been completed, separate invoices must be issued for any such partial deliveries. The following details must be specified: consignor, consignee, description, quantity and price of the goods delivered or services performed.

The supplier must indicate the amount of the VAT on the invoice and specify the price without VAT for each item on the invoice.

A credit note must be issued for goods returned to offset an issued invoice. This rule also applies where the supplier allows a price reduction after the issue of the invoice, provided that the reduction is not a discount.

The supplier must file copies of invoices, credit notes and cash vouchers.

Where an invoice or a cash voucher covers both taxable and non-taxable supplies, the invoice must specify the taxable supplies. Such supplies must be listed and added up separately.

Invoices for cross-border trade of goods between taxable persons within European Union Member States must show both the supplier's and the customer's VAT number and each number must be identified with the nationality prefix (for Denmark the prefix is DK).

For a description of compliance and administrative obligations on European Union trade see section 7.6 of the Introduction to the European Union.

9.4   VAT Returns
Within one month and ten days after the end of each taxation period, a taxable person must submit to the customs and tax authorities a return of the amounts of VAT payable, VAT calculated on intra-Community acquisitions and VAT receivable for the period and the amount of sales which are exempt with credit. Amounts have to be shown in Danish kroner, fractions thereof being disregarded. Such returns, which must be signed by the responsible manager(s) of the enterprise, must be submitted on special forms which should also be used for settlement of the net VAT balance.

Taxation periods must be calendar quarters. Filing on a monthly basis is normally not possible. For enterprises registered as farmers, fishermen, etc, the period is six months.

If the VAT return for any tax period is filed late, the tax liability for that period is increased by 1% (minimum DKK500, maximum DKK1,100), and if the VAT is not paid on time, interest is to be paid at the rate of 1.3% per month (minimum DKK50).

The authorities are entitled to estimate the VAT to be paid if no return is received.

9.5   VIES Statements
VIES statements ('Sales Listings') must be submitted by the taxable person to the local tax office where he is registered for VAT on a quarterly basis together with the VAT return (see section 7.9.2 of the Introduction to the European Union).

9.6   INTRASTAT
Traders who supply goods to other Member States or who acquire goods from other Member States must provide monthly details of the goods movement if their sales exceed DKK800,000 and their acquisitions exceed DKK500,000 (see section 7.9.3 of the Introduction to the European Union).

9.7   Registers
Certain registers of goods movements must also be kept (see section 7.9.4 of the Introduction to the European Union).

9.8   Powers of Authorities

The customs and tax authorities are authorised to inspect premises used in connection with the operations of enterprises which are required to register and to inspect the stocks held by such enterprises, their books of account, other records, correspondence, etc.

At the request of the customs and tax authorities, the books and records must be surrendered or filed with the customs and tax authorities.

On request, suppliers to enterprises which are required to register have to provide the customs and tax authorities with information about goods and services delivered to such enterprises.

9.9   Objection/Appeal

Any disputes with the customs and tax authorities may be submitted to a board of appeal of six members, who should possess a general knowledge of administrative and business matters. The board has the final power to make administrative decisions on:

- questions concerning the scope of VAT liability
- questions concerning taxable value
- questions concerning the scope of the exemptions
- questions relating to VAT deductibility items
- questions as to how public utility deliveries have to be defined
- appeals against estimated assessments made by the customs and tax authorities.

The final decisions are made by the Court of Justice.

10   SPECIAL REGIMES

10.1 Split Registration

On application, an entrepreneur carrying on export may become subject to a special split registration regime.

A split registration means that the entrepreneur's business is divided into two sectors (A and B – a fictitious transaction), and the entrepreneur may then invoice his export orders in the following three steps:

1   an export order is invoiced from sector A to sector B of the company, and VAT is levied on this transaction. Sector B of the company may then recover this VAT amount as input VAT on a monthly basis
2   the export order is invoiced without VAT
3   the output VAT is paid on a quarterly basis on the invoice mentioned under the first step.

By means of this special regime, it is possible for the entrepreneur to benefit from an interest free loan from the authorities as long as the export business continues.

10.2 Second-Hand Goods

A special second-hand goods scheme came into effect on 1 July 1994 in accordance with the Seventh VAT Directive and applies to sales of works of art, antiques and collectors' items and passenger motor vehicles.

VAT will be charged on the margin between buying and selling prices only.

For cross-border transactions the rules apply from 1 January 1995.

11   FURTHER READING

Momsvejledningen, Told-& Skattestyrelsen

Momsloven med Kommentarer og Eu-henvisnigner, AF Lars Loftager Jorgensen, Borge Aagaard Pedersen og Lars Rasmussen

Moms' loose-leaf binders, A/S Skattekartotekets Informationskontor

Contributor: Mogens Krewald
                  Ernst & Young A/S
                  Tagensvej 86
                  DK-2200 Copenhagen N
                  Denmark
                  Tel: +45 35 824848
                  Fax: +45 35 0824710

FINLAND

1 GENERAL BACKGROUND

Finland introduced a Value Added Tax (VAT) on June 1 1994 which superseded the old Turnover Tax. The VAT system closely followed the EC VAT Directives in anticipation of Finland joining the European Union on 1 January 1995.

VAT in Finland is levied by the regional tax authority (lääninverovirasto). There are 11 County Tax Offices in Finland. VAT on imports is levied by the Finnish Customs Office and is paid in conjunction with customs duties.

1.1 The Single Market – Intra-Community Acquisitions
As a Member State of the European Union Finland applies the rules for VAT applicable to the Single Market and, in particular, the transitional arrangements which apply in respect of intra-Community supplies during the transition period which commenced on 1 January 1993.

For ease of reference and to reduce repetition the transitional arrangements are set out in detail in section 7 of the Introduction to the European Union which precedes this section of the book.

It is recommended that this chapter is read in conjunction with the transitional arrangements.

2 WHO IS TAXABLE?

2.1 General
Any physical or legal person (limited company, partnership, etc) who delivers taxable goods or renders taxable services in the course of business is liable to VAT.

Small entrepreneurs are not subject to VAT if their annual invoicing does not exceed FIM50,000. From 1 January 1995 the method of calculating the limit changed. In addition to annual invoicing some exempt income is taken into account such as, for example, rental income from real estate and financial income.

Charitable organisations are subject to VAT only if they are subject to income tax or if their activity otherwise is considered to be a business activity.

2.2 Transactions with Branch/Subsidiary
A subsidiary is always registered separately for VAT purposes. Exchange of goods or services between a parent company and its subsidiary is usually taxable. Services supplied between branches of the same legal entity are not subject to VAT. Thus services supplied between a branch and its head office or another branch are not taxable even if one of the

This chapter reflects the law on VAT in Finland as at 1 January 1995.

parties is situated outside Finland. However, the importation of goods (see section 2.9 below) and the intra-Community acquisition of goods by a branch (see section 2.10) are taxable events.

2.3   Government Bodies

Government entities are taxable if they deliver goods or services in competition with private entities. Even cost-price sales are taxable.

Government entities do not pay VAT if the sales price is remarkably below cost price. They are also taxable persons in respect of intra-Community acquisitions (see section 7.2.4 of the Introduction to the European Union).

2.4   Fiscal Unity/Group Registration

Group registration is not available in Finland between enterprises. Each taxable person (individual or legal body) must account for VAT individually.

Group registration is, however, available for banks and insurance companies and to enterprises closely linked to them. For example, a data processing service company can be a part of a group with a bank and sell exempt services inside the group.

2.5   Foreign Entrepreneurs

A foreign entrepreneur is liable for VAT if he sell goods or services in Finland so long as the sale is a part of his business activity carried on abroad.

However, if a non-resident entrepreneur without a regular place of business in Finland, or without voluntary registration for VAT, sells goods or certain taxable services in Finland, the reverse charge is applicable. The purchaser of the goods or services has to account for VAT. If the purchaser is another foreign entrepreneur or an individual, the seller has to account for VAT. If the purchaser is the State, VAT is not payable.

2.6   Representative Offices

Representative offices (for example, dependent agents who provide services of a supporting or auxiliary nature such as marketing services) generally do not qualify as permanent establishments for either corporate tax or VAT purposes.

2.7   VAT Representatives

If a non-resident has a permanent establishment in Finland, and if he sells goods or services, he must register for VAT. In general, a VAT representative is not needed for this VAT registration. However, a VAT representative accepted by the tax county office of Uusimaa (situated in Helsinki) is needed for voluntary registration for VAT. The VAT representative is obliged to keep books and take care of other administrative matters, but is not responsible for the payment of VAT.

2.8   Reverse Charge Mechanism

A resident customer is liable to pay VAT when he purchases goods or certain services from a non-resident supplier if the seller does not have a permanent establishment or VAT registration in Finland.

Reverse charge mechanism is also applicable to services other than personal transport and teaching, educational services, cultural, entertainment and sport occasions.

2.9   Importers

Goods brought into Finland from other than European Union-countries are subject to VAT at customs clearance. The tax is paid by the importer. Likewise, a private individual is liable to pay VAT on importation of goods. No registration is required in this case.

Imported goods are taxed at the same rate as if the goods were supplied within Finland.

2.10   Acquirers of Goods from the European Union

The movement of goods from one Member State to another is an acquisition. If there is an acquisition by a Finnish business, the supplier in the other European Union Member State is not obliged to register. If there is a 'fictitious acquisition' (because, for example, there is no change in title) VAT registration in Finland will be required for the supplier (see section 7 of the Introduction to the European Union).

2.11   Supplier of New Means of Transport

Any person who undertakes on an occasional basis intra-Community supplies of new means of transport which are dispatched or transported from Finland to another Member State is regarded as a taxable person (see section 7.2.6 of the Introduction to the European Union).

2.12   Non-Taxable Legal Persons – Taxable Persons with No Right to Recover VAT and Farmers Benefiting from Notional Refunds

Such persons are considered as outside the scope of VAT when during the civil year and the preceding one their yearly intra-Community acquisitions are below FIM50,000. As soon as an acquisition puts them above this threshold they are subject to common intra-Community rules and must pay VAT on their acquisitions. They must therefore obtain an identification number and submit VAT returns.

The same persons may opt to be subject to common rules even for acquisitions below the threshold. The option takes effect the first day of the month in which it is exercised and expires on 31 December of the second year following the option; the option is renewable for periods of two years unless renounced two months before the two-year period expires.

3   WHAT IS TAXABLE?

Finnish VAT is levied on the supply of taxable goods and services in Finland and on the import and intra-Community acquisition of goods.

The customer is liable to VAT in some cases under the reverse charge mechanism.

3.1   Supply of Goods

The term 'supply' means the transfer of goods for compensation. The term 'goods' applies to all tangible properties. Utilities, such as electricity, gas, heat and similar intangibles qualify as goods. Land and buildings are considered goods but are not subject to VAT.

3.2   Imports of Goods

VAT must be paid not only on taxable supplies in Finland but also on imports of taxable goods. This applies regardless of the purpose of the import and irrespective of the transaction on which the import is based. Tax on imports is assessed by the customs office in accordance with procedures laid down for customs clearance. The customs office is also the authority to be consulted regarding VAT on imports.

3.3   Intra-Community Acquisition of Goods

Intra-Community acquisition is defined as the acquisition of the right to dispose as owner of movable, tangible property dispatched or transported to the person acquiring the goods by or on behalf of the vendor or the person acquiring the goods to a Member State other than that from which the goods are dispatched or transported.

Intra-Community acquisitions of goods for consideration are subject to VAT when they are performed by a taxable person acting as such or by a non-taxable legal person where:

- the vendor is a taxable person acting as such who is not eligible for the tax exemption as a small undertaking
- the goods are not installed by or on behalf of the vendor
- the vendor is not involved in distance selling (see sections 7.2 and 7.3.4 of the Introduction to the European Union).

3.4   Distance Sellers

Persons who supply goods from another Member State to non-VAT registered persons in Finland may be taxable in respect of such supplies (see section 7.4.2 of the Introduction to the European Union).

3.5   New Means of Transport

The transfer to Finland from another Member State of new means of transport is always taxable as an intra-Community acquisition regardless of the status of the supplier or the purchaser (see section 7.2.6 of the Introduction to the European Union).

3.6   Contract Work

If a VAT-registered person in another Member State sends goods to Finland to be processed there and the processed goods are not returned to the original Member State, then the owner of the goods will have to register and account for VAT in Finland (see section 7.2.5 of the Introduction to the European Union).

3.7   Excise Products

In certain circumstances a non-registered acquirer of excise products may have to register and account for VAT on acquisitions of products which are subject to excise duty (see section 7.2.7 of the Introduction to the European Union).

3.8   Assembly/Installation

A supply of goods takes place in Finland if the specific goods to be supplied are located in Finland. This applies even if an overseas entrepreneur has no place of business in Finland. However, the liability of supply of assembled or installed goods may be passed to the Finnish customer under the reverse charge mechanism (see section 2.8 above).

3.9   Supply of Services

Anything which is not considered a good and which can be sold in a business form is considered a service. Only a few services are exempt. These include:

- financing services
- insurance services
- education which is based on law
- health care and medical treatment
- social care.

3.10 Self-Supply of Goods/Services

VAT is also charged on withdrawal by the owner of goods from his own business when the goods and services are for private use or for purposes which fall outside the scope of the Act. VAT is also payable on a self-supply of services.

4 PLACE OF SUPPLY

4.1 Supply of Goods

The place of supply is in Finland if the commodities are delivered within the country.

Goods which are sold to a Finnish customer before importation are not taxable in Finland. The customer has to pay VAT if he imports the goods into Finland.

Goods which are delivered abroad (exports) are zero-rated with right to deduction.

Where goods are supplied on board ships, aircraft or trains during that part of a passenger's journey which is effected in the European Union, the supply is deemed to take place at the point of departure of the transport.

Special rules also apply to the so-called regime of distance selling (see section 7.4.2 of the Introduction to the European Union).

4.2 Intra-Community Acquisitions

As a general rule, the place where an intra-Community acquisition of goods takes place is deemed to be the place where the goods are when transportation to the person acquiring the goods ends.

To make a zero-rated intra-Community supply followed by a taxed intra-Community acquisition on which the VAT may be deducted by the acquirer, the VAT identification numbers of the parties involved must be stated on the invoice.

If, for any reason, the goods eventually arrive in a Member State other than that which issued the VAT number to the acquirer, the latter is deemed to acquire the goods in the Member State of arrival of the goods. In this case double taxation could occur, since the purchaser must account for VAT both in the Member State which issued the VAT number to him and in the Member State of arrival of the goods.

The presumption is that the place of acquisition is the country which issued the VAT number to the acquirer; however, if the acquirer can show that he has paid VAT in the Member State of arrival of the goods he will not be liable for payment of acquisition VAT in his own Member State.

4.2.1 Chain Transactions

'Triangulation' involves the situation where three parties in three different countries are involved in selling and purchasing the same goods. For example, *A* in France sells goods to *B* in Belgium who sells the goods to *C* in Finland and the goods are sent directly from *A* to *C* (see section 7.4.1 of the Introduction to the European Union).

4.2.2 Goods Placed on Board Ships, Aircraft or Trains During Transport
When goods are supplied for consumption on board ships, aircraft or trains during transport and the place of departure and destination are within the territory of the European Union, the place of supply is the place where the goods are at the time of departure of the transport.

4.3 Supply of Services

4.3.1 General Rule
The rules in Finnish VAT legislation follow the place of supply rules of the Sixth VAT Directive.

With certain exceptions, a service is deemed to be sold in Finland if it is delivered from a permanent establishment situated in Finland. Otherwise it is deemed to be sold in Finland if the seller's domicile is in Finland.

4.3.2 Exceptions
■   leasing service of hauling equipment is deemed to be supplied in Finland if it is de facto used solely in Finland. If the service is de facto used in countries outside the European Union it is deemed to be supplied abroad and is outside the scope of VAT
■   services directed to real estate are deemed to be sold in Finland if real estate is situated in Finland
■   goods transport within the European Union is deemed to be supplied in Finland if the transport begins in Finland. However, if the purchaser uses a VAT number given in Finland the transport is deemed to be supplied in Finland in spite of where it actually takes place. Transport to countries other than EU-countries, together with related services (unloading, loading, forwarding services, etc),are zero-rated.

The following services are supplied in Finland if they are performed in Finland:

■   teaching and educational services, cultural, entertainment and sports occasions, together with services closely connected with the organisation of such services
■   unloading of cargo, loading and other equivalent services in connection with goods transportation
■   valuation of movable goods
■   work performances directed to movable goods.

Certain services, 'intangible services', are deemed to be sold in Finland if the purchaser has a permanent establishment in Finland to which the service is delivered. If the service is not delivered to a permanent establishment in Finland or abroad the service is deemed to be sold in Finland if the purchaser's domicile is in Finland. These services include:

■   delivery of copyright, patent, licence, trademark and other intellectual rights
■   advertising and publicity services
■   consultancy, product development, planning, bookkeeping, auditing, writing, drawing, translating services, juridical services, etc
■   data processing, planning or programming of computer programs or computer systems

- delivery of information
- notarial work, collection and other services relating to financing
- leasing of harbour
- leasing of movable property excluding leasing of hauling equipment
- obligation to refrain partly or wholly from use of intellectual property rights listed above
- acquiring the above services in the name and on behalf of another.

In addition, the Act includes a list of services which are considered as supplies of services outside Finland and which are zero-rated with right to deduction:

- **Transportation services:** however, as far as intra-Community transport of goods is concerned (ie transport where the place of departure and the place of arrival are situated within the territories of two different Member States), the place of supply is deemed to be the place of departure. By derogation from this rule, the place of supply of intra-Community transport of goods rendered to customers identified for VAT purposes in a Member State other than that of the departure of the transport is deemed to be within the territory of the Member State which issued the customer with the VAT number under which the service was rendered to him (see section 7.4.4 of the Introduction to the European Union).
- **Services ancillary to intra-Community transport of goods:** as far as activities ancillary to intra-Community transport of goods are concerned, the place of supply of these services is deemed to be the territory of the Member State which issued the customer with the VAT number under which the services were rendered to him, provided the services rendered to a customer who is identified for VAT purposes in a Member State other than that within the territory of which the services are rendered materially (see section 7.4.5 of the Introduction to the European Union).
- **Services provided by brokers and other intermediaries:** the place of supply of services which form part of an intra-Community transport of goods by intermediaries and brokers is the place of departure of the transportation – once again a compulsory reverse charge is applied if the supplier and the customer are in different Member States (see section 7.4.6 of the Introduction to the European Union).
- **Other services rendered by brokers and other intermediaries:** with regard to all other services rendered by brokers and other intermediaries (except those mentioned above and except those relating to supplies of intangible services such as advice, transfer of patent rights, etc – Article 9.2(e) of the Sixth VAT Directive) the place of supply is where the services are carried out, unless the services are rendered under the VAT identification number of a customer registered in a Member State other than that of the intermediary. Such services are deemed to take place in the Member State which issued the VAT identification number and the customer in that Member State must account for the VAT (see section 7.4.7 of the Introduction to the European Union).
- **Work on movable goods:** the place of supply of services on movable goods (eg, repair and valuation) is where the services are actually performed. However, there is a derogation which shifts the VAT liability on a reverse charge basis to the customer in circumstances where the supplier and the customer are in different Member States and the customer is registered for VAT (see section 7.4.8 of the Introduction to the European Union).

4.4   Reverse Charge Mechanism

In the case of supplies of services mentioned in section 2.8 above, the supply is treated as being made where the recipient of the supplies belongs. Thus the 'importation' into Finland of such services is subject to the reverse charge (self-supply to and by the customer). The 'export' of such services to a person in his business capacity elsewhere in the European Union or to any person in a third country is treated as outside of the scope of Finnish VAT.

5   BASIS OF TAXATION

5.1   Supplies within Finland

VAT is payable on the entire amount billed to the purchaser for goods or taxable services. This amount includes delivery, packaging, insurance, other taxes, etc regardless of whether these are included in the sales price or invoiced separately.

Discounts and credits given to the purchaser are deducted from the taxable amount.

5.2   Self-Supplies

VAT due on self-supplies is calculated on the basis of the purchase price of the goods. In the case of goods manufactured by an entrepreneur for his own business or services performed by the entrepreneur himself, the basis for the tax is the direct and indirect expenses of producing the goods or the service.

5.3   Imports

The basis for the calculation of VAT on imported goods is the customs value for the goods. This includes customs duties and all other duties except VAT. When goods are reimported after repair abroad the taxable value is the cost of such repair with the addition of the cost of transport to and from Finland.

5.4   Acquisitions

The value used is the contract price, which may include commission, packing and transport. If the acquisition is fictitious, then there is no change of ownership and the VAT value is the purchase price, cost price or value of similar goods. The value of acquisitions must also be shown separately on the VAT return.

5.5   Chargeable Event/Time of Payment

VAT has to be paid monthly. VAT on a supply is chargeable in the month during which the goods were delivered, services were performed, or the possession of the goods was taken. The tax is due within one month and 15 days of the end of the month. A taxable person has one month and 15 days to pay the VAT due.

VAT chargeable on the intra-Community acquisition of goods shall be due on the fifteenth day of the month following the month during which the intra-Community acquisition occurred (see section 7.5.2 of the Introduction to the European Union).

If an invoice is issued prior to the fifteenth day by the supplier the tax shall be due when the invoice is issued.

A taxable person/entrepreneur accounts for VAT on an intra-Community acquisition by reporting the acquisition VAT on his periodic VAT return. If he is entitled to full deduction of VAT he deducts the acquisition VAT as input tax on the same return. However, if the taxable person/entrepreneur is not entitled to full or partial deduction he must pay to the tax authorities the difference between the VAT on the acquisition and the amount he is entitled to deduct.

VAT in respect of fictitious intra-Community acquisitions becomes due at the time the acquisition of the goods was made.

Practising professionals pay VAT on the basis of payments accrued.

5.6   Credit Notes/Bad Debts

If the entrepreneur gives a credit and issues a credit note he is allowed to reduce his VAT liability accordingly. The customer, on the other hand, has to reduce his input tax deduction.

When a taxable person believes a debt will not be paid, he can recover the VAT paid on the supply when the bad debt is entered as such in the books. The related VAT will be refunded.

6   TAX RATES

The rates are as follows:

0%:   newspapers and magazine subscriptions, sale and lease of certain ships and aeroplanes and the transfer of a business

6%:   passenger transportation, accommodation, theatre, music, circus and dance performances

12%:   books, movie theatre performances, leasing of sports facilities (golf, squash, tennis, swimming pools, ice hockey, field sports, etc), medicines

17%:   groceries and foodstuffs, animal food (from 1 January 1998 – 12%)

22%:   all other goods and services which are not exempt or liable at the 0%, 6%, 12% or 17% rates.

7   EXEMPTIONS

7.1   Exemptions with Credit for Input Tax

The zero rate operates in the same manner as exemption with credit.

While supplies of banking, financial and insurance services are exempt from VAT if the recipient of these services is resident or established outside the European Union, input credit attributable to such supplies is recoverable.

7.2   Exemption without Credit for Input Tax

The following goods or services are exempt without credit for input VAT:

- health care and medical treatment
- social care

- education based on law
- financing services
- insurance services.

7.3 Exempt Importation

The importation of goods which is followed by an intra-Community supply may be exempt (see section 7.7.2 of the Introduction to the European Union).

7.4 Non-Taxable Transactions

7.4.1 Transactions within the Same Legal Entity

Supplies within the same legal entity are not taxable when the branch and its head office are both established in Finland. However, supplies made between a foreign head office and its branch in Finland are taxable.

Transactions within a municipality are not taxable. The same applies to transactions within the State departments.

7.4.2 Transfer of Business

Selling goods and services when transferring a business or a part of a business is exempt. The exemption requires that the transferee continues the same business activity.

7.4.3 Subsidies, Penalty Payments and Compensation

Subsidies, penalty payments and compensation are outside the scope of VAT, provided they are not to be qualified as payments for taxable supplies.

7.5 Election to be Subject to VAT

In certain cases, it is possible to apply for tax liability. The qualifying applicants are:

- a blind person (who has no assistance other than his spouse or children under 18) who makes taxable supplies
- an entrepreneur whose annual invoicing with certain exempt income does not exceed FIM50,000
- an owner or lessor of real estate in respect of his leasing of real estate
- a society for the public good, vocational education institutions and social shelter work
- distance sellers (see section 3.4)
- non-taxable legal persons and government bodies who acquire goods from other European Union Member States (see section 7.2.4 of the Introduction to the European Union).

8 CREDIT/REFUND FOR INPUT TAX

8.1 General Rule

According to the general rule a taxpayer can deduct the input tax of purchased goods and services if acquired for his taxable activities. However, the following are not deductible:

- self-supplies of goods
- private cars and some other motor vehicles and their fuels and maintenance and

repairs if the motor vehicle is not used exclusively for business purposes
- cost of employees' travel between home and work where these are compensated by the employer
- private use by the taxable person or his staff of real estate used for private use or hobbies and purchases related to that real estate
- representational expenses
- goods to be donated.

8.2   Adjustment of Entitlement to Credit

When goods are used for both deductible and non-deductible purposes the amount of tax suffered which is attributable to non-deductible purposes has to be excluded from the input tax deduction. The proportion has to be estimated at the start of the accounting year on the basis of the use for the two purposes.

Changes in the use of the goods will lead to additional credits or additional tax liabilities depending on whether the use of the goods changes from exempt to taxable transactions or vice versa. This must be recalculated at the end of the accounting year.

8.3   Partial Exemption

Entrepreneurs making both taxable and exempt (without credit) supplies are allowed to recover only the input VAT relating to taxable supplies, calculated on a pro rata basis.

A partially exempt enterprise can deduct input tax based on the previous year's turnover for the different parts of the business. The allocation is based on the financial statements of the company.

8.4   Time of Recovery

Deductible tax may be reclaimed in the month when goods or services are received. Normally the deductible tax is less than the tax amount of the sales in the same month. If it is more, the excess will be transferred into the next month's tax return.

8.5   Refund For Foreign Entrepreneurs

A foreign entrepreneur can apply for a refund of the VAT suffered on his purchases in Finland. The application must be made on a specific form, in Finnish, to:

> Uudenmkan Laaninveronrasto
> Rataplihantie 11, pl 88
> 00521 Helsinki
> Finland

A foreign entrepreneur is entitled to the refund if the acquisition was made in connection with:

- an activity which would be taxable or zero-rated if performed in Finland
- a sale in Finland where a purchaser is liable to VAT.

To be entitled to the refund a foreign enterprise must not be a taxable person in Finland or have a permanent establishment or VAT registration in Finland.

The VAT can be reclaimed back for periods of three months. The applicant has to submit the application within six months from the end of the year to which the claim belongs.

A VAT refund procedure is also applicable to countries which do not have equivalent procedures. VAT is refunded to diplomatic missions on a reciprocal basis.

The minimum amount for refund is FIM1,200. If the application is made for the whole calendar year or the last part of the calendar year the minimum amount is FIM150.

9   ADMINISTRATIVE OBLIGATIONS

9.1   Registration

All entrepreneurs who deliver taxable goods or render taxable services in the course of business have to register at the County Tax Office. The registration is done on a special form which has to be submitted before commencing business. It is also possible to register voluntarily.

9.2   Books and Records

All taxable persons have an obligation to keep books and records in a way which makes it possible to assess the VAT liability.

9.3   Invoices

An invoice or a voucher has to indicate the following matters:

- the VAT liability of the seller
- the amount of VAT
- the exemption if the supply is not taxable.

VAT registration numbers need not be shown on invoices in Finland except in the case of intra-Community transactions, goods transport within the European Union, agency services, work on movable goods, etc within the European Union.

There are special requirements for invoices with regard to intra-Community transactions. For example, in a triangulation where the goods are transported directly to a customer in a Member State other than Finland, and the goods are invoiced by a Finnish purchaser who further invoices the final customer, special rules apply. If the first purchaser is in Finland, he has to include in his invoice to the final customer his VAT number, the customer's VAT number and a statement indicating that he is involved in triangulation (see section 7.3.3 of the Introduction to the European Union).

If a Finnish entrepreneur sells work on movable goods to an entrepreneur in another Member State which is exempt from VAT, the VAT number of the purchaser has to be included in the invoice (see section 4.3.2).

9.4   Returns

Returns have to be filed monthly, at the latest within a month and 15 days after the month in question. The obligation is the same for small companies. A yearly return must also be submitted on 15 February of the following year. In the yearly return a taxable person must identify the amount of VAT due during the year. Where several VAT rates are involved, the different rates have to be separated.

9.5 VIES

A European Union sales list (VIES) has to be submitted quarterly within one month and 15 days after each quarter. In VIES a taxable person reports his sales of goods to other Member States (see section 7.9.2 of the Introduction to the European Union).

9.6 INTRASTAT

INTRASTAT details have to be submitted within ten days after each month. This details the movement of goods between European Union countries (see section 7.9.3 of the Introduction to the European Union).

9.7 Registers

Taxable persons must also keep a register of certain goods which have been transported or dispatched to another Member State such as materials dispatched for contract work (see section 7.9.4 of the Introduction to the European Union).

9.8 Powers of Authorities

If the tax has not been paid in time an additional 30% of the amount of tax payable may be imposed. In addition, annual interest of 12% will be charged on the amounts not paid in due time.

If a return has not been filed in time the County Tax Office may assess the tax payable and charge an increase.

If an enterprise has given wrong or erroneous information to avoid taxes, the tax payable may be doubled.

Neglected taxes can be assessed and imposed for a period of three years from the end of the accounting period in question.

In addition, there is a special fine of between FIM500 and FIM10,000 if a taxable person neglects the obligation to provide the VIES or yearly return.

9.9 Objections/Appeals

Decisions of the County Tax Office may be appealed against to the County Tax Court up to three years from the end of the accounting period to which the decision relates. An appeal against the decision of the County Tax Court may be made to the Supreme Administrative Court.

10 SPECIAL VAT REGIMES

10.1 Farmers and Retailers

Primary producers became liable to VAT from 1 January 1995. Finland does not apply a flat-rate scheme for farmers. The VAT rate on primary producers is 17% during a transitional period. From the beginning of 1998 the VAT rate will be lowered to 12%.

10.2 Second-Hand Goods

A tax-liable purchaser is entitled to deduct the amount of an imputed input tax when purchasing second-hand goods from a seller who is not liable to pay VAT if the purchaser resells the goods in Finland. If the goods are sold to a European Union country or a country outside the European Union, the special deduction is not available. The further distribution of second-hand goods is taxable in Finland at the 22% rate (see section 7.10.2 of the Introduction to the European Union).

10.3 Real Estate

Leasing of buildings and real estate and sales of old buildings are not subject to VAT. Construction of new buildings and all kinds of construction work services related to land or building are subject to VAT.

Old buildings are those in respect of which the owner has not deducted the input VAT, in those which have been acquired or brought into use before the new VAT Act was introduced on 1 June 1994. If the input VAT of a building has been deducted after the introduction of the new Act and if the building is sold or taken into other than a deductible purpose within five years from the end of the year when the building was taken into use or when the constructing work was finished, the owner has to repay to the VAT authorities the VAT he has deducted. After five years the building can be sold or taken into use for a purpose other than a deductible purpose without any VAT consequences.

The lessor of real estate can opt for taxation.

If the leasing of real estate is for temporary purposes such as a camping site, sports facilities, hotel rooms or parking, the leasing is subject to VAT.

10.4 Arts

Paintings, water colours, sculptures, etc are exempt from VAT when sold directly by the artists as also is agency of art (for example, art galleries).

Contributor: Paivi Taipalus
                 Tilintarkastajien Oy
                 Oy Ernst & Young Ab
                 Kaivokatu 8
                 00100 Helsinki
                 Finland
                 Tel: +358 0 172771
                 Fax: +358 0 6221323

FRANCE

1   GENERAL BACKGROUND

A tax on consumption was first introduced in France in 1920. This tax was gradually modified and finally called 'value added tax,' in French 'taxe sur la valeur ajoutée (TVA)' in 1968. Important modifications were made to harmonise the French legislation with the Sixth Council Directive on VAT with effect from 1 January 1979.

The term 'French territory' means France including Corsica and Monaco. VAT is also applicable in the overseas departments of Martinique, Guadeloupe and Reunion, although special rules apply there. In particular, transactions between France and these departments are treated as exports or imports (see section 8.5 'Refund for Foreign Entrepreneurs').

VAT in France is administered by the Income Tax authorities, with the exception of VAT levied on imports which is administered by Customs (Administration des Douanes).

1.1   The Single Market – Intra-Community Acquisitions
As a Member State of the European Union France applies the rules for VAT applicable to the Single Market and, in particular, the transitional arrangements which apply in respect of intra-Community supplies during the transition period which commenced on 1 January 1993.

For ease of reference the transitional arrangements are set out in detail in section 7 of the Introduction to the European Union which precedes this section of the book. It is recommended that this chapter be read in conjunction with the transitional arrangements.

2   WHO IS TAXABLE?

2.1   General
Any person supplying taxable goods or services in the course of business, whether on a regular or occasional basis is taxable (assujetti). The term 'business' applies to all the activities of producers, traders and suppliers of services which are carried out independently. The activities of employees are outside the scope of VAT.

Since the legal status of the person is irrelevant VAT applies equally to corporate bodies, individuals, liberal professions, residents and non-residents.

Entrepreneurs whose turnover for the preceding year was below FF70,000 are exempt. They may, however, choose to be subject to tax to be able to recover input VAT. This exemption does not apply to real estate transactions subject to VAT.

2.2   Transactions with Branch/Subsidiary
VAT is not due on transactions within the same legal entity. Supplies of services between a branch and its foreign head office are therefore not subject to VAT. On the contrary, services

---

This chapter reflects the legislation on VAT in France as at 1 January 1995.

supplied by a foreign company to its French subsidiary, or vice versa, will be a taxable supply.

2.3 Government Bodies

Government bodies are not subject to VAT in respect of their activities of an administrative, social, sporting or cultural nature. However, they are liable to VAT in respect of their commercial activities or their activities which are deemed to be in competition with other commercial concerns. They may have to be identified for VAT if they have made intra-Community acquisitions (during the current civil year or the preceding year) in excess of FF70,000 (see section 7.2.4 of the Introduction to the European Union).

Government bodies are compulsorily subject to VAT notably for transactions such as supply of goods manufactured by them for sale, distribution of gas, electricity and thermal energy, transport of goods (except those carried out by the post office), transportation of persons, services provided in ports and airports, supply of water in communes of more than 3,000 inhabitants, organisation of fairs of a commercial nature, etc.

2.4 Fiscal Unity/Group Taxation

The concept of fiscal unity does not exist in French VAT law. Each taxable person (individual or legal body) must account for the tax independently of any other taxable person. It is not possible for a group of taxable persons to file joint returns.

2.5 Foreign Entrepreneurs

Entrepreneurs without an establishment in France but delivering goods in France or supplying services which are taxable in France are subject to VAT. A foreign entrepreneur is taxable in France when he acts as the importer of goods or when he makes a taxable acquisition in France.

Generally, a non-resident entrepreneur is considered as having an establishment for VAT purposes if he keeps in France a regular place of activity such as an office, shop, factory or simply a fixed domicile from which the activity is exercised. Any centre of activity from which a taxable person (assujetti) carries out taxable transactions on a regular basis should be regarded as a permanent establishment. Real estate located and let in France is not considered as constituting a permanent establishment.

A non-resident entrepreneur with an establishment in France is treated as a local company and should comply with all the rules applicable to French entrepreneurs, including having to obtain an identification number and file regular returns. However, he will be able to offset input VAT against output VAT on his domestic return.

2.6 Representative Office

Representative offices of foreign entrepreneurs are not regarded as taxable persons when they only carry out activities of a preparatory or auxiliary nature. The foreign entrepreneur is entitled to ask the French VAT authorities to refund the input VAT incurred in France through its representative office (see section 8.5 'Refund for Foreign Entrepreneurs').

2.7 VAT Representative

Foreign entrepreneurs making direct taxable supplies in France (without an establishment in France) are required to appoint a VAT representative who will be responsible for fulfilling the administrative obligations and for payment of the tax due by the foreign entrepreneur. A VAT representative is jointly liable for any tax or penalty due by the foreign entrepreneur.

2.8   Reverse Charge Mechanism

Foreign entrepreneurs who supply in France, services mentioned under Article 9.2 (e) of the Sixth VAT Directive (such as copyrights, patents, hiring out of movable goods, advertising services, consultancy, provision of staff, financial services, etc) do not have to account for VAT in France since the tax on such services is due by the recipient (see section 4.3 'Reverse Charge Mechanism').

However, the reverse charge does not apply when the same services are supplied by a non-European Union supplier to a non-entrepreneur in France (for example, an individual) who uses the services in France. The foreign entrepreneur established outside the European Union will be liable to VAT in France and the appointment of a VAT representative is compulsory.

2.9   Importers

Goods brought into France from non-European Union countries are liable to VAT at customs clearance. The tax is due by the importer. If the goods are sent directly by the foreign firm to the final customer in France who appears as the actual importer, VAT due on imports will be payable by the French customer.

2.10   Acquirers of Goods from Other European Union Member States

The movement of goods from one Member State to another is an acquisition. If there is an acquisition by a French business, the business in the other European Union Member State is not obliged to register. If there is a 'fictitious acquisition' (because, for example, there is no change in title) VAT registration in France will be required for the business in the other European Union Member State (see section 7.2 of the Introduction to the European Union).

2.11   Non-Taxable Legal Persons – Taxable Persons with No Right to Recover VAT and Farmers Benefiting from Notional Refunds

Such persons are considered as outside the scope of VAT when during the civil year and the preceding one their yearly intra-Community acquisitions are below FF70,000. As soon as an acquisition puts them above this threshold they are subject to common intra-Community rules and must pay VAT on their acquisitions. They must therefore obtain an identification number and submit VAT returns.

The same persons may opt to be subject to common rules even for acquisitions below the threshold. The option takes effect the first day of the month in which it is exercised and expires on 31 December of the second year following the option. The option is renewable for periods of two years unless renounced two months before the two-year expiring period.

2.12   Supplier of New Means of Transport

Any person who undertakes on an occasional basis intra-Community supplies of new means of transport that are dispatched or transported from France to another Member State is regarded as a taxable person (see section 7.2.6 of the Introduction to the European Union).

3   WHAT IS TAXABLE?

VAT is due on the supply in France of goods and services, as well as on the importation of goods and acquisition of goods.

To be taxable a supply must be made for consideration. The consideration is usually the price paid for the goods or the services. It may also be goods or services received in exchange for the supply. Supplies made at cost are taxable.

To fall within the scope of VAT and, therefore, be taxable, a transaction must fulfil the direct link criterion which implies that the two following conditions are met:

■   the transaction must provide a distinct benefit to the beneficiary. This condition is met even if the supply is collective, difficult to assess with precision, or is part of a legal obligation
■   the counterpart (ie, whether the price is paid for the goods or services or goods or services received in exchange for the supply) must be directly linked with the benefit provided for by the transaction.

The counterpart may not be the normal value of the transaction and can be paid by a third party.

3.1   Supply of Goods
The term 'supply' (delivery) usually refers to the actual transfer of the right to dispose of the goods as an owner from one person to another against payment. It can be effected by a sales deed but in the absence of any legal documents the handing over of the goods is also treated as a supply. This is the case in:

■   hire purchase contracts
■   seizure of goods by legal officers
■   sales with retention of ownership until full payment
■   exchange of goods
■   contribution in kind to a corporate body.

From 1 January 1993 certain other transactions are also considered as supplies of goods (see section 7.2.2 of the Introduction to the European Union).

The term 'goods' applies to all tangible movable properties. Intangible properties are treated as services. Utilities such as electricity, gas, heat or refrigeration qualify as 'goods'. Land and buildings are subject to special rules.

3.2   Importation of Goods
The introduction of goods to the territory of France triggers liability for import VAT when the goods come from a non-European Union country. Under certain circumstances payment of VAT can be delayed until the goods are finally put onto the French market (see section 10.7 'Bonded Warehouses'). In limited cases, the importation of goods into France is exempt from VAT (see section 7.3 'Exempt Imports'). Payment of the tax may be postponed for 30 days ('Credit d'enlevement') after a number of requirements have been fulfilled.

3.3   Distance Sellers
Persons who supply goods from another Member State to non-VAT registered persons in

France may be taxable in respect of such supplies (see section 7.4.2 of the Introduction to the European Union).

3.4 New Means of Transport
The transfer to France from another Member State of new means of transport is always taxable as an intra-Community acquisition regardless of the status of the supplier or the purchaser (see section 7.2.6 of the Introduction to the European Union).

3.5 Contract Work
If a VAT registered person in another Member State sends goods to France to be processed there and the processed goods are not returned to the Member State from which the goods for process originated, then the owner of the goods will have to register and account for VAT in France (see section 7.2.5 of the Introduction to the European Union).

3.6 Excise Products
In certain circumstances a non-registered acquirer of excise products may have to register and account for VAT on acquisitions of products which are subject to excise duty (see section 7.2.7 of the Introduction to the European Union).

3.7 Assembly/Installation
A supply of goods takes place in France if the specific goods to be supplied are located in France. This applies even if an overseas entrepreneur has no place of business in France. However, the liability of supply of assembled or installed goods may be passed to the French customer under the reverse charge mechanism (see section 2.8 'Reverse Charge Mechanism').

3.8 Supply of Services
The term 'services' applies to all transactions which are not treated as supplies of goods.

The transfer of intangible property such as rights on trademarks, patents, know-how, software, etc is regarded as supply of services. The following transactions also qualify as services:

- leasing, renting
- transport of persons or goods
- commissions
- building construction work
- research and expertise
- agreement to refrain from an activity
- food and drink consumed on the spot
- change transactions
- certain transactions on securities.

3.9 Self-Supplies of Goods/Services
In certain cases which are specified by law, an entrepreneur is deemed to supply goods to himself and is therefore liable for VAT on the goods.

A self-supply is deemed to occur:

- when goods acquired in the course of a business and giving rise to an input tax credit are finally used, appropriated or devoted to non-business purposes. This is the case, for example, where goods are appropriated by the directors, or employees of a company for their personal use

- when goods are extracted, manufactured, built or transformed by the entrepreneur himself for the needs of his business or when goods are bought, imported or acquired (intra-Community acquisitions). There is a self-supply even if the manufacturing, building or transformation is carried out by a third person at the request of the entrepreneur.

This rule is intended to avoid distortion of competition by preventing an entrepreneur from obtaining goods free of VAT when he would not have any or only a limited right of recovery either because he is not making any taxable supplies or because recovery of the input VAT is disallowed. A self-supply is always taxable when it concerns capital assets. It is taxable only in limited cases when it concerns other goods. A self-supply is taxable, for instance, if goods other than capital goods have given rise to a deduction of input VAT to be finally devoted to an exempt or out-of-scope sector of activity.

Further to the 1989 Finance Act, self-supplies of services are taxable when an entrepreneur performs, himself or with the help of a third party, services using the company's goods or means if the two following conditions are met:

- the services are performed for purposes outside the company's business, and
- input tax on the goods, or means used to provide these services, was partly or fully recoverable.

4   PLACE OF SUPPLY

VAT is chargeable in France only if the supply of goods or services takes place in France. The rules for determining the place of supply are different for goods and services.

4.1   Supply of Goods

Where the goods are to be transported, the rules are as follows:

- if the goods to be delivered are in France before transportation, then the supply is taxable in France (with the important exception of export sales)
- if the goods to be delivered are abroad before transportation, then the supply is subject to VAT in France at the point of importation if the goods are coming from a non-European Union country; the VAT is either payable by the foreign supplier or by the final customer in France
- if dispatch or transportation of the goods to the person acquiring them ends in France and the goods are coming from another European Union country, the acquisition will be taxable in France. The terms 'person acquiring the goods' covers: the person to whom the goods are sold, the person receiving in France contract work executed in another European Union State, the person transferring goods from his undertaking in another Member State to France, the taxable person acting in his own name but for the account of a principal (known as a commissionaire).

Where the goods are not transported, the supply is taxable in France if the goods are in France when they come into the power and possession of the purchaser.

If the foreign entrepreneur is importing the goods from outside the European Union, VAT is due upon importation on the value of the goods; the value of the total supply is then subject to VAT under deduction of the tax paid upon importation. The appointment of a fiscal representative is also compulsory in such a case.

4.1.1 Triangulation

In application of the Simplification Directive, France has implemented the following rules when three operators identified in three different European Union countries are involved in successive sales. Three situations may arise in a situation where entrepreneur A sells to entrepreneur B who sells to entrepreneur C:

The goods are transported from European Union Member State 1 to France (Member State 3):

The intra-Community acquisition is being made for the purpose of a further sale of goods by Entrepreneur B to C in France. B must not be established and must not have appointed a VAT representative in France, and he must not be established in Member State 1.

The goods are transported directly to C. C is a taxable person or a non-taxable legal entity identified for VAT. B issues an invoice to C showing his identification number in country B, the identification number of C in France, and the statement: 'Application de l'article 28 quatre titre E section 3 de la directive 77/388/CEE modifiée'. The invoice does not bear any VAT.

The goods are transported from European Union Member State 1 to Member State 3; entrepreneur B gives his identification number in France:

Despite the use of his VAT number in France, no VAT will be due in France if the following conditions are fulfilled: B is established in France (or has appointed a fiscal representative); he is established neither in Member State 1 nor in Member State 3. B makes an acquisition in Member State 3 for the purposes of a subsequent sale to C identified for VAT in that State. The goods are dispatched directly from A to C. B should deliver to C an invoice with no VAT but mentioning 'Application de l'article 28 quatre titre E section 3 de la directive 77/388/CEE modifiée'. B should indicate on the invoice received from A that it relates to a triangular transaction subject to the simplification rules. C is liable for the payment of the VAT in Member State 3 for the goods he purchased from B.

The goods are dispatched from France to Member State 3:

Entrepreneur A makes an exempt intra-Community supply when the required conditions are met. A declares in his INTRASTAT report the identification of his client B in Member State 2 and indicates Member State 3 as country of destination of the goods.

4.1.2 Consignment Stock

Stock transferred by a foreign European Union entrepreneur in execution of a consignment sale agreement does not constitute a taxable acquisition upon arrival of the goods in France if the following conditions are fulfilled:

- the foreign European Union supplier sells the goods to his French client in the premises where they are stored
- the transfer of ownership takes place no later than three months from the date of arrival of the goods in France.

95

If these conditions are fulfilled at the date title passes, the French client is deemed to make an intra-Community acquisition. If the conditions are not fulfilled, the foreign European Union supplier has to declare an intra-Community acquisition at the time the three-month period expires and he must tax the sale to his client in France as a domestic transaction. He will need to appoint a VAT representative.

When stock is transferred from France to a foreign European Union entrepreneur it is accepted that the supplier is seen as not making a deemed supply as long as the country of destination considers that there is no fictitious acquisition. The intra-Community supply will take place when title passes. A pro forma invoice should be established when the goods leave France and the transfer should be declared on the INTRASTAT return (see section 9.6 INTRASTAT Returns). The proper invoice will be issued at the time of the chargeable event, ie at transfer of ownership.

4.1.3 Distance Sales
The rules relating to distance sales are as follows:

- Distance sales from France: the place of supply is not in France but in the European Union Member State of arrival of the goods which the seller has effected during the preceding year or for the current year distance sales to a non-taxable or private person for an amount exceeding the threshold fixed by the Member State (ie ECU35,000 for Belgium, Denmark, Finland, Greece, Ireland, Italy, Portugal, Spain and Sweden, and ECU100,000 for Austria, France, Germany, Luxembourg, The Netherlands and the United Kingdom).

  The French supplier may opt to be subject to VAT in the country of arrival, even if his distance sales are below the above thresholds. The option should be exercised in France, separately for each Member State. It is valid for two years and tacitly renewable unless renounced two months before the two-year expiring period.

- Distance sales into France: the place of supply is in France if the foreign European Union supplier has realised in France during the preceding year or during the current civil year a total amount of distance sales exceeding ECU100,000 (FF700,000). Below that threshold, the foreign European Union supplier may opt in his Member State to be subject to VAT in France for his distance sales. In either case, the appointment of a fiscal representative is compulsory.

4.1.4 Sales Subject to Trial Runs
Sales made under the condition precedent of successful trial runs are not treated as intra-Community supplies or acquisitions until the condition precedent is fulfilled and the transfer of ownership effected.

4.2   Supply of Services

4.2.1 General Rule
The general rule is that the place where services are deemed to be supplied is the place where the entrepreneur supplying the services has his place of business, his permanent establishment or his usual place of residence from which the services are supplied.

4.2.2 Exceptions
There are a number of exceptions to the general rule:

- services connected with real estate, such as the services of estate agents, architects, etc, are deemed to be supplied where the real property is located
- transport of goods and persons (except intra-Community transport of goods) is taxable for the distance covered in France. Only transport which takes place in France is taxable. Closely related services such as loading and unloading are taxable if executed in France. Exemptions apply to international transport and to exported goods (see section 7.1 'Exemptions with Credit for Input Tax'). A new European Union directive proposes to substitute the criteria of place of departure to that of the distance covered for the transport of persons
- renting means of transport is deemed to be supplied in France:
    - if the lessor is established in France and the services are used by the lessee in France or in another European Union country
    - if the lessor is established outside the European Union and the services are used in France by the lessee
- cultural, artistic, sporting, scientific, educational and entertainment services are supplied where they are physically carried out
- works and expertise on tangible movable goods. These works (such as repair, maintenance, transformation) and expertise are taxable in France when they are physically carried out in France
- Intellectual services: the following are deemed to be supplied where the recipient of the services usually resides or has a fixed establishment:
    - transfers and assignments of trade marks, licences, copyright, patents
    - advertising services
    - services of consultants, engineers, chartered accountants, consultancy offices
    - data processing and supply of information
    - financial, banking and insurance services
    - supply of staff
    - acceptance to refrain from carrying out an activity or exercising any right
    - renting of movable properties (apart from the renting of means of transport).

According to this rule no VAT will be due in France when the recipient of these services is established outside France. However, the tax will be due in France if the services are provided by a supplier established in France to a non-entrepreneur located in another European Union country. VAT will also be due in France if the services are provided by a non European Union supplier to a non-taxable recipient who uses the services in France.

- *intermediaries:* the services of intermediaries or agents, acting in the name and for the account of principals in transactions concerning goods, are taxable in France when the place of the transaction in which they are involved is situated in France, unless the recipient of the services has given to the agent a VAT identification number in another European Union Member State. It is taxable in France if the recipient of services established outside France has given to the agent a French VAT identification number.
- *intra-Community transport of goods and ancillary services:* the domestic leg of an intra-Community transport of goods which precedes or ends such a transport follows the rules of place of supply of intra-Community transportation (see section 7.4.4 of

the Introduction to the European Union). The conditions of the exemption are the same as for works and expertise on tangible movable goods (see below)

■ ***transport of goods for exportation and ancillary services:*** the domestic leg of a transport of goods destined to exportation is exempt. The same exemption applies to ancillary services such as loading, unloading and handling. The conditions of the exemption are the same for works and expertise on tangible movable goods (see below)

■ work (such as repair, maintenance and transformation) and expertise relating to tangible movable goods are taxable in France when they are physically carried out in France. However, they are exempt of French VAT, even if realised in France, if the following conditions are fulfilled:

– the recipient of the services must be a taxable entrepreneur not established in France who would be entitled to a full recovery of the input tax

– the recipient must give his identification number (in a country other than France) to the supplier

– the recipient must provide the supplier with a certificate of taxable person

– the supplier must issue an invoice without French VAT but including the statement: 'Exonération TVA, Article 262 qinquies du CGI', as well as the VAT identification numbers of both supplier and recipient.

(See section 7.4.8 of the Introduction to the European Union.)

4.3 *Reverse Charge Mechanism*
A foreign supplier without a fixed establishment in France who provides the following services to a French taxable entrepreneur will not have to charge French VAT since the liability for the tax is shifted to the French recipient. These services are:

■ transfers and assignments of trade marks, licences, copyright, patents
■ advertising services
■ services of consultants, engineers, chartered accountants, consultancy offices
■ data processing and supply of information
■ financial, banking and insurance services
■ supply of staff
■ acceptance to refrain from carrying out an activity or exercising any right
■ renting of movable properties (apart from the renting of means of transport).

In the case of a foreign supplier established outside the European Union who provides these services to a non-entrepreneur in the State, French VAT will be due by the foreign supplier if the services are used in France. The appointment of a VAT representative will then be necessary.

5   BASIS OF TAXATION

5.1 *Supplies within France*
VAT is assessed on the total price received (or to be received) from the client or a third party as consideration for the supply of the goods or services. Ancillary expenses, additional payments, commissions, packaging expenses, insurance charged by the seller and customs

duties are part of the taxable basis. If no monies are received, VAT must be assessed on the total value of the goods or services received in exchange for the supply.

If cash discounts are granted on the invoice, it is the net amount which is subject to VAT.

5.2 Self-Supplies

VAT due on self-supplies is calculated on the basis of the purchase price of the goods or otherwise on the cost to the supplier. In the case of goods manufactured by an entrepreneur for his own business, the cost will include the value of the raw materials, of the services used in the manufacture and/or the salary expenses if the work was carried out by the entrepreneur's own employees.

The purchase price or the cost is determined at the time the tax becomes due.

5.3 Imports

VAT due on the importation of goods is assessed on the value determined for customs purposes, to which should be added freight and insurance costs to the first place of destination in the country, as well as the taxes or duties paid upon importation, except for VAT. Ancillary costs (such as commission, packaging, transportation and insurance) to the first place of destination within France should also be added to the taxable basis. Discounts and rebates come as a deduction to the taxable basis.

Imported software is taxed on the total value (in the case of standard software) or on the sole value of the carrier (in the case of specific software). The value of the information is treated as a service (see section 4.2.2 'Intellectual Services').

5.4 Intra-Community Transfer of Goods

Where stock or capital goods are transferred from one Member State to another, VAT is due on the purchase price of the goods or of similar goods or, in the absence of such a price, on the cost price.

5.5 Contract Work

When contract work fulfils the definition given by the law, the taxable basis is the value of the service supplied by the contract manufacturer.

5.6 Chargeable Event/Time of Payment

Different rules apply to goods and to services. VAT on goods becomes due when title passes or when the right to dispose of the goods as an owner is transferred. This is the case even if the corresponding invoices have not been issued. The full VAT will be due even if the price has not been paid for the goods or if it is paid by instalments. When the transaction is made under a condition precedent, the transfer of ownership occurs upon realisation of the condition precedent.

VAT on services is normally due when the services are performed. However, it is payable under the general rule upon receipt of the payment from the customer, thus allowing the supplier to delay the payment of the tax until he has been fully paid by his customer. However, entrepreneurs supplying both goods and services may find it simpler to declare their taxable transactions using the same rule for both. They can therefore opt to pay VAT on services at the same time as VAT on goods ('option pour les debits') which normally coincides with the invoicing. A letter should be addressed to the tax authorities to inform them that this option is being exercised.

Construction works are deemed to be services. VAT is therefore due according to the above rules.

VAT due on imported goods is payable at the time of customs clearance.

VAT due is paid every month on the goods delivered and the monies received for services during the previous month (see section 9.4 'VAT Returns').

5.7   Credit Notes/Bad Debts

A refund of VAT can be obtained by an entrepreneur who issues a credit note to his customer.

VAT on uncollected debts can be recovered by the supplier provided a special procedure is followed.

6   TAX RATES

The following main rates currently apply in France:

2.1%:   newspapers and certain medicines

5.5%:   food, water, medicine, certain products from agriculture and fishing, transport of persons, books, lodgings, hotel accommodation, original works of art, equipment for the handicapped, services of lawyers in case of juridical assistance, renting of camping space, services relating to the press, transfer of copyrights by the authors or artists, transfer of copyright on books, meals supplied in canteens or hospitals, subscriptions for supply of water, gas, heating, etc

9.5%:   for the overseas departments of Martinique, Guadeloupe and Réunion

18.6%:   all other supplies of goods or services which are not exempt or not subject to another specified rate.

7   EXEMPTIONS

A transaction is considered as exempt when, while being within the scope of VAT, it is excluded from being subject to the tax by a special provision of the law. As a rule, exempt supplies prevent an entrepreneur from recovering the tax incurred on purchases made in connection with these exempt supplies. However, the law provides that a number of exempt supplies are entitled to input credit.

7.1   Exemptions with Credit for Input Tax

The following exemptions are with credit for input tax:

■   goods transported out of France by a resident or non-resident entrepreneur
■   delivery of goods to be placed under customs duty suspensions
■   services connected with goods under customs duty suspensions, such as transportation, handling, warehousing and packaging

- insurance expertise on exported goods
- work and repairs performed for the account of a foreign client on goods to be exported
- services connected with the importation of goods, the cost of which has already been included in the amount on which tax at importation was based
- sale and renting of ships and aircraft engaged in international trade or professional fishing
- repair, transformation and maintenance performed on ships and aircraft as mentioned above
- international transport of persons or goods
- equipment subsidies granted by the government or municipalities
- financial and banking services when supplied to non-European Union recipients
- insurance and reinsurance services when supplied to non-European Union recipients
- certain importations and intra-Community transactions
- services of travel agents relating to services performed outside the European Union.

Exporters may purchase in France, free of VAT, goods and related services which they intend to export up to a limit equal to their export transactions of the preceding year (implementation of Article 16.2 of the Sixth VAT Directive).

7.2   Exemption without Credit for Input Tax
The following exemptions are without credit for input tax:

- medical care or services provided by hospitals, doctors, dentists and laboratories
- collection, storage and supply of human blood, milk or organs
- social or cultural services of associations or foundations
- educational services provided by schools, universities and private teachers
- state postal services
- insurance and reinsurance transactions (input tax may be creditable in certain cases)
- financial and banking services (input tax may be recovered in limited cases)
- reimbursement of joint expenses by members of independent groups of persons exempt or not subject to VAT
- leasing of unfurnished residential or commercial buildings
- subsidies obtained for non-taxable transactions
- supply of goods and services by non-profit making organisations (under certain conditions).

7.3   Exempt Imports
Limited exemptions apply to goods introduced into France by travellers. Personal and household belongings are not taxed when someone is setting up his main residence in France. VAT relief is also available under certain conditions for goods which are temporarily imported or which are re-imported after repair abroad. The importation of goods which is followed by an intra-Community supply may be exempt (see section 7.7.2 of the Introduction to the European Union).

7.4   Non-Taxable Transactions

7.4.1 Transactions within the Same Legal Entity
Supplies within the same legal entity are not taxable. Supply of services made between a

foreign head office and its branch in France (or vice versa) are treated as internal non-taxable transactions.

7.4.2 Transfer of Business

The transfer of a business or of a complete and independent branch of activity is not subject to VAT. This exemption does not prevent the recovery of the input VAT paid in relation to the transfer.

7.4.3 Subsidies/Penalty Payments/Compensation

Subsidies granted by government bodies are generally liable to VAT when they are directly linked to the cost of a taxable supply, or when they purport to offset operating losses.

Subsidies granted by one company to another (often referred to as a waiver of debt) are liable to VAT when the two companies have commercial links. The tax is due by the beneficiary of the subsidy if he is established in France. When the links are only financial no VAT is due on the amount of the subsidy.

Generally the VAT status of subsidies is a difficult area and professional advice should be obtained to ensure that it is correctly treated.

Penalty payments made for premature termination of contracts are normally liable to VAT.

Monies paid in compensation for damage caused are not subject to VAT. Careful analysis is nevertheless required to establish that the compensation cannot be considered as being part of a taxable operation.

7.5   Election to be Subject to VAT

Taxable persons making certain exempt supplies may elect to be subject to VAT. Election will enable them to charge VAT and correspondingly recover the input tax relating to these supplies. Election may be made for the following activities:

- leasing of agricultural property
- leasing of unfurnished real property for business purposes
- supply of certain services by municipalities (for example, supply of water)
- banking and financial services (election is possible only for a limited number of specified translations)
- farming
- distance sellers (see section 3.3)
- non-taxable legal persons, government bodies, etc (see section 2.3).

8   CREDIT/REFUND FOR INPUT TAX

8.1   General Rule

The principle is that all the VAT paid on goods and services by a French entrepreneur is recoverable.

However, this principle applies only if the input tax was incurred with a view to achieving taxable transactions. This important restriction prevents entrepreneurs from recovering input VAT on:

- goods and services obtained for exempt supplies. However, exports and international trade transactions are allowed a full deduction even though they are exempt from VAT
- goods and services used for private consumption. This also applies to hotel accommodation, travel and restaurant expenses paid by companies for their employees or third parties
- goods or services used to provide goods or services free of charge or at a price very much below market price (with the exception of gifts of a very small value).

No credit is available for input tax on:

- private cars even when used in the course of business. The same restriction applies to services obtained in connection with private cars such as repairs, transport and renting. Van-type cars are subject to the 18.6% standard rate and input tax is recoverable
- petrol
- leisure boats
- cycles and motorcycles
- private planes and helicopters
- transport of persons (by road, air, railway, etc) and ancillary services such as reservations
- hotel accommodation, entertainment expenses
- services connected to goods for which input tax recovery is not allowed (car repairs, commissions, etc).

8.2   Adjustment of Entitlement to Credit

A credit for input VAT obtained in respect of capital assets may have to be adjusted if one of the following events occurs before the beginning of the fourth year (for movable goods) or the ninth year (for immovable goods) following purchase:

- transfer of the capital assets (for consideration or free of charge), if the transaction is not subject to VAT on the total value of the transaction
- transfer of the capital assets from a taxable to an exempt sector of activity
- termination of business
- termination of all taxable activities.

Part of the input tax will have to be repaid on a pro rata time basis.

In a similar way, if credit for input VAT was not available or only partially available at the time of the acquisition of the asset, an additional credit may be obtained if the asset goods are sold within the same period (four or nine years) and if the sale is subject to VAT on the total price and not only on the margin.

8.3   Partial Exemption

Entrepreneurs may realise transactions which are within the scope of VAT (whether taxable or exempt) as well as transactions outside the scope of VAT. The recovery of the input tax will depend on the analysis of these various types of transactions. A law of 30 December 1993 has introduced new rules for deduction. The analysis must be made in two steps as described below.

- ■ ***Transactions Outside the Scope of VAT:*** only the tax incurred on goods or services used for taxable transactions can be recovered (unless a specific disallowance exists). The input tax incurred for transactions outside the scope of VAT cannot be recovered. Goods and services used for both outside the scope transactions and within the scope transactions allow a deduction of input tax in proportion of their 'physical' allocation to the taxable transactions. The allocation can be made transaction by transaction or by using an appropriate allocation key for all the expenses concerned, using for instance the information provided by analytical accountings.
- ■ ***Transactions within the Scope of VAT (Taxable and Exempt):*** If the goods or services purchased can be attributed to being used for taxable supplies the credit for input VAT will be fully allowed. On the other hand, if attribution is made to exempt supplies, it will be totally disallowed.

The allocation rule is used for goods other than capital goods. As far as capital goods are concerned, the Tax Administration considers them to have a mixed allocation (exempt and taxable transactions). Their creditable input tax is calculated by applying the ratio of the turnover relating to taxable supplies over the total turnover. However, the position of the Tax Administration could be challenged on the basis of a decision of the Supreme Administrative Court.

The applicable ratio is calculated for each calendar year. During the year a provisional ratio is used either based on that of the previous year or, in the case of a new business, on anticipated sales. The final ratio must be determined at the latest by 25 April of the following year and the credit obtained for the previous year must be adjusted accordingly.

8.4   Time of Recovery
Input VAT cannot be recovered before it has actually been accounted for by the supplier. Consequently it becomes creditable normally as soon as the goods are supplied and the services have actually been performed.

The delay of one month which was applicable in France for recovery of VAT on all supply of goods and services (except capital goods) was replaced on 1 July 1993 by the rule mentioned above.

However, France allows payment of VAT on services at the time they are actually paid. The time of recovery for the client is therefore postponed until payment has occurred.

When recoverable input VAT is in excess of output VAT an application can be made to the tax authorities to obtain a refund of the excess.

8.5   Refund for Foreign Entrepreneurs
Foreign entrepreneurs not established in France and who do not supply goods or services in France may obtain a refund of the VAT paid on goods or services purchased in France, as well as of the VAT incurred at the time of importation under the Eighth or Thirteenth Council Directives.

Claims for refunds must be requested on a special form addressed to:

> DSGI – Service de Remboursement de TVA
> 9 Rue d'Uzes
> 75084 PARIS CEDEX 02
> France

The claim must be completed in French and filed at the latest before 30 June following the end of the calendar year during which the VAT was paid in France. The original invoices and/or import documents must accompany the claim together with a certificate (provided by the foreign tax authorities) establishing that the foreign entrepreneur is a taxable person in his country. In the case of refunds concerning services, proof of the payment by the client must also be supplied (this is due to the special rule permitting payment of the VAT only upon settlement of the invoice). The claim may be submitted directly by the foreign European Union entrepreneur; no VAT representative is required.

Entrepreneurs from outside the European Union must prove (in addition to the above requirements) that the VAT for which they are claiming a refund was paid in order to market their products in France or to supply certain services (such as 9.2 (e) services). Non European Union entrepreneurs must appoint a VAT representative in France to file the claim in their names.

For the purpose of refund, the French overseas departments (Martinique, Guadeloupe, Reunion, and Guyana), the Canary Islands, Ceuta and Melilla are considered to be members of the European Union.

No recovery is available for a number of items (see section 8.1 'General Rule').

9   ADMINISTRATIVE OBLIGATIONS

9.1   Registration
An entrepreneur who is engaged in an industrial, commercial or professional activity is subject to VAT whatever his annual turnover may be (see section 10.1 Exemption for Small Businesses and Artists/Interpreters).

Within the first two weeks of starting operations, entrepreneurs must register with their local Income Tax office. A VAT identification number will be attributed to them.

9.2   Books and Records
Entrepreneurs who are subject to VAT must keep adequate accounting books to justify all their transactions. When they are charging different VAT rates, their corresponding sales must be accounted for separately. In the same way, transactions which are exempt from VAT must be accounted for separately.

9.3   Invoices
The issue of an invoice is compulsory for all transactions made with taxable entrepreneurs as well as with non-taxable legal bodies. A document containing all the information on an invoice must also be issued for payments on account when they trigger a tax point. Invoices (or documents equivalent to an invoice) must also be issued for all exempt intra-Community supplies or transfers.

Invoices must contain the following information:

- the date and number of the invoice
- the name and address of the supplier
- the name and address of the customer

- the date of the transaction (if different from the date of invoice)
- for each good or service: the quantity, nature, unit price exclusive of tax and rate of the VAT
- for each rate of VAT: the total due exclusive of VAT and the total corresponding VAT
- the amount of rebates and discounts.

It is compulsory for an invoice to be issued for every distance sale taxable in France, even if the purchaser is not an entrepreneur.

Specific details are required in the following cases:

- the intra-Community VAT identification numbers of the supplier and recipient must be mentioned on all invoices concerning intra-Community transactions
- the note: 'Exonération de TVA - Article 262 ter-I du CGI' must be stated in the case of exempt intra-Community supply or transfer
- the note: 'Application de l'article 28 quatre titre E§ 3 de la directive 77/388/CEE modifiée' must be given in cases of triangulation.

Apart from these specific VAT requirements, the invoices issued must show all the compulsory information required by commercial law: supplier's name or corporate name, form of the company (sa, sarl, etc), address, registration number and share capital.

Failure to comply with these requirements prevents the recovery of input VAT and may trigger fines.

9.4   VAT Returns

Every month, the entrepreneur must file a VAT return to declare his taxable transactions of the preceding month. The date of filing may differ from one entrepreneur to another but all filing must take place between the fifteenth and twenty-fourth days of the month following the transactions declared.

Small entrepreneurs (see section 10.1 'Special VAT Regimes' for a definition) are allowed to submit quarterly returns whatever the amount of VAT due by them in the course of a month or calendar year ('forfait'). When they are taxed under the simplified method ('regime simplifié') they may submit a quarterly return so long as their total annual VAT is below FF12,000.

When the return shows a VAT credit, ie an excess of input over output VAT, it can be carried forward and used until completely offset against output VAT. A refund can also be obtained at the end of each civil quarter.

Entrepreneurs whose turnover in the preceding civil year was in excess of FF100 million must compulsorily pay the VAT by bank order.

Upon request, entrepreneurs paying on a monthly basis may be authorised to pay provisional amounts (of at least 80% of the actual tax due) which are regularised the following month.

9.5   VIES Statements

VIES statements must be submitted by entrepreneurs to the Centres Inter Regionaux de Saisie Bonnees on a quarterly basis (see section 7.9.2 of the Introduction to the European Union).

9.6 INTRASTAT Returns

Since 1 January 1993, a new report of all intra-Community transactions has to be filed by traders.

This report ('Déclaration d'Echanges de Biens' - DEB) has a tax and statistical purpose. It must be filed every month either in a detailed or simplified form depending on the volume of intra-Community transactions. Failure to submit these reports triggers a fine of FF5,000 (rising to FF10,000 if not filed within 30 days of an official request to do so). Each omission or mistake triggers a fine of FF100 per error or omission with a maximum of FF10,000.

9.7 Registers

Certain registers of goods movements must also be kept (see section 7.9.4 of the Introduction to the European Union).

9.8 Powers of the Authorities

The tax authorities may estimate the tax to be paid if an entrepreneur has failed to file VAT returns within 30 days of a formal request to do so.

The tax authorities have a period of three years to correct a VAT transaction. The period ends on 31 December of the third year following the transaction when the fiscal year coincides with the calendar year.

An input credit which has been omitted from a VAT return can still be claimed until the end of the second calendar year following the omission.

Failure to submit returns in time entails the payment of interest at the rate of 0.75% per month. Misdeclarations entail an interest charge of 0.75% of the tax due plus a penalty of 40% in case of bad faith or 80% in case of fraud.

Late payment of tax entails the payment of interest at the rate of 0.75% per month plus a penalty of 5%.

9.8.1 Control of the Rules of Invoicing

A new procedure for control was introduced on 1 January 1993. Under the new procedure tax controllers may visit an entrepreneur unexpectedly and request to see all invoices, inventories, books and records as well as all documents relating to transactions for which invoices have been issued. They may ask questions and justifications of the transactions. This procedure is not a tax audit. At the end of the control a report is drawn up detailing the mistakes or errors but no assessment can be made; only penalties for misdeclaration in the register of contract work can be imposed. Where numerous mistakes are found in invoices, the tax authorities can initiate a proper tax audit.

9.9 Objections/Appeals

An entrepreneur may request a reduction or a repayment of his tax if it was wrongly assessed. Claims must be filed with the local tax authorities before the end of the second calendar year following assessment or payment of VAT.

Appeals are heard by the trial court (tribunal administratif) within two months of the tax authorities' refusal. Further appeal is possible before the Administrative Appeal Court and the Supreme Court (Conseil d'Etat).

10   SPECIAL VAT REGIMES

Special VAT rules apply to a number of activities. The general outlines of the main special regimes are summarised below.

10.1 Small Businesses

Small entrepreneurs whose turnover is below FF500,000 (suppliers of goods) or FF150,000 (suppliers of services) may account for VAT according to a simplified procedure ('Forfait'). The amount of VAT due for the year is assessed on the value of the taxable transactions after deduction of input VAT. The taxable basis is negotiated with the tax authorities.

Small entrepreneurs whose turnover is below FF3,500,000 (suppliers of goods) or FF1 million (suppliers of services) may file their return according to a simplified method (regime simplifié).

Small entrepreneurs whose turnover of the preceding year was below FF70,000 are exempt (franchise). They may nevertheless elect to be subject to tax.

Authors, artists and interpreters can benefit from a special VAT exemption if the sale of their works and/or transfer of the rights on their works resulted in a turnover during the preceding civil year below FF245,000. They may elect to be subject to VAT even if they are below that figure.

Small entrepreneurs, authors and artists must be registered with the tax authorities even if they are under the 'franchise'. They do not have to produce VAT returns but must be able to justify at all times through their accounting records that they are eligible for a special exemption. They cannot invoice VAT to their clients and cannot recover any input VAT.

10.2 Farmers

The term 'farmers' should be understood to include all the activities relating to agricultural as well as livestock production.

They may be classified into three categories:

- farmers compulsorily subject to VAT. This applies when their average income over two years exceeds FF300,000
- farmers who have elected to be subject to VAT. Election may be limited to part of their activity or apply to all their activities. It is valid for three years
- farmers who are not taxable to VAT. They all benefit from a lump sum refund intended to compensate for the non-creditable input VAT incurred on the acquisition of goods and services. The refund is made on an annual basis.

10.3 Banking and Financial Institutions

Most of the transactions of these institutions are exempt from VAT (see section 7 'Exemptions') under article 13 B (d) of the Sixth VAT Directive.

They are however taxable, particularly for the following transactions:

- debt collection
- factoring
- management and safekeeping of shares, interests in companies or associations, debentures and other securities

- transactions on gold, silver or other metal coins or bank notes which are not normally used as legal tender or coins of numismatic interest
- commissions received for advice, studies of a financial nature.

They may elect to be subject to VAT for a number of specified transactions, notably:

- credit transactions
- certain transactions in securities
- certain transactions concerning deposit and current accounts
- transactions in shares, interests in companies or associations
- management of special investment funds
- transactions relating to the financing of exportations.

Transactions subject to VAT by law (or upon election) and banking and financial transactions made to the profit of non-European Union recipients or relating to exportations give rise to a deduction of the related input tax.

10.4 Second-Hand Goods

All second-hand capital goods are subject to VAT. This new provision is applicable since 1 January 1990. However, when no input tax could be recovered at the time of the purchase, such goods are exempt when sold after use.

When the sale of second-hand capital goods is subject to VAT, no adjustment of the input tax credit need be made. Partially exempt entrepreneurs who only recovered part of the input tax at the time of purchase can obtain an additional deduction.

Second-hand goods sold by traders are subject to VAT either on the total price or on the margin. If VAT is paid only on the margin, the trader is limited in the recovery of the input tax.

See also section 7.10.2 of the Introduction to the European Union.

10.5 Arts and Antiques

Artistic items such as paintings, water colours, sculptures, tapestries, etc are subject to VAT when sold directly by the artists (see above for special exemption for turnover below FF245,000). The VAT is due at the reduced rate of 5.5%.

When art pieces are sold by traders, the taxable basis may either be the margin or the sale price.

Imports of artistic items are subject to VAT at the reduced rate on the customs value. Importations for auction sales by a taxable person are exempt. intra-Community acquisitions of artistic items are taxable under the normal rules.

10.6 Travel Agencies

A special regime applies to travel agents who hold a professional licence and who act in their own capacity and not for the account of their customers.

The services they provide are exempt from VAT in respect of that part which is used outside the European Union. Travel agents are taxed at the rate of 18.6% on the difference between the payments received and the related expenses incurred during a given period (month or half year). They cannot recover the input VAT relating to their expenses.

10.7 Bonded Warehouses

Goods imported from non-European Union countries into bonded warehouses do not have to pay VAT and customs duty until they are removed for sale in the Community. Importation of goods into a type A, B, C, D or F warehouse is subject to the prior approval of the Customs authorities. The agreement specifies the conditions in which the goods are to be kept. Only minor processes are allowed for goods in bond (packing, handling, etc).

10.8 Free Ports

Free ports allow entrance of non-European Union goods in suspension of VAT and customs duty. All transactions or modifications of the goods in these free ports are subject to customs control. The following free ports are located on the French territory: free ports of Bordeaux, Le Havre, Marseille, Guadeloupe and the free ports of the Chamber of Commerce and Industrie at Longwy and Mulhouse.

10.9 Real Estate

10.9.1 VAT Regime Applicable During the Construction of the Building

The acquisition of land used for construction is subject to VAT at a rate of 18.6%. Builders can normally deduct VAT paid on land and construction work. They can also obtain a refund of tax credits under certain conditions.

10.9.2 VAT Regime Applicable at the Time of Transfer of the Building

VAT or transfer duties on buildings are due depending on whether or not the building involved is new.

If the building is sold before its completion, sales are always subject to VAT at a rate of 18.6%.

If the building is sold within five years following its completion, the first sale (or the second one if the first one was made by an estate broker (marchand de biens)) which takes place during this period is subject to VAT at a rate of 18.6% whether the building is commercial or private.

If the building is sold more than five years after its completion, it is always subject to transfer duties at a rate of approximately 18% (commercial property) or 8% (private dwellings).

10.9.3 VAT Regime Applicable While the Building is Rented

Rented unfurnished private dwellings are never subject to VAT.

Furnished residential buildings let occasionally, permanently or seasonally are not normally subject to VAT. No option to be subject to tax exists for these type of leases. However, some leases of furnished private dwellings are subject to tax when a number of conditions are fulfilled.

Unfurnished commercial buildings are not normally subject to VAT, but the lessor may opt to pay VAT at a rate of 18.6% even if the lessee is not a taxable person; the option must be mentioned in the lease agreement.

10.9.4 Recovery of Input VAT Paid on the Purchase of the Building
If the owner of the building uses it to carry out a taxable activity, he can deduct the VAT paid on the building.

If the owner leases the building he can deduct VAT if the rental income is subject to VAT.

Contributor: Anne Ermel
                      Ernst & Young
                      Cedex 21
                      92095 Paris La Defense 2
                      France
                      Tel: +33 1 46 93 60 00
                      Fax: +33 1 47 67 01 06

GERMANY

1   GENERAL BACKGROUND

The Value Added Tax Law (Umsatzsteuergesetz) came into effect on 1 January 1968. Before this Germany had a cumulative all-stage turnover tax which had been in effect for nearly fifty years. From 1 January 1980 the Value Added Tax Law was amended so as to bring the German legislation into conformity with the requirements of the Sixth and Eighth VAT Directives of the European Community. On 1 January 1993 the transitional VAT system of the Sixth VAT Directive was transferred into national VAT law (for a description of the transitional VAT regime see the Introduction to the European Union). Exceptions to the transitional system in German law are described in this chapter.

The VAT is administered by the tax office responsible for all the tax affairs of the enterprise, ie normally the place where the enterprise is located. VAT matters of foreign enterprises without a branch or fixed establishment in Germany are handled by the Bundesamt für Finanzen in Bonn or by specially determined tax offices responsible for non-resident entrepreneurs.

VAT on imports is dealt with by the customs duty office. Since 1 January 1993 imports are defined as supplies from third countries.

1.1   The Single Market – Intra-Community Acquisitions
As a Member State of the European Union, Germany applies the rules for VAT applicable to the Single Market and, in particular, the transitional arrangements which apply in respect of intra-Community supplies during the transition period which commenced on 1 January 1993.

For ease of reference the transitional arrangements are set out in detail in section 7 of the Introduction to the European Union which precedes this section of the book.

It is recommended that this chapter is read in conjunction with the transitional arrangements.

2   WHO IS TAXABLE?

2.1   General
An entrepreneur (taxable person) is any person who independently carries on a commercial or professional activity. The enterprise comprises the entire commercial or professional activity of the entrepreneur. Any activity whose purpose is to obtain income on a continuing basis is commercial or professional even if there is no intention to make profits or if it is an association acting only vis-à-vis its members. VAT is levied on taxable transactions carried out in Germany by an entrepreneur, regardless of whether he is a citizen or resident of Germany or has a place of management in Germany.

This chapter represents the law on VAT in Germany as at 31 December 1994.

The taxable person or entrepreneur may be:

- a legal person
- an individual
- an association of individuals
- a combination of legal persons
- any other economic entity (ie public bodies as far as they act as an entrepreneur).

Private persons who engage in an occasional transaction are not deemed to be entrepreneurs within the meaning of the VAT law.

Registration is required as soon as the definition of entrepreneur is satisfied. VAT is not levied where the previous year's total turnover (inclusive of VAT) in Germany did not exceed DM25,000 and the current year's turnover will probably not exceed DM100,000. If an entrepreneur applies this rule he is not allowed to show VAT on his invoices. Consequently input tax would not be deductible. However, this treatment can be waived, the waiver binding the entrepreneur for at least five calendar years.

2.2 Transactions with Branch/Subsidiary

Any supplies of goods or services between the head office and a branch of the same company are internal transactions and therefore are outside the scope of the tax even where the head office and branch are in different countries. On the other hand, supplies between a foreign company and its German subsidiaries are regarded as transactions inside the scope of the tax. Under the transitional system this does not apply to transfers of goods from the head office to its branch in another Member State and vice versa. Such transfers are treated as fictitious intra-Community supplies of goods.

2.3 Public Bodies

Juridical persons under public law (the state and municipalities) are not liable to VAT as long as they fulfil governmental functions only. However, if they are engaged in commercial or professional activities, they will qualify as entrepreneurs. They are also entrepreneurs if they make intra-Community acquisitions (see section 7.2.4 of the Introduction to the European Union).

2.4 Fiscal Unity/Group Registration

Under certain conditions, a parent company and its controlled subsidiary company which are financially, economically and organisationally integrated, can be regarded as a single fiscal unit (Organschaft) for VAT purposes, and group taxation may apply. Details of the sales and services of the controlled company are then reported on the returns of the parent company. This applies also to exempt and partially exempt entrepreneurs. Transactions between the parent company and the controlled subsidiary company are considered to be internal transactions and therefore outside the scope of the tax.

The application of fiscal unity (Organschaft) for VAT purposes is determined by the circumstances. A special application to the tax authorities is not necessary.

According to the Sixth VAT Directive, the concept of fiscal unity is limited to transactions between those parts of the group which are located in Germany. All members of the group are registered in the name of the parent. If the parent is resident outside Germany, the registration is made in the name of the most important part of the enterprise in Germany.

Nevertheless, each controlled subsidiary company may receive on request a unique VAT identification number. In such cases, the parent in the above example or the most important part of the enterprise in Germany is liable to account for the total VAT.

2.5   Foreign Entrepreneurs

Non-resident entrepreneurs who do not have their registered office or branch office in Germany become liable to VAT if the place of supply of the goods or services is in Germany. Generally the non-resident entrepreneur performing taxable supplies in Germany has to register with the German tax authorities and pay his VAT liability.

Non-residents who have a domicile, branch or place of management or lease or who let immovable property in Germany have to register with the tax authorities in the same way as a domestic entrepreneur.

2.6   Representative Offices

Representative and information offices of foreign entrepreneurs which only perform activities of a preparatory or similar nature do not qualify as a fixed establishment for VAT purposes (for refund of VAT see section 8 'Credit/refund for input tax').

2.7   VAT Representatives

The appointment of a fiscal representative is not yet necessary in Germany but the subject is currently under discussion at official level.

2.8   Reverse Charge Mechanism

A special provision applies where taxable work supplies (such as supply and installation contracts) (Werklieferungen) or supplies of services (such as intra-Community transport services) by non-resident entrepreneurs are concerned. The recipient of the work supply or the service is obliged to withhold the VAT from consideration and to pay it to his own tax office, provided he is an entrepreneur or a juridical person in public law. Depending on the personal circumstances the recipient may claim this VAT as an input tax (reverse charge mechanism).

In order to simplify the reverse charge mechanism the zero arrangement (Null-Regelung) will apply, provided that the recipient of the supply is an entrepreneur who would be entitled to a full credit if this input tax were billed to him and the non-resident entrepreneur does not show any VAT on his invoice. In this case the recipient of the supply need not withhold any tax.

2.9   Importers

VAT on imports from non-European Union countries becomes due when goods are imported into Germany and cleared by the customs. The importer (transporter, entrepreneur or individual) is liable for payment of the tax.

2.10 Acquisitions

The movement of goods from a Member State to Germany is treated as an intra-Community acquisition in Germany. If there is an acquisition by a German business, the supplier in the other Member State is not obliged to register. If there is a 'fictitious acquisition' (because, for example, goods are transferred at the disposal of the foreign entrepreneur to Germany)

VAT registration will be required for the non-German supplier. Special rules apply for goods transferred by a supplier from another Member State to his German sales commissionaire. At the time the goods are transferred to Germany, an intra-Community acquisition is deemed to be carried out by the commissionaire (see section 7.2 of the Introduction to the European Union).

2.11 Non-Taxable Legal Persons – Taxable Persons with no Right to Recover VAT and Flat-Rate Scheme Farmers

Such persons are not considered to be carrying out intra-Community acquisitions when during the calendar year their yearly intra-Community acquisitions are below DM25,000 and this amount is expected not to be exceeded in the current year. If an acquisition puts them above this threshold they are subject to common intra-Community rules and must pay VAT on their acquisitions (beginning from the calendar year after that year). They must therefore obtain an identification number and submit VAT returns.

The same persons may opt to be subject to the common rules even for acquisitions below the threshold. The option takes effect on the first day of the month in which it is exercised and can be withdrawn on 31 December of the second year following the option. The option applies for a minimum period of two years.

2.12 Supplier of New Means of Transport

Any person who undertakes on an occasional basis intra-Community supplies of new means of transport that are dispatched or transported from Germany to another Member State is regarded as a taxable person (see section 7.2.6 of the Introduction to the European Union).

3 WHAT IS TAXABLE?

Both the supply of goods or services made by an entrepreneur within Germany for a consideration and the intra-Community acquisition and the importation of goods are subject to VAT.

3.1 Supply of Goods

Supplies of an entrepreneur are activities by which he, or a third party acting on his behalf, enables the customer or a third party acting on his behalf to dispose of an object in his own name (procurement of the right of disposal).

A supply of goods includes the transactions between the principal and the commission agent in the case of a commission agency, and a work supply, if the entrepreneur has undertaken the treatment of processing of an item using material which he procures himself, unless such materials are merely of an accessory or ancillary character.

3.2 Imports of Goods

The importation of goods from third countries into Germany is generally a taxable event. Some exemptions apply, for example, for personal luggage of travellers, household goods of persons moving to Germany, goods to be re-exported after a certain period of time, and for goods in situations where the subsequent supply is an intra-Community supply by the importer.

The time for payment of VAT on imports may be deferred if the goods are brought into a bonded warehouse or a free port. In this case VAT will become due if and when the goods are dispatched for free circulation in Germany.

3.3 Intra-Community Acquisition

For the general rules of intra-Community acquisitions see section 7 of the Introduction to the European Union.

3.4 Distance Sellers

Persons who supply goods from another Member State to private persons and persons mentioned in section 2.11 above in Germany may be taxable in respect of such supplies (see section 7.4.2 of the Introduction to the European Union). The threshold for distance sales to Germany is DM200,000 per calendar year.

3.5 New Means of Transport

The transfer to Germany from another Member State of new means of transport is always taxable as an intra-Community acquisition regardless of the status of the supplier or the purchaser (see section 7.2.6 of the Introduction to the European Union).

3.6 Contract Work

In Germany contract work (see section 7.2.5 of the Introduction to the European Union – 'contract work as processing of goods') is defined as operations in which a principal dispatches materials from one Member State to another Member State, where the materials are processed by a contractor, after which the processed products are returned for disposal by the principal to another Member State. This type of contract work is only treated as an intra-Community supply by the contractor (followed by an intra-Community acquisition by the principal in the Member State where the goods are returned to) in circumstances where the function of the goods has been changed by the process.

3.7 Excise Products

In certain circumstances a non-registered acquirer of excise products may have to register and account for VAT on acquisitions of products which are subject to excise duty (see section 7.2.7 of the Introduction to the European Union).

3.8 Assembly/Installation

A supply of goods takes place in Germany if the specific goods to be supplied are located in Germany. This applies even if an overseas entrepreneur has no place of business in Germany. However, the liability for VAT on the supply of assembled or installed goods may be passed to the customer under the reverse charge mechanism (see section 2.8 'Reverse Charge Mechanism').

3.9 Supply of Services

Services are activities which do not qualify as a supply of goods. They may also comprise omission or toleration of an act or of a situation.

Services also include transfers of patents, trademarks, licences, granting of loans, renting of property, staff hire, legal and technical assistance, transportation services, advertising, data processing, granting of licences, etc.

3.10 Self-Supplies of Goods/Services

The application by a taxable person of goods forming part of his business assets for his private use or that of his staff, or more generally, the application of such goods for purposes other than those of his business, is a taxable consideration. The same applies where goods forming part of the business assets are applied to the private use of the taxable person or his staff and to the supply of services carried out free of charge by the taxable person for his private use or that of his staff.

The self-supply of goods and services for which no input VAT was paid (and therefore no deduction is possible) is not a taxable self-supply. The Ministry of Finance has given this interpretation in a decree dated 29 September 1993 in accordance with the judgment of the European Court of 25 May 1993 (C-193/91). Additionally, certain expenses which are not deductible according to the income tax law are deemed to be a taxable supply (for example, gifts to customers with a value of more than DM75 per annum and per customer, expenses for entertainment with customers if the relating accounting requirements are not fulfilled, etc).

3.11 Special Arrangements for the Supply of Goods and Services to Diplomatic and Consular Arrangements to International Organisations Recognised as Such and to NATO Forces

Under the present German VAT law there is no intra-Community acquisition if the goods are delivered from another European Union- Member State to Germany and the customer is an institution described in Article 15.10 of the Sixth VAT Directive. In consequence, a supply of goods which is sent by a supplier from another Member State to such an institution in Germany has to be treated for VAT purposes as a distance sale. If the supplier is beyond the threshold of DM200,000 of its distance sale supplies to Germany in the current year, the place of supply is in Germany.

Under the rules of Article 67.3 NATO treaty (NATO ZAbK) the supplies are exempt. The most important condition of this treaty is that the order for the supply must have been given by an official department of the relevant NATO force and be proved by the official paper, 'Abwicklungsschein'.

Under the conditions of Article 67.3 NATO ZAbK, services which take place in Germany are also exempt.

4 PLACE OF SUPPLY

The supply of goods or services is only taxable in Germany if the place of supply or intra-Community acquisition is in Germany. Therefore, it is important to determine the place of supply.

4.1 Supply of Goods

In German VAT law there was no change in the place of supply rules when the transitional VAT system of the Sixth VAT Directive was transferred into national VAT law.

A supply is executed at the place where the goods are located at the time of the procuration of the right of disposal. This means that, if the goods are physically present in Germany at the time of supply, the transaction is taxable in Germany. However, exports and intra-Community supplies are exempt.

Where the goods are located outside Germany at the time of supply, the supply is not taxable in Germany. Subsequent import into Germany, however, will qualify for VAT on importation.

If the goods are dispatched or transported either by the supplier, by the recipient or by a third person then the place of supply is the place where the goods are located at the time when dispatch or transport to the person to whom they are supplied begins.

If goods are supplied for consumption on board ships, aircraft or trains during transport the place of transaction is in the territory of consumption (see also section 4.2.2).

Special provisions may apply if the goods are shipped to the customer or on his behalf to a third party from abroad into Germany or into another European Union Member State. In this case the place of supply is in the importing country, provided that the supplier or his agent is the debtor for the VAT to be paid upon the importation.

4.1.1 Chain Transactions/Triangulations

The general rules also apply in case of chain transactions. Each entrepreneur within the chain is deemed to have carried out a taxable transaction in the form of a simultaneous supply of goods at the moment of transfer of the power of disposal by the first entrepreneur in the chain to the last recipient. The place of supply for each entrepreneur is determined by the rules explained above.

4.2 Place of Supply Intra-Community Acquisitions

The place of intra-Community acquisition of goods shall be deemed to be the place where the goods are at the time when dispatch or transport to the person acquiring them ends.

4.2.1 Intra-Community Chain Transactions – Goods

There are some exceptions for chain transactions within the European Union (intra-Community chain transactions). Germany still has a different VAT treatment from the other Member States for chain transactions.

For intra-Community chain transactions in Germany the basic rule for the place of intra-Community acquisition is not applicable. The German government has ruled that if an invoice is addressed to a customer in a chain transaction who is registered for VAT in another Member State, the transaction covered by that invoice is deemed to be an intra-Community acquisition in that Member State. Consequently the subsequent supply of that customer is deemed to be an intra-Community supply in his Member State followed by an intra-Community acquisition in the Member State of arrival (A-B-C– contract).

In the other Member States the EC-Simplification rule no.92/111/EEC is applicable provided that an A-B-C– contract takes place. For more details see section 7.4.1 of the Introduction to the European Union. To avoid collisions with other Member States in case of triangulation according to the EC Simplification rule no.92/111/EEC the German Ministry of Finance advises the application of both the German rules and the simplification rule of Directive no.92/111/EEC analogously.

4.2.2 Goods Placed on Board Ships, etc

When goods are supplied for consumption on board ships, aircraft or trains during transport and the place of departure and destination are within the territory of the European Union, the place of supply is the place where the goods are at the time of departure of the transport.

4.3   Supply of Services

4.3.1   General Rule
As a general rule, the place where a service is supplied is the place where the supplier has established his business or has a fixed establishment from which the service is supplied.

4.3.2   Exceptions
There are various exceptions to this general rule:

- the place of the supply of services closely connected with immovable property including the services of estate agents and experts, architects etc is the place where the property is situated
- the place of supply of services relating to cultural, artistic, scientific, educational, entertainment or similar activities, including the activities of the organisers of such activities, is the place where those services are physically carried out.
- The place of supply of the services listed below when supplied to entrepreneurs is deemed to be where the customer has established his business or has a fixed establishment to which the service is supplied. If the customer is a non-entrepreneur resident outside the European Union, then the place of supply of services is the place where the recipient has his permanent address or where he usually resides. Where the customer is a non-entrepreneur resident within the European Union, the general rule applies. The services are:
  - transfers and assignments of patents, copyrights, trademarks and similar rights;
  - services such as advertising or public relations, including the services of advertising contractors and advertising agencies;
  - the services of lawyers, patent lawyers, tax advisers, accountants, experts, engineers, members of the board of directors as well as the legal, economic and technical advice given by other entrepreneurs;
  - data processing;
  - the grant of information including industrial processes and experiences;
  - certain financial transactions and services connected with the trade of gold, silver and platinum (excluding coins and metals made from these precious metals);
  - the supply of staff;
  - the relinquishment of the exercise of the right mentioned in the first item above;
  - the complete or partial relinquishment of the exercise of professional or commercial activities;
  - the procurement of the other services denominated under the points above;
  - the hiring out of movable tangible property, other than means of transport.
- In order to avoid double taxation, non-taxation or the distortion of competition, a special regulation applies to the supply of services by entrepreneurs not resident within the European Union. Thus, if an entrepreneur who operates his business from a place outside the territory of the European Union:
  - supplies one or more of the 11 services listed above to juridical persons under public law in Germany not qualifying as an entrepreneur; or
  - any other services for which the general rule (4.3.1) applies
    then the supply of such services is deemed to be rendered in Germany if the effective use and enjoyment of it take place in Germany.

■ ***Goods transport services:*** the place where goods transport services are supplied is the place where the transport takes place. Cross-border transport to a third country is exempt.

Intra-Community goods transport rules are described in section 7.4.4 of the Introduction to the European Union.

The basic rule for intra-Community goods transport is that the place of supply is where the transport begins. This rule does not apply when the customer has the VAT status of an entrepreneur and uses the VAT identification number of another Member State for the transport service rendered to him. In this case the transport service takes place in the other Member State and is taxable there.

■ ***Services ancillary to goods transport services:*** the same applies to ancillary services (such as handling and storage) connected with transport services as long as they are not linked to an intra-Community transport service. The basic rule is that such services are deemed to be made where they are carried out physically.

■ ***Domestic goods transport and services related thereto directly linked to intra-Community goods transport:*** in principle, the place of these services is where the transport or the related services take place. However, if such services are directly connected with intra-Community goods transport and the customer uses a VAT identification number of another Member State, these services are exempt with credit.

■ ***Work on movable goods:*** the work on movable tangible property and valuations of movable tangible property take place where the services are provided. The services on movable tangible property for an entrepreneur with a VAT identification number of another European Union Member State is exempt (see section 7.4.8 of the Introduction to the European Union).

■ ***Services of intermediaries/brokers:*** for the place of supply of services provided by brokers or other intermediaries, see section 7.4.6 and 7.4.7 of the Introduction to the European Union.

4.4   Reverse Charge Mechanism
Under certain conditions the liability to VAT for taxable work supplies or the supply of services is transferred from the foreign entrepreneur to the recipient of the supplier (see section 2.8 'Reverse charge mechanism').

5   BASIS OF TAXATION

5.1   Supplies within Germany
The basis of taxation in respect of supplies of goods and services is the consideration which has been or is to be obtained for such supplies. The provisions with respect to the basis of taxation are governed by the exchange principle. The consideration must be connected directly with the performance rendered. Consideration is defined as everything which the recipient of goods or services expends in order to obtain the supply, reduced, however, by the VAT itself. The taxable amount does not include amounts received by a taxable person from his purchaser or customer for expenses paid in the name and for the account of the customer and which are entered in his books on a suspense account (transitory items).

The taxable person may not deduct any tax (eg excise duties) which may have been charged on these transactions.

5.2 Self-Supplies

Self-supplies are taxable even without payment of consideration. The application of goods or use of goods for purposes other than those of a taxable business are assessed on the purchase price plus ancillary expenses. If no purchase price is available the basis of taxation is the cost price, the full cost or the expenditure incurred.

5.3 Imports

The basis of taxation of imports is the value of the imported goods according to the provisions of the customs law. Different treatment is applied to imports of equipment used for electronic data processing and containing data or computer programs.

If imported goods are not liable to customs duty, the basis of taxation is the consideration paid. Where no consideration is payable the value for customs purposes is the basis of taxation.

The basis of taxation includes transportation costs, duties and other levies but not German VAT on importation.

5.4 Acquisitions

The value used is the contract price, which may include commission, packing and transport. If the acquisition is fictitious, then there is no change in ownership and the VAT value is the purchase price, cost price or value of similar goods. The value of acquisitions is also separately shown on the VAT return (see section 7.2 of the Introduction to the European Union).

5.5 Chargeable Event/Time of Payment

As a general rule, VAT becomes due at the end of the month in which the goods are supplied or the services are completed. The due date for payment is ten days after the month concerned, irrespective of the time of receipt of the consideration. A one-month extension for payment may be achieved upon application if one-eleventh of the prior year's tax liability was paid in advance to the tax authorities.

Where the goods are not supplied and the services are not completed but a partial consideration is received, liability to VAT arises at the end of the month in which the partial consideration was received.

VAT on imports becomes due at the time the imported goods enter Germany. On application a deferment of import VAT payable may be allowed to the fifteenth day of the month following the month of importation. A security payment is not necessary if the importing entrepreneur is entitled to a full input tax credit.

Furthermore, deferral of payment can be obtained while the goods are stored in a bonded warehouse. In this case VAT will become due when the goods are dispatched for free circulation in Germany.

VAT chargeable on the (fictitious) intra-Community acquisition of goods shall be due at the issuance of the invoice, at the latest at the end of the month following the month during which the intra-Community acquisition occurred (see section 7.5.2 of the Introduction to the European Union).

A taxable person/entrepreneur accounts for VAT on an intra-Community acquisition by reporting the acquisition VAT on his periodic VAT return. If he is entitled to full deduction of VAT he deducts the acquisition VAT as input tax on the same return. However, if the taxable person/entrepreneur is not entitled to full or partial deduction he must pay to the tax authorities the difference between the VAT on the acquisition and the amount he is entitled to deduct.

5.6   Cash/Invoice Basis
Small enterprises with a taxable turnover in Germany not exceeding DM250,000 in the previous year may account for VAT on a cash basis.

5.7   Credit Notes/Bad Debts
If the entrepreneur gives a credit and issues a credit note he is allowed to reduce his VAT liability accordingly. The customer has to reduce his input tax deduction.

The VAT calculation can also be adjusted if the entrepreneur does not or only partially receives payment and proper evidence to prove this can be submitted.

6   TAX RATES

The rates which apply in Germany are:

7%:   foodstuffs, books, services of dental technicians, theatres, orchestras, circus presentations, etc

15%:   all other supplies of goods and services which are not exempt or taxable at the 7% rate

7   EXEMPTIONS

7.1   Exemptions with Credit for Input VAT (Zero Rate)
Where an entrepreneur makes exempt supplies he is not allowed to charge VAT (for exceptions see section 10.5 'Election for taxable supplies') nor is he entitled to reclaim input tax suffered. However, a credit for input VAT incurred in connection with certain exempt activities can be obtained for the following:

- the export of goods;
- the procurement of exports, cross-border transportation services, etc;
- navigation and air traffic services;
- certain cross-border transportation services;
- supplies of gold to central banks;
- certain supplies by the Federal Railway Company;
- under certain conditions supplies to NATO and the Army of Russia in Germany (see section 3.11);
- while supplies of banking, financial and insurance services are exempt from VAT if

the recipient of these services is resident or established outside the European Union, input credit attributable to such supplies is recoverable.

7.2 Exemptions without Credit for Input VAT

The following supplies are exempt from output tax and do not qualify for credit of related input VAT incurred:

- financial transactions such as the granting and negotiation of credits, transactions as to monetary claims, transactions in the deposit business, sale of shares, etc. However, this does not extend to custody and administration of securities (for exceptions see section 7.1 and 8 'Credit/refund for input tax');
- transactions falling under the Real Estate Acquisition Tax Law;
- insurance transactions, including related services performed by insurance brokers and insurance agents;
- the leasing or letting of immovable property except leasing in the hotel sector, the letting of premises and sites for parking vehicles, short term leasing of camping sites or letting of permanently installed equipment and machinery;
- transactions resulting from activities as physician, dentist, etc.

7.3 Exempt Importation

The importation of goods which is followed by an intra-Community supply may be exempt (see section 7.7.2 of the Introduction to the European Union).

7.4 Non-Taxable Transactions

7.4.1 Transactions within the Same Entity

Transactions within the German part of a fiscal unity for VAT purposes, and transactions between head office and branch (disregarding the location), are treated as internal transactions and therefore outside the scope of VAT (see also section 2.2).

7.4.2 Transfer of Business

The transactions within the scope of a sale of a business or a part thereof to another entrepreneur which are carried out for the enterprise of the transferee are not subject to VAT. The requirements of a sale of a business are fulfilled if an enterprise or a part thereof conducted separately within the organisational structure of an enterprise, whether for consideration or not, is conveyed or contributed to a company as a whole.

7.4.3 Subsidies, Penalty Payments and Compensation

Certain transactions are deemed to be outside the scope of VAT because the payments received are not treated as a consideration for a supply. This applies to the receipt of investment grants, the payment of damage claims according to Civil Law, the receipt of subsidies, etc.

7.5 Election to be Subject to VAT

In the case of exemptions without credit, any related input VAT paid in connection with the output transaction becomes a cost factor. There are a limited number of circumstances in which the entrepreneur has the right to waive the tax exemption and opt to tax the supply in order to qualify for input VAT credit. The entrepreneur can opt for each supply separately.

The following exemptions benefit from this option provided the supply was made to other entrepreneurs:

■   certain financial transactions;

■   supplies falling under the Real Estate Acquisition Tax Law to the extent that the recipient uses the supplies exclusively for activities chargeable for VAT;

■   supplies of immovable property provided the property is not used for habitation or non-entrepreneurial purposes and the recipient uses the property exclusively for activities chargeable for VAT;

■   certain supplies relating to the use of common property by apartment owners;

■   activities of blind persons who do not employ more than two persons.

Certain other persons/bodies may also elect to become taxable persons:

■   distance sellers (see section 3.4);

■   non-taxable legal entities and government bodies – (see section 7.2.4 of the Introduction to the European Union).

For more details see section 10.4 below.

8   CREDIT/REFUND FOR INPUT TAX

8.1   *General Rule*

The entrepreneur can deduct the following input tax:

■   tax suffered on supplies of goods or services which were carried out for his enterprise (not for private purposes), provided the input tax is shown separately in the invoice;

■   VAT paid in respect of goods imported for his enterprise (VAT on import);.

■   VAT paid on intra-Community acquisition.

8.2   *Exceptions*

Excluded from input tax deductions is the VAT paid on supplies of goods and services, on intra-Community acquisitions and on imports which the entrepreneur uses for the execution of the following supplies:

■   tax-exempt transactions;

■   transactions carried out abroad which would be tax-exempt if executed within Germany;

■   supplies of goods and other services carried out without consideration which would be tax-exempt if executed for consideration.

This exclusion from input tax deduction does not apply if the related transaction is or would be:

■   a tax-exempt export of goods;

■   a tax-exempt supply of certain financial services and related directly to goods exported into a territory outside the European Union;

■   a tax-exempt supply of certain financial services where the recipient of the services is resident outside the European Union, or the recipient is resident in a European

Union country but the service is directly related to an export of goods in a non-European Union country.

8.3 Adjustment of Entitlement to Credit

An adjustment of entitlement to input tax credit will be made on a pro- rata basis if the circumstances governing the tax deduction in the first calendar year of use changes within the first five years (ten years in the case of immovable property). This will lead to additional credits or additional tax liabilities depending on whether the use of the goods changes from exempt to taxable transactions or vice versa.

8.4 Partial Exemption

As regards purchases of goods and services which are used by a taxable person – both for supplies in respect of which VAT is deductible and supplies in respect of which VAT is not deductible – such proportion of the VAT suffered shall be non-deductible as it is economically attributable to supplies which lead to exclusion from input tax deduction. The entrepreneur may estimate this proportion in an appropriate way.

8.5 Time of Recovery

Input credit can be claimed for the month in which the supply was made if the entrepreneur is in possession of the appropriate invoice. If the input tax exceeds the output VAT the balance will be refunded upon application.

8.6 Refund to Foreign Entrepreneurs

Non-resident entrepreneurs who have neither their registered office nor branch office in Germany and who do not make taxable supplies in Germany or whose supplies are taxed under the reverse charge mechanism are entitled to recover VAT billed to them by applying a special refund procedure. The non-resident entrepreneur has to register with:

> Bundesamt für Finanzen
> Postfach
> 53225 Bonn
> Germany

or with a responsible district tax office.

The refund must be claimed by using special forms common to all European Union Member States which indicate the aggregate amount of input tax to be refunded. The request must be sent, together with a certificate indicating that the applicant is registered as an entrepreneur in his country of residence and with the original invoices showing the amount of VAT, not later than six months after the end of the calendar year concerned. An extension to the last date for filing may be applied for prior to the end of the six-month period.

The period of time for which a refund of input VAT may be claimed can vary but cannot be for less than three months (unless it is the end of the calendar year) or more than one calendar year. The minimum amount of refunds claimed must be DM400. However, if the period of time for which the refund is claimed is equal to a calendar year, or if the refund is claimed for the last part of the calendar year, the amount claimed must be at least DM50. The tax authorities will issue a tax assessment notice indicating the amount of refund. Repayment of VAT takes about three to six months.

The refund may be claimed by entrepreneurs resident both within and outside the European Union.

It is not necessary to appoint a fiscal representative for VAT purposes; however, for practical reasons it is advisable to authorise a tax adviser to handle the formalities.

Where the non-resident entrepreneur provides taxable supplies of goods in Germany he has to register with the competent tax office and to file monthly/quarterly/yearly VAT returns. A surplus of input tax will be refunded.

9   ADMINISTRATIVE OBLIGATIONS

9.1   Registration

Every entrepreneur who carries out taxable transactions in Germany must register with the local tax office where the enterprise is located irrespective of the amount of turnover. Since 1 March 1995, however, there is one central competent tax office for a foreign entrepreneur, depending on which country he is established. After registration the entrepreneur will get a tax number (Steuernummer) under which the necessary VAT returns must be filed. For transactions within the European Union every entrepreneur needs a VAT Identification Number (VAT-ID-No). An entrepreneur registered in Germany may obtain this number on request at:

> Bundesamt für Finanzen
> Außenstelle
> Industriestraße 6
> 66740 Saarlouis
> Germany

However, a non-resident entrepreneur who exclusively performs taxable supplies where the reverse charge mechanism applies is not obliged to register or file tax returns.

9.2   Books and Records

The entrepreneur must keep accounts in sufficient detail to permit the proper application of the VAT Law and inspection by the tax authorities.

The accounts must include:

- the consideration for the supplies and services separated into taxable and tax-exempt transactions;
- taxable transactions recorded separately where different tax rates are applied;
- consideration received for supplies not yet executed (payment in advance);
- if the entrepreneur is entitled to only partial input tax deduction, the allocation method has to be verified;
- the basis for the assessment of VAT on imports as well as the amount of import tax;
- the basis for the assessment of VAT on intra-Community acquisitions and the related VAT amount.

A special register must be kept of the goods the entrepreneur has temporarily moved to or received from another Member State, eg materials dispatched for contract work (see section 7.6 of the Introduction to the European Union).

These records must be kept for a period of ten years. The tax authorities may carry out a tax audit and inspect the accounts and outgoing and incoming invoices. This can be done as long as the statutes of limitation have not expired, generally four years after the end of the year in which the VAT return was filed.

9.3   Invoices

Every entrepreneur is on request obliged to issue an invoice in respect of all goods and services supplied by him to another entrepreneur and must keep a copy. The invoice must contain the following information:

- the name and the address of the supplying entrepreneur;
- the name and the address of the recipient of the supply;
- the quantity and description of the supplied goods or the type and volume of services;
- the date of the supply of goods or services;
- the consideration for the supply of goods or services;
- the tax amount relating to the consideration;.

It is not necessary to show the tax number (Steuernummer) of the supplier.

In the case of intra-Community supplies it is necessary to show the VAT ID number of the customer.

9.4   VAT Returns

Preliminary returns have to be filed monthly if the tax liability in the preceding calendar year was more than DM6,000; quarterly if the last year's tax did not exceed DM6,000; or annually if the last year's tax did not exceed DM1,000. Both the preliminary returns and the tax liability are due on the tenth day after the end of the respective month or quarter. A one-month filing extension may be allowed if a down payment of one-eleventh of the tax liability of the prior year is made. In addition, the entrepreneur has to submit an annual tax return which is due on 31 May of the following year. Permission for extension of filing of the annual tax return may be obtained upon application. Any tax liability resulting from the annual tax return is due one month after it is filed.

9.4.1 Correction of Returns

As long as the VAT returns are preliminary ones, an application for correction can be filed. The monthly returns are preliminary as long as a tax assessment notice was not issued by the tax authorities. Additionally, the tax authorities may declare a tax assessment notice to be preliminary.

9.5   Sales Listing (VIES)

Entrepreneurs who make intra-Community supplies have to submit a recapitulative statement. This statement should be drawn up for each calendar quarter and must usually be submitted within ten days of the end of the quarter. An entrepreneur has only to submit the statement yearly if his annual turnover of the previous year does not exceed DM400,000 and his intra-Community supplies did not exceed DM30,000 in the previous calendar year and it is unlikely that this amount will be exceeded during the current year (see section 7.9.2 of the Introduction to the European Union).

The statement has to be sent to:

> Bundesamt für Finanzen
> Außenstelle
> Industriestraße 6
> 66740 Saarlouis
> Germany

9.6 INTRASTAT

Entrepreneurs with intra-Community transactions have to report them on a special report to the 'Statistisches Bundesamt' in Wiesbaden. Goods which arrive in Germany have to be reported separately from those leaving Germany for another Member State. For each record the threshold is DM200,000 (see section 7.9.3 of the Introduction to the European Union).

The INTRASTAT has to be sent to the following address:

> Statistisches Bundesamt
> Außenhandelsstatistik
> Postfach 55 28
> Wiesbaden
> Germany

9.7 Registers

Certain registers of goods movements must also be kept (see section 7.9.4 of the Introduction to the European Union).

9.8 Powers of the Authorities: Estimate of Tax Paid (Estimated Assessment)

If the VAT returns are not filed until the due date, the tax authorities will issue tax assessment notices and will assess an estimated tax liability. The period of limitation for assessment of taxes is four years from the end of the year during which the tax return was filed.

9.9 Objections/Appeals

The taxpayer has the right to file an appeal with the tax authorities against a VAT assessment notice within one month of receiving it. Further appeals are possible to the District Tax Court or to the Supreme Tax Court if the tax authorities do not amend the tax assessment notice as requested.

9.10 Penalties for Late Filing/Payment

The penalty (Verspätungszuschlag) for failure to file a tax return in time can be up to 10% of the amount of tax as finally determined (subject to a maximum of DM10,000). The penalty is reduced or not collected if the delay is excusable.

The percentages of the tax amount payable for late filing are as follows:

up to 1 month late	1%-3%
up to 2 months late	2%-4%
up to 3 months late	3%-5%
more than 3 months	4%-8%
in special cases	9%-10%

A default surcharge (Säumniszuschlag) for failure to pay the tax in time has to be paid at a rate of 1% of the deficiency for every month or fraction thereof. No default surcharge is due if the tax liability is paid not later than five days after the due date.

10   SPECIAL VAT REGIMES

10.1   Agricultural and Forestry Enterprises
A special tax treatment with reduced tax rates applies to certain determined transactions in the agricultural and forestry section. Special provisions also relate to the percentage of input tax credit to be allowed as well as provisions on other tax reductions. As a result these supplies are often taxed at 0%. On application the entrepreneur can apply the general tax rules.

10.2   Fishing
The import of fish caught by fishermen resident in Germany and imported on German vessels is exempt from VAT on importation.

10.3   Banking/Financial Activities
Under the general conditions, banking and financial activities are VAT-exempt and input taxes connected with these transactions are not deductible. However, the tax exemption can be waived.

An exception applies to input taxes in connection with financial transactions supplied to customers resident outside the European Union. Therefore, it is advisable to review the transactions of banks or bank representative offices very carefully in order to determine the percentage of deductible input tax.

10.4   Small Entrepreneurs
Small traders resident in Germany whose turnover in the previous year did not exceed DM25,000 and the current year's turnover will probably not exceed DM100,000 do not have to pay VAT. They need not show any VAT in their invoices. Consequently the input tax is not deductible. However, they may elect for taxation. This option is binding on five years.

10.5   Elections for Taxable Supplies as a Tax Planning Idea
As described in section 7 'Exemptions' above, there are a number of cases in which the entrepreneur has the option to waive an exemption if the supply is made to other entrepreneurs. Such a waiver would allow the supplier to deduct the connected input tax. There is no disadvantage for the recipient of the goods or services if he is entitled to a full input tax credit.

The review of this provision is very important where supplies such as the sale or lease of real estate are concerned. The waiver of tax exemptions can enable the supplier to deduct input taxes connected with the construction of a building which would otherwise be lost.

The waiver of the tax exemption can only be effective to the extent that the sub-lessee (the end consumer) exclusively uses the property for taxable supplies subject to VAT. This rule was adopted to prevent the situation where an intermediate taxable company created by the lessor, leases the property to a third party who uses it for dwelling purposes.

The restriction set out in Article 9.2 UStG is allowed by Article 13C of the Sixth VAT Directive.

However, this entitlement to input tax credit will be reviewed over a period of ten years (see section 8 'Credit/refund for input tax'). Therefore, one should avoid making a lease liable to VAT and then selling the real estate on a tax-exempt basis within ten years.

10.6 Free Port Areas

Generally the free port areas are not part of the German territory for German VAT purposes. Nevertheless, under the rules of Article 3.2 Sixth VAT Directive the free port areas are part of German territory. In consequence a supply from a German entrepreneur (U1) to another German entrepreneur (U2) to the free port followed by a supply to a French entrepreneur to France (U3) leads to an intra-Community supply from U2 to U3, whilst the supply from U1 to U2 is treated as a domestic supply in Germany as long as U2 does not use a VAT-identification number of another Member State for this transaction. As a result free port areas are disregarded for intra-Community transactions. Consequently the free port areas are only of importance for transactions from or to a third country.

Therefore, if the place of supply is a free port area the supply is not taxable. However, German VAT law has determined a number of activities where the place of supply is deemed to be in Germany and consequently the supply is taxable.

These are inter alia:

■ supplies of goods designated for use or consumption within such duty free zones;
■ supplies of goods used for the maintenance of private means of transport, provided they are not supplies for the enterprise of the customer;
■ private use in these areas;
■ supplies of goods which are, from an import tax point of view, in free movement, etc.

10.7 Second-Hand Goods, Works of Art, Collectors' Items and Antiques

A special regulation has applied since 1 July 1990 for the taxation of the supply of second-hand cars whenever a commercial car dealer acquires a car from a person and VAT is not due on the transaction. The person transferring the car may be a private person, public body, an entrepreneur supplying the car tax-free or a small entrepreneur whose transactions are exempt. When the second-hand cars are subsequently sold to customers, the car dealers will be taxed on the difference between the retail price and the acquisition price of the cars.

On 14 February 1994 the Council of the European Community adopted Directive 94/5/EC. This Directive comprises special arrangements for second-hand goods, works of art, collectors' items and antiques. According to Article 26a(B) of the Sixth Directive Member States must apply special arrangements for taxing the profit margin made by a taxable dealer of the items described above. Germany has transferred the rules of the Sixth Directive according to Article 26a (B) into national VAT law.

From 1 January 1995 the supply of all second-hand goods, works of art, collectors' items and antiques in Germany are taxable under the same scheme as already described above for second-hand cars. For each transaction the retailer has an option to apply either the margin scheme or the normal VAT arrangement. The margin scheme is not applicable for precious stones and precious metal (ie gold).

There are special rules for intra-Community transactions of second-hand goods, works of art, collectors' items and antiques.

10.8 Travel Agency
Special rules exist for the taxation of services rendered by travel agencies to a non- entrepreneur. Travel services to entrepreneurs are taxed according to the general rules.

11 FURTHER READING

Beck, *Umsatzsteuer Textsammlung*, CH Beck

Birkenfeld/Forst *'Das Umsatzsteuerrecht im Europäischen Binnenmarkt'*, Erich Schmidt Verlag

Bunjes/Geist, *Umsatzsteuergesetz*, CH Beck

Forst/Treptow, *Umsatzsteuer-Handausgabe*, Stollfuss

Hartmann/Metzenmacher, *Umsatzsteuergesetz*, Erich Schmidt

Noll/Rödder *'Das neue Umsatzsteuerrecht des Exports und Imports'*, IdW-Verlag

Plueckebaum/Malitzky, *Umsatzsteuergesetz*, Carl Heymanns

Rau, *Umsatzsteuergesetz 1980*, Otto Schmidt

Rau/Dürrwächter, *Die Mehrwertsteuer*, Otto Schmidt

Rondorf *'Das Umsatzsteuer-Binnenmarktgesetz'*, CH Beck

Schule/Teske/Wendt, *Kommentar zur Umsatzsteuer*, Forkel

Schuhmann, *Umsatzsteuergesetz 1980*, Forkel

Solch/Ringleb/List, *Umsatzsteuer*, CH Beck

Stadie, *Das Recht des Vorsteuerabzugs,* Otto Schmidt

Vogel/Reinisch/Hoffmann, *Kommentar zum Umsatzsteuergeset*, Rodolf Haufe

Völkel/Karg, *ABC-Führer Mehrwertsteuer*, Schaffer

Worner, *Umsatzsteuer in nationaler und europäischer Sicht,* Otto Schmidt

Contributor: Christa Breucha
                  Schitag Ernst & Young
                  Mittlerer Pfad 15
                  70499 Stuttgart-Weilimdorf
                  Federal Republic of Germany
                  Tel: +49 711 9885244
                  Fax: +49 711 9885228

GREECE

1   GENERAL BACKGROUND

Value added tax (VAT) was introduced in Greece with effect from 1 January 1987 and replaced a number of indirect taxes, the most important of which were the turnover tax and stamp tax. For VAT purposes, the territory of Greece excludes the area of Mount Athos.

VAT in Greece is administered by the income tax authorities. However, VAT on import is controlled by the Customs Department of the Ministry of Finance.

1.1   The Single Market – Intra-Community Acquisitions
As a Member State of the European Union, Greece applies the rules for VAT applicable to the Single Market and, in particular, the transitional arrangements which apply in respect of intra-Community supplies during the transition period which commenced on 1 January 1993.

For ease of reference and to reduce repetition the transitional arrangements are set out in detail in section 7 of the Introduction to the European Union which precedes this section of the book.

Only the exceptions to the transitional arrangements are set out in this chapter. It is therefore recommended that this chapter be read in conjunction with the transitional arrangements.

2   WHO IS TAXABLE?

2.1   General
Any person supplying goods or services in the course of business, whether on a regular or occasional basis is a taxable person. Employees are outside the scope of VAT. There is no minimum monetary limit for liability for VAT.

2.2   Transactions with Branch/Subsidiary
VAT is due on transactions within the same legal entity. Services supplied to a branch in Greece by its foreign head office and vice versa are therefore subject to VAT. If goods are involved the rules concerning intra-Community acquisitions or imports apply. Crossborder supplies between a foreign parent company and its subsidiary in Greece are taxable supplies.

2.3   Government Bodies
The Greek State, municipalities, communities and other organisations governed by public law are not considered taxable persons in respect of activities in which they engage in pursuance of their objectives, even where they collect dues, fees or contributions. These bodies, however, are considered to be taxable persons when they engage in such activities as telecommunications, supply of gas, electricity and thermal energy, transport of goods,

---

This chapter reflects the law on VAT in Greece as at 31 December 1994.

port and airport services, passenger transport, running of trade fairs and exhibitions, and making acquisitions from other Member States (see section 7.2.4 of the Introduction to the European Union).

2.4   Fiscal Unity/Group Registration
This concept does not exist in Greece.

2.5   Foreign Entrepreneurs
Entrepreneurs with no establishment in Greece but who deliver goods in Greece or supply services which are taxable in Greece are subject to VAT.

A foreign entrepreneur is regarded as delivering goods in Greece when he acts as the importer of the goods.

A non-resident entrepreneur with an establishment in Greece is treated as a local company and should comply with all the rules applicable to a Greek entrepreneur.

2.6   Representative Office
Representative offices of foreign entrepreneurs are not within the scope of VAT when they carry out preparatory or auxiliary activities.

2.7   VAT Representative
Foreign entrepreneurs with no permanent establishment in Greece who conduct business transactions in Greece are required to appoint a VAT representative who will be responsible for fulfilling the administrative obligations and for payment of the tax due.

2.8   Reverse Charge Mechanism
Where certain services are rendered to a Greek subject the recipient shall account for Greek VAT. The services concerned are:

- transfers and assignments of copyrights, patents, licences, trademarks and similar rights
- advertising services
- services of consultants, engineers, consultancy bureaux, lawyers, accountants and other similar services, data processing and provision of information (but excluding any services relating to land)
- acceptance of any obligation to refrain from pursuing or exercising, in whole or in part, any business activity, etc
- banking, financial and insurance services (including reinsurance, but excluding the provision of safe deposit facilities)
- the supply of staff
- the letting or hire of goods other than means of transport
- the services rendered by one person to another in procuring for the other any of the services mentioned in the preceding sections.

In all the above cases, the liability for the tax is shifted to the recipient of the services.

2.9   Importers
Import VAT is due on the supply of goods effected for consideration by a third country supplier to a Greek subject.

2.10 Intra-Community Acquisitions

During a transitional period which began on 1 January 1993 and which will continue until 31 December 1996 at the earliest, special rules apply to the transfer of goods between Member States of the European Union. These rules are set out in detail at section 7.2 of the Introduction to the European Union.

2.11 New Means of Transport

Any person who undertakes on an occasional basis intra-Community supplies of new means of transport that are dispatched or transported from Greece to another Member State is regarded as a taxable person (see section 7.2.6 of the Introduction to the European Union).

3 WHAT IS TAXABLE?

3.1 Supply of Goods

The term 'supply of goods' means the transfer of the right to dispose of tangible movable or immovable property.

The term 'movable goods', includes energy which may be the subject of a transaction, eg electricity, gas, refrigeration and heat.

3.2 Imports of Goods

Importation of goods means the entry of goods from a third country into the Greek territory.

3.3 Intra-Community Acquisition of Goods

The acquisition (import) of goods from another Member State of the European Union is a taxable transaction (see section 7 of the Introduction to the European Union).

3.4 Distance Sellers

Persons who supply goods from another Member State to non-VAT-registered persons in Greece may be taxable in respect of such supplies (see section 7.4.2 of the Introduction to the European Union).

3.5 New Means of Transport

The transfer to Greece from another Member State of new means of transport is always taxable as an intra-Community acquisition regardless of the status of the supplier or the purchaser (see section 7.2.6 of the Introduction to the European Union).

3.6 Contract Work

If a VAT-registered person in another Member State sends goods to Greece to be processed there and the processed goods are not returned to the Member State from which the goods for process originated, then the owner of the goods will have to register and account for VAT in Greece (see section 7.2.5 of the Introduction to the European Union).

3.7 Excise Products

In certain circumstances a non-registered acquirer of excise products may have to register and account for VAT on acquisitions of products which are subject to excise duty (see section 7.2.7 of the Introduction to the European Union).

3.8 Assembly/Installation

A supply of goods takes place in Greece if the specific goods to be supplied are located in Greece. This applies even if an overseas entrepreneur has no place of business in Greece.

3.9 Supply of Services

A supply of services is defined as any transaction which does not constitute a supply of goods. This wide definition allows a large number of transactions to be classified as 'services'. Such transactions may include, inter alia:

■ assignments of intangible property, such as the transfer of rights over know-how and trademarks
■ obligations to refrain from an act or to tolerate an act or situation
■ the exploitation of hotels, furnished rooms and houses, camping grounds and similar installations, parking places, means of transport and caravans, the leasing of industrial sites and of safes
■ the sale of food and drink by restaurants, provision of entertainment and other similar activities
■ the use of goods forming part of the assets of a business for the private use of the taxable person or his staff or, more generally, for purposes other than those of the business, where the VAT on such goods is deductible
■ supply of services carried out free of charge by the taxable person for his own private use or that of his staff or, more generally, for purposes other than those of his business
■ application by a taxable person of his own services for the purpose of his business where the tax on such services, had they been acquired from another taxable person, would not have been deductible.

3.10 Self-Supplies of Goods/Services

A taxable supply of goods or services is deemed to occur in the following situations:

■ goods are extracted, manufactured, built or transformed by the entrepreneur himself for the use of his own business or for the private use of directors, employees, or third parties
■ services are provided free of charge to directors, employees or third parties
■ when assets of an entrepreneur are used for private purposes by the owner or his staff or more generally when used for purposes other than those of the business.

In such cases, the entrepreneur has to issue a specific document to report these self-supplies to the tax authorities. The VAT is payable by the entrepreneur on the cost of the goods or services provided.

4 PLACE OF SUPPLY

4.1 Supply of Goods

The place of supply of goods is deemed to be in Greece if, at the time the tax becomes chargeable, the goods are within Greek territory.

In cases where a transfer of the right to import goods is effected, the place of supply is considered to be within Greek territory although the goods may be outside the country.

With regard to transfers of goods to or from another Member State of the European Union (see section 7 of the Introduction to the European Union).

4.2   Intra-Community Acquisitions

As a general rule, the place where an intra-Community acquisition of goods takes place is deemed to be the place where the goods are when transportation to the person acquiring the goods ends.

To make a zero-rated intra-Community supply followed by a taxed intra-Community acquisition on which the VAT may be deducted by the acquirer, the VAT identification numbers of the parties involved must be stated on the invoice.

If for any reason the goods arrive finally in a Member State other than that which issued the VAT number to the acquirer, the persons purchasing the goods acquire the goods in the Member State of arrival of the goods. In this case double taxation could occur, since the purchaser must account for VAT both in the Member State which issued the VAT number to him and in the Member State of arrival of the goods.

The presumption is that the place of acquisition is the country which issued the VAT number to the acquirer; however, if the acquirer can show that he has paid VAT in the Member State of arrival of the goods he will not be liable for payment of acquisition VAT in his own Member State.

4.2.1 Chain Transactions

'Triangulation' involves the situation where three parties in three different countries are involved in selling and purchasing the same goods. For example, A in France sells goods to B in Belgium who sells the goods to C in Greece and the goods are sent directly from A to C (see section 7.4.1 of the Introduction to the European Union).

4.2.2 Goods Placed on Board Ships, Aircraft or Trains During Transport

When goods are supplied for consumption on board ships, aircraft or trains during transport and the place of departure and destination are within the territory of the European Union, the place of supply is the place where the goods are at the time of departure of the transport.

4.3   Supply of Services

4.3.1 General Rule

The place of supply of services is considered to be Greece if, at the time the tax becomes chargeable, Greece is the country where the supplier has established his business, or has a fixed establishment from which the service is supplied or, in the absence of such a place of business or fixed establishment, he has a permanent address or habitual residence.

4.3.2 Exceptions

Greece is considered to be the place of supply of services in the case of:

■   services connected with immovable property situated in Greece, including the services of estate agents and experts, engineers, architects and firms providing on-site supervision

■   transport services, if the transport takes place within Greece. The rules relating to international transport depend on the distance covered within the country (see section 7.4.4 of the Introduction to the European Union with regard to intra-Community goods transport services)

■ services connected with the establishment or assembly of imported goods if the related work is performed in Greece by the supplier of such goods who is established outside Greece

■ services connected with the hiring of all forms of transport if the lessor is established in Greece and the lessee uses the asset in Greece or in another member State of the European Union, or if the lessor is established in a country outside the European Union and the lessee uses the asset within Greece

■ services supplied in Greece relating to cultural, artistic, sporting, scientific, educational, entertainment or similar activities, including the activities of the organisers of such activities and the supply of ancillary services

Certain other services are treated differently:

■ *goods transport services:* when supplied in connection with intra-Community transport, services of goods may be zero-rated (see section 7.4.4 of the Introduction to the European Union)

■ *services ancillary to intra-Community goods transport services:* services such as loading, unloading and similar activities may also be zero-rated (see section 7.4.5 of the Introduction to the European Union)

■ *work on movable property:* repairs, valuations, etc of movable tangible property may also be zero-rated (see section 7.4.8 of the Introduction to the European Union)

■ *services provided by brokers or other intermediaries:* the supply of such services which form part of an intra-Community transport of goods – the place of supply is the European Union Member State which issued the VAT identification number of the customer (see section 7.4.6 of the Introduction to the European Union)

■ *services rendered by brokers or other intermediaries:* certain services provided by brokers or other intermediaries which do not come within the scope of Article 9.2(e) of the Sixth VAT Directive – the place of supply is the Member State of the customer which issued his VAT registration number (see section 7.4.7 of the Introduction to the European Union).

4.4 Reverse Charge Mechanism

When a foreign entrepreneur provides for business purposes the following services to a Greek entrepreneur he will not have to account for Greek VAT since the tax will be payable by the Greek recipient. This special rule (the 'reverse charge mechanism') applies to the 'importation' of:

■ transfers and assignments of copyrights, patents, licences, trademarks and similar rights

■ advertising services

■ services of consultants, engineers, consultancy bureaux, lawyers, accountants, data processing and supply of information

■ acceptance to refrain from pursuing or exercising a business activity or a right relating to copyrights, patents, trademarks, etc

■ the supply of staff

- banking, financial and insurance services
- the services of an agent when procuring any of the above mentioned services.

This rule does not apply if the services are provided for private or non-business use.

5 BASIS OF TAXATION

5.1 Supplies within Greece

The taxable amount in respect of supplies of goods and services is the consideration which has been or is to be obtained by the supplier of goods or services.

Incidental expenses, such as commissions, packing, insurance, transport and customs duties are part of the taxable basis.

5.2 Self-Supplies

The taxable basis of self-supplies of goods or services is the cost. Cost of goods may easily be determined as it is deemed to be the cost of raw materials plus labour costs. It is more difficult to establish cost in the case of services.

5.3 Imports

VAT due on the importation of goods is assessed on the value paid by the importer to the supplier. The taxable amount also includes all taxes, duties, levies and contributions paid to the State by other third parties, and also commission, transport and insurance costs, with the exception of VAT.

5.4 Intra-Community Acquisitions of Goods

The rules during the transition period are set out in section 7.5 of the Introduction to the European Union.

5.5 Chargeable Event/Time of Payment

VAT becomes due when the goods have been supplied, imported or acquired and the services performed. The actual payment of the tax is made at the time the VAT return is filed. For filing dates see section 9.4 'VAT returns'.

5.6 Credit Notes/Bad Debts

VAT can be recovered by a Greek entrepreneur who issues a credit note to his client. A court decision is necessary to establish that a debt cannot be recovered.

6 TAX RATES

The current VAT rates are:

4%: books and magazines

8%: products regarded as basic necessities

18%: all other goods or services.

7   EXEMPTIONS

7.1   Exemptions with Credit for Input Tax

There is no zero-rating in Greece but exemption with credit has a similar effect. Supplies which are exempt but which carry the right to recovery of input tax are:

■   export of goods from Greece, provided that the tax authorities are satisfied that the goods have in fact been exported

■   insurance and reinsurance services rendered to non-European Union residents, including related services performed by insurance brokers and insurance agents.

7.2   Exemptions without Credit for Input Tax

Certain activities are not subject to VAT and do not carry a right to recovery of input tax. They are:

■   services supplied by lawyers, doctors, dentists, veterinarians, nurses and physiotherapists

■   the supply of educational services by public or private educational institutions

■   tuition given privately by teachers at all levels of education

■   the income (rent) from buildings, excluding the exploitation of hotels, furnished rooms, parking places, etc

■   hospital and medical care and the supply of goods incidental thereto provided by bodies governed by public law or by other institutions which operate under conditions comparable to those applicable to bodies governed by public law

■   air, sea and rail transport of passengers from within the country to a destination outside Greece and vice versa, and services closely connected with such transport

■   delivery of gold to the Bank of Greece.

7.3   Exempt Importations

The importation of goods which is followed by an intra-Community supply may be exempt (see section 7.7.2 of the Introduction to the European Union).

7.4   Non-Taxable Transactions

7.4.1   Transfer of Business

The transfer of a complete business as a going concern is not subject to VAT.

7.4.2   Subsidies/Penalty Payments

Subsidies received from the Greek government (essentially by exporters or investors) are never subject to VAT. Subsidies granted by an entrepreneur to another entrepreneur may be subject to VAT depending on the nature of the subsidies. Subsidies which take the form of reimbursement of expenses are not subject to VAT.

Penalty payments are not subject to VAT.

7.5   Option to be Subject to VAT

Transactions are either subject to VAT or exempt. It is not possible to opt to pay VAT when an exemption normally applies. However, distance sellers (see section 3.8) and non-taxable legal persons and government bodies may elect to be taxable persons (see section 7.2.4 of the Introduction to the European Union).

8   CREDIT FOR INPUT TAX

8.1   General Rule

An entrepreneur is, in principle, entitled to recover VAT paid on the purchase of goods and services, the importation of goods from a country outside the European Union, and on the acquisition of goods from other Member States of the European Union (see section 7.8 of the Introduction to the European Union) provided such goods are acquired in connection with a taxable activity. However, irrespective of a person's VAT status no credit is granted for input tax on:

- purchase or import of tobacco products
- purchase or import of alcoholic beverages to the extent that these have been utilised in non-taxable transactions
- banquets, entertainment and hospitality expenses
- accommodation, food, drink, transport and entertainment expenses for personnel or company representatives
- purchase or import of passenger cars with up to nine seats for private use, motor-bicycles and mopeds, vessels and aeroplanes for private use or sporting activities, as well as the related fuel, repair, maintenance, rental and circulation expenses generally.

8.2   Adjustment of Entitlement to Credit

The input VAT recovered on capital assets has to be adjusted if the assets are sold within five years. Repayment of the input VAT will be one-fifth for each year the assets were not used by the entrepreneur.

8.3   Partial Exemption

Entrepreneurs making both taxable and exempt supplies are entitled to recover only that input tax related to their taxable supplies. When goods and services are attributable to the taxable activity, VAT can be recovered in full.

When goods and services are used for both taxable and non-taxable activities, the creditable input tax is calculated on the ratio between taxable supplies and total supplies.

The applicable ratio is determined at the time each VAT return is filed.

8.4   Time of Recovery

Input VAT incurred in a VAT period (one month, two months or a quarter (see section 9.4 'VAT returns')) can be offset against the output VAT for the same period.

When input VAT is in excess of output VAT, a refund can be obtained on application.

8.5   Refund for Foreign Entrepreneurs

Foreign entrepreneurs with no fixed establishment in Greece may apply for a refund of the VAT they incur in Greece.

9   ADMINISTRATIVE OBLIGATIONS

9.1   Registration

Registration with the tax office in the district in which the business is located is required by any person who makes or intends to make taxable supplies. There are no monetary limits below which registration is not required.

9.2   Books and Records

Proper books and records as provided by the Tax Records Code should be kept by any entrepreneur who makes taxable supplies. Purchases and sales should be accounted for on the basis of the applicable VAT rate.

For European Union trade, special accounts for intra-Community acquisitions or other transfers of goods must be kept (see section 7.6 of the Introduction to the European Union).

9.3   Invoices

VAT invoices must contain the following information:

- name and address of the supplier
- name and address of the customer
- the tax number of the supplier
- description of the supply
- price of goods or services, excluding VAT
- rate of VAT and corresponding amount of VAT.

9.4   Returns

During the year temporary VAT returns are filed. The date of filing is determined by the category of books of account the entrepreneur must keep. Entrepreneurs whose turnover is below Drs15 million (category A) are required to keep purchase books only and have to file VAT returns on a quarterly basis on the fifteenth of the month following the end of the quarter.

Entities whose turnover is between Drs15 million and Drs180 million (category B) are required to keep income and expenditure books and must file their VAT returns on the twentieth of the month following the end of a two-month period.

Corporations, limited liability companies, foreign companies and any other entity with a turnover above Drs180 million (category C) have to keep full sets of books (journal, general ledger, etc) and their VAT returns have to be filed monthly on the twenty-fifth of the following month. A final VAT return for the entire year is filed within two months from the end of the accounting year. Payment of VAT is made to the tax authorities directly or to the post office upon filing of the VAT returns.

There are additional compliance and administrative obligations in respect of intra-European trade (see section 7.9 of the Introduction to the European Union).

9.5   VIES Statements

VIES statements must be submitted by taxable persons to the regional Inland Revenue office on a quarterly basis (see section 7.9.2 of the Introduction to the European Union).

9.6 INTRASTAT

Traders who supply goods to other Member States or who acquire goods from other Member States must provide monthly details of the goods movement if their sales exceed Drs1,500,000 and their acquisitions exceed Drs5 million (see section 7.9.3 of the Introduction to the European Union).

9.7 Registers

Certain registers of goods movements must also be kept (see section 7.9.4 of the Introduction to the European Union).

9.8 Powers of the Authorities

The following are some of the fines imposed under the Greek tax laws in case of offences (whether committed wittingly or not):

OFFENCE		FINE
(a)	Late filing of VAT returns	5% of tax per month
(b)	Non-filing or filing of inaccurate VAT returns	500% of the non-declared tax

The tax authorities may correct any VAT transactions during a ten-year period.

Taxpayers have a period of three years to correct their VAT returns or to apply for a reduction or repayment of VAT when it was wrongly assessed.

9.9 Objections/Appeals

When an entrepreneur is reassessed by the tax authorities he has to settle 30% of the VAT assessment even if he wants to dispute it. Within 20 days of the tax authorities' report, the entrepreneur may appeal to a first instance court or agree to a compromise with the tax authorities. If the court's decision is in favour of the tax authorities the full amount of the reassessment has to be paid immediately, although further appeal is possible to a higher court and possibly to the Supreme Court.

10 SPECIAL VAT REGIMES

10.1 Farmers

The special arrangements for farmers provide for the return of tax charged on their purchases of goods and services. This return is effected by applying a flat rate percentage increase to the price, exclusive of tax, of the agricultural products and services delivered by the farmers.

Under these arrangements, farmers do not file returns and cannot claim deductions of tax on any of their purchases. The special arrangements do not apply to farmers who carry on their agricultural operations through any form of company.

As in the case of small enterprises, farmers may elect to be included under the normal VAT arrangements.

10.2 Small Enterprises

Small enterprises are defined as those whose annual income does not exceed Drs15 million and which, under the provisions of the Tax Records Code, either do not keep books or keep books of the first category. Excluded from the definition are farmers for whom other special arrangements apply and enterprises which derive at least 60% of their income from wholesale or export sales.

Small enterprises whose annual income does not exceed Drs1 million are exempted from the obligation of filing returns or the payment of tax. This exemption, however, does not apply to enterprises which commence business for the first time. Exempted enterprises cannot claim deduction of tax on their purchases (see section 8.1 'General rule') and invoices issued by them must not include VAT.

The income of small enterprises, other than those which are exempted, is determined on a deemed basis by the application of gross profit coefficients to the cost of their purchases excluding VAT. The coefficients are determined by the Ministry of Finance. These enterprises must file returns in the same way as all other enterprises.

Small enterprises may elect to be included under the normal VAT arrangements and exempted enterprises may elect to be included under the status of small enterprises or under normal arrangements.

10.3 Travel Agents

Special arrangements apply to travel agents who, for the purpose of providing travel facilities to their customers, use the supply of goods and services of other taxable persons. All transactions performed by a travel agent in respect of a journey are treated as a single service by the travel agent to the traveller. This service is taxable in Greece if the place of establishment of the travel agent from which the service is provided is in Greece.

The taxable amount in these cases is the difference between the amount paid by the travel agent's customer, exclusive of VAT, and the actual cost to the travel agent of supplies and services, including tax, provided by others where these supplies are for the direct benefit of the customer.

The tax charged to the travel agent by other taxable persons on the above transactions is not recoverable.

The above provisions do not apply to agents who are acting only as intermediaries paid by commission.

Contributor: George Vassalakis
                Ernst & Young
                Athens Tower
                23rd Floor
                2 Messogion Street
                GR-115 27 Athens
                Greece
                Tel: +30 1 77597840
                Fax: +30 1 7759790

IRELAND

1   GENERAL BACKGROUND

Value added tax (VAT) was introduced in Ireland on 1 November 1972 replacing a combined retail and wholesale tax system which had been in operation for the preceding nine years.

Ireland acceded to membership of the European Union on 1 January 1973.

Control of VAT is vested in the Revenue Commissioners. Internally, administration of VAT is exercised in conjunction with the administration of income tax, corporation tax and capital gains tax by Inspectors of Taxes; at the point of importation it is administered by Customs and Excise.

The VAT Act 1972 is the principal legislation governing VAT. It has been amended by subsequent Finance Acts and is supported by various regulations and Statutory Instruments. It was harmonised with the Sixth VAT Directive of the European Union by the VAT Amendment Act 1978.

1.1   *The Single Market – Intra-Community Acquisitions*
As a Member State of the European Union, Ireland applies the rules for VAT applicable to the Single Market and, in particular, the transitional arrangements which apply in respect of intra-Community supplies during the transition period which commenced on 1 January 1993.

For ease of reference and to reduce repetition the transitional arrangements are set out in detail in section 7 of the Introduction to the European Union which precedes this section of the book.

It is recommended that this chapter be read in conjunction with the transitional arrangements.

2   WHO IS TAXABLE?

2.1   *General*
There is no equivalent in Irish tax law of the term 'entrepreneur' although the term 'taxable person' as used in Ireland serves a similar purpose. Any person, other than somebody acting as an employee, who supplies taxable goods or services within the State in the course or furtherance of business and whose annual turnover exceeds, or is likely to exceed, IR£20,000 from services or IR£40,000 from goods must account for VAT. These thresholds only apply to taxable persons established in Ireland and are not available to taxable persons who do not have an establishment in Ireland. A profit motive is not required; thus, certain non-profit making organisations are subject to VAT in accordance with the general principles.

This chapter reflects the law on VAT in Ireland as at 1 March 1995.

A person who disposes of certain taxable interests in property must also register and account for VAT (see section 10.6 'Real Property').

Any person who disposes of a taxable person's goods in satisfaction of a debt must register and account for VAT. This applies to receivers and liquidators. The legislation also requires the registration of banks which dispose of goods when enforcing their security under mortgages or debentures, although this is not always enforced in practice.

2.2 Transactions with Branch/Subsidiaries

Subsidiaries of foreign firms which supply taxable goods and services in Ireland are treated in the same manner as other taxable persons, even where the goods and services are supplied to the parent company situated outside the State. Services supplied between branches of the same legal entity are not subject to VAT. Thus services supplied between a branch and its head office or another branch are not taxable even if one of the parties is situated outside Ireland. However, the importation of goods (see section 2.9), and the intra-Community acquisition of goods (see section 2.10) by a branch are taxable events.

2.3 Government Bodies

Except in regard to intra-Community acquisitions from other European Union Member States (see section 7.2.4 of the Introduction to the European Union) and certain imported services, for example leasing from abroad, the State and local authorities are not taxable persons in respect of any of their other activities unless the Minister of Finance makes an order to this effect. To date no order has been made. State and local authorities are of course liable to VAT at the point of importation in respect of all goods imported by them.

2.4 Fiscal Unity/Group Taxation

The term 'fiscal unity' is not used in Irish legislation but there is provision whereby several taxable persons, including individuals, may be regarded as one for the purposes of VAT. Where the Revenue Commissioners are satisfied that it would be in the interests of efficient administration, and that no loss of tax would be involved, they may treat a group of taxable persons as a single taxable person. This facility has been extended with effect from 1 September 1989 to include exempt and partially exempt incorporated companies. However, group registration will not be permitted for taxable persons without an establishment in Ireland, therefore cross-border VAT groups are not permitted.

Under this system, with the exception of certain dealings in property, intra-group transactions may be ignored for VAT purposes. One member of the group, the 'remitter', will submit a single 'group' VAT return. The remitter's return will show output tax and input tax for the external transactions of the group. All members of the group will be jointly and severally liable to comply with the VAT obligations of each member.

The Inspector must be advised of any proposed change to a VAT group structure, for example, a subsidiary being sold off and leaving the group or another taxable person wishing to join the group. When a company which has been a member of a VAT group is sold off, the other members will still be liable for group VAT debts incurred while it was a member of the group.

2.5 Foreign Firms

Foreign firms which supply goods or services in Ireland are obliged to register and account for VAT irrespective of the value of those supplies unless they have an establishment in Ireland, in which case the registration thresholds apply (see section 2.1).

Foreign firms which do not supply taxable goods or services in Ireland are not permitted to elect to register for VAT.

2.6   Representative Office

A representative office of an overseas business such as the sales office of a foreign manufacturer which does not make supplies in Ireland is not required to register for VAT in Ireland unless it makes taxable supplies in Ireland.

Where a foreign firm sends goods to an agent or representative in Ireland for distribution in Ireland the foreign firm must register and account for VAT. The agent or representative (but not an employee) of the foreign firm should also register and account for VAT on the services he provides to the foreign firm.

However, a foreign firm which makes an intra-Community acquisition of goods in Ireland and makes a subsequent supply of those goods to a taxable person in Ireland can avoid registration under simplification measures whereby:

■   the intra-Community acquisition is disregarded;
■   the person to whom the goods are supplied is deemed to have made the supply.

The VAT arising on the deemed supply by the person to whom the goods are supplied is accounted for by using the reverse charge mechanism. In practice, the Revenue Commissioners will only permit this to apply where the foreign company has no more than one customer.

2.7   VAT Representatives

A foreign firm is not obliged to appoint a representative or responsible person to act on its behalf if it is making taxable supplies in Ireland. However, the Revenue has power, by notice in writing, to substitute for the foreign firm any agent or manager who has acted on behalf of the foreign firm or any person who has allowed such supplies to be made on land owned, occupied or controlled by him, and hold that person accountable in respect of the foreign firm's liabilities.

2.8   Reverse Charge Mechanism

Persons who receive from abroad, for business use, certain services (such as copyrights, patents, hiring of movable goods, advertising, consultancy and certain financial services) are obliged to account for VAT on the value of the services. The recipient of such services is regarded as supplying the services to himself (see section 4.4 'Reverse charge mechanism').

2.9   Importers

Persons who import goods into Ireland from outside the European Union (including a branch importing goods from another branch or head office) are subject to VAT at the same rate as applies to the supply of those goods within Ireland.

Non-resident entrepreneurs who import goods (ie from outside the European Union) into Ireland through an agent or representative are generally obliged to register for VAT and are liable for VAT on the importation of such goods. They are deemed to import the goods themselves, the agent merely acting on their behalf. A true agency relationship must, of course, actually exist: many traders who act as principals – for example, sole concessionaires or distributors but who are commonly referred to as agents – incur liability for VAT in their own right. Non-resident entrepreneurs delivering goods directly to Irish customers are not liable for VAT on this transaction. In this instance, it is the customer who is the importer and who is therefore liable to pay the tax.

The place of supply of services may be deemed by VAT law to be outside the State (see section 4.4 'Reverse Charge Mechanism').

2.10 Acquirers of Goods from Other European Union Member States

The supply of goods from one Member State to another is treated as an acquisition in the Member State to which the goods are dispatched. If there is an acquisition by an Irish business, the business in the other European Union Member State is not obliged to register in Ireland. If there is a 'fictitious acquisition' (ie an inter-branch transfer where there is no change in title) the 'acquiring' branch will have to 'account' for VAT in Ireland which may involve registration if the branch is not already registered (see section 7.2 of the Introduction to the European Union).

2.11 Supplier of New Means of Transport

Any person who undertakes on an occasional basis intra-Community supplies of new means of transport that are dispatched or transported from Ireland to another Member State is regarded as a taxable person (see section 7.2.6 of the Introduction to the European Union).

2.12 Non-Taxable Legal Persons – Taxable Persons with no Right to Recover VAT and Flat Rate Farmers

Such persons are considered to be outside the scope of VAT when, during any continuous period of 12 months, the total value of their acquisitions has not exceeded or is not likely to exceed IR£32,000. As soon as an acquisition puts them above that threshold they are subject to common intra-Community rules and must pay VAT on their acquisitions. They must therefore obtain an identification number and submit VAT returns.

The same persons may opt to be subject to common rules even for acquisitions below the threshold. The option takes effect the first day of the VAT period in which it is exercised. The option applies until it is cancelled in writing.

Persons who are not otherwise liable to VAT but who are required (or elect) to register for VAT in Ireland in respect of intra-Community acquisitions become subject to VAT in respect of all their other taxable supplies. This does not apply in the case of farmers, fishermen, racehorse trainers and Government departments.

3 WHAT IS TAXABLE?

VAT liability arises:

- on the taxable supply of goods or services in Ireland for consideration by a taxable person in the course or furtherance of any business carried on by him
- on the importation of goods into Ireland from outside the European Union

■ on the intra-Community acquisition of goods by a taxable person in Ireland and the intra-Community acquisition of a new means of transport by any person.

3.1 Supply of Goods

A taxable supply of goods means a voluntary or involuntary transfer of ownership whether by delivery of the goods or otherwise. The term 'goods' includes not only new and second-hand goods but also buildings and land which have been developed or are being developed.

Gifts of taxable goods made by a taxable person in the course or furtherance of business are liable to VAT unless their cost to the donor is IR£15 or less. This de minimus limit does not apply to a series or succession of gifts made to one person.

Industrial samples or advertising goods given free for business use to trade customers such as advertising mirrors, beer mats and industrial samples, etc are not taxable even where the value of the goods exceeds IR£15. The normal rules for input credits will apply but, as this area can give rise to disagreement with the Inspector on interpretation, expert advice should be sought.

The disposal of assets (including capital assets) used in a business in respect of which a VAT input credit has been obtained is a taxable supply and VAT must be accounted for. There is no reduction in the amount of VAT payable because of the time period during which the goods were used in the taxable business. Ireland does not operate the capital goods scheme provided for in Article 20 of the Sixth VAT Directive. Taxable persons are entitled to immediate recovery of VAT on the purchase, acquisition or importation of capital goods (see section 8.1).

A taxable supply of goods includes:

■ the transfer of ownership of goods by agreement
■ the handing over of goods under a hire purchase contract
■ the handing over by a contractor of goods made up from materials supplied in whole or part by his customer
■ the application or appropriation of materials or goods by a taxable person to some private or exempt use, ie self-supply
■ the seizure of goods by a sheriff or other person acting under legal authority
■ the provision of electricity, gas, and any form of power, heat, refrigeration or ventilation
■ the transfer of goods by a person from his business undertaking in Ireland to his business undertaking in another European Union Member State (with certain exceptions).

3.2 Importations of Goods

In principle, the mere importation of goods is a taxable event irrespective of the status of the importer or the nature of the importation (but see section 7 'Exemptions'). Goods imported into a bonded warehouse are liable to VAT (with the exception of alcohol products). The tax is assessed on the value for customs purposes excluding any duties which are not being paid at the time of entry for warehousing.

3.3 Intra-Community Acquisitions

From 1 January 1993 VAT is charged, levied and paid on the intra-Community acquisition of goods (other than new means of transport) effected within Ireland for consideration by a taxable person, and on the intra-Community acquisition of new means of transport effected by anyone within Ireland for consideration (see section 7 of the Introduction to the European Union).

3.4 Distance Sellers

Persons who supply goods from another Member State to non-VAT registered persons in Ireland may be taxable in respect of such supplies (see section 7.4.2 of the Introduction to the European Union).

3.5 Contract Work

If a VAT registered person in another Member State sends goods to Ireland to be processed there, and the processed goods are not returned to the Member State from which the goods for process originated, then the owner of the goods will have to register and account for VAT in Ireland (see section 7.2.5 of the Introduction to the European Union).

3.6 Excise Products

In certain circumstances a non-registered acquirer of excise products may have to register and account for VAT on acquisitions of products which are subject to excise duty (see section 7.2.7 of the Introduction to the European Union).

3.7 Assembly/Installation

A supply of goods takes place in Ireland if the specific goods to be supplied are located in Ireland. This applies even if an overseas entrepreneur has no place of business in Ireland.

3.8 Supply of Services

A supply of services can be defined as any supply in the course of business which is not a supply of goods. It includes an agreement to refrain from engaging in a particular activity or the toleration of a commercial activity carried on by others. Food and drink provided in the course of operating such businesses as hotels, restaurants, cafes, public houses, catering businesses or businesses providing facilities for the consumption of food and drink and vending machines are treated as supplies of services rather than supplies of goods.

3.9 Self-Supplies of Goods/Services

A self-supply of goods occurs when a person diverts to private or exempt use goods which he has imported, purchased, manufactured or otherwise acquired and in respect of which he is entitled to a VAT deduction.

The provision of catering services for employees by an employer is regarded as a self-supply of services and VAT must be paid on the cost to the supplier. This is the only self-supply of services provided for in the Irish legislation.

3.10 Mixed Goods and Services Transactions

Where a contract is essentially an agreement for the supply of services but includes goods (eg a part used in repairing a photocopier) the transaction is treated as a single supply of goods if the value of the goods exceeds two-thirds of the contract price (excluding VAT). Otherwise the transaction is treated as a single supply of services.

Where multiple supplies of goods only, services only, or goods and services together are made for one price, special rules apply (see section 6.2 'Package rule').

4   PLACE OF SUPPLY

4.1   *Supply of Goods*

The place where goods are supplied is deemed for the purposes of VAT to be:

■   the place where the transportation begins, if the supply of goods requires their transportation

■   in the case of intra-Community acquisitions, the place of supply is where the goods are when the dispatch or transportation ends

■   in any other case the place where the goods are located at the time of the supply.

Assembly, installation and incorporation of goods into other goods in Ireland is taxable in Ireland irrespective of their transportation from abroad.

Distance sales of goods by European Union suppliers to unregistered customers in Ireland are subject to Irish VAT if the value of such sales exceeds IR£27,000 per annum, ie the place of supply of the goods is the place where the transportation of the goods ends (see section 4.1.2).

4.1.1   Chain Transactions

Where there is a series of agreements for the sale of the same goods from vendor to purchaser to sub-purchaser, etc and all parties to the agreements agree that the goods should be delivered directly by the vendor to the last sub-purchaser, each seller in this chain is deemed to have made a supply of goods to the next sub-purchaser and is accordingly liable for VAT. The net effect, of course, will be that if all sub-purchasers sell in the course of business, all will be entitled to an input tax credit exactly equal to the amount of VAT charged to them. If, however, one of them is not selling in the course of his business and is not, therefore, registered for VAT, his sub-purchaser will not pay VAT on the purchase. If this sub-purchaser sells in the course of his business he will nevertheless have to charge his purchaser VAT and account for it to the Revenue.

4.1.2   Distance Sellers

The place of supply of goods (other than new means of transport) dispatched or transported directly or indirectly by the supplier either:

■   from the territory of another Member State to a non-taxable person in Ireland, or

■   from Ireland to a person in another Member State who is not registered for VAT there

is the place where the goods are when the dispatch or transportation ends. Non-taxable persons include private persons, fully exempt persons and flat rate farmers.

For full details see section 7.4.2 of the Introduction to the European Union.

4.2   *Intra-Community Acquisitions*

As a general rule, the place where an intra-Community acquisition of goods takes place is deemed to be the place where the goods are when transportation to the person acquiring the goods ends.

To make a zero-rated intra-Community supply followed by a taxed intra-Community acquisition on which the VAT may be deducted by the acquirer, the VAT identification numbers of the parties involved must be stated on the invoice.

If for any reason the goods arrive finally in a Member State other than that which issued the VAT number to the acquirer, the person purchasing the goods acquires the goods in the Member State of arrival of the goods. In this case double taxation could occur, since the purchaser must account for VAT both in the Member State which issued the VAT number to him and in the Member State of arrival of the goods.

The presumption is that the place of acquisition is the country which issued the VAT number to the acquirer. However, if the acquirer can show that he has paid VAT in the Member State of arrival of the goods he will not be liable for payment of acquisition VAT in his own Member State.

4.2.1 Chain Transactions
Triangulation involves the situation where three parties in three different countries are involved in selling and purchasing the same goods. For example, *A* in France sells goods to *B* in Belgium who sells the goods to *C* in Ireland and the goods are sent directly from *A* to *C* (see section 7.4.1 of the Introduction to the European Union).

4.2.2 Goods Placed on Board Ships, Aircraft or Trains During Transport
When goods are supplied for consumption on board ships, aircraft or trains during transport, and the place of departure and destination are within the territory of the European Union, the place of supply is the place where the goods are at the time of departure of the transport.

4.3 Supply of Services

4.3.1 General Rule
The general rule is that the place where services are deemed to be supplied for VAT purposes is the place where the person supplying the service has his establishment or (if he has more than one) the establishment of his which is most concerned with the supply or (if he has no establishment) his usual place of residence.

4.3.2 Exceptions
Services carried out for any work connected with real estate and certain other services, ie teaching, sports, transport, ancillary transport activities (loading, unloading, handling, etc), are exceptions to the above and are taxable at the place where the real estate is located or where the services are performed.

When the recipient is established outside the EU the place of supply of the following services is deemed to be where the recipient is established. When the recipient is established in the EU the place where the services are supplied is deemed to be where the supplier is established when the services are received for a non-business use and where the recipient is established when the services are received for a business use:

■   transfers and assignments of copyrights, patents, licences, trademarks and similar rights
■   transfers and assignments of goodwill, and obligations to refrain from engaging in a

particular business activity or from exploiting a right referred to above

■ advertising services. However, advertising services connected with the letting and exploitation of immovable property in Ireland which is held for business purposes and performed by an Irish entrepreneur for an entrepreneur resident within the European Union (but outside Ireland) are considered to be supplied in Ireland and, therefore, taxable transactions for the purposes of Irish VAT. This is because, as explained above, the service is deemed to be rendered at the location of the immovable property

■ intellectual services performed within the ordinary course of their professional activity by consultants, accountants, engineers and those engaged in the supply of similar services

■ financial transactions engaged in by banks and other financial institutions, with the exception of the renting of safes

■ the supply of staff

■ the activities of agents in relation to the above-mentioned services

■ the leasing of movable tangible property other than means of transport

Certain other services are treated differently

■ *Intra-Community goods transportation, ie the transportation of goods from one Member State to another:* the basic rule is that the place of supply is the place of departure (Article 28bC Sixth VAT Directive). However, if the customer is registered for VAT in a different Member State to the supplier, the place of supply is deemed to be the Member State of the customer, who must account for VAT on the reverse charge basis (see section 7.4.4 of the Introduction to the European Union).

■ *Services ancillary to intra-Community goods transport:* the place of supply of services ancillary to intra-Community transport of goods is not the country of the supplier where the customer is VAT-registered in another Member State. In these circumstances the supply is within the territory of the Member State which issued the customer with the VAT registration number and under the reverse charge mechanism the customer must account for the VAT (see section 7.4.5 of the Introduction to the European Union).

■ *Services provided by brokers or other intermediaries:* the place of supply of such services, where they form part of an intra-Community transport of goods, is the Member State which issued the VAT identification number of the customer (see section 7.4.6 of the Introduction to the European Union).

■ *Services rendered by brokers or other intermediaries:* the place of supply of certain services provided by brokers or other intermediaries (which do not come within the scope of Article 9.2(e) of the Sixth VAT Directive) is the Member State of the customer which issued to him his VAT registration number (see section 7.4.7 of the Introduction to the European Union).

■ *Work on movable goods:* the place of supply of services on movable goods (such as repairs and valuations) is the Member State of the customer where the customer is registered for VAT in a different Member State to that of the supplier. Under the reverse charge mechanism the supply is not subject to VAT in the country of the supplier and the customer must account for VAT (see section 7.4.8 of the Introduction to the European Union).

4.4   Reverse Charge Mechanism

The place of supply of the following services such as copyrights, patents, hiring of movable goods, advertising, consultancy and financial services, provision of staff and some others is generally where the recipient of the services has his business. This gives rise to the 'reverse charge' concept in that the recipient is held to be liable to VAT on the value of the services he has received and will be entitled to the normal input VAT deduction if he is a taxable person. Thus a fully taxable person will ultimately not have to pay VAT, but an exempt person is obliged to register and is not entitled to input credit in respect of such services.

5   BASIS OF TAXATION

5.1   Supplies within Ireland

Where the consideration takes the form of money, the amount on which tax is chargeable is normally the total sum paid or payable to the person supplying the goods or services including all taxes, commissions, costs, and charges whatsoever but excluding the VAT chargeable in respect of a transaction. VAT must therefore be returned on the VAT exclusive price.

Where goods or services are supplied, and the consideration does not consist of or does not consist wholly of an amount of money, and where certain goods are supplied free of charge, the amount on which tax is chargeable is the open market or arms-length value of the goods or services supplied.

5.2   Self-Supplies

Self-supplies of goods, ie the use of goods for which refund of VAT has been obtained by a taxable person in respect of an exempt or non-business activity, are liable to VAT, on the basis of their cost to the supplier. The provision of catering services for employees, by an employer, is regarded as a self-supply of services. Tax in respect of self-supplies becomes due when the goods are appropriated or when the services are supplied.

VAT must be paid on the cost of the goods or service to the taxable person. In practice, the input credit taken is recovered or disallowed; however, there are exceptions with regard to property and expert advice should be sought.

5.3   Importations

The value of imported goods (ie from outside the European Union) for the purposes of VAT is the value for customs purposes, plus any taxes, duties, and other charges levied either outside or by reason of importation, inside the State (excluding VAT) on the goods and not already included. Where the value is expressed in a foreign currency the amount must be converted to the national currency in accordance with European Union rules.

However, goods imported into a warehouse are taxed on the 'short price', ie the value exclusive of any duty payable. When removed from a bonded warehouse by a taxable person VAT will not be payable on any duty paid.

5.4   Intra-Community Acquisitions

The value used is the contract price, which may include commission, packing and transport. If the acquisition is fictitious, then there is no change in ownership and the VAT value is the purchase price, cost price or value of similar goods. The value of acquisitions is also separately shown on the VAT return.

5.5   Chargeable Event/Time of Payment

5.5.1   Domestic Supplies – Supplies within Ireland
Liability to tax arises at the time when taxable goods or taxable services are supplied.

In dealings between taxable persons tax becomes due on the date of issue of the invoice (which must be issued within 15 days of the end of the month during which the taxable supply took place) or on the receipt of a payment in advance of the issue of an invoice. However, if the advance payment is received from a taxable person an invoice must be issued within 15 days of the end of the month.

The time when tax is due can be summarised as follows:

- in dealings with taxable persons tax is due on the earlier of:

  - the date on which the invoice was issued, or the date on which the invoice should have been issued;
  - the date on which payment is received in advance of the date on which the tax would normally be due;

- in dealings with unregistered persons tax is due when the taxable goods or services have been supplied.

5.5.2   Intra-Community Acquisitions
A chargeable event occurs when the intra-Community acquisition of goods is effected. Tax is due on intra-Community acquisitions on the fifteenth day of the month following the month during which the intra-Community acquisition occurred. If the supplier's invoice is issued prior to this date the tax is due on the intra-Community acquisition on the date of issue of the notice.

5.5.3   Imports
Tax is normally payable on imports at the time of importation. However, a deferred payment scheme may be authorised which will defer payment of the tax to the fifteenth day of the month following that in which the goods are imported.

5.6   Cash/Invoice Basis
VAT due must normally be accounted for on the basis of the value of invoices issued in the appropriate VAT period. However, where a taxable person supplies goods or services to the value of 90% or more of his annual turnover to non-registered customers (for example, a retail shop) or his turnover from supplies to VAT registered persons does not and is not likely to exceed £250,000 per annum, he may elect in writing to account for VAT on the basis of moneys received. The cash basis provides automatic bad debt relief. VAT is payable at the rate applicable at the time of the supply notwithstanding that the rate may have changed between the date of the supply and the date the cash is received.

5.7   Credit Notes/Bad Debts
A registered person may adjust his liability for tax in respect of goods returned to him,

discounts or other price adjustments allowed or bad debts written off by him subsequent to his having paid the appropriate tax. A registered person must prove to the Inspector's satisfaction that the debt was pursued through the usual commercial channels and was then written off. A credit note should not be issued and the debtor is entitled to retain the VAT input credit shown on the original invoice.

Where a price reduction has been allowed by one registered person to another after the issue of an invoice showing VAT, and a corresponding tax adjustment is actually made, the person who has issued the invoice is required to issue a credit note showing the amount of tax by which his liability has been reduced.

However, where both the issuer and recipient are taxable persons and they both agree not to make any change in the amount of tax shown on the original invoice, a VAT credit note need not be issued.

6   TAX RATES

6.1   Rates
The following rates apply:

0%:   exported goods, certain animal feedstuffs and fertilisers, books, food and drink excluding alcoholic and soft drinks, bottled mineral waters, oral medicines, children's clothing and footwear, medical equipment for the handicapped; services related to the export of goods such as docking, landing, loading or unloading facilities including the provision of customs clearance directly in connection with the disembarkation or embarkation of passengers or the importation or exportation of goods from outside the European Union

2.5%:   live cattle, sheep, goats, pigs, deer, horses and greyhounds

12.5%:   developed property, building services, newspapers, hotel accommodation, tour guide services and certain car and boat hire, restaurants, cinema, cabaret, museum and art gallery admission, health studios, the disposal of waste material, certain agricultural services, works of art and certain services of auctioneers, solicitors, estate agents in connection with the sale of agricultural land, electricity, fuel, gas (excluding motor fuel), repair and maintenance or alteration of movable goods (including cars), certain personal services and the professional services of veterinary surgeons

21%:   goods or services not subject to one of the specified rates or exempt from tax, including rent where the exemption has been waived (see section 10.6).

6.2   Package Rule (Cocktail Rule)
If an article comprising goods taxable at different rates is sold for a single price – for example, a book (0%) and cassette (21%) – tax is payable on the entire amount at the rate applicable to the higher or highest VAT-rated item included. In the examples given the package would be liable to VAT at 21%. The same provision applies to services liable at different rates or to a mixture of goods and services (see section 3.10 'Mixed Goods and Services Transactions').

7 EXEMPTIONS

7.1 *Exemption with Credit for Input Tax (Zero Rate)*

In all cases the zero rate referred to above works as an exemption with credit because the suppliers of zero-rated goods and services are entitled to input credit under the normal rules. However, the following activities which are exempt from VAT also carry an entitlement to recovery of VAT:

- international passenger transport
- financial or insurance services supplied outside the European Union.

7.2 *Exemption without Credit for Input Tax*

The supply of certain goods and services is exempt for VAT, with the result that the suppliers of such goods or services are not permitted to charge VAT and an input credit will not be allowed where it is attributable to the purchase or importation of any of the goods or services.

They include:

- betting and lotteries
- catering services to patients of a hospital or to students of a school where they are supplied in the hospital or in the school
- charities – certain services of non profit-making organisations
- services for the protection of children
- cultural activities and admissions to plays, concerts, ballet and circuses
- education
- financial services – lending money or providing credit, any dealings in stocks, shares, debentures, the operation of current, deposit or savings accounts, management of certain unit trusts
- funeral undertaking
- collection, storage and supply of human organs, human blood and human milk
- insurance services and insurance agents
- medical and dental services and hospital care together with welfare and social security services provided by non-profit-making organisations
- national broadcasting and television services
- postal services – non-postal services supplied by An Post have been liable to VAT since 1 January 1992
- property – short term letting of property
- sport – promotion of and admission to sporting events and provision of sporting facilities by non-profit-making organisations
- travel agencies and tour operators.

7.3 *Exempt Imports*

Certain importations are exempt from VAT, such as personal effects of travellers, personal goods imported on permanent transfer of private residence, goods used in a business on the permanent transfer of that business to Ireland, temporary imports, goods reimported after being repaired abroad, goods in transit and raw materials for the manufacture of goods which will be exported. Certain restrictions and qualifications apply to some of these items.

The importation of goods which is followed by an intra-Community supply may be exempt (see section 7.7.2 of the Introduction to the European Union).

7.4 Transactions Outside the Scope of VAT or Non-Taxable

7.4.1 Transactions within the Same Legal Entity
Transactions between members of a VAT group are not taxable. Intra-Community transfers between branches are, however, taxable. Input credit will be allowed subject to the normal rules.

7.4.2 Transfer of Business
The transfer of a business or part thereof and the transfer of goodwill or other intangible assets of a business in connection with the transfer of a business or part thereof between two taxable persons is not regarded as a taxable activity. Credit for input tax will be allowed where appropriate in respect of such transactions. It is important to note that the business transferred does not have to amount to a going concern to qualify.

7.4.3 Subsidies/Penalty Payments/Compensation/Waiver of Debt
Subsidies, penalties, grants and compensation payments will be regarded as outside the scope of VAT and thus not taxable if it is clear that they are not received in respect of a supply of taxable goods or services. Premature lease termination payments are however regarded as taxable. A price subsidy is generally taxable and a waiver of debt may be regarded as a price reduction. Expert advice should be sought when dealing with any payments or waivers of this nature.

7.4.4 Intra-Group Lending and Bank Deposit Interest
In practice, interest from inter-group lending, for example, between holding and subsidiary companies, is not regarded as exempt and there is no restriction of input credit unless the holding company is a bank or lending institution. Credit for input tax will be allowed where appropriate. Similarly, bank or building society interest earned by a taxable person will not normally be regarded as exempt income and recovery of input VAT will not be affected.

7.5 Election to be Subject to VAT
The following persons are not obliged to register for VAT but may do so if they wish:

- farmers
- fishermen
- persons in receipt of rents from lettings under a lease for a period of less than ten years
- persons whose turnover from activities which are otherwise taxable does not exceed IR£40,000 per annum (in the case of a supply of goods) or IR£20,000 per annum (in the case of a supply of services)
- European Union suppliers whose turnover from supplies of goods to unregistered Irish customers does not exceed IR£27,000 per annum (see section 3.4)
- non-taxable legal persons and government bodies whose intra-Community acquisitions do not and are not likely to exceed IR£32,000 per annum (see section 7.2.4 of the Introduction to the European Union).

If a person in any of the above categories also has other taxable activities he may of course be obliged to register for VAT in respect of all his activities.

8 CREDIT/REFUND FOR INPUT VAT

8.1 General Rule
In computing the amount of tax payable by him a taxable person may deduct the tax relating to most goods and services purchased, acquired or imported by him which are used for the purposes of his taxable business. No deduction may be made for the tax paid on goods and services used for any other purposes. To be entitled to the deduction the registered person must have a proper VAT invoice or suitable evidence of import VAT paid, eg a copy of the entry or, if payment has been deferred, the monthly control statement from Customs & Excise. There is a special scheme for exporters of goods (see section 10.7).

8.2 Exceptions
As an exception to the general rule, input tax suffered in relation to certain activities which are exempt or outside the scope of VAT is deductible including:

- transport outside the State of passengers and their accompanying baggage
- certain financial and insurance services supplied outside the European Union or directly in connection with the export of goods to a place outside the European Union
- supplies of goods and services outside the State which would be taxable supplies if made within the State
- transfer of a business (see above)
- inter-group lending (see above).

Dealers in second-hand motor vehicles may take an imputed credit in respect of the purchase of a motor vehicle from a private individual or a registered person who did not qualify for an input credit. The amount of the imputed credit is 17.35% of the purchase price.

A deduction is not permitted in respect of tax suffered on any of the following:

- food and drink
- accommodation
- personal services for the benefit of an employee even if the expense is incurred for business purposes
- entertainment expenses
- purchase and hire of passenger cars (except in the case of a garage or car hire trader)
- petrol (otherwise than as stock in trade).

8.3 Adjustment of Entitlement to Credit
There are no special rules with regard to the review of apportioned input credits in respect of capital goods as provided for in Article 20(2) of the Sixth VAT Directive.

8.4 Partial Exemption
Persons who make taxable and other supplies such as exempt supplies and supplies which are outside the scope of VAT are entitled to recover VAT incurred in making the taxable supplies only.

Where the purchases, intra-Community acquisitions or imports are used in making both taxable and exempt/outside the scope supplies, an apportionment of the input VAT is allowed. The allowable input tax credit is usually calculated by reference to the ratio of the turnover of taxable supplies to the total turnover of all supplies. Alternatively, the ratio may be determined on any other basis which may be agreed between the taxable person and the local Inspector of Taxes. Thus, for example, some registered persons may claim that areas, assets, number of employees, employees' time, employees' remuneration, etc which are attributable to taxable supplies represents a more equitable basis for calculating the allowable input credit. This apportionment is normally calculated on an annual basis.

8.5   *Time of Recovery*
A taxable person is entitled to recovery of input tax subject to the rules of entitlement outlined above when he has a valid VAT invoice or suitable evidence of the payment of import VAT. It is not necessary that he has paid for the goods or that the supplier has paid the output tax to the authorities.

The claim to input tax credit should be made in the VAT return for the period in which the invoice or import documents are issued.

8.6   *Refund to Foreign Businesses*
Any person who is engaged in business outside Ireland and who does not supply taxable goods or services within the State may reclaim tax suffered in Ireland on certain goods and services acquired in Ireland and tax suffered on certain goods imported. These may arise in connection with attendance at exhibitions, training courses, the costs of a representative office, agency services, etc.

Refunds will not be made in respect of tax which is not recoverable by registered persons in Ireland (see section 8.1) or in respect of goods or services where the foreign firm's business would be regarded as exempt if carried on in Ireland.

Claims should be submitted within six months of the end of the relevant calendar year but they will normally be entertained for up to ten years. The claim form must be supported by the appropriate original Irish VAT invoices and suitable evidence of import VAT paid to the Customs authorities. European Union claimants must also produce a certificate that the claimant is an entrepreneur in his own country. The scheme also applies to persons engaged in business outside the European Union. It is not necessary for the foreign business to appoint an agent or fiscal representative in Ireland. Claims for refunds should be addressed to:

> VAT Repayments Section
> Revenue Commissioners
> Government Offices
> Kilrush Road
> Ennis
> Co Clare
> Ireland

9   ADMINISTRATIVE OBLIGATIONS

9.1   *Registration*

Any person who supplies taxable goods or services within Ireland in the course of his business or who elects to become taxable (see section 2 'Who is Taxable?' and section 7.5 'Election to be subject to VAT') must register at the VAT office in the district in which his main place of business is situated. This includes persons who supply zero-rated goods and services but excludes persons who make exempt supplies only.

Provisional registration of an intending trader is permitted. When the registration application has been approved a VAT number will be allocated by the Inspector. This will normally be the same number as that allocated to the taxable person for corporation or income tax.

The registration will be cancelled if it transpires that the person is not or has ceased to be a taxable person. The Inspector must be informed of any relevant changes to the business in this regard.

Branches of the same legal entity may in certain exceptional circumstances be permitted to register separately. This will not, however, interfere with the overall liability of the legal entity. Application in writing must be made to the local Inspector.

A person who is obliged to register but fails to do so does not avoid a liability to VAT even where VAT has not been charged to his customers.

9.2   *Books and Records*

Registered persons, including foreign firms registered for VAT, must keep full records for a period of six years of all business transactions which may affect their liability to VAT. The records must be kept up-to-date and must be sufficiently detailed to enable a trader accurately to calculate his liability and the Inspector of Taxes to check the calculation if necessary. Failure to keep proper records could result in a penalty of IR£1,200. A foreign firm may keep its books and records outside Ireland but must produce them for inspection in Ireland whenever requested to do so.

9.3   *Invoices*

An inadequate invoice will deprive the recipient of his right to deduct VAT.

Invoices and credit notes must contain:

- the VAT registration number of the person issuing the invoice with the national prefix for Ireland ('IE')
- the date of supply
- the name and address of the taxable person supplying the goods or services
- the name and address of the person to whom the goods or services are supplied and, in the case of a VAT registered customer in another European Union Member State, the customer's VAT number in that Member State
- a full description of the goods or services supplied
- the quantity or volume of goods supplied
- the consideration (exclusive of VAT)
- the rate or rates of tax and amount of tax at each rate chargeable.

Care should be taken when issuing invoices in respect of zero-rated or exempt activities, or activities which are outside the scope of VAT, that no tax is shown on the invoice. VAT incorrectly stated on an invoice is payable to the Revenue Commissioners.

Where the zero rate applies it should be shown on the invoice as follows: 'VAT @ 0% = nil'. An invoice or credit note issued for VAT purposes in amounts expressed in a foreign currency must contain the corresponding figures in Irish punts – the net and total consideration and the VAT charged must be shown separately in Irish punts.

9.4   VAT Returns
Each taxable person must, by the nineteenth day of the month following the end of each two-month taxable period (Jan/Feb, March/April, etc), file a return with the Revenue Commissioners showing the amount of input tax deductible and output tax payable by him for the period and must pay the tax due by the same date. The return must be in Irish punts.

The Inspector of Taxes may allow some variation in the legal requirement to make returns on a strict Jan/February, March/April, etc basis where, because of problems in a particular trade, the registered person may have difficulty in assembling, for the second month in a period, all the data necessary for the submission of their VAT return by the due date. Any such variation does not permit a postponement of tax due.

A registered person who is in a continuous repayment position, ie an exporter or a supplier of zero-rated goods, may also apply to the appropriate Inspector of Taxes for permission to make VAT returns on a monthly basis which will improve cash flow. Annual accounting is available for certain registered persons (see section 10.1 'Annual Accounting').

An Annual Return of Trading must be completed and filed with the July/August return each year covering the year from the previous September. This declaration is merely a summary of sales and purchases trading figures, in addition to intra-Community acquisitions and imports, at each VAT rate.

9.5   Monthly Control Statement
Taxable persons in Ireland whose turnover from supplies of goods to other taxable persons in Ireland exceeds IR£2 million per annum are required to send each taxable customer a detailed Monthly Control Statement showing the total value of supplies to the customer, details of the allowances and rebates paid to the customer, and the value of gifts and benefits given to the customer (though there is a IR£600 per annum threshold for gifts).

9.6   Advance Payments of VAT
An advance payment of VAT is required on 10 December each year by traders whose annual VAT liabilities for the year to the previous June exceed £1 million. The advance payment amount is either one-twelfth of the total liability for the year to June or the actual VAT liability for the month of November.

Where there is a repayment due to a registered person this will be made by way of cheque or set-off against tax outstanding to the Revenue Commissioners.

9.7   VIES Statements
VIES statements ('sales listings') must be submitted by taxable persons on a quarterly basis to the following address:

VIMA
Newry Road
Dundalk
Co Louth
Ireland

See section 7.9.2 of the Introduction to the European Union.

9.8   INTRASTAT
Traders who supply goods to other Member States, or who acquire goods from other Member States, must provide monthly details of the goods movement if those supplies exceed IR£500,000 and their acquisitions exceed IR£100,000 (see section 7.9.3 of the Introduction to the European Union).

9.9   Registers
Certain movements of goods must be recorded in a register (see section 7.9.4 of the Introduction to the European Union).

9.10   Correction of Returns
If a return needs to be amended this must be done without unreasonable delay. A supplementary return should be filed for the period during which the error or omission occurred and any additional tax paid. Interest will arise from the original due date. Where the supplementary return involves a repayment of tax it will be repaid without the addition of interest.

9.11   Powers of the Authorities
Authorised Revenue officers have extensive powers in regard to the inspection and seizure of records and there are penalties if an authorised officer is impeded in his duty by the registered person or his employees. The officers will normally review the VAT position for a period of two to three years preceding the audit date. However, the statutory limit is ten years except in the case of fraud or neglect where there is no limit.

The Revenue Commissioners may defer repayment of all or part of any tax refundable to any taxable person where they consider that the business activities of that person and of others are so interlinked that it would have been expedient to have applied a group registration to all the persons concerned, and where any of the persons so interlinked has not filed all VAT returns or paid all VAT due.

The Inspector may refuse to allow a group registration or may cancel a group registration without explanation. As group registration is totally at the discretion of the Inspector his decision may be queried but cannot be appealed against (see section 9.13 'Appeals').

Where a taxable person fails to make a VAT return the authorities may issue an estimated assessment of the tax due. This can be displaced only by making a proper return or by proving that one is not a taxable person.

Where the Inspector is of the opinion that a taxable person has underpaid the VAT properly due he may issue an assessment based on the correct figures or an estimate. This assessment may be appealed against. Assessments can be made at any time up to ten years from the end of the appropriate tax period.

VAT is a preferential debt in bankruptcy or liquidation. Tax payable in respect of a 12- month period prior to the commencement of proceedings in bankruptcy or liquidation ranks equally with most other taxes and certain other preferential debts in priority to all other debts.

The Revenue Commissioners may formally determine whether or not a particular activity is an exempt activity and the rate at which tax is chargeable in relation to the supply of goods or services.

9.12 Penalties

The penalty for late filing of returns is IR£1,200. If the person concerned is a body of persons (eg a company whose members have limited liability), the secretary is liable to a separate penalty of IR£750.

The penalty for failing to produce records or obstructing a Revenue officer in the exercise of his powers is IR£1,000.

The penalty for late payment of VAT is an interest charge of 1.25% for each calendar month or part of a month for which the payment is late. This applies also to VAT by way of assessment. The due date for the payment of tax charged by assessment is the nineteenth day of the month following the latest month included in the assessment.

9.13 Appeals

Where a person is dissatisfied with any formal determination of the Revenue Commissioners, with any assessment of the payable amount made on him, or with any refusal or restriction of a repayment claim made by an Inspector of Taxes he may appeal to the Appeal Commissioners, in writing, within 21 days of the notification of determination, assessment or refusal.

The Appeal Commissioners, who are independent from the Revenue Commissioners, are the first Court of Appeal. They hear arguments from the appellant or his representative and from the Inspector of Taxes. If either person is dissatisfied with the Appeal Commissioners' decision he may appeal to the ordinary courts.

9.14 Language

All forms of communications with the Revenue Commissioners, including forms, replies, submissions and appeals may be expressed in either the Irish or English language.

10 SPECIAL VAT REGIMES

10.1 Annual Accounting

This facility is only available to traders who are selected by the Revenue Commissioners. The basis of selection or the criteria used to make such selections has not been disclosed by the Revenue Commissioners but it appears that small net payers of VAT on an annual basis are likely to be selected. Under this system a selected trader must make one annual return for VAT for the year ending 31 August prior to 19 September of that year. The Revenue Commissioners have retained the right to demand payments on account during the annual accounting period.

A direct debit scheme is available for all traders. A trader can, therefore, agree with the Revenue Commissioners to make twelve equal instalment payments starting in September each year. The amount, which is paid by direct debit from the trader's bank account is based on his pattern of payments for the previous year. An annual return must be completed for the year to August and any balancing payment must be made with the return by 19 September.

10.2 Art
Works of art, including paintings, drawings, etchings, sculptures, etc irrespective of age, which have been executed by hand are liable at 12.5%. All mass-produced copies are liable at 21%. Exported originals or copies are zero-rated. (See section 10.14 for details of the margin scheme.)

10.3 Farmers
Farmers are not obliged to register for VAT but may do so if they wish. Farmers who do not register are compensated for the tax they are charged on their purchases by means of a 2.5% flat rate addition to the prices at which they sell their produce and services, etc to VAT-registered persons (they are known as 'flat-rate' farmers). The VAT registered person who buys produce or services from non-registered farmers may claim input credit of the 2.5% addition to the price paid.

Farmers are required to register for VAT if their turnover from supplies of non-farming goods and services exceed IR£40,000 and IR£20,000. Farmers are also required to register if the value of their intra-Community acquisitions exceeds IR£32,000 per annum or they are in receipt of any specified services from abroad (see section 4.4). Farmers who opt to (or are required to) register because of intra-Community acquisitions or are required to register because they are receiving specified services from abroad can, in effect, limit their registration status to these activities and retain their 'flat-rate' status for their ordinary farming activities, ie they will continue to receive the 2.5% flat rate addition.

10.4 Horses
Live horses are regarded as livestock and liable to VAT at 2.5%.

Racehorse training services are chargeable at 21%. The amount on which tax is chargeable is the amount of fees which relates to training only and not those amounts which relate to associated services such as keeping, feeding, minding and generally looking after an animal's well-being. In the practical administration of the tax the Revenue Commissioners are prepared to accept as a general, but not invariable, rule that approximately 10% of the total charge made by trainers relates exclusively to training.

10.5 Postal Services
The provision of public postal services by the Irish post office (An Post) is specifically exempted by the VAT Act. Certain non-postal services supplied by the Irish post office (An Post) are liable to VAT in the normal way.

10.6 Real Property
A VAT liability arises on the disposal of a taxable interest in property in the course or furtherance of business. A taxable interest consists of either a freehold interest or a leasehold interest for a period of at least ten years. The property must have been developed after 31

October 1972 and the person disposing of the property must have been entitled to input tax credit on the development or acquisition costs. The term 'development' is widely defined and includes construction, demolition, extension, alteration or reconstruction of buildings as well as operations on land which materially alter its use. There is no registration limit for property dealings.

The outright sale of a taxable property is liable to VAT at 12.5% of the sale price.

A person who creates and disposes of a lease in a taxable property for a period of at least ten years is liable to account for VAT at 12.5% on the value of the lease. The regulations provide for specific methods of valuation of leasehold interest of at least ten years which are based on the expected rent yield. He must also account for VAT on the value (if any) of the reversionary interest, as a self-supply. The reversionary interest has no value where the lease is for a period in excess of 20 years.

Where a taxable property is developed and leased for a period of less than ten years there is a deemed self-supply of the property and the lessor must account for VAT at 12.5% on the cost of the property (ie purchase price and development costs). Input VAT credit is not allowed in such circumstances. However, to avoid a self-supply liability and where the tenants are taxable persons the lessor should consider waiving his exemption on rents, in which case he should charge VAT at 21% on the rent and will additionally be entitled to claim input credits in respect of the ongoing maintenance costs. This right to waiver does not require the approval of the lessee.

10.7 Relief for Authorised Exporters
Exporters whose turnover from intra-Community supplies and exports (ie outside the European Union) exceed 75% of their total turnover can apply for an authorisation (known as a section 13A authorisation) to zero-rate purchases of goods and services in Ireland as well as imports from outside the European Union. The application must be accompanied by an audit certificate. The scheme is of considerable benefit to exporters, effectively putting them in a neutral position for VAT purposes and avoiding pre-financing large outstanding VAT repayment claims.

10.8 Retailers
Retailers whose supplies consist of goods chargeable to VAT at more than one rate may avail themselves of one of four schemes for the calculation of their output VAT which are approved for different businesses by the Revenue authorities. These schemes are based on the level of resale purchases at each rate but a taxable person may propose any other scheme so long as it is approved before use.

10.9 Retail Sales Exports Scheme
Non-European Union visitors are entitled to relief from tax on certain purchases in retail outlets of goods which are taken abroad by them.

Additionally, in designated tax-free shops, sales up to specified limits to travellers departing the State for European Union and non-European Union countries can be zero-rated.

10.10 Second-Hand Goods and Antiques
Car dealers who purchase motor vehicles from non-registered persons are entitled to an imputed VAT credit (see section 8.2 'Exceptions').

10.11 Shannon Customs-Free Airport and Ringaskiddy Free Port
VAT is not payable on importation of goods from outside the State into the Shannon Customs-Free Airport and Ringaskiddy Free Port. Goods supplied within (but not outside) the Customs-Free area to a registered person at Shannon Airport by a registered person from outside the airport qualify for zero-rating. Goods supplied to a registered person at Ringaskiddy do not qualify for zero-rating.

Goods supplied by a registered person at Shannon Airport to another registered person who is trading within the Shannon Customs-Free Area or Ringaskiddy Free Port also qualify for zero-rating but goods going in the opposite direction do not qualify for zero- rating.

The supply of taxable services to persons within the Customs-Free Area, whether or not they are registered, does not qualify for zero-rating.

10.12 Small Enterprises
Small traders whose turnover does not exceed the statutory limit and who are supplying taxable goods or services may elect to become taxable persons, in which case all the rights and obligations of taxable persons come into operation.

10.13 Travel Agencies and Tour Operators
Travel agents and tour operators are exempt from VAT and cannot recover any VAT suffered.

10.14 Second-Hand Goods
With the adoption of the Seventh European Union VAT Directive new rules were introduced, effective from 1 January 1995, with regard to the sale of second-hand goods, antiques, collectors' items and works of art. Essentially, where any of these items were purchased from unregistered suppliers and subsequently sold by dealers, the amount on which VAT is charged is the dealer's margin thereby giving the dealer an imputed credit for the residual VAT which is still included in the original purchase price.

Globalisation arrangements are available for low value goods which are generally bought in bulk (see section 7.10.2 of the Introduction to the European Union).

11   FURTHER READING

Jim Somers, *Irish Value Added Tax*, Butterworths

Jim Somers, *VAT Acts*, Butterworths

Contributor: Jim Somers
                  Ernst & Young
                  Ernst & Young Building
                  Harcourt Centre
                  Harcourt Street
                  Dublin 2
                  Tel: +353 1 475 0555
                  Fax: +353 1 475 0599

ITALY

1   GENERAL BACKGROUND

VAT was introduced in Italy on 1 January 1973 replacing another general tax on consumption, IGE (general tax on revenues). The Italian name for VAT is IVA (Imposta sul Valore Aggiunto). The harmonisation of Italian legislation with the Sixth European Council Directive was achieved on 1 April 1979.

VAT is levied on the supply of goods and services in Italy made by entrepreneurs and professionals on intra-Community acquisitions and on all imports of goods. For VAT purposes, Italy means the whole territory subject to the sovereignty of the Italian Republic with the exception of the municipalities of Campione d'Italia and Livigno.

VAT is administered by the Ministry of Finance which also administers direct taxes. Within the Ministry of Finance, VAT due on importation is administered by the Customs Department, all other VAT is administered by a specific department through a network of local VAT offices.

1.1   The Single Market – Intra-Community Acquisitions
As a Member State of the European Union, Italy applies the rules for VAT applicable to the Single Market and, in particular, the transitional arrangements which apply in respect of intra-Community supplies during the transition period which commenced on 1 January 1993.

For ease of reference, the transitional arrangements are set out in detail in section 7 of the Introduction to the European Union which precedes this section of the book. It is recommended that this chapter is read in conjunction with the transitional arrangements.

2   WHO IS TAXABLE?

2.1   General
Entrepreneurs and professionals are taxable persons and therefore liable to tax. The definition of an 'entrepreneur' is very broad and includes anyone conducting an industrial, commercial or agricultural activity on a regular and independent basis, including the exploitation of intangible assets. The same can be said with respect to professionals in relation to professional and artistic activities. These definitions imply that:

- occasional supplies of goods and services are not subject to tax
- employees are not taxable persons
- the legal status of the entity qualifying as entrepreneur or professional is completely irrelevant in principle. In other words, entrepreneurs can be either resident or non-resident in Italy, can be an individual or an association of individuals (for example, partnership), a legal entity with profit aim (for example, limited responsibility

---

This chapter reflects the law on VAT in Italy as at 1 January 1995.

companies) or a legal entity pursuing public purposes (for example, the State, municipalities and so on).

There is no income limit below which a taxable person can avoid registration for VAT purposes.

2.2 Transactions with Branch/Subsidiary

Transactions between a branch and its head office are not explicitly regulated. They are usually subjected to tax. According to the draft of a new VAT law currently being discussed, these transactions are considered to be non-taxable. However, the law is not yet in force.

A subsidiary is considered to be an autonomous Italian resident entity and VAT is therefore applicable according to general rules.

2.3 Government Bodies

Special rules apply to non-profit organisations including government bodies such as the State or municipalities. These rules are intended to distinguish between the entrepreneurial activities and non-entrepreneurial activities which are usually conducted by these entities. In any case, in order to avoid distortion of competition, certain supplies are treated as taxable even if not made in the course of an entrepreneurial activity.

If the public entities acting as such take part in intra-Community transactions they are treated as private persons and pay the VAT according to the origin principle (see section 7.2 of the Introduction to the European Union). In the other Member State the supplier will therefore charge VAT on his supplies to public bodies as if they were domestic supplies (see section 7.2.4 of the Introduction to the European Union).

However, if a public body, acting in its capacity as a public body, purchases goods in another Member State for an annual amount exceeding a threshold of L16 million, or if this threshold has been exceeded in the previous calendar year, or when it opts to be treated as a taxable person, the public body is treated as such and such purchases are deemed to be intra-Community acquisitions, taxed in the country of destination.

2.4 Fiscal Unity/Group Taxation

To a limited extent, group taxation may be permitted for VAT purposes. The group can only comprise a holding company together with all the limited liability companies (spa and srl) in which it holds, directly or indirectly, the majority of voting share capital from the beginning of the taxable year prior to the one in which the consolidation takes place.

No consolidation is possible for individuals and partnerships, and no foreign entity can be part of a group.

The election for this special regime must be made each year before 5 March. Group taxation enables the holding company to offset VAT credit and debit positions. Each member of the group remains independent in all respects except for the payment or reimbursement, either periodical or annual. Transactions within the group remain taxable and VAT is computed by each company according to general rules.

There is, therefore, no particular advantage in including an exempt entity in the group (although this is nonetheless possible). The holding company is jointly and severally liable for the VAT due by any member of the VAT group.

2.5   Foreign Entrepreneurs

In principle, foreign entrepreneurs become liable to tax when supplying goods or services in Italy according to special rules (see section 4 'Place of Supply').

A permanent establishment of a foreign entrepreneur in Italy is subject to tax in Italy as if it were an independent entity. Supplies made by and to the permanent establishment are considered to be made by or to an Italian taxable person.

VAT law does not provide for the definition of permanent establishment, nor does Income Tax law. The OECD definition is usually used.

2.6   Representative Office – VAT Representative

A representative office in Italy (as opposed to a permanent establishment) is not subject to VAT. The manager of the representative office may be appointed as the VAT representative. The VAT representative is jointly and severally responsible with the foreign enterprise for the fulfilment of all the duties imposed by VAT law.

2.7   Reverse Charge Mechanism

In certain cases liability to VAT is shifted from the supplier to the recipient. This applies in the case of a number of services which are considered to be rendered in Italy when the beneficiary of them is an Italian resident entity. The foreign entrepreneur may elect to have a VAT representative in Italy who will issue the relevant invoice, but, if no election is made, the Italian entity will pay VAT by issuing a so- called 'self-invoice' replacing the one which could have been issued by the VAT representative.

2.8   Importers

VAT liability arises on clearance of the goods by the competent customs authority. Importers are those who qualify as such according to customs law. It can well be a private person, ie, neither an entrepreneur nor a professional. VAT is levied according to the rules applicable to Customs duties.

2.9   Acquirers of Goods from Other European Union Member States

The movement of goods from one Member State to another is an acquisition. If there is an acquisition by an Italian business, the business in the other European Union Member State is not obliged to register. If there is a 'fictitious acquisition' (because, for example, there is no change in title) VAT registration in Italy will be required for the business in the other European Union Member State (see section 7.2 of the Introduction to the European Union).

2.10   Non-Taxable Legal Persons – Taxable Persons with No Right to Recover VAT and Farmers Benefiting From Notional Refunds

Such persons are considered as outside the scope of VAT when, during the civil year and the preceding one, their yearly intra-Community acquisitions are below a threshold of L16 million. As soon as an acquisition puts them above that threshold they are subject to common intra-Community rules and must pay VAT on their acquisitions. They must therefore obtain an identification number and submit VAT returns.

The same persons may opt to be subject to the common rules even for acquisitions below the threshold. The option takes effect from the first day of the year (if it is exercised in the VAT declaration form of the previous year), or from the day in which it is exercised (at the beginning of business or during the year but before performing any purchase) and expires on 31 December of the second year following the option. The option is renewable for periods of two years except if renounced two months before the two-year period expires.

2.11   Supplier of New Means of Transport

Any person who undertakes on an occasional basis intra-Community supplies of new means of transport that are dispatched or transported from Italy to another Member State is regarded as a taxable person (see section 7.2.6 of the Introduction to the European Union).

3   WHAT IS TAXABLE?

VAT is levied on the supply of goods or services effected for consideration within the country and on the import of goods.

3.1   Supply of Goods

Supply of goods means the actual transfer of ownership of tangible assets, which includes movables, immovables and utilities such as electricity, gas, etc. The following are also considered as supplies of goods even if they do not comply with the general definition in all respects:

- hire purchases which are taxable on handing over of the goods, though ownership is transferred when the last instalment is paid
- rents of goods when it is provided that, at the end of the period agreed in the contract, the ownership will be transferred
- the transfer of goods made by buying or selling agents acting in their own name but for the account of third parties
- supplies of goods usually manufactured or traded by the entrepreneur made without consideration, ie gifts and self-supplies
- assignment of goods used to perform the business activity to the entrepreneur or to the professional (excluding goods for which VAT on the purchase was not deductible).

A number of supplies are considered non-taxable transactions even if they comply with the general definition in most respects (see section 7.4 'Non-Taxable Transactions').

3.2   Imports of Goods

Importation of goods means the introduction of goods coming from non-European Union countries into free circulation in Italy. This situation is referred to as a 'final importation'. Importations are taxed as such, irrespective of the legal status of the importer. Temporary importations are not subject to VAT. VAT is levied when Customs clearance is obtained. Bonded warehouses are available to defer the payment of VAT while keeping the goods in stock in Italy. Goods in bonded warehouses are not considered as imported, ie they do not qualify as national goods. The situation relating to European Union goods is discussed below.

3.3   Intra-Community Acquisitions

From 1 January 1993 VAT is charged, levied and paid on the intra-Community acquisition of goods (other than new means of transport) effected within Italy for consideration by a taxable person, and on the intra-Community acquisition of new means of transport effected by anyone within Italy for consideration (see section 7 of the Introduction to the European Union).

3.4 Distance Sellers

Persons who supply goods from another Member State to non-VAT-registered persons in Italy may be taxable in respect of such supplies (see section 7.4.2 of the Introduction to the European Union).

3.5 New Means of Transport

The transfer to Italy from another Member State of new means of transport is always taxable as an intra-Community acquisition regardless of the status of the supplier or the purchaser (see section 7.2.6 of the Introduction to the European Union).

3.6 Contract Work

If a VAT registered person in another Member State sends goods to Italy to be processed there and the processed goods are not returned to the Member State from which the goods for process originated, or to another Member State, but they stay in Italy, the processor must charge VAT and then the owner of the goods will have to register and account for VAT in Italy in order to recover it (see section 7.2.5 of the Introduction to the European Union).

3.7 Excise Products

In certain circumstances a non-registered acquirer of excise products may have to register and account for VAT on acquisitions of products which are subject to excise duty (see section 7.2.7 of the Introduction to the European Union).

3.8 Assembly/Installation

A supply of goods takes place in Italy if the specific goods to be supplied are located in Italy. This applies even if an overseas entrepreneur has no place of business in Italy. However, the liability of supply of assembled or installed goods on behalf of a European Union supplier may be passed to the Italian customer under the reverse charge mechanism (see section 2.7 'Reverse Charge Mechanism').

3.9 Supply of Services

Services are broadly defined as obligations to perform, refrain from or tolerate an act or situation for a consideration.

The following are also considered to be supplies of services if made for consideration:
- leasing and hiring of movables and immovables
- lending of money and securities
- transfers and licences of copyrights, patents and know-how
- the assignment of contracts (see section 7.4 'Non-Taxable Transactions').

3.10 Self-Supplies of Goods/Services

A self-supply of goods is the application by an entrepreneur or professional of goods forming part of his business assets for his private use or for purposes other than those of his business, including liquidation and allotment to shareholders or partners. These transactions are subject to VAT in any case, irrespective of whether a VAT credit was granted for the relevant self-supplied goods at the moment of purchase or manufacture.

In principle, self-supplies of services are not taxed. Exceptions include:

■   services constituted by transfers or licences of intangible assets (such as copyrights, know-how, etc)
■   leasing and hiring of movables and immovables
■   assignment of contract.

These are treated as self-supplies of services when rendered without consideration to shareholders or partners.

4   PLACE OF SUPPLY

VAT applies to supplies of goods and services taking place in Italy. It is therefore necessary to have a clear understanding of the territoriality rules.

4.1   Supply of Goods

Transactions concerning immovables are deemed to take place in Italy when the immovables are situated in Italy.

Transactions concerning movables are subject to VAT when such movables are physically present in Italy at the moment the relevant transaction takes place. According to wording used by customs legislation, this means that the goods must be national, nationalised (ie finally imported from abroad) or subject to temporary importation in Italy. Therefore, a supply of goods in view of their exportation is subject to VAT, even if this is a case of exemption with credit (see section 7 'Exemptions').

4.1.1 Chain Transactions

A special rule applies if several entrepreneurs enter into subsequent transactions involving the same goods (chain transactions). Then each entrepreneur within the chain is deemed to have made a taxable supply, even if the actual ownership is transferred directly from the first entrepreneur to the last recipient in the chain. However, when these transactions involve transportation of the goods from a place outside the Union to a place within Italy, all transactions which took place before customs clearance are considered outside the scope of Italian VAT. The importation is subject to Italian VAT and any subsequent sale is ruled by Italian VAT law. With regard to intra-Community chain transactions, see section 7.4.1 of the Introduction to the European Union.

4.1.2 Distance sales

The place of supply of goods (other than new means of transport) dispatched or transported directly or indirectly by the supplier either:

■   from the territory of another Member State to a non-taxable person in Italy, or
■   from Italy to a person in another Member State who is not registered for VAT there

is the place where the goods are when the dispatch or transportation ends. Non-taxable persons include private persons, fully exempt persons and flat rate-farmers.

For full details see section 7.4.2 of the Introduction to the European Union.

4.2 Intra-Community Acquisitions

As a general rule, the place where an intra-Community acquisition of goods takes place is deemed to be the place where the goods are when transportation to the person acquiring the goods ends.

To make a zero-rated intra-Community supply followed by a taxed intra-Community acquisition on which the VAT may be deducted by the acquirer, the VAT identification numbers of the parties involved must be stated on the invoice.

If, for any reason, the goods arrive finally in a Member State other than that which issued the VAT number to the acquirer, the person purchasing the goods acquires the goods in the Member State of arrival of the goods. In this case double taxation could occur, since the purchaser must account for VAT both in the Member State which issued the VAT number to him and in the Member State of arrival of the goods.

The presumption is that the place of acquisition is the country which issued the VAT number to the acquirer. However, if the acquirer can show that he has paid VAT in the Member State of arrival of the goods, he will not be liable for payment of acquisition VAT in his own Member State.

4.2.1 Chain Transactions

'Triangulation' involves the situation where three parties in three different countries are involved in selling and purchasing the same goods. For example, *A* in France sells goods to *B* in Belgium who sells the goods to *C* in Italy and the goods are sent directly from *A* to *C* (see section 7.4.1 of the Introduction to the European Union).

4.2.2 Goods Placed on Board Ships, Aircraft or Trains During Transport

When goods are supplied for consumption on board ships, aircraft or trains during transport, and the place of departure and destination are within the territory of the European Union, the place of supply is the place where the goods are at the time of departure of the transport.

4.3 Supply of Services Not Ruled by European Union VAT Law

4.3.1 General rule

Services are deemed to be rendered in Italy if the supplier has his domicile (registered office) or a permanent establishment (from which the service is supplied) within the territory of the State.

4.3.2 Exceptions

The following are exceptions to the general rule:

- services connected with immovable property are deemed to be rendered where in Italy when the property is situated there
- services connected with movable tangible property; ancillary transport activities (when not qualified as European Union services); cultural, artistic, sporting, scientific, educational and entertainment activities are deemed to be rendered in Italy when those services are physically carried out there
- services derived from the hiring out of movable tangible property other than means of transport transfer and assignment of copyrights, patents, licences, trademarks and

similar rights (please note that transfer of software will be discussed in the specific section concerning European Community rules); advertising services; services of consultants, engineers, consultancy bureaux, lawyers, accountants and other similar services, as well as data processing and the supply of information, banking, financial and insurance transactions; the supply of staff; the services of agents who act (either in their own name or in the name of the principal) to procure for their principal the services referred to under this point. Obligations to refrain from pursuing or exercising a business activity or a right referred to above are deemed to be supplied in Italy when the recipient has his domicile in Italy or an Italian permanent establishment. Unless the services provided are used or enjoyed outside the European Union. If the recipient is a non-entrepreneur established in the European Union the place of supply shall be deemed to be in Italy.

When the following services are rendered to entities established outside the EU, the place of supply is deemed to be Italy when the effective use and enjoyment take place in Italy. This applies to the transfer and assignment of copyrights, advertising services, banking, financial and insurance transactions, supply of staff, services of agents relating to those services, and obligations to refrain from pursuing a business activity or exercising a right. This last rule, referring to the place of effective use or enjoyment, is specific to Italy.

■   *hiring of forms of transport are deemed to be supplied in Italy:*

  –   if the recipient is outside the European Union and the services are used or enjoyed in Italy
  –   if the supplier is outside the European Union and the relevant services are used in Italy.

■   *transport services:* the supply of transport services is treated as taking place in Italy to the extent that the journey is within Italy, although there are exceptions. The transport of passengers outside Italy or to or from a place outside Italy is zero-rated. The transport of freight from or to Italy to a place outside the European Union is zero-rated. The VAT liability of transport and ancillary services directly linked to a movement of goods between Member States provided by a Italian supplier may be shifted to the Member State of the customer on production of an European Union VAT registration number (other than an Italian number) and thus become outside of the scope of Italian VAT unless the purchase of the transport service is subject to VAT in Italy. Difficulties occasionally arise as a matter of practice, including conflicts with the jurisdiction of other Member States.

■   *cultural, artistic, sporting, entertainment services, etc:* generally, the place of supply is treated as the location at which the performance or service takes place. However, such services have been included in the list of specified services under which the Italian recipient would account for VAT under the reverse charge mechanism (see section 2.7 'Reverse Charge Mechanism') when the foreign performer has not a VAT representative in Italy.

■   *work on movable goods:* as noted above, work on movable goods may constitute a supply of goods rather than a supply of services, in which event the supply is made where the treatment or process is applied. In contrast, services of work on goods such as valuation and repair works is not a supply of goods but of services. The general place of supply rule is where the service takes place. However, with effect from 1 September 1993 the charge may be made without a VAT charge, providing certain criteria are met.

■ *services provided by brokers or other intermediaries:* the place of supply of such services which form part of an intra-Community transport of goods is the European Union Member State which issued the VAT identification number of the customer (see section 7.4.6 of the Introduction to the European Union).

■ *services rendered by brokers or other intermediaries:* certain services provided by brokers or other intermediaries which do not come within the scope of Article 9.2(e) of the Sixth VAT Directive shall not be Italy if the services provided are used or enjoyed by the recipient outside the European Union. If the recipient is a non-entrepreneur established in the European Union, the place of supply shall be deemed to be in Italy (see section 7.4.7 of the Introduction to the European Union).

4.4 Reverse Charge Mechanism

A very important aspect to be considered is how to charge VAT on supplies made by foreign entities who have no permanent establishment in Italy and have not appointed a VAT representative in Italy (see section 2 'Who is Taxable?'). In this situation, the reverse charge mechanism applies. The taxable person resident in Italy must account for the supplies received as if he had made the supply himself. In other words, he replaces the foreign entity. At the same time, according to the general rules, he may recover the VAT charged as input tax (see section 8 'Credit/refund for input tax'). This is achieved by the recipient issuing a 'self-invoice'.

5 BASIS OF TAXATION

5.1 Supplies within Italy

The taxable basis is everything which constitutes the consideration received or to be received by the supplier from the customer (or from a third party) in connection with a certain supply. Such consideration does not include:

■ price reductions by way of discounts provided for in the relevant invoice
■ packing expenses, when packages must be returned to the supplier
■ late payment interest
■ amounts due by the customer as reimbursement for expenses paid by the supplier in the name and for the account of the former.

When the consideration is denominated in a foreign currency, the exchange rate to be used is that on the date on which the chargeable event has occurred (see section 5.5 'Chargeable event/Time of Payment'). When no consideration exists or it is in kind, VAT is assessed taking into account the open market value of the supply.

5.2 Self-Supplies

In case of self-supplies, the tax basis is the open market value of the goods or services at issue. The taxable event occurs at the moment of appropriation.

5.3 Imports

VAT due on import of goods is charged on the value assessed for customs purposes, plus freight costs to the first place of destination in the country, plus customs duties paid on the importation itself. As to the goods that were transferred before customs clearance from the importer to another taxable person, the taxable basis for VAT purposes is the consideration of the last supply.

5.4 Intra-Community Acquisitions

The amount on which tax is chargeable on the acquired goods is the total consideration. The consideration is the total amount or, in so far as the compensation is not in money, the total value of the compensation charged on the supply, including all taxes, commissions, costs and charges whatsoever, but excluding the VAT chargeable in respect of that acquisition. If more is actually paid than has been agreed, the taxable amount is the amount actually paid.

If the invoice is in foreign currency, the applicable exchange rate will be the rate on the day on which the transaction takes place (if it is indicated in the invoice). If there is no such indication, the buyer will use the rate of the date of invoice.

The transfer by a person of goods from his undertaking in Italy to another Member State for the purposes of his business is deemed to be a supply of goods, with certain exceptions. The taxable amount is the fair value of the goods (see 7.5.1 of the Introduction to the European Union).

5.5 Chargeable Event/Time of Payment

As a general rule, a taxable event occurs:

- for immovable goods: when the transfer deed is signed
- for movable goods: when supplied or dispatched
- for services: when the relevant price (or consideration) is paid
- for importation: when the goods are released from customs.

There are a number of exceptions which take into account specific situations (eg, goods to be resold on commission, supplies to the State and other public bodies, situations where delivery does not coincide with the actual transfer of ownership).

In principle, an invoice must be issued when a chargeable event occurs. In any case, if an invoice is issued or the price or an advance payment is received prior to the date of the taxable event, VAT becomes nonetheless due.

The rules governing the issue of invoices are explained in section 9 'Administrative Obligations'.

The ordinary rule is that VAT charged to customers is offset against input tax on a monthly basis (see section 10.9 'Small Entrepreneurs'). The net balance, if any, must be paid by the eighteenth of the month after the month of reference. Invoices issued but not yet registered in the VAT sales book and not yet settled must also be taken into account.

Regular exporters may be entitled to make purchases without paying VAT either on internal supplies or on imports (see section 7.1 'Exemption with Credit for Input Tax').

5.6 Credit Notes/Bad Debts

If the taxable amount is modified after the issue of the relevant invoice, or if the supply is cancelled, a credit note may be issued by the supplier to offset the sum and to reimburse the customer for VAT paid. The original supplier deducts the reimbursed VAT. When the partial or total annulment of the transaction is due to an agreement entered into after the performance of the original transaction, a credit note cannot be issued if more than a period of one year has elapsed.

No particular procedure governs the case of uncollectable invoices (bad debts). Even when it is possible to issue a credit note, this rarely happens because it could jeopardise the collection of the debt because of civil law and income tax complications.

6   TAX RATES

The present rates are as follows:

2%:   certain basic consumption goods (eg bread)

4%:   certain consumption goods, sales of buildings qualifying as 'non-luxury immovables' and services relating to their sale

9%:   other important consumption goods (eg electric power)

13%:   software and other goods and services

19%:   all other goods and services which are not exempt or not taxable at the 2%, 4%, 9% or 13% rates.

Services relating to the construction of goods and financial leasing are subject to the same rate as that applicable to the sale of the goods themselves.

7   EXEMPTIONS

7.1   *Exemptions with Credit for Input Tax*
This regime applies to supplies of goods for intra-Community acquisition, exports of goods outside the European Union, the sale of aircraft and ships and 'international services', ie services related to import-export.

It works like the zero-rate regime in other countries and it is intended to permit the taxation of goods in the country of destination. All the formal VAT requirements must be met but no VAT is charged and input tax is recoverable in full.

The most important international services are as follows:

■   transport of goods intended for import or export; leasing of means of transport in order to perform such transport services
■   forwarding agent services with respect to the above-mentioned transport
■   loading, unloading, maintenance, handling and storage relating to goods intended for export or import.

These services are exempt in case of imported goods provided that their cost is included in the tax basis of VAT to be paid on import. Since none of these exempt transactions bears any tax, the entrepreneur performing them on a regular basis (regular exporter) ends up in a permanent credit position due to input tax paid. The refund of this credit tends to be rather slow in Italy.

In order to partially avoid this effect, regular exporters and sellers involved in European Union transactions are entitled to ensure that their purchases do not exceed the total exports and/or intra-Community sales made during the previous calendar year or 12 months, according to the exporter's choice. From the supplier's viewpoint, this is another case of exemption with credit.

7.2   Exemption without Credit for Input Tax

Exempt transactions do not bear any VAT. Nonetheless, all the formal requirements provided by the VAT law must be met (for exceptions see section 10.2 'Banking and Financial Activities' and section 10.7 'Retailers'). Input VAT incurred in connection with these kinds of transactions is not recoverable (see section 8 'Credit/Refund for Input Tax').

The most important exempt transactions are as follows:

- the granting and negotiation of credit and financing, including the discounting of bills of exchange and cheques and any dealings in credit guarantees
- insurance and reinsurance transactions
- transactions concerning currency, bank notes and coins used as legal tender in a foreign country (transactions concerning Italian money and those concerning deposits, current accounts and other financial items are non-taxable transactions)
- transactions (except management and safe keeping) concerning shares, interests in companies, debentures and other securities, excluding documents establishing title to goods
- the leasing of immovable property, excluding financial leasing (to which the same rate applies as for actual negotiation), leasing of commercial buildings which cannot be used as houses (standard rate), leasing of houses performed by real estate companies (4% rate) and leasing taking place in the context of a business lease (standard rate)
- many activities performed in the public interest (such as medical assistance, transactions involving human blood, milk or organs, and educational services provided by qualified bodies).

7.3   Exempt Importation

The importation of goods which is followed by an intra-Community supply may be exempt (see section 7.7.2 of the Introduction to the European Union).

7.4   Non-Taxable Transactions

Non-taxable transactions are as follows:

- transactions which would be subject to tax as a consequence of the general definition but which are nonetheless excluded by a specific provision. With respect to these transactions no VAT obligation exists and they do not affect the deductibility of input tax incurred in conjunction with transactions subject to VAT. In Italy, these non-taxable transactions are also referred to as being outside the scope of VAT. Exempt transactions are considered within the scope of VAT.
- the transactions which do not comply with the definition of taxable supplies.

The most important non-taxable transactions are:

- transfers of currency and credits
- transfers of a business as a going concern

- contribution of goods in exchange for shares or quotas
- transfer of goods in the context of company reorganisations or mergers
- transfer of land intended for agriculture
- the supply of staff, provided the consideration does not exceed the cost incurred
- the supplies of goods with respect to which input tax was not recoverable at the time of purchase because of specific regulations, such as cars and luxury goods, (see section 8 'Credit/refund for input tax')
- exploitation of copyright by the author.

In many cases, these transactions are subject to RegistrationTax.

7.4.1 Subsidies/Penalty Payments/Compensation
These are not taxable unless they represent a consideration for a supply. It may, however, be difficult to determine the exact nature of the payments and professional advice should be obtained in each specific situation.

7.5 Election to be Subject to VAT
Election to be subject to VAT is available to distance sellers (see section 3.4) and to non-taxable legal persons and government bodies in certain circumstances (see section 7.2.4 of the Introduction to the European Union) if the amount of the sales does not exceed Lit54 million during the calendar year. If the amount of the sales is in excess of the above, and in certain other specific circumstances, the foreign entity must appoint a VAT representative in Italy.

8 CREDIT/REFUND FOR INPUT TAX

8.1 General Rule
Taxable persons have the right to recover input tax incurred for the purposes of their taxable transactions. This means that input VAT paid in relation to exempt transactions (discussed in section 7.2 'Exemption without Credit for Input Tax') cannot be deducted. The same applies to supplies obtained for private consumption or intended to be used for non-commercial purposes. VAT is not recoverable on a number of expenses which are deemed to be usually incurred for private consumption, ie:

- purchase or import from non-European Union countries of means of transport intended to be used both for goods and persons provided they are not the object of the primary activity of the taxable person or a primary instrument of that activity; services related to such means of transport are subject to the same condition
- purchase or import of goods subject to the 19% rate when they are considered luxury goods or, for some goods, unless they are the object of the primary activity of the taxable person. Services related to such goods are subject to the same condition. Recovery is disallowed for liberal professions
- purchase or import of cars or motorcycles intended for personal transport and exceeding a given cylinder capacity which do not constitute the primary activity of the taxable person, up to 31 December 1996. Services (ie, maintenance) relating to such goods are subject to the same conditions. The purchase or import of fuels and lubricants in relation to means of transport which do not give title to deduct VAT is subject to the same limitation

- hotel and restaurant services
- motorway tolls
- transport services concerning individuals.

8.2   Adjustment of Entitlement to Credit

Deductible input tax on depreciable assets whose depreciation rate is lower than 25% must be adjusted if, in each of the four years subsequent to the one of purchase, the partial exemption ratio has changed by more than 10%. The effect of this adjustment is an additional credit or a partial repayment for the year of the adjustment.

8.3   Partial Exemption

Entrepreneurs making both taxable and exempt supplies are entitled to recover input VAT attributable to both, but only for that part which relates to taxable supplies. This is achieved by computing the ratio between the amount of taxable supplies and the amount of total supplies, including exempt transactions but excluding non-taxable transactions. No other criteria are allowed by the VAT authorities.

For the purpose of the ratio, exempt transactions do not include occasional exempt supplies (for example, the sale of shares in a subsidiary by a manufacturing company). The supply of capital goods (ie depreciable assets) is not included in the turnover and therefore has no impact on the determination of this ratio. The entrepreneur can make an election to compute a separate ratio for each sector of his business provided that each sector is separately accounted for.

8.4   Time of Recovery

The general rule is that input VAT can be recovered when the relevant invoice is accounted for in the VAT books (see section 9 'Administrative Obligations'). Input VAT on invoices recorded in a given month (or quarterly as the case may be) is offset against VAT charged to customers on invoices issued (even if not recorded) in the same period. If the former exceeds the latter, the balance (credit) is carried forward to the next period.

8.5   Refund for Foreign Entrepreneurs

Foreign entrepreneurs without a permanent establishment in Italy do not qualify as taxable persons. Nonetheless, they may incur an input VAT on supplies made to them by a taxable person. To recover such VAT they have two possibilities:

- they may appoint a VAT representative in Italy who will file an annual return and claim the refund according to general rules, or
- they may apply directly to the VAT authorities in Rome. This is only possible for European Union residents who have performed no transactions in Italy (apart from exempt international services) and excluding VAT on immovables. The application must be made on a specific form and addressed to:

VAT office
Via Canton 10
00144 Rome
Italy

The original invoices giving rise to the claim must be attached to the form, together with a certificate from the VAT authorities of the applicant's country confirming that he is a taxable person in that country. The refund may be applied for quarterly or annually. In any case, applications must be received by the authorities before 30 June of the year following the one for which the refund is required. It is also possible to have the relevant refund remitted abroad to a given bank account nominated by the claimant.

9   ADMINISTRATIVE OBLIGATIONS

9.1   Registration
Each taxable person must register with the local VAT office and get his own VAT number. This applies even to very small undertakings, since no income or revenue limit exists in Italy. The application must be filed on a specific form within 30 days from the start of the activity. When changes in the data communicated to the VAT authorities occur, the taxable person must inform the authorities within 30 days. At the moment of registration, a tax amounting to Lit100,000 (individuals) or to Lit250,000 (companies, VAT representatives excluded) must be paid. The same amount must be paid every year by 5 March.

9.2   Books and Records
Supply invoices must be accounted for in a specific book within 15 days of the date of issue. Invoices received from suppliers must be recorded in a second book before the end of the month following the one of receipt. Taxable persons entitled not to issue invoices must record payments collected in a third book. Specific rules are provided for intra-Community transactions.

Before they are used, all VAT books must be 'validated' by a VAT office or a notary public. All the pages are stamped and numbered and the total number of pages is indicated on the last one. In the absence of these formalities, book entries are void.

9.3   Invoices
In principle, each VAT transaction must be documented by an invoice containing at least the following elements:

- date of issue
- chronological number
- identification data of the customer, including VAT number (if any)
- description of the transaction
- consideration, rate of VAT, VAT amount and total amount. In the case of exempt transactions, reference must be made to the specific legal provision granting the exemption.

Invoices must be issued when chargeable events occur. As a derogation, a unique invoice can be issued for the supplies of goods of a given month before the end of the following one, provided that the delivery of the related goods is documented by special transport documents (such as delivery notes) regulated by VAT law.

In some cases (for example, retailers, banks and insurance companies) the issue of invoices is not mandatory unless expressly asked for by customers.

Taxable persons who, in the conduct of their business or profession, make taxable purchases (either of goods or services) in respect of which the issue of the invoice is mandatory, must ensure that they receive such an invoice.

If, after four months from the date of the supply, no invoice is received, the customer must go to the competent VAT office within 31 days, pay the VAT due (if any) and show two copies of a document which is intended to replace the invoice. One copy of it will be returned by the VAT authorities and will be registered in the customer's books.

If an invoice received is not in accordance with the law, the customer must go to the VAT office within 15 days from the date on which the invoice was recorded and pay the additional VAT due (if any). Again, two copies of a document which is intended to replace the invoice must be shown to the VAT office, which will return one copy for the records.

Heavy fines are imposed on customers in cases of non-compliance.

9.4 IVA (Advance Payment)

By 27 December of every year all taxable persons must make an advance payment for VAT referred to the last month or the last quarter. According to the ordinary method, the sum must represent 88% of the amount paid (or which should have been paid) for the corresponding month or quarter of the previous year. In any event it must not be less than 88% of the amount due at the end of the period (the last month or the last quarter).

9.5 VAT Return

VAT returns must be filed annually not later than 15 March of the year following the one of reference. The general rule is that VAT must be paid on a monthly basis, ie the net VAT due for a given month is payable by the eighteenth day of the following one.

Where the input VAT exceeds the output VAT the excess is carried forward to the subsequent period. Any additional VAT demanded (usually as a result of adjustments of exemption ratio) is paid in connection with the annual return. If an excess of input VAT over output VAT arises, it can be either carried forward or reimbursed. Small undertakings (whose annual turnover must not exceed Lit360 million for entrepreneurs performing services, and Lit1 billion in all other cases) and liberal professions (whose annual turnover must not exceed Lit360 million) can pay VAT on a quarterly basis with interest of 1.5%.

9.6 INTRASTAT

Traders who supply goods to other Member States or who acquire goods from other Member States must provide separately details of the intra-Community sales and purchases performed, either for VAT purposes or for statistical purposes (see section 7.9.3 of the Introduction to the European Union).

The sales/purchases listings must be submitted by taxable persons to the competent customs authorities, making reference to the registered office of the taxable persons or of the person which is delegated to sign them. The frequency of submission depends on the amount of the sales/purchases:

■   on a monthly basis, if the respective amount exceeds Lit150 million (submission must be made before the fifteenth working day of the following month)

■   on a quarterly basis, if the respective amount is between Lit 50 million and Lit150 million (submission must be made before the end of the month following the current quarter)

■ on a yearly basis, if the respective amount does not exceed Lit50 million (submission must be made before the end of the month following the current year).

The periodicity of the presentation of INTRASTAT must be ascertained for sales and purchases separately.

9.7 Registers
Certain registers of goods movements must also be kept (see 7.9.4 of the Introduction to the European Union).

9.8 Powers of Authorities
VAT authorities are entitled to check that VAT provisions are respected. Should the VAT return not be filed, they can make an estimated assessment. The same applies if the return is not signed, mandatory records have not been kept, or the VAT authorities can show that the taxable person's records are not reliable. Returns filed within 30 days from the due date are considered valid, though penalties apply for late filing.

If the return is filed within 90 days from the due date, the taxable person avoids criminal penalties but he is subject to the penalties for absence of filing: between two and four times the VAT due for the calendar year.

No correction of the annual return can be made. It is only possible to file a new return within the above mentioned term of 30 days after the due date. Input VAT not claimed in the annual return for the year in which it should have been recorded is lost forever. In case of late payment of the balance shown by the annual return, the penalties are 50% of the amount due plus the annual 6% interest. In the case of late payment of the periodic amounts, either monthly or quarterly, the penalties are between two and four times the amount due, plus interest.

The VAT authorities are entitled to check VAT returns up to four years after the end of the one of reference. They have a further year in case of estimated assessments.

9.9 Objections/Appeals
Disputes of any kind are settled before tax courts (Commissioni Tributarie). The claim must be raised within 60 days from the date on which the tax assessment is notified. There are four degrees of judgment. Even if the taxable person challenges the assessment, one-third of the tax assessed must be paid at once. Penalties are imposed only at the end of the whole procedure. Disputes concerning VAT on importations are settled under customs provisions.

10 SPECIAL VAT REGIMES

10.1 Agricultural Enterprises
The supply of certain agricultural products by the producer is subject to a special regime with respect to the determination of input tax, ie input tax is computed in such a way as to be in any case equal to the VAT charged to customers. VAT due on the purchase of depreciable assets can be recovered to the extent that it exceeds deductible input tax according to the mentioned automatic system.

Agricultural products which are eligible are contained in a list which also contains some fishing products. For this purpose, agricultural producers are those thus defined by the Civil Code.

Where supplies qualifying for this regime are made in conjunction with non-qualifying supplies, input tax relating to the latter is computed according to the ratio between them and the total supplies.

Agricultural producers with very low supplies (less than Lit10 million) are excluded from all VAT formalities except for the obligation to keep received invoices.

In any case, agricultural producers may elect to compute VAT pursuant to ordinary rules. This election is binding for three years.

10.2 Banking and Financial Activities
Most transactions performed by banking and financial institutions are exempt without credit. They do not have to issue invoices unless their customers explicitly ask for them.

These entities may elect to give up their right to recover input VAT in respect to taxable transactions, in which case their administrative obligations are simplified. This election is binding for three years.

Special provisions apply with respect to the issue of invoices, accounting and VAT payments.

10.3 Different Activities Conducted by the Same Entity
Entrepreneurs conducting different activities may elect to account separately for each one. Notice to the VAT office must be given in the annual return concerning the previous year and it is binding for three years. The validity of the election is longer if depreciable assets are purchased with respect to which the adjustment of entitlement to credit applies (see section 8 'Credit/Refund for Input VAT').

Separate accounting is usually adopted when exempt transactions take place together with taxable ones (for example banking activity and leasing activity), so that input tax attributable to taxable transactions can be recovered fully. Allocation of input tax among the various activities does not take place according to definite criteria, but on a case by case approach. There are certain cases in which separate accounting is mandatory (for example agricultural and retailing activities). Supplies of goods and services from a taxable activity to an exempt one (or to an activity such as agriculture or entertainment with a special regime concerning input tax) must take place at the open market value.

10.4 Entertainment Activities
The VAT tax basis for entertainment activities is the same as for Entertainment Tax and is collected according to the rules governing this latter tax. Input tax is equal to two-thirds of output tax and no obligation exists with respect to issue of invoices, accounting for VAT, or the annual returns. Entertainment entrepreneurs may however elect to be subject to VAT according to the general rules. This election is binding for three years. Where a sponsored activity is performed together with the entertainment activity the deduction is increased by one-tenth of the amount collected.

10.5 Sales of Books and Newspapers
General rule is that VAT is based on the sale price with respect to the number of copies sold or delivered less copies returned. The amount of copies returned is fixed by law and, for 1995, is equal to 60% of the amount delivered for sale.

10.6 Free Port Areas
The municipalities of Campione d'Italia and Livigno on the Swiss border, though part of the Italian Republic, are outside the customs border so that the goods brought there from abroad are not considered as imported goods.

10.7 Retailers
Retailers are entitled not to issue invoices unless expressly asked for by their customers. Some of them must, nonetheless, issue a special fiscal receipt if no other evidence of the tax is available. This applies to restaurants and hotels.

Retailers can record payments received, including VAT, in a special book. When goods for sale are subject to different rates, it is necessary to distinguish payments relating to the various goods.

Nonetheless, the Ministry of Finance has authorised certain categories of retailer (notably pharmacies, food and dress shops) to record sales without reference to the different rates. Total supplies are then attributed to the various rates in the same proportion as purchases. Once the various categories have been determined, output VAT is computed by applying specific ratios to the recorded payments.

10.8 Second-Hand Goods
A special regime applies to second-hand goods, objects of art and antiques in conformity with the Council Directive on second-hand goods (see section 7.10.2 of the Introduction to the European Union).

10.9 Small Entrepreneurs
Small entrepreneurs are those taxable persons whose total supplies do not exceed Lit360 million (for services) and Lit1 billion (in all other cases) in the calendar year prior to the one of reference. Total supplies comprise exempt transactions and exclude non-taxable transactions. Small entrepreneurs are entitled to simpler formalities with regard to the issue of invoices and records. They may also pay VAT on a quarterly rather than a monthly basis (although a further 1.5% interest must be paid).

10.10 Foreign Travellers
Foreign travellers resident outside the European Union are entitled to a VAT refund on goods purchased in Italy and taken outside the European Union if the amount paid is higher than Lit300,000 (net of VAT). The procedure is fixed by a Ministerial Decree which provides that the foreign traveller must obtain a stamp by the customs authorities on the purchase invoice and send it to the Italian shop within three months. The shop is entitled to grant the reimbursement directly to the foreign traveller. The minimum amount which may be reimbursed is Lit57,000. Usually this service is performed by Italian banks.

10.11 Travel Agencies

A special regime applies for travel and tourist agencies which do not act in the name and for the account of their customers. In this case, the supply is considered as taking place directly between the final supplier and the customer and is regulated by general rules.

Conversely, when travel agencies act in their own name and for the account of their customers, a unique supply of services is taxable if carried out within the European Union, while considered as exempt (with credit) otherwise.

The tax basis is the difference between the consideration paid by the customer and the expenses, (including VAT), incurred by the third parties to the customer. Special provisions exist for supplies made partly inside and partly outside the EU. Travel agencies cannot deduct VAT on supplies made by third parties to their customers.

Travel agencies do not have to issue an invoice for their services unless it is expressly asked for by the customer before or at the time of the taxable event. The taxable event is the payment of the consideration or the beginning of the journey, if it happens prior to the payment. In any case, customers are not entitled to deduct VAT paid in connection with such services.

There are specific provisions regulating books and records of travel agencies, as well as the determination of the VAT payments during the year and at the end of the year. A special form must be submitted together with the annual return.

11   FURTHER READING

Mandò, *Imposta sul Valora Aggiunto*, 1993, ed IPS0A

Reggi, *L'Imposta sul Valore Aggiunto*, 1994, ed Pirola

Centore, *IVA intracomunitaria*, 1994, ed IPSOA.

Contributors: Gian Paolo Giannini, Maurizio Bottoni and Paolo Comuzzi
Ernst & Young
Studio Associato Legale Tributario
Via Cornaggia 10
20123 Milan
Italy
Tel: +39 2 85141
Fax: +39 2 89010199

LUXEMBOURG

1   GENERAL BACKGROUND

In 1969 the Grand Duchy of Luxembourg adopted value added tax (VAT) which replaced a cumulative Turnover Tax with effect from 1 January 1970. The law of 12 February 1979 implemented the Sixth Council Directive which lays down a uniform basis for assessment of VAT. This law came into force on 1 January 1980. The further amendments by the Sixth VAT Directives 77/388/EEC, 92/111/EEC and 94/5/EEC were implemented by the laws of 18 December 1992, 13 March 1993 and 23 December 1994.

VAT in Luxembourg is administered by the 'Administration de l'Enregistrement et des Domaines' and is known as 'taxe sur la valeur ajoutée' (TVA).

1.1   The Single Market – Intra-Community Acquisitions

As a Member State of the European Union, Luxembourg applies the rules for VAT applicable to the Single Market and, in particular, the transitional arrangements which apply in respect of intra-Community supplies during the transition period which commenced on 1 January 1993.

For ease of reference and to reduce repetition, the transitional arrangements are set out in detail in section 7 of the Introduction to the European Union which precedes this section of the book.

It is recommended that this chapter is read in conjunction with the transitional arrangements.

2   WHO IS TAXABLE?

2.1   General

Any person who carries out independently, in any place, any economic activity is considered as a taxable person including:

- persons making exempt supplies only
- small entrepreneurs
- flat-rate farmers.

'Economic activities' comprise all activities of producers, traders, persons supplying services and include agriculture, mining activities and activities of the liberal professions. The exploitation of tangible or intangible property for the purpose of obtaining income is also considered an economic activity.

Anyone who carries out on an occasional basis a transaction relating to the activities referred to above may also be treated as a taxable person.

This chapter reflects the law on VAT in Luxembourg as at 31 January 1995.

Persons only occasionally supplying new means of transport are always treated as taxable persons.

The use of the word 'independently' excludes employed and other persons from the tax in so far as they are bound to an employer by a contract of employment or by any other legal ties creating the relationship of employer and employee.

Small entrepreneurs whose turnover is less than LUF400,000 are not liable to VAT. They are, however, required to register for VAT purposes.

2.2 Transactions with Branch/Subsidiary

Branches and subsidiaries of foreign companies supplying taxable goods or services in Luxembourg are treated in the same way as other entrepreneurs.

Supplies of goods or services between a subsidiary and the parent company are within the scope of VAT. Services supplied between a Luxembourg branch and its foreign head office or vice versa are treated as internal supplies and are, therefore, outside the scope of VAT.

2.3 Government Bodies

Government bodies are not subject to VAT on their activities of an administrative, social or cultural nature.

However, commercial activities or activities which are deemed to be in competition with other commercial companies are subject to VAT.

2.4 Fiscal Unity/Group Taxation

The concept of fiscal unity does not exist in Luxembourg VAT law. Each taxable person (individual or legal body) must account for the tax independently in the same way as any other taxable person. It is not possible for a group of taxable persons to file joint returns.

2.5 Foreign Entrepreneurs

Foreign entrepreneurs who have no establishment in Luxembourg are subject to VAT and corresponding registration in Luxembourg when they deliver goods in Luxembourg or supply services which are taxable in Luxembourg and not subject to the reverse charge.

For VAT purposes, foreign entrepreneurs are considered as having an establishment if they keep a regular place of activity (office, factory, etc) in Luxembourg. Non-resident entrepreneurs with an establishment in Luxembourg are treated as local entrepreneurs. Registration of foreign entrepreneurs is made with the:

> Administration de l'Enregistrement et des Domaines
> Bureau d'imposition 10
> Boîte Postale 31
> L-2010 Luxembourg
> Tel (352) 44 905 451

2.6 Representative Office

Representative offices of foreign entrepreneurs who only carry out activities of a preparatory or an auxiliary nature are not treated as taxable persons. VAT incurred in Luxembourg can be recovered by foreign entrepreneurs (see section 8.5 'Refund for Foreign Entrepreneurs').

2.7 VAT Representatives

Foreign entrepreneurs who do not maintain a fixed establishment in Luxembourg by making taxable supplies within Luxembourg, and branches of foreign companies which are not owners of real estate located within Luxembourg, are required to pay a deposit or to produce a letter of guarantee issued by a bank established in Luxembourg to the VAT authorities. The amount of the guarantee must be equal to six months' liability.

If this obligation is not fulfilled, the appointment of a VAT representative who will be responsible for fulfilling the administrative obligations and for payment of the VAT due by the foreign entrepreneur or by the branch is required.

2.8 Reverse Charge Mechanism

If certain specified services are supplied by a non-resident entrepreneur who does not maintain a fixed establishment in Luxembourg, the liability for payment of VAT moves to the taxable recipient of the service. The services are:

- intra-Community goods transportation services
- services ancillary to intra-Community goods transport services
- services provided by brokers and intermediaries related to intra-Community goods transport
- transfers and assignments of copyright, patents, licences, trademarks and similar rights
- advertising services
- services of consultants, engineers, consultancy bureaux, lawyers, accountants and other similar services; data processing and provision of information (but excluding from this head any services relating to land and buildings)
- acceptance of any obligation to refrain from pursuing or exercising, in whole or part, any business activity or any such rights as are referred to in this section
- banking, financial and insurance services (including reinsurance, but excluding the provision of safe deposit facilities)
- the supply of staff
- the letting or hire of goods other than means of transport
- services rendered by one person to another in procuring for that other person any of the services mentioned in this section.

2.9 Imports

Goods imported into Luxembourg by resident entrepreneurs or by foreign entrepreneurs with a fixed establishment in Luxembourg are liable to VAT. The tax is not due until the next VAT return has to be filed and it can be recovered by taxable entrepreneurs within the same return.

This rule also applies to foreign entrepreneurs who do not have a fixed establishment in Luxembourg if they can prove that they are registered in Luxembourg and if the customs documents show that they are the recipient of the goods.

Goods imported into Luxembourg by persons who are not registered for VAT purposes are liable to VAT at customs clearance.

2.10 Intra-Community Acquisitions

The movement of goods from one Member State to another is an acquisition in the Member

State to which the goods are dispatched. If there is an acquisition by an Luxembourg business, the business in the other European Union Member State is not obliged to register in Luxembourg. If there is a 'fictitious acquisition' (ie in an inter-branch transfer where there is no change in title) VAT registration in Luxembourg will be required for the business in the other European Union Member State (see section 7.2 of the Introduction to the European Union).

2.11 Supplier of New Means of Transport
Any person who undertakes on an occasional basis intra-Community supplies of new means of transport that are dispatched or transported from Luxembourg to another Member State is regarded as a taxable person (see section 7.2.6 of the Introduction to the European Union).

2.12 Non-Taxable Legal Persons – Taxable Persons with No Right to Recover VAT and Flat-Rate Farmers
Such persons are considered to be outside the scope of VAT when, during the previous or current year, at the moment of acquisition the total value of their acquisitions has not exceeded LUF400,000. As soon as an acquisition puts them above that threshold they are subject to common intra-Community rules and must pay VAT on their acquisitions. They must therefore obtain an identification number and submit VAT returns.

The same persons may opt to be subject to common rules even for acquisitions below the threshold. The option is binding for a minimum period of two calendar years (see section 7.2.4 of the Introduction to the European Union).

3   WHAT IS TAXABLE?

VAT is levied on the supply of goods and services in Luxembourg and on importation of goods.

3.1 Supply of Goods
The term 'supply' means the transfer of the right to dispose of tangible property as owner. Generally, the transfer is effected by sale. The remittance of goods is also treated as a supply.

The term 'goods' applies to all tangible movable properties. Utilities such as electricity, gas, heat and similar intangibles qualify as goods. Land and buildings are not subject to VAT (see section 10.4 'Real Estate').

3.2 Imports of Goods
'Import' means the entry into Luxembourg of goods which are not considered as being in free circulation in the European Economic Community. In limited cases, the importation of goods into Luxembourg is exempt from VAT (see section 7.1 'Exemptions with Credit for Input Tax').

Goods imported into bonded warehouses are not subject to VAT until they are removed for sale (see section 10.3 'Bonded Warehouses').

3.3 Intra-Community Supplies of Goods
Intra-Community supplies of goods follow the rules of the transitional system, including the

simplified triangulation methods according to Council Directive 92/111/EEC and the simplification measures related to the supply of services on movable goods, such as repairs (see section 7 of the Introduction to the European Union).

3.4 Distance Sales/Mail Order

The threshold for compulsory registration for distance sales is LUF4,200,000. Optional registration for a minimum period of two years is possible if the threshold is not reached (see section 7.4.2 of the Introduction to the European Union).

3.5 Contract Work

If a VAT-registered person in another Member State sends goods to Luxembourg to be processed there and the processed goods are not returned to the Member State from which the goods for process originated, then the owner of the goods will have to register and account for VAT in Luxembourg (see section 7.2.5 of the Introduction to the European Union).

3.6 Excise Products

In certain circumstances a non-registered acquirer of excise products may have to register and account for VAT on acquisitions of products which are subject to excise duty (see section 7.2.7 of the Introduction to the European Union).

3.7 Assembly/Installation

A supply of goods takes place in Luxembourg if the specific goods to be supplied are located in Luxembourg. This applies even if an overseas entrepreneur has no place of business in Luxembourg.

3.8 Supply of Services

The term 'services' applies to all transactions which are not treated as a supply of goods.

The transfer of intangible properties such as patents, know-how, software, etc, is considered as a supply of services.

Services also include:

- leasing, renting
- transport of persons and goods
- commissions
- research and expertise
- agreements to refrain from certain activities.

3.9 Self-Supply of Goods/Services

A taxable self-supply of goods is deemed to arise if:

- goods acquired in the course of a business and giving rise to an input tax credit are used for non-business purposes
- goods are extracted, manufactured, built or transformed by the entrepreneur himself for the use of his business. A self-supply also arises if the manufacturing, building or transformation is carried out by a third party at the request of the entrepreneur.

The rule of taxable self-supply is designed to avoid distortion of competition caused by the fact that otherwise an entrepreneur making exempt supplies would make a saving by not paying non-deductible VAT if he manufactured certain goods himself instead of acquiring them from third parties.

Self-supply of services is normally not deemed to constitute a taxable supply.

4   PLACE OF SUPPLY

VAT is chargeable in Luxembourg only when goods and services are supplied or deemed to be supplied in Luxembourg.

4.1   Supply of Goods

If the goods are dispatched or transported:

- the place of supply is in Luxembourg if the goods are in Luxembourg when dispatch or transport either by the supplier or by the person to whom they are supplied or by a third person begins
- if the goods are installed or assembled in Luxembourg, with or without a trial run, by or on behalf of the supplier, the place of supply is in Luxembourg.

If the goods are not transported:

- the place of supply of goods which are not dispatched or transported is deemed to be in Luxembourg if the goods are in Luxembourg when the supply takes place.

4.1.1 Chain Transactions

Where there is a series of agreements for the sale of the same goods from vendor to purchaser to sub-purchaser, etc and all parties to the agreements agree that the goods should be delivered directly by the vendor to the last sub-purchaser, each seller in this chain is deemed to have made a supply of goods to the next sub-purchaser and is accordingly liable for VAT. The net effect, of course, will be that if all sub-purchasers sell in the course of business, all will be entitled to an input tax credit exactly equal to the amount of VAT charged to them. If, however, one of them is not selling in the course of his business and is not therefore registered for VAT, his sub-purchaser will not pay VAT on the purchase. If this sub-purchaser sells in the course of his business he will nevertheless have to charge his purchaser VAT and account for it to the VAT authorities.

4.1.2 Distance Sellers

The place of supply of goods (other than new means of transport) dispatched or transported directly or indirectly by the supplier either:

- from the territory of another Member State to a non-taxable person in Luxembourg, or
- from Luxembourg to a person in another Member State who is not registered for VAT there

is the place where the goods are when the dispatch or transportation ends. Non-taxable persons include private persons, fully exempt persons and flat-rate farmers.

For full details see section 7.4.2 of the Introduction to the European Union.

4.2 Intra-Community Acquisitions

As a general rule, the place where an intra-Community acquisition of goods takes place is deemed to be the place where the goods are when transportation to the person acquiring the goods ends.

To make a zero-rated intra-Community supply followed by a taxed intra-Community acquisition on which the VAT may be deducted by the acquirer, the VAT identification numbers of the parties involved must be stated on the invoice.

If the goods for any reason arrive finally in a Member State other than that which issued the VAT number to the acquirer, the person purchasing the goods acquires the goods in the Member State of arrival of the goods. In this case double taxation could occur, since the purchaser must account for VAT both in the Member State which issued the VAT number to him and in the Member State of arrival of the goods.

The presumption is that the place of acquisition is the country which issued the VAT number to the acquirer. However, if the acquirer can show that he has paid VAT in the Member State of arrival of the goods he will not be liable for payment of acquisition VAT in his own Member State.

4.2.1 Chain Transactions

'Triangulation' involves the situation where three parties in three different countries are involved in selling and purchasing the same goods. For example, A in France sells goods to B in Belgium who sells the goods to C in Luxembourg and the goods are sent directly from A to C (see section 7.4.1 of the Introduction to the European Union).

4.2.2 Goods Placed on Board Ships, Aircraft or Trains During Transport

When goods are supplied for consumption on board ships, aircraft or trains during transport and the place of departure and destination are within the territory of the European Union, the place of supply is the place where the goods are at the time of departure of the transport.

4.3 Supply of Services

4.3.1 General Rule

Services are normally considered to be supplied at the place where the entrepreneur supplying the services is established or has a fixed basis from which the services are supplied.

4.3.2 Exceptions

There are a few exceptions to the general rule:

- services connected with real estate (real estate agents, architects, etc) are supplied where the real estate is situated
- transport of goods and persons is subject to VAT where it effectively takes place; thus, only transport within Luxembourg is subject to VAT
- the place of supply of the following services is deemed to be where they are physically carried out:
  - cultural, artistic, sporting, scientific, educational and entertainment services
  - ancillary transport activities, such as loading, unloading, handling and similar activities

- – valuations of movable tangible property
- – work on movable tangible property
■ the following services are deemed to be supplied at the recipient's place of business if he is a registered entrepreneur:
- – transfers and assignment of trademarks, licences, copyrights and patents
- – advertising services
- – services of consultants, engineers and accountants
- – data processing and supply of information
- – financial, banking and insurance services
- – supply of staff
- – hire of movable property other than means of transport
- – agreeing to refrain from carrying out an activity or exercising rights.

■ *intra-Community goods transportation, ie the transportation of goods from one Member State to another:* the basic rule is that the place of supply is the place of departure (Article 28bC Sixth VAT Directive). However, if the customer is registered for VAT in a different Member State to the supplier the place of supply is deemed to be the Member State of the customer, who must account for VAT on the reverse charge basis (see section 7.4.4 of the Introduction to the European Union).

■ *services ancillary to intra-Community goods transport:* the place of supply of services ancillary to intra-Community transport services of goods is not taxable in the country of the supplier where the customer is VAT-registered in another Member State. In these circumstances the supply is within the territory of the Member State which issued the customer with the VAT registration number and under the reverse charge mechanism the customer must account for the VAT (see section 7.4.5 of the Introduction to the European Union).

■ *services provided by brokers or other intermediaries:* the supply of such services which form part of an intra-Community transport of goods: the place of supply is the Member State which issued the VAT identification number of the customer (see section 7.4.6 of the Introduction to the European Union).

■ *services rendered by brokers or other intermediaries:* certain services provided which do not come within the scope of Article 9.2(e) of the Sixth VAT Directive: the place of supply is the Member State of the customer which issued his VAT registration number (see section 7.4.7 of the Introduction to the European Union).

■ *work on movable goods:* the place of supply of services on movable goods (eg repairs and valuations) is the Member State of the customer where the customer is registered for VAT in a different Member State to that of the supplier. Under the reverse charge mechanism the supply is not subject to VAT in the country of the supplier and the customer must account for VAT in his country (see section 7.4.8 of the Introduction to the European Union).

4.4   Reverse Charge Mechanism

The liability for payment of VAT on certain services supplied by a non-resident entrepreneur who does not maintain a fixed establishment in Luxembourg will normally fall on the taxable recipient (see section 2.8).

5   BASIS OF TAXATION

5.1   Supplies within Luxembourg and Intra-Community Acquisitions

VAT is calculated on the total consideration obtained for the supply of the goods or services, including ancillary expenses, transport, insurance and subsidies received as complementary consideration.

If a larger amount is received than invoiced, VAT is payable on the amount received.

5.2   Self-Supplies

VAT due on self-supplies is calculated on the basis of the purchase price of the goods or on the cost of the supplies. In the case of goods manufactured by an entrepreneur for his own business, the cost will include the value of the raw materials, the services obtained for the manufacturing, and the salary expenses if the work was carried out by the entrepreneur's own staff.

Self-supply of services is not a taxable transaction.

5.3   Imports

The basis of taxation on importation of goods is the value for customs purposes determined in accordance with the Community provisions in force. The basis includes, as far as they are not already included, taxes, duties, levies and other charges due outside Luxembourg as well as incidental expenses such as commission, packing, transport and insurance.

5.4   Intra-Community Acquisitions

The value used is the contract price, which may include commission, packing and transport. If the acquisition is fictitious, then there is no change in ownership and the VAT value is the purchase price, cost price or value of similar goods. The value of acquisitions is also separately shown on the VAT return.

5.5   Chargeable Event/Time of Payment

VAT becomes due at the time the goods are supplied or the services are rendered or when goods are imported into Luxembourg.

If there is an obligation to issue an invoice, tax becomes due on the fifteenth day following the supply of goods or services, or at the date the invoice is issued prior to that date.

Tax is also due on payments received on account relating to non-exempt supplies of goods or services before their delivery or performance.

The tax payable falls due on the fifteenth day of the month after the end of the tax period and must be remitted together with the VAT return (see section 9.4 'VAT Return').

5.6   Credit Notes/Bad Debts

If an entrepreneur gives a credit, he is allowed to reduce his VAT liability accordingly, provided a credit note is issued to the customer.

When evidence exists that the payment cannot be obtained from a customer, the output VAT paid on the supply can normally be recovered by the supplier. An adjustment should be made in all cases where the payment is not received after two years.

6 TAX RATES

The following rates are applicable under Luxembourg VAT law:

3%: (super reduced rate) applies to certain goods considered as essential, mainly food, pharmaceutical products, sale and borrowing of books, children's shoes and clothes, restaurants, hotels, transport of persons, concerts, theatres, residential buildings (see section 10.9)

6%: (reduced rate) applies to supplies of gas (for heating, lighting and engines), electricity, works of art – a special rate (see section 10.7)

12%: (intermediary rate) applies to:
- wine from fresh grapes of less than 13% vol (excluding sparkling wines, liquors and aperitifs)
- fuels
- lead free gasoline
- washing powders
- leaflets for advertisements
- tobacco
- advertising, advisory and similar services (lawyers, accountants, auditors)
- services provided by travel agencies and tour operators
- management of credit and of credit guarantee by a person other than the person who granted the credit
- custody or management of stocks and shares

15%: (standard rate) applicable to all supplies of goods and services not exempt or subject to another specified rate.

7 EXEMPTIONS

7.1 Exemptions with Credit for Input Tax
The main exemptions with credit for input tax are:
- export of goods
- sales by tax-free shops in airports
- supplies of goods to taxable persons within the Community
- supplies of new means of transport within the Community
- intra-branch transfers of goods within the Community
- distance sales taxable in another European Union country
- certain intra-Community acquisitions by foreign entrepreneurs
- import of goods destined to an intra-Community supply
- work and repairs performed for the account of a foreign client on goods to be exported
- supplies of goods and services to aircraft and ships engaged in international trade
- supplies of gold to public bodies
- supplies of goods and services to specified international institutions or embassies
- services connected with exports of goods
- services connected with imports of goods the cost of which is already included in the taxable basis of goods imported

- international transport of persons
- services of intermediaries related to certain exempt activities
- financial or insurance services supplied outside the European Union.

7.2 Exemptions without Credit for Input Tax

An entrepreneur engaged in exempt activities is not permitted to charge VAT and is not entitled to a credit for VAT incurred on expenditure made in connection with those activities.

The main exemptions are:

- medical care or services provided by hospitals, doctors, dentists and laboratories
- transactions on human blood, milk and organs
- social and cultural services
- educational services provided by schools and universities
- public postal services
- insurance and reinsurance transactions (input VAT may be recovered in certain cases)
- financial and banking services (input VAT may be recovered in certain cases)
- supply and leasing of real property (for exceptions see section 10.4 'Real Estate')
- supply of gold bars, ingots and coins used as legal tender
- transactions of shares.

7.3 Non-Taxable Transactions

7.3.1 Transactions within the Same Legal Entity

Supplies within the same VAT entity are considered to be outside the scope of VAT (see section 2.2 'Transactions with Branch/Subsidiary').

7.3.2 Transfer of Business

Transfer of a business or an independent part thereof is not subject to VAT provided the transferee continues to use the assets in carrying on the business.

The exemption does not prevent the recovery of the input VAT paid on other services related to the transfer of the business.

7.3.3 Subsidies

Subsidies are subject to VAT when the payments constitute in fact a complementary consideration for supplies of goods and services made by the recipient.

Subsidies are not subject to VAT when the payments provided by the government are not directly connected with the price of the supplies made.

7.4 Election to be Subject to VAT

Entrepreneurs making certain exempt supplies may elect to be subject to VAT. Election will enable them to charge VAT and to recover the input tax relating to these supplies.

Election is possible for:

- small entrepreneurs
- agricultural and forestry enterprises
- supply and leasing of real property

- distance sellers (see section 3.4)
- non-taxable legal persons and government bodies whose intra-Community acquisitions do not exceed LUF400,000 (see section 7.2.4 of the Introduction to the European Union).

8   CREDIT FOR INPUT TAX

8.1   General Rule

Generally, all the VAT paid on goods and services by a Luxembourg entrepreneur within the course of business is recoverable.

No credit is granted for input tax on:

- goods and services used for non-business purposes
- goods and services used for exempt transactions, with the exception of input tax related to exempt banking and financial and insurance transactions, provided the recipient of these services is established outside the European Community
- expenditure for private purposes (for example hotel accommodation, travel and restaurant expenses, expenses for food, for goods and services for maintaining a private lifestyle or for other private purposes).

8.2   Adjustment of Entitlement to Credit

Throughout a period of four book years for movable depreciable goods and nine book years for immovable goods following the year of purchase, the entitlement to a credit for input tax may be adjusted on a pro rata basis, depending on whether the use of the goods changes from use for exempt transactions to use for taxable transactions and vice versa.

8.3   Partial Exemption

An entrepreneur making taxable and exempt supplies is allowed to recover only the input tax relating to those taxable supplies.

If the goods or services can be attributed to being used for taxable supplies, the credit for input VAT will be fully allowed. If the attribution is made to exempt supplies, it will be totally disallowed.

If the goods or services are used for taxable and exempt supplies, the creditable input tax is calculated in the ratio of the turnover of supplies entitled to credit to the total turnover.

The ratio is established according to the available data at the time the entrepreneur started to use the goods or services. In the final VAT return of the year, an adjustment for creditable input tax must be made according to the information available for the entire year.

On request, the entrepreneur may be allowed to use another ratio if this gives a fairer split (for example actual use of the purchased goods).

The tax authorities may also oblige the entrepreneur to use a ratio other than the turnover ratio.

8.4   Time of Recovery

A credit for input tax can be claimed in the VAT return for the tax period (calendar year, quarter or month) during which the supplier made the supplies. Repayment is made on request if the tax credit exceeds LUF50,000 or if the tax credit at year's end exceeds LUF100.

8.5 Refund for Foreign Entrepreneurs

Foreign entrepreneurs not established in Luxembourg and who do not supply goods or services in Luxembourg may obtain a refund of VAT paid on goods or services purchased in Luxembourg.

Claims for refund must be requested on a form addressed to:

> Administration de l'Enregistrement et des Domaines
> Bureau d'imposition 11
> Boîte Postale 31
> L - 2010 LUXEMBOURG

Claims must be filed within six months following the end of the calendar year during which VAT was incurred in Luxembourg.

Claims must be accompanied by the original invoices and a certificate confirming the status as a taxable person issued by the tax authorities of the European Union Member State where the applicant is established. Minimum amounts for claims are LUF9,000 per quarter or LUF1,100 per year. Luxembourg law permits refunds to non-European Union entrepreneurs on the principle of reciprocity. Claims by non-European Union entrepreneurs can only be made on a yearly basis, the minimum amount per claim being LUF4,500.

9   ADMINISTRATIVE OBLIGATIONS

9.1   Registration

An entrepreneur engaged in any industrial, commercial or professional activity must register with the VAT authorities within the 15 days following the date of the beginning of his activities.

9.2   Books and Records

An entrepreneur is obliged to keep accounts in sufficient detail to permit application of the VAT and inspection by the tax authority. The records must be kept for a period of ten years.

9.3   Invoices

Invoices must be issued for each supply before the fifteenth day following the end of the month in which the supply was made.

All invoices must contain the following information:

- the date of the invoice
- the name and address of the supplier and the purchaser
- the date on which the supply of goods or services has taken place
- the quantity and designation of the goods or description of the services
- the price of the goods or services excluding VAT
- if different VAT rates are applied, the basis and the corresponding VAT applying to each VAT rate

- the VAT rates and the corresponding VAT due
- reason for any VAT exemption.

9.4   VAT Returns

Entrepreneurs are required to file monthly or quarterly VAT returns before the fifteenth day of the month after the end of the taxation period, or annual VAT returns before 1 March of the year following the taxation period.

The option of filing monthly, quarterly or annual VAT returns depends on the annual turnover realised during the year prior to the taxation year as follows.

Annual Turnover Excluding Tax

LUF1 – 4,500,000	annual return
LUF4,500,001 – 25 million	quarterly returns
> LUF25 million	monthly returns

9.5   VAT Identification Number

The VAT identification number contains ten digits: LU + 8 numbers.

This number is different from the VAT registration number which consists of 11 numbers.

9.6   VIES/Recapitulative Statements

Quarterly recapitulative intra-Community sales listings have to be filed with the VAT administration before the fifteenth day following the end of the quarter, indicating per customer the VAT identification number and the amount invoiced in relation to:

- intra-Community supplies and deemed supplies of goods
- goods dispatched for processing
- supplies of goods made in another Member State according to triangulation simplification measures.

If the annual intra-Community supplies of goods do not exceed LUF600,000 (excluding supplies of new means of transport) and the annual turnover of the taxpayer is between LUF1,800,000 and LUF4,500,000 the recapitulation statement can be submitted yearly.

If total turnover is less than LUF1,800,000 and intra-Community supplies do not exceed LUF600,000 a simplified listing has to be filed.

9.7   INTRASTAT

INTRASTAT formalities are kept separate from VAT obligations and have to be submitted to the Statec (Governmental office for statistics).

The statistics must list all intra-Community supplies of goods as well as all intra-Community acquisitions.

No statement has to be filed if the annual total of both movements (acquisitions and supplies) of goods does not exceed LUF4,200,000.

A simplified statement is allowed if the annual total of both movements is between LUF4,200,000 and LUF10 million.

A detailed statement must be submitted for both movements if the acquisitions or supplies exceed LUF10 million.

The detailed statement has to contain the following information:

■ the Member State of origin or of destination
■ the identification of the economic operator
■ the identification of the declaring third party, if any
■ the month or year of reference
■ the quantity of goods in volume and units*
■ the supplementary statistic unity, if any*
■ the statistical value of the goods*
■ the nature of the transaction*
■ the terms of supply*
■ the presumed transport form*.

9.8 Registers
Certain registers of goods movements must also be kept (see section 7.9.4 of the Introduction to the European Union).

9.9 Interest
Punitive interest at a rate of 12% per annum is payable from the date of notification of the formal recovery proceedings.

9.10 Powers of Authority
If a tax return is not filed after expiration of the time limit for submission, the tax authorities may issue an assessment for an estimated amount.

Penalties of between LUF2,000 and LUF200,000 may be fixed if legal obligations are not met. Penalties for late payment not exceeding 10% of the tax due may be fixed.

The statute of limitations is five years from the end of the calendar year in which the VAT liability arose.

9.11 Objections/Appeals
An appeal against an assessment of tax must be lodged within three months of receipt of the notice of assessment.

Further appeals are possible within three months to the District Court and to the Supreme Court (Conseil d'Etat).

10 SPECIAL VAT REGIMES

10.1 Agricultural and Forestry Enterprises
Agricultural and forestry enterprises are excluded entirely from VAT. They are not entitled to a credit for input tax but an option to be taxed as a normal entrepreneur can be made.

In the case of simplified statements, the information marked * may be ignored.

10.2 Banking and Financial Institutions

Most of the activities carried out by banking and financial institutions are exempt. In practice some activities which are taxable or deemed to take place outside the European Union, allow the recovery of a relatively low input tax.

10.3 Bonded Warehouses

Goods imported into bonded warehouses are not subject to VAT and customs duty until they are removed for sale in the European Union. Imports of goods into a bonded warehouse are subject to the prior approval of the Customs authorities.

10.4 Real Estate

10.4.1 Land

The acquisition of land is not subject to VAT but to a transfer duty at the rate of 7% or 10%* of the acquisition price.

10.4.2 Transfer of buildings

The acquisition of a building before its construction is subject to VAT. The rate is 15% of the acquisition price.

The acquisition of a building during its construction is subject to:

■   transfer duty at a rate of 7% or 10%* for the finished part
■   VAT at a rate of 15% for the part that is not yet finished.

The transfer of a building after completion is subject to transfer duty at a rate of 7% or 10%* of the total price.

An entrepreneur purchasing a building for business purposes may obtain a refund of VAT in so far as acquisition was subject to VAT by option.

10.4.3 Rental of Buildings

Rental income of a residential building is not subject to VAT.

Rental income for buildings used for business purposes is not normally subject to VAT. However, if the lessor and the lessee are both taxable persons, they may both opt for a taxable lease on condition that the building is assigned for more than 50% to an activity entitled to recover VAT. This option request has to be signed by both parties and will allow refund of input tax related to the leased building.

10.5 Small Entrepreneurs

Entrepreneurs whose annual turnover is less than LUF400,000 are not subject to VAT (see section 2.1 'General') and are not entitled to input tax credit. However, small entrepreneurs may opt for the application of the normal regime.

Special tax reductions are given to other small entrepreneurs whose annual turnover is less than LUF1 million.

---

* depending on the location and/or the nature of the building

10.6   Travel Agencies

Special rules apply to activities carried out by travel agencies.

10.7   Profit Margin Taxation on Second-Hand Goods, Works of Art, Collectors' Items and Antiques

Profit margin taxation applies to taxable dealers selling second-hand goods, works of art, collectors' items and antiques supplied to them by:

- non-taxable persons
- taxable persons making exempt supplies when the goods did not qualify for recovery of input VAT
- small entrepreneurs involving capital assets
- another taxable dealer under profit margin taxation.

'Taxable amount' is the difference between the sales and purchase price reduced by the VAT calculated on this same margin.

The taxable dealer making supplies of works of art, collectors' items and antiques:

- imported by himself
- supplied to him by their creator or successors in title
- supplied to him by a taxable person other than a taxable dealer when that supply was subject to reduced rate

may opt for application of profit margin taxation. This option has to cover a period of two years.

Under the profit margin scheme, input VAT is not deductible and invoices may not show any VAT.

A special globalisation regime is possible for goods whose purchase price is below LUF10,000.

Option for normal scheme is possible.

The special rate of 6% for works of art is applicable on:

- imports
- supplies made by:
  - their creator or his successor in title
  - a taxable person on an occasional basis who imported the goods himself from the creator or his successor who was entitled to full deduction.

10.8   Goods on Consignment

Goods transferred on consignment to or from Luxembourg are considered as intra-Community supplies or acquisitions. The owner of the goods transferred to Luxembourg has to register in Luxembourg.

10.9   Procedure Concerning Application of 3% Rate to Residential Buildings

The application of the 3% rate on residential building is subject to specific requests for reimbursement of 12% (difference between 15% normal rate and 3% specific rate) of VAT paid on:

- new constructions
- transformation or renovation of residential buildings within the three years of purchase or after 20 years

up to a maximum amount of VAT to be recovered of LUF1,500,000. In the case of sale or change of use or assignment of the building, one-tenth of the VAT recovered may be adjusted for each year remaining of a ten-year period.

Contributor: Thierry Fleming
Ernst & Young
PO Box 351
L-2013 Luxembourg
Tel: +352 42 11241
Fax: +352 45 123201

THE NETHERLANDS

1   GENERAL BACKGROUND

A general indirect tax on consumption of the value added tax type (VAT) – in Dutch 'Belasting over de Toegevoegde Waarde' (BTW) – was introduced on 1 January 1969. The VAT Act is supported by two Statutory Instruments: the Royal VAT Decree and Ministerial VAT Orders. Following European Community tax harmonisation, the VAT Act was amended to comply with the Sixth VAT Directive from 1 January 1979.

It should be noted that the exact wording of the Sixth Directive has not been incorporated into the Dutch legislation and there are many derogations which must be taken into account. Council Directive of 16 December 1991 (supplementing the common system of VAT and amending the Sixth VAT Directive with a view to the abolition of fiscal frontiers (91/680/EEC)) and Council Directive 92/111/EEC of 14 December 1992 (amending the Sixth VAT Directive and introducing simplification measures with regard to VAT) have also been adopted in the Dutch legislation.

Where the VAT Act refers to 'the Netherlands' it means the European territory of the Kingdom of the Netherlands, thereby excluding the Netherlands Antilles, Aruba and the Dutch part of the Continental Shelf.

VAT is administered by the various VAT Inspectors throughout the country in so far as the tax is not levied on importation. VAT due on importation is dealt with by the Inspectorate of Customs and Excise, unless the postponed accounting system is applied.

1.1   The Single Market – Intra-Community Acquisitions
As a Member State of the European Union, the Netherlands applies the rules for VAT applicable to the Single Market and, in particular, the transitional arrangements which apply in respect of intra-Community supplies during the transition period which commenced on 1 January 1993.

For ease of reference and to reduce repetition the transitional arrangements are set out in detail in section 7 of the Introduction to the European Union which precedes this section of the book.

It is recommended that this chapter is read in conjunction with the transitional arrangements.

2   WHO IS TAXABLE?

2.1   General
An entrepreneur supplying goods and services or making an intra-Community acquisition of goods (see section 7.2 of the Introduction to the European Union) within the Netherlands is liable to the tax. An entrepreneur is 'anyone who conducts a trade or business (or a

---

This chapter reflects the law on VAT in the Netherlands as at 1 January 1995.

liberal profession) independently'. A profit motive, however, is not necessary. Persons making supplies exclusively free of charge do not qualify as entrepreneurs. Generally, a person who makes an occasional transaction is not deemed an entrepreneur liable to VAT. An employee is not a taxable person for VAT purposes.

A 'trade or business' includes the exploitation of tangible or intangible goods (for example, copyrights, patents and trademarks) in order to derive income from them on a regular basis.

The taxable person is determined by economic and social considerations rather than legal concepts. The entrepreneur can be resident or non-resident, an individual, an association of individuals (for example, a partnership), a legal person, a combination of legal persons or any other economic entity.

2.2 Transactions with Branch/Subsidiary

Branches and subsidiaries of foreign companies from which supplies of goods and services are made in the Netherlands are treated in the same way as other entrepreneurs. Cross-border supplies of goods between a subsidiary and the parent company abroad or vice versa are within the scope of VAT.

When goods are transferred from a business in the Netherlands to another Member State to be used in the other Member State in the course or furtherance of the business, there is deemed to be an (exempt) intra-Community supply in the Netherlands followed by an intra-Community acquisition in the other Member State. Such a fictitious intra-Community transaction necessitates that the business which transfers the goods to another Member State must register there and fulfil all other administrative obligations required in the Member State of arrival of the goods.

There are several exceptions to this rule, the effect of which is to treat the specified transfers as being neither intra-Community supplies of goods in the Netherlands nor intra-Community acquisitions in the other Member State, and vice versa. Such transfers therefore should not be recorded as a supply on the VAT return or VIES sales list (recapitulative statement) with one exception, namely the transfer of goods/materials for the purpose of having contract work carried out on them should be recorded on the sales list.

Cross-border supplies of services between a branch and its foreign head office are, however, outside the scope of VAT and thus not taxable, since these are internal transactions within the same VAT entity.

2.3 Government Bodies

Public entities such as the State and municipalities may also be subject to VAT. These entities may, in fact, act in three different capacities, ie as 'government', non-entrepreneur or entrepreneur. When fulfilling a governmental function (ie which they are required to perform under public law) they do not act as entrepreneurs. Public entities making supplies can be deemed to qualify as entrepreneurs regarding certain supplies which may distort competition in relation to commercial enterprises.

If the public entities acting as such take part in intra-Community transactions they are treated as private persons and pay the VAT according to the origin principle (see section 7.2 of the Introduction to the European Union). In the other Member State the supplier will therefore charge VAT on his supplies to public bodies as if they were domestic supplies (see 7.2.4 of the Introduction to the European Union).

If a public body acting as such, however, purchases goods in another Member State for an annual amount exceeding a threshold of Hfl23,000 or, if this threshold has been exceeded in the previous calendar year, or when it opts to be treated as a taxable person, the public body is treated as such and such purchases are deemed to be intra-Community acquisitions, taxed in the country of destination.

2.4 Fiscal Unity/Group Taxation

The requirements for a fiscal unity are different for VAT purposes and corporate tax purposes.

Two or more Dutch resident entrepreneurs or fixed establishments constitute a fiscal unity for VAT purposes if they are so closely connected by financial, organisational and economic links that they form one single taxable entity. This is determined on the facts and circumstances. However, a formal decision from the tax inspector is required if they are to be recognised as a single taxable entity. Entrepreneurs can also request such a decision. The fiscal unity will have consequences from the first day of the month following the tax inspector's decision.

All members of the fiscal unity are normally registered under the name and number of a representative member of the group. One single VAT return is filed by the representative member.

Fiscal unities for VAT and corporate tax purposes do not necessarily have the same members.

Internal transactions between members of a fiscal unity are disregarded for VAT purposes. In particular, when (partly) exempt entities form part of a fiscal unity, this creates an advantage since it prevents irrecoverable VAT from being incurred on charges for internal transactions, in proportion to the extent that the fiscal unity as a whole is engaged in taxable transactions. Special care must also be taken with reorganisations (which may result in breaking up the fiscal unity).

A disadvantage of fiscal unity is that each member of the fiscal unity is jointly and severally liable for the VAT payable by the fiscal unity, irrespective of from whom the liability arose.

If the requirements for a fiscal unity are no longer met because of changing facts and circumstances, then the entrepreneur must inform the tax inspector. If he is not notified, the several liability for each of the previous members of the fiscal unity will continue.

Only taxable persons/entrepreneurs can form part of a fiscal unity. A company whose only activity consists of holding shares in other companies is not considered to be a taxable person/entrepreneur since the mere holding of shares is not an economic activity as defined in Article 4.2 of the Sixth VAT Directive. Therefore, 'pure' holding companies cannot participate in a fiscal unity.

2.5 Foreign Entrepreneurs

Non-Dutch entrepreneurs become in principle liable to VAT when supplying goods and services within the Netherlands in the course of their business unless the reverse charge mechanism is applied (see section 2.8).

If the foreign entrepreneur has a fixed establishment in the Netherlands from which supplies to third parties are made (for example, a workshop, plant, sales office or central depot), it is treated as a domestic entrepreneur. Registration requirements apply as for Dutch entrepreneurs.

Note that the concept of fixed establishment for VAT purposes is not the same as that of the permanent establishment for corporate and income tax purposes. It is normally necessary for supplies to be made from the fixed establishment in order to be recognised as such for VAT purposes.

2.6 Representative Offices

Representative and information offices of foreign entrepreneurs whose activities are limited to those of a preparatory or auxiliary nature do not normally qualify as fixed establishments for VAT purposes. The same generally applies for branches taxed on a cost-plus basis for corporate tax purposes. As a consequence, the Dutch VAT incurred will have to be recovered under the 'mutual recovery procedure' (see section 8.5 'Refund for Foreign Entrepreneurs'), instead of the normal procedure of claiming a credit when filing the quarterly or monthly VAT returns.

2.7 VAT Representatives

Except in cases of distance sales subject to VAT in the Netherlands, foreign entrepreneurs making supplies within the Netherlands do not have to employ a tax representative or appoint someone who is severally and jointly liable for the tax.

A fiscal representative may be appointed with either a general licence or a limited licence. In the latter case the representation is restricted to importation and subsequent intra-Community supplies.

2.8 Reverse Charge Mechanism

If no fixed establishment exists, a special provision shifts the VAT liability for the supply of both goods and services from the foreign entrepreneur to the Dutch resident recipient, provided the latter is an 'entrepreneur' or 'entity' as defined by the General Act on Taxation. Registration by the foreign entrepreneur is then not required.

This specific provision avoids problems connected with the Dutch tax authorities having to maintain administrative and financial connections with foreign entrepreneurs who have no fiscal presence in the Netherlands.

Under this so-called reverse charge mechanism, the Dutch resident entrepreneur must account for the supplies as if he had made the supply himself. At the same time he may recover the VAT due in full as input tax. As a result, no VAT is actually payable unless the Dutch resident entrepreneur is wholly or partially exempt.

The reverse charge mechanism does not apply if the recipient of the goods and services is a non-resident entrepreneur who does not maintain a fixed establishment in the Netherlands or is a non-entrepreneur who does not qualify as an entity under the General Act on Taxation (for example, a private person). In this case, VAT is still due and payable to the tax authorities by the foreign entrepreneur and registration with the Inspectorate of Customs and Excise in Heerlen is compulsory.

Contrary to most other European Union countries this reverse charge mechanism is not restricted to certain specific services.

2.9 Importers

VAT liability arises when goods are brought into the Netherlands from a third country and cleared by Customs. VAT due must be paid by the importer (entrepreneur or private individual) in the same way as if it were an import duty, before the goods are released by the Customs authorities. For resident entrepreneurs and foreign entrepreneurs with a fixed establishment in the Netherlands who regularly import goods, a deferral scheme (postponed accounting system) may delay the VAT from becoming due until the next VAT return is filed (see section 5.4 'Chargeable Event/Time of Payment').

It is not necessary actually to own the goods in order to declare them for importation. It is not uncommon for the goods to be imported by an authorised (forwarding) agent, who will report the VAT due on importation. These amounts are subsequently charged through to his customer, who may credit this VAT as input VAT.

2.10 Acquirers of Goods from Other European Union Member States

The movement of goods from one Member State to another results in an acquisition. If there is an acquisition by a Dutch business, the business in the other European Union Member State is not obliged to register. If there is a 'fictitious acquisition' (because, for example, there is no change in title) VAT registration in the Netherlands will be required for the business established in the other European Union Member State (see section 7.2 of the Introduction to the European Union).

2.11 Non-Taxable Legal Persons – Taxable Persons with No Right to Recover VAT and Flat-Rate Scheme Farmers

Such persons are not subject to VAT when the annual value of their yearly intra-Community acquisitions is below Hfl23,000. As soon as an acquisition puts them above this threshold they are subject to common intra-Community rules and must pay VAT on their acquisitions. They must then obtain an identification number and submit VAT returns.

The same persons may opt to be subject to the common rules even for acquisitions below the threshold. The option takes effect on the first day of the month in which it is exercised and expires on 31 December of the second year following the option; the option is renewable for periods of two years except if renounced two months before the two-year expiring period.

2.12 Supplier of New Means of Transport

Any person who undertakes on an occasional basis intra-Community supplies of new means of transport that are dispatched or transported from the Netherlands to another Member State is regarded as a taxable person (see section 7.2.6 of the Introduction to the European Union).

3   WHAT IS TAXABLE?

VAT is levied on the supply of goods and services for consideration in the Netherlands, the intra-Community acquisition of goods by a taxable person or by another legal entity (not being a taxable person – see section 7.2.4 of the Introduction to the European Union), on the intra-Community acquisition of a new means of transport (see section 7.2.6 of the Introduction to the European Union) and on the importation of goods. The distinction between a supply of goods and services is important, because of the different rules governing the time and place of supply. The decision may influence whether or not the supply is taxable and which VAT rate is applicable.

3.1   Supply of Goods

Generally, a supply of goods includes any transaction resulting in a transfer of title or possession of goods which then cease to form part of an entrepreneur's business assets. In addition to an outright sale of goods (including sale through a commission agent or by auction), this includes, for example:

- the handing over under a hire-purchase, conditional sale or credit-sale agreement
- the handing over by a manufacturer who produces goods from materials provided by the customer
- the transfer of goods under an agreement to install or incorporate them into other goods.

All tangible goods qualify as goods. Electricity, gas, heat, refrigeration and similar intangibles are deemed to be tangible goods.

The establishment, transfer, amendment, and cessation of rights relating to real property (with the exception of mortgages and ground rents) are also considered to be a supply of goods.

When goods are transferred from a business in the Netherlands to another Member State to be used in the other Member State in the course or furtherance of the business there is deemed to be an (exempt) intra-Community supply in the Netherlands followed by an intra-Community acquisition in the other Member State (see section 7.2.2 of the Introduction to the European Union).

3.2   Importation of Goods

'Importation of goods' is the introduction of goods from third countries (or territories of the European Union where VAT is not applied) into free circulation in the Netherlands. Importation is a taxable event unless exempt (see section 7.1 'Exemptions with Credit for Input Tax'), irrespective of whether the importer is a private individual or an entrepreneur. Payment of VAT may be deferred by provisionally storing the goods in a bonded warehouse (see section 10.6 'Free Port/Bonded Warehouse').

The input VAT due at importation can be credited by the person for whom the goods are destined (ie the addressee). The entitlement to the credit must, however, be evidenced with proper documentation.

3.3   Intra-Community Acquisitions

From 1 January 1993 VAT is charged, levied and paid on the intra-Community acquisition of goods (other than new means of transport) effected within the Netherlands for consideration by a taxable person, and on the intra-Community acquisition of new means of transport effected by anyone within the Netherlands for consideration (see section 7 of the Introduction to the European Union).

3.4   Distance Sellers
Persons who supply goods from another Member State to non-VAT registered persons in the Netherlands may be taxable in respect of such supplies (see section 7.4.2 of the Introduction to the European Union). Fiscal representation is required.

3.5   New Means of Transport
The transfer to the Netherlands from another Member State of new means of transport is always taxable as an intra-Community acquisition regardless of the status of the supplier or the purchaser (see section 7.2.6 of the Introduction to the European Union).

3.6   Contract Work
If a VAT registered person in another Member State sends goods to the Netherlands to be processed there and the processed goods are not returned to the Member State from which the goods for process originated, then the owner of the goods will have to register and account for VAT in the Netherlands (see section 7.2.5 of the Introduction to the European Union).

3.7   Excise Products
In certain circumstances a non-registered acquirer of excise products may have to register and account for VAT on acquisitions of products which are subject to excise duty (see section 7.2.7 of the Introduction to the European Union).

3.8   Assembly/Installation
A supply of goods takes place in the Netherlands if the specific goods to be supplied are located in the Netherlands. This applies even if an overseas entrepreneur has no place of business in the Netherlands. However, the liability of supply of assembled or installed goods may be passed to the Dutch customer under the reverse charge mechanism (see section 2.7 'Reverse Charge Mechanism').

3.9   Supply of Services
For VAT purposes a service is any transaction for consideration which does not otherwise qualify as a supply of goods. When there is no consideration, the service is not taxable. Services include:

■   the outright transfer of rights, such as patent rights, trademarks, licences, securities, etc
■   the providing of management, staff hire, the leasing of goods, granting of (sub) licences
■   agreements to refrain from certain activities or to tolerate activities of others.

If the service is rendered as a gift, the related input VAT may be disallowed (see section 8.1 'Credit – General Rule').

3.10   Self-Supply of Goods/Services
VAT is normally not charged on self-supplies. However, a taxable supply of goods is deemed to arise if:

- goods are produced or acquired in the course of business activities and are appropriated permanently for other than business purposes (for example, personal use)
- goods are manufactured within the enterprise and used for business purposes, but only if the entrepreneur is not (or only partially) entitled to a credit for the input tax had he purchased the goods instead of manufacturing them.

The latter provision aims at avoiding distortion of competition where an entrepreneur making, for example, exempt supplies (and thus not entitled to a credit for input tax) could avoid paying non-deductible VAT by manufacturing the goods in-house rather than acquiring them from third parties. For example, a builder who builds houses which are subsequently rented out free of VAT.

When, upon request of the entrepreneur, a third person produces goods from goods belonging to that entrepreneur, the goods so produced are deemed to be goods manufactured in the entrepreneur's own enterprise. Land also qualifies as 'goods' for this purpose.

Although the VAT Act enables the Ministry of Finance to prescribe similar rules for the self-supply of services, no such order has, as yet, been made. Consequently, the self-supply of services is not taxable.

Donations of goods and services for business purposes (ie, gifts) are not liable to VAT. However, in some cases the credit for related input VAT may be disallowed (see section 8.1 'Credit – General Rule').

4   PLACE OF SUPPLY

It is essential to determine the place of supply since VAT is imposed only when goods and services are supplied or deemed to be supplied, or goods are acquired or deemed to be acquired in the Netherlands.

4.1   *Supply of Goods*
The place where a supply is deemed to take place is:

- if the goods are transported in connection with the supply, the place where such transport begins
- in all other cases, the place where the goods are at the time of the supply.

4.1.1   *Chain Transactions*
A special rule applies if several entrepreneurs enter into subsequent transactions involving the same goods (chain transactions). In such cases each entrepreneur within the chain is deemed to have made a taxable supply even if the actual ownership is transferred directly from the first entrepreneur to the last recipient in the chain. When these transactions involve transportation of the goods from a place outside the Union to a place within the Netherlands, all transactions are deemed to be in the Netherlands and thus subject to Dutch VAT. A zero rate applies to the transactions preceding the supply made by the actual importer. With regard to intra-Community chain transactions, see section 7.4.1 of the Introduction to the European Union.

4.1.2 Consignment

If a non-resident consignor holds stock in the Netherlands, he is required to register as a non-resident company for Dutch VAT purposes for making a taxable fictitious intra-Community acquisition (when moving his products to the Netherlands) and performing administrative obligations. The sale by the non-resident consignor to the Dutch consignee and the subsequent sale by the consignee to a customer are considered taxable domestic supplies in the Netherlands.

However, according to a ruling of the Dutch tax authorities, a non-resident consignor does not have to register for VAT purposes in the Netherlands. According to the ruling, the acquisition by the consignor in the Netherlands resulting from placing the goods in consignment can be outside the scope of Dutch VAT. The supply made by the consignor to the consignee which takes place when the consignee supplies the goods to the recipient is at that moment deemed to be an intra-Community supply which should be reported as such by the non-resident consignor in his own country. The Dutch consignee is deemed to make a taxable intra-Community acquisition and, subsequently, a taxable supply to the customer.

If consignment goods are transported from outside the European Union into the Netherlands, VAT will be due on importation by the consignee. A ruling allows the consignee to deduct the import VAT. When the goods are resold, a supply is made simultaneously by the non-resident consignor to the consignee in the Netherlands, since the goods were already imported. However, on the basis of a departmental ruling, this supply can remain outside the scope of the VAT.

4.1.3 Distance Sales

The place of supply of goods (other than new means of transport) dispatched or transported directly or indirectly by the supplier either:

- from the territory of another Member State to a non-taxable person in the Netherlands, or
- from the Netherlands to a person in another Member State who is not registered for VAT there

is the place where the goods are when the dispatch or transportation ends. Non-taxable persons include private persons, fully exempt persons and flat-rate farmers.

For full details see section 7.4.2 of the Introduction to the European Union.

4.2 Intra-Community Acquisitions

As a general rule, the place where an intra-Community acquisition of goods takes place is deemed to be the place where the goods are when transportation to the person acquiring the goods ends.

To make a zero-rated intra-Community supply followed by a taxed intra-Community acquisition on which the VAT may be deducted by the acquirer, the VAT identification numbers of the parties involved must be stated on the invoice.

If, for any reason, the goods arrive finally in a Member State other than that which issued the VAT number to the acquirer, the person purchasing the goods acquires the goods in the Member State of arrival of the goods. In this case double taxation could occur, since the purchaser must account for VAT both in the Member State which issued the VAT number to him and in the Member State of arrival of the goods.

The presumption is that the place of acquisition is the country which issued the VAT number to the acquirer. However, if the acquirer can show that he has paid VAT in the Member State of arrival of the goods, he will not be liable for payment of acquisition VAT in his own Member State.

4.2.1 Chain Transactions

'Triangulation' involves the situation where three parties in three different countries are involved in selling and purchasing the same goods. For example, *A* in France sells goods to *B* in Belgium who sells the goods to *C* in the Netherlands and the goods are sent directly from *A* to *C* (see section 7.4.1 of the Introduction to the European Union).

4.2.2 Goods Placed on Board Ships, Aircraft or Trains During Transport

When goods are supplied for consumption on board ships, aircraft or trains during transport and the place of departure and destination are within the territory of the European Union, the place of supply is the place where the goods are at the time of departure of the transport.

4.2.3 Work on Movable Goods

The place of supply of services on movable goods (eg, repair and valuation) is where the services are actually performed. However, there are special rules where such services are performed for a customer who is VAT registered in another Member State (see section 7.4.8 of the Introduction to the European Union).

4.3 Supply of Services

4.3.1 General Rule

Services are normally considered to be supplied where the entrepreneur supplying the services is established or has a fixed establishment from which the services are supplied. There are, however, various exceptions.

4.3.2 Exceptions

The exceptions to the general rule are as follows:

- services with respect to real estate (rendered by real estate agents, architects, etc) are supplied where the real estate is situated
- transport of persons takes place where the actual transport occurs. Only transport within Dutch territory is subject to Dutch VAT
- transport of goods is deemed to take place where the transport begins. However, in cases of intra-Community transport this service is deemed to be rendered at the place of the recipient of the service under whose VAT identification number the service is rendered. (Transport of goods for exportation or to the place of destination after importation qualifies for the zero rate – see section 7.4.4 of the Introduction to the European Union)
- services consisting of cultural, artistic, sporting, scientific, educational, entertainment or similar activities are supplied where the activity is physically carried out. This rule also applies to services consisting of loading, unloading or similar activities in

connection with transport. However, in cases of intra-Community transport these services are deemed to be rendered in the Member State which issued the VAT identification number to the recipient (see section 7.4.5 of the Introduction to the European Union). Services supplied in respect to tangible movable goods, including examination by experts, are also supplied where the activity is physically carried out, but if such services are rendered to a person under his VAT identification number in another Member State these services are zero-rated (see section 7.4.8 of the Introduction to the European Union)

■ transfer and assignment of copyrights, patents, licences, etc' advertising' advisory and similar services (such as those of lawyers, accountants), data processing and supply of information; the leasing of tangible movable goods (with the exception of means of transport – to which the general rule applies), banking, financial and insurance services, supply of staff, and the obligation to refrain, partly or fully, from pursuing a professional activity or from a transfer or assignment of copyrights, patents, etc are all supplied where the recipient of the services resides provided that he qualifies as entrepreneur in another Member State or is resident outside the European Union territory

When, based on the above mentioned rule, the services are taxable outside the European Union but actually used and enjoyed within the Netherlands by a non-taxable legal person, the services are taxable within the Netherlands. Furthermore, the hiring out of means of transport to any non-taxable persons is taxable within the Netherlands when the means of transport is used and enjoyed within the Netherlands.

4.4 Reverse Charge Mechanism

In the case of supplies of services mentioned in section 2.8 above, the supply is treated as being made where the recipient of the supplies belongs. Thus the 'importation' into the Netherlands of such services is subject to the reverse charge (self-supply to and by the customer). The 'export' of such services to a person in his business capacity elsewhere in the European Union or to any person in a third country is treated as outside of the scope of Dutch VAT.

5 BASIS OF TAXATION

5.1 Supplies within the Netherlands

VAT is calculated on the total amount charged. If this amount is not expressed in monetary terms VAT is charged on the total value of the consideration. If a larger amount is received than invoiced, VAT is payable on the amount actually received.

Some amounts are excluded from the tax basis, eg cash discounts, certain incidental charges (such as itemised insurance costs which the entrepreneur supplying the goods pays to another entrepreneur), certain transitory amounts, import duties and other taxes paid on behalf of the recipient.

For second-hand goods and works of art sold by a taxable dealer the margin scheme applies (see section 7.10.2 of the Introduction to the European Union).

5.2 Self-Supplies

For the self-supply transactions and the permanent appropriation of goods produced or acquired in the course of business for non-business purposes (see section 3.3 'Self-Supply of Goods/Services'), the basis of taxation is the actual cost of purchasing or producing the goods, ie the price, exclusive of VAT, for which the goods can be acquired, or the costs of manufacturing (including overheads but excluding fixed general costs, interest and profit mark-up). Self-supply of services is not a taxable transaction.

5.3   Importation

VAT on importation is calculated on the customs value. Carriage, insurance and freight costs until importation and transportation costs until the place of destination in the Netherlands are included in the customs value in addition to any taxes, duties or other charges (such as import duty, excises and agricultural levies but excluding the VAT) levied on the goods.

VAT due on the importation of carriers of information (eg cassette tapes, diskettes), under certain conditions, may be limited to the value of the carrier, excluding the value of the information. The information is taxable as a service.

5.4   Intra-Community Acquisitions

The amount on which tax is chargeable on the acquired goods is the total consideration. The consideration is the total amount or, in so far as the compensation is not in money, the total value of the compensation charged on the supply, including all taxes, commissions, costs and charges whatsoever, but excluding the VAT chargeable in respect of that acquisition. If more is actually paid than has been agreed, the taxable amount is the amount actually paid.

If the invoice is in foreign currency, the applicable exchange rate will be the last published selling rate at the time the VAT becomes due.

As a general rule, the transfer by a person of goods from his undertaking in the Netherlands to another Member State for the purposes of his business is deemed to be a supply of goods. The taxable amount is the (historical) purchase or cost price (see 7.5.1 of the Introduction to the European Union).

5.5   Chargeable Event/Time of Payment

Generally, the VAT becomes due at the time the goods are supplied or the services are rendered or when goods are imported into the Netherlands. If the entrepreneur is obliged to issue an invoice, the VAT becomes due at the time the invoice is issued or, if this does not happen in time, at the time the invoice has to be issued. If the consideration is received at an earlier time, the VAT becomes due at that moment.

The tax payable falls due one month after the end of the taxation period and must be remitted together with the VAT return.

Tax is payable even if the customer has not yet paid the invoice. When VAT is accounted for on a cash basis, the tax is only payable in so far as the consideration was received.

Where VAT arises on the importation of goods, the tax must normally be paid before the goods are released by the Customs authorities. However, a resident entrepreneur regularly importing goods can defer payment until the moment he has to file his periodic VAT return. He can normally claim a credit for the tax in the same return. This postponed accounting or deferral scheme ('verleggingsregeling') thus avoids any cash flow problems and will be granted together with a special VAT code number by the tax inspector upon request.

Non-resident entrepreneurs who do not maintain a fixed establishment in the Netherlands do not have this possibility of deferral, unless they import specifically designated goods, mainly raw materials and non-consumables. They will, therefore, normally have to pay the VAT on importation and subsequently set off this amount in a domestic return or request a refund at the Inspectorate for Foreign Entrepreneurs in Heerlen. Payment of VAT may, however, be deferred by provisionally storing the goods in a Customs warehouse.

VAT chargeable on the intra-Community acquisition of goods is due on the fifteenth day of the month following the month during which the intra-Community acquisition occurred (see section 7.5.2 of the Introduction to the European Union).

If an invoice is issued prior to the fifteenth day by the supplier the tax is due when the invoice is issued.

A taxable person/entrepreneur accounts for VAT on an intra-Community acquisition by reporting the acquisition VAT on his periodic VAT return. If he is entitled to full deduction of VAT he deducts the acquisition VAT as input tax on the same return. However, if the taxable person/entrepreneur is not entitled to full or partial deduction he must pay to the tax authorities (Belastingdienst) the difference between the VAT on the acquisition and the amount he is entitled to deduct.

VAT in respect of fictitious intra-Community acquisitions becomes due at the time that the acquisition of the goods was made.

5.6   Cash/Invoice Basis
The liability for VAT is normally linked with the issue of the invoice. Invoices must be issued before the fifteenth day after the month in which the supply was made. An entrepreneur is obliged to issue an invoice for supplies made to other entrepreneurs. No invoice is required for supplies made to non-entrepreneurs.

Certain designated entrepreneurs (retailers, etc) can account for VAT on a cash basis. VAT then becomes due at the time the consideration for the supply is actually received. However, even when VAT is accounted for on a cash basis, invoices need to be issued for supplies made to entrepreneurs.

5.7   Credit Notes/Bad Debts
Entrepreneurs accounting for VAT on the invoice basis who do not receive or only partially receive payment, or to whom the consideration was repaid because a discount was given or the goods were returned, can have their VAT liability adjusted on application. The application must be filed with the tax inspector together with the normal VAT return, over the period in which the entitlement to refund arises. It is generally not possible to set off this amount against the VAT due. Proof that the amount will not or cannot be paid by the customer must, however, be provided. Entrepreneurs accounting for VAT on a cash basis automatically obtain bad debt relief.

If the entrepreneur gives a credit, he is also allowed to claim a refund of VAT provided a credit note is issued to the customer. The customer, in turn, must repay to the tax authorities the VAT stated on the credit note in his next VAT return.

6 TAX RATES

There are at present three tax rates:

0%: exports; supplies of sea-going vessels and aircraft used in international transport, services rendered in connection with the supplies referred to above, such as loading, unloading and repair of sea-going vessels, transport of imported goods to their place of destination, international passenger transport by sea-going vessels and aircraft. The zero rate in the Netherlands, specifically mentioned in the VAT Act, is a technical zero rate which works as an exemption with credit (see section 7.1 'Exemptions with Credit for Input Tax') for the exportation of goods and services related to export and import, for example, the supply of goods from outside the Netherlands which are not (yet) imported. The zero rate is in general applied to intra-Community supplies of goods (see section 7.7.1 of the Introduction to the European Union). An entrepreneur/taxable person applying the zero rate must be able to prove his entitlement to do so on the basis of books and documents, for example, bills of lading, payments from abroad, Customs documents, VAT identification numbers of the customers, etc.

6%: in general, supplies subject to the reduced rate are basic primary necessities (for example, all foodstuffs), medical goods (medicines, medical aids), cultural goods (books, paintings), goods and services for use by the agricultural sector, and certain other supplies such as passenger transport, and hotel accommodation.

17.5%: all supplies of goods and services not exempt or subject to the reduced rate of 6% or to 0%.

7 EXEMPTIONS

7.1 Exemptions with Credit for Input Tax
Generally no credit for input VAT is available for exempt supplies. However, an exception applies to Dutch input VAT incurred in connection with exempt banking, financial and insurance transactions, provided the recipient of these services is resident or established outside the territory of the European Union. Also, the zero rate works as an exemption with credit (see section 6 'Tax Rates').

Exemptions may also apply to the importation of goods, for example, personal effects of travellers, goods imported by diplomats, packing containers and means of transport which will be re-exported, certain goods for educational institutions, household contents of persons moving into the Netherlands from outside the Union, certain goods to be imported temporarily, and goods re-imported after having been repaired abroad.

7.2 Exemptions without Credit for Input Tax
An entrepreneur engaged in exempt activities is not permitted to charge VAT. Moreover, he is not entitled to a credit for VAT incurred on expenditure made in connection with such activities. The main exemptions are:

- supply and leasing of real property, with certain exceptions (see sections 10.11 'Supply of Real Property' and 10.12 'Rental of Real Property')

- certain supplies of goods and services in the medical, social and cultural areas (such as those provided by doctors, hospitals, youth organisations, museums, etc)
- insurance, financial and banking transactions (with the exceptions discussed above), management of special investment funds
- non-commercial activities of public radio and television broadcast organisations. Television commercials are, however, taxable
- public postal, telephone (until 1 January 1996) and telegraph services
- certain educational services
- supply of goods which have been used exclusively for exempt activities or are otherwise not eligible for input credit.

7.3   Exempt Importation
The importation of goods which is followed by an intra-Community supply may be exempt (see section 7.7.2 of the Introduction to the European Union).

7.4   Non-Taxable Transactions

7.4.1 Transactions within the Same Legal Entity
Supplies within the same VAT entity (internal transactions) are disregarded since they are considered to be outside the scope of VAT, for example, supplies of goods and services between members of a fiscal unity or supplies of services between a foreign head office and its Dutch branch or vice versa.

7.4.2 Transfer of a Business
No VAT is due if an enterprise or an independent part thereof is sold or otherwise transferred as a 'going concern', provided the transferee continues to use the assets in carrying on the enterprise. The fact that this is a non-taxable transaction does not, however, affect the entitlement to a credit for input tax on, for example, the expenditure incurred in connection with transferring the business.

7.4.3 Subsidies/Penalty Payments/Compensation
This is a rather complex area and expert advice should always be obtained. Subsidies and grants are subject to VAT when these payments:

- constitute the consideration for supplies made by the recipient or
- are directly connected with the price of the supplies (price subsidies), for example, subsidies paid by the government to entrepreneurs in compensation for charging too low prices to their customers (eg agricultural products).

Other subsidies are outside the scope of VAT – in particular, subsidies provided by the government for, for example, certain (or all) activities of some institutions performed in the general public interest. Also, 'operational' subsidies are considered outside the scope of VAT. These are subsidies granted to cover budget deficits for which the grantor of the subsidy does not request a supply in return and which are performed purely with the object of giving the respective entity assistance.

Payment for damage claims (compensation) normally does not fall within the scope of VAT since these payments are not made as a consideration for a supply.

Penalty payments, for example, to compensate for premature termination of lease agreements are, however, subject to VAT.

7.5   Election to be Subject to VAT

Entrepreneurs making certain exempt supplies may elect to be subject to VAT, in which case they will be entitled to recover the input tax incurred in connection with these supplies. Election is possible for:

- supply and leasing of real property (see sections 10.11 'Supply of Real Property' and 10.12 'Rental of Real Property')
- agricultural and forestry enterprises (see section 10.1 'Agricultural and Forestry Enterprises')
- distance sellers (see section 7.4.2 of the Introduction to the European Union)
- flat-rate farmers, public bodies and exempt persons (see section 7.2.4 of the Introduction to the European Union).

8   CREDIT/REFUND FOR INPUT TAX

8.1   General Rule

An entrepreneur is in principle entitled to recover VAT payable on goods and services, intra-Community acquisitions and importation of goods within the course of business. However, no credit is granted for input tax on:

- goods and services used for non-business purposes (for example, private use)
- goods and services used for exempt transactions (with the exception of input tax related to exempt banking and financial and insurance transactions, provided the recipient of these services is resident or established outside the European Union territory)
- restaurant and catering expenditure for meals and drinks, goods and services for maintaining a certain private lifestyle, gifts, supplying employees with food, housing, private transport, remuneration in kind or facilities for sport and entertainment or for other private purposes.

For certain categories of expenditure, a specific rule is applied:

Input tax is disallowed on gifts if given to those who, if they are or should be charged with VAT on goods or services, would not at all or not for more than 50% be entitled to a credit for input tax. If the total of the purchase, production or cost price (excluding VAT) incurred for the same person on the categories of expenditure referred to above does not exceed Hfl500 – in one book year, the disallowance of the input credit can be disregarded.

8.2   Adjustment of Entitlement to Credit

During a certain period (four book years for movable depreciable goods and nine book years for immovable goods following the year of purchase) the entitlement to a credit for input tax at the time of purchase may be adjusted on a pro-rata basis, depending on whether the use of the goods changes from use for exempt transactions to use for taxable transactions or vice versa. This may result in either additional credit or liability for further tax.

8.3 Partial Exemption

Entrepreneurs making both taxable and exempt supplies are entitled to recover input tax related only to their taxable supplies. The creditable input tax is calculated on the ratio between taxable supplies and total supplies. In some cases, to obtain a more reasonable proportion, another ratio may be negotiated with the tax authorities on the basis of, for example, actual use of the purchased goods and services in relation to time spent, employees, floor space, number of transactions, etc.

The ratio is established according to the data available at the time the entrepreneur started to use the goods and services. In the last VAT return of the book year, an adjustment for creditable input tax must be made according to the information available for the entire book year.

8.4 Time of Recovery

A credit for input tax can normally be claimed in the VAT return for the declaration period (normally a calendar quarter or month) during which the supplier made his supply, as shown on the invoice. If the VAT liability for a particular declaration period is less than the VAT credit, the difference will be refunded on application.

8.5 Refund for Foreign Entrepreneurs

Non-resident entrepreneurs who are not liable to Dutch VAT need not register. Nevertheless, they may incur Dutch input VAT, for example, on importation, costs incurred by representative offices in the Netherlands (for example, office lease, cars, computers, exhibitions, etc) or by employees for courses/conferences in the Netherlands. This Dutch input tax cannot be credited in another European Union Member State. A refund of the tax can, however, be obtained under the so-called 'mutual recovery procedure', on special application to:

> Belastingdienst/Particulieren/Ondernemingen
> Buitenland
> Postbus 2865
> 6401 DJ Heerlen
> The Netherlands

Entrepreneurs resident outside the European Union can also obtain this refund. The application must be completed in Dutch on a special form (OB, BU) and submitted by 30 June of the year following the year in which the VAT was incurred.

Claims should not cover a period of less than three months (unless the claim relates to a remainder of the calendar year) or more than a calendar year.

It often takes at least six months before first refund claims are dealt with by the tax authorities. Subsequent claims are normally handled more quickly.

Foreign entrepreneurs who are (partly) refused a refund have the right to lodge an appeal to the VAT authorities within six weeks after the decision. Claimants should lodge appeals to the Court within six weeks after the decision by the VAT authorities on the first appeal.

Only VAT in excess of Hfl470 may be reimbursed for a claim period of more than three months but less than a calendar year. If the application relates to a calendar year or a period shorter than three months, VAT claims in excess of Hfl60 can be granted.

It is not necessary for a foreign entrepreneur to use an agent or fiscal representative in the Netherlands for refund claims.

VAT on certain kinds of expenditure is excluded from the credit/refund (see section 8.1 'General Rule').

9   ADMINISTRATIVE OBLIGATIONS

9.1   *Registration*
Registration is required at the VAT office in the district in which the taxable person's business is located as soon as the definition of entrepreneur is satisfied and liability to VAT arises (see section 2 'Who is Taxable?'). There is no monetary limit below which registration is not required.

Foreign entrepreneurs who do not maintain a Dutch place of business and whose liability is not shifted to the recipient of the supply (see section 2.8 'Reverse Charge Mechanism') will have to register with Belastingdienst/Particulieren/Ondernemingen Buitenland in Heerlen, (Foreign Entrepreneurs Department). It is not necessary to appoint a VAT agent, but this may be more practical.

Provisional registration as a 'starting entrepreneur' is possible. After a registration form has been completed, the Tax Inspector will normally grant the entrepreneur a VAT registration number.

9.2   *Books and Records*
The entrepreneur is obliged to keep detailed records and accounts of the supplies made by and to him, as well as his imports and exports. Failure to do so may result in a maximum penalty of Hfl5,000. The records must be kept for a period of ten years.

9.3   *Invoices*
Invoices must be issued before the fifteenth day after the month in which the supply was made. Normally, an invoice must contain the following information:

- the VAT registration number of the supplier (in intra-Community transactions the VAT registration numbers of both the supplier and the customer – see section 7.9.1 of the Introduction to the European Union)
- the date of supply
- the name and address of the entrepreneur supplying the goods and services
- the name and address of the entrepreneur to whom the goods and services are supplied
- a clear description of the goods and services supplied
- the quantity of goods supplied
- the consideration (excluding VAT)
- the amount of VAT due.

Where no liability to VAT arises, no VAT should be stated on the invoice. This is of importance not only for the non-entrepreneur, but also for the foreign entrepreneur whose liability to VAT is shifted to the recipient of the supplies under the reverse charge mechanism (see section 2.8 'Reverse Charge Mechanism'). The latter may consider stating on the invoice, 'VAT liability shifted to recipient under article 12, para. 2, VAT Act'.

Incorrectly stated VAT will, nevertheless, be due to the tax authorities. Furthermore, an inadequate invoice will normally jeopardise the right to claim a credit for input tax by the recipient.

9.4   VAT Returns

The entrepreneur is obliged to file a tax return (including remittance of any VAT due) within one month of the end of each calendar quarter.

The tax inspector can require that a tax return be filed monthly or the entrepreneur may elect for monthly filing if this is more favourable for him (ie, when his input tax regularly and significantly exceeds his output tax). Filing annually is only possible with approval from the tax authorities.

9.5   VIES Statements

VIES statements ('Opgaven Intra-Communautaire Leveringen') must be submitted by entrepreneurs/taxable persons to the Central Unity ICT on a quarterly basis at the following address:

> Centrale Eenheid ICT
> Pikeursbaan 11
> PO Box 5054
> 7400 GD Deventer
> The Netherlands

See 7.9.2 of the Introduction to the European Union for further details.

9.6   INTRASTAT

Traders who supply goods to other Member States or who acquire goods from other Member States must provide monthly details of the goods movement if their sales exceed Hfl400,000 and/or their acquisitions exceed of Hfl400,000 on a yearly basis (see section 7.9.3 of the Introduction to the European Union).

9.7   Registers

Certain registers of goods movements must also be kept (see 7.9.4 of the Introduction to the European Union).

9.8   Powers of Authorities

If no VAT return is received after expiry of the time limit for submission of the return, the tax authorities will issue an assessment for an estimated amount.

Failure to file, late filing or late payment will result in penalties in the form of additional assessments. In principle, the fines can be 100% of the additional tax due. However, the penalty is normally reduced to 10%, 25% or 50%, depending on the circumstances.

The statute of limitations for additional assessments is five years from the end of the calendar year in which the VAT liability arose. The VAT authorities will also audit the records of the five preceding years to check whether the VAT due has been collected.

9.9   Objection/Appeal

An appeal can be made to the tax inspector against:

- an additional tax liability assessed on a VAT return
- the inspector's decision regarding the reduction of a fine
- his refusal to grant a refund

so long as it is made within six weeks from the date of assessment or decision. Further appeals are possible to the Court of Appeal and, if necessary, the Supreme Court, the time limit again being six weeks.

9.10 Liability for Managers

Under certain conditions, managers or persons/legal entities acting as such can be held liable for the VAT due.

10 SPECIAL VAT REGIMES

10.1 Agricultural and Forestry Enterprises

These enterprises are excluded entirely from VAT with respect to their transactions performed for 'agricultural' production in the strict sense. At the same time, they are not entitled to a credit for input tax. However, they can, if they wish, opt to be taxed as an ordinary entrepreneur. This may be advantageous where substantial investments are made.

Entrepreneurs purchasing agricultural goods and services from these qualifying agricultural and forestry enterprises can, however, claim a fixed 5.6% of the amounts paid as input tax.

10.2 Art and Antiques

A special regime applies to objects of art and antiques in conformity with the Council Directive on second-hand goods (see section 7.10.2 of the Introduction to the European Union).

10.3 Building Construction

A special provision shifts the liability for VAT from the sub-contractor to the main contractor. The main contractor must account for the supplies as if he had made the supply himself. At the same time this VAT can be recovered as input tax.

10.4 Financial Institutions

No special regimes (for example, election to become subject to VAT) apply to financial institutions such as banks and insurance companies. A credit is, however, allowed for Dutch input tax incurred in relation to exempt banking, financial and insurance transactions, provided the recipient of these services is resident or established outside European Union territory.

10.5 Fishing Enterprises

A special zero rate applies to the importation and supply of fish to a fish auction.

10.6 Free Port/Bonded Warehouse

No free port facilities apply in the Netherlands. However, there is a bonded warehousing system where goods can be stored without being subject to import duties and VAT. The goods may be sorted and tested, etc while stored in a bonded warehouse, and even assembly is possible under certain conditions.

10.7 Retailers
Certain designated entrepreneurs, such as retailers, can account for VAT on the cash basis instead of an invoice basis.

10.8 Small Entrepreneurs
A special tax reduction is given to small entrepreneurs who are either individuals or associated groups of individuals (for example, partnerships) and who owe an amount of VAT of no more than Hfl4,150 per year after credit for input VAT.

10.9 Travel Agencies
Special rules exist for the tax treatment of activities of travel agencies involving trips, organised transport, the supply of food and beverages during the trips, commissions on sales of organised trips, and the letting of holiday bungalows and apartments.

10.10 Transfer and Leasing of Real Property
The VAT treatment of property transactions is rather complex, and great care needs to be taken when acquiring or disposing of any real property interest (freehold or leasehold). Expert advice should, therefore, always be obtained.

10.11 Supply of Real Property
The transfer of real property constitutes a taxable supply from the moment of construction until two years after it has been taken into use for the first time. Subsequent transfers will be exempt from VAT unless both the buyer and the seller make a joint election for a taxable supply.

Election for a taxable transfer may be advantageous, depending on the circumstances. The question of whether or not an option will be favourable is closely related to the nine-year adjustment period following the year of purchase during which the entitlement to a credit is reviewed (see section 8.2 'Adjustment of Entitlement to Credit').

The adjustment is made on the legal assumption that the supplying entrepreneur continues to use the property supplied within the course of his business until the end of the adjustment period:

- exclusively for exempt transactions, when the supply of the property is exempt, or
- exclusively for taxable transactions, when the supply of the property is taxable.

For example, a selling entrepreneur (such as a bank or insurance company) who is not entitled to credit the VAT which has been paid upon acquisition of the property, but who opts for a taxable transfer may recover a proportionate amount of the previously uncreditable VAT. In contrast, an entrepreneur who is entitled to deduct the VAT, and who opts for a taxable transfer may find that the proportionate amount of previously credited VAT becomes uncreditable.

Election for a taxable transfer must, however, be made jointly and thus requires the co-operation of the buyer, whose VAT position and interest may not coincide with those of the seller. Also, where a joint election for a taxable transfer has been made, a special provision shifts the liability for VAT due by the seller to the buyer, who will have to declare this VAT due on his VAT return. To the extent that entitlement to a credit exists, he can again credit this VAT.

Note that the transfer of the economic ownership of real property is considered to be a supply for VAT purposes.

In addition to VAT, the buyer will also have to consider the fact that the transfer of real property may be subject to a 6% Transfer Tax.

Generally the buyer can claim an exemption from Transfer Tax if the transfer is also subject to VAT but, even so, double taxation does sometimes occur.

The exemption from Transfer Tax does not apply if the following two conditions are met simultaneously:

- the entrepreneur supplying the real property has used it as a business asset in the course of his business, and
- the acquirer qualifies as an entrepreneur who will use the real property in the course of his business for VAT-taxable transactions and who is therefore entitled to a full (or partial) refund of VAT charged to him on acquisition.

In general, if the buyer is not entitled to a credit for input tax, an election for a taxable transfer is not likely to be favourable for him, as this will result in an uncreditable 17.5% VAT charge, although the transfer of real property will then be exempt from Transfer Tax. If, however, the buyer is entitled to a credit, he may be inclined to co-operate in an election for a taxed transfer. The 17.5% VAT can be credited and the only charge will be the 6% Transfer Tax, which can then not be avoided.

10.12 Rental of Real Property
The hiring and letting of real property is normally exempt from VAT except for:

- the renting of machines and business installations
- the rental of accommodation within the framework of the hotel business to persons who only stay there for a short period
- the rental of parking space for motor vehicles and boats, etc
- the rental of safe deposit boxes
- the rental of real property, other than buildings or parts thereof used as a dwelling.

The lessor and lessee of real property may opt for a taxable lease by filing a joint request provided it will not be used as a dwelling. The advantage of such an option for the lessor may be that it will enable him to claim a refund of input tax. If the lessee is an entrepreneur who is in a position to credit input tax charged to him, an option for a taxable lease will be more advantageous than an exempt lease.

Contributor: Prof. Dr B. J. M. Terra
                 Moret Ernst & Young
                 PO Box 7883
                 1008 AB Amsterdam
                 The Netherlands
                 Tel: +31 20 5497333
                 Fax: +31 20 6462553

PORTUGAL

1   GENERAL BACKGROUND

Value added tax (VAT) was introduced in Portugal on 1 January 1986 to overcome certain deficiencies in the tax system on consumption and also to comply with the requirements of the European Union following the accession of Portugal from 1 January 1986.

Harmonisation with the Sixth VAT Directive was achieved in 1989.

Portugal comprises the continental territory plus Madeira and the Azores. Because of the existence of lower VAT rates applicable to supplies in Madeira and the Azores, operations relating to supplies in Madeira, the Azores and mainland Portugal must be treated and reported separately.

Administration of VAT has been given to a central service in Lisbon. VAT at the point of importation is collected by the Customs.

1.1   *The Single Market – Intra-Community Acquisitions*
As a Member State of the European Union, Portugal applies the rules for VAT applicable to the Single Market and, in particular, the transitional arrangements which apply in respect of intra-Community supplies during the transition period which commenced on 1 January 1993.

For ease of reference and to reduce repetition the transitional arrangements are set out in detail in section 7 of the Introduction to the European Union which precedes this section of the book.

It is recommended that this chapter is read in conjunction with the transitional arrangements.

2   WHO IS TAXABLE?

2.1   *General*
Broadly speaking a taxable person is defined as any entity under whose name is carried on, independently and regularly, an economic activity. The word entity can mean an individual, a company, a legal body or a fund.

The following are also considered to be taxable persons:

- anyone performing occasional transactions qualified as commercial by the law (excluding purchase for resale)
- anyone performing an operation in connection with an economic activity, no matter where performed
- anyone importing goods

This chapter reflects the VAT legislation in Portugal as at 31 December 1994.

- any person quoting VAT on an invoice
- any person making intra-Community acquisitions of new means of transport
- any person making intra-Community supplies of new means of transport.

2.2 Transactions with Branch/Subsidiary

No special regulation applies to transactions between a branch and its foreign head office. They are considered to be two independent taxpayers and therefore supplies between them are normally subject to VAT. There are, however, special rules with regard to intra-branch movements of goods cross-border within the European Union (see section 7.2 of the Introduction to the European Union).

2.3 Government Bodies

The State and other public entities are taxable persons in respect of onerous transactions which do not constitute mere acts resulting from their powers of authority.

When performing intra-Community acquisitions of goods of an amount higher than PTE1,800,000 per annum the government bodies are always considered to be taxable persons (see section 7.2.4 of the Introduction to the European Union).

2.4 Fiscal Unity/Group Taxation

The fiscal unity concept is not applicable in Portugal.

2.5 Foreign Entrepreneurs

Foreign entrepreneurs with no establishment in Portugal are subject to VAT when they make taxable supplies which are considered to be supplied in Portugal. This is the case when foreign entrepreneurs import goods into Portugal. This also applies when they perform services which are deemed to be supplied in Portugal, or when they sell in Portugal goods previously imported to or purchased in Portugal by them.

2.6 Representative Office

Representative offices of foreign entrepreneurs are not regarded as liable to VAT when they only carry out activities of a preparatory or auxiliary nature. The foreign entrepreneur will be able to claim from the Portuguese VAT authorities a refund of the input VAT incurred in Portugal (see section 8.5 'Refund for Foreign Entrepreneurs').

2.7 VAT Representatives

Foreign entrepreneurs performing operations which are considered to be supplied in Portugal must register for VAT purposes. The registration must be made through a VAT representative who must be resident in Portugal.

Compliance with all the administrative obligations in the VAT Code must also be made through the VAT representative. The VAT representative is jointly and severally liable for compliance with all the VAT obligations.

2.8 Reverse Charge Mechanism

Foreign entrepreneurs who supply the services indicated under article 9.2(e) of the Sixth VAT Directive (royalties, advertising, consultancy, etc) to Portuguese VAT taxpayers do not account for VAT in Portugal. Instead, the tax is due by the recipient entrepreneur.

This rule also applies in the case of intra-Community transport services of goods; services ancillary to transport services, and intermediary services supplied by a taxable person established in another European Union Member State (see section 7.4 of the Introduction to the European Union).

Foreign entrepreneurs who make other kinds of supplies in Portugal must register for VAT purposes. When this rule is not complied with, the Portuguese taxpayer acquiring the goods or services is responsible for the payment of the VAT due. However, this does not extinguish the foreign entrepreneur's obligations.

2.9 Importers
Goods brought from third countries into Portugal are subject to VAT at Customs clearance. The tax is payable by the importer.

2.10 Acquisitions – European Union Trade
Cross-border transactions between enterprises in the 15 European Union Member States are not treated as imported goods, but as intra-Community acquisitions (see section 7 of the Introduction to the European Union).

2.11 Non-Taxable Legal Persons – Taxable Persons with No Right to Recover VAT and Farmers Benefiting from Notional Refunds
Such persons are considered as having no obligation to comply with VAT law when, during the civil year and the preceding one, their yearly intra-Community acquisitions are below PTE1,800,000. As soon as an acquisition puts them above this threshold they are subject to the common intra-Community rules and must pay VAT on their acquisitions.

The same persons may opt to be subject to the common rules even for acquisitions below the threshold. The option is made by presenting a return during the month of January, is valid from the first day of the same month and must be kept for a period of at least two years. To be renounced a return must be presented during the month of January of the year to which it refers.

2.12 Supplier of New Means of Transport
Any person who undertakes on an occasional basis intra-Community supplies of new means of transport that are dispatched or transported from Portugal to another Member State is regarded as a taxable person (see section 7.2.6 of the Introduction to the European Union).

3 WHAT IS TAXABLE?

The following are subject to VAT:

- supplies of goods and services effected for consideration within Portugal by a taxable person acting as such
- imports of goods
- intra-Community transactions effected within Portugal (see section 7 of the Introduction to the European Union).

3.1 Supply of Goods

In accordance with the VAT Code a supply of goods is considered to happen when a tangible good is transferred for consideration in a way corresponding to the use of the right of property.

Electricity, gas, heat and refrigeration are considered as tangible goods.

In addition to the above definition there are certain events that are considered to be supplies of goods such as:

- the delivery of goods by way of a leasing contract which has a clause, applicable to both parties, providing for the transfer of the ownership at the end of the contract
- the delivery of a movable good as a result of a contract of purchase and sale where the transfer of ownership is only made when the price is either totally or partially paid
- the delivery of movable goods produced or assembled as a result of contract work.

When goods are delivered as a result of a commission contract, taxable fictitious supplies of goods are considered to happen between the commissionaire and the principal as well as between the commissionaire and the client.

The transfer of the ownership of a business or of such a part of it that may become an independent business is considered neither a supply of goods nor a supply of services when the recipient is a partly or wholly taxable person.

3.2 Imports

Broadly speaking importation of goods is a concept applicable to goods coming from third countries. The liability to tax happens when the goods are cleared by the Customs.

Goods under Customs control are not considered as imported.

3.3 Acquisitions

VAT is accounted for as an acquisition on the VAT return as output tax and will be recoverable subject to the normal rules.

Provided that Portuguese businesses quote their VAT registration number, complete with the national prefix, the supplies of goods from other Member States may be effectively zero-rated to the Portuguese purchaser.

3.4 Distance Sellers

Persons who supply goods from another Member State to non-VAT-registered persons in Portugal may be taxable in respect of such supplies (see section 7.4.2 of the Introduction to the European Union).

3.5 New Means Of Transport

The transfer to Portugal from another Member State of new means of transport is always taxable as an intra-Community acquisition regardless of the status of the supplier or the purchaser (see section 7.2.6 of the Introduction to the European Union).

3.6 Contract Work

If a VAT-registered person in another Member State sends goods to Portugal to be processed there, and the processed goods are not returned to the Member State from which the goods for process originated, then the owner of the goods will have to register and account for VAT in Portugal (see section 7.2.5 of the Introduction to the European Union).

3.7 Excise Products

In certain circumstances a non-registered acquirer of excise products may have to register and account for VAT on acquisitions of products which are subject to excise duty (see section 7.2.7 of the Introduction to the European Union).

3.8 Assembly/Installation

A supply of goods takes place in Portugal if the specific goods to be supplied are located in Portugal. This applies even if an overseas entrepreneur has no place of business in Portugal.

3.9 Supply of Services

The concept of supply of services given by the Portuguese VAT Code has a residual nature; thus any operation not being either a supply of goods or an import of goods or an intra-Community acquisition of goods is a supply of services.

3.10 Self-Supplies of Goods/Services

The following self-supplies of goods and services are subject to VAT:

- the free supply of goods belonging to an undertaking when the input VAT was deducted upon their acquisition (excluding samples and low value gifts)
- the permanent allocation of goods belonging to an undertaking to the private use of the owner or of its employees, when the input VAT was deducted upon their acquisition
- the free use of goods of an undertaking by its owner or employees when the input VAT was deducted upon their acquisition
- the free supplies of services performed by an undertaking to meet the private needs of its owner or the employees.

Self-supplies are also taxable in the case of a partially taxable person, using the system of direct attribution for deducting input tax, when goods are transferred from the taxable sector to the exempt sector of the business.

4 PLACE OF SUPPLY

When considering the important concept of supply, it is necessary to divide Portugal into the following three areas:

- The mainland
- Madeira
- The Azores

In these circumstances, the concept of supply is also important for the purpose of defining in which part of Portugal a transaction is considered to have been carried out for taxation and reporting purposes.

4.1   Supply of Goods

4.1.1   General
A supply of goods is considered to have occurred:

■   at the place of departure of the transport to the client
■   when the supply does not involve any transport, at the place where the delivery is actually made.

When the importer and the subsequent acquirers sell goods before their importation these operations are considered to take place in Portugal. In this case the rules above must be used to define in which particular part of Portugal the transaction takes place.

4.1.2   Distance sales
Where a supplier dispatches or transports goods (other than new means of transport) directly or indirectly either:

■   from the territory of another Member State to a non-taxable person in Portugal, with an annual sales value of PTE6,300,000, or
■   from Portugal to a person in another Member State who is not registered for VAT there with an annual sales value which exceeds the threshold set by the country of destination

the place of supply is the place where the goods are when the dispatch or transportation ends. Non-taxable persons include private persons, fully exempt persons and flat-rate farmers.

For full details see section 7.4.2 of the Introduction to the European Union.

4.1.3   Supplies on Board Ships, Aircraft and Trains
When the supplies are made on a ship, aircraft or train, during an intra-Community transport of persons, the place of supply is at the place of departure of the transport.

4.2   Supply of Services

4.2.1   General rule
The supply of services in Portugal is taxable when and where the supplier has his head office or the fixed place of business from which the service is supplied.

4.2.2   Exceptions
The following are exceptions to the general rule:

■   services connected with real estate, including those performed by estate agents, architects, etc are deemed to be supplied at the place where the property is located
■   cultural, artistic, sporting, scientific, educational and entertainment services, including those performed by the organisers of those activities and those performed by the suppliers of services ancillary to those activities are deemed to be supplied where the events are physically carried out
■   renting of means of transport is taxable in Portugal:

–   when the lessor is established in Portugal

– when the lessor is established in third countries and the goods are effectively used in Portugal.

When the supplier is not VAT registered in Portugal the following services are deemed to be supplied in Portugal if the recipient is a Portuguese VAT-taxable person:

- transfers and assignments of trade marks, licences, copyright
- patents, advertising services
- services of consultants, engineers, chartered accountants, consultancy offices
- data processing and supply of information
- financial, banking and insurance services
- supply of staff
- acceptance to refrain from carrying out an activity or exercising any rights
- renting of movable properties (apart from the renting of means of transport)
- services of intermediaries in these activities.

On the other hand, when these same services are performed by a Portuguese VAT-taxable person they are not taxable when:

– the recipient is in a third country
– the recipient is a VAT-taxable person in another European Union country

- Contract work performed on an intra-Community basis and goods delivered by a supplier in Portugal to a customer in another Member State on behalf of a buyer in a third Member State is treated in the same manner as triangulation (see section 7.4.1 of the Introduction to the European Union).
- **Work on movable goods:** such work is deemed to be supplied in the place where it is actually performed. However, special rules apply if services are provided by recipients established outside Portugal (see section 7.4.8 of the Introduction to the European Union).
- **Transportation services:** the general rule regarding transport services is that they are taxable in Portugal only in regard to the distance covered in Portugal. However, since enforcement of this rule would be in practice impossible, there are numerous exceptions and exemptions that are applicable to transport services. As a result, transport services are taxable:

  – when performed inside the Mainland
  – when performed inside each island of the Azores and Madeira
  – when related to intra-Community transactions (see section 7.4.4 of the Introduction to the European Union).

- **Services ancillary to transport services:** when supplied in connection with intra-Community transport of goods services, such services may be zero-rated (see section 7.4.5 of the Introduction to the European Union).

- **Services provided by brokers or other intermediaries:** the place of supply of such services which form part of an intra-Community transport of goods is the European Union Member State which issued the VAT identification number of the customer (see section 7.4.6 of the Introduction to the European Union).

- **Services rendered by brokers or other intermediaries:** the place of supply of certain services provided by brokers or other intermediaries (which do not come within the scope of Article 9.2(e) of the Sixth VAT Directive) – is the Member State of the customer which issued to him his VAT registration number (see section 7.4.7 of the Introduction to the European Union).

4.3 Reverse Charge Mechanism

See section 2.8 above.

5 BASIS OF TAXATION

5.1 Supplies within Portugal

VAT is assessed on the total price received, or to be received, as consideration for the supplies of the goods or services by the supplier from the purchaser, the customer or a third party.

The following are considered as included in the basis of taxation:

■ taxes, duties, levies and charges, excluding the VAT itself
■ incidental expenses such as commission, packing, transport and insurance costs charged by the supplier to the purchaser or customer
■ subsidies directly linked to the price of the supplies.

The taxable amount shall not include:

■ price discounts and rebates allowed to the customer
■ interest for late payment
■ the amounts received as indemnities when declared by the court
■ the amounts received by a taxable person from his purchaser or customer as repayment for expenses paid out in the name and for the account of the latter and which are entered in his books in a suspense account.

The taxable person may opt to consider the subsidies received as subject to VAT even when they are not directly linked to the price of the supplies. When this option is not exercised the subsidies (excluding those granted in relation to the purchase of equipment) are treated as if they were resulting from exempt supplies without credit for input VAT.

Where information for determining the taxable amount is expressed in a foreign currency the exchange rates to be used are the rates for the sale of a currency, either as published by the Bank of Portugal or as practised by any bank established in Portugal. The taxable persons may opt either to use the rate of the day when the tax becomes chargeable or the first working day of the corresponding month.

5.2 Self-Supplies

VAT due on self-supplies of goods must be calculated, as the case may be:

■ on the purchase price, or
■ on the cost price

at the moment when the operation takes place.

VAT due on self-supplies of services must be calculated on the open market value of the services.

5.3 Importation of Goods

The taxable amount on the importation of goods is the Customs value as defined by the applicable European Union regulations, and shall include the following elements when they are not already included in it:

- import duties and any other taxes due on importation, excluding the VAT to be levied
- chargeable expenses, such as commission, packing, transport and insurance costs incurred up to the first place of destination within the Portuguese territory, excluding transport expenses between the islands making up the Autonomous Regions of Madeira and the Azores, and between these and Continental Portugal and vice versa.

5.4 Acquisitions

The value used is the contract price, which may include commission, packing and transport.

If the acquisition is fictitious, then there is no change in ownership and the VAT value is the purchase price, cost price or value of similar goods. The value of acquisitions is also separately shown on the VAT return.

5.5 Chargeable Event/Time of Payment

5.5.1 Supply of Goods

The taxable event happens and the VAT is chargeable at the moment when the goods are delivered to the customer. However:

- when the supply is made only after the installation or the assembly of the goods, the taxable event happens when either the installation or the assembly are completed
- when the supply is made in accordance with a contract for a permanent supply, and the payment of the supplies is fixed to happen with reference to fixed periods, the taxable event happens at the end of each period
- when the property of the goods is transferred only when a certain condition is met the taxable event happens when the condition is met
- when the supply is made through a commissionaire, the fictitious operation between the principal and the commissioner is considered to happen at the same moment that the goods are delivered either to the customer or to the principal.

5.5.2 Supply of Services

The taxable event occurs and the VAT is chargeable at the moment when the supply of the service is completed. However:

- when the supply is made in accordance with a contract for a permanent supply and payment for the supply is made on a periodic basis, the taxable event happens at the end of each period
- when the supply is made through a commissionaire, the fictitious supply made by the principal to the commissioner is considered to happen at the same moment as the supply to the customer.

The above rules have the following exceptions:

235

   –   when any amount is received or invoiced before the date of the taxable event the VAT is chargeable immediately

   –   where there is an obligation to issue an invoice, the VAT is due at the moment when the invoice is issued. Otherwise, the VAT is chargeable at the end of the legal period in which the invoice should have been issued

■   VAT is due on intra-Community acquisitions at the same moment as defined above; however, the tax only becomes chargeable on the fifteenth day of the month following the one where the taxable event happened, unless an invoice was issued earlier (see section 7 of the Introduction to the European Union).

As a rule, the payment of VAT by taxpayers included in the normal regime is made together with the return with respect to the period when the tax became chargeable (see section 9.4).

5.6   *Credit Notes/Bad Debts*
When a credit note is issued cancelling all or part of an invoice, the entrepreneur may deduct the VAT shown on the credit note from output VAT when filing his VAT return. VAT paid on uncollected debts can be refunded when the debts qualify as bad debts.

6   TAX RATES

Currently there are two rates in mainland Portugal:

5%:   basic foodstuffs, pharmaceuticals, books, newspapers, agricultural inputs, diesel, electricity, etc

17%:   all other goods and services which are not exempt or taxable at the reduced rate.

However, where operations are considered to have been performed in Madeira and the Azores the rates are 4% and 13% respectively.

7   EXEMPTIONS

7.1   *Exemptions with Credit for Input Tax*
Exemptions with credit allow the taxable person to reclaim from the State the full VAT incurred on his purchases of goods or services.

These exemptions apply to the following:

■   exports and similar transactions
■   general financial transactions and services supplied by insurance brokers and insurance agents when the recipient is established outside the European Union
■   international transport of persons or goods
■   supplies of services included in the taxable basis of the importation of goods
■   supplies of goods and services exempt under international agreements
■   delivery of goods to be placed under Customs duty suspensions
■   services connected with goods under Customs duty suspensions.

7.2 Exemptions without Credit for Input Tax

These exemptions do not give the taxable person the right to deduct, or reclaim from the State, the VAT incurred on his purchases.

Examples of these exemptions are:

- the medical and paramedical professions, hospitals, centres for medical treatment, etc
- educational establishments within the national education system
- public postal services
- general financial transactions and services supplied by insurance brokers and insurance agents, when the recipient is not established outside the European Union
- the renting and the sale of immovable property.

7.3 Exempt Importation

The importation of goods which is followed by an intra-Community supply may be exempt (see section 7.7.2 of the Introduction to the European Union).

7.4 Non-Taxable Transactions

7.4.1 Transactions within the Same Legal Entity

Supplies within the same legal entity are not taxable when the branch and its head office are both established in Portugal. However, supplies made between a foreign head office and its branch in Portugal are treated as taxable transactions.

7.4.2 Transfer of Business

The transfer of a business or of a complete and independent branch of an activity is not subject to VAT unless the recipient is a non-taxable or wholly exempt person.

When the recipient is a partially exempt company it must account for VAT taking into account its deductible proportion.

7.4.3 Subsidies/Penalty Payments/Compensation

Subsidies are generally subject to VAT when they are directly linked to the cost of a taxable supply (see section 5.1).

7.5 Election to be Subject to VAT

Besides real estate (see section 10 'Special VAT Regimes') taxpayers carrying on the following activities can opt to be subject to VAT under normal terms when carrying on the following activities:

- certain centres for medical treatment
- agricultural, husbandry and forestry activities.

Distance sellers (see section 3.4), non-taxable legal persons and government bodies (see section 7.2.4 of the Introduction to the European Union) may also elect to be taxable persons.

8   CREDIT/REFUND FOR INPUT VAT

8.1   The General Rule

The principle is that all the VAT incurred upon the acquisition of goods or services by a Portuguese taxable person is recoverable.

This rule has some important exceptions. Thus the VAT incurred upon the acquisition of the items indicated below is not deductible:

- acquisition, manufacture, importation, rental, use, transformation or repairing of passenger cars, yachts, helicopters, planes, motor-bicycles and motorcycles
- acquisition of fuel used by vehicles, excluding diesel oil; only 50% of the input VAT on diesel oil used in passenger cars is deductible
- expenses of transport and business travel of the taxpayer
- expenses relating to accommodation, meals, drinks and tobacco
- expenses relating to entertainment and luxury goods and services.

8.2   Adjustment of Entitlement to Credit

The credit for input VAT obtained on capital assets may have to be adjusted if one of the following events occurs before the end of the fourth year (for movable goods) or the ninth year (for immovable goods) following the year when they began to be used:

- transfer of the capital assets (for consideration or free of charge), if the transaction is not subject to VAT
- transfer of the capital assets from a taxable to an exempt sector of activity
- termination of business
- termination of all taxable activities.

The deduction of the input tax regarding fixed assets must also be adjusted when the owner is a partially exempt person and certain conditions are met during the above defined period of adjustment.

8.3   Partial Exemption

Taxable persons who make both taxable and exempt (without credit) supplies are allowed to recover only that input VAT relating to taxable supplies, calculated on a pro rata basis.

The deductible proportion is calculated according to Article 19 of the Sixth VAT Directive.

The amount of the subsidies not included in the taxable amount must be included in the denominator of the fraction.

8.4   Time of Recovery

When a taxable person has a VAT credit in excess of his VAT liability, a refund can be claimed in the periodic VAT returns when the net credit is higher than PTE1,500,000.

The refund can also be claimed when during a period of 12 months there is a permanent credit higher than PTE50,000.

Reimbursements must be made by the end of the third month following the claim. This period is reduced to 30 days for taxpayers in a permanent credit situation. Reimbursements to non-resident taxpayers must be made within six months of the filing of the claim.

In practice, since 1993 the recovery period has been longer as a result of the introduction by the government of artificially complicating administrative controls.

8.5   *Refund for Foreign Entrepreneur*

Foreign entrepreneurs not registered for VAT purposes in Portugal are entitled to a refund of the VAT incurred in Portugal provided that:

- they do not have a residence or a permanent establishment in Portugal
- they have not effected any sale of goods or rendered any services which are deemed to be supplied in Portuguese territory, except:

    - transport and related services connected with imports and exports or entry into duty free zones
    - rendering of services for which the tax is due in Portugal by the recipient entrepreneur.

The reimbursable VAT must be capable of being deducted/recovered by a Portuguese entrepreneur acting under the same conditions.

The reimbursement to non-European Union entrepreneurs is only made when it is certified by the country where they are established that:

- they are subject to a turnover tax in that country
- their country applies a reciprocal treatment to Portuguese taxpayers.

In addition to this, non-European Union entrepreneurs can only claim for the reimbursement of the VAT through a resident representative.

The claim must be filed, at the latest, before 30 June following the end of the calendar year during which VAT was incurred in Portugal. The original invoices must accompany the claim. The amount to be reimbursed cannot be lower than PTE4,000.

Quarterly claims can be filed when the amount to be reimbursed is over PTE32,000.

9   ADMINISTRATIVE OBLIGATIONS

9.1   *Registration*

Taxpayers must register and submit a declaration before beginning their activity.

9.2   *Books and Records*

Accounting and bookkeeping must be organised so as to facilitate the production of clear and unequivocal information to complete and remit the correct amount of tax and to verify the operation of VAT.

In order to comply with the above requirements the taxable persons must register separately the following:

- the supplies of goods and services performed by the taxable person
- the imports of goods performed by the taxable person in order to meet the need of its undertaking
- the acquisitions of goods and services performed by the taxable person.

A record of supplies of goods and services must be prepared in such a way that the following is recorded:

■　the value of the non-exempt supplies, excluding VAT, at each VAT rate
■　the value of the supplies exempt without credit
■　the value of the supplies exempt with credit
■　the value of the VAT charged, at each rate.

Imports and acquisitions must be recorded in such a way that the following information is available:

■　the value, net of VAT, of the operations where the input VAT is totally or partially deductible
■　the value, including VAT, of the operations where the input VAT is totally non-deductible
■　the value of the acquisitions of diesel
■　the value of the deductible VAT at each rate.

The Portuguese Official Plan of Accounts (POC) is organised in order to allow taxpayers to comply with the above.

The compliance with the POC is compulsory for all the companies subject to the Portuguese Law. The books have to be kept in Portuguese and in Portuguese currency.

All the accounting documents (internal and external) and the accounting records must be kept for a period of ten years. Under certain conditions microfilming is allowed.

Small-scale taxable persons are not obliged to follow the POC and can comply with the above VAT rules through the use of a simplified set of books specified in the VAT Code. However, it is also possible to avoid using these books by using computers which must contain all the information in the prescribed format. To do this the taxpayer must obtain prior permission from the tax office.

9.3　Invoicing

Invoices must be issued within five working days from the date when the taxable event happens (see section 5.5). An option is available to invoice globally referring to periods equal to or shorter than one month.

As a general rule the invoicing paper must be pre-printed and pre-numbered by printers authorised by the Minister of Finance. As an exception to this rule, a taxable person may invoice using normal (not pre-numbered) paper provided that the invoice is prepared using a computer invoicing program. However, the VAT Office must be informed by the taxable person before he uses this invoicing method.

At least two paper copies of the invoices must be prepared, the original to be sent to the customer and a copy to be kept by the supplier with its accounts.

Invoices must be numbered sequentially and the chronological order must be respected.

All the forms of cancelled invoices must be kept by the taxable person, this means that neither the original nor the copy of a cancelled invoice can be destroyed.

In addition to those indicated above the invoices must contain the following elements:

- the date when the invoice was issued
- the legal name (not just the commercial designation), address, VAT number and the data relating to the registration at the Commercial Register (if appropriate)
- the legal name and address of the purchaser
- the purchaser's VAT number (when applicable, ie when the customer is an entity registered for VAT purposes in Portugal and in the case of intra-Community supplies of goods, when the recipient is a VAT-taxable person in any European Union Member State)
- volume and description of the goods/services which enables the supply to be correctly identified and that the application of the VAT rates and/or exemptions may be verified by the VAT Inspection
- the price (without VAT) and any other item having an influence in the computation of the taxable amount
- VAT rate(s) and the reason why any exemption is applicable
- VAT amount.

All goods in transit must be accompanied by two copies of the delivery note, invoice, or similar document, except:

- goods obviously for personal or domestic use by the owner
- goods from retailers acquired by the final consumer
- goods from agricultural producers
- goods from fishing
- tobacco, matches and fuel.

9.4   VAT Returns

The following forms are to be taken into account:

- the periodic return
- the annex to the periodical return
- the annex regarding the intra-Community supplies of goods (the 'recapitulative statement' – see section 7.6 of the Introduction to the European Union)
- the annual return
- the annex to the annual return.

9.4.1 Periodic Return

Depending on the annual turnover being higher or lower than PTE40 million, the return must be sent to the VAT Office for monthly or quarterly periods.

When the return relates to monthly periods it must be sent by mail to the VAT Office before the end of the second month following the month to which the return relates. When it refers to quarterly periods it must be sent by mail to the VAT Office by the fifteenth day of the second month following the end of each quarter.

The return and the corresponding VAT payment (see section 5.5 above) are deemed to be received in time if it was posted three weekdays before the due date.

9.4.2 Annex to the Periodic Return

When the declarant performs operations which are considered to be supplied in an area other than the one where he is registered for VAT purposes, one or two annexes must be attached to the periodic return which disclose the operations performed in those areas. For example, the declarant may be registered in the Mainland but also perform operations which are considered to be supplied in Madeira and in the Azores.

In addition to the periodic return two annexes must be filed: one regarding Madeira and another one regarding the Azores.

9.4.3 Annex Regarding the Intra-Community Supplies of Goods
When the declarant performs intra-Community supplies of goods this annex must be attached to the periodic return (see section 7.6 of the Introduction to the European Union).

9.4.4 Annual Return
The annual return must be filed by 31 May of the year following the one to which it refers.

9.4.5 Annex to the Annual Return
The annex to the annual return must be sent to the VAT Office together with the annual return. It must be used in the same circumstances as an annex to the periodic return (see section 9.4.2).

9.5 VIES Statements/Recapitulative Statement
In this return (to be attached to the annual return (see section 9.4.4)) the declarant must identify the entities which were supplied by him during the previous year with goods of an amount higher than PTE500,000, together with the corresponding amounts.

This return can be filed either in paper or electronically.

9.6 INTRASTAT
Traders who supply goods to other Member States or who acquire goods from other Member States must provide monthly details of the goods movement if their sales exceed PTE17 million and their acquisitions exceed PTE12 million (see section 7.9.3 of the Introduction to the European Union).

9.7 Registers
Certain registers of goods movements must also be kept (see section 7.9.4 of the Introduction to the European Union).

9.8 Powers of Authorities
The tax authorities are authorised to inspect premises used in connection with the operations of taxable persons, and to inspect their stocks, books of accounts, documents, etc.

VAT returns or transactions can be corrected by the tax authorities over five years.

VAT paid unduly can be corrected by the taxable persons during the year following the date of the transaction without prior authorisation from the tax authorities. VAT paid unduly and not corrected within this period may still be recovered within five years provided that the approval of the tax authorities is obtained.

Late payment of tax entails the payment of interest at a rate of 24% per annum.

9.9   Objections/Appeals
Taxable persons who are individually or jointly responsible for payment of the tax may contest the VAT liability according to the terms of the Tax Procedural Code.

9.10   Annulment of VAT by the Tax Authorities
This may occur whenever VAT is assessed in excess of that due and if the amount to be cancelled exceeds PTE500. The right to a refund expires after five years.

9.11   Compensatory Interest
If the above situation occurs and it can be proved that the error is the responsibility of the tax authorities, taxable persons are entitled to receive compensatory interest at the rate of 18% per annum.

10   SPECIAL VAT REGIMES

10.1   Bonded Warehouses
Goods imported into bonded warehouses are not liable to VAT and Customs duty until they are removed for sale in Portugal. Importing of goods into a bonded warehouse is subject to the prior approval of the Customs authorities. The agreement applies for a limited period of time and specifies the conditions in which the goods are to be kept.

10.2   Free Zones
There are two free zones in Portugal: the Island of Madeira and the Island of Santa Maria in the Azores.

10.3   Real Estate
Transactions on real estate are exempt (see section 7.2 'Exemptions without Credit for Input Tax'). However, entrepreneurs may elect to become liable. As a consequence they have to charge VAT on their transactions but they can claim input VAT incurred on their acquisitions.

10.4   Second-Hand Goods
VAT is due on second-hand goods sold by a VAT taxpayer and is assessed on the difference between the purchase and sales prices. Input VAT related to these sales cannot be recovered (see section 7.10.2 of the Introduction to the European Union).

10.5   Small Entrepreneurs
Retailers whose total amount of purchases does not exceed PTE7,500,000 are covered by a special regime. VAT is assessed on 25% of the total VAT paid on purchases. The VAT included in their invoices is not recoverable by the purchasers.

There is an exemption regime applicable to:

- retailers who have a turnover below PTE2 million per annum
- any taxpayer with a turnover below PTE1,500,000 per annum who is not making either imports or exports and not obliged to follow the POC.

10.6 Travel Agencies

This regime follows the rules of the Sixth VAT Directive whereby the taxable amount is the difference between the price paid by the customers and the costs of the expenses paid by the agent to third parties (airlines, hotels, etc). Input VAT included in these expenses is not recoverable. The special regime for travel agencies is not applicable to services rendered by travel agencies and operators acting in the name and on behalf of their clients.

11   FURTHER READING

J Pinto Fernandes and J. Cardoso do Santos, *VAT Code (commented)*
Emanuel Vidal Lima, *VAT Code (commented)*
VAT Code, VAT State Department Edition

Contributor: Virgilio Manso
                  Ernst & Young
                  Av. da Republica, 90 - 3°
                  1600 Lisbon
                  Portugal
                  Tel: +351 1 791 2000
                  Fax: +351 1 795 7587

SPAIN

1   GENERAL BACKGROUND

As a consequence of Spain's entry into the European Community, value added tax (VAT) came into force in Spain on 1 January 1986. A new Law was introduced in 1992 which clarified some ambiguous aspects of the regulations and introduced provisions required by the 'single market'.

From a territorial point of view, VAT is applicable on the Spanish mainland, the Balearic Islands (including Spanish territorial sea to a limit of 12 miles), but not in the Canary Islands, Ceuta or Melilla (North African areas under Spanish sovereignty). The VAT Act 37/1992 of 28 December and regulations approved by Royal Decree 1624/1992 of 29 December are the main legislation governing VAT.

VAT is administered in Spain by the tax authorities except for the VAT levied on imports which is collected by Customs. They are both parts of the Ministry of Finance.

1.1   Single Market – Intra-Community Acquisitions
As a Member State of the European Union, Spain applies the rules for VAT applicable to the Single Market and, in particular, the transitional arrangements which apply in respect of intra-Community supplies during the transition period which commenced on 1 January 1993.

For ease of reference the transitional arrangements are set out in detail in section 7 of the Introduction to the European Union which precedes this section of the book.

It is recommended that this chapter is read in conjunction with the transitional arrangements.

2   WHO IS TAXABLE?

2.1   General
An entrepreneur ('empresario o profesional') acting as either an individual or an entity who supplies taxable goods or services in the course of business, whatever the purposes or results of that business, is a taxable person.

Non-entrepreneurs that carry out onerous intra-Community acquisitions of new means of transport are taxable persons for that operation.

Trading companies are always considered to be entrepreneurs. Generally, a person who makes an occasional transaction is not deemed to be an entrepreneur liable to VAT. Employees are outside the scope of VAT.

There is no threshold below which VAT is not chargeable.

This chapter reflects the law on VAT in Spain as at 1 March 1995.

2.2 Transactions with Branch/Subsidiaries

Subsidiaries of foreign firms which supply taxable goods and services in Spain are treated in the same manner as other taxable persons, even where the goods and services are supplied to a parent company situated outside the State. Services supplied between branches of the same legal entity are not subject to VAT. Thus services supplied between a branch and its head office or another branch are not taxable even if one of the parties is situated outside Spain. However, the importation of goods (see section 2.9) and the intra-Community acquisition of goods (see section 2.10) by a branch are taxable events.

2.3 Government Bodies

State, regional and local government bodies are not subject to VAT in respect of the activities which they carry out without consideration or which are remunerated by the payment of a tax. However, these bodies are always considered taxable persons in relation to the following activities:

- telecommunications
- supply of water, gas, electricity and steam
- transport of goods and passengers
- port and airport services
- supply of new goods manufactured for sale
- transactions of agricultural intervention agencies in respect of agricultural products regulated by the common European Union agricultural policy
- running of trade fairs and exhibitions
- warehousing
- activities of commercial publicity bodies and travel agencies
- running of staff shops, co-operatives, industrial canteens and similar institutions
- commercial activities of radio and television
- intra-Community acquisitions (see section 7.2.4 of the Introduction to the European Union).

2.4 Fiscal Unity/Group Taxation

Entrepreneurs may apply to the tax authorities for permission to file a joint tax return. Conditions will be established in the corresponding authorisation.

2.5 Foreign Entrepreneurs

If a foreign entrepreneur or an entrepreneur from the Canary Islands, Ceuta or Melilla supplies goods or services in Spain without having a permanent establishment for VAT purposes, tax is charged via the reverse charge mechanism.

If the foreign entrepreneur has a fixed establishment within Spain from which supplies to third parties are made, it is treated as a local entrepreneur and should comply with all the rules applicable to an established entrepreneur. Generally, a non-resident entrepreneur is regarded as having a fixed establishment for VAT purposes if he keeps a regular place of business in the Spanish VAT territory such as a branch, office, shop, factory, warehouse, installations, workshop, etc, where an entrepreneurial activity is performed.

2.6 Representative Office

A representative office of a foreign entrepreneur which only performs activities of a preparatory or auxiliary nature is not considered to be a fixed establishment. The services supplied to its head office are not subject to VAT. Input VAT of the representative office can be claimed by the head office according to a procedure established for foreign entrepreneurs based on the Eighth and Thirteenth VAT Directives (see section 8.5 'Refund for Foreign Entrepreneurs').

2.7   Reverse Charge Mechanism

Foreign entrepreneurs with no establishment in Spain supplying to other entrepreneurs (whether Spanish or not) goods or services which are deemed to be supplied in Spain are not liable to VAT in Spain since the tax in these cases is due by the recipient (see section 4 'Place of Supply').

The system also applies for intra-Community acquisitions.

2.8   Importers

The importer of goods is always the taxable person and the tax is due at customs clearance.

2.9   Acquisitions of Goods

The movement of goods from one Member State to another is an acquisition. If there is an acquisition by a Spanish business, the business in the other Member State is not obliged to register. If there is a 'fictitious acquisition' (because, for example, there is no change in title) VAT registration in Spain will be required for the business in the other Member State (see section 7.2 of the Introduction to the European Union).

2.10   Non-Taxable Legal Persons – Taxable Persons with No Right to Recover VAT and Farmers Benefiting from Notional Refunds

Such persons are considered to be outside the scope of VAT when, during the civil year and the preceding one their yearly intra-Community acquisitions are below ESP1,300,000. As soon as an acquisition puts them above this threshold they are subject to common intra-Community rules and must pay VAT on their acquisitions. They must therefore obtain an identification number and submit VAT returns.

The same persons may opt to be subject to common rules even for acquisitions below the threshold. The option takes effect the first day of the month in which it is exercised and expires on 31 December of the second year following the option; the option is renewable for periods of two years unless renounced before the end of the two-year expiring period.

2.11   Supplier of New Means of Transport

Any person who undertakes on an occasional basis intra-Community supplies of new means of transport that are dispatched or transported from Spain to another Member State is regarded as a taxable person (see section 7.2.6 of the Introduction to the European Union).

3   WHAT IS TAXABLE?

VAT is levied on the supply of goods and services in Spanish VAT territory, on intra-Community acquisitions and on the import of goods.

3.1 Supply of Goods

'Supply of goods' means the transfer of the right to dispose of tangible property.

Gas, heating, refrigeration, electric current, etc are considered tangible property.

The following are also treated as supplies of goods:

■ the establishment, extension and transfer of rights in rem over real property, excluding mortgages
■ the transfer of the ownership of property by order of a public authority or in pursuance of the law
■ the handing over of goods under a hire purchase contract
■ sales with retention of ownership until full payment
■ contribution in kind to a corporate body
■ the delivery, on a contract work basis, by a contractor of movable property made or assembled from materials supplied in whole or in part by a customer, when the cost of the materials supplied by the contractor exceeds 20% of the taxable amount
■ the self-supply of goods
■ the sale of standard software
■ the transfer of goods between a principal and an undisclosed agent.

3.2 Imports

'Importation of goods' means the entry of goods into Spanish VAT territory, irrespective of their destination or the status of the importer. Imports of goods are in general taxable. However, in certain cases, a number of exemptions are applicable (see section 7.3 'Exempt Imports').

Services rendered in connection with the import of goods are exempt provided that the value of services is included in the taxable amount of the import.

3.3 Intra-Community Acquisitions

From 1 January 1993 VAT is charged, levied and paid on the intra-Community acquisition of goods, other than new means of transport, effected within Spain for consideration by a taxable person, and on the intra-Community acquisition of new means of transport effected by anyone within Spain for consideration (see section 7 of the Introduction to the European Union).

3.4 Distance Sellers

Persons who supply goods from another Member State to non-VAT registered persons in Spain may be taxable in respect of such supplies (see section 7.4.2 of the Introduction to the European Union).

3.5 New Means of Transport

The transfer to Spain from another Member State of new means of transport is always taxable as an intra-Community acquisition regardless of the status of the supplier or the purchaser (see section 7.2.6 of the Introduction to the European Union).

3.6 Contract Work

If a VAT-registered person in another Member State sends goods to Spain to be processed there and the processed goods are not returned to the Member State from which the goods for process originated, then the owner will have to register and account for VAT in Spain (see section 7.2.5 of the Introduction to the European Union).

3.7   Excise Products

In certain circumstances a non-registered acquirer of excise products may have to register and account for VAT on acquisitions of products which are subject to excise duty (see section 7.2.7 of the Introduction to the European Union).

3.8   Assembly/Installation

A supply of goods takes place in Spain if the specific goods to be supplied are located in Spain. This applies even if an overseas entrepreneur has no place of business in Spain. However, the liability of supply of assembled or installed goods may be passed to the Spanish customer under the reverse charge mechanism (see section 2.7 'Reverse Charge Mechanism').

3.9   Supply of Services

Supply of services means any supply which does not constitute a supply of goods.

It also applies to:

- transfer of intangible property such as rights to trademarks, patents, know-how, tailor-made software, etc
- leasing, renting
- agreements to refrain from certain activities
- contract work when it is not a supply of goods
- commission charged by a disclosed commissionaire
- transport
- transfer of a lease contract of a business premises
- self-supply of services.

3.10   Self-Supply of Goods/Services

The supply of goods is deemed to be a self-supply of goods when:

- goods are transferred by an entrepreneur from his business to his personal use or for consumption
- goods are supplied to third parties without charge
- goods are acquired or produced by an entrepreneur and used in his business as capital assets or transferred from one area of his business to another in which the entitlement to input VAT credit differs by 50%.

The supply of services is deemed to be a self-supply of services when:

- goods or rights are transferred from the business for personal consumption and are not any of those goods listed under section 5.2 'Self-Supplies'
- business goods are used for private purposes
- services are rendered without charge.

4   PLACE OF SUPPLY

VAT is chargeable in Spain only if the supply of goods or services takes place in Spanish VAT territory.

4.1   Supply of Goods
The general rule is that the place of supply is where the goods are physically located at the time of supply.

Special rules apply when:

- goods are transported: the place of supply is where the transport begins. If transport of goods begins outside Spanish VAT territory, the place of supply by the importer and the place of any subsequent supplies are deemed to be Spain
- goods are installed or assembled: the place of supply is where they are installed or assembled
- immovable property is supplied: the place is where it is situated
- goods are delivered to train, boat or airplane passengers in a transport that begins in Spanish territory and whose destination is in another Member State: the delivery takes place in Spain
- in a distance sales scheme the place of supply is Spain where the foreign entrepreneur has either exceeded sales of ESP4,550,000 in Spanish territory or has opted to have its operations subject to Spanish tax.

4.1.1 Chain Transactions
A special rule applies if several entrepreneurs enter into subsequent transactions involving the same goods (chain transactions). In such cases each entrepreneur within the chain is deemed to have made a taxable supply even if the actual ownership is transferred directly from the first entrepreneur to the last recipient in the chain. When the transaction involves transportation of the goods from a place outside the Union into Spain to a place within Spain, all the transactions are deemed to be in Spain and thus subject to Spanish VAT. A zero rate applies to the transactions preceding the supply made by the actual importer. (With regard to intra-Community chain transactions, see section 7.4.1 of the Introduction to the European Union.)

4.1.2 Distance Sales
The place of supply of goods (other than new means of transport) dispatched or transported directly or indirectly by the supplier either:

- from the territory of another Member State to a non-taxable person in Spain, or
- from Spain to a person in another Member State who is not registered for VAT there

is the place where the goods are when the dispatch or transportation ends. Non-taxable persons include private persons, fully exempt persons and flat-rate farmers.

For full details see section 7.4.2 of the Introduction to the European Union.

4.2   Intra-Community Acquisitions
As a general rule, the place where an intra-Community acquisition of goods takes place is deemed to be the place where the goods are when transportation to the person acquiring the goods ends.

To make a zero-rated intra-Community supply followed by a taxed intra-Community acquisition on which the VAT may be deducted by the acquirer, the VAT identification numbers of the parties involved must be stated on the invoice.

If the goods for any reason arrive finally in a Member State other than that which issued the VAT number to the acquirer, the person purchasing the goods acquires the goods in the Member State of arrival of the goods. In this case double taxation could occur, since the purchaser must account for VAT both in the Member State which issued the VAT number to him and in the Member State of arrival of the goods.

The presumption is that the place of acquisition is the country which issued the VAT number to the acquirer. However, if the acquirer can show that he has paid VAT in the Member State of arrival of the goods he will not be liable for payment of acquisition VAT in his own Member State.

4.2.1 Chain Transactions
'Triangulation' involves the situation where three parties in three different countries are involved in selling and purchasing the same goods. For example, *A* in France sells goods to *B* in Belgium who sells the goods to *C* in Spain and the goods are sent directly from *A* to *C* (see section 7.4.1 of the Introduction to the European Union).

4.2.2 Goods Placed on Board Ships, Aircraft or Trains During Transport
When goods are supplied for consumption on board ships, aircraft or trains during transport and the place of departure and destination are within the territory of the European Union, the place of supply is the place where the goods are at the time of departure of the transport.

4.2.3 Work on Movable Goods
The place of supply of services on movable goods (eg repair and valuation) is where the services are actually performed. However, there are special rules where such services are performed for a customer who is VAT-registered in another Member State (see section 7.4.8 of the Introduction to the European Union).

4.3   Supply of Services

4.3.1 General Rule
The place of supply is where the supplier has established his business or has a permanent establishment from which the service is supplied or, in the absence of such a place of business or permanent establishment, where he has his registered office or permanent address.

For these purposes, the definition of 'permanent establishment' is that of the OECD for Corporation Tax purposes plus:

- installations exploited by an entrepreneur for the keeping and delivery of goods
- centres for the purchase of goods or services, and
- rented or exploited real estate.

4.3.2 Exceptions
The following exceptions apply:

- services connected with immovable property: the place of supply is the place where the property is located
- transport services: the place of supply is the place where the transport takes place, considering distances covered. Only transport supplied within Spanish territory is taxable (national air space and territorial waters included)
- the place of supply of services relating to the following is where they are physically carried out:

  - cultural, artistic, sporting, scientific, educational, entertainment or similar activities
  - ancillary transport activities such as loading, unloading, handling, storing and similar activities
  - television viewing services
  - lotteries
  - work on movable tangible property
  - valuation of movable tangible property
  - hotel and restaurant services

- the place of supply of renting means of transport is where the lessor is established.

The place of supply of the following services is the place where the recipient of the services has established his business or has a fixed establishment to which the services are supplied or, in the absence of such a place, where he has his registered office or permanent address:

- transfers and assignments of copyrights, patents, licences, trademarks and similar rights
- transfer or concession of goodwill, exclusivity rights or right to practise certain professional activity
- advertising services
- services of consultants, engineers, auditors, tax experts, lawyers, accountants and other similar services
- data processing services and the supplying of information
- delivery of commercial information services
- services of translation or correction of texts
- banking, financial and insurance transactions, including reinsurance
- company management
- the supply of staff
- dubbing of films
- the hiring out of movable tangible property, with the exception of means of transport and containers
- obligation to refrain from pursuing or exercising, in whole or in part, a business activity or a right referred to above
- the services of agents who act in the name and for the account of another, when they procure for their principal the services referred to above.

This rule does not apply when the recipient is a non-entrepreneur resident in a European Union country. In such a case, VAT is charged by the Spanish supplier.

- ***Intra-Community goods transportation:*** (ie transport where the place of departure and the place of arrival are situated within the territories of two different Member

States), the place of supply is deemed to be the place of departure (see section 7.4.4 of the Introduction to the European Union)

- *services ancillary to intra-Community goods transport:* the place of supply of services ancillary to intra-Community transport services of goods is not the country of the supplier when the customer is VAT-registered in another Member State. In these circumstances the supply is within the territory of the Member State which issued the customer with the VAT registration number, and under the reverse charge mechanism, the customer must account for the VAT (see section 7.4.5 of the Introduction to the European Union)

- *intermediaries/brokers:* the place of supply of services rendered by intermediaries acting in the name and for the account of other persons, when such services form part of transactions (other than those for which the place of supply is deemed to be where the recipient of the service is located and to the extent that those transactions take place within the European Union), is the place where the main transactions for which the intermediary services are performed are deemed to take place.

By derogation from this rule, where the customer is identified for VAT purposes in a Member State other than that within the territory of which the main transactions are deemed to take place, the place of supply of services rendered by the intermediaries is deemed to be within the territory of the Member State which issued the customer with the VAT number under which the service was rendered to him by the intermediary (see section 7.4.6 of the Introduction to the European Union).

- *work on movable goods:* where the customer is registered for VAT in a different Member State to that of the supplier, the place of supply is the Member State of the customer. Under the reverse charge mechanism the supply is not subject to VAT in the country of the supplier and the customer must account for VAT (see section 7.4.8 of the Introduction to the European Union).

4.4 Reverse Charge Mechanism

The reverse charge mechanism applies when, according to the above rules, supplies of goods and services are made within Spanish VAT territory by a foreign entrepreneur not established in Spain to another entrepreneur. The taxable person is not the supplier but the recipient entrepreneur. Tax self-charged by the recipient will be deductible in the same VAT return. Should the recipient of the service or good not be established in Spain, the reverse charge mechanism would not apply.

5   BASIS OF TAXATION

5.1   Supplies within Spanish Territory

With regard to supplies of goods and services, the taxable amount is the total consideration which has been or is to be obtained by the supplier, including:

- commissions, containers, packing, transport, insurance, interest and any other amount charged to the customer
- interest for late payments
- subsidies directly linked to the price
- taxes, duties, levies and charges on the same supply, excluding VAT.

Not included are:

- indemnities
- discounts and rebates
- expenses incurred in the name and on behalf of the customer.

When the consideration is not payable in cash, or is not wholly formed by cash, the open market value is applied.

In the case of transactions between related parties at a price lower than the market price, the taxable basis cannot be lower than the full cost to the supplier.

5.2   Self-Supplies
For self-supply of goods, the basis of taxation is the historical cost (excluding VAT) of the goods or services purchased or used to produce the goods. In respect of self-supply of services, the taxable basis is the full cost incurred by the taxable person in providing the services.

5.3   Imports
With regard to the importation of goods, the taxable basis is the customs value, plus the following items, in so far as they are not already included in the customs value:

- taxes, duties, levies and other charges due by reason of importation, excluding VAT
- incidental expenses such as commissions, packing, transport and insurance incurred up to the first place of destination within Spanish VAT territory.

5.4   Intra-Community Acquisitions
The amount on which tax is chargeable on the acquired goods is the total consideration. The consideration is the total amount or, in so far as the compensation is not in money, the total value of the compensation charged on the supply including all taxes, commissions, costs and charges whatsoever, but not including the VAT chargeable in respect of that acquisition. If more is actually paid than has been agreed, the taxable amount is the amount actually paid.

If the invoice is in foreign currency, the applicable exchange rate will be the last published selling rate at the time the VAT becomes due.

In general, the transfer by a person of goods from his undertaking in Spain to another Member State for the purposes of his business is deemed to be a supply of goods. The taxable amount is the (historical) purchase or cost price (see section 7.5.1 of the Introduction to the European Union).

5.5   Chargeable Event/Time of Payment
VAT becomes chargeable when the goods are delivered or the services are performed. For supplies of electricity, gas, etc, and supplies of services which give rise to successive payments, VAT is chargeable at the time each payment becomes due for the period.

However, where a payment is to be made on account before the goods are delivered or the services are performed, the tax becomes chargeable on receipt of the payment and on the amount received.

VAT is due on imports when the importers apply for the clearance of the goods from the customs.

VAT chargeable on the intra-Community acquisition of goods shall be due on the twentieth day of the month following the quarter or month during which the intra-Community acquisition occurred (see section 7.5.2 of the Introduction to the European Union).

A taxable person/entrepreneur accounts for VAT on an intra-Community acquisition by reporting the acquisition VAT on his periodic VAT return. If he is entitled to full deduction of VAT he deducts the acquisition VAT as input tax on the same return. However, if the taxable person/entrepreneur is not entitled to full or partial deduction he must pay to the tax authorities the difference between the VAT on the acquisition and the amount he is entitled to deduct.

VAT in respect of fictitious intra-Community acquisitions becomes due at the time the acquisition of the goods was made.

5.6   Credit Notes/Bad Debts

Taxable amounts can be adjusted in the case of:

- re-usable containers and packaging returned to the supplier
- discounts and rebates subsequent to supplies
- total or partial cancellation.

In these cases, a new invoice should be issued indicating the changes or modifications to the original transaction and identifying the invoices modified.

VAT charged on invoices which remain unsettled may be recovered in cases of receivership or bankruptcy. For these purposes, an express authorisation from the Ministry of Finance is needed.

6   TAX RATES

The rates are as follows:

4%:   supplies, intra-Community acquisitions and imports of:
- bread
- yeast and cereals for the preparation of bread
- milk, including hygienised, sterilised, concentrated, without cream, evaporated and powdered
- cheeses
- eggs
- natural fruits, greens, vegetables and tubers not transformed
- books, magazines and newspapers without a prevalent advertising content
- pharmaceutical specialities
- vehicles for the handicapped and wheel chairs, including their repair
- prostheses
- official protection housing

7%:   supplies, intra-Community acquisitions and imports of:
- food (excluding alcoholic and refreshment beverages) for humans and animals
- animals, vegetables and products suitable for the elaboration of food
- goods or products used for farming, stock breeding and forestry
- water for humans and animals and irrigation
- pharmaceutical specialities for veterinary purposes
- devices to replace human or animal physical deficiencies
- housing
- mopeds of less than 50 cc
- overland transport for passengers and their baggage
- hotels, camping and restaurant services
- certain farming, stock breeding and forest accessory services
- performances by artists in films, plays and musical comedies
- urban cleaning and rubbish collection
- theatres, circuses, parks, concerts, libraries, museums, zoological parks, cinemas, exhibitions and similar entries
- radio and television services rendered to non-entrepreneurs and amateurs through payment of a fee
- non-exempt social assistance
- funeral services
- non-exempt health assistance
- amateur sport entertainment
- commercial fairs and exhibitions
- housing construction

16%:   all other supplies, imports and intra-Community acquisitions not taxable at another specified rate or exempt.

7   EXEMPTIONS

7.1   *Exemptions with Credit for Input Tax*
The following exemptions are with credit for input tax:

- exports and intra-Community supplies of goods
- services rendered in connection with exports and the above-mentioned deliveries (transport, storage, custody, etc)
- services rendered by agents connected with the above-mentioned operations
- transport of passengers and their baggage by air or sea from Spain to foreign countries or the Canary Islands, Ceuta and Melilla and vice versa.

While supplies of banking, financial and insurance services are exempt from VAT if the recipient of these services is resident or established outside the European Union, input credit attributable to such supplies is recoverable.

7.2   *Exemptions without Credit for Input Tax*
The following exemptions, amongst others, are without credit for input tax:

- public postal services

- services connected with health care (hospitals, medical assistance, dentistry, etc)
- mandatory education
- services rendered by social security
- insurance and reinsurance
- banking and other financial transactions
- conveyances of rural land and second or successive transfers of buildings
- real estate rentals (except ground rent for parking, storage of goods and lease of business premises which are taxable)
- gambling, games and lotteries
- supplies of goods in which input VAT could not be deducted when they were acquired
- supplies of pictures, sculptures, etc made by the artist.

7.3   Exempt Imports

Imports of goods are usually taxable. However, in certain cases exemptions are applicable. For example:

- imports of goods which would be exempt if supplied within Spanish territory
- imports of goods under a declaration for transit arrangements or by recognised international organisations
- imports of goods to be placed in temporary storage or under free zone arrangements.

Services rendered in connection with the importation of goods are exempt provided that the value of services is included in the taxable amount of the import.

The importation of goods which is followed by an intra-Community supply may be exempt (see section 7.7.2 of the Introduction to the European Union).

7.4   Non-Taxable Transactions

7.4.1 Transactions within the Same Legal Entity
Transactions between a head office and its branch both located within Spanish territory are not taxable because they are taking place within the same legal entity. However, cross-border goods transactions are treated according to general VAT rules and are taxable.

7.4.2 Transfer of Business
When an entrepreneur transfers his entire business (assets and liabilities), it is considered that no supply of goods has taken place provided that the recipient continues with the same business. This rule also applies to the transfer of 'branches of activity' made according to Law 29/91 which implements the European Community Merger Directive.

7.4.3 Subsidies/Penalty Payments/Compensation
Subsidies are liable to VAT when they are directly linked to the price of taxable supplies. The amount should be included by the beneficiary in the taxable amount of the supplies to which they are linked.

Penalty payments for breach of contracts are liable to VAT when they relate to taxable transactions.

Sums of money paid by way of compensation are not subject to VAT.

7.5   Election to be Subject to VAT

Entrepreneurs with the right of full deduction of their input VAT may elect to have an exempt purchase of real estate subject to VAT and not to 6% Real Estate Transfer Tax.

Distance sellers (see section 3.4 above) and non-taxable legal persons and government bodies (see section 7.2.4 of Introduction to the European Union) also may elect to become taxable persons.

8   CREDIT/REFUND FOR INPUT TAX

8.1   General Rule

A taxable person may claim input VAT relief in respect of VAT borne on supplies and intra-Community acquisitions of goods and services received and in respect of VAT paid on the import of any goods, in so far as these goods or services are used or are to be used for the purpose of a taxable business carried out or to be carried out by him.

If deductible input VAT exceeds, in a tax period, the amount of output VAT due, the excess can be carried forward to the following period, except in the case of exporters who can claim a VAT refund monthly in the proportion of their zero-rated operations to their total turnover.

Input VAT cannot be claimed on the following items:

- cars, motorcycles, leisure aircraft or boats and related expenses when the vehicle is not exclusively used for business purposes
- travel, hotels, restaurant or entertainment services (although travel, hotel and restaurant expenses may be deductible in a business trip)
- antiques, jewels, pearls and gold objects
- gifts to clients, employees or third parties.

8.2   Adjustment of Entitlement to Credit

VAT paid on capital goods can be deducted in the same way as any other input VAT. However, during a period of four years for movable property and nine years for immovable property, starting from the time when the goods are first used, the entitlement to a credit for input tax at the time of purchase must be adjusted when the deductible proportion (in respect of a partially exempt person) for any of these years, differs by more than 10% from that for the year in which the goods were acquired. This may result in an additional credit or a VAT repayment.

8.3   Partial Exemption

When a taxpayer makes both exempt (with no tax credit) and taxable supplies, only a proportion of the non-attributable input VAT may be deducted.

The general rule for calculating the deductible proportion is as follows:

ratio = total value of taxable supplies x 100 ÷ total value of all supplies.

The following items are not included in the formula:

- VAT
- sales of capital goods used in the business

- financial and real estate operations, unless they are the activity of the taxpayer
- self-supplies of goods and services.

A special rule applies when a company carries out activities which are clearly different and to which special VAT rules apply. This special rule allows the deduction of the input VAT incurred on the acquisition of goods and services for taxable activities but disallows the deduction of the input VAT for the exempt activities. The input VAT borne for the acquisition of goods and services used in both activities may be deducted by applying the standard ratio.

8.4 Time of Recovery

Input VAT is deductible when the invoice has been received by the taxable person or when VAT is due on imports. The claim to input tax credit should be made in the VAT return for the period in which input VAT is allowed.

If at the end of the year input VAT exceeds output VAT, the taxpayer may request a refund for the balance at the time the last return is filed (end of January of the following year).

Exporters and entrepreneurs that carry out intra-Community supplies of goods included in the Special Register (exports exceeding ESP20 million a year), may request refunds on their monthly returns. The refund is limited to 16% of the value of exports and intra-Community supplies of goods made in the same period.

8.5 Refund for Foreign Entrepreneurs

There is a special procedure for refund to entrepreneurs established in the Canary Islands, Ceuta, Melilla and other Member States as well as in non-European Union Member States.

8.5.1 European Union Entrepreneurs

The activity of the foreign entrepreneur must be subject to VAT or other similar tax in his country.

He should not have made any supplies of goods or services within Spanish VAT territory other than the following:

- transport and ancillary exports and imports
- deliveries and services in which the reverse charge mechanism applies.

Refund of VAT cannot be claimed if the input VAT refers to goods or services for which an input credit is not allowed (see section 'General Rule').

Refund of VAT over ESP25,000 may be claimed for either a quarter or a year and must be claimed within a period of six months from the last day of the period to which it refers.

Refunds between ESP3,000 and ESP25,000 may be claimed when they refer to the whole year.

The documents to be filed are the following:

- official claim form: the form may be that of any European Union country but it should be completed in Spanish
- certificate issued by the tax authorities of the country of residence of the applicant indicating that the applicant is a VAT taxpayer

■   original invoices and import documents evidencing the Spanish VAT paid.

8.5.2 *Non-European Union Entrepreneurs*

The procedure and requirements are the same as for European Union entrepreneurs except for the following points:

■   it is necessary to prove reciprocity for Spanish entrepreneurs in the country of the applicant

■   a VAT representative must be appointed.

9   ADMINISTRATIVE OBLIGATIONS

9.1   *Registration*

All entrepreneurs who commence activities which are subject to VAT within the Spanish VAT territory must use the official form to register with their tax office before the date of commencement. The right to claim input VAT credit is conditional upon this registration.

9.2   *Books and Records*

The following books must be kept by a taxable person:

■   book of invoices issued
■   book of invoices received
■   book of assets (only if the pro rata method of recovery of VAT is applicable)
■   book of certain intra-Community operations (certain contract work operations and transfers of goods).

9.3   *Invoices*

Every taxable person must issue an invoice for each supply, even in the case of exemption or self-supply. It is also possible to issue a single invoice for all the supplies made to the same person during a month.

When the recipient is an entrepreneur, the invoice should be issued within 30 days from the date of the chargeable event. It should be sent to the recipient within another 30 days. However, when the recipient is a private individual, the invoice should be issued and sent the moment the supply is made.

Invoices must incorporate the following information:

■   an identifying number
■   the name, address and fiscal identification number of the supplier
■   the name, address and fiscal identification number of the recipient
■   description of the supply
■   the total amount payable, excluding VAT
■   tax rate and tax due
■   place and date of issuance
■   if the invoice corresponds to a payment in advance, it should be clearly indicated.

Failure to comply with these requirements may prevent the recovery of input VAT.

Every taxable person is obliged to keep all invoices received for a period of five years (nine years for real estate purchased by a company where recovery of VAT is calculated on a pro rata basis).

9.4 VAT Returns

VAT returns have to be submitted every three months, although in the following cases the return must be filed monthly:

- when sales in the previous year exceeded ESP1,000 million
- when the taxpayer is included in the exporter register (exports have to exceed ESP20 million)
- when the taxpayer elects to file a monthly return.

VAT returns must be submitted no later than 20 days after the end of the period to which they relate, with the exception of the return for the last period of the year which can be submitted within the following 30 days and the one of July that may be filed up to 20 September.

9.5 VIES Statements

VIES statements ('Declaration recapitulativa de operaciones intra communitarias') must be submitted by entrepreneurs/taxable persons to the Ministry of Finance office of the place where the taxable person is resident.

For more details see 7.9.2 of the Introduction to the European Union.

9.6 INTRASTAT

Traders who supply goods to other Member States or who acquire goods from other Member States must provide monthly details of the goods movement if their sales or acquisitions exceed ESP14 million (see section 7.9.3 of the Introduction to the European Union).

9.7 Registers

Certain registers of goods movements must also be kept (see section 7.9.4 of the Introduction to the European Union).

9.8 Basque Country and Navarra

The Basque Country and Navarra are autonomous territories within Spain which have their own tax legislation.

Basically, the VAT rules concerning the Basque Country and Navarra are as follows:

- entrepreneurs who carry out activities only within one of these territories are taxed by the administration of that territory
- entrepreneurs who carry out activities in the Basque Country and/or Navarra and the rest of the Spanish VAT territory are taxed by the administration of their registered office or permanent address if their previous year sales were lower or equal to ESP300 million
- if the activities are carried out in both territories and the previous year sales were higher than ESP300 million, VAT must be paid to the administrations of all the territories involved according to the percentage of operations made in each territory. There are specific rules to determine in which territory a supply is made.

9.9   Powers of the Authorities

9.9.1 Estimate of Tax Paid
The tax authorities may estimate the tax to be paid if an entrepreneur has failed to file VAT returns within the period prescribed and a formal request to do so is not complied with.

9.9.2 Statute of Limitations
The statute of limitation is five years from the filing date.

9.9.3 Correction of Returns
Input credit which has been omitted on a VAT return can still be claimed for a period of one year from the date on which the VAT became chargeable or import VAT was paid.

If a return needs to be amended, a supplementary return should be filed and any additional tax paid with surcharge from the original due date. If the supplementary return involves a refund of tax unduly paid it is necessary to file a request to the tax authorities.

Excess VAT may be paid back within the statute of limitations.

Failure to submit returns in time entails the payment of a 10% surcharge if made within the quarter or 50% if made later. If the payment is requested by the tax authorities and output VAT was charged to the customer, a minimum penalty of 150% of the VAT due is applicable.

Late payment of tax when an application for deferred or partial payment has not been made and payment is requested by the authority, is punished by a penalty of 20% of the tax due plus late payment interest.

9.9.4 Objections/Appeals
Appeals to the tax authorities or to the Regional Administrative Court (Tribunal Economico-Administrativo-Regional) must be made within 15 days from the date of notification of an assessment or a disputed decision. In certain cases, the decision of the trial court may be appealed against to the Central Administrative Court (Tribunal Economico-Administrativo-Central). Further appeals are also possible to the Territorial Justice Court (Audiencia Territorial), the National Justice Court and the Supreme Court (Tribunal Supremo).

A special procedure applies when a dispute arises between the supplier and the recipient concerning the VAT to be charged.

10   SPECIAL VAT REGIMES

10.1 Agricultural, Livestock and Fisheries Activities
There is a special scheme for agricultural, forestry, livestock and fishing enterprises. Entrepreneurs are compensated for the VAT they are charged on their purchases by means of a 4% flat-rate addition to the price at which they will sell their products to VAT taxable persons. Taxable persons to whom the goods or services are supplied are obliged to pay that compensation and may claim input credit in respect of it.

10.2 Real Property Transactions
Specific rules apply to real property transactions, which are considered to be supplies of

goods. The supply is deemed to be rendered at the place where the real property is located.

The place of the supply of services connected with immovable property, such as leases, services of estate agents and experts, services for preparing and co-ordinating construction work, services of architects and engineers, mediation in real property transactions, etc is the place where the property is situated.

The following transactions are exempt from VAT (although certain entrepreneurs may elect to have the first two made subject to VAT):

■   second and subsequent supplies (after that made by the promoter) of buildings or parts thereof, and of the land on which they stand. (In this case, transfer tax is due at a rate of 7% by the purchaser)
■   supplies of country land
■   letting of buildings or parts thereof for housing, including garages and other accessory sections if they are let together with the building.

The reduced VAT rate of 7% is applicable to:

■   supplies of buildings or parts thereof to be used for housing, including garages and other accessory sections (if they are sold together)
■   building constructions for housing, including premises and garages.

This rate may be reduced to 4% in the delivery of government protected or promoted houses by the promoters.

10.3 Retailers
There are two special schemes with regard to retailers:

■   The optional scheme for retailers supplying goods chargeable to VAT at more than one rate. This is the usual scheme for big department stores. The taxable base is determined according to the level of purchases at each rate.
■   The equivalent increase scheme. This scheme is obligatory for individual retailers, with certain exceptions. Entrepreneurs who supply goods to retailers must charge an additional 4%, 1%, or 0.5% rate (depending on whether the general, reduced, or super-reduced rate is applicable) on all supplies. The entrepreneur must pay the additional percentage to the administration. The 4%, 1% or 0.5% also applies to imports and intra-Community acquisitions made by retailers.

The retailer does not have to pay VAT to the Administration nor can he claim repayment of any input VAT suffered. The retailer must charge his customers VAT at the appropriate rate corresponding to the goods supplied without adding the additional VAT charged to him under this scheme.

10.4 Second-Hand Goods, Antiques and Art Goods
There are special optional schemes for second-hand traders and antique dealers under which the taxable person may choose how to determine the taxable base. It can either be 30% of the total consideration or the difference between the sales price and purchase price. In the latter case the taxable base can never be lower than 20% of the total consideration. An option for one of these alternatives applies to all supplies of this nature.

See section 7.10.2 of the Introduction to the European Union for further details.

10.5 Small Entrepreneurs

Individual entrepreneurs who carry out certain specified activities and whose previous year's sales were lower than ESP50 million may opt for a simplified procedure for charging and collecting the VAT. The VAT due is determined by applying certain indices or formulae approved by the tax authorities.

10.6 Travel Agencies

A special scheme applies to travel agents and tour operators who deal with customers in their own name and use the supplies and services of other taxable persons in the provision of travel facilities. The taxable base is the travel agent's margin, that is to say, the difference between the total amount to be paid by the traveller, exclusive of VAT and the actual cost to the travel agent of supplies and services (including VAT) provided by other taxable persons when these supplies are for the direct benefit of the traveller.

Travel agents' services are exempt when transactions entrusted to other taxable persons, for the benefit of the traveller and used for travelling purposes, are performed by such persons outside the European Union. Where these transactions are performed both inside and outside the European Union, only that part of the travel agent's service relating to transactions outside the European Union is exempt. This exemption entitles the entrepreneur to input credit.

11   FURTHER READING

Julio Banacloche, *El IVA y las Operaciones Intracomunitarias*, Editorial Revista de Derecho Privado
José Antonio Serrano Sobrado, Alberto Monreal, *Todo IVA 1993*, Editorial Praxis
Manuel Sánchez González, *Impuesto sobre el Valor Añadido, Operaciones Sujetas, comentarios a la nueva Ley*, Editorial Aranzadi
Impuesto sobre el Valor Añadido, Editorial Lex Nova 1993

Contributor: Juan Jose Terraza
Ernst & Young
L'Illa Avda. Diagonal
575, 7th Floor
08029 Barcelona
Spain
Tel: +34 3 4106707
Fax: +34 3 4053784

Currently Juan Jose is on secondment to the Spanish Tax Desk at Ernst & Young International, New York:

Ernst & Young
787 Seventh Avenue
New York, NY 10019
USA
Tel: +1 212 773 1234
Fax: +1 201 773 5582

SWEDEN

1   GENERAL BACKGROUND

Value added tax (VAT) was first introduced into Sweden in 1969. A new VAT law came into effect on 1 July 1994 which contained the main amendments necessary to harmonise the Swedish VAT system with the European VAT Directives. Further amendments have been introduced since Sweden joined the European Union on 1 January 1995. Even if the new legislation harmonises with the European Union legislation, the VAT treatment of supplies in the cultural sphere (artists, concerts, theatre and similar shows) and supplies by non-profit organisations has not yet been harmonised fully with the provisions of the Sixth VAT Directive but will most probably be amended in the middle of 1995. The treatment of second-hand goods and operations by tourist agencies will be brought into line with the Sixth VAT Directive as amended by the second-hand goods directive at a later date.

The new law from 1 January 1995 may be summarised as follows:

- the main amendments relate to and expand the basis of assessment (tax base)
- all supplies of goods and services are subject to VAT, unless they are considered to be exempt supplies. In order to modify the Swedish VAT law to the European Union rules, some of the present exemptions will be abolished
- the terms 'import' and 'export' are restricted to the movement of goods to and from third territories
- the Swedish VAT return has been supplemented to include seperate details of goods purchased from or sold to other Member States
- taxable persons engaging in intra-Community transactions must file a VAT return every month instead of bi-monthly as previously
- previously, the self-supply of goods was subject to VAT only when the price of the transaction was below the fair market price. However, according to the new rules, the self-supply of goods is subject to VAT when the transfer is free of charge or when the price is below purchase price or the manufacturer's cost. Similar limitations have been introduced for the supply of services
- the previous rules regarding deductions of input VAT generally remain the same. However, there are some amendments for intra-Community transactions, investments related to capital goods, and for invoices for less than SEK200
- the tax rates which earlier included a reduced rate of 21% on restaurant services and 12% on postal services are increased to the standard rate of 25%.

1.1   The Single Market – Intra-Community Acquisitions
As a Member State of the European Union Sweden applies the rules for VAT applicable to the Single Market and, in particular, the transitional arrangements which apply in respect of intra-Community supplies during the transition period which commenced on 1 January 1993.

This chapter reflects the law on VAT in Sweden as at 1 January 1995.

For ease of reference the transitional arrangements are set out in detail in section 7 of the Introduction to the European Union which precedes this section of the book.

It is recommended that this chapter is read in conjunction with the transitional arrangements.

2   WHO IS TAXABLE?

2.1   General

According to the basic rule, the liability to pay tax arises whenever supplies of a taxable commodity or service occurs in Sweden in commercial activity. Any physical or legal person (limited company, incorporated association, etc) conducting a taxable activity in an independent manner is liable to pay tax. Therefore, if a person has two or more distinct enterprises, each is normally subject to separate VAT.

Any person whose turnover per year, including VAT, is over SEK200,000 (ECU15,400) must be registered for VAT. However, independently of the limit, a turnover under SEK200,000 must be reported separately in the ordinary Income Tax return. Under certain circumstances it is possible to be registered for VAT even if the turnover is below the limit. That applies to export business, business in a start-up period and business with zero-rated supplies.

Special rules apply to general partnerships ('handelsbolag'). They are subject to VAT, although each owner is taxed individually for Income Tax purposes. A single business partnership ('enkeltbolag') is normally regarded as a trading company and is subject to VAT. A single partnership in the building business, however, is not taxable per se; rather each partner is taxable individually, both for Income Tax and VAT purposes. For VAT purposes, however, the partners can decide that only one of them should do the accounting for the tax authorities.

Estates of deceased persons, estates in bankruptcy and commission companies also qualify as taxable persons.

2.2   Transactions with Branch/Subsidiary

A subsidiary will always have its own registration. Supplies between parent and subsidiary are always taxable, although cross-border supplies may be viewed as exports or imports. A branch will have its own registration only if the activity in the branch is seen as a different line of business income for the company.

Services supplied between branches of the same legal entity are not subject to VAT. Thus services supplied between a branch and its head office or another branch are not taxable even if one of the parties is situated outside Sweden. However, the importation of goods (see section 2.9) and the intra-Community acquisition of goods (see section 2.10) by a branch are taxable events.

2.3   Government Bodies

Government entities are taxable if they deliver goods or provide services to anyone other than government entities.

The VAT liability will remain. However, within the present VAT system, the Municipal and the County Councils are entitled to repayment of input VAT incurred by them even when the VAT is related to exempt supplies. These rules will be abolished and the repayment will be regulated in a separate document. The possibility of voluntary registration for VAT purposes when letting real estate to a municipality will remain unchanged except for real estate which is sub-let by a Municipality to be used in business activities which are not subject to VAT, or is used as a private home.

Government bodies may also be treated as taxable persons if they make intra-Community acquisitions (see section 7.2.4 of the Introduction to the European Union).

2.4 Fiscal Unity/Group Taxation

There are no special rules for taxation of companies as a group or fiscal unity. It is possible to credit VAT incurred in one company in the group by charging the VAT to another company of the group. The ownership must, however, amount to more than 90% of the shares and the charged company must not supply the refunding company with taxable services.

2.5 Foreign Entrepreneurs

Non-resident entrepreneurs are deemed to carry on a commercial activity if it is conducted in a commercial manner either inside or outside Sweden.

Supplies of goods in Sweden occur if the goods are physically in Sweden when the transport starts by the seller, the buyer, the forwarding agent of the seller or of the buyer, or an independent forwarding agent.

Foreign entrepreneurs may thus incur tax liability under the Value Added Tax Act even if they are not liable for income tax in Sweden.

2.6 Representative Offices

Representative offices (for example, dependent agents who provide services of a supporting and/or auxiliary nature, such as marketing services, etc) generally do not qualify as a permanent establishment for either Corporate Tax purposes or VAT purposes.

2.7 Vat Representatives

A foreign person is only liable to VAT when taxable supplies are made in Sweden. If this foreign person has no permanent establishment in Sweden, he must register through a representative who is responsible for fulfilling the administrative obligations, but not for paying the tax. The representative must be approved by the regional tax office.

2.8 Reverse Charge Mechanism

When certain services are 'imported' for business purposes, the customer in Sweden must account for Swedish VAT as if he had made a supply of the services to himself. The services in question are as follows:

- publicity services
- data services, including the supplying of information and automatic data processing
- services relating real estate in Sweden, eg supplying or selling
- writing services
- translation services
- the granting or transferring of the right to patents, the right of use to a construction or invention, design rights, trade mark rights, copyright to literary and artistic works or the right to use a system or programs for automatic data processing

- the testing or analysis of goods
- other services of a financial, juridical, administrative or other similar nature, for example legal, auditing or consultancy business

2.9 Importers

The term 'importation' is restricted to the movement of goods from a third territory, ie from a non-Member State. The tax liability is incurred when an application for Customs duty is made for goods imported from a third territory.

2.10 Acquirers of Goods from the European Union

The movement of goods from one Member State to another is an acquisition. If there is an acquisition by a Swedish business, the seller is not obliged to register. If there is a 'fictitious acquisition' (because, for example, there is no change in title) VAT registration will be required (see section 2.5 'Foreign Entrepreneur' and section 7.2 of the Introduction to the European Union).

There is a concession available for 'call-off' (consignment) stock whereby VAT registration is not required if the stock is located at the Swedish business's premises and falls under its control, even though title has not passed.

2.11 Supplier of New Means of Transport

Any person who undertakes on an occasional basis intra-Community supplies of new means of transport that are dispatched or transported from Sweden to another Member State is regarded as a taxable person (see section 7.2.6 of the Introduction to the European Union).

3   WHAT IS TAXABLE?

VAT is levied whenever a turnover of taxable goods or services occurs within Sweden.

3.1 Supply of Goods

In the VAT system in general, all goods and services are taxable, except those specially exempted by the VAT Act (see section 7 'Exemptions').

'Supply' means a delivery of goods and services.

The term 'goods' refers primarily to tangible objects which do not constitute real property. Goods are taxable unless specifically exempt from the tax. Both raw materials and semi-finished goods, etc, as well as finished consumer and capital goods, are subject to tax. It is of no consequence whether the commodity is new or used. The right to lease farmland, patents and the supply of standard computer software are also considered to be a supply of goods.

3.2 Imports of Goods

VAT must be paid not only on taxable turnover in Sweden, but also on imports of taxable goods from a non-Member State. This applies regardless of the purpose of the import and irrespective of the transaction on which the import is based. Tax on imports is levied by the

Customs Office in accordance with procedures laid down for Customs clearance. The Customs Office is also the authority to be consulted regarding VAT on imports.

3.3   Intra-Community Acquisition of Goods

'Intra-Community acquisition' is defined as the acquisition of the right to dispose as owner of movable, tangible property dispatched or transported to the person acquiring the goods by or on behalf of the vendor, or the person acquiring the goods to a Member State other than that from which the goods are dispatched or transported.

Intra-Community acquisitions of goods for consideration are subject to VAT when they are performed by a taxable person acting as such or by a non-taxable legal person where the vendor is a taxable person acting as such who is not eligible for the tax exemption as a small undertaking, where the goods are not installed by or on behalf of the vendor, and where the vendor is not involved in distance selling (see sections 7.2 and 7.4.2 of the Introduction to the European Union).

3.4   Distance Sellers

Persons who supply goods from another Member State to non-VAT-registered persons in Sweden may be taxable in respect of such supplies (see section 7.4.2 of the Introduction to the European Union).

3.5   New Means of Transport

The transfer to Sweden from another Member State of new means of transport is always taxable as an intra-Community acquisition regardless of the status of the supplier or the purchaser (see section 7.2.6 of the Introduction to the European Union).

3.6   Contract Work

If a VAT-registered person in another Member State sends goods to Sweden to be processed there, and the processed goods are not returned to the Member State from which the goods for process originated, then the owner of the goods will have to register and account for VAT in Sweden (see section 7.2.5 of the Introduction to the European Union).

3.7   Excise Products

In certain circumstances a non-registered acquirer of excise products may have to register and account for VAT on acquisitions of products which are subject to excise duty (see section 7.2.7 of the Introduction to the European Union).

3.8   Assembly/Installation

A supply of goods takes place in Sweden if the specific goods to be supplied are located in Sweden. This applies even if an overseas entrepreneur has no place of business in Sweden. However, the liability of supply of assembled or installed goods may be passed to the Swedish customer under the reverse charge mechanism (see section 2.7 'Reverse Charge Mechanism').

3.9   Supply of Services

All services are taxable when they are not specifically exempted by law.

3.10 Self-Supply of Goods/Services

The term 'self-supply' means that a taxable person takes goods or services from his taxable activity for which he is entitled to either an input VAT credit or a refund and puts those goods or services to private use.

Self-supplies are taxable even if the service is not sold on the open market for consideration. Further, when a person supplies a service to himself for private use, irrespective of whether goods are self-supplied or not with the service, the service is taxable as from 1 January 1995.

Self-supplies are subject to VAT when the transfer is free of charge or the price is below the purchase price or manufacturer's cost.

4   PLACE OF SUPPLY

4.1 Supply of Goods

The place of supply is in Sweden when the goods, including commodities, are delivered within the country.

Goods which are sold to a Swedish customer before importation are not taxable in Sweden. Goods which are delivered to a non-Swedish country (export) are taxable in Sweden, but are zero-rated.

Goods which are sold to a non-resident entrepreneur's warehouse in Sweden are taxable.

4.2 Intra-Community Acquisitions

As a general rule, the place where an intra-Community acquisition of goods takes place is deemed to be the place where the goods are when transportation to the person acquiring the goods ends.

To make a zero-rated intra-Community supply followed by an intra-Community acquisition on which the VAT charged may be deducted by the acquirer, the VAT identification numbers of the parties involved must be stated on the invoice.

If, for any reason, the goods arrive finally in a Member State other than that which issued the VAT number to the acquirer and the person purchasing the goods acquires the goods in the Member State of arrival of the goods this could cause double taxation, since the purchaser must account for VAT both in the Member State which issued the VAT number to him and in the Member State of arrival of the goods.

The presumption is that the place of acquisition is the country which issued the VAT number to the acquirer. However, if the acquirer can show that he has paid VAT in the Member State of arrival of the goods he will not be liable for payment of acquisition VAT in his own Member State.

4.2.1 Chain Transactions

'Triangulation' involves the situation where three parties in three different countries are involved in selling and purchasing the same goods. For example, A in France sells goods to B in Belgium who sells the goods to C in Sweden and the goods are sent directly from A to C (see section 7.4.1 of the Introduction to the European Union).

4.2.2 Goods Placed on Board Ships, Aircraft or Trains During Transport

When goods are supplied for consumption on board ships, aircraft or trains during transport and the place of departure and destination are within the territory of the European Union, the place of supply is the place where the goods are at the time of departure of the transport (see section 7.4.3 of the Introduction to the European Union).

4.3 Supply of Services

4.3.1 General Rule

The main rule is that a service is supplied in Sweden if the supplier has his permanent establishment there.

4.3.2 Exceptions

Special rules for certain types of services are as follows:

- Services in connection with real estate are supplied in Sweden if the property is situated there.
- Transportation services are supplied in Sweden if the service is physically performed in the territory of Sweden. However, if the services are performed both in Sweden and outside Sweden, the total service will be regarded as supplied abroad when the transport goes directly to or from a third territory. This relates to:

  - the transportation of goods or passengers in Sweden
  - the transportation of goods or passengers to a non-Member State
  - passenger transport to and from a Member State.

- Consultancy services, transfers and assignments of copyrights, advertising services, banking, financial and insurance transactions, supplies of staff, agency services (other than those related to transport) and the hiring out of movable tangible property supplied by a non-resident supplier are supplied in Sweden if the customer has his permanent establishment there. However, if the customer is a private person, the services are supplied in the Member State where the supplier lives or has his permanent establishment.
- Services related to cultural, artistic, sporting, scientific, education, entertainment or similar activities, etc are supplied in Sweden if they are physically carried out there.
- *Goods transportation services:* transportation of goods from Sweden to another Member State is supplied in Sweden when the transport of the goods departs from Sweden, This applies to all supplies to private persons.

  However, if the customer of the transport service, supplied by a Swedish carrier is registered for VAT purposes in another Member State and he is using his VAT registration number, the service is supplied in the State where he is registered. If the carrier and the customer are both registered in Sweden, the carrier will be liable for the VAT on the supply. In addition, if the customer in not registered in Sweden or in another Member State of the European Union, the carrier must account for VAT in the country where the transport commenced (see also section 7.4.4 of the Introduction to the European Union).

- *Intermediary goods transport services:* the above rules are also applicable to intermediary services in relation to the transportation of goods between Member States (see also section 7.4.6 of the Introduction to the European Union).

271

- *Services ancillary to goods transport:* storage, loading and unloading of goods and similar services provided in connection with the intra-Community transport and agency services related thereto are supplied in Sweden if they are performed there (see section 7.4.5 of the Introduction to the European Union).
- *Work on movable goods:* valuation of and work on movable tangible property are supplied in Sweden if those services are physically carried out there.

4.4 Reverse Charge Mechanism

The concept of a reverse charge mechanism, as applicable in European Union countries exists in Sweden from 1 January 1991 for both individuals and entities (see section 2.8).

5 BASIS OF TAXATION

5.1 Supplies within Sweden

According to the basic rule, the taxable base consists of the entire payment exclusive of VAT.

In cash sales, 'payment' refers to payment received, ie the cash price less applicable cash discounts. The value of a commodity given in exchange is regarded as the equivalent of cash payment. Bills of exchange and other promissory instruments of debt do not constitute cash payment.

In the case of credit sales, payment is the price on which the buyer and seller have agreed when entering into their agreement, as evidenced by an invoice or other document made at the time. Such payments shall also include instalment payment charges, financing charges and all other price increments with the exception of interest which is payable by the customer under the agreement.

If a bill of exchange or other instrument of debt is made out for payment in connection with the agreement, the agreed price consists of the amount payable according to such a document plus any cash payment made over and above this amount. This applies even if a lower price is stated in an invoice or similar document.

For taxable goods and services the taxable base includes:

- the received consideration, exclusive of VAT
- other taxes imposed
- any additional charges, except interest.

5.2 Self-Supplies

The self-supply of goods will be taxed on the basis of the cost price or, if that is not available, the manufacturer's price at the time of use. The self-supply of services will be taxed on the basis of the purchase cost.

5.3 Imports

The taxable base is the value of the goods plus Customs duty and other state taxes or charges, exclusive of VAT.

5.4 Acquisition

The value used is the contract price, which may include commission, packing and transport.

If the acquisition is fictitious, then there is no change in ownership and the VAT value is the purchase price, cost price or value of similar goods. The value of acquisitions is also separately shown on the VAT return.

5.5 Chargeable Event/Time of Payment

The basic rule is that tax liability arises in connection with supply at the time of delivery of a commodity or provision of a service. Liability arises prior to delivery or provision of a service when advance payment or payment on account is received.

For importation the liability arises when importation has taken place.

According to the Accounting Act 1972 the recording of payables and receivables may be made either on a current basis periodically, by notation in lists, or by recording them at the end of the fiscal year. As a result of these alternatives, a bookkeeping-based form of VAT reporting is carried out according to one of two methods, the 'invoicing method' or the 'final accounts methods'.

However, turnover under SEK200,000 is reported in the ordinary annual Income Tax return, which coincides with the bookkeeping method. Because of this, the final accounts method is normally used by VAT-registered persons.

The final accounts method is used primarily by taxpayers who during the current year, only record entries for cash receipts and disbursements.

The invoicing method is applied in the first instance by taxpayers whose bookkeeping system provides for chronological recording of items in original books of entry (daybook) or who have a bookkeeping system with lists kept on a current or periodical basis.

5.6 Credit Notes/Bad Debts

If a loss arises on a supply for which the taxpayer has previously reported VAT payable, a deduction may be made in the amount of the corresponding lost VAT. The deduction is made by reducing the figure for VAT payable. To qualify for the deduction, the loss must be an actual or formally declared loss on accounts receivable. If payment is received for a previously deducted loss, VAT must once again be reported for the payment received.

If a bonus discount (with the exception of so-called conditional discounts) has been paid in arrears and VAT has been previously reported, an adjustment may be made for the tax accruing on such a discount, etc. The deduction is made by a reduction of the tax received. No reduction of the taxable base is permitted for a 'conditional discount', ie a discount awarded if payment is made within a certain period of time.

A credit note is a requirement for the seller to be entitled to reduce his tax received.

6   TAX RATES

Currently there are four rates:

0%:   exports of goods, newspapers, printing of zero-rated newspapers, medicines on prescription or provided to hospitals, aircraft fuel and aviation paraffin

12%:   hotel and camping services and passenger transportation

21%:   food and restaurant services

25%:   all other goods and services which are not taxed at the 0%, 12% or 21% rates or are not exempt.

7   EXEMPTIONS

7.1   Exemption with Credit for Input Tax

The zero rate effectively acts in a manner similar to 'exempt with credit'.

Some services in Sweden which contain a 'foreign element' are regarded as export services. As a consequence, the entrepreneur need not charge VAT, but will nevertheless be allowed a refund for input VAT. They are:

- delivery within Sweden if the goods are to be taken directly out of Sweden by a forwarder or carrier
- delivery to a foreign entrepreneur who himself collects the goods to take them directly out of Sweden, if the goods are intended for activity conducted by the entrepreneur outside Sweden
- delivery of goods in a free port, provided the goods are not intended for use in the free port
- delivery of goods to or for use or trade on board a ship or aircraft in international service
- delivery of beer, wine, spirits and tobacco products for sale in a tax-free shop
- delivery of a passenger car or motorcycle which is included in an exported vehicle list
- delivery of goods to a foreign entrepreneur who is not liable to pay tax in Sweden, provided the delivery takes place under the terms of a warranty commitment made by the foreign entrepreneur
- service performed on a commodity which has been brought into Sweden exclusively for this service and which is subsequently taken out of Sweden*
- procurement of goods on behalf of a foreign client*
- transport of goods directly to or from a foreign country
- transport or other taxable service in Sweden which relates to an imported or exported commodity and which a forwarder or carrier provides for a foreign client in connection with import or export*
- loading, unloading or other services in a trading port or airport which relates to an imported or exported commodity from a foreign entrepreneur
- testing or analysis of a commodity for a foreign client*
- storage of a commodity for a foreign client*
- service on behalf of a foreign client which results only in a report, minutes, etc*
- service on board a ship or aircraft in international service, or a service relating to equipment or other goods for use on such ships or aircraft
- product development, project planning, drawing, designing, construction or other similar services for a foreign principal*
- the granting or transfer to a foreign user of:
  - permission to use a design or invention relating to a taxable commodity
  - design rights, trademark rights, copyright to literary and artistic works and photographic pictures
  - the right to use a system or program for automatic data processing*

- data services and the supplying of information on behalf of a foreign client*
- writing services and translating services for a foreign client*
- other services of a financial, juridical or administrative nature for a foreign client*
- traffic tolls on a bridge or a tunnel between Sweden and another country.*
- while supplies of banking, financial and insurance services are exempt from VAT if the recipient of these services is resident or established outside the European Union, input credit attributable to such supplies is recoverable.

The following supplies of goods are exempt with credit:

- ships for lifesaving and parts, spare parts or equipment for such ships, on condition that the ship is placed at the disposal of the Swedish Society for the rescue of shipwrecked persons (Svenska Sällskapet för Räddning af Skeppsbrutna)
- ships for commercial shipping trade and commercial fishing, ships for tugs and salvage. Aircraft related to commercial transportation of goods or people, and services related to such a ship or aircraft. Also parts, spare parts and equipment for such a ship or aircraft.

7.2 Exemption without Credit for Input Tax

The following activities are exempt without credit for input tax with the result that the supplier cannot recover VAT on the purchase of goods or services attributable to these activities:

- hospital treatment, dental treatment or social care: this is classified as treatment which qualifies for compensation for medical expenses
- educational services, excluding education, information or training which the vendor arranges in connection with the supply of goods or services which are liable to taxation
- banks and financing services, share transactions, bonds, promissory notes, gift vouchers and similar documents of value, excluding trust operations, debt collecting services, renting out of safe-deposit boxes, etc plus financing companies' sale of recovered goods
- insurance services: services which are classified as a re-selling enterprise which is carried out by insurance brokers, etc but excluding an insurance company's sale of goods which have been taken over in connection with settlement of claims
- works of art, literary works, cinema, circus, theatre, opera and ballet performances, concerts, library and museum enterprises. However, works of art and literary works are tax-exempt only when the grant or the transfer is carried out by the originator himself or his estate
- transfer or grant of the right to real estate, excluding voluntary tax liability for the renting of business premises, for agricultural leases, renting of hotel rooms, etc renting of parking spaces, the use of harbours or airports and safe-deposit boxes, publicity or advertising services, and letting of places for animals
- postage stamps, bank notes and coins which are, or have been, the means of payment (not collectors' items)

---

* In order for export to be deemed to have taken place, the client must conduct business outside Sweden which would entail tax liability under the Swedish Value Added Tax Act if the business were conducted in Sweden. The client should be able to prove that he conducts business activity outside Sweden by, for example, presenting registration documents or equivalent proof.

- periodical membership publications or employees' publications (internal newsletters)
- the inserting or acquisition of advertisements in exempt publications as per periodical membership publications above
- the fee-financed productions of radio and television programmes by the Swedish Radio Group
- human organs, blood and breast milk
- lotteries, including betting and other types of gambling
- stock-in-trade inventory and other assets of a business if transferred or taken over through a sale of the entire business or part thereof to someone who is liable for VAT, upon a merger or similar transaction
- services related to the opening or the care of a grave provided by public cemeteries
- providing premises for sport purposes: including all types of leasing of tracks or entrance fees to sports centres, etc. Accessories to the business or other equipment which is included in the grant of enjoyment may also be tax-exempt
- the supply of gold to the Bank of Sweden.

7.3 Non-Taxable Transactions

7.3.1 Transactions Within the Same Legal Entity
Transactions within the same legal entity are not taxable as they are not regarded as turnover. Thus, transactions between a foreign head office and a branch in Sweden or vice versa are not regarded as turnover.

7.3.2 Transfer of Business
Assets and other goods are exempted from VAT when they are included in a transfer of a business. In order to be exempt, the transfer must concern the whole business or a certain independent part of it.

7.3.3 Subsidies/Penalty Payments/Compensation
Subsidies, penalty payments and compensation are outside the scope of VAT, provided they are not to be qualified as payments for taxable supplies.

7.4 Election for Taxable Supplies
The government may, upon request, rule that tax liability also applies, until further notice, to a person rendering a service which is not specified by law, for example, for forwarding agents accounting for VAT at import. Distance sellers (see section 3.4), government bodies (see section 2.3) and non-taxable legal persons may in certain circumstances elect to register for VAT.

8 CREDIT/REFUND FOR INPUT VAT

8.1 General Rule
A person who is liable to report VAT is entitled to claim a deduction in his tax return for tax paid on purchases, acquisitions and imports used for the purposes of his taxable business. The right to deduction is essentially general in nature, ie it covers all types of acquisitions(with a few exceptions). No credit is allowed for VAT incurred on the following transactions:

- dwelling houses
- personal cars and motorcycles for purposes other than a passenger transport undertaking dealing in such vehicles or renting them. The right to a deduction for tax paid on the cost of rental (leasing) of a passenger car is limited to 50%
- VAT on entertainment and representation (deductible for income tax purposes). (Representation is entertainment expenses occurring in the operation of business, both external and internal, for example restaurant expenses, meeting expenses, etc.)

Some special rules are in force:

- it is possible to credit VAT charged from one company to another in a group where one Swedish company owns more than 90% of the shares of one or more Swedish companies in the group. This can be seen as the concept of fiscal unity in the Sixth VAT Directive
- an entrepreneur liable to VAT is entitled to a credit for fictitious VAT when he buys taxable goods from a non-taxable person or company. The credit is the amount of VAT which would have been charged by the seller if he had been liable to VAT in the transaction. For example, if a foreign entrepreneur liable for VAT in Sweden buys equipment from a Swedish insurance company (which is not taxable), he can deduct 20% of the price as VAT, even though VAT was not charged.

8.2   Adjustment of Entitlement to Credit
A partially exempt enterprise deducts input tax based on the previous year's turnover for the different parts of the business. An adjustment must be made when the annual accounts become final.

8.3   Partial Exemption
If part of the turnover concerns activities which do not lead to liability for VAT, the input tax must be split between purchases relating to taxable and exempt (no credit) transactions. The input tax may be divided on the basis of the ratio of taxable and non-taxable transactions of total turnover. Other allocation methods are also permitted, for instance, on the basis of how the floor space of the business premises is used or on the ratio between the employees in the different parts of the business.

8.4   Time of Recovery
A person who has to report VAT in the ordinary income tax return (see section 2.1 'General') must follow the same rules as for income tax, ie, the rules regarding tax arrears are applicable when payment is overdue. The payment dates are the same as those for income tax. If the total amount to be paid exceeds SEK20,000, supplementary payments must be made by 18 February of the year after the fiscal year. If the total amount to be paid does not exceed SEK20,000, the last payment date will be 30 April. However, the tax arrears charge (ie the penalty) is only payable if payment is not made, at the latest, by 30 April.

When the invoicing method is applied, the right to claim deductions for VAT paid commences at the time that the business transactions on which the right to the deduction is based is entered into the books, or when it is recorded in a list.

This means that a person filing a return for a certain reporting period is entitled to a deduction (in addition to deductions for VAT on cash purchases) for VAT on unpaid invoices which have been entered into the books or recorded during the period, and which relate to deliveries of goods or provision of services made.

The right to claim deductions when applying the final accounts method commences during the current fiscal year when cash payment is made. Debt instruments (bills of exchange and promissory notes) are not considered the equivalent of cash payment. Therefore, deductions may not be made until the debt instrument is traded or redeemed. VAT which has been charged on unpaid payables may not be deducted until the return for the final reporting period of the tax year.

8.5   Refund for Foreign Entrepreneurs
A foreign businessman who is not liable for VAT in Sweden is entitled to repayment of VAT provided that:

- the VAT relates to business which he carries on abroad
- the business would have involved liability for VAT if it had been carried on in Sweden
- the VAT would in that case have been deductible.

The right to repayment is thus limited to what would have been deductible input VAT for a company operating in Sweden.

A foreign businessman who procures goods or a service on behalf of a client is entitled to repayment of VAT. This applies only if the client would have been entitled to repayment if he had bought the goods or service without an intermediary.

The right to repayment relates only to VAT which a Swedish taxpayer has debited, not to 'notional tax'.

The right to repayment of VAT arises when goods have been delivered to or imported into Sweden or when a service has been provided.

Foreign businessmen wishing to recover VAT should fill in a special application form (RSV 5801). The application must cover a period of at least three successive calendar months during one calendar year, and not more than one calendar year.

The applicant must enclose invoices specifying the VAT together with a certificate or other documents showing the type of business carried on abroad.

Application forms are available from county tax offices and from local tax offices. Applications must be sent to:

> Skattemyndigheten i Kopparbergs län
> 771 83 Ludvika
> Sweden

9   ADMINISTRATIVE OBLIGATIONS

9.1   Registration
All persons or entities liable for Swedish VAT must be registered with the local tax authority

and must report the VAT on the ordinary VAT return. However, anyone who is only liable for VAT because of the acquisition of new means of transport or excisable goods does not have to be registered, although they still have to file a VAT return in accordance with each purchase.

Individuals and smaller entities with a turnover below SEK200,000 per year can report the VAT on their ordinary Income Tax return. However, small enterprises who buy or sell to or from other Member States must register in the ordinary way and file a VAT return.

Entrepreneurs who are not registered because their turnover does not exceed SEK200,000 per year will be registered automatically when they report the VAT on their ordinary Income Tax return.

An entrepreneur must register for domestic transactions and must also register separately for intra-Community transactions.

9.2 Books and Records
The basic principle is that liability to report VAT commences when a person becomes liable to record a business transaction entailing tax liability in his books of account. Similarly, the right to deduction commences when an acquisition is entered into the books. Certain exceptions have been made from this accrual basis principle.

For bookkeeping and tax purposes the books and records must be kept for ten years. If no books and records are kept, a penalty is likely to be imposed and the VAT liability will be based on an estimate.

9.3 Invoices
All taxable persons must issue an invoice, settlement or corresponding document for each taxable transaction. There are certain exceptions to this rule.

The invoice, settlement statement or corresponding document must indicate the amounts of payment and tax, as well as other information of relevance for determining tax liability and the right to deductions such as the amount of VAT, the name of the purchaser and the seller, the registration number for VAT and a specification of what has been supplied. Under Swedish bookkeeping rules, which are also applicable for VAT accounting, the invoice must be issued as soon as possible after the supply has been made.

The retail trade has been exempted from compulsory invoicing, as have persons who perform services which are principally directed to the general public, for example, in the restaurant sector.

9.4 VAT Returns
The general reporting period is every second month. However, for companies that sell or buy to or from other Member States the tax period is monthly. If the turnover does not exceed SEK200,000 and the sales to and from Member States are less than SEK120,000 per year the reporting period can be one year. However, if it is a split financial year, the calendar year cannot be used as the reporting period. The tax return shall be filed the fifth day of the second month after the end of the reporting period, annually or monthly.

9.5   VIES Statements

VIES statements ('Sales listings') must be submitted by taxable persons to the local tax authority on a quarterly basis (see 7.9.2 of the Introduction to the European Union for further details).

9.6   INTRASTAT

Traders who supply goods to other Member States or who acquire goods from other Member States must provide monthly details of the goods movement if their sales exceed SEK900,000 and their acquisitions exceed SEK900,000 (see section 7.9.3 of the Introduction to the European Union).

9.7   Registers

Certain registers of goods movements must also be kept (see section 7.9.4 of the Introduction to the European Union).

9.8   Powers of Authorities

If the tax cannot be reliably computed on the basis of the return, or if no return has been filed, the county administration will determine the tax on reasonable grounds by way of assessment. Additional assessments can be imposed up to six years following the calendar year during which the tax year expired.

Once the tax return has been submitted, it constitutes a final statement of the tax for the period and shall constitute the basis for the tax assessment. It is, of course, possible to correct errors that may have been made in a return which has already been submitted. The most convenient procedure in such a case is simply to replace the incorrect return by a corrected return for the same reporting period. A return form for this purpose may be ordered from the county administration VAT section. If a corrected return is received by the county administration, a new assessment will be made.

An additional 20% of the tax amount will be charged if incorrect information is provided in a tax return or other document.

9.9   Objections/Appeals

VAT is assessed for each reporting period. Once a return has been filed on time, the tax declared is deemed to have been assessed automatically. No formal notice is given to the taxpayer. If the taxpayer does not think that he can resolve a tax issue in mutual agreement with the county administration, he may appeal against the county administration's decision to the County Fiscal Court of Appeal. In order to do this, he must request a final assessment from the county tax administration. The final assessment can then be appealed. The request for the final assessment must be made within six years following the end of the calendar year during which the tax year expired.

The ruling of the County Fiscal Court of Appeal may be appealed against to the Fiscal Court of Appeal and subsequently (after special permission) to the Supreme Administrative Court. The appeal must be made within two months after the decision from the County Fiscal Court of Appeal has been received.

10   SPECIAL VAT REGIMES

10.1   Agricultural and Forestry Enterprises

Growing woodland, crops and other vegetation where sales take place independently of the conveyance of the land are regarded as taxable goods. So also are the rights of:

- agricultural leases
- timber rights or other comparable rights
- the right to extract earth, stone and some other natural products.

10.2   Financial Institutions

Financial activities are normally outside the scope of VAT. Generally, financial companies are liable for VAT in respect of the sale of items which have been repossessed by the company under the terms of a purchase. Trust operations, debt collecting services, renting out of safe-deposit boxes, etc are taxable.

10.3   Fishing Enterprises

No special rules for VAT liability apply to fishing companies and they can buy fishing boats without VAT because these are exempt.

10.4   Free Ports/Bonded Warehouses

There are free ports in two places in Sweden: Stockholm and Gothenburg. Provided the goods are not intended for use in the free port, delivery of goods in a free port is regarded as export.

It is possible to have bonded warehouses in Sweden. They do not have to be situated in the free port area. Customs duty will be paid when goods are taken out of the warehouse.

10.5   Real Property Transactions

Real property is not subject to tax. The term 'real property' is highly important in the application of the VAT rules since there are, in the real property area, special rules governing such questions as to which goods and services are subject to tax, when the liability to report VAT commences, and how the taxable base is determined. For the purpose of VAT real property includes, first of all, everything which is defined to be real property under the Code of Land Laws. It also includes buildings, conduits, fences and similar facilities which have been installed in or above the ground for permanent use and which are owned by a person other than the owner of the land. Items added to a building are generally regarded as building fixtures if they are designed for permanent use and relate to the general function of the building.

Building fixtures are not subject to VAT.

Industrial fixtures which have been procured for direct use in a particular specified business are deemed to be goods, even if they have been permanently installed in the building.

Business fixtures procured for direct use in a particular business are defined as goods. Equipment for plumbing, sanitation, heating, electricity and the like which is defined by the Land Laws as part of the building shall, however, always be regarded as real property if the equipment is of the type normally used to equip a building for residential housing purposes.

Upon application, the county administration may rule that the owner of real estate shall be liable to pay tax on the rental of business premises used in an activity which is itself subject to VAT. A lease with rights to a tenant-owner's flat ('bostadsratt') is considered the equivalent of rental in this case. This possibility does not extend to second-hand rentals.

The aim here is to allow the property owner to deduct the tax he has paid on construction costs, etc. To do this he must charge tax to the tenant who can subsequently deduct it through his tax return. Once tax liability has been granted, there are certain possibilities for retroactive deductions. There are also regulations on restoring deductions for tax paid if circumstances are altered, for example if the property is sold.

10.6 Retailers
There are special rules for retailers.

10.7 Second-Hand Goods/Arts and Antiques
Second-hand goods are treated as normal goods. Works of art are exempted from VAT when the artist or his estate is the seller. For antiques and artistic work (not sold by the artist) there is one important special rule: no businessman who exports antique goods or artistic work is entitled to a credit for input tax.

10.8 Small Entrepreneurs
Small entrepreneurs are taxable under the common rules, but can report the VAT in the ordinary Income Tax return.

10.9 Travel Agencies
VAT is levied on commission earned by Swedish travel agents for selling passenger tickets, etc for domestic flights and travelling in Sweden. VAT is not payable on commission for international flights and travelling outside Sweden or to and from Sweden.

11   FURTHER READING

Handledning, Mervardeskatt 1993
Nils Mattsson, Mervardeskatten
Peter Melz, Mervardeskatten
Hans Fink, Momsboken
Jan Kleerup and Peter Melz, Handbok i Mervardeskatt

Contributor: Jan Kleerup
                   Ernst & Young
                   Adolf Frederiks Kyrkogata 2
                   Box 3143
                   103 62 Stockholm
                   Sweden
                   Tel: +46 8 6139000
                   Fax: +46 8 7917511

THE UNITED KINGDOM

1   GENERAL BACKGROUND

Value Added Tax (VAT) was introduced into the United Kingdom with effect from 1 April 1973 in conjunction with admission to the European Union on 1 January 1973. An indirect tax, it plays a significant part in the raising of revenue in the United Kingdom. The yield, at about £40 billion per year, is roughly half the yield of the direct taxes.

For VAT purposes, the United Kingdom comprises England, Wales, Scotland, Northern Ireland and (effectively) the Isle of Man, but it does not include the Channel Islands, which are not only outside the United Kingdom, but also outside the European Union.

United Kingdom VAT legislation is for the most part contained in the Value Added Tax Act 1994 (VATA 1994), and subsequent primary legislation, but much detailed legislation is contained in Statutory Instruments. Substantial amendments were made to the original legislation with effect from 1 January 1978 in order to make the United Kingdom position correspond more closely with that set out in the Sixth VAT Directive. There have been further major changes to the legislation as a result of the creation of the Single Market on 1 January 1993.

VAT is administered by Her Majesty's Customs & Excise ('Customs'), whilst the direct taxes such as Corporation Tax, Income Tax, etc, are administered by the Inland Revenue. Although it is permitted, there is currently little interchange of information between the two government departments but this is slowly changing. Their procedures are in many respects markedly different. This contrasts with the position in many other Member States.

1.1   The Single Market – Intra-Community Acquisitions
As a Member State of the European Union the United Kingdom applies the rules for VAT applicable to the Single Market and, in particular, the rules which apply in respect of intra-Community supplies during the transitional period which commenced on 1 January 1993.

For ease of reference, the transitional arrangements are set out in detail in section 7 of the Introduction to the European Union which precedes this section of the book.

It is recommended that this chapter is read in conjunction with the chapter on the transitional arrangements.

2   WHO IS TAXABLE?

2.1   General
A 'taxable person' is any person (individual, company, partnership, etc) who makes or intends to make taxable supplies while he is or is required to be registered under the provisions of

---

This chapter reflects the legislation on VAT in the United Kingdom as at 1 January 1995.

VATA 1994. A 'taxable supply' is a supply of goods or services (other than an exempt supply) made in the United Kingdom in the course or furtherance of any business.

The concept of 'business' is fundamental in considering whether or not a liability to VAT arises. Certain supplies are deemed always to be 'business', for example, subscriptions to clubs, but the definition of 'business' in the VAT legislation is not intended to be exhaustive. There is case law on the subject, and in general 'business' is more all-embracing than the equivalent 'trading' test for direct taxation. The word 'entrepreneur' is not used in the United Kingdom VAT legislation, but broadly speaking a person carrying on a business is very similar to an 'entrepreneur' in other Member States.

Notification of a liability to be registered for VAT is required to be made to Customs within the next 30 days when taxable supplies are in excess of or expected to exceed £46,000 per annum (with effect from 30 November 1994).

A non-VAT registered business acquiring goods from the European Union is also required to notify liability to register if the value of acquisitions exceeds, or is expected to exceed within the next 30 days, £46,000 (with effect from 1 January 1995).

There is a requirement to be VAT registered if a European Union business makes distance sales to non-VAT registered persons or to private purchasers in the United Kingdom where the value exceeds £70,000 (1994 figures) in the year commencing 1 January (see section 7.3.4 of the Introduction to the European Union).

The registration threshold is usually increased each year (in November) broadly in line with inflation. Stiff penalties exist for late notification of a liability to be registered, and this matter is dealt with further below.

Businesses are able to register for VAT voluntarily when taxable supplies are below the registration limits, and such registrations are in fact commonplace. (Registration is also possible for representative offices of overseas businesses – see section 2.6 below.) Where a business makes taxable supplies exclusively or predominantly to other businesses that are registered for VAT, no loss of competitiveness arises; registration enables the business to reclaim as input tax VAT arising on expenditure which is attributable to its own taxable supplies of goods and services (but not when they are exempt or unrelated to business) and the fact that a business is registered for VAT (demonstrated by a VAT number on invoices) can add credibility to the business.

2.2   Transactions with Branch/Subsidiary
If a branch of an overseas business (as opposed to a subsidiary company of an overseas business) is registered for VAT, any supplies of services between the branch and head office or other branches are outside the scope of the tax; this is important where the United Kingdom branch is partly exempt but is importing certain services from abroad.

2.3   Government Bodies
Special provisions enable local authorities and certain other bodies, including certain government bodies, to recover VAT on supplies made to them. They are also obliged to charge VAT on certain supplies made, particularly when in competition with the private sector. They may also be treated as taxable persons if they make intra-Community acquisitions (see section 7.2.4 of the Introduction to the European Union).

2.4   Fiscal Unity/Group Transactions

Although the concept of fiscal unity is widely known throughout the business community in the United Kingdom, the phrase itself is totally unknown. Instead, the legislation refers to group registration. This facility allows all bodies corporate (but not individuals, partnerships, etc) under common control and resident or established in the United Kingdom to be treated as one, with just one VAT return submitted to Customs by the representative member. There are several tests for common control but, to put it simply, if one company has a majority of the voting rights then both companies are eligible for group registration.

The facility is entirely optional; any combination of United Kingdom-resident established companies may be group-registered. However, in order to protect their revenue, Customs have power to refuse group registration, and they will exercise this power where an avoidance motive is suspected. From 3 May 1995 there is an equivalent power aimed at preventing de-grouping. There are many advantages and disadvantages to group registration, but it should be emphasised that there are considerable planning opportunities associated with the facility. In particular, there are significant numbers of businesses in the United Kingdom which are partly exempt (see section 8.3 'Partial Exemption'), and group registration prevents the unnecessary generation of irrecoverable VAT on cross-charges between companies under common control.

Where companies are group-registered, a joint and several liability to United Kingdom VAT arises for each of them. Where the potential liability is material in any instance, the existence of the VAT group registration is normally recorded by way of note to the accounts.

2.5   Foreign Businesses/VAT Representatives

Foreign businesses which supply goods or services in excess of the registration limits in the United Kingdom must notify Customs of their liability to be registered in the United Kingdom, in the same way as national suppliers.

Customs may direct that a tax representative is appointed for registration purposes, but otherwise it is not necessary. Commercially, however, there is much reluctance for businesses to act as such because Customs contend that the tax representative is liable for the VAT debts of his overseas principal. Whilst in theory this problem could be obviated through the use of bank guarantees, the practical problems are such that overseas businesses often register directly with a special unit of Customs, lodging an appropriate bank guarantee, as necessary.

2.6   Representative Office

A representative office of an overseas business is eligible for United Kingdom VAT registration even when it makes no taxable supplies in the United Kingdom. This allows it to recover input tax on expenditure. However, registration is limited to those circumstances where the supplies of the business overseas would be taxable supplies if made in the United Kingdom.

2.7   Reverse Charge Mechanism

Where certain services are 'imported' into the United Kingdom by way of business, the importer must account for United Kingdom VAT as if he had made the supply to himself. The services in question are as follows:

- transfers and assignments of copyright, patents, licences, trademarks and similar rights
- advertising services
- services of consultants, engineers, consultancy bureaux, lawyers, accountants and other similar services; data processing and provision of information (but excluding any services relating to land)
- acceptance of any obligation to refrain from pursuing or exercising, in whole or part, any business activity or any such rights as are referred to in the first subsection above
- banking, financial and insurance services (including reinsurance, but excluding the provision of safe-deposit facilities)
- the supply of staff
- the letting on hire of goods other than means of transport
- the services rendered by one person to another in procuring for the other any of the services mentioned in the preceding sections
- any service not described above when supplied to a recipient who is registered for United Kingdom VAT.

The importation of such services constitutes taxable turnover for registration purposes and might mean, for example, that a business otherwise making only exempt supplies would have to register for United Kingdom VAT if the importations exceeded the registration limits. These provisions, which accurately implement Article 9.2(e) of the Sixth VAT Directive, are an exception to the normal rule for establishing the place of supply of services where the supplier is established, the tax charge arising instead in the hands of the customer importing these mainly intellectual services from overseas. The charge only sticks when the importer is unable to reclaim all his input tax (ie if he is exempt or partly exempt).

The last indent in the above list provides for the so-called 'tax shift' mechanism where a non-resident business provides services which would normally have their place of supply in the United Kingdom, but the business has no permanent establishment. It places responsibility for accounting for the VAT in the hands of the resident VAT-registered customer, rather than the non-resident supplier.

The reverse charge does not apply to services which are either zero-rated or exempt, or to the provision of services between parts of a single legal entity (eg branches of the same business) or within a group registration.

Although the supply of installed goods in the United Kingdom is a supply of goods, it may be treated as a supply of services for the purposes of operating the reverse charge mechanism.

2.8   Importers

A non-European Union business is not obliged to register for VAT if title to the imported goods passes outside the United Kingdom, and the customer himself imports the goods.

Furthermore, if a non-European Union business maintains a stock of goods in the United Kingdom, those goods can be imported under the VAT registration number of an import agent, who will then charge VAT as appropriate to the United Kingdom customer. The only complication here is that the import agent will have to charge the non-European Union business VAT on his commission, which will be irrecoverable; this problem can be avoided if the foreign business is separately registered either through a VAT agent (who could be the import agent), or through the special unit mentioned above (see section 2.5 'Foreign Business').

2.9   Acquirers of Goods from the European Union

The movement of goods from one Member State to another is an acquisition. If there is an acquisition by a United Kingdom business, the European Union business is not obliged to register. If there is a 'fictitious acquisition' (because, for example, there is a movement of stock) VAT registration will be required for the European Union business (see section 2.5 'Foreign Business' and section 7.2 of the Introduction to the European Union).

There is a concession available for 'call-off' (consignment) stock whereby VAT registration is not required if the stock is located at the United Kingdom business's premises and falls under its control, even though title has not passed. The transaction is treated as an acquisition in the United Kingdom and the fictitious acquisition disregarded.

2.10   Non-Taxable Legal Persons – Taxable Persons with No Right to Recover VAT and Farmers Benefiting from Notional Refunds

Such persons are considered as outside the scope of VAT if on an annual basis their yearly intra-Community acquisitions are below £46,000. As soon as an acquisition puts them above that threshold they are subject to common intra-Community rules and must pay VAT on their acquisitions. They must therefore obtain an identification number and submit VAT returns.

The same persons may opt to be subject to the common rules even for acquisitions below the threshold. The option takes effect the first day of the month in which it is exercised and expires on 31 December of the second year following the option; the option is renewable for periods of two years except if renounced two months before the two-year expiring period.

2.11   Supplier of New Means of Transport

Any person who undertakes on an occasional basis intra-Community supplies of new means of transport that are dispatched or transported from the United Kingdom to another Member State is regarded as a taxable person (see section 7.2.6 of the Introduction to the European Union).

3   WHAT IS TAXABLE?

Taxable supplies are all supplies made by way of business which are of a type which would be standard-rated at 17.5%, or zero-rated when made by a person who is registered or registrable. Exempt supplies are specifically not taxable supplies.

3.1   Supply of Goods

The transfer of the whole property in goods is a supply of goods for VAT purposes. The distinction between a supply of goods, on the one hand, and a supply of services, on the other, is sometimes difficult to grasp, but the legislation specifies that the following (inter alia) are supplies of goods:

- the application by one person of a treatment or process to another person's goods
- the supply of any form of power, heat, refrigeration or ventilation
- the granting, assignment or surrender of a major interest in land.

The transfer or disposal of assets of a business, including free gifts over £10, is treated as a supply of goods, whether or not there is consideration.

3.2   Imports of Goods

VAT is either payable upon importation, or, more usually, a debit is made to the importer's bank account on the fifteenth day of the month following removal from the port or airport (deferred duty system). Input tax relief is then available to the importer in the same way as with normal supplies. It is not possible to place goods which are not liable to VAT at importation in a Customs or bonded warehouse.

Exceptionally, postal imports of goods worth less than £2,000 are dealt with by postponed accounting, whereby payment of tax upon importation is postponed until completion of the importer's next VAT return.

In all instances, it is important that the importer has the correct documentation before claiming input relief.

3.3   Acquisitions

VAT is accounted for as an acquisition on the VAT return as output tax and will be recoverable subject to the normal rules (see section 8 'Credit/Refund Input Tax').

Providing United Kingdom businesses quote their VAT registration number, complete with GB prefix, the supplies of goods from other Member States will be zero-rated.

3.4   Distance Sellers

Persons who supply and are responsible for delivery of goods from another Member State to non-VAT registered persons in the United Kingdom may be taxable in respect of such supplies (see section 7.4.2 of the Introduction to the European Union).

3.5   New Means of Transport

The transfer to the United Kingdom from another Member State of new means of transport is always taxable as an intra-Community acquisition, regardless of the status of the supplier or the purchaser (see section 7.2.6 of the Introduction to the European Union).

3.6   Contract Work

If a VAT-registered person in another Member State sends goods to the United Kingdom to be processed there, and the processed goods are not returned to the Member State from which the goods for process originated, then the owner of the goods must register and account for VAT in the United Kingdom (see section 7.2.5 of the Introduction to the European Union).

3.7   Excise Products

In certain circumstances a non-registered acquirer of excise products may have to register and account for VAT on acquisitions of products which are subject to excise duty (see section 7.2.7 of the Introduction to the European Union).

3.8   Assembly/Installation

A supply of goods takes place in the United Kingdom if their supply involves installation or assembly at a place in the United Kingdom to which they are removed. This applies even if an overseas entrepreneur has no place of business in the United Kingdom. However, the liability of supply of assembled or installed goods may be passed to the United Kingdom customer under the reverse charge mechanism (see section 2.7 'Reverse Charge Mechanism').

3.9 Supply of Services

Anything which is not a supply of goods but is done for a consideration (including the granting, assignment or surrender of any right) is a supply of services.

3.10 Self-Supply of Goods/Services

There are a number of circumstances when a business has to account for VAT on supplies made to it, rather than by it, in addition to the case of certain imported services (see section 2.7 'Reverse Charge Mechanism').

Where a partly exempt or unregistered manufacturer of business stationery or car dealer produces business stationery or cars for its own use, or where it self-supplies construction services or building land, special rules apply to the 'value added' element. This is to prevent unfair competition with manufacturers of these goods.

Where the self-supply is of construction services relating to the construction of new buildings or a major extension or enlargement, VAT must be accounted for on the open market value of the construction services when this exceeds £100,000 or more. This provision was introduced from 1 April 1989, and applies to in-house construction services, including those provided within a VAT Group.

A self-supply charge used to apply also to commercial building developments generally, but has been abolished from 1 March 1995 with provision for phasing out arrangements for existing projects by 1997.

The provision applied where a building or civil engineering work whose value was not less than £100,000 was developed by a partly exempt person for his own occupation but not using in-house labour or when there was to be an exempt disposal of the building or work (for example, a long leasehold rather than a freehold sale). The self-supply charge arose when the building or work was first used other than for a fully taxable purpose. The value of the self-supply was the aggregate of the historical value of the land on which it stands and the value of all standard rate supplies made or to be made in connection with it. This self-supply was introduced from 1 August 1989.

Where the self-supply is of a car, VAT must be accounted for on the VAT exclusive cost of the vehicle. The tax point is created when the car is transferred from the new car sales floor.

Where the self-supply is of stationery, VAT must be accounted for on the full cost of production of the stationery including overheads. The tax point is created when there is a clear intention to use the stationery in the business. It should be noted that some stationery supplies may be zero-rated.

4   PLACE OF SUPPLY

4.1   Supply of Goods

The place of supply rules for goods have been amended since the introduction of the Single Market. The following general rules apply but are not exhaustive.

The place of supply of any goods which does not involve their removal from or to the United Kingdom is treated as being in the United Kingdom if the goods are physically in the United Kingdom, and otherwise as being outside the United Kingdom. If the supply of any goods involves their removal from the United Kingdom, they should be treated as supplied in the United Kingdom. If it involves their removal to the United Kingdom from outside the European Union they should be treated as supplied outside the United Kingdom.

4.2   Intra-Community Acquisitions

As a general rule, the place where an intra-Community acquisition of goods takes place is deemed to be the place where the goods are when transportation to the person acquiring the goods ends.

To make a zero-rated intra-Community supply followed by a taxed intra-Community acquisition on which the VAT may be deducted by the acquirer, the VAT identification numbers of the parties involved must be stated on the invoice.

If for any reason the goods arrive finally in a Member State other than that which issued the VAT number to the acquirer, the person purchasing the goods acquires the goods in the Member State of arrival of the goods. In this case double taxation could occur, since the purchaser must account for VAT both in the Member State which issued the VAT number to him and in the Member State of arrival of the goods.

The presumption is that the place of acquisition is the country which issued the VAT number to the acquirer. However, if the acquirer can show that he has paid VAT in the Member State of arrival of the goods, he will not be liable for payment of acquisition VAT in his own Member State.

4.2.1 Chain Transactions and Triangulation

'Triangulation' involves the situation where three parties in three different countries are involved in selling and purchasing the same goods. For example, A in France sells goods to B in Belgium who sells the goods to C in the United Kingdom and the goods are sent directly from A to C (see section 7.4.1 of the Introduction to the European Union).

4.2.2 Goods Placed on Board Ships, Aircraft or Trains During Transport

When goods are supplied for consumption on board ships, aircraft or trains during transport and the place of departure and destination are within the territory of the European Union, the place of supply is the place where the goods are at the time of departure of the transport.

4.3   Supply of Services

4.3.1 General Rule

Under the normal rule, supplies of services are treated as being made where the supplier 'belongs', ie where the seat of his business is established, or where there is some other fixed establishment or, failing that, his usual place of residence. Where a supplier has establishments in more than one country, the supply is treated as being made by the establishment most directly concerned with making the supply. The same test is used to determine where the recipient of a service belongs.

4.3.2 Exceptions

The following are exceptions to the general rule:

- Land and property: services closely related to land and property are treated as being made where the land or property is situated. This includes construction, repair and maintenance services and the services of architects, estate agents, auctioneers and similar professionals involved in matters relating to land.
- Transport services: the supply of transport services is treated as taking place in the United Kingdom to the extent that the journey is within the United Kingdom, although there are exceptions. The transport of passengers outside the United Kingdom or to or from a place outside the United Kingdom is zero-rated. The transport of freight from or to the United Kingdom to a place outside the European Union is zero-rated. The VAT liability of transport and ancillary services directly linked to a movement of goods between Member States provided by a United Kingdom supplier may be shifted to the Member State of the customer on production of a European Union VAT registration number (other than a United Kingdom number) and thus become outside of the scope of United Kingdom VAT. Difficulties occasionally arise as a matter of practice, including conflicts with the jurisdiction of other Member States.

  The supply of passenger transport services within the United Kingdom is also zero-rated with certain exceptions (eg taxis and 'fun' rides).

- Cultural, artistic, sporting, entertainment services, etc: generally, the place of supply is treated as where the performance or service takes place. However, such services are included in the list of specified services under which the United Kingdom recipient would account for VAT under the reverse charge mechanism (see section 2.7 'Reverse Charge Mechanism'). A business supplying such services may still register for United Kingdom VAT if it wishes.
- Work on movable goods: as noted above, this may constitute a supply of goods rather than a supply of services when the effect is to alter the character of the goods, in which event the supply is made where the treatment or process is applied. By contrast, services involving work on goods, eg valuation and repair works, are not a supply of goods but of services. The general rule is that the place of supply is where the service takes place. However, with effect from 1 September 1993 the charge may be made without a VAT charge, providing certain criteria are met.
- Services provided by brokers or other intermediaries: the place of supply of these services which form part of an intra-Community transport of goods the Member State which issued the VAT identification number of the customer (see section 7.4.6 of the Introduction to the European Union).
- Services rendered by brokers or other intermediaries which do not come within the scope of Article 9.2(e) of the Sixth VAT Directive: the place of supply of these services is the Member State of the customer which issued to him his VAT registration number (see section 7.4.7 of the Introduction to the European Union).

4.4   *Reverse Charge Mechanism*
In the case of supplies of services mentioned in section 2.7 above, the supply is treated as being made where the recipient of the supplies belongs. Thus the 'importation' into the United Kingdom of such services is subject to the reverse charge (self-supply to and by the customer). The 'export' of such services to a person in his business capacity elsewhere in the European Union or to any person in a third country is treated as outside of the scope of United Kingdom VAT (the supply of such services to a person in the European Union not in a business capacity is subject to United Kingdom VAT). It should be noted that Customs require the supplier of such services to be able to demonstrate that the European Union (non-United Kingdom) recipient of the service is in business. This may be best evidenced by quoting the VAT number of the recipient's Member State on the supplier's invoice, although in the case of a government department or other public body, it may also be necessary to show that this service is received in a business capacity. This rule does not apply to services relating to land or property in the United Kingdom.

5   BASIS OF TAXATION

5.1   *Supplies within the United Kingdom*
In the simplest of cases, the consideration for a supply is the cash passing. However, where barter trading is involved, the consideration is deemed to be the value of the goods or services tendered in exchange. Where the consideration does not consist or does not wholly consist of money, VAT is charged on the equivalent in monetary terms. Free supplies of services (where there is genuinely no consideration in return) do not give rise to a VAT liability, but it should be noted that, where goods or a succession of goods are given away in the course of business, or where a gift of goods is made and their cost to the donor is more than £10 (exclusive of VAT), then there is deemed to be a supply of the goods. VAT is paid on the cost of the goods.

Special anti-avoidance provisions apply to supplies between connected persons which allow Customs to impose open market value when they believe the price has been artificially depressed; these apply most especially to circumstances where the recipient of the supply is partly exempt or not registered for VAT.

5.2   *Self-Supplies*
VAT is due on certain self-supplies of goods or services and the basis for the VAT value/tax point depends on certain rules (see section 3.10 'Self-Supplies').

5.3   *Imports*
The value for calculating VAT on importations follows normal GATT principles. Where customs duty is payable, the VAT is calculated by reference to the price plus duty.

5.4   *Acquisitions*
For calculating the VAT on acquisitions, the value used is the contract price, which may include commission, packing and transport. If the acquisition is fictitious, then there is no change in ownership and the VAT value is the purchase price, cost price or value of similar goods. The value of acquisitions is also separately shown on the VAT return.

5.5 Chargeable Event/Time of Payment

The time of supply depends on whether a supply of goods or a supply of services is involved. In the case of a supply of goods, the time of supply is the earliest of the following:

- the date the goods are removed to give effect to the contract
- the date the supplier raises a VAT invoice
- the date when the supplier receives consideration.

Where there is an acquisition or a supply for acquisition, the tax points are the same, being the earlier of:

- the fifteenth day of the month following that in which the removal to or from another Member State occurred; or
- the date of a tax invoice.

In the case of the supply of services, the time of supply is the earliest of:

- the date of completion of the services
- the date a VAT invoice is issued
- the date when the supplier receives consideration.

A large number of special rules cover particular circumstances including:

- supplies of goods on approval
- sale of goods on sale or return
- goods for private use
- imported services
- supplies of any form of power, heat, refrigeration or ventilation
- continuous supplies of services
- supplies in the construction industry.

5.6 Cash/Invoice Basis ('Cash Accounting')

Special relief is available to businesses making supplies of less than £350,000 per annum whereby those opting to use the relief can account for tax by reference to the date of cash payment rather than by reference to the date of issue of invoices. The Cash Accounting Scheme is particularly useful to those small businesses whose customers take extended credit for settling their debts. Furthermore, the effect of using the scheme is to give automatic VAT bad debt relief. More generally, suppliers within the retail industry have always been able to elect to account for tax by reference to the date of receipt of cash.

5.7 Credit Notes/Bad Debts

A credit note may only be used to correct a genuine mistake; it may not be issued in circumstances where a customer has failed to pay for a supply, for whatever reason. Relief for VAT on bad debts is limited, and generally only applied in the past where the customer was insolvent. However, bad debts with tax points arising after 31 March 1989 will be eligible for relief when they are six months old and have been written off in the registered person's accounts. Before 1 April 1993 and in relation to supplies made prior to 1 April 1992, the qualifying period was one year.

6   TAX RATES

The present rates are as follows:

0%:   food (with exceptions), sewerage services and water (other than to industry), books, talking books for the blind and handicapped and radio and cassette players for the blind, construction of dwellings and certain other non-commercial buildings, etc (see section 10.5 'Real Property'), protected buildings, certain international services, passenger transport, caravans and house-boats, gold, bank notes, drugs, medicine and aids for the handicapped, exports, certain supplies by and to charities, clothing and footwear for young children. Many of the zero-rated reliefs have qualifying criteria

2.5%:   importations of works of art, antiques and collectors' items

8%:   supplies of fuel and power to domestic consumers and other (mainly charitable) limited categories

17.5%:   all other supplies of goods and services which are not exempt or taxed at the 0%, 2.5% or 8% rates.

7   EXEMPTIONS

7.1   Exemptions with Credit for Input Tax (Zero Rate)
The United Kingdom has more zero-rated supplies than almost any other European Union State. In effect, zero-rating is exemption with credit since it allows the attributable input tax to be recovered.

While supplies of banking, financial and insurance services are outside the scope of VAT if the recipient of these services is resident or established outside the European Union, input credit attributable to such supplies is recoverable.

7.2   Exemptions without Credit for Input Tax
Land (with certain exceptions such as holiday accommodation, parking and sporting rights), supplies subject to the option to tax (see section 10 'Special VAT Regimes'); insurance, postal services, betting, gaming and lotteries, finance, education, health and social welfare, burial and cremation, trade unions and professional bodies, sports competitions, transfers of works of art, etc to museums in satisfaction of tax, and fund raising events put on by charities and similar bodies which are not part of a series or regular run of similar events.

Certain imports are not subject to VAT, such as personal effects of travellers, personal goods imported on permanent transfer of private residence, temporary imports, goods re-imported after being repaired abroad, and goods in transit. Certain restrictions and qualifications apply to some of these items.

7.3   Exempt Importation
The importation of goods which is followed by an intra-Community supply may be exempt (see section 7.7.2 of the Introduction to the European Union).

7.4 Non-Taxable Transactions

For a variety of reasons, certain transactions do not give rise to a liability to VAT, but the justification for this situation varies according to the circumstances, and it is difficult to categorise the situations under any neat headings. Nonetheless, the following specific items are worthy of note:

- supplies between members of the same VAT group
- supply of an employee's services under a contract of employment
- supplies of services for no consideration
- supplies made outside of the United Kingdom
- supplies not made in the course of business
- supplies not made by a taxable person.

7.4.1 Transactions within the Same Legal Entity or VAT Group

These are outside the scope of VAT and include transactions between branches and head office, between different corporate bodies which are members of the same VAT group, and transactions between separately registered divisions of the same corporate body, irrespective of geographical location worldwide. Transactions between different corporate bodies which are members of the same United Kingdom VAT group are also outside the scope of VAT.

7.4.2 Transfer of Business

Provided certain detailed requirements are met, a transfer of a business as a going concern, or of part of a business which is operational in its own right, is neither a supply of goods nor a supply of services. Both parties to the transaction must be (or become) VAT registered and there must be an intention (and ability) to carry on the business in the same way as before the transfer. An anti-avoidance provision exists whereby, if the transfer is into a partly exempt VAT group, the transferee has to account for VAT under a special self-supply rule on the value of all assets less than three years old, except to the extent that there was a partial exemption restriction on the original purchase of the goods. This provision does not apply to goodwill.

7.4.3 Subsidies/Penalty Payments/Compensation

Each payment must be treated on its own merits but, by and large, a subsidy or donation does not represent the consideration for any supply if it is 'no strings attached'. The question to be asked is whether the payment is made, in reality, for anything which is done (or not done, including giving up a right) by the recipient. If it is, then VAT will be chargeable.

The question of the VAT treatment of compensation payments has recently been subject to review by Customs and it should not be assumed that any payment which is described as compensation will not be subject to VAT. In general, out-of-court settlements and liquidated damages (for example, for a breach of contract) are outside the scope of VAT, but this is an area where care is needed.

Sponsorship payments towards the support of sporting or cultural events, etc will be treated as taxable if the sponsor receives in return tangible benefits such as publicity and promotion of his product.

7.4.4 Dividends

Dividends represent the distribution of profits, and are not the consideration for any supply.

7.4.5 Disposals of Motor Cars (for a Consideration Less than the Purchase Price)
As a general rule, this is not a supply liable to VAT, primarily because input tax would have been blocked on the original acquisition of the car, and its subsequent disposal does not give rise to any 'added value'. (There is a blocking of input tax recovery on the purchase of cars by a business, except for certain categories, for instance, motor dealers for resale, taxis, driving schools, hire of cars on a short-term basis and other cases where the use of the car is wholly business. The same exemptions apply to long-term leasing. From 1 August 1995 blocking does not apply to the purchase of a motor car wholly for business use (eg for onward leasing).

7.5 Election to be Registered for VAT
A person who makes taxable supplies where the value of these supplies is less than the registration limits may nevertheless register for VAT in order to reclaim input tax on expenditure. The person must, however, be making taxable supplies in the course or further-ance of a business.

An election to register option is also available to distance sellers (see section 3.4) and to non-taxable legal persons and government bodies (see section 7.2.4 of the Introduction to the European Union).

8   CREDIT/REFUND FOR INPUT TAX

8.1   General Rule
A registered business is entitled to claim credit in its quarterly VAT Return for input tax suffered on the expenditure by way of offset against output tax. Where input tax regularly exceeds output tax, it is entitled to submit returns monthly. Customs normally make repayments of the tax in question within 14 days of the submission of a return to Southend-on-Sea. Customs are liable to pay a repayment supplement of 5% (or £50 if greater) if repayment is not made within 30 days from the date of receipt by Customs.

There are a few exceptions to the general principle that a fully taxable business can claim input relief for all VAT suffered on its expenditure. The most notable exceptions are the outright purchase of motor-cars for mixed business and private use and on entertainment expenditure; input relief is also blocked in the case of private and non-business expenditure.

8.2   Adjustment of Entitlement to Credit
The provisions of Article 20.2 of the Sixth VAT Directive (ie the provision relating to adjustments for capital items) was introduced from 1 April 1990. This has created a serious administrative complication for the partly exempt sectors of British industry and commerce (most notably the financial and insurance sectors). In order to minimise administrative complications, adjustment is required only for computers and computer equipment valued at £50,000 or more and land and buildings (or parts of buildings) valued at £250,000 or more. The input tax recovery is adjusted over a five-year period in the case of computers and computer equipment, and ten years in the case of land and buildings to take account of changes in the partial exemption recovery position of the business concerned.

8.3   Partial Exemption

A partly exempt business may have its entitlement to input relief restricted to the extent that it makes exempt supplies. Before 1 April 1987 different rules applied, but since that date the legislation follows the principles of the Sixth VAT Directive, more especially Articles 17 and 19. The basic principle is that input tax must be directly attributed as far as possible to taxable activities on the one hand and exempt and non-business activities on the other. The former input tax can be recovered in full, but the latter cannot be recovered. Any residual input tax which cannot be attributed directly in this way can be recovered according to a fair and reasonable apportionment. The standard method for such an apportionment is based on the value of supplies made; alternatively, a special method may be agreed with (or directed by) Customs based on some other calculation, provided it produces a fair and reasonable result.

Provided that the input tax attributable to exempt activities is very small, certain de minimis limits will apply, and the business can treat itself as fully taxable. A partly exempt business will almost certainly need professional guidance in negotiating an appropriate partial exemption method with Customs, and securing an agreement in writing. Many such agreements include a provision whereby input relief is provisionally claimed on a quarterly basis, depending on the circumstances prevailing at that time. Subsequently, an 'annual adjustment' will be called for, whereby the input tax provisionally reclaimed will be adjusted having regard to the facts of the year as a whole. This 'annual adjustment' must be distinguished from adjustments to entitlement to credit (see section 8.2 'Adjustment of Entitlement to Credit').

8.4   Time of Recovery

Businesses may claim input relief by reference to the supplier's tax-point although, in practice, in the absence of a purchase day book, input relief will be claimed by reference to the date of payment. Claims for input relief should normally be made in the quarter in which the expenditure is incurred.

8.5   Refunds for Foreign Businesses

Foreign businesses are entitled to claim relief for VAT suffered on United Kingdom expenditure pursuant to the Eighth and Thirteenth VAT Directives. Businesses registered for VAT in another Member State have been able to claim refunds since 1 January 1981 under the Eighth VAT Directive, and businesses established outside the European Union since 1 January 1988 under the Thirteenth VAT Directive. The reclaim procedure is known as mutual recovery, and the detailed provisions are to be found in Customs Notice 723.

It is important to note that claims must be submitted to Customs within six months of the end of the relevant accounting year; thus claims by European Union businesses must be submitted by 30 June for VAT suffered in the previous year to 31 December, whilst non-European Union businesses must submit their claims by 31 December in respect of the previous 12 months ended on 30 June.

Claims should be sent to:

> HM Customs & Excise
> Overseas Repayments
> 8th/13th Directive
> Customs House, PO Box 34
> Londonderry, BT38 7AE
> Northern Ireland

9   ADMINISTRATIVE OBLIGATIONS

9.1   Registration

Any person who makes or intends to make taxable supplies in excess of the registration limits is required to notify Customs of that fact.

The current turnover limit of £46,000 per annum has already been referred to above, as have the concepts of voluntary registration and group registration (see sections 2.1 'General' and 2.4 'Fiscal Unity/Group Transactions').

Further points to note about registration for VAT are as follows:

■   exemption from registration: it is possible for businesses with taxable supplies over the registration limits to be granted exemption from registration. (It is still necessary to notify Customs of the obligation to register when the registration turnover limit is first exceeded.) This is the case where a business can demonstrate that, if it were registered for VAT, its input tax would always exceed its output tax. The provision is therefore only of interest to businesses with an overwhelming preponderance of zero-rated supplies, and it does, of course, mean foregoing recovery of input tax.

■   divisional registration: A company organised into a number of self-accounting units is able to opt to have each of these divisions separately registered for VAT. This facility is very seldom encountered in practice, but may be of use where there are practical difficulties in completing one return for the entire company. This facility is not available to persons who are partly exempt.

9.2   Books and Records

Books and records of a business must be retained for a minimum of six years in order to facilitate the conduct of control visits by Customs officers.

There are additional compliance and administrative obligations in respect of intra-Community trade (see section 7.6 of the Introduction to the European Union).

9.3   Invoices

All businesses making supplies of goods or services at the standard rate are obliged to issue a tax invoice where the customer is a taxable person. A tax invoice must contain a number of points of information, although the requirements are less onerous in the case of certain supplies costing less than £100.

The statutory regulations require that a tax invoice shall show:

■   an identifying number, the date of the supply, the date of the issue of the document, the name, address and registration number of the supplier and the person to whom the goods or services are supplied, the type of supply, eg, sale, loan, hire purchase, etc, a description of the goods or services supplied, for each description the quantity of the goods or the extent of the services, the rate of tax and the amount payable (including tax), the gross total amount payable (excluding tax), the rate of any cash discount offered, each rate of tax chargeable, the amount of tax chargeable at each such rate and the total amount of tax chargeable. All figures must be expressed in Sterling.

If a United Kingdom VAT-registered person issues a tax invoice to a person in another Member State in connection with a movement of goods between Member States the additional information below shall be shown also:

- the letters GB as a prefix to a VAT registration number
- the VAT registration number of the recipient of the supply of goods and services, including the alphabetical code of the Member State, the gross amount payable excluding tax and, where the supply is of a new means of transport, a description sufficient to identify it as such and the values expressed in Sterling.

9.4   Returns

VAT returns must reach Customs Headquarters at Southend-on-Sea, together with a cheque in settlement of the liability where appropriate, by the end of the month following the quarterly period of account. (Monthly returns are normally used for repayment claims but, exceptionally, where a monthly return shows a liability due to Customs, the same deadlines apply as for quarterly returns.) It is also possible to agree special accounting periods with Customs. An extension of seven days is permissible where the business agrees to make settlement through the Bank Giro system, rather than through the post, although this needs Customs' prior written consent.

Separate returns concerning intra-Community movement of goods are required during the transition period (see section 7.6 of the Introduction to the European Union).

9.5   European Union Sales Lists

European Union sales lists showing intra-Community supplies must be made by registered businesses making supplies of goods to businesses registered for VAT in other Member States on Form VAT 101. Traders with a low turnover of European Union sales may not need to do so, but must seek exemption from their local VAT offices. The completed list must normally be sent to the following address:

> The Controller
> VAT Central Unit
> HM Customs & Excise
> 21 Victoria Avenue
> Southend-on-Sea XSS 991
> England

See 7.9.2 of the Introduction to the European Union.

9.6   INTRASTAT

Traders who supply goods to other Member States or who acquire goods from other Member States must provide monthly details of the goods movement if their arrivals of goods from or despatches of goods to other Member States exceed £150,000 (see section 7.9.3 of the Introduction to the European Union).

9.7   Registers

Certain registers of goods movements must also be kept (see 7.9.4 of the Introduction to the European Union).

9.8 Powers of the Authorities

Given that VAT is administered by the same government department (HM Customs and Excise) that seeks to control drug and other smuggling, it is perhaps not surprising that it should have very extensive powers for collecting VAT. Whilst these powers were re-defined in 1985, they remain very extensive indeed, and prison sentences are applicable in the most serious circumstances.

9.9 Estimated Assessments

Where VAT returns are not submitted to Southend-on-Sea within the prescribed time limits, the Customs' computer will automatically issue an estimated assessment. The submission of the return in question will serve to cancel the assessment, but in the absence of the return, the estimated tax assessed must be paid.

There is provision in the legislation for registered businesses to estimate net tax due to Customs, but this requires Customs' prior consent, which is not easily obtained.

9.10 Periods of Limitation

Except in cases of fraud, wilful neglect, etc, there are strict time limits within which Customs must raise assessments covering mistakes discovered during the course of their control visits.

The time limits for making an assessment depend on the provision under which it is made, the conduct giving rise to the assessment and whether the assessment is made before or after the person's death.

Basically, Customs are not entitled to go back more than six years prior to the date of the assessment, nor more than two years where they take more than 12 months to issue an assessment having become aware of sufficient facts as to enable them to issue an assessment in the first instance.

9.11 Correction of Returns

Although VAT has been in operation in the United Kingdom since 1973, it is rather surprising that the legal position surrounding the manner in which errors in earlier returns should be corrected has only recently been settled. Following court decisions unfavourable to Customs' argument that repayments of tax overpaid in past return periods were entirely at their discretion, legislation was passed in 1989 which established a statutory basis for recovery of overpaid tax, except where the claimant would be unjustly enriched (for example, when he had collected VAT from his customers but would not be refunding it to them on receiving the overpayment due to himself).

Errors of VAT under £2,000 may be adjusted on the current VAT return. Errors in excess of this should be notified to Customs.

9.12 Penalties

9.12.1 Late Submission of Returns and Late Payment

A number of automatic civil penalties have been introduced for such offences.

In the case of late submission of returns and/or payments a default is recorded and after a written warning a surcharge of 2% for the first subsequent offence is imposed, rising on a sliding scale to 15%. These surcharges are not allowable for direct taxation purposes.

A surcharge will not be imposed where there is a repayment due or a nil return submitted or a return submitted late where the tax has been paid by the due date.

9.12.2 Late Registration
Penalties have applied since 25 July 1985 for failure to notify an obligation to register for VAT on time. The penalties are on a sliding scale according to the length of time involved: 10% of the net tax due for up to nine months, 20% for a period over nine months but not exceeding 18 months, and 30% for a period over 18 months.

9.12.3 Default Interest
From 1 April 1990 interest has been imposed on assessments made by Customs to correct earlier mistakes. However, Customs should not now impose interest where there is no tax loss to the revenue. Again, such interest is not deductible for direct taxation purposes.

9.12.4 Misdeclarations, etc
In the case of large errors detected by Customs (rather than voluntarily disclosed by the registered business) a misdeclaration penalty of 15% of the tax which would have been lost if the error had not been discovered will be imposed in specified circumstances, subject to objective tests.

This penalty may be avoided if the error is found and voluntarily disclosed to Customs by the registered person; but interest will still be payable. A similar persistent misdeclaration penalty of 15% of the net tax wrongly declared is imposed in prescribed circumstances.

These penalties are not imposed when there is judged to be a reasonable excuse, but the criteria for such an excuse are tightly circumscribed by law.

9.13 Appeals
A wide variety of matters can be taken before a VAT Tribunal on appeal, including assessments for tax due. Whilst it is possible to appeal directly to a VAT Tribunal, in practice most registered businesses ask for the point of dispute to be locally reviewed by senior Customs personnel. Such a review may lead to the settling of the dispute without the cost and inconvenience of proceeding to formal litigation. The time for making an appeal to a VAT Tribunal is limited to 30 days. This can sometimes be extended, and the time should not run whilst a local review is underway. However, this should be confirmed with Customs in writing.

Throughout the United Kingdom, the VAT Tribunal deals with all appeals in the first instance. In England and Wales, subsequent appeals are to the High Court, the Court of Appeal, and the House of Lords, in turn. In Scotland, however, an appeal from the VAT Tribunal is direct to the Court of Session, and then to the House of Lords. Any court can refer a matter of difficulty to the European Court of Justice. VAT appeals all the way to the House of Lords are rare, perhaps one a year; appeals to the VAT Tribunal are, however, much more commonplace.

10   SPECIAL VAT REGIMES

10.1   Annual Accounting
This enables a business with turnover of less than £300,000 per annum (see section 5.6 'Cash/Invoice Basis') to submit just one VAT return a year, with provisional payments on account being made during the interim by way of direct debit to the bank account of the business, calculated by reference to estimates of liabilities.

10.2   Financial and Insurance Institutions
A wide variety of special rules apply to supplies made by banks, insurance companies, insurance brokers, Lloyd's managing agents and syndicates, and unit trust management companies.

10.3   Free Zones
A free zone is a designated enclosed area in which goods may remain without payment of VAT arising at importation. Each free zone is run by an independent commercial operator. Customs do not control free zone goods until they leave the free zone. The United Kingdom government has designated a number of free zone areas of which only Liverpool, Southampton and Tilbury, Ronaldsway (Isle of Man) and Birmingham International Airports are operational.

10.4   Oil Industry
Special treatment is accorded to oil companies involved in exploration activities.

10.5   Real Property
As a result of the defeat of the United Kingdom government in its case against the European Commission before the European Court of Justice, substantial changes have been made to the legislation that governs the VAT liability of construction services and property transactions.

Some zero-rating remains but its scope has been greatly reduced; for instance, buildings whose construction and sale qualifies for zero-rating are confined to dwellings and qualifying residential and charitable buildings.

Generally speaking, freehold sales of commercial buildings and civil engineering works are automatically standard-rated within three years of completion. The freehold sale of qualifying buildings remains zero-rated if the freehold is sold by the person who constructed the building; the freehold sale of qualifying buildings by other persons is exempt. All other freehold and leasehold disposals of land or buildings are exempt with the option to tax.

The option to tax applies to the sale or lease of any land or any non-residential building (for example, not qualifying for zero-rating) and is at the vendor's or landlord's discretion and on a building-by-building basis (though it currently includes all the buildings in a complex or precinct of buildings). From March 1995, the rules governing the option were relaxed to some extent, allowing 'selective' options to tax on buildings in a shopping mall or industrial estate or discrete areas of agricultural land. The option may not be exercised if the vendor or landlord is connected (within the meaning of section 839 of the Taxes Act) with the purchaser or tenant, and one of those parties is not a fully taxable person. This is designed to prevent VAT avoidance through lease and leaseback schemes involving connected parties.

Leases granted in connection with qualifying buildings fall into two categories; those exceeding 21 years' duration granted by a builder are zero-rated in respect of the premium, if any, or the first payment of rent, and exempt thereafter: other leases are exempt from the outset though certain supplies of interests in land are standard-rated (for example, car parking and holiday accommodation). Leases granted in connection with commercial buildings are exempt, irrespective of duration (with the option to tax).

10.6 Retail Export Schemes
Visitors to the United Kingdom from outside the European Union are entitled to export certain retail products free of VAT under special rules.

10.7 Retail Industry
A variety of different accounting schemes apply, according to the individual circumstances of the retailer.

10.8 Second-Hand Goods
Following the implementation of the Seventh VAT Directive on 1 January 1995, a margin scheme of accounting for VAT applies to sales of all second-hand goods except for precious metals and gemstones. Under this scheme, dealers in such goods account for VAT on the difference between the buying and selling price, and, as a simplification, can do so under a simplified method known as Global accounting. As its name suggests, this allows business dealing in low volume second-hand goods to account for VAT on the difference between total purchases and sales rather than on an item by item basis.

From May 1995, a lower rate of 2.5% applies to importations of works of art, antiques and collectors' items (which were previously relieved for import VAT).

See also section 7.10.2 of the Introduction to the European Union.

10.9 Tour Operators
VAT is imposed only by reference to the margin on trading of anyone acting as a principal in putting together and selling tours and holidays, for example, package holidays. The VAT incurred in buying-in the ingredients of such tours, etc (whether in the United Kingdom or elsewhere in the European Union) is not recoverable, and the supply by the tour operator is seen as a single supply from the place where it has established its business or the fixed establishment from which the supply is made. The margin is currently standard-rated in respect of the standard-rated elements in the package, and zero-rated in respect of the zero-rated elements, but this is due to change from 1 January 1996 when the margin will be standard-rated for all elements supplied within the European Union.

10.10 Distance Sellers
During the transitional period a distance seller is a taxable person who supplies goods to a non-taxable individual or entity in another Member State and who arranges the transportation of those goods to the Member State of the customer. If the value of such distance sale supplies exceeds a threshold set by the Member State of the non-VAT registered customer then the supplier must register and account for VAT in that country (see section 7.3.4 of the Introduction to the European Union).

11   FURTHER READING

Tolley's Value Added Tax, Tolley
Tolley's VAT Planning, Tolley
Tolley's VAT on Construction, Land and Property, Tolley
De Voil, *Value Added Tax*, Butterworths
Mainprice British Value Added Tax Reporter, CCH Editions Limited
Croner's Reference Book for VAT, Croner
Relf and Preston *VAT Guide*, Oyez.

Contributor: Peter Jenkins
                 National Tax Partner
                 Ernst & Young
                 Becket House
                 1 Lambeth Palace Road
                 London SE1 7EU
                 England
                 Tel: +0171 928 2000
                 Fax: +0171 931 1120

EUROPE – OTHER

CYPRUS

1   GENERAL BACKGROUND

Value added tax (VAT) was introduced in Cyprus with effect from 1 July 1992.

Although Cyprus is not a member of the European Union, the VAT Laws are largely based on the principles of the EU Directives. Cyprus VAT legislation is contained in the Value Added Tax Act 1990 and subsequent legislation and in additional rules, orders and notifications.

VAT on internal transactions and on imports is administered by the Customs & Excise Department.

2   WHO IS TAXABLE?

2.1   General
A taxable person is any person (individual, company, partnership, etc) who makes or intends to make taxable supplies in the course or furtherance of business.

The term 'business' means an economic activity which is exercised in an independent manner, notwithstanding the objectives or the results of this activity. It includes the exercise of any trade, profession or vocation, but excludes the rendering of salaried services.

A person is required to register for VAT when taxable supplies exceed C£12,000 per annum.

2.2   Government Bodies/Local Authorities
Government bodies and local authorities are not taxable persons in respect of their activities. They are, however, obliged to charge VAT on certain supplies which are specified in the legislation and are liable to pay VAT on local purchases and importation of goods.

2.3   Group Taxation
There are no provisions for fiscal unity and group registration in the Cyprus VAT legislation. Each company is separately registered and liable to VAT and all transactions between group companies are subject to VAT in the normal way.

2.4   Foreign Businesses
Foreign businesses which supply goods or services in Cyprus in excess of the registration limits are liable to register for VAT in the same way as local businesses.

2.5   VAT Representatives
Foreign businesses which are liable to register for VAT in Cyprus may appoint a represen-

---

This chapter reflects the law on VAT in Cyprus as at 31 December 1994.

tative in Cyprus to be responsible for all the Cyprus VAT liabilities of the foreign business. Alternatively they may provide a bank guarantee to the satisfaction of the authorities.

2.6   Reverse Charge Mechanism

Where a person receives certain services from abroad for business use, he is regarded as having supplied the services to himself and must account for VAT on the value of the services on the date of payment. At the same time this amount is deductible as input tax. This treatment only affects businesses which make exempt supplies and are unable to reclaim all their input tax. The services in question are as follows:

- transfers and assignments of copyrights, patents, licences, trademarks and similar rights
- acceptance of any obligation to refrain from pursuing or exercising, in whole or in part, any business activity or any such rights as are referred to above
- advertising services
- services of consultants, engineers, architects, real estate agents, consultancy bureaux, lawyers, accountants and other similar services as well as data processing and provision of information
- the supply of staff
- the hire of any movable items, but excluding means of transport.

The importation of these services constitutes taxable turnover for registration purposes and might mean that a business which otherwise makes only exempt supplies would have to register for VAT if the total value of the services exceeds the registration limits.

2.7   Importers

A foreign business is not obliged to register for VAT if title to the imported goods passes outside Cyprus and the customer himself imports the goods. If a foreign business imports goods to Cyprus through an agent who acts as principal in Cyprus, the goods can be imported under the VAT registration number of the import agent who will then charge VAT as appropriate to the Cyprus customer.

3   WHAT IS TAXABLE?

'Taxable supplies' are all standard-rated or zero-rated supplies of goods or services made in Cyprus by a taxable person in the course or furtherance of any business carried on by him and the importation of goods into Cyprus.

3.1   Supply of Goods

For VAT purposes, 'supply of goods' is defined as the transfer of the whole property in goods for a consideration. The legislation specifies that the following are also supplies of goods:

- the supply of immovable property
- the execution of works on immovable property, whether or not the materials are provided by the contractor
- the application by one person of a treatment or process to another person's goods
- the supply of any form of power, heat, refrigeration or ventilation.

3.2   Supply of Services

Any supply in the course of business which is not a supply of goods but is done for a consideration is a supply of services, and includes food and drink supplied in the course of catering, the operation of hotels, furnished rooms and houses, camping sites, parking places, and the leasing of factories and safe deposit boxes.

3.3   Self-Supplies of Goods

Where a person in the course or furtherance of a business produces, imports or purchases certain goods which are not supplied to another person but are used for the purpose of that business, then the business has to account for VAT on the supplies made to itself. This 'self-supply' treatment applies only to motor cars and, in the case of partly exempt persons, to stationery.

3.4   Imports of Goods

The importation of goods into Cyprus is subject to VAT at the same rate as that applying to the sale of similar goods within Cyprus. VAT is payable at the time of importation and is levied as if it were a customs duty.

Goods imported into a bonded warehouse or free zone are not liable to VAT while they remain under these customs regimes.

If the importer is a taxable person he is entitled to claim back input tax in the same way as local suppliers provided that he has the correct customs documentation.

4   PLACE OF SUPPLY

4.1   Supply of Goods

A supply of goods which does not include their removal from or to Cyprus is treated as taking place in Cyprus. If the supply of goods involves their removal from Cyprus, the goods are treated as supplied in Cyprus and, if it involves their removal to Cyprus, they are treated as supplied outside Cyprus.

4.2   Supply of Services

The place of supply of services is the place where the supplier has his establishment or, if he has establishments in more than one country, the establishment which is most connected with the supply. If he has no establishment, the place of supply is his usual place of residence.

4.3   Reverse Charge Mechanism

The place of supply of the services referred to in section 2.6 above is where the recipient of the services belongs. Thus the importation into Cyprus of such services is subject to the reverse charge treatment. The export of such services to a person outside Cyprus is exempt.

5   BASIS OF TAXATION

5.1   Supplies within Cyprus

Where the consideration for a supply is wholly in money, VAT is chargeable on the amount upon which, if the VAT is added, would be equal to the total sum paid or payable. Where the consideration does not consist or does not wholly consist of money, the value of the supply shall be taken to be its open market value.

Special provisions apply to supplies of goods between connected persons where the prices have been artificially depressed. There are special rules for second-hand goods, package holidays, etc.

Goods given away in the course or furtherance of business whose cost exceeds 0.75% of the annual gross income of the business are deemed to be taxable supplies of goods.

5.2   Imports
The value of imported goods for calculating VAT is the customs' value (including all other duties and charges levied on importation).

5.3   Chargeable Event/Time of Supply
In the case of a supply of goods, the time of supply is the earliest of the following:

- the date of delivery of the goods, or
- the date the supplier issues an invoice, or
- the date the supplier receives payment.

In the case of a supply of services the time of supply is the earliest of the following:

- the date of completion/performance of the services, or
- the date the supplier issues an invoice, or
- the date the supplier receives payment.

If an invoice is issued within 14 days from the delivery of the goods or the performance of the services, then the invoice date is the tax point, unless overridden by earlier payment. The period of 14 days may be extended with the approval of the VAT Commissioner.

Special rules apply to continuous supplies of services, supplies in the construction industry, etc.

5.4   Cash/Invoice Basis
There is no provision for cash accounting in the Cyprus VAT legislation.

5.5   Credit Notes/Bad Debts
Where goods have been returned or a price reduction has been allowed, a registered supplier may adjust his VAT liability by issuing a credit note. A credit note may not be issued for writing off a bad debt.

Relief for bad debts is only available when the customer has become bankrupt or insolvent.

6   TAX RATES

The following rates apply:

0%: food (except for food supplied in the course of catering), water (except bottled water), medicines, fertilisers, insecticides and agricultural machinery; gas in cylinders, books, newspapers and magazines, urban and rural bus services, air and sea transport abroad, children's clothing and footwear, export of goods, services regarding the management of sea-going vessels, commission received from abroad for the arrangement of imports/exports of goods.

8%: all supplies of goods and services unless they are specifically exempt or zero-rated.

7 EXEMPTIONS

7.1 Exemptions with Credit for Input Tax

The effect of zero-rating is similar to exemption with credit in that the supplier, while not obliged to charge output VAT, is entitled to recover input VAT.

The supplies of goods within customs regimes (free zones, bonded warehouses, etc) are exempt from VAT but carry the entitlement to recovery of input tax.

7.2 Exemptions without Credit for Input Tax

The following supplies are exempt from VAT:

- sale and rental of land and buildings (except holiday accommodation, parking, etc)
- financial and insurance services
- postal services
- lotteries
- education
- health and social welfare
- trade unions
- certain services when supplied to an overseas person (eg advertising, services of consultants, engineers, architects, lawyers, accountants).

8 CREDIT/REFUND FOR INPUT TAX

8.1 General Rule

A taxable person is entitled to claim credit for input tax suffered on goods or services purchased or imported which are used or intended to be used for the purposes of his taxable supplies. To be entitled to the credit the registered person must have a proper VAT invoice or the customs' entry form. Deductible input tax is offset against output tax in the quarterly VAT return.

8.2 Refund of Excess Input Tax

Where at the end of a tax period input tax exceeds output tax, the excess is carried forward to be set off in the next quarter, except in the following cases, where it is refunded immediately:

- it relates to zero-rated supplies
- it was incurred on capital expenditure
- in cases where under the circumstances it is impossible for the excess to be set off by

the end of the following year
- three years have elapsed since the end of the quarter during which the excess resulted.

8.3 Exceptions

A credit is not allowed for VAT suffered on any of the following:

- goods or services used for construction works on immovable property
- entertainment expenses
- food, drink, accommodation, transportation and entertainment for the employees and representatives of the business
- purchase or importation and running expenses of saloon cars and ships or aircraft for private use
- purchase or importation of smoking materials or alcoholic drinks not intended for resale.

8.4 Adjustment of Entitlement to Credit

There are no provisions for adjustment of input tax credits in respect of capital goods.

8.5 Partial Exemption

Where a taxable person makes both taxable and exempt supplies, the input tax deduction is restricted by the extent that it relates to the exempt supplies. Input tax directly attributed to taxable supplies can be fully recovered. Input tax directly attributed to exempt supplies cannot be recovered. Any input tax which cannot be directly attributed must be apportioned. The standard method described in the rules is based on the ratio of taxable supplies to total supplies. An alternative method may be agreed with the authorities. If input tax attributable to exempt activities is within certain de minimis limits, the business can recover all the input tax.

8.6 Time of Recovery

A taxable person may make a claim for input tax deduction in the VAT return for the period in which the supplier's tax point falls, although a claim can only be made when he has a valid tax invoice. Input tax deduction cannot be claimed by reference to the date of payment.

8.7 Refunds for Foreign Businesses

Cyprus does not operate a refund scheme for foreign businesses incurring VAT in Cyprus.

9 ADMINISTRATIVE OPERATIONS

9.1 Registration

Any person who makes or intends to make taxable supplies in excess of the registration limits (currently C£12,000 per annum or C£3,000 quarterly) is required to notify the authorities within 30 days. Businesses, which make taxable supplies below the registration limits, may register for VAT voluntarily, but they must remain registered for a period of at least three years.

Divisional or group registrations are not permitted.

9.2   Books and Records

Taxable persons must maintain detailed and up-to-date books and records which must be retained for seven years.

9.3   Invoices

Registered businesses must issue tax invoices when making standard-rated supplies to another taxable person. A tax invoice must contain certain specified information, although a less detailed invoice may be issued by retailers for supplies amounting to less than C£50.

9.4   VAT Returns

VAT returns must be submitted by the tenth day following the end of the month which follows the end of every tax period. Each tax period covers three months, but a taxable person who is usually in a repayment position may apply for permission to file monthly returns.

9.5   Correction of Returns

Where a taxable person discovers that output tax or input tax has been under/overstated in a previous period, he may make the appropriate corrections to this tax account and include them in the VAT return of a later tax period, provided that he is not under investigation.

9.6   Powers of the Authorities

The VAT Commissioner has extensive powers in relation to a number of matters including the power to:

- raise assessments for VAT due where a return has not been submitted or where there are grounds to believe that the submitted return is incomplete or incorrect
- require deposits or guarantees
- demand the presentation of records and information
- search business premises and persons present in such premises
- obtain samples.

9.7   Penalties

There are a number of automatic penalties in the legislation dealing with offences, including:

- a fine of C£30 per month for late submission of the VAT return
- a 10% fine on the due amount for late payment of tax due and, if the omission continues for more than 30 days, a further 9% interest on the tax due and on the fine
- a fine of C£50 per month for failure to notify the obligation to register for VAT.

Penalties (including imprisonment) may also be imposed by a court of law for fraudulent evasion of tax, using or making of a false statement, failure to register/deregister for VAT purposes, failure to submit a tax return or to pay the tax, and failure to maintain proper books and records.

9.8   Appeals

Any taxable person who is dissatisfied with a decision, order, notice or other act of the Commissioner, may appeal to the Minister of Finance within 30 days of the notification of the decision.

The Minister shall not deal with the appeal unless the Commissioner certifies that the person submitting the appeal has submitted all the tax returns required and paid all the tax due. The Minister must examine the appeal and give his decision within 60 days from the date of appeal. If the appellant disagrees with the decision he may appeal to a court of law.

10   SPECIAL VAT REGIMES

10.1   Retailers
Three schemes are available to retailers for calculating their output tax. A retailer may select the one most appropriate to his circumstances.

10.2   Second-Hand Goods
Special schemes apply to sales of the following second-hand goods whereby VAT is accounted for only on the margin between buying and selling prices: motor cars, works of art, antiques and collectors' pieces, motor-cycles, caravans, boats and outboard motors, electronic music organs, aircraft, firearms.

10.3   Tour Operators
Tour operators acting as principals in organising and selling holidays are subject to a special regime whereby VAT is imposed only on the margin which is the difference between the selling price of the package and the costs paid by the tour operator to third parties. Input tax incurred on these expenses is not recoverable.

10.4   Farmers
Farmers do not fall under the provisions of the VAT law regarding supplies made by them of goods or services which consist of agricultural products produced by them or the supply by them of agricultural services. However, if a farmer makes other taxable supplies in the course or furtherance of a business, then he must register for VAT purposes and he will be a taxable person with regard to the supplies of goods or services made in the course of his other business. Notwithstanding this, a farmer may elect to be registered for VAT purposes.

Contributor: Christia Rossidou
                 Ernst & Young
                 Nicosia Tower Centre
                 36 Byron Avenue
                 Nicosia (162)
                 Cyprus
                 Tel: + 357 2 467000
                 Fax: + 357 2 476613

CZECH REPUBLIC

1   GENERAL BACKGROUND

Value added tax (VAT) was introduced into the Czech Republic on 1 January 1993 replacing the single-stage turnover tax inherited from the previous planned economy, which consisted of 1,506 different tax rates on manufactured and imported goods.

The Czech VAT is a two-rate structure, with most goods liable to VAT at the rate of 22%, and most services liable to VAT at the rate of 5%. There is a desire to adopt a VAT system which is compatible with the Czech Republic's eventual membership of the European Union. As such, future amendments should bring the current system more into line with the Union's rules.

Control of VAT is vested in the Financial Authority.

2   WHO IS TAXABLE?

2.1   General
'Taxable persons' who make 'taxable supplies' are required to charge VAT.

'Taxable persons' are essentially individuals or legal entities who systematically conduct on an independent basis a commercial activity for the purposes of making a profit. Consequently, a private individual will not usually be a 'taxable person' and hence will pay VAT on his purchases without being able to claim a refund of the tax.

Registration by taxable persons is mandatory where Czech turnover exceeds certain limits set out in the legislation – see section 9.1 below. Failure to register on time could lead to penalties relating to both late payment of tax and late filing of returns.

A 'taxable supply' includes the delivery of goods and the transfer of real estate property (excluding the transfer of land) involving a change of ownership, the provision of services, and the transfer or exploitation of rights ensuring from industrial or other intellectual property, within the framework of a business enterprise. It also includes the provision of goods, services, buildings and structures, and the transfer and exploitation of certain rights – (see section 3 below).

2.2   Government Bodies
As the activities of government bodies fall outside the definition of taxable persons, supplies made by them are outside the scope of the VAT Act.

2.3   Group Taxation
There are no provisions to enable businesses under common control to be grouped under the same VAT registration. Thus, transactions between such entities are liable to VAT in the

This chapter reflects the law on VAT in the Czech Republic as at 31 December 1994.

same way as those between unconnected parties, irrespective of how closely they are connected in terms of common management.

2.4 Foreign Firms

Foreign firms which supply goods and services in the Czech Republic are obliged to register and account for VAT if their Czech turnover is in excess of the appropriate limits.

Foreign firms which do not supply taxable goods and services in the Czech Republic are not permitted to register for VAT.

2.5 Branch Offices

A representative office of a foreign entity which makes taxable supplies in the Czech Republic and whose Czech turnover exceeds certain limits is obliged to register and account for VAT on the supplies which it makes.

In practice, however, the financial authorities will not register a branch or representative office of a foreign entity unless the representative office is registered in the Companies Register, as no VAT agent exists within the jurisdiction of the authority.

2.6 Importers

VAT is due on the importation of goods, either permanent or temporary, into the Czech Republic and is payable at the point of entry. Generally, imported goods are liable to VAT at the same rate as those supplied within the Czech Republic.

If the person importing the goods is an agent for an overseas supplier, the import agent is obliged to charge tax to the buyer, without the right to a deduction.

Goods that are only imported temporarily are subject to taxation at the rate of 3% per month (even if incomplete) of the tax which would have been payable on the goods if they were to be released into free circulation.

3   WHAT IS TAXABLE?

VAT liability arises on all taxable supplies made in the Czech Republic for or without consideration, including supplies in kind.

3.1 Supply of Goods

A 'taxable supply of goods' means the delivery of goods and the transfer of real estate property, including the delivery of buildings, structures and building works even in the form of a lease contract with a subsequent purchase of the leased goods, involving a change of title. The transfer of land is not considered to be a supply of goods.

The term 'goods' is defined as tangible movable assets, including thermal and electric energy, gas and water.

3.2 Supply of Services

A 'supply of services' is the provision of activities or materially tangible results of activities, which are not goods.

3.3 Self-Supply of Goods and Services
The following self-supplies are also be considered as taxable supplies:

- the provision of goods, services, buildings and structures, transfer and exploitation of rights by taxpayers for private use if the taxpayer is a private person
- the provision of goods, services, buildings and structures, transfer and exploitation of rights for purposes not connected with business activities, in the case of supplies which, in the event of business activities, are not subject to tax
- the provision of goods, services, buildings and structures, transfer and exploitation of rights for purposes not connected with business activities, if a tax deduction has been received for those goods.

The self-supply of passenger cars and returnable glass containers which were manufactured by the taxpayer is considered to also be a taxable supply in circumstances where the taxpayer is not entitled to claim a tax deduction on these goods.

3.4 Imports
The mere importation of most goods gives rise to a taxable supply. Imported goods which are exempt from duty (such as software) shall be exempt from VAT, subject to certain exceptions.

'Imported goods' are defined as:

- goods cleared for free circulation in the Czech Republic
- goods cleared and registered for temporary circulation in the Czech Republic, to enable further processing, modification or repair before being returned abroad
- re-exported goods cleared and registered for temporary circulation in the Czech Republic for the purpose of temporary use
- goods cleared for temporary use.

4 PLACE OF SUPPLY

4.1 Supply of Goods
For the purposes of the VAT Act, the place where goods are supplied shall be:

- the place where the goods are located at the time when the process of their transport or despatch begins, provided that the delivery of the goods is connected with their transport or despatch, regardless of who is effecting the transport or despatch of the goods
- the place where the goods are installed or assembled, if the delivery of the goods includes such installation or assembly, or
- the place where the goods are located at the time of their delivery, if the delivery is effected without their transport or despatch.

If real estate is transferred, or a building or structure is delivered, the place of the taxable supply shall be the place where the real estate or the structure concerned is located.

4.2 Supply of Services and Transfer of Rights
The place of taxable supply is generally the place where the person providing the service or

effecting the transfer and exploitation of rights has its seat or its permanent establishment where it provides the services. If the provider has no seat or permanent establishment, it shall be the place of the person's residence or the place where the person is usually staying.

4.2.1 Exceptions

The exceptions to this general rule are as follows:

- In the case of services relating to real property, including services provided by real estate agencies, assessors, architects and construction repairers, the place of supply is the place where the real property is located.
- If transport services are provided, the place of supply is the place where the transport originates.
- For services associated with cultural, artistic, sporting, scientific, educational, entertainment or similar events, including agency, organisational and auxiliary services relating to such activities, the place of supply is the place where the services are actually provided.
- For services related to travel agency, accommodation, catering, consultancy, financial services, insurance, commercial and agency services, legal services, information and translation services and educational activities, the place of supply is the place where the services are actually provided.

5   BASIS OF TAXATION/CHARGEABLE EVENT

5.1   Supplies within the Czech Republic

Where the consideration takes the form of money the amount on which tax is chargeable is normally the total sum paid or payable to the person supplying the goods or services including all taxes, commission, costs and charges whatsoever but not including the VAT chargeable in respect of the transaction. VAT must, therefore, be returned on the VAT-exclusive price.

Where goods or services are supplied and the consideration does not consist or does not consist wholly of an amount of money and where certain goods are supplied free of charge, the amount on which tax is chargeable is the open market or arms length value of the goods or services supplied.

5.2   Imports

The value for VAT purposes of imports is the value taken for customs duty purposes plus the customs duty and any Consumption Tax payable on the goods.

5.3   Chargeable Event

A tax liability is established on the day the taxable supply is realised. A taxable supply is considered as having been realised at the following times:

- in the case of a sale of goods under a sales contract, the date specified in the contract and, in other cases, the day the goods are delivered or paid for, whichever is the earlier
- in the case of the transfer of real estate, the day when ownership of the property is assumed or the right of management is transferred
- for the provision of services, the day when the services are rendered or paid for, whichever is the earlier

- in the case of the transfer and exploitation of rights, the date on which the contract becomes effective
- in the case of a taxable supply provided without consideration, the date specified in the relevant contract, or the day when delivery of the taxable supply without consideration is effected or such a supply is provided, depending on which occurs earlier
- in the case of taxable supplies made for personal consumption by a taxpayer who is a natural person and for purposes not related to business activities, the day of the receipt of the goods or services
- in cases not listed above, on the day of payment.

Taxable supplies realised through vending machines, and in cases where payments for taxable supplies are made with credit cards and other means of payment replacing money, shall be considered as having being realised on the day the taxable person removes the money or tokens from the relevant machines or equipment, or ascertains in a different manner the amount of sales.

In the case of lease contracts and contracts for work where the taxable supply is carried out in the form of a partial supply or a recurrent supply, every partial or recurrent supply shall be considered to be a separate taxable supply. For this purpose, the taxable supply is deemed to be realised on the last day of the taxable period in which it is provided.

The payment of an advancement is not considered to be a realisation of a taxable supply.

5.4   Imports
Tax is normally payable on imported goods at the time of importation.

6   TAX RATES

The following rates apply:

5%:   on most services and certain goods: (including most foodstuffs but excluding confectionery, fuels and pharmaceuticals)
22%:   on most goods and certain services: (including restaurant and public catering, repairs and maintenance, tourist travel services, accommodation services, commercial and agency services, and various works of a manufacturing nature).

7   EXEMPTIONS

7.1   Exemption with Credit for Input Tax
The following supplies are exempt from tax liability, although the taxpayer providing the supplies is entitled to claim a tax deduction on the inputs for that supply:

- international transport: international transport of goods, money and scheduled international transport of passengers, and services related to international transport. 'International transport' is understood to mean transport from a place abroad to another place abroad via the Czech Republic; or from a place abroad to a place in the Czech Republic; or from a place in the Czech Republic to a place abroad; or between two places in the Czech Republic as part of international air and river transport

- export of goods: goods cleared in accordance with the export regime whose final delivery abroad is certified on the respective tax document by the customs authority
- goods supplied to foreign aviation companies designed for sale aboard their planes, goods sold by duty-free stores, and goods sold to foreign diplomats and other persons who enjoy privileges and immunities under international treaties
- services provided abroad, provided such services are not used in the Czech Republic. Final use, consumption or exploitation of the service rendered and its exclusive provision in relation to activities abroad, is decisive for the exemption
- cultural performances, management consultancy services, commercial and agency services, if provided to persons not having their permanent establishment, seat or permanent residence in the Czech Republic, shall always be considered as the provision of services to other countries.

7.2   Exemption without Credit for Input Tax

The supply of certain goods and services is exempt from VAT. The suppliers of such goods or services are not permitted to charge VAT nor will an input credit be allowed where it is attributable to the purchase or importation of any of these goods or services. They include:

- postal services
- radio and television broadcasting
- financial operations
- insurance business
- transfer and lease of land and building sites (an option to tax exists)
- training and education
- health services and goods
- social welfare
- lotteries and similar games
- the sale of an enterprise

Most property transactions are exempt from VAT (including the transfer of buildings acquired more than two years prior to transfer), with the result that the vendor or landlord cannot recover VAT on costs. However, there is an option for taxation in the case of commercial property (see section 10.4 below).

The practical difficulty with these provisions is determining exactly what transactions fall within the definitions, particularly regarding the financial sector.

7.3   Exempt Imports

In general, imported goods are exempt from VAT provided that they are also exempt from customs duty.

However, VAT always applies to:

- the import of goods intended for educational, scientific and cultural purposes and the import of scientific apparatus and instruments
- the import of religious objects unless they were donated
- goods exempt from customs duty provided within the framework of the general system of preferential tariffs.

8   CREDITS/REFUNDS FOR INPUT VAT

8.1   General Rule
Taxable persons are entitled to deduct VAT if the purchased goods, structures, transferred real estate property, accepted service or transferred and exploited rights will be used to obtain turnover from taxable supplies.

No deduction may be claimed unless the taxpayer has a proper VAT invoice to prove the claim.

8.2   Exceptions
VAT incurred on the purchase of passenger cars (unless the purchaser's business consists of buying and selling cars) and returnable glass bottles is specifically not deductible.

A taxable person whose business activity is that of purchasing second-hand passenger cars for the purpose of their resale shall be entitled to a tax deduction of the input tax on the purchase of such cars.

8.3   Partial Exemption
Persons who make taxable supplies and other supplies such as exempt supplies are entitled to recover VAT on the exempt supplies only. In such cases, only a proportion of the business's total input VAT may be recovered. The amount of allowable input tax which may be deducted from the total input tax for the period is determined by multiplying the total input tax by the following co-efficient:

$$\frac{\text{Total taxable supplies for the period (exclusive of VAT)}}{\text{Total of all supplies for the period (exclusive of VAT)}}$$

The calculated co-efficient is rounded upwards to four decimal places.

Further, there are de minimus limits so that, if the co-efficient calculated exceeds 0.95, the entire amount of the input tax for the period may be deducted by the taxpayer. However, if the calculated co-efficient amounts to less than 0.05, none of the input tax incurred for the period may be deducted.

No alternative calculations are allowed.

Proceeds from the sale of an enterprise, rent and taxable activities carried out abroad under certain legislation are not included in the total income in the denominator.

The ratio should be calculated separately for each tax period. At the end of the calendar year the calculation is repeated to compute the overall recovery rate for the whole year. Any difference between the calculation for the whole year and the calculation for each month is accounted for in the tax return for the last tax period of the year.

8.4   Excess Deductions
Refund of an excess tax deduction is payable within 30 days from when the return on which it is claimed is lodged. This is dependent on whether the taxpayer claiming the refund has any tax liabilities outstanding. In such a case, the refund will be applied to that other liability.

8.5   Bad Debts

In many cases, VAT charged to customers must be paid to the financial authorities before payment is received. No arrangements exist whereby this VAT may be recovered in the event of non-payment, if the supply has been made. This will result in a cost to the supplier, as credit notes may not be issued in such circumstances.

9   ADMINISTRATIVE OBLIGATIONS

9.1   Registration

Registration for VAT is mandatory where turnover exceeds CZK750,000 (approximately US$D25,000) in the three previous months.

Persons who exceed this threshold are obliged to apply for registration not later than 20 days after the end of the month in which they exceeded the turnover limit.

Taxpayers may apply for cancellation of their registration one year after the effective date shown on their certificate of registration in cases where their turnover for the three preceding consecutive months did not exceed CZK1,500,000, and at the same time their turnover for the 12 preceding consecutive months did not exceed CZK6 million (approximately US$200,000).

No provisions exist to enable businesses under common control to be grouped under the same VAT registration.

Individuals are also required to register if they make taxable supplies on the basis of an association agreement or another similar contract with other individuals and the total of all the supplies made under the association exceeds CZK750,000 in the three previous months. A taxable person, who is not a taxpayer, who concludes a contract of association with a taxpayer will be considered as a taxpayer from the date of conclusion of the contract. This person is required to lodge his own return and fulfil his own tax duty.

A person who is obliged to register and does not do so may be fined up to CZK1 million (approximately US$33,000).

9.2   Books and Records

Taxpayers are required to keep all documents necessary for the assessment of tax for ten years from the end of the calendar year in which the tax liability arose.

Furthermore, these records must be kept according to received and issued tax documents, as well as debit and credit notes. For received taxable supplies, records must list separately supplies from abroad and from the Czech Republic according to the individual tax rates. In the case of taxable supplies made, taxpayers are obliged to keep records listing separately supplies exempt from taxation, supplies designed for exportation and domestic supplies divided according to the individual tax rates, and also supplies which do not represent taxable supplies.

9.3   Invoices

Where a taxpayer makes a taxable supply, he is required to supply a 'tax document' within 15 days after the day of making the taxable supply. The tax document is required to show the following:

- commercial name, seat or permanent residence, place of enterprise and tax identification number of the taxpayer
- commercial name, seat or permanent residence, place of enterprise and tax identification number of the taxpayer for whose benefit the taxable supply is made
- serial number of the document
- designation and quantity of the respective goods or the scope of the taxable supply
- date of issue of the document
- date of realisation of the taxable supply
- total amount of the price before tax
- rate of the tax
- total amount of the tax rounded up to the next ten hellers or, as the case may be, stated also in hellers.

Where a tax document refers to a number of supplies with different rates, or a mixture of exempt and taxable supplies, the total amount of each category and the tax applicable to each category must be listed separately.

Taxpayers who make taxable supplies on a commission basis as part of travel agency services are not obliged to issue a tax document on behalf of the person for whom they are providing the supply. However, they must issue a document of payment which includes :

- commercial name, seat or permanent residence, place of enterprise and tax identification number of the taxpayer
- the commercial name of the taxpayer for whose benefit the taxable supply has been made
- the serial number of the document
- the date of realisation of the taxable supply
- the price including tax
- a note specifying that the price mentioned above includes VAT.

9.4   VAT Returns

Taxpayers are required to submit a tax return within 25 days from the end of the tax period which is generally each calendar month, even if the return is negative. Payment of any tax due must also be made at that time.

If the taxable person's turnover for the proceeding calendar year or the assumed annual turnover is less than CZK10 million (approximately US$330,000), the taxable period shall be the taxable quarter.

Quarterly taxpayers may opt for a monthly tax period at the beginning of the next calendar year. This also applies to monthly taxpayers who choose to have a calendar quarter as their tax period.

9.5   Correction of Returns

Provisions exist to enable a taxpayer who has incorrectly calculated a tax liability or a refund to lodge an additional return to the financial authorities. Such a return must be lodged within six months of the tax payment date in situations where a taxpayer's liability is to be decreased, or an excess deduction is to be increased. The additional return is only required to specify the differences against the tax return submitted originally.

9.6 Powers of the Authorities

The Tax Administrator monitors the accuracy and completeness of tax returns.

In general, taxpayers are required to calculate the tax in the tax return. However, the Tax Administrator may determine the tax base and the tax due by using any available method if any of the following apply:

- the tax return is not filed on time
- the tax return is not corrected within the time limit specified in a notice by the Tax Administrator
- the tax return includes incorrect or incomplete information with respect to matters that are crucial for the determination of tax.

If the Tax Administrator makes a determination concerning the tax base and the amount of tax, he informs the taxpayer of the determination through a request for payment. This document explains the grounds for the Tax Administrator's determination.

Taxpayers may appeal tax assessments. The taxpayer may appeal against the tax base and the tax determined by the Tax Administrator and also against other decisions specified or not excluded by law. An appeal against a decision by the Tax Administrator may be filed within a 30-day period which begins the day after the date on which the decision is delivered.

Tax may not be assessed and a refund may not be claimed more than three years after the end of the applicable tax year. If the tax assessment is under review, however, the authorities may renew the three-year period by notifying the taxpayer of such action before the end of the period. However, tax may not be assessed more than ten years after the end of the applicable tax year.

VAT is a preferential debt in bankruptcy or liquidation.

9.7 Penalties

If a taxpayer fails to meet correctly and in time his registration obligation, or to file a tax return at all, the Financial Authority shall impose a fine of up to CZK1 million (approximately US$33,000).

In the case of errors in computing the amount of VAT payable, the penalty is 100% of the error if this is discovered by the financial authorities, and 20% of the error if this is corrected by the taxpayer himself and included in an additional tax return.

Late payment penalties are imposed at the rate of 0.1% per day. This applies to the errors noted above as well as to late payment penalties.

Late filing of returns is subject to a penalty equal to 10% of the liability for the period.

10 SPECIAL VAT REGIMES

10.1 Money

Goods shall also be deemed to include bank notes and coins of Czech currency at the moment when they are delivered by their manufacturer to the Czech National Bank or when they are imported by the Czech National Bank, as well as bank notes, currency notes and coins of

Czech and foreign currencies sold as collector's items at a price higher than their nominal value or higher than the conversion of their nominal value into Czech currency.

10.2 Travel Agents

Where travel services are provided on behalf of an operator under a commission arrangement, the travel agent is liable to 22% VAT on the commission included in the price of the ticket or tour (with the exception of international air and bus transport). The value of this commission may either be calculated by reference to the selling price of the service, or it may be calculated as the actual commission earned. The actual commission earned may be calculated as the difference between the actual costs and sales realised for each transaction individually, or for the total transactions for a particular period, which must not exceed one calendar year.

Services connected with scheduled international transport of passengers are exempt from the liability to tax. As such, travel agents have no liability to tax on the commission from the sale of international air and bus tickets.

10.3 Car Dealers

Registered car dealers are entitled to claim refunds of VAT incurred on passenger cars purchased for resale.

A taxable person whose business activity is that of purchasing second-hand passenger cars for the purpose of their resale in an unchanged condition shall be entitled to a tax deduction of input tax on the purchase of such cars. Where the cars are purchased from persons who are not taxpayers, the tax base shall be the difference between the purchase price from the person who is not a taxpayer and the resale price without tax.

10.4 Property

While most property transactions are exempt from VAT, there is an option to elect for taxation. The options allow the vendor or landlord to recover VAT on costs, but he must then charge VAT on sales and lettings. Most business tenants and purchasers will be able to recover this VAT from the tax authorities, but occupiers with exempt or non-business activities will suffer at least some of it as a cost. Since these include the finance and insurance sectors the option to tax can have an adverse impact on rents and values, particularly in the financial districts of major cities. VAT can also create a significant cash flow cost, even where a purchaser or tenant can recover it in full.

The option to tax is not permanent. However, once a business has opted to tax a building or site, it must inform the fiscal authorities and is obliged to comply with such a decision at least till the end of the year following the year in which the decision was delivered to the fiscal authority.

Contributors: Dirk Kroonen and Greg Hill
Ernst & Young
Vinohradska 184
130 52 Prague 3
Czech Republic
Tel: +42 2 6713 30 10
Fax: +42 2 6713 30 72

ESTONIA

1   GENERAL BACKGROUND

VAT was introduced in Estonia in 1991 and came into force on 10 January 1991. The latest VAT law amendments came into effect on 1 January 1994. VAT is administered by the tax authorities, with the exception of VAT levied on imports which is administrered by Customs.

2   WHO IS TAXABLE?

2.1   General
A taxable person is any person making a taxable supply as a result of entrepreneurship defined as an independent economic activity of a person, in the course of which gainful or gratuitous alienation of a good or a service takes place. 'Persons' may be either individual or legal persons. Working under a labour contract is not treated as entrepreneurship.

Any taxable person with an annual turnover of more than EEK130,000 (US$10,000) has to register with the tax authorities. A person may, however, also elect to be registered if his taxable turnover is less than EEK130,000.

2.2   Transactions through a Branch/Subsidiary
Subsidiaries of foreign companies supplying taxable goods and services are taxed in the same manner as other taxable persons.

Transactions between the head office and its branch are exempt from VAT, unless the branch or head office is located in a foreign country, in which case the transaction is treated either as an export or import.

2.3   Government Bodies
State and local authorities are not liable to VAT as long as they fulfil governmental functions only. If they are engaged in commercial activities, they are treated as taxable persons.

2.4   Fiscal Unity/Group Registration
The authorities have the right to register as one person taxable enterprises (such as a fiscal unity or group) whose taxable supply, if calculated separately, does not exceed EEK130,000 in a calendar year, provided that they are owned, wholly or partially, by one person or have common management.

This provision only applies to legal persons.

A company with one or more subsidiaries is not automatically regarded as one entity, but may request to be registered as one taxable person.

This chapter reflects the legislation on VAT in Estonia as at 31 December 1994.

2.5   Foreign Entrepreneurs

Non-resident entrepreneurs become liable to VAT if the place of supply of goods or services is in Estonia. In principle, the non-resident entrepreneur performing taxable supplies in Estonia has to register itself with the tax authorities and to pay VAT.

2.6   Representative Offices

Representative offices are taxable persons if they make taxable supplies. If they are merely representative or information offices which only carry out activities of a preparatory or an auxiliary nature, they are not treated as taxable persons.

A foreign entrepreneur has no right to a refund of the input VAT incurred in Estonia through its representative office.

A representative office may voluntarily apply for registration for VAT purposes.

2.7   VAT Representative

VAT law does not contain any special provisions for VAT representatives.

2.8   Reverse Charge Mechanism

Imports of services are exempt from VAT.

2.9   Importers

Taxable persons and all other persons importing goods to Estonia must pay VAT on the imports in accordance with the customs law.

Imported goods are taxed at the same rate as that applying to sales within Estonia.

Import of goods by a natural person is exempt from VAT within the limits established by the Ministry of Finance regarding the value and amount of imports.

Import of goods by persons with diplomatic status, representations of foreign diplomatic and consular missions, representations of international organisations and intergovernmental programmes of co-operation for use in the exercise of their official functions is not subject to VAT, provided that the government of the foreign country grants reciprocal rights to the respective persons and institutions of Estonia.

3   WHAT IS TAXABLE?

For VAT purposes the term 'taxable supply' means the supply of goods located in Estonia, the supply of services rendered in Estonia and the import of goods.

3.1   Supply of Goods

The term 'goods' includes all movable and tangible property, animals, liquids, gases, electric and thermal energy.

Immovables, money and securities are not treated as goods.

The term 'supply' means:

■   the sale, exchange or alienation on leasing terms of goods or services
■   the gratuitous alienation of goods or services

- the consumption of goods and services by any person liable to tax
- hiring or leasing.

3.2 Supply of Services

VAT law treats services as any benefits sold by way of entrepreneurship, and which are not covered by the term goods.

3.3 Self-Supply of Goods/Services

In general, transfer of goods or services within an enterprise is not subject to VAT.

The consumption of goods and services within an enterprise is treated as a taxable supply in the following circumstances:

- goods given and services rendered to natural persons in the form of salaries, bonuses and other payments
- production of goods and rendering of services to be used as lottery prizes by a person arranging the lottery
- goods and services used for the purpose of entertaining guests and catering and accommodation for the staff of an enterprise
- motor fuel consumed for one's own use.

No input VAT is creditable in respect of the purchase of the above goods and services.

Furthermore, the input VAT on the purchase of automobiles not directly related to entrepreneurship cannot be deducted from the VAT calculated on the taxable supply.

3.4 Importation of Goods

Importation is a taxable event. However, in some cases goods may cross the border without VAT if, for example, they are in transit or if they are held in a bonded warehouse. In addition, goods can be imported without VAT if they are to be re-exported after processing.

4 PLACE OF SUPPLY

The supply of goods and services is subject to VAT only if it takes place in Estonia.

4.1 Supply of Goods

A supply of goods is treated as taking place in Estonia if the goods are being imported into Estonia, are delivered or made available to the recipient in Estonia, or are being exported from Estonia.

4.2 Supply of Services

The general rule is that the place of supply of services is Estonia if the entrepreneurship of the person providing the service is carried out in Estonia. This means that all services are taxed at the rate of 18% except in cases when the supply of services can be treated as an export of services which is zero-rated or a service which is exempt.

4.3 Reverse Charge Mechanism

Services imported into Estonia are exempt from VAT, with the exception of the hiring or leasing of goods imported into Estonia. The taxable basis will be the amount payable under a contract and the lessee must calculate and pay the VAT to the Customs Board.

5 BASIS OF TAXATION

5.1 Supplies within Estonia

The value of a taxable supply shall be the selling price of the goods or services to which all charges payable by the recipient to the seller have been added.

5.2 Self-Supplies

The taxable basis for self-supplied goods and services is the 'fair market price' which is the taxable value for any goods or services exchanged or alienated without payment or for partial payment.

5.3 Imports

The taxable value for any import of goods shall be the customs value of the goods, including all taxes on import, but excluding VAT.

Until the Law of Customs Value comes into effect, the value of an export-import transaction, including packaging, loading, transport and insurance costs up to the Estonian customs border, shall be regarded as the customs value of the goods.

5.4 Chargeable Event/Time of Payment

The supply shall be treated as having taken place on the earliest of the following events:

- when the goods are delivered or made available to the purchaser or the service is provided
- when the invoice is issued
- when payment is made.

When goods are imported, the tax is paid to the customs authorities at the time of importation.

The taxable person must issue an invoice within the seven days following the sale.

5.5 Credit Notes/Bad Debts

When a credit note is issued cancelling all or part of an invoice, the entrepreneur may deduct the VAT stated thereon from output VAT and enter the reduced amount on his VAT return.

VAT paid on uncollected debts may not be deducted from output VAT.

6 TAX RATES

The current tax rates are as follows:

0%: – export of goods and services
      – subscriptions to periodicals published and printed in Estonia
      – theatre tickets of theatres registered in Estonia

The following services are treated as exports:

- rendering a service to a legal person of a foreign country outside the customs territory of Estonia
- lease of movables, provided that the leased property is permanently used outside the customs territory of Estonia
- transport services relating to the international conveyance of goods
- storage of goods in a warehouse on the account and in the name of a natural or legal person of a foreign country
- rendering services on board water and air transport vessels outside the customs territory of Estonia
- transport abroad of passengers and their personal luggage by water, air, rail and road
- rendering services to passengers bound for a trip abroad in areas of airports and harbours accessible after the passport and customs control
- harbour services relating to maintenance of vessels making trips abroad
- services relating to maintenance of aircraft making trips abroad
- maintenance and repair of vessels of water and air transport making trips abroad
- booking and selling accommodation for hotels in a foreign country
- the value of a tour package (voucher) sold outside the customs territory of Estonia for rendering services to foreign tourists arriving to Estonia, as well as selling tour packages to be used by tourists leaving Estonia for a foreign country outside the customs territory of Estonia
- construction and repair of buildings and construction outside the customs territory of Estonia, and drawing up the plans of a building or construction to be built outside the customs territory of Estonia including that of interior design
- rendering services to a legal or natural person of a foreign country pertaining to applications, keeping in effect documents for protection of objects of intellectual property, and services pertaining to protection of rights relating to such objects
- rendering consultation and advertising services to a legal person of a foreign country
- rendering information services to information agencies of a foreign country
- carrying out scientific research on the basis of an order placed by a legal person of a foreign country
- arranging theatrical performances, variety shows, cinema shows, concerts, sports events and exhibitions outside the customs territory
- processing or repair of goods belonging to a person of a foreign country, if the processed or repaired goods will be transported to its owner outside the customs territory
- use inside the customs territory of Estonia of mobile telephones registered outside Estonia
- acting as intermediary for a transaction carried out between the seller and purchaser of goods or services provided that these are being consumed outside the customs territory of Estonia
- making warranty repairs on goods produced by a person of a foreign country
- providing catering services outside the customs territory of Estonia.

7 EXEMPTIONS

A transaction is considered as exempt when certain goods and services are excluded from being subject to VAT by a special provision of the VAT law. As a rule, the supplier is unable to recover the input tax paid in connection with these exempt supplies.

7.1 Exemptions with Credit for Input Tax

Input tax may be deducted from output tax when the entrepreneur makes a zero-rated supply.

7.2 Exemption without Credit for Input Tax

The supply of the following goods and services is exempt without credit for input tax:

- elementary, basic, secondary and higher education, together with advanced training and continuing education
- public postal services
- medical services under health insurance and medical requisites
- funeral requisites and services
- organisation of gambling
- lottery tickets
- letting of housing
- medicines and equipment for health and medical diagnostics
- treating dangerous waste.

7.3 Non-Taxable Transactions

7.3.1 Transactions within the Same Entity

Supplies within the same entity are not taxable. Transactions between a head office and its branch are not subject to VAT unless the branch or the head office is situated in a foreign country. A transaction between a domestic and a foreign person is treated either as an export or as an import.

Transactions between a parent company and its subsidiary are a taxable supply, unless registered jointly.

7.3.2 Transfer of Business

The sale of shares is not subject to VAT. Non-monetary contributions made by shareholders directly to the share capital of an enterprise in accordance with the foundation documents are not a taxable supply. The alienation of goods and services in the course of liquidation or reorganisation of an enterprise is subject to VAT.

The transfer of goods in the course of privatisation of state and municipal property and transfer of property from state ownership to municipal ownership is exempt from VAT.

7.3.3 Subsidies/Penalty Payments/Compensation

Subsidies, penalties, grants and compensation payments will be regarded as being outside the scope of VAT if they are not received in respect of a supply of goods or services.

8   CREDIT FOR INPUT TAX

8.1   *General Rule*

In computing the amount of tax payable, a taxable person may deduct the tax relating to goods and services, purchased or imported, that are used for the purposes of his taxable business.

A credit is not allowed for VAT paid on:

- goods and services used for purposes of exempt transactions
- goods and services related to the entertainment of guests, and to catering and accommodation for staff
- automobiles not directly related to entrepreneurship
- motor fuel consumed for one's own use.

8.2   *Adjustment of Entitlement to Credit*

The VAT paid by a person upon the purchase of fixed assets acquired for his entrepreneurship shall be adjusted according to the actual use of the fixed assets over a period of three calendar years.

Where a registered person uses the fixed asset for both taxable and exempt supplies, the deduction of VAT shall be carried out in accordance with the proportion of the taxable use of the asset. The adjustment will be made at the end of the calendar year. If the entrepreneur ceases to use the fixed asset in his entrepreneurship, he is liable for the VAT on the residual value of the asset.

8.3   *Partial Exemption*

Entrepreneurs making both taxable and exempt supplies are allowed to recover the input VAT relating to the taxable supply. However, deduction of the input VAT is limited by the ratio of the taxable supply to the total supplies, calculated for each calendar year. During the year a provisional ratio is used based either on that of the previous year or on the expected ratio of the current year.

8.4   *Time of Recovery*

Input credit can be claimed for the month in which the supply was made and an invoice received. If the input exceeds the output VAT, the difference will be refunded upon application.

8.5   *Refund for Foreign Entrepreneurs*

Input VAT can be refunded only to persons registered with a tax office.

A foreign entrepreneur making a taxable supply may register itself for VAT. Foreign entrepreneurs who do not make taxable supplies may not claim back input VAT which they have paid.

9   ADMINISTRATIVE OBLIGATION

9.1   Registration
Any person whose taxable supply exceeds EEK130,000 (US$10,000) during a calendar year must apply for registration with the tax office.

The tax authorities will independently register a person who has failed to apply for registration.

A person who supplies 'taxable' goods or services but who is not obliged to register for VAT because his turnover is below the limit for compulsory registration may elect to become a taxable person.

9.2   Books and Records
A registered person is required to keep accounts and, in chronological order, copies of all invoices issued by him, all invoices certifying payment of VAT on all purchases of goods and services and bills of entry certifying payment of VAT on imports, for a period of seven years.

9.3   Invoices
A registered person must issue an invoice within seven days after the time of supply which contains the following information:

- name of the seller, his address and registration number
- number of the invoice and date of issue
- name and address of the purchaser
- description, quantity and selling price of the good or service
- price excluding VAT
- taxable value, if different from the selling price
- amount of VAT and
- date of delivery, if different from the issuing date of the invoice.

9.4   VAT Returns
The tax period is a calendar month and all VAT returns must be filed by the twentieth day of the month following each tax period. However, the Ministry of Finance has the right to establish a period other than a calendar month. Usually for small entrepreneurs the Ministry of Finance will permit quarterly filing of returns.

9.5   Power of Authorities
The tax authorities are authorised to inspect premises used in connection with business activities and to inspect the stock held, their books of account, invoices, records, etc.

On the request of the tax authorities all books and records must be surrendered or sent to the tax or customs office.

9.6   Objection/Appeal
The taxpayer has the right to file an appeal with the tax authorities against a VAT assessment within one month after having received a notice from the tax authority. Further appeals may be made to the National Tax Board, or to the court if the tax authorities do not amend the tax assessment notice as requested.

10   SPECIAL VAT REGIMES

10.1   Retailers
Retailers can account for VAT on a cash basis instead of an invoice basis and, in this case, the tax rate shall be 15.25% of the selling price including VAT.

10.2   Second-Hand Goods and Auction Sales
In case of commission sales of second-hand goods, the agent shall pay VAT on the commission.

On the supply of auction sales the auctioneer shall pay the VAT on the payment received for acting as an intermediary in the sale of goods.

10.3   Bonded Warehouses
Goods imported into bonded warehouses are not liable to VAT and customs duty until they are removed for sale in Estonia. Goods in the bonded warehouses are under the control of the Customs authorities.

10.4   Real Estate
Immovables are not treated as goods and the sale of immovables is not a taxable supply. VAT paid on purchase of repair and construction services in regard to buildings and construction used in entrepreneurship is deductible. If the building is being used partly in entrepreneurship and partly as a home, the VAT is deductible only for that proportion of the building being used for the entrepreneurship.

Contributor: Tonis Jakob
                 Ernst & Young
                 Ravi 27
                 EE 0007 Tallinn
                 Estonia
                 Tel: +372 2 683513
                 Fax: +372 2 6310611

HUNGARY

1   GENERAL BACKGROUND

Value added tax (VAT), in Hungary – Általanos Forgalmi Adó (ÁFA), was introduced in Hungary on 1 January 1988, replacing the previous single stage Consumption Tax. The Act covers the territory of the Republic of Hungary.

VAT is administered by the Hungarian tax authority (APEH). The Customs authorities are responsible for VAT on importation.

2   WHO IS TAXABLE?

2.1   General
Every natural or legal person and business association with or without legal personality, qualifies as a taxable person for the purposes of VAT if, while not acting as an employee, he (or it) sells goods or renders services in his own name, independently on a regular and not occasional basis, for the purpose of collecting revenue or covering expenses, and not on a charitable basis. A profit motive is not required. For the purposes of VAT construction projects are considered to be goods. In general, taxable persons include State-owned companies, co-operative companies and other enterprises, special production groups of co-operatives, artisans and retailers. Budget organisations such as health, educational and scientific organisations, owner-occupied condominiums or holiday houses, associations, societies, foundations and individuals may be taxable persons if they make regular supplies. In certain circumstances certain internal activities such as small business units within a taxable enterprise may be regarded as a separate taxable person.

2.2   Transactions with Subsidiaries/Branches
Transactions between a parent company and its subsidiary are treated as transactions between independent parties. Transactions within the same legal entity are not regarded as taxable supplies.

2.3   Government Bodies
The government and local authorities are regarded as taxable persons in respect of taxable activities which they supply and which are not deemed to be supplied in connection with their public administration responsibilities.

2.4   Fiscal Unity/Group Registration
There are no facilities for fiscal unity/group registration in the Hungarian VAT legislation.

This chapter reflects the law on VAT in Hungary as at 31 October 1994.

2.5   Foreign Entrepreneurs

A non-resident entrepreneur who establishes a facility in Hungary to supply goods or services continuously is liable for VAT on the supplies. A non-resident entrepreneur who does not have an establishment in Hungary and who supplies goods or services on a continuous basis may opt to become a taxable person. Where a Hungarian taxable person receives taxable supplies from a non-resident taxable person who has not opted to be liable to Hungarian VAT, the recipient is liable to VAT (see section 5.3 'Importations').

Foreign traders liable to VAT in Hungary must correspond with:

> Tax Supervision Offices of the Tax and Financial Control Authority
> (Adó- és Pénzügyi Ellenőrzési Hivatal, APEH)
> Haller Pál u 3-5
> 1096 Budapest
> Hungary

Foreign taxable persons who are liable to VAT in Hungary have the same rights and obligations as Hungarian taxable persons. If goods or services are supplied for amounts in foreign currency, the foreign taxable person may (and must if specifically requested by the customer) charge the amount of VAT in Hungarian currency. The forint amount of VAT must be indicated even if the total value of goods or services is paid in foreign currency. Settlements with tax authorities may only be effected in forints. For this purpose the taxable person must open a forint account solely for the purposes of paying VAT with a bank properly authorised by the National Bank of Hungary.

2.6   Representative Offices

A representative office of a foreign enterprise providing services of a supporting and auxiliary nature (for example, taking in orders) may, even if no supplies are made in Hungary, apply for voluntary registration. This enables it to obtain a refund of VAT on local purchases of goods or services without having to go through the mutual recovery system outlined in section 8.6 'Refunds to foreign traders'. This facility, however, is not available for representative offices of enterprises carrying out activities which are exempt from VAT in Hungary.

2.7   VAT Representatives

A foreign firm is not obliged to appoint a representative or responsible person to act on its behalf if it is making taxable supplies in Hungary.

2.8   Reverse Charge Mechanism

Persons who receive from abroad for business use any taxable service are obliged to account for VAT on the value of the service. The recipient of the service is regarded as supplying the service to himself.

2.9   Importers

Goods are regarded as liable to VAT at importation if they are imported under a valid foreign trading contract by a person with a foreign trading licence. Other goods, such as personal belongings imported into Hungary, are not subject to VAT.

3   WHAT IS TAXABLE?

Hungarian VAT is levied when taxable persons supply goods or services in Hungary, receive goods or services from outside Hungary, or supply goods and services for export.

3.1   Supply of Goods
On the basis of the VAT Act, VAT is levied on all goods, new and used, when the right to use such goods has been transferred or when services have been rendered.

For VAT purposes this includes goods and services supplied free of charge and self-supplies. Goods purchased under a hire purchase agreement are also regarded as a supply of goods. Goods are referenced to the statistical register of the Central Statistical Office. The transfer of title of buildings is regarded as a supply of goods whether the building is entirely new or has already been completed.

3.2   Supply of Services
'Services' means everything not included in the category of 'goods'. Services have been categorised by the Central Statistical Office and these categories, which have been adopted for VAT, are liable at one of three rates unless they are exempt.

Where a contractor processes goods which have been supplied by his principal (and which remain the property of the principal) the supply is not regarded as a sale of goods but as a supply of services.

3.3   Self-Supply of Goods and Services
There is a self-supply of goods and services when a person diverts to private or exempt use goods which are imported, purchased, manufactured or otherwise acquired and in respect of which he is entitled to a VAT deduction.

There is a self-supply of goods and services where goods which he has manufactured are used in an end product which is not liable to VAT. VAT must be paid on the cost of the supply of goods or services to the supplier.

4   PLACE OF SUPPLY

4.1   Place of Supply of Goods
The place where goods are supplied is defined as the location of the goods at the same time of sale except for importation of goods where the place of supply is deemed to be in Hungary.

4.2   Place of Supply of Services

4.2.1   General Rule
The general rule is that the place where services are deemed to be supplied for VAT purposes is the place where the person supplying the service has his headquarters or offices. In the absence of such headquarters or offices the permanent or habitual residence of the supplier is considered the place of supply.

4.2.2 *Exceptions*

The exceptions are:

- services deemed to be rendered where actually performed:

    - transportation
    - cultural, scientific, educational, entertainment and sports services
    - assembling, maintenance and repair of capital equipment
    - consultation directly connected or related to products

- services directly connected to a building or construction project are deemed to be supplied where the building or facility is located. These services include:

    - architectural design
    - construction work
    - general contracting consultancy work for the construction industry
    - protection of immovable property
    - rental of buildings, partial or total

- services deemed to be rendered at the head office of the user:

    - renting articles (except buildings and real estate)
    - transfer of rights, patents, trade marks and other intangibles
    - promotional and propaganda services
    - engineering, legal accounting, tax and other consulting services
    - processing and provision of data and information
    - financial services
    - provision of personnel.

4.3 *Reverse Charge Mechanism*

In respect of certain services and in certain circumstances goods received from abroad VAT must be accounted for by the recipient as if he himself had supplied the service (see section 2.8 'Reverse charge mechanism').

5   BASIS OF TAXATION

5.1 *Supplies within Hungary*

Where the consideration takes the form of money, the amount on which tax is chargeable is normally the total sum paid or payable to the person supplying the goods or services including all levies, transportation and packaging costs, etc. If cash discounts are granted on the invoice it is the net amount which is subject to VAT.

VAT must be expressed in Hungarian forints even though the price may have been expressed in foreign currency. In order to define the taxable base, therefore, the official exchange rate of the National Bank of Hungary applicable at the time liability to VAT was incurred must be taken into consideration.

If the consideration is not in money, for example, if the consideration for the supplies takes the form of goods or services, the taxable base is the commercial value of such supplies.

5.2   Self-Supplies

VAT on self-supplies is calculated on the basis of the purchase price of the goods or otherwise on the cost to the supplier. In the case of goods manufactured by an entrepreneur for his own business the cost will include the value of the raw materials and of the services used in the manufacture and/or the cost of remuneration if the work was carried out by the entrepreneur's own employees. The purchase price or the cost is determined at the time the goods are first put into use.

5.3   Importations

In the case of importations the taxable base is the customs value plus customs duty and the customs clearance fee.

VAT must be paid to the customs authorities on the day the goods are cleared through customs. Deferred payment arrangements are available. The VAT paid may be recovered on the next periodic VAT return or by refund for certain foreign entrepreneurs (see section 8.6 'Refunds to foreign traders').

When services are imported the taxable base is the equivalent value of the services.

5.4   Chargeable Event/Time of Payment

Liability to VAT arises on the day of delivery of the goods or rendering of the service, as substantiated by the invoice but:

■   if payment is made in cash, the chargeable event is on the day of payment. Payments using cash substitutes are also considered as cash payments, for example, postal banking accounts, regular cheques and credit certificates

■   in the case of importation of services the chargeable event is on the day the supplier's invoice is received or if no invoice is issued on the day of payment.

5.5   Cash/Invoice Basis

VAT due must normally be accounted for on the basis of the amount of invoices issued in the appropriate VAT period. However, some entrepreneurs with low turnovers may settle their tax liability after they have been paid for the goods or services they have supplied, ie on a cash receipts basis. Such entrepreneurs include:

■   business associations without legal personality

■   industrial service and agricultural co-operatives and those operating universities or colleges

■   partnerships of private individuals with legal personality (other than legal partnerships) provided their annual turnover is less than 25 million forints

■   craftsmen, retailers, private individuals and small-scale agricultural producers with annual sales revenue of at least 2 million forints.

Such entrepreneurs may deduct VAT only when they have paid the invoices of their suppliers.

6   TAX RATES

The current rates are as follows:

0%:   exported goods and services and the supply of medicine. Because of the non-convertibility of the forint, certain domestic sales are also considered exports for VAT purposes – such as sales by diplomat shops selling items solely for convertible currency

10%:   certain products and services including agricultural and food industry products, transportation, and hotels and catering

25%:   all other goods and services.

6.1   The Package Rule (Cocktail Rule)

For the purposes of VAT the rate of VAT to be applied to ancillary services such as packaging, warehousing, loading or unloading which are closely linked to the sale of goods or rendering of services is the rate of VAT specified for such sales or services if such services are linked to the sale of one's own goods or the supply of one's own services.

7   EXEMPTIONS

7.1   Exemption with Credit for Input Tax

The zero rate (see section 6 'Tax Rates') works as an exemption with credit because the suppliers of zero-rated goods and services are entitled to input credit under the normal rules.

7.2   Exemption without Credit for Input Tax

The supply of certain goods and services is exempt from VAT. The suppliers of such goods or services are not required to charge VAT nor will an input credit be allowed where the purchase or importation is attributable to any of these goods or services.

They include:

- sale of land
- sale of housing, except for sale prior to the conclusion of building works, and first sale following conclusion of building works
- renting of students' hostels
- mail service
- financial services and related additional services, except for financial leasing and safe guarding
- transfer of ownership rights representing money or moneys worth reflecting creditor or owner (member) relations
- housing services and related additional services, except for garage services
- renting out and leasing of real estate
- management of housing property
- solicitors' and legal representatives' activities, and legal documentation activities
- organisation of scientific events
- public administration compulsory social insurance

- teaching related to the population
- human health care, except extermination of rodents and parasites outdoors
- social provisions, except social catering
- other communal and social services
- radio and television services
- news agency related services
- library, archival, museum and other cultural services except zoos and botanic gardens, the presentation of protected natural resources
- sports and leisure services, except competition and professional sports
- gambling services.

7.3   Option to Become Exempt

Retailers and restaurateurs may opt to be treated as exempt entities if their projected sales revenues are below 1 million forints. Where a taxable person is both a retailer and a restaurateur the same limit applies. Other suppliers of taxable activities may also opt to be treated as exempt entities where their annual projected sales revenue is below 500,000 forints. As of 1 January 1995 this threshold is increased to 1 million forints. Where a business activity is commenced during a year the above amounts are reduced proportionally.

If the limit is exceeded in the course of the year, exemption ceases immediately and liability to VAT arises with respect to the entire amount in excess of the limit for that year.

7.4   Exempt Importations

There is no liability to VAT on imports where:

- the goods are temporarily imported for processing and will afterwards be re-exported. The processing is treated as a service provided in Hungary
- the imports are going to a duty free zone
- the goods are sent to a bonded warehouse
- the imports are personal effects.

7.5   Waiver of Exemption

Suppliers of goods and services which are deemed to be exempt may not waive their exemption and elect to become taxable, with the exception of those taxable persons who have elected to become exempt.

7.6   Non-Taxable Transactions

7.6.1 Transactions within the Same Legal Entity

Transactions (including cross-border transactions between branches of the same legal entity) are not taxable.

7.6.2 Transfer of Business

Where a State-owned company is transformed into a type of business association, or one type of business association is transformed into another type, the successor company does not incur liability to VAT in respect of the items of property transferred.

8   CREDIT/REFUND FOR INPUT VAT

8.1   General Rule

In computing the amount of tax payable by him, a taxable person may deduct the tax relating to most goods and services purchased or imported by him which are used for the purpose of his taxable business.

No deduction may be made for the tax paid on goods and services used for any other purposes. To be entitled to the deduction the registered person must have a proper VAT invoice or a stamped copy of the customs entry. The excess of VAT charged to a taxable person over the amount of VAT charged by him on taxable supplies of goods or services will be refunded by the tax administration.

A taxable person using a cash basis accounting method is not entitled to recover VAT paid until he has paid his supplier.

Deduction is not permitted in respect of VAT payable on any of the following:

■   cars, except for resale;
■   fuel, except diesel fuel for non-personal vehicles and fuel for resale;
■   local and long haulage taxi services;
■   coffee, alcoholic beverages, mineral waters, soft drinks, tobacco products and tea for personal consumption or entertainment purposes and similar catering services.

VAT paid on goods prior to starting a business and charged as costs during the operation of the business may be deducted by private individuals who are liable to VAT provided the period between procurement and the start of the business is less than three years.

8.2   Partial Exemption

Persons who make taxable and other supplies are only entitled to recover the VAT incurred in making the taxable supplies.

Where the purchases or imports are used in making both taxable and exempt supplies an apportionment of the input VAT is required. The allowable input tax credit is calculated in the ratio of the turnover of taxable supplies to the aggregated turnover of taxable and exempt supplies. The taxable person is given the option of using figures from the current year or the previous year, but if the previous year is used the deduction must be corrected at the end of the year by using the data for the current year.

8.3   Adjustment of Entitlement to Credit

The taxable person is entitled to an apportioned credit in respect of immovable property or fixed assets that are partially used in taxable VAT supplies and partially in exempt supplies. The deductible proportion must be monitored for four years after the year of purchase (nine years in case of buildings). Unlike many other countries, an adjustment will only be made if the difference in the original recovery rate differs by more than 10%, for example:

where VAT incurred on immovable property = 400,000 forints
the recovery rate is:

Year of purchase   -   20%

    Year 1   -   22%

    Year 2   -   28%

    Year 3   -   34%

    Year 4   -   40%.

Therefore, the recovery of VAT is as follows:

    Year of purchase 400,000 x 20% = 80,000

    Year 1   Nil

    Year 2   Nil

    Year 3   400,000 x (34% - 20%) ÷5 = 11,200

    Year 4   400,000 x (40% - 20%) ÷5 = 16,000

    TOTAL RECOVERY = 107,200 forints

8.4   Time of Recovery

A taxable person is entitled to a recovery of input tax using the rules to entitlement outlined above when he has a valid VAT invoice or stamped and paid customs entry document. If he is accounting for VAT on a cash receipts basis he must have paid for the goods or services before he can recover the VAT.

8.5   Foreign Businesses

A non-resident entrepreneur may become liable to Hungarian VAT if he falls under the category of taxable person (see section 2 'Who is taxable?').

8.6   Refunds to Foreign Traders

Non-resident entrepreneurs are entitled, on a reciprocity basis, to reclaim the VAT incurred on some of their purchases for business purposes of goods and services in Hungary. This applies at present to Austria, Belgium, France, Germany, Luxembourg, The Netherlands, Sweden and the United Kingdom.

Only invoices containing VAT of at least 2,000 HUF may be submitted for refund.

Claims for refunds must be submitted to the tax authorities by 30 June of the year following the year in which the VAT was incurred. Refunds in excess of 20,000 HUF may be made on a quarterly basis. Claims for refunds must be submitted on a special form and should be addressed to:

    Adó- és Pénzügyi Ellenôrzési Hivatal
    Fôvárosi Adófelügyelôsége
    H-1096 Budapest, Haller Pál u. 3-5
    Hungary

The claim for a refund must be accompanied by a special form, the original invoices and a certificate of status from the tax authority of the claimant's country certifying that the non-resident entrepreneur was a taxable person for the purpose of VAT in that country. Non-resident entrepreneurs must also state that they did not have a permanent establishment in Hungary. The tax authorities issue a statement within 30 days of receipt of the application indicating the amount of the refund, against which appeals may be submitted. The refunded VAT will be deposited in a forint account at:

> Inteltrade
> Budapest,
> Csalogány u. 6-10.
> Hungary
> Tel: (36-1)156 9800
>   (36-1) 156 9974

Because of the non-convertibility of the forint, the tax administration will also indicate the amount of the refunded VAT which may be converted into foreign currency. This amount will be related to the amount paid by the foreign entrepreneur in foreign currency or with forints obtained by exchanging convertible currency (as certified by a foreign exchange certificate made out in his name which should also be attached to the refund claim).

Refunds of VAT paid with respect to commercial accommodation may, however, only be claimed in forints by a non-resident entrepreneur regardless of how he has paid for those services.

9   ADMINISTRATIVE OBLIGATIONS

9.1   Registration
A taxable person must register with the APEH office that has jurisdiction over the headquarters or permanent residence of the taxable person and that office will assign the tax identification number.

9.2   Books and Records
All persons registered for Hungarian VAT purposes must keep full records for five years of all business transactions which may affect their liability to VAT. The records must be kept up to date and must be sufficiently detailed to enable the taxpayer accurately to calculate his liability and the tax administration to check the calculation if necessary. The records which must be maintained are:

- invoices received and issued by the taxable person arranged in numerical order
- documents and vouchers used as substitutes for invoices which substantiate liability to VAT and entitlement to refunds
- itemised records based on invoices and substitute invoices received and issued which contain identification data, the taxable base, the amount of VAT included in the invoices as substitutes and the amount invoiced
- separate records of liability to VAT, entitlements to refunds and satisfaction thereof based on the invoices and vouchers.

9.3   Invoices
Taxable persons must issue appropriate VAT invoices in respect of all their supplies. If payment is made in cash the supplier may issue a simplified invoice if the customer so requests.

For VAT purposes an invoice must contain:

- serial number
- name and address and tax identification number of the issuer
- date
- date of sale of goods or rendering of services
- name and address of customer
- statistical code number of the goods or services supplied
- description and features of the goods or services
- unit price of the goods or services without VAT
- the unit of measurement and total quantity
- rate of tax in per cent charged on the goods or services or a statement that they are exempt
- value of goods or services in the invoice without VAT
- amount of VAT charged on goods and services in the invoice
- total value of goods and services in the invoice with VAT.

9.4 VAT Returns

As a general rule taxable persons are obliged to make a monthly return by the twentieth day of the month following the end of the tax month.

As of 1 January 1995 taxpayers who paid less than 1 million forints of VAT in 1994 are permitted to file quarterly VAT returns.

An annual return must be filed by 15 February of the year following the tax year.

9.5 Penalties

There are various penalties for late filing, negligence, late payment, etc. The penalty for late filing is 5% of the tax if the return is up to 15 days late, 20% up to the thirtieth day and 30% over 30 days. A penalty of 5% may be levied on the outstanding tax liability and interest of twice the National Bank's rate may be charged for late payment. Currently the National Bank's rate is 22% a year. The authorities may issue notices of the underpayments of VAT and they may add penalties and fines to these notices. The tax administration may calculate the correct amount of VAT due by a taxable person in circumstances where an incorrect return or incorrectly calculated and self-assessed amount of tax has been submitted.

9.6 Appeals

Taxable persons have recourse to a multiple-tier system of appeals against VAT assessments.

10 SPECIAL VAT REGIMES

10.1 Agricultural Production

Private individuals engaged in agriculture are obliged to register for VAT depending on the level of their activities:

- annual sales from agriculture less than 500,000 forints – the individual does not qualify as a taxable person under any circumstances;
- private individuals with annual sales from agriculture in excess of two million forints

or with annual sales between 500,000 and two million forints but who are otherwise registered with the tax authorities as entrepreneurs qualify as taxable persons.

10.2 Freelancers
Freelancers such as artists, designers, industrial designers, consultants, and legal advisers are classified as either taxable or non-taxable persons.

Generally, artists selling their work either directly or through a gallery are regarded as taxable persons. Non-taxable persons are those rendering exempt services such as doctors, freelance teachers, lawyers, etc.

10.3 Second-Hand Goods
When purchasing second-hand goods or new goods from a non-taxable person a taxable person may deduct the imputed VAT contained in the all-inclusive price paid.

10.4 Small Enterprises
Taxable persons who opt to be treated as exempt (see section 7.3 'Option to become exempt'), but who have sales in excess of the annual turnover limit, do not have to register in accordance with the general rules and there is a simplified method of calculation used for their VAT payments.

The tax payable on annual sales of commercial accommodation of less than 1.5 million forints may be calculated by applying an average rate of 5.8%. Input recovery of VAT incurred is not allowed.

None of the above methods is mandatory and the taxable person may also opt to use the general rules.

10.5 Retail Trades
In addition to all the other options, retail trades may calculate the amount of VAT payable by use of a special retail scheme.

10.6 Travel Agencies
Taxable persons supplying services in the tourist industry may use either of the following methods of calculating VAT:

■ the services rendered are assumed to be homogenous and the taxpayer charges VAT on the full amount of service rendered. When defining the taxable value the value of services utilised abroad may be disregarded. When using this method a taxable person may deduct VAT paid on services ordered from third parties and utilised by the tourists

■ VAT is charged only on the mark-up and VAT incurred on inputs may not be recovered.

Contributor: Fred Ritzmann
                Ernst & Young Kft
                1146 Budapest
                Hermina út 17
                Hungary
                Tel: +36 1 252 8333
                Fax: +36 1 142 7552

ICELAND

1 GENERAL BACKGROUND

Iceland, which is not a member of the European Union, introduced value added tax (VAT) on 1 January 1990 through the Value Added Tax Act No. 50/1988. It replaced the former Retail Sales Act which had been in force since 1960.

VAT is levied on all stages of production and trade except where specific exemptions apply. VAT on supplies made within Iceland is controlled by a regional tax office in every county. VAT on imports is levied by the Icelandic Customs Office and is paid according to the same procedure as customs duties.

2 WHO IS TAXABLE?

2.1 General
The liability to pay VAT arises whenever turnover of a taxable commodity or service occurs in Iceland in a commercial activity. Any physical or legal person (limited company, corporation, partnership or individual) who carries on a business or trade which involves the supply of taxable goods and/or services is liable to pay tax.

Co-operatives and other societies supplying taxable goods and/or services (even if they are tax-exempt according to Act 75/1981 (Income Tax and Corporation Tax) and other special Acts), are liable to VAT if they sell goods and services in competition with other enterprises. This also applies if they sell only members' goods and services, or even if they sell only to members. Also liable are public utility enterprises supplying taxable goods and services, auctioneers, agents and other representatives of foreign-owned enterprises.

2.2 Government Bodies
Central Government, county and municipal institutions and public enterprises in competition with commercial undertakings are liable to VAT.

2.3 Foreign Entrepreneurs
Agents and other representatives of foreign-owned enterprises are taxable.

2.4 VAT Representatives
Non-residents without an office or a fixed place of business in Iceland must appoint a local representative for VAT purposes if they provide taxable supplies in Iceland.

This chapter reflects the law on VAT in Iceland as at 31 December 1994.

3   WHAT IS TAXABLE?

VAT is levied on all goods and services unless specifically exempted, with the result that tax will be paid on the increase in value added to the products at any individual stage of production.

3.1   Supply of Goods

The tax applies to all goods (new or used) including electricity, heating and other forms of energy, animals and plants but not immovable property. Share certificates, debt instruments and items of similar value are not considered taxable as long as their primary function is that of evidencing a right. As soon as the inherent value ceases to represent a right but simply becomes printed matter, VAT applies. Bills and coins are considered taxable goods when converted to collectors' items. Taxable goods can, in certain circumstances, qualify for exemption (see section 7.2).

3.2   Supply of Services

All services are taxable with the exception of exempt services listed in section 7.2.

3.3   Self-Supply of Goods/Services

The Minister of Finance has the power to determine that entities not normally subject to VAT must pay VAT on goods and services produced or rendered solely for their own use. This may occur, for instance, where the taxable goods and/or services of an enterprise are used for the purpose of constructing a building for the personal use of its owner or if the enterprise uses specified resources to construct a building or buildings when such a building(s) are used for purposes other than those related to the sale of taxable goods or provision of taxable services, or if such immovable property is later to be sold, rented or leased (see section 5.2).

4   PLACE OF SUPPLY

4.1   Supply of Goods

Supply of goods which are physically located in Iceland at the time of supply are liable to VAT. Goods which are imported into Iceland are also liable to VAT at the point of importation. Goods which are delivered outside Iceland are zero-rated.

4.2   Supply of Services

4.2.1   General Rule

A service is deemed to be rendered at the place where the activities are carried out.

4.2.2   Exceptions

The supply of certain services in Iceland to an enterprise which is neither domiciled nor has a place of business in Iceland may, in certain instances, be exempt from taxable turnover.

The supply of these services may be considered to have been 'exported' if:

- the service is for use outside Iceland
- the buyer could (if his business activity were domiciled in Iceland and should, therefore, be registered) apply the VAT arising from the purchase of the service as

input tax. In this case the seller must obtain from the buyer a certificate issued by the appropriate authority in his home country outlining the nature of his business enterprise. Normally such services would be those provided by consultants and intermediaries (representatives), advertising services, the rental of movable property, etc. Certain services, such as those applicable to real estate, transportation of goods, etc do not qualify for the exemption.

5   BASIS OF TAXATION/CHARGEABLE EVENT

5.1   Basis of Taxation
The taxable base includes the following:
- charge for the delivery of the goods or services
- taxes (excluding VAT) and charges which have already been levied at previous stages of business
- costs of packing, transportation, insurance, etc whether such costs are included in the price or charged separately
- charges for connecting-up, installation charges, and other amounts payable by the buyer
- agents' commission, etc, and auctioneers' fees
- cash discounts and other discounts which are subject to conditions that have not yet been satisfied at the time of delivery (invoicing). Unconditional discounts given at the time of delivery of goods and services are, however, deducted from the selling price in order to determine the taxable base (see section 5.7.3).

Excluded from the taxable base are, however, interest and interest-related charges levied at any time on the unpaid balance of the purchase price, provided that the amount of such interest or interest-related charges can be ascertained from the hire-purchase contract or from payment vouchers and service charges which are not included in the price.

5.2   Self-Supplies
When the owner of an enterprise uses goods or services of the enterprise in a private capacity or for purposes other than in connection with the turnover of the enterprise, such use is a taxable supply which is valued for VAT purposes on the basis of the price generally charged exclusive of VAT (see section 3.3).

5.3   Non-Arm's Length Transactions
In the case of transactions which are not conducted at arm's length (ie transactions between parties having a community of interests such that one party holds a financial interest in the other party's enterprise), the taxable value may be determined as the general selling price of the goods or services concerned.

5.4   Used Vehicles
When a used vehicle is sold by an entity for business purposes VAT is due on 80.32% of the dealer's selling price (inclusive of VAT) minus the entity's buying price. This applies when the invoice for a sale contains no indication of a tax or any other value on the basis of which the tax may be calculated. No tax liability arises if the entity's selling price (inclusive of VAT) does not exceed his buying price.

5.5   Chargeable Event

VAT is payable by a registered enterprise at all stages of the commercial turnover of goods. This includes:

- the sale or delivery of goods against payment and the provision of labour and services against payment
- the value of taxable goods and services sold or produced by an enterprise or taken for private use by an owner
- the value of taxable goods and services used by an enterprise for purposes other than the sale of taxable goods and services
- the sale or delivery of machinery, equipment and other factors of production
- inventories, machinery, equipment and other factors of production on hand at the time of an enterprise's deregistration.

When an invoice is issued in connection with the delivery of goods or services, that delivery is deemed to have taken place on the date stated on the invoice provided such invoice is made out before or soon after the completion of delivery. Conversely, if payment is received in part or in full prior to actual delivery, 80.32% of the amount actually received shall be included in taxable turnover for the taxation period during which payment is made if the good or the service is taxable at the 24.5% tax rate. If the good or the service delivered is taxable at the 14% tax rate then 87.72% of the amount actually received shall be included in the taxable turnover for the taxation period during which payment is made.

5.6   Special Rules

An election may be made to include goods delivered on commission or consignment in either the taxable turnover made during the period in which such deliveries took place, or in the taxable turnover of the period in which settlement with the commission agent or the consignee is effected. In this case, the invoice may not be made out until settlement is effected.

5.7   Adjustment to Taxable Turnover

5.7.1 Returned Goods

When a seller credits a buyer in respect of returned goods, the seller is entitled to deduct 80.32% (ie the amount returned net of VAT included therein) of the credited amount from its taxable turnover if the goods are taxable at the 24.5% tax rate. If the goods returned are taxable at the 14% tax rate then the enterprise is entitled to deduct 87.72% of the credited amount from its taxable turnover.

5.7.2 Bad Debts

Enterprises may deduct from their taxable sales 80.32% of losses (ie the amount lost net of VAT included therein) due to bad debts which arise out of transactions involving goods delivered and services performed when the goods or services are taxable at the 24.5% tax rate. When the goods or services are taxable at the 14% tax rate, then the enterprise may deduct from its taxable sales 87.72% of the losses. If such debts are subsequently paid, whether in full or in part, then 80.32% of the amounts recovered shall be added to the enterprise's taxable turnover for goods or services where the 24.5% tax rate applies and 87.72% for goods or services where the 14% tax rate applies.

5.7.3 Discounts

When, subsequent to delivery, a discount is given to a business entity which is entitled to deduct the value of the VAT from its input tax, the discount may only be included in the calculation for credit if a credit note is actually issued showing the amount of the discount. The value of the VAT to be claimed as credit is also to be shown on the credit note.

6   TAX RATES

The present rates are as follows:

14%:   –   rental of hotel rooms and accommodation in guest houses
        –   books, newspapers, magazines and periodicals (local or national) in the Icelandic language, subscriptions to radio and television stations
        –   warm water, electricity and fuel oil used for the heating of houses and of swimming pools
        –   most food. This rate does not apply to restaurants.

24.5%: –   all other taxable goods and services which are not specifically exempt or liable at the 14% rate.

7   EXEMPTIONS

7.1   Exemptions with Credit for Input Tax

The sale of a variety of goods and services is exempt (ie output tax is not payable). The sale of the following goods and services, while said to be 'zero-rated' if they fulfil certain conditions, are in fact exempt supplies with entitlement to credit for input tax:

■   exportation of goods and services
■   sale of goods and services to the Iceland Defence Force at Keflavik International Airport, but excluding sales to individual members of the Defence Force
■   international goods transportation, and transportation within Iceland if such transportation is part of a contract covering the movement of goods to or from Iceland
■   provisions, fuel and equipment delivered for use in ships and aircraft engaged in international traffic, but excluding Icelandic fishing vessels transporting their catch abroad, boats under six metres in length, pleasure boats and private airplanes
■   sales and rentals of ships and aircraft and the repair and maintenance services rendered to ships and aircraft but excluding boats under six metres in length, pleasure boats and private airplanes
■   work performed by an enterprise on goods when the work is done for the account of a non-resident client who, eventually, exports the goods
■   project planning, design, and other services relating to buildings and other immovable property, when such property is located outside Iceland.

7.2   Exemptions without Credit for Input Tax

The following activities qualify for VAT exemption:

- health services, such as treatment in hospitals, maternity wards and sanatoriums. Services provided by the medical community, physicians, dentists, nurses, etc are specifically excluded from VAT
- social services including those provided by day care centres, nursery schools, school day centres, temporary care centres, etc
- educational activities including those provided on a commercial basis, driver instruction, flight instruction and dance instruction, primary, secondary, and university education, re-education, vocational training and refresher courses, language and music training. Certain activities do not, however, qualify for exemption and are, therefore, taxable eg horse riding instruction
- cultural activities, including museums, libraries, zoological gardens, etc including admission to concerts, the showing of Icelandic films, theatre and ballet (provided that such activities are not connected with other activities that may be deemed to be of a commercial nature and not VAT exempt or combined with restaurant services)
- sports activities and rental of sport accommodation, including the use of public swimming pools, ski-lifts and admission to sport competitions, sport shows and health spas
- passenger transport
- postal services, but excluding parcel post services
- real estate rental, including the letting of parking spaces, but excluding short-term rental of restaurants or meeting facilities; the sale of rights to hunt or fish
- insurance services, including valuations and appraisal services when carried out in conjunction with insurance services
- banking and other financial services, including financial brokerage
- lotteries
- activities of authors and composers and similar artistic activities including translators' services provided in connection with the artistic activities of authors and composers
- services of travel agencies
- services provided by undertakers and church activities in direct connection with funerals
- artists selling their own works of art (provided that such works are covered by Customs Code numbers 9701.1000 – 9703.0000) and auctioneers selling such works at auctions
- enterprises engaged in a business with an annual turnover of less than ISK185,200 (1993) the amount used to determine VAT exemption is indexed and is revised annually on the basis of the Building Cost Index. However, as soon as the 12 months' turnover is expected to exceed the minimum, the exemption no longer applies and registration is required
- scientific institutions, libraries, and official institutions on the importation of reports, technical publications, and other printed matter which they receive free of charge (Regulation 71/1993). The same exemption applies to other persons that receive free of charge the publications listed above as long as the FOB-value in ISK does not exceed SDR.50 or its equivalent
- services rendered by non-profit organisations where the proceeds accrue in their entirety to charity.

7.3   Non-Taxable Transactions

The transfer of inventories, machinery and other equipment is not to be included in the tax base when such transfer takes place as a direct result of a change in the ownership of an enterprise, or a part of an enterprise, provided that the new owner is engaged in a registered business. The seller must inform the appropriate tax authorities of such transfers (sales) and their value not later than eight days after they take place.

8   CREDIT/REFUND FOR INPUT TAX

8.1   General Rule

Output tax is defined as the VAT applicable to taxable sales or deliveries made by taxable enterprises during a taxation period. Input tax applicable to a taxation period is the VAT shown on invoices issued by suppliers to a taxable enterprise for that period as well as the VAT incurred by the enterprise for imports for the period.

No credit is allowed for VAT included in certain business expenses which contain an element of private consumption:

- the operation of canteens and employee cafeterias
- the acquisition and operation of housing accommodation for the enterprise's owners or employees
- remuneration in kind to owners or employees
- the acquisition and operation of recreation centres, holiday homes, summer cottages, day care centres, etc for the use of owners or employees
- entertainment expenses and gifts
- acquisition, operation and rental of passenger vehicles for nine persons or less except in the case of car dealers and car hire businesses.

8.2   State and Municipalities

Public enterprises, when in competition with the private sector, may claim credit for that part of the input tax which is directly related to the sale of taxable goods and services. In addition, State agencies and municipalities will receive a refund on VAT paid on the purchase of the following goods and services:

- refuse collection, including the actual collection of refuse, transportation, burying and elimination/incineration. The VAT is not refunded on recycling or reprocessing activities.
- cleaning
- snow removal
- rescue activities and security arrangements arising from natural disasters and civil defence operations
- services of engineers, technicians, architects, lawyers, certified public accountants and other, similar, specialists.

8.3   Credit and Refunds

If the input tax claimable by an enterprise for a particular taxation period exceeds the output tax payable for that same period, then the excess tax will be refunded to the enterprise.

If the enterprise owes taxes, then only that amount of the VAT credit which exceeds the amount of taxes owed shall be paid to the enterprise. The balance of taxes owed means any and all taxes, duties and penalties that have been applied because of late filing or late payment.

8.4   Residential Housing

An individual who engages tradesmen to construct for him a dwelling for his private and personal use is entitled to a credit for that part of the VAT incurred which represents the cost of labour expended at the construction site. This also applies to renovations and repairs to residential housing.

8.5   Heating of Houses and Swimming Pools

Utilities which sell warm water and/or electricity for the purpose of heating houses or swimming pools receive a partial credit so that VAT paid is 11% or less than the weighted average price on kWh for these services.

8.6   Foreign Tourists

Foreign tourists are entitled to partial credit for VAT. The credit amounts to between 60% and 75% of the VAT amount paid depending on the value of goods purchased according to a special table appended to Regulation 500/1989.

Only a foreign national domiciled outside Iceland is eligible. The tourist must export the goods bought within one month from the date of purchase. The goods in question shall be sealed and released to the buyer upon his departure from Iceland. The buyer must produce his repayment check with the relevant data attached in order to claim the exempted goods at time of departure.

8.7   Embassies and Foreign Diplomats

The sale of goods to embassies or diplomatic agents does not constitute an export and must include VAT.

Embassies and diplomats are, however, entitled to repayment of the VAT (except on food purchases) on condition that the goods are for the exclusive use of an embassy or the personal use of a diplomatic agent and his family.

Applications for repayment must be made to the Ministry for Foreign Affairs with the original invoice or bill of sale (minimum ISK10,000) which clearly indicates that VAT has been paid.

8.8   Foreign Enterprises

Foreign enterprises can recover VAT repayment on the following:

■   the purchase, processing/preparation, storage and transportation of goods which they have exported from Iceland in their own name and the purchase of related services
■   repairs, installation, storage and transportation of equipment and machinery sold to Iceland. Pertinent costs must have been included in the dutiable value of such equipment and machinery at the time of importation to Iceland.

The VAT repayment may be made to any foreign enterprise which would qualify for registration in Iceland if it were domiciled in Iceland, and which would, therefore, need to be registered. This means that such enterprises as travel agencies, insurance companies, banks and financial institutions do not qualify for VAT repayment. A further prerequisite is that the enterprise shall have had no sales of goods and taxable services in Iceland in the period to which the application refers.

9   ADMINISTRATIVE OBLIGATIONS

9.1   *Registration*

Any entrepreneur who satisfies the requirements of a taxable person must register his business activity with a regional Director of Taxes no later than eight days prior to the commencement of that activity. Any change in the nature of the business activity or change of address or ownership must be reported to the appropriate authorities within eight days. When a registered business is liquidated or is sold to another registered business, the previous registration is cancelled.

When an entrepreneur carries on a taxable business for a limited period, the business may be registered for a predetermined period of time. Temporary registration must be no less than one-fourth of a month and may not exceed two months.

9.2   *Special Registration and Optional Registration*

The sale and rental of immovable property is VAT exempt (see section 7.2). Entrepreneurs engaged in construction for the purpose of selling real estate to taxable enterprises may apply for special registration. This type of registration gives a builder the right to claim input tax incurred on all materials related to immovable property sold to a registered enterprise. Special registration may also apply to a builder prior to the actual sale of immovable property, but in such cases a bond must be posted to cover the VAT to be repaid.

The owners of immovable property (or parts thereof), who do not fulfil the criteria of taxable persons and who, in the course of business, rent or lease such property to a taxable enterprise have the option to register. Once registered the entrepreneur must remit VAT on the rental fee. This in turn, entitles the entrepreneur to receive credit for the input tax on all taxable goods and services purchased which relate to the rented or leased property covered by the optional registration.

Optional registration is not granted for a period of less than two years.

9.3   *VAT Returns*

Taxable enterprises must submit periodic returns and the difference between input tax and output tax charged during each taxation period. If the input tax claimed by an enterprise for a particular tax period exceeds the output tax payable for the same period, then the excess tax will be refunded to the enterprise. The tax periods are generally two months: January/February, March/April, etc.

Enterprises whose output tax is regularly lower than its input tax may apply to a regional tax office for a shortened taxation period of one month. If the output tax is regularly less than 50% of the input tax, an enterprise can apply for a further reduction in the taxation period of less than one month, but not less than one week.

■   *Multiple Activities:* an enterprise engaged in more than one taxable activity may, subject to the approval of a Regional Tax Office, submit a separate return for each activity. If the enterprise is engaged in more than one type of trade or industry, a separate return must be filed for each type.

■   *Fishing:* an enterprise engaged in the processing of fish can apply to a Regional Tax Office to file a special preliminary (interim) return applicable to the input tax on purchases of raw materials (fish) for processing. The taxation period applicable to such instances will be one week, Monday to Sunday.

- *Agriculture:* tax periods applicable to those engaged in agriculture are six months, January to June and July to December. Due dates for VAT payable are 1 September for the former period and 1 March (in the following year) for the latter. A regional Director of Taxes may, upon application, authorise an extraordinary filing for those engaged in agriculture if it is apparent that they are entitled to a substantial VAT credit as a result of their purchase of durable and/or operating goods.

9.4   Assessment and Collection

Payment of tax falls due and must be remitted one month and five days after the end of the tax period. If the fifth day falls on a weekend or a general holiday, payment may be made on the next working day.

9.5   Records

Purchases and sales of taxable goods and services by a registered enterprise must be recorded in a manner which facilitates the calculation of the enterprise's tax liability and the control of the amount of tax due.

All records and bookkeeping data, including relevant invoices, statements and cash register tapes must be kept for a minimum of six years after the end of the accounting year.

If an enterprise keeps ordinary books of accounts, they must contain separate accounts for:

- the tax payable (output tax)
- the tax deductible (input tax)
- VAT control
- output tax on payments on account.

The general rule is that the VAT is applied directly to the appropriate account, output tax or input tax. The alternative is to maintain a control account for each two-month tax period, income and expense accounts are discounted for VAT and the resulting amounts (input tax and output tax) applied to their respective accounts.

VAT exempted sales (such as exports) must be recorded in a separate account. The total of this account is reported in its entirety on the VAT return for each tax period. Separate accounts shall also be kept for purchases and imports of taxable goods and services that are taxed at different tax rates. The same applies to sales of taxable goods and services at different tax rates.

In cases where an enterprise does not maintain ordinary books of account, the accounts should be kept in a ledger of adequate quality for accounting purposes.

Farmers are not required by law to maintain a detailed double-entry accounting system. Those who do not must, however, maintain simplified records which are as a minimum acceptable requirement, sufficient to allow the Tax Authorities to verify subsequent returns.

9.6   Invoices/Credit Notes/Deposit Vouchers

Registered enterprises are, in general, required to issue invoices to their customers for all taxable goods and services supplied by them. In the case of partial (advance) payments, or payments on account, separate invoices must be issued by the supplier for every such payment. When goods are returned to the supplier, the supplier shall issue a credit note for the returned goods. The credit note shall contain a reference to the original invoice. The same applies to discounts given, or adjustments made, after the issuance of the original invoice.

If a transaction covers both taxable and non-taxable supplies, the invoice must clearly state transactions for each category as specified by the Act.

The issue of invoices is not required in the case of retail sales to private consumers although sales must be reported through cash register tapes. If a retail sale is made to a taxable enterprise, an invoice must be issued.

Invoices issued by a taxable enterprise must be in triplicate and sequentially pre-numbered. The enterprise's name, national identification number and VAT registration number must be pre-printed on the invoice. The following must also appear on the invoice:

- date of issue
- name and national identification number of the consignee. The name and national identification number need not appear on the invoice when selling for cash to private consumers
- description of the transaction
- quantity, unit price and total value of the goods or service supplied
- amount of VAT and tax rate.

The invoice must indicate clearly whether or not its total value includes VAT. If the VAT value is not specifically indicated on the invoice, the invoice must contain the information to the effect that VAT may be calculated by applying 19.68% to the invoice total if the goods or services are taxed at the 24.5% tax rate. For goods or services taxed at the 14% tax rate the calculation can be performed by applying 12.28% to the invoice total.

Invoices involving sales to taxable purchasers must always indicate the actual VAT amount and the tax category. The same invoice may be used for taxable and non-taxable transactions (see section 7.2.2). The same invoice may also be used for transactions that are taxable and partly taxable.

A credit note must be issued whenever goods are returned or when discounts are given or other adjustments made after the issue of the original invoice if the effect of such returns, discounts or adjustments is to reduce the taxable turnover. The credit note must always include a reference to the original invoice.

Deposit vouchers are, in certain instances, equivalent to invoices. This would, for instance, be the case with branches or agencies where such enterprises might receive merchandise for processing or resale. A deposit voucher issued by the recipient of goods for processing or resale must contain all the information contained in an invoice together with the VAT registration number of the buyer.

9.7   *Power of the Authorities*
If the tax return for any period is late, if the tax is not remitted in time in full, or any other discrepancy exists in the return and payment process, the Regional Director of Taxes will assess the amount payable and subsequently advise the appropriate agent acting on behalf of the State Treasury of his assessment. If a return is received in time (see section 8.2.1) and the balance shown thereon indicates that a refund is due to the enterprise, the refund will then be paid not later than 15 days after the filing of the return.

If the Regional Director of Taxes is unable to properly evaluate the accuracy of the return, the 15-day period is extended by the number of days it takes the Regional Director of Taxes to verify it.

9.8 Additional Tax, Interest and Penalties

If the return or the tax due is not remitted on time, a penalty may be applied. The increase in tax liability is 2% per day of the amount owed up to a maximum of 20% (there is no minimum penalty).

The appropriate agent of the State Treasury may, with the aid of the Police Authorities, cause an enterprise to cease its operations if the enterprise has failed to remit the tax in full along with any and all penalties that have been applied to arrears, or has failed to keep proper records.

If an enterprise has filed a proper return indicating a balance due by reason of the input tax having exceeded the output tax (see section 8.3) the enterprise is entitled to receive late payment interest on the amount due if it has not been received within one month of the due date.

9.9 Appeal Procedure

If a Regional Tax Director's VAT assessment prove unsatisfactory to an entrepreneur, he may file a complaint with the Director. The complaint must be filed in writing within 30 days of the assessment, clearly stating the reason(s) why the assessment is being contested. The Regional Director of Taxes then has to respond to the complaint within 30 days and must advise the entrepreneur of his decision by registered mail.

If the entrepreneur is not satisfied with the decision, he has the option to file an appeal with the State Internal Revenue Board (Yfirskattanefnd) whose decision is final. The appeal to the Board must be filed within 30 days of the date of issue of the Regional Tax Director's decision.

10 SPECIAL REGIMES

10.1 Agriculture

Special rules apply to the filing of tax returns by agricultural activities. The tax period is six months, January to June and July to December. The due date for VAT payable for the former period is 1 September and for the latter, 1 March. Those entrepreneurs whose business turnover from activities other than farming equals or exceeds 60% must file their returns bi-monthly (see section 8.1).

10.2 Imports

Tax on imports is levied at the same rate as for supplies of goods within Iceland, based on the taxable value as determined in accordance with the rules for customs duties. Payment of VAT must be made to the Customs Authorities not later than the due date in the period following the date of importation.

Importers engaged in a taxable activity may be allowed postponement on the VAT payment.

The taxable value of imported goods is the dutiable price in addition to customs duties including freight charges, insurance costs and all charges incurred up until the goods reach their first destination in Iceland.

Imports may, in certain circumstances, be exempt from VAT. This applies to goods that are free of, or exempt from, customs duties. Examples of such goods are those that are imported to Iceland on a temporary basis for the purpose of being used at exhibitions or trade shows and goods that are imported as repair parts with the provision that the repaired item(s) are to be exported from Iceland without having been used in Iceland in any manner whatsoever.

The chief rule applying to tax-exempt goods is that they must be re-exported from Iceland.

11   FURTHER READING

VAT in Iceland, Director of Internal Revenue in Iceland

Contributor: Margret Flovenz
                  Endurskodun & Radgjof HF
                  Ernst & Young International
                  Skeifan 11 A
                  PO Box 8693
                  108 Rejkjavik
                  Iceland
                  Tel: +354 1 685511
                  Fax: +354 1 689585

LATVIA

1   GENERAL BACKGROUND

Value added tax (VAT) came into force on 1 January 1992. Since then several changes have been introduced into VAT law, although the latest, which came into force in 1995, have not been taken into account in this chapter. VAT is administered by the tax and customs authorities.

2   WHO IS TAXABLE?

2.1   General
VAT must be paid by legal persons who independently run a business. Natural persons who deal with economic activities are not taxable persons.

2.2   Transactions with Branch/Subsidiary
Transactions between a parent company and its subsidiary are treated as transactions between independent parties.

2.3   Government Bodies
Government bodies are not subject to VAT in respect of their activities of an administrative, social or cultural nature.

2.4   Fiscal Unit/Group Registration
If an enterprise consists of more than one unit, division or branch, taxation as one single enterprise is required. VAT law does not contain a special provision for group registration.

2.5   Foreign Entrepreneurs
Foreign entrepreneurs who wish to carry out economic activities are required to establish a subsidiary, and register it according to the Enterprise Law.

2.6   Representative Office
Representative offices of foreign entrepreneurs are not regarded as taxable persons when they merely carry out activities of a preparatory of auxiliary nature. As a rule, a representative office may not supply goods or services.

2.7   VAT Representatives
VAT law contains no provisions concerning VAT representatives.

2.8   Reverse Charge Mechanism
The import of services is not taxable.

This chapter reflects the legislation on VAT in Latvia as at 31 December 1994.

2.9 Importers

Goods imported into Latvia are liable to VAT. The tax which is due by the importer, has to be paid to the customs authorities.

3 WHAT IS TAXABLE?

VAT is levied on the supply of goods and services and on the import of goods.

3.1 Supply of Goods

Supply of goods means the actual transfer of ownership of movables. Money and securities are not treated as goods. The following are treated as supply:

- selling of goods
- processing of goods
- self-supply of goods.

3.2 Supply of Services

Supply of services means any supply which does not constitute supply of goods.

It also applies to:

- leasing, renting
- commission
- transport
- self-supply of services
- construction and any other work which is not a supply of goods.

3.3 Self-Supply of Goods/Services

In certain cases specified by law, self-supplies are subject to VAT (for example, use of goods or services for private consumption or for purposes not related to the taxable activity of the enterprise). In general, transfers of goods and services within an enterprise are not subject to VAT.

3.4 Importation of Goods

Importation of goods is a taxable event irrespective of the legal status of the importer. VAT is levied when the customs clearance has been made.

4 PLACE OF SUPPLY

VAT applies to supplies of goods and services taking place in Latvia.

4.1 Supply of Goods

When the goods at the time of supply are located outside Latvia, the supply is not taxable in Latvia.

4.2 Supply of Services

VAT law does not contain special rules regarding the place of supply of services. As a general rule, the place where the service is supplied is the place where the supplier has established his business.

4.3   Reverse Charge Mechanism

VAT law does not contain a reverse charge mechanism for transferring the liability to VAT from a non-resident supplier to the recipient.

5   BASIS OF TAXATION

5.1   Supplies within Latvia

VAT is charged on the total amount of consideration paid by the buyer. The exchange of goods and services is also a taxable supply.

5.2   Self-Supply

The tax basis for self-suppliers and private use is the purchase price or the actual cost of production.

5.3   Imports

VAT due on the importation of goods is assessed on the value determined for customs purposes, to which taxes and duties paid on the importation should be added.

5.4   Chargeable Event/Time of Payment

Liability to tax arises at the time when taxable goods or services are supplied. Advance payments received from customers are also taxable.

The time of supply is:

- time of delivery of goods, or
- time of rendering services, or
- time when payment is made.

Tax is payable on imports at the time of importation.

5.5   Credit Notes/Bad Debts

When a credit note is issued cancelling all or part of an invoice, the entrepreneur may deduct the VAT shown on the credit note from output VAT when filing his VAT return.

VAT paid on uncollected debts cannot be refunded.

6   TAX RATES

Currently there is only one tax rate, ie 18%.

7   EXEMPTIONS

A person who supplies exempt goods or services may not recover any input tax.

7.1   Exemption with Credit for Input Tax

Exports of goods and services are exempt. Input tax relating to goods and services used for export is recoverable.

The following exemptions also carry a right to credit for input tax:

■   sale of goods for water or air transport vessels connected with international transport for sale or consumption during the journey
■   specified food for children who are younger than 1 year old
■   rental of residence
■   tourist services for foreign tourists.

7.2   Exemptions without Credit for Input Tax

The following exemptions are without credit for input tax:

■   medicines, medical services, medical requisites
■   religious and funeral services
■   catering for staff provided by employer; catering provided by educational, medical and social care institutions
■   cultural activities, including cinema and theatre performances; radio and television transmissions
■   movies
■   banking and insurance services
■   transit transport services
■   maintenance of parks, etc.

7.3   Non-Taxable Transactions

7.3.1   Transactions within the Same Legal Entity
Transactions within the same legal entity are considered to be internal transactions and are not subject to VAT.

7.3.2   Transfer of Business
Transfer of business is wholly taxable.

7.3.3   Subsidies/Penalty Payments
Generally, the VAT status of subsidies is a difficult area because VAT law does not explain taxation of subsidies. Usually subsidies granted by government bodies are not liable to VAT when they are not directly linked to the cost of supplying goods or services.

Penalty payments are not usually liable to VAT.

8   CREDIT/REFUND FOR INPUT VAT

8.1   General Rule
The entrepreneur can deduct the input tax paid on goods and services and on the importation of goods used for his business.

No credit is allowed for input tax on:

- goods and services used for non-business purposes
- goods and services used for exempt transactions
- expenditure for private purposes
- purchase of fixed assets.

8.2 Adjustment of Entitlement to Credit

There are no adjustments for VAT on fixed/capital assets because VAT paid on the purchase of fixed assets is not refundable.

8.3 Partial Exemption

When goods and services are used for both taxable and non-taxable activities, the creditable input tax is calculated on the basis of the ratio between the taxable supplies and total supplies.

8.4 Time of Recovery

Input credit can be claimed for the month in which the supply was made and VAT, indicated separately on the invoice, was paid. If the input tax exceeds the output VAT, the balance will be refunded upon application.

8.5 Refund to Foreign Entrepreneurs

A foreign entrepreneur who is not established in Latvia may not obtain a refund of VAT paid on goods or services purchased in Latvia.

9 ADMINISTRATIVE OBLIGATIONS

9.1 Registration

An entrepreneur engaged in an industrial, commercial or professional activity has to register with the local tax authorities if his taxable supplies exceed LVL7,500 (approximately US$14,000) during a calendar year.

A person whose taxable supply is less than the registration limit may voluntarily register itself for VAT. Refund of the input VAT is allowed only if he has taxable supply.

9.2 Books and Records

Entrepreneurs who are subject to VAT must keep adequate accounting books to justify all their transactions.

9.3 Invoices

Invoices issued must show all the compulsory information required by accounting law. The VAT due has to be indicated separately.

9.4 VAT Return

Every month the entrepreneur must file a VAT return to declare his taxable transactions for the preceding month. The date of filing is the fifteenth day of the month following that in which the transactions occurred.

If the VAT payable is less than LVL500 (approximately US$900) per month, tax returns may be filed quarterly.

9.5 Powers of the Authorities
The tax authorities may enforce the tax if an entrepreneur has failed to file a VAT return. Enforced tax may be 110 % of the tax of the previous tax return. This can only be avoided by making a proper return.

9.6 Penalties
The penalty for filing of inaccurate VAT returns is 30% of the non-declared tax.

9.7 Objections/Appeals
The taxpayer has the right to file an appeal with the tax authorities against a VAT assessment notice. If he is dissatisfied with their decision, he may appeal to the court.

10 SPECIAL VAT REGIMES

10.1 Agricultural and Fishery Activities
Agricultural and fishing enterprises have to be registered with the local tax authorities if their taxable supply exceeds LVL30,000 (approximately US$55,000) during a calendar year.

10.2 Second-Hand Goods
In the case of auctions of second-hand goods offered for sale by private persons, the auctioneer may request that his activities be treated as supply of service instead of sale of goods.

10.3 Supply of Real Property
The transfer of real property is exempt from VAT. The purchaser of real property may not deduct the input VAT paid on the purchased fixed assets and construction services.

10.4 Rental of Real Property
The rental of land and residential buildings is exempt from VAT.

Contributor: Tonis Jakob
                Ernst & Young
                Ravi 27
                EE 0007 Tallinn
                Estonia
                Tel: +372 2 683513
                Fax: +372 2 6310611

NORWAY

1   GENERAL BACKGROUND

Norway introduced value added tax (VAT) in 1970 through the Value Added Tax Act of 19 June 1969. The territory of Norway for VAT purposes does not include the areas of Svalbard and Jan Mayen.

VAT is the principal indirect tax in Norway and is largely based on the same principles as those applying in the European Union. Norway has adopted the European Union's Second VAT Directive.

The local VAT authority is the regional County Tax Office ('fylkesskattekontoret') or the Customs Authorities ('tolldistriktssjefen') for imported goods. The Tax Directorate is the overall superior authority. The Customs and Excise Directorate is the overall authority for import VAT.

A special tax on investment, etc was introduced on 1 January 1970 in conjunction with the VAT system and is called Investment Tax.

The Acts of 19 June 1969 No.66 and No.67 relating to VAT and Investment Tax (IT) have not been changed significantly in recent years. However they have both been amended by subsequent Acts and are supplemented by a number of regulations issued by the Ministry of Finance and Tax Directorate. The rates of VAT and IT are stipulated annually by the Parliament ('Storting').

VAT on imports is levied by the Norwegian Customs Offices ('tolldistriktskontoret') and is paid according to the same procedure as customs duties.

2   WHO IS TAXABLE?

2.1   General
The basic rule is that liability to pay VAT arises whenever turnover of taxable goods or services occurs in Norway through commercial activity. Any physical or legal person (limited company, partnership, etc) conducting a taxable activity is liable to pay VAT. Special rules apply for certain partnerships, trading companies, corporate groups, estates of deceased persons and estates in bankruptcy.

A business must register for VAT once its taxable sales exceed a certain limit (at present NOK30,000) in the previous 12-month period (not necessarily the calendar year). For charitable and non-profit institutions and organisations the limit is NOK70,000. All entrepreneurs supplying goods and services subject to VAT must be registered in the VAT register. This is done by completing a specially prescribed form and submitting it to the County Tax Office in the county in which the entrepreneur has his permanent place of business.

This chapter reflects the VAT and Investment Tax legislation in Norway as at 31 December 1994.

2.2   Transactions with Branch/Subsidiary

Transactions between a head office and a branch are deemed not to be a supply because they are looked upon as the same tax subject if the supply is within the same legal entity. Transactions between companies are deemed not to be a supply if the companies are registered as one single entrepreneur (see section 2.4).

2.3   Government Bodies

Government bodies are liable to VAT if they supply goods or services in competition with private entities.

2.4   Fiscal Unity/Group Taxation

Several activities operated by the same owner (corporate or personal) are, as a general rule, regarded as a single taxable entity for VAT purposes, provided they are not established as separate legal entities. If separate accounts are kept for one or more of these activities, they may upon application be registered separately in the VAT register.

Affiliated joint-stock companies may upon application be treated as a single entity for VAT purposes when at least 85% of the capital in each company is held by the same owner or owners. Goods or services may then be transferred between the companies without charging VAT. The companies will, moreover, be entitled to a combined deduction for input VAT on goods and services for operating buildings, machines and other operating assets. Such companies may have the right to deduct input VAT relating to such buildings, machinery, etc even if it has been transferred to a separate real-estate company not engaged in activities liable to VAT (for example, because it operates a purely rental business). An entity which is renting out real estate is individually unable to be registered in the VAT register. But as affiliated joint-stock companies they could be registered together and make a full deduction for input VAT.

If part of an entrepreneur's business consists of activities for which no credit is allowed (for example, sales of real-estate), VAT paid on purchases and imports must be split between those related to transactions which benefit from the right to a credit (taxable transactions) and those which do not benefit (non-taxable). The VAT paid on purchases must, however, be apportioned to reflect the transactions carrying the right and those not carrying a right to a credit. The attribution of input tax to taxable supplies has to be determined by Regulation 18 of 20 December 1969.

2.5   Foreign Entrepreneurs

Foreign enterprises supplying taxable services or selling goods in Norway are fully liable to VAT in the same way as Norwegian enterprises. Such foreign suppliers must be registered in the VAT register and are subject to the tax and accounting rules for VAT purposes. Application for registration is made to the County Tax Office where the foreign enterprise's representative has a place of business, registered office or residence. The foreign trader will then be given a registration number and become entitled to claim credit for input tax if this has been paid, for instance, on importation.

A foreign entrepreneur who makes no taxable supplies in Norway has no right to deduct input VAT.

If a foreign supplier who is making taxable supplies in Norway fails to register, the Norwegian customer may be liable for the VAT if the customer is not qualified to deduct the input VAT. Foreign entrepreneurs may thus incur VAT liability under the Value Added Tax Act even if they are not liable for income/corporation tax in Norway.

2.6   Representative Office
The supplies of a representative office in Norway are treated in the same way as an ordinary entrepreneur and the supplier has the same rights and obligations.

2.7   VAT Representatives
Where the foreign supplier does not maintain a place of business or registered office in Norway, registration and remittance of VAT must be undertaken through a representative. Registration, invoicing and VAT return filing procedures are determined by Regulation 71 of 31 March 1977.

2.8   Reverse Charge Mechanism
The reverse charge mechanism is not used in Norway but in some cases the importer of services relating to business equipment will be charged for Investment Tax of 7% (see section 2.5 'Foreign Entrepreneurs' and section 11 'Investment Tax').

2.9   Importers
The main rule is that VAT is payable on all imports of goods.

Regulations for the calculation and collection of VAT on imports were issued in December 1975 with several subsequent amendments.

A customs clearance agent may pay the VAT due on importation on behalf of the importer, and pass the cost on to the importer.

3   WHAT IS TAXABLE?

3.1   Supply of Goods
Sales of all goods are liable to VAT unless otherwise provided by the Act. 'Sales' is defined in the Act as the supply of goods or the performance of services against payment, including the exchange of goods and services.

A sale or a service in a chain transaction is looked upon as an individual supply for VAT purposes. If the transaction in the chain is, for instance, exported, it is only the last transaction which is exempt from VAT.

3.2   Supply of Services
VAT is payable also on the sale of services, but only on those services expressly specified in the Act.

The following are the main taxable services:

- services relating to goods or real property
- the renting of goods, including machinery, mechanical and electrical equipment connected with real property
- the transport and storage of goods except transport of goods to foreign countries

- the assignment of patents, licences, trademarks
- advertising, including arranging advertising contracts or space for advertisements
- technical assistance such as project planning, drawing, construction and other technical assistance relating to services supplied in connection with works on goods or real property, by persons such as architects
- typewriting, copying, office services, mass mailing and computer services
- telecommunication services, including telephone, telegraph and telex
- catering in (or from) hotels and other catering establishments.

3.3 Self-Supply of Goods/Services

VAT is also charged on the withdrawal by the owner of goods and services from his own business when such goods and services are for private use or for purposes which fall outside the scope of the Act.

Tax shall be paid on a self-supply basis when goods and services from the entrepreneur concerned are used:

- for the accommodation and 'in kind' remuneration of the entrepreneur, his management, employees and pensioned staff
- in work on and management of real property covering housing needs, leisure time, holiday or other recreational needs, including movables and equipment for such property
- for entertainment purposes
- for gifts and for publicity purposes
- for the transport of persons, including costs of acquisition and running expenses of passenger vehicles, without regard to the use to which the vehicles are put. The only exemption is passenger cars used in rental services.

No tax shall be paid on services rendered free of charge by an individual direct to charitable and non-profit institutions and organisations.

3.4 Importation of Goods

VAT must be paid not only on taxable supplies in Norway but also on imports of taxable goods. This applies regardless of the purpose of the import and irrespective of the transaction on which the import is based. Tax on imports is assessed by the Customs Office in accordance with procedures laid down for customs clearance. The Customs Office is also the authority to be consulted regarding VAT on imports.

4   PLACE OF SUPPLY

4.1 Supply of Goods
The following rules apply:

- goods which are sold to a Norwegian customer before importation are not taxable in Norway. The customer has to pay VAT if he brings the goods into Norway
- goods which are delivered abroad (exported) are not taxable in Norway
- goods which are supplied to a non-resident entrepreneur's warehouse in Norway are normally taxable.

4.2 Supply of Services

4.2.1 General Rule
The supply of services is based on the territoriality principle, but instead of a place of supply regulation (such as Article 9 of the Sixth VAT Directive of the European Union), a service is deemed to be rendered at the place where the activities are physically carried out, or where the effective use take place. Some services which contain a 'foreign element' are exempted as export services.

4.2.2 Exemptions
VAT exemption applies to services supplied by registered Norwegian suppliers for use abroad or for use on foreign ships and aircraft provided that the service is either performed abroad or on the foreign ship or aircraft, or is performed in Norway for a customer resident abroad, and provided the effective use takes place abroad. In the case of work on goods, such as repairs to a machine, exemption is also dependent upon the goods being dispatched through customs by the enterprise supplying the service.

5   BASIS OF TAXATION

5.1   Supplies within Norway
The main rule is that output VAT must be calculated on the basis of the consideration. The ordinary basis is the amount the business in question demands for its goods or services in the normal course of its operations.

The basis shall include all costs and incidental expenses, including:

■   cost of packing, transport, insurance, etc included in the price, or for which separate payment is demanded
■   customs duties and other excises
■   selling charges, fees, commissions and other expenses incurred in connection with the supply but excluding VAT.

Discounts and bonuses agreed upon and given are deducted from the sales value.

When charitable and non-profit institutions and organisations demand an exceptionally high level of profit on their supplies, the basis for calculating the output VAT should not include that part of the remuneration which exceeds the ordinary sales value.

5.2   Self-Supplies
When goods or services are exchanged in circumstances where a commonality of interests might lead to an artificially low consideration, or when they are withdrawn from a business for private use, the sales value on which VAT is charged must not be lower than the sales value of similar goods and services sold by the enterprise.

5.3   Importations
The basis for the calculation of VAT on imported goods is the customs value for the goods. This includes customs duties and all other duties except VAT. When goods are re-imported after repair abroad the taxable value is the cost of such repair with the addition of the cost of transport to and from Norway.

VAT on imports is payable when the goods pass through customs. It is calculated and collected by the customs authorities.

5.4 Chargeable Event/Time of Payment

VAT on the supply of taxable goods and services becomes due as soon as the taxable goods or services have been delivered.

VAT returns must be submitted for each two-calendar-month period. The VAT due for each period is payable within one month and ten days after the end of the VAT period.

5.5 Credit Notes/Bad Debts

Where a debtor fails to pay the full amount due for a taxable supply, and the registered supplier has already reported and accounted for VAT, a deduction may be made of an amount corresponding to the VAT paid. The deduction is made by reducing the figure for output VAT. To qualify for the deduction, the loss in question must be an actual or formally declared loss on accounts receivable. If payment is received for a previously deducted loss, VAT must be reported for the payment received.

6   TAX RATES

There are at present two rates of VAT:

0%: – newspapers; books and periodicals at the last stage of the sale process
– vehicles covered by the resolution made by the Storting prescribing excise tax on re-registration, providing the vehicles have been registered in Norway
– services concerned with the planning, projecting, building, repair and maintenance of public roads at the last stage of the sales process

23%: All other supplies and imports of taxable goods and services.

7   EXEMPTIONS

A person who sells exempt goods or services does not incur VAT liability and is not entitled to deduction for tax paid on acquisitions for the business.

7.1 Exemptions with Credit for Input Tax

The following supplies are exempt from VAT but carry the right to recovery of input VAT. They are not liable to VAT at the zero rate but the effect is similar.

- goods supplied to foreign countries and to Svalbard and Jan Mayen
- goods for use in sea areas outside Norwegian territorial waters, in connection with the exploration and exploitation of submarine resources
- goods supplied to foreign ships and aircraft
- goods supplied to Norwegian ships over a certain limit and aircraft used in international transport
- services to foreign ships and aircraft
- services to Norwegian ships over a certain limit and aircraft used in international transport

- international transport services
- supply of services to non-registered suppliers of services to investments in sea-areas outside Norwegian territorial waters.

These exemptions are with credit, ie the entrepreneur is allowed a credit for the VAT imposed on him. Credit for previously paid VAT is available only to an entrepreneur engaged in trade or business. The input VAT is only deductible if it relates to purchases of goods and services for use in the registered enterprise.

It is of no consequence whether the goods are new or used.

The following goods and services which are normally taxable are treated as being exempt with credit when supplied in Norway:

- supplies of goods in a free port, provided the goods are not intended for use in the free port
- supplies of goods to or for use or trade on board a ship or airplane in international service
- supplies of beer, wine, spirits and tobacco products for sale in a tax-free shop
- advertising or other publicity services on behalf of a foreign client
- transport of goods directly to or from a foreign country.

7.2   Exemptions without Credit for Input Tax
The following services are exempt without credit for input tax:

- renting of real property
- passenger transportation
- banking, financial and insurance services
- education
- health services
- legal, auditing and book-keeping services.

7.3   Transactions Outside the Scope of VAT
The main transactions which are outside the scope of VAT are:

- works of visual art when the artist himself or his estate is the seller
- products for personal use at importation
- postage stamps
- showing of motion picture films
- medical services.

7.4   Election to be Subject to VAT
A person supplying the following exempt services may elect for voluntary registration within regulations issued by the Ministry of Finance:

- commercial agents
- shipbrokers
- bookkeeping and public accounting firms
- news agencies
- shipping and airline companies

- lessors of agricultural property
- private planning consultants
- lessors of buildings and plant used by VAT-liable lessees.
- soil and ground testing activities
- marine positioning activities

Through voluntary registration suppliers can obtain the right to deduct input VAT on purchases made for their activities, but they are then subject to the rules governing IT (see section 11 'Investment tax'). Furthermore, VAT becomes chargeable on the relevant services supplied by the voluntarily registered supplier even though, normally, such services are not chargeable to VAT under the Act.

8 CREDIT/REFUND FOR INPUT VAT

8.1 General Rule
An entrepreneur who is liable to account for VAT is entitled to claim a deduction in his tax return for VAT paid on acquisitions and imports for the purpose of his taxable business. The right to deduction is essentially general in nature, that is, it covers all types of acquisitions with a few exceptions.

No credit is allowed for VAT suffered on the following:

- meals, food and drink and other benefits for use by the owner or his employees
- housing, accommodation and recreational purposes
- entertainment, gifts and handouts for advertising purposes (with a threshold of NOK50)
- costs of acquisition and running expenses of passenger vehicles – without regard to the use to which the vehicles are put. The only exemption is passenger cars used in rental services.

8.2 Adjustment of Entitlement to Credit
There are no special rules with regard to the review of apportioned input credits in respect of capital goods as provided for in Article 20(2) of the Sixth VAT Directive of the European Union.

8.3 Partial Exemption
Where part of the turnover consists of supplies which are not liable to VAT, the input tax attributable to purchases which are used for the purposes of the non-taxable activities may not be claimed.

VAT paid on purchases which are used for the purposes both of taxable and exempt supplies must be apportioned so as to reflect the supplies which carry the right to input credit and those which do not.

8.4 Time of Recovery
A taxable person is entitled to recovery of input tax (subject to the rules of entitlement outlined above) when he has a valid VAT invoice or stamped customs entry. It is not necessary for him to have paid for the goods or for the supplier to have paid the output tax to the authorities.

The claim to input tax credit should be made in the VAT return for the period in which the invoice or import documents are issued.

8.5   *Refund for Foreign Entrepreneurs*

Norwegian VAT suffered by foreign entrepreneurs who do not make taxable supplies in Norway cannot be recovered.

9   ADMINISTRATIVE OBLIGATIONS

9.1   *Registration*

All taxable enterprises which supply taxable goods or services have to register at the regional tax office when their turnover exceeds NOK30,000 in a 12-month period. For charitable and non-profit institutions and organisations the limit is NOK70,000.

Entry in the VAT register is made by notifying, on a specially prescribed form, the County Tax Office in the county in which the enterprise has its permanent place of business.

When an enterprise is entered in the VAT register, it is obliged to collect and remit VAT, and is entitled to deduct input VAT.

Voluntary registration (ie electing to be subject to VAT services which are otherwise exempt) is also possible (see section 7.4).

9.2   *Books and Records*

The VAT Act requires registered enterprises to organise their bookkeeping in such a manner that the VAT authorities may at any time check sales, withdrawals (if any), purchases, output and input VAT and the accuracy of the VAT calculation.

Regulations relating to the keeping of accounts were issued by the Director of Taxes on 20 August 1969 with amendments on 15 December 1977.

9.3   *Invoices*

Regulations relating to the contents of sales documents, etc which are to serve as evidence for the calculation and collection of VAT were issued on 14 October 1969 by the Ministry of Finance.

VAT registered persons must always issue a written sales document (ie a note, invoice or bill) when selling goods and services to other VAT registered persons. A contract note or other voucher issued by a purchaser may also be regarded as evidence of sale. Sales documents must include the following information:

■   invoice number and date
■   name and address of both seller and buyer
■   VAT registration number of the seller
■   clear description of the goods or services supplied
■   price.

It must be produced in duplicate and one copy must be kept by the supplier.

For sales between registered persons, sales documents must indicate the price excluding VAT and the VAT amount separately ('open invoicing'). If sales documents cover both taxable and non-taxable sales, the figures relating to the taxable sales must be shown and summarised separately.

A non-VAT registered person may not show a VAT amount on his sales document.

All books of accounts kept by a taxable person, together with vouchers, notes, contracts, correspondence, invoices and other account documents, must be retained for at least ten years.

9.4   VAT Returns

All VAT registered suppliers must submit a sales and turnover return ('omsetningsopp-gave') to the County Tax Office for each VAT period. The return must be made on a special form and contain details of total supplies (and withdrawals, if any) in the VAT period, a calculation of the output VAT, deductible input VAT, and shall state the difference between the output and input VAT amounts. Supplies of VAT exempt goods and services must also be shown.

The figures must normally be based on the invoicing principle, ie both output and input VAT must be included in the return for the VAT period during which the supply or purchase was invoiced by or to the taxable person. The accounting records of the taxable person must be arranged accordingly (accounting basis). Advance or part payments shall be included in accordance with special regulations issued by the Ministry of Finance on 9 September 1974.

If deductible input VAT in any one VAT period exceeds payable output VAT, the excess is refunded by the taxation authorities to the taxable entity.

A claim for refund automatically arises when the tax return shows a negative VAT amount. The claim need not, therefore, be submitted separately. If the refundable VAT amount regularly exceeds the VAT liability on supplies by more than 25%, the administration may shorten the VAT period to one month. If the refundable VAT regularly exceeds VAT on supplies by more then 50%, the tax administration may shorten the VAT period further, but never to less than one week.

The Act requires that the taxation authorities ensure that refunds are made within three weeks of the receipt of the tax return. The taxable person is entitled to interest on any overdue refund.

If no refund has been made within the three-week time limit, the taxable person is entitled to deduct the refundable amount in its subsequent returns.

As the final date for submitting the tax return is one month and ten days from the end of the VAT period, one month and ten days plus a further twenty-one days may thus pass before a refund takes place. In any case, the enterprise may shorten the refund period by submitting its return as early as possible after the end of the VAT period.

9.5   Powers of the Authorities

VAT is administered in each county by the County Tax Office ('fylkesskattekontoret'). The office conducts the day-to-day administration and control of the tax system and makes decisions in the first instance where authority has not expressly been vested in others. The County Tax Office also maintains the VAT register.

The central administration of the tax system lies with the Tax Directorate ('Skattedirektoratet') in Oslo.

Appeals over decisions made by the County Tax Office lie with the Tax Directorate. The time limit for submitting appeals is three weeks from the date the decision is communicated to the person or company in question.

If the Tax Directorate has made the decision in the first instance, the appeal lies with the Ministry for Finance.

The Customs and Excise authorities collect the VAT on imports of goods and services and function as a tax authority of first instance. Decisions made by the customs authorities may be appealed against to the Customs and Excise Directorate ('Toll- og Avgiftsdirektoratet') in Oslo within the same three weeks time limit.

A special Appeals Board (the VAT Board of Appeals) has been established to deal with certain appeals, such as where VAT has been arbitrarily assessed because returns have not been filed ('omsetningsoppgave' – Chapter XIII of the Act). The Board is appointed by the Ministry for Finance who has power to reverse the Board's decision.

9.6   Penalties

Any person who wilfully gives wrong or insufficient information in a tax return or in any other form of information given to the tax authorities and, by those means, withholds tax or obtains an incorrect deduction for input tax, is punishable by fines or imprisonment according to the provisions of the Act of Punishment.

Any person who wilfully fails to register or to file returns when required to do so, or who violates the regulations concerning bookkeeping, accounting and information, is liable to fines or imprisonment for a period of up to three months. The same applies to violations of the regulations issued under the VAT Act. If the intention was to withhold tax or to obtain an incorrect deduction, the punishment may be imprisonment for a period up to three years, as well as fines; accessories to a wrongdoing are liable to the same punishment.

If violations of the Act occur through negligence, the taxpayer is only liable to a fine.

These provisions apply where the offence is not covered by more stringent penal provisions.

Any person who wilfully or negligently contravenes the Act or any regulations issued pursuant to the VAT Act, with the result that the Treasury has been or could have been deprived of tax, may be ordered to pay an additional tax of up to 100% over and above the tax assessed according to the procedure for discretionary assessment. Such an order may be made up to ten years after the expiry of the period in question.

If payment is not made on the due date, interest is due on the delayed tax at 1.75% per month or part of a month until the tax is paid. Very often the interest will be as large as the additional tax, especially when the assessment covers a long period of time. Interest of less than NOK100 can be ignored.

When VAT returns have not been rendered in time or in the prescribed form, a demand for the net VAT due for the period(s) concerned may be issued by the authorities. This assessment may be made up to three years after the expiration of the period concerned.

Even though a return has been rendered in time and in the prescribed form, an assessment for additional VAT may be issued by the authorities for the three preceding periods if the account books, etc have not been submitted, made available, or sent, upon request, to the tax authorities.

10   SPECIAL REGIMES

10.1   Non-Profit Organisations
Special rules apply to charitable and non-profit organisations if they make taxable supplies.

The limit for VAT registration of charitable and non-profit institutions and organisations is NOK70,000. No VAT shall be paid on services rendered free of charge by an individual directly to charitable and non-profit institutions and organisations. Charitable and non profit institutions and organisations which provide advertisements in their own publications are VAT exempted for this activity, provided that they do not publish more than four publications containing advertisement sections annually. When charitable and non-profit institutions and organisations demand a very large profit on sales, output tax should not be calculated on that part of the remuneration which exceeds the ordinary sales value. Charitable and non-profit institutions and organisations with a gross turnover not exceeding NOK200,000 in a 12-month period are entitled, on application, to file one VAT return annually.

10.2   Agents
Agents who do not own the goods and services they supply are not mentioned in the Act as being liable to taxation. An agent may, however, apply for voluntary registration. If the agent does not only bring together a supplier and buyer, but also sells goods on his own account, he is liable to taxation for this business activity.

A commission agent – a person who acts in his own name on behalf of a third person in the supply of goods – is liable to registration. Both the commission agent and the principal are considered as independent persons for the VAT liability and sales on commission are considered as sales by both the principal and the commission agent.

10.3   Auctioneers
Auctioneers are liable to register and account for VAT under the normal rules. Output tax is due on the selling price and no credit is given as usually no input tax is paid. If, however, the seller of the goods is registered, input tax will be paid by the auctioneer and credit will be given for the tax thus paid. In other words, the owner and the auctioneer are treated for VAT purposes as though the owner sells the goods to the auctioneer. Sales by auction in execution of a legal judgment are not subject to VAT.

10.4   Small Entrepreneurs
If turnover in a 12-month period does not exceed the registration limit of NOK30,000 the entrepreneur need not be registered. Voluntary registration is not possible for such small entrepreneurs.

11   INVESTMENT TAX (IT)

11.1   Introduction
The special tax on investments, etc was introduced on 1 January 1970 in conjunction with the VAT system. It is levied on durable items of business equipment and is payable by entrepreneurs which are registered under the VAT Act. Investment Tax does not carry any right of deduction and is therefore finally borne by the enterprises.

11.2   The Tax Rate
The rate of IT is stipulated annually by the Parliament in connection with the annual budget. The rate is at present 7%. Enterprises engaged in industrial manufacturing and mining are zero-rated. The zero rate also applies to certain kinds of business equipment which the owner uses in industrial manufacturing and mining.

11.3   Entrepreneurs Liable to IT
Only entrepreneurs which must be registered under the VAT Act and those voluntarily registered, are liable to IT. However, although such enterprises as banks and insurance companies are not liable to IT, they must pay VAT on all VAT-liable purchases, without being entitled to deduct input VAT.

11.4   Items Subject to IT
The tax is levied on purchases of and work on durable business equipment for use in VAT-liable activities. A number of detailed regulations apply to IT as a result of its close connection with the VAT Act.

IT is chargeable on goods purchased by the enterprise for use as business equipment and for use in the manufacture of such equipment, provided that the enterprise is entitled to deduct the input VAT on such purchases. It is also chargeable on goods which the business itself manufactures for the same purpose.

11.5   Imports
Goods imported as business equipment are subject to IT to the same extent as domestic purchases. IT is calculated on the customs value.

Equipment rented from abroad is IT-liable. This ensures equal treatment with domestic suppliers of business equipment for rental.

Where certain services are imported into Norway for business use, the importer must account for Norwegian IT. Such services relate to work on business equipment for use in VAT-liable activities.

11.6   Use of Own Goods
IT is also levied if the entrepreneur takes into use as business equipment goods which are normally intended for sale, or for use as raw materials or semi-manufactures.

11.7   Exemptions for Non-Durable Equipment
The Act provides that non-durable equipment should be exempt from IT and the Ministry of Finance is authorised to draw the distinction between durable and non-durable equipment. Under the regulations of 18 November 1969 (No.10), the following have been exempted from IT:

- fuel, electric power, gas and water
- motor fuel (but not petrol), lubricating oil and lubrication grease
- soap, detergents and cleaning agents
- advertising material for use abroad
- goods intended for sale which in accordance with trade custom are taken into use as samples or for demonstration purposes and which thereafter are returned to store to be sold in the normal course of business.

For enterprises engaged in the manufacturing industry or in work on goods and real property, including buildings and plants, the IT exemption is more extensive. Such enterprises are not liable to IT in respect of goods used as non-durable business equipment in the production of goods for sale or for use in the enterprise itself, or in respect of work on goods, real property, buildings or plant for others.

The regulations define 'non-durable' equipment as goods normally consumed or considerably depreciated by being used once or a few times in the course of normal manufacturing operations or during work on goods, etc. This means that business equipment consumed in the course of manufacturing, the processing of goods, or construction activities is IT-free.

Repairs, maintenance and cleaning of an entrepreneur's business performed by his own employees, is not liable to IT. However, materials, etc consumed during the work are IT-liable.

11.8 Basis for Calculations of IT
The main rule is that IT is levied on the purchase price excluding VAT. The taxable value is therefore the same as for VAT purposes. Freight, customs value, taxes other than VAT and other delivery costs must be included.

11.9 Refund of IT on Re-Export
On 27 July 1970 the Ministry of Finance issued regulations regarding the refund of IT on the re-export of equipment imported for hire or loan. The enterprise may claim a refund of the IT charged upon import, less 5% for each month or part thereof. Thus, no refund may be claimed after 20 months. The claim for refund is included in the return for the tax period during which the equipment is re-exported.

No refund of IT may be claimed on the re-export of taxable objects other than those which have been hired or borrowed from abroad.

12   FURTHER READING

Thor Refsland, *Merverdiavgiftsloven Del I*
Thor Refsland, *Merverdiavgiftsloven Del II*
Thor Refsland, *Investeringsavgiften*
Thor Refsland, *Praktisk merverdiavgift og investeringsavgift*
Ole Gjems Onstad and Tor S. Kildal, *Merverdiavgift for næringsdrivende.*

Contributor: Eivind Bryne
Ernst & Young
Tullins Gate 2.
P.O Box 6834
St Olavs Plass
N- 0130 Oslo
Norway
Tel: +47 22 03 60 00
Fax: +47 22 11 00 95

POLAND

1 GENERAL BACKGROUND

Poland introduced value added tax on 5 July 1993 through the Act on Goods and Services Tax and Excise Tax of January 1993. Further amendments were introduced on 1 January 1994 and as of 1 and 16 January 1995, and legislation has been supplemented by a number of decrees issued by the Minister of Finance. Although the full name of the tax is the Tax on Goods and Services ('Podatek od towarów i us_ug'), the abbreviation 'VAT' is commonly used.

VAT is administered by the tax authorities with the exception of VAT levied on imports which is collected by the Customs authorities. VAT replaced the old Turnover Tax.

2 WHO IS TAXABLE?

Taxable persons are: legal persons, entities without legal personality and natural persons:

- whose registered office or place of domicile is in the territory of the Republic of Poland and who carry out taxable activities on their own behalf and on their own account in circumstances which indicate their intention to carry them out on a regular basis, even if they have been performed only once, as well as where they consist of a single transaction of sale of anything specifically acquired for that purpose, or
- who carry out brokerage services, services arising from the management of investment trust funds, services provided under agency contracts, order contracts and contracts of sale on commission, and similar services, or
- who are obliged to pay customs duty on the basis of separate regulations, irrespective of whether the goods are exempt from customs duty or whether the duty has been suspended, or
- whose registered office, place of domicile or place of residence is located abroad, but they carry out taxable activities in Poland in person, through an authorised agent, through employees, or by means of a permanent establishment or vehicle set up for production, commerce or services, or
- who are recipients of imported taxable services.

In general, a person who makes an occasional transaction is not liable to VAT. Employees are outside the scope of VAT. There is an exemption from VAT payments granted in 1995 for taxpayers whose turnover in 1994 did not exceed PLN80,000 [1]. This turnover limit is to be amended every year to account for inflation.

This chapter reflects the legislation on value added tax in Poland as at 16 January 1995.

[1] There was a change in Polish currency on 1 January 1994. Thus PLN1 (new Zloty) = PLZ10,000 (old Zloty). All examples in this chapter are shown in new Zlotys.

Any person who provides taxable services or sells taxable goods and who is not exempt from VAT should register and account for VAT.

2.1   Transactions with a Branch/Subsidiary

No special regulations apply to transactions between a branch and its foreign head office. They are considered to be two independent taxpayers and therefore supplies between them are subject to VAT.

2.2   Government Bodies

State and local authorities do not carry out taxable activities and therefore cannot create any output VAT. Their purchases are burdened with VAT. State and local authorities are liable to VAT at the point of importation in respect of goods imported by them. However, a customs and VAT exemption applies to goods imported by the State sector provided that the goods in question are designated for their statutory use and were obtained by them free of charge.

2.3   Fiscal Entity

The concept of a fiscal entity does not exist in Poland.

2.4   Foreign Entrepreneurs

Foreign entrepreneurs with no establishment in Poland may be liable to VAT if they perform taxable activity within Polish territory. Such entrepreneurs may register for VAT at the appropriate tax office and will then be treated in the same way as any other VAT taxpayer. The possibility of registration is currently being reviewed by the tax authorities.

2.5   Representative Office

Representative offices of foreign entrepreneurs are not regarded as liable to VAT if they only carry out activities of a preparatory or auxiliary nature. Gaining a refund of input VAT incurred by representative offices is, therefore, not possible. However, if a representative office carries out services other than of a preparatory or auxiliary nature on the basis of a permit granted by the Polish authorities, it may register for VAT purposes and obtain VAT refunds.

2.6   VAT Representatives

The concept of a VAT representative does not exist in Poland.

2.7   Reverse Charge Mechanism

If services are provided in Poland by a foreign entity which is not a registered VAT taxpayer in Poland, then the obligation to pay the VAT falls on the recipient of the service. The VAT paid on the 'imported service' is treated as output VAT and is not recoverable but may be treated as a cost for Corporate Tax purposes.

2.8   Importers

The VAT on imports becomes due when goods are imported into Poland and are finally cleared by the Customs authorities. The tax obligation rests with the importer.

3   WHAT IS TAXABLE?

The supply of goods and services in Poland is taxable. The import and export of goods and services is also subject to taxation, although exports are generally taxed at the zero rate.

3.1   Supply of Goods
The following activities are treated as taxable supplies of goods:

- the sale of goods
- the giving over of goods for advertising and representation purposes
- the giving over of goods for the taxpayer's own use, or the use of partners, shareholders, members of co-operatives, employees and former employees, members of associations, members of legislative bodies and corporate bodies, and the taxpayer's employees and former employees, or other kinds of donations
- the exchange of goods, including the exchange of services for goods and goods for services
- giving over of the goods as a form of debt settlement
- giving over of the goods as a substitute for cash payment
- preparing a compulsory stock-take of goods and products processed by a natural person at the moment of termination of his/her economic activity or by a company without legal personality at the moment of dissolving the company.

Several groups of goods are exempt from VAT, including low-processed foodstuffs, agricultural products, animal husbandry and certain imported goods.

The term 'goods' includes not only goods but also all forms of energy, houses, buildings and parts of buildings.

3.2   Mixed Transactions
The Polish VAT regulations do not include special provisions for mixed transactions.

3.3   Supply of Services
The supply of the following services is subject to VAT:

- the rendering of services for payment
- services rendered for advertising and representation purposes
- services rendered for the taxpayer's own use, or the use of partners, shareholders, members of co-operatives, employees and former employees, members of associations, members of legislative bodies and corporate bodies and the taxpayer's employees and former employees
- the exchange of services, including the exchange of services for goods and goods for services
- services rendered free of charge
- performing services as a form of a debt settlement
- rendering the services as a substitute for cash payment.

Certain groups of services are exempt from VAT, eg agricultural services, forestry services, inspection of water, air and soil, municipal services (with a few exceptions), services in the field of State administration, services in the field of finance and insurance, services in the field of culture and arts, education and sport, etc.

3.4   Self-Supplies of Goods/Services

There is a self-supply of goods when a person diverts to private or exempt use any goods which he has imported, purchased, manufactured or otherwise acquired and in respect of which he is entitled to a VAT deduction.

Polish VAT regulations consider as a self-supply of goods and services, goods and services given over for the purposes of representation or advertising or for the taxpayer's own use or that of partners, shareholders, fellow-members of co-operative associations and their families, members of boards of companies, members of associations, and employees and former employees. This is the only instance of a self-supply of goods and services provided for in the Polish VAT law.

3.5   Import of Goods

By the term 'import of goods' the Polish VAT Law refers to the delivery of goods from abroad, irrespective of how they are introduced into Polish customs territory. Basically, the import of goods is VAT-liable irrespective of the status of the importer. The VAT obligation arises with the final customs clearance. Goods imported into a bonded warehouse or duty-free zone are not liable to VAT.

The basis of assessment of VAT on imported goods is the customs value of the goods increased by the customs duty due, 6% import tax and excise tax (where applicable).

4   PLACE OF SUPPLY

4.1   Supply of Goods

The place where goods are supplied is deemed for the purposes of VAT to be the place where the goods are located at the time of the supply.

4.1.1 Chain Transactions

Where several persons are involved in the sale of the same goods in such a way that one person dispatches the goods directly to the final recipient, but in reality the transaction passes through more persons, each party actually involved in the sale will be deemed to have made a sale and is therefore liable for VAT.

4.2   Supply of Services

The general rule is that the place where services are deemed to be supplied for VAT purposes is the place where they are actually rendered.

4.3   Reverse Charge Mechanism

The place of supply of imported services is generally the place where the recipient of the services has his business. This gives rise to the 'reverse charge' concept in that the recipient is held to be liable to VAT on the value of the services he has received. The VAT paid on such services is not deductible. The only exception is services which are exempt from VAT due to their particular nature.

The exemption given to certain entities due to the character of their particular business does not apply in this case.

5 BASIS OF TAXATION

5.1 Supplies within Poland

Where the consideration takes the form of money, the amount on which VAT is chargeable is normally the amount due from the sale of goods or services reduced by the amount of tax. Where advances, prepayments or instalments have been collected, turnover also includes the amount of the advances, prepayments or instalments received, reduced by the tax in respect of them.

Where goods or services are supplied and the consideration does not consist of or does not consist wholly of an amount of money, and where certain goods are supplied free of charge, the amount on which tax is chargeable is the value of goods and services calculated on the basis of prices used in trade with the main customer or, if there is no main customer, the average prices prevailing in the given locality on the date when the transaction took place, reduced by tax. The amount due encompasses the total value of the goods in question due from the buyer.

The above principle applies to the goods and services given over to the taxpayer's own use, given over for the purposes of representation and advertising as well as donations of goods, exchanges of goods, exchanges of services, exchanges of services for goods and goods for services.

The principle also applies to the giving over of goods and performing of services as a form of debt settlement, or as a substitute for cash payment or to preparing a compulsory stock-take of goods and products proposed by a natural person at the moment of stopping his/her economic activity or by a company without legal personality at the moment of dissolving the company.

5.2 Self-Supplies

The self-supply of goods is liable to VAT. The basis of assessment is the price used in trade with the main customer, or the average market price if there is no main customer.

5.3 Importations

The value of imported goods for the purposes of VAT is the value specified in the SAD (customs clearance) document, ie the value for customs purposes increased by customs duty due, import tax and excise tax (when applicable).

Import tax is currently equal to 6% of the customs value increased by the customs duty due. Excise tax is calculated on the basis of the customs value increased by the customs duty at the basic rate and import tax. However, goods imported into a bonded warehouse are not subject to VAT.

5.4 Chargeable Event/Time of Payment

Liability to VAT arises when taxable goods are released (supplied), delivered, exchanged or donated, or taxable services are rendered. In particular:

- If the sale of goods or rendering of services has to be proved by an invoice, the tax obligation arises when the invoice is issued, and in any event not later than seven days after the delivery of the goods or rendering of the service.
- In the case of the export of goods, the tax obligation arises when the border Customs

office confirms that the goods have left Polish Customs territory. In the case of the import of goods, the tax obligation arises when the goods have been admitted for trade in Polish Customs territory as defined by the Customs Law.

■   Where payment of at least 50% of the price has been made as an advance prepayment or instalment before the goods are delivered or the service rendered, the tax obligation relating to the amount paid arises at the time of the receipt of payment.

■   In the case of goods and passenger transport by car, train, plane, ship or boat, shipping and trans-shipping services, sea and commercial harbour services as well as building and assembling services, liability to tax arises at the moment of receiving full or part payment, but in any case not later than 30 days after the services were rendered.

■   The liability to tax on imported services arises at the moment of making full or part payment, but in any case no later than 30 days after the services were rendered.

■   The liability to tax on leasing, rental or similar services in Poland arises at the moment of receiving full or part payment, but in any case no later than the date payment is due.

■   The liability for tax on the delivery of energy, gas, communication and radio-communication services arises when the payment falls due.

■   The liability for tax on the press and the sale of books occurs at the moment of the receipt of payment or after issuing the final invoice which takes into account the returns.

■   The liability for tax on exportation of services occurs when the payment or part payment is received.

■   The tax obligation on tourist services occurs when the invoice or simplified bill is issued but in any case no later than 15 days after the service has been rendered.

■   The tax obligation on some kinds of scrap occurs when whole or part payment is made but in any case no later than 20 (or in some cases 30) days after the scrap is dispatched.

5.5 *Invoices*

VAT due must normally be accounted on the basis of invoices issued in the appropriate period. Issuing an invoice gives rise to a VAT obligation whether or not the invoice has been issued correctly. If, by mistake, a VAT-exempt entity issues a VAT invoice, it is obliged to pay the VAT included on the invoice.

5.6 *Correcting Invoices/Bills*

When a change in price occurs after the goods have been released and the invoice has been issued, a correcting invoice should be issued which includes the amount of the price difference and, in particular, the decrease or increase in VAT due. Correcting invoices are treated in the same way as a regular invoice for the purposes of VAT settlement.

6   TAX RATES

6.1 *Rates*

Currently, there are three rates of VAT:

0%:   – export of goods
      – services related to the export of goods such as packing, storage, loading, unloading, controlling, weighing, supervising the security of transport, etc
      – services rendered on the basis of agency, and broker's commission or similar

agreements relating to exported goods
- building, technological and urban planning services, consultancy services, notarial and solicitors' services if rendered on behalf of foreign business entities
- basic and supplementary medicines, goods sold to customs-free zones in airports or sea and river harbour border crossings
- international transport
- newspapers and books (certain conditions apply until 31 December 1995)
- various other goods and services.

7%: – goods connected with agriculture and forestry, such as certain machinery and equipment, fertilisers and foodstuffs
- goods connected with health care, such as medical materials, optical glass, hearing aids
- food (unless VAT exempt)
- selected children's goods (baby wear, children's wear, children's shoes, cosmetics for children, school stationery)
- musical instruments and accessories, music, maps, press publications, books
- road and bridge building and maintenance, personal transport services, telecommunication and radio-communication services, tourist services, catering services (except for the sale of alcohol, tea and coffee)
- electricity and heating services, gas, gas fuels and heating oils
- some building materials and building services.

22%: all other goods and services.

7   EXEMPTIONS

7.1   Exemption with Credit for Input Tax (Zero Rate)
Generally, only input VAT incurred on the purchase of goods and services attributable to taxable supplies (including those which are zero-rated) may be fully recovered by the taxpayer. However, as an exception, the purchase of certain goods (primarily machines and equipment for the food industry) attributable to VAT-exempt supplies carries an entitlement to recover input VAT paid.

7.2   Exemption without Credit for Input Tax
The supply of certain goods and services is exempt from VAT. Input VAT incurred on purchases relating to the supply of VAT-exempt goods and services is not recoverable.

VAT-exempt goods and services include:

- products of animal husbandry
- certain low-processed agricultural products (meat, dairy produce, etc)
- folk and artistic handicrafts
- products of forestry and hunting
- agricultural services
- forestry services
- Post Office services
- inspection of water, sewage, air and soil, testing and measuring services
- certain municipal services

- housing services
- services in the field of science and technology
- services in the field of education
- services in the field of culture and the arts
- services in the field of health and social welfare
- services in the field of physical education and sport
- services in the field of State administration, local government, administration of justice, national defence and public security, excluding advocate's services and notarial services
- financial and insurance services, excluding the sale and purchase of foreign currency, leasing services and insurance brokerage services
- services rendered by political organisations, trade unions and other self-governing organisations created by legislation
- television and film services (excluding advertising services)
- services relating to holidays and gratuitous incidental services rendered by an employer to their employees or employees' families
- meals sold in milk bars, and in canteens and snack bars attached to institutions (provided the canteen or snack bar is not open to the general public)
- regenerative and preventive meals
- financial services relating to securities performed by stockbrokers and institutions managing investment funds
- import of telecommunication services
- the resale of used goods by the user, and the donation of such goods, on condition that the goods neither are nor have been part of the assets of the user's business activity
- certain services financed by money obtained from abroad as a result of the initiatives of foreign governments or international organisations.

7.3   Exempt Imports
Certain imports are exempt from VAT, such as the personal effects of travellers, temporary imports of goods other than capital assets, goods donated by international organisations or foreign governments, and personal goods imported by a person taking up permanent residence in Poland. A number of varying restrictions and qualifications apply to the import of these items.

7.4   Transactions Outside the Scope of Polish VAT or Non-Taxable

7.4.1 Transactions within the Same Legal Entity
Transactions within the same legal entity are not taxable when the branch and its head office are located within Polish territory. However, branches of legal entities which prepare separate balance sheets may also be VAT taxpayers, subject to the agreement of the tax office. Cross-border transactions between branches of the same legal entity are subject to VAT.

7.4.2 Transfer of Business
The sale of a business or its coherent parts is outside the scope of VAT.

7.4.3 Gaming
Gaming is not subject to VAT if it is subject to gaming tax on the basis of separate legislation.

7.4.4 Illegal Activities
No VAT liability arises from activities which cannot be the subject of a legally binding contract.

7.4.5 Land/Intangible Property Rights
The transfer of land or intangible and legal assets (eg copyrights, contractual rights) is outside the scope of VAT.

7.5 Election to be Subject to VAT
The following persons (entities) are not obliged to register for VAT but may choose to do so:

- persons whose turnover did not exceed PLN80,000 in the previous fiscal year
- persons who pay income tax in a lump sum in accordance with the relevant legislation
- persons who commence taxable activity, provided the declared value of their turnover during the fiscal year does not exceed PLN80,000 proportionally to the period of carrying out sales.

In general, any Polish entity may register for VAT.

8 CREDIT/REFUND FOR INPUT VAT

8.1 General Rule
The taxpayer has the right to deduct input tax which was imposed when goods and services were purchased from the amount of output tax due.

The following conditions should be met in order to make a deduction:

- the registered person must have a proper VAT invoice, a correcting VAT invoice or a stamped copy of a Customs clearance document (SAD). Simplified bills do not give the right to deduct any VAT included on them
- the reduction of output tax should take place either in the month in which the taxpayer received the invoice or Customs clearance document or in the following month.

If the taxpayer did not carry out any taxable activity during a specified month, the input tax for such period is accounted for in the next period in which taxable activity is undertaken, but cannot be later than 36 months from the end of the month in which the taxpayer received the invoice or Customs documents.

8.2 Exceptions
Generally, registered taxpayers whose activities are tax exempt are entitled to recover input tax if they purchase or import specified goods used for exempt activities such as:

- slaughter machinery
- machinery used for milk processing
- new buses, trolley buses, trams and subway cars used in city transportation.

Under certain very limited conditions, the refund of input tax paid on the purchase of investment goods charged with the standard VAT rate may be made before the tax obligation arises in the form of an advance payment (see section 10.2).

In general, the deduction or refund of tax differences does not apply to purchases by a taxpayer of:

■ goods and services for manufacturing or the resale of goods or the provision of services which are exempt from tax
■ personal cars and their component parts, unless their onward sale is a normal part of the taxpayer's business, or if the purchaser buys parts in order to manufacture personal cars or to perform repairs or service such cars
■ goods and services which are used in such a way as to preclude the expenditure from being treated as a cost of gaining income as defined by corporate tax law
■ goods and services for which the purchase:

– was documented with a simplified bill or incorrectly submitted invoice
– was made due to a donation or non-payable delivery of services.

The reduction of output tax or the refund of tax differences does not apply to taxpayers who have not registered or who have been removed from the register.

8.3   Partial Exemptions

A taxpayer who sells both goods which are subject to tax and goods which are exempt is obliged to record separately the input tax paid in respect of taxable sales and exempt sales.

The taxpayer may deduct only input tax related to taxable supplies from the amount of tax due on such supplies. If it is not possible to wholly or partially separate these sums, the taxpayer may subtract from the output tax due that part of input tax paid which corresponds to the value of the sale of taxable goods as a percentage of total sales.

8.4   Credits and Returns

If the amount of input tax is higher than the amount of output tax in the settlement period, the taxpayer has the right to reduce the tax due for the following periods accordingly.

If the whole or part of a taxpayer's sale is taxed at rates lower than the standard rate the difference should be returned by the tax office. However, if the amount of input tax exceeds 22% of the total turnover taxed at these rates, the tax office may limit the refund due in a given month to this lower amount. The period of this limitation cannot exceed three months.

If all sales are taxed at the standard rate, the amount of the returned difference shall not exceed the value of input tax in respect of the purchase of goods and services which became part of the taxpayer's fixed assets and intangible and legal assets which are subject to depreciation.

8.5   Time Limit and Method of Refund

The refunded tax difference shall be paid into the taxpayer's bank account within 25 days from the date when the taxpayer submits his declaration. This declaration should be submitted before the twenty-fifth day of the month following the month in which the situation necessitating the refund arose. On the special request of the taxpayer, the tax office is obliged to refund the tax difference within 15 days from the date of submitting the VAT declaration, so long as the taxpayer has settled all his/her tax obligations on time during the last 12 months.

8.6   Refund to Foreign Businesses

VAT refunds in Poland are only applicable to taxpayers registered in Poland for VAT purposes.

8.7   Purchases Financed from International Sources

The taxpayer who purchases (imports) goods using money obtained from foreign aid (including the initiatives of foreign governments or international organisations) is entitled to apply for a refund of input tax paid on such purchases.

9   ADMINISTRATIVE OBLIGATIONS

9.1   Registration

Generally, any entity performing taxable activities within Poland, whether Polish or foreign, is a taxpayer and therefore is liable to register for VAT. The only exceptions to this are where an entity performs sales of exclusively VAT-exempt goods or where, because of its level of turnover in the previous tax year, the entity does not exercise its option to elect to register for VAT (the current turnover threshold is PLN80,000).

A VAT registration form should be submitted to the appropriate tax office (determined by the district in which taxable activities are performed) at least one day before performing the first taxable activity. In practice it is advisable to make the appropriate application in advance, before the first purchase charged with VAT is made.

When a taxpayer commences taxable activities during a tax year, he may elect for exemption from VAT if the estimated value of his sales does not exceed the specified threshold level, proportional to the period of carrying out sales. If a taxpayer chooses exemption and then his sales exceed the threshold amount, the exemption is annulled at the moment when the threshold is exceeded and the VAT obligation arises on the amount exceeding the threshold.

Registration will be cancelled if the taxpayer stops performing taxable activities, becomes insolvent or ceases to exist. The taxpayer is obliged to inform the tax office of such events.

Subject to the agreement of the tax office, branches or divisions of the same legal entities which prepare separate balance sheets may register for VAT separately.

An entity who is obliged to register but does not do so, does not avoid a liability to VAT even when VAT has not been charged to its customers.

9.2   Books and Records

Taxpayers, other than those exempt from tax or those carrying out exclusively VAT-exempt activities, are obliged to keep full records containing the essential information for describing the entity, subject of taxation, basis of assessment of VAT, amounts of output and input tax, amounts of tax which should be paid or refunded, and other information necessary to draw up a proper tax declaration. These records must be kept for a period of five years.

Penalties may be imposed if the taxpayer fails to keep appropriate records and, as a result:

- if the subject and basis of assessment cannot be described, the tax authorities will estimate the value of unrecorded sales, impose tax at the 22% rate and increase the amount of estimated tax by 100%

■ if the value of input tax paid is overestimated, the amount of output tax is increased by three times the overestimation.

Taxpayers exempt from VAT are obliged to record sales for a given day before any sales are undertaken on the following day. If it is ascertained that a taxpayer does not record a sale in the appropriate way, or records it negligently, the value of his sales may be estimated by the tax authorities and taxed at 22%, without the right to deduct any input VAT.

9.3   Invoices
An incorrectly drawn-up invoice deprives the recipient of the right to deduct input VAT. VAT invoices can be issued only by VAT-registered taxpayers who have obtained a VAT identification number and are not VAT-exempt or do not perform exclusively VAT-exempt activities.

According to Polish VAT law only the following entities are entitled to receive VAT invoices:

■ VAT-registered taxpayers who have an identification number (ie taxpayers who are entitled to issue VAT invoices)
■ purchasers of energy, gas and telecommunication services
■ purchasers of exported goods and services
■ consulates and embassies and their personnel.

A proper VAT invoice must contain:

■ the name and address of the taxpayer supplying the goods or services
■ the company stamp of the seller, unless data concerning the seller is in some other way permanently included on the invoice
■ the name and address of the taxpayer to whom the goods or services are supplied
■ the VAT registration numbers of the seller and the buyer
■ the date of issuing the invoice
■ the number of invoice and the term – 'faktura VAT'
■ the date of sale
■ a full description of the goods or services supplied
■ the individual prices of goods or services, excluding VAT
■ the rates and amounts of VAT
■ the value of sold goods or services, excluding VAT
■ the value of sold goods or services including VAT
■ the amounts due, including due VAT expressed in numbers and words
■ the full names and signatures of persons authorised to issue and receive invoices
■ a statistical code (SWW/KU) if goods or services are subject to the 7% or 0% rate or are VAT-exempt
■ the term 'orygina' or 'kopia'.

Special care should be taken when issuing VAT invoices because, if the sale is not subject to tax, or is exempt from tax, or the amount of tax given on the invoice is higher than the correct amount due, any VAT incorrectly stated is payable to the State budget and can not be recovered.

In cases where a taxpayer is not obliged to issue VAT invoices, he may issue simplified bills.

9.4   VAT Returns

Taxpayers are obliged, without being requested by the tax office, to calculate the tax due for each month by the twenty-fifth day of the month following the month in which the tax obligation arose, and to pay the due tax into the account of the appropriate tax office. Within the same period, taxpayers are obliged to submit appropriate tax declarations. The obligation to submit tax declarations does not apply to those taxpayers who are VAT-exempt or exclusively perform VAT-exempt activities, unless they are entitled to receive a refund of their input VAT.

9.5   Correction of Returns

In general, the possibility of correcting VAT declarations is not directly covered by the Polish VAT regulations. However, in practice such corrections are possible through agreement with the local tax office.

9.6   Powers of the Authorities

Tax authorities have extensive powers with regard to the inspection and seizure of records required to be kept by VAT taxpayers. During routine tax controls they usually examine a taxpayer's monthly VAT declarations, invoices issued and received, and the evidence of sales and purchases. They cannot in any way be impeded in their duties by the taxpayer or his employees during the inspection.

Tax authorities are entitled to remove the taxpayer from the register and cancel the VAT number if the taxpayer stops performing taxable activities. The tax authorities are also entitled to make assessments of the tax due when the taxpayer fails to submit monthly VAT declarations or does not correctly keep the required records.

9.7   Penalties

If the taxpayer does not keep appropriate records and, as a consequence, the subject and basis of assessment cannot be described, the unrecorded sales are taxed at 22% and the estimated tax is increased by 100%. If the input tax is overestimated the amount of output tax due is increased by three times the overestimation.

If tax declarations are not submitted to the tax office, an estimated assessment of the tax due can be made by the tax authorities, with the application of the 22% VAT rate and no right to make input tax deductions. Furthermore, the amount of output tax due will be treated as tax arrears which are subject to penal interest of 0.18% for each day of delayed payment plus a penal fee, the size of which is determined individually by the tax office.

9.8   Appeals

If a taxpayer is dissatisfied with any of the tax authority's decisions concerning VAT, he can appeal in writing against their decision within 14 days to the higher authority through the tax office who issued this decision. The taxpayer's appeals must be considered within two months. Final appeals are made to the Superior Administrative Court.

10   SPECIAL REGIMES

10.1   Cash Registers

Taxpayers who provide services, including general trading and catering, to private persons not engaged in business are obliged to keep a record of turnover and tax due by means of cash registers. Those who do not fulfil this obligation lose the right to reduce output tax by the input tax paid on acquiring goods and receiving services for the period in which a cash register is not installed.

The technical criteria which cash registers should meet are specified in separate regulations and include a fiscal memory which facilitates the permanent recording and multiple read-out of data which cannot be removed without destroying the whole mechanism. The fiscal memory should be capable of storing the relevant data for five years and should contain a mechanism preventing the records from being destroyed.

10.2   Refund of Tax Paid on the Purchase of Investment Assets before Starting Taxable Activity

Taxpayers who have made investments before commencing taxable activities may, under certain conditions, obtain a refund of input tax paid on goods treated as fixed assets and intangible legal assets which are subject to amortisation, before any tax liability arises.

These conditions are:

■   the entity is registered at the tax office and has an identification number
■   it has so far not carried out any taxable operations
■   investment purchases have already exceeded PLZ5 billion (exclusive of VAT)
■   the entity has fully settled all amounts due (ie purchase price and all taxes) in respect of the investment purchases made
■   the entity submits an invoice specifying the amount of VAT paid
■   the entity makes a statement that:

    –   it will not choose exemption from VAT from the beginning of its activities subject to VAT until three years after the year in which the investment was made
    –   it will not apply to the tax office to pay tax in a lump sum
    –   it keeps proper evidence of purchases
    –   the goods are to be used in a taxable activity
    –   the first taxable operations will not take place until six months after the first investment purchase.

The refund is made in the form of an advance and is made upon the taxpayer's application to the tax office. It is paid in two equal instalments for quarterly periods, directly into the applicant's bank account. The first instalment will be paid within 60 days of the quarter in which the application was submitted, the second within 60 days of the first instalment.

10.3   Special Methods for Calculating VAT

Taxpayers who provide services, including general trading and catering services, may calculate the amount of output tax due by reference to the value of sales multiplied (tax inclusive) by 18.03% or 6.54%. The latter rate applies to goods subject to the reduced 7% rate. The method of calculation is 'in 100'.

10.4 VAT on Expenditure for Representation and Advertising Purposes

The transfer of goods and the provision of services for representation and advertising purposes is liable to VAT in the same way as the sale of goods and services.

The VAT provisions clearly specify the scope of taxation of expenditure for representation and advertising purposes with respect to the following:

- the transfer of own goods for representation and advertising purposes
- the transfer of acquired goods for representation and advertising purposes
- the provision of own services.

Consequently, both the transfer of goods and the provision of own services for representation and advertising purposes is subject to VAT. It is not important whether the taxpayer designates self-manufactured goods or previously purchased assets for these purposes. In relation to services, the taxpayer's own services and external services purchased by him have to be clearly distinguished. Only a taxpayer's own services, rendered for representation and advertising purposes, are subject to VAT. Consequently the purchasing of 'external' services is not equivalent to rendering one's own services for representation and advertising purposes and therefore should not result in a tax obligation.

10.5 Used Goods

Polish VAT regulations define 'used goods' as goods which have been in use for at least six months and, in the case of houses and other buildings, at least five years from the end of the year when construction was completed. The resale of used goods is VAT-exempt provided that it is made by the user and that the resold goods neither are nor have been part of the assets of the user's business activity.

10.6 Personal Cars

The VAT treatment of personal cars is quite unfavourable since input VAT paid on purchases by the taxpayer of personal cars and their component parts cannot be recovered unless their onward sale is a normal part of the taxpayer's business activity or if the purchaser buys parts in order to manufacture personal cars or service such cars.

Furthermore, if a personal car is hired, rented or leased, VAT charged on the agreed instalments cannot be recovered.

10.7 Consultancy 'Expertise' Services

Consultancy services are treated very favourably by the Polish VAT regulations since under certain conditions they may be subject to the zero rate. The Polish VAT system has been rigidly based on the territorial concept according to which services effectively performed in Poland cannot benefit from the zero export rate. However, consultancy services are one of the few exceptions to this rule.

In order to benefit from this favourable treatment the following requirements have to be met:

- the services have to be provided for the benefit of a foreign party which is not a registered Polish VAT taxpayer
- the taxpayer has evidence that the service has been paid for in foreign currency and transferred to their account in a bank in Poland.

The scope of the category of 'consultancy or expertise services' is quite broad and includes financial advisory services, preparation of business plans, technical reports, quality reports, technological expert studies and cash flows.

This advantageous treatment of such services is of particular importance for service companies based in Poland, providing in the main support and development services to, and being predominantly financed by, their parent companies.

10.8 Legal and Advisory Services
Entities rendering legal and advisory services are obligatorily VAT taxpayers regardless of the value of their turnover.

Contributor: Derek Chrusciak
                  Ernst & Young
                  ul. Wspolna 62
                  00-684 Warsaw
                  Poland
                  Tel: +48 2 625 5477
                  Fax: +48 22 294263

ROMANIA

1   GENERAL BACKGROUND

Value added tax (VAT) was introduced in Romania on 1 July 1993 by Ordinance 2/1992 under the economic and financial reform programme.

Ordinance No.3/1992 stipulated that VAT should be applied from 1 January 1993 but, in Law 130/1992 the Romanian Parliament decided that the provisions of Ordinance 2/1992 should come into force on a date to be determined by a special law. This law turned out to be Law 32/1993 which provided that VAT should be applied with effect from 1 July 1993.

VAT replaces the Tax on Goods Circulation, although this tax continues to be applied to domestically produced oil and gas. Additional control is enforced through the regulations regarding excise duty on goods manufactured in or imported to Romania.

In legal terms, VAT is 'an indirect tax to be applied on the transfer of goods ownership as well as on services provided'.

It is a general tax applied at each stage of the manufacturing process on the value added by each intermediary and the final producer, as well as on the distribution up to its transfer to the final consumer. The final consumer is the only one not to be credited by the State, being subject to pay in full the VAT due for the finished item.

The Ordinance No.3/1992 was modified and supplemented by new regulations and methodological norms which clarify certain ambiguous items in the original text.

2   WHO IS TAXABLE?

2.1   *General*
The following persons are liable to VAT:

- private persons (as individuals or in associations) authorised to carry on an independent economic activity (as per Decree-Law 54/1991), or legal persons registered as economic agents (including autonomous State bodies, commercial companies, privately owned farming partnerships, profit-orientated associations and other economic agents, foreign capital companies), that supply goods deliveries or services within the territory of the country
- most legal or private persons, whether or not they are registered as economic agents, who import taxable goods or services.

Generally, private and legal persons must pay VAT on imports which are subject to custom duties, irrespective of the destination of the goods and services.

This chapter reflects the legislation on VAT in Romania as at 31 December 1994. Significant changes are expected to occur in the near future.

VAT is also due on imports which are exempt from customs duty if the VAT legislation does not provide specific exemption.

2.2   Government Bodies and Public Institutions

Public Institutions (which are legal persons according to the public law), non-profit associations, religious, political and civil organisations and trade unions are liable to VAT if they supply goods or provide services within the country, but only if they are regularly carrying on taxable transactions, either directly or through subsidiaries, in order to obtain profit.

2.3   Foreign Investors

Foreign investors (whether private or legal persons) are taxable when:

- they invest capital in a Romanian company set up in association with Romanian private or legal persons or with foreign capital
- they carry on commercial activities in Romania, with the legal status of a foreign person and are acknowledged as a legal foreign person, under the conditions stipulated by Romanian Law.

Foreign investors enjoy a series of facilities under Law 35/1991 (amended) such as VAT exemption and, under certain circumstances, zero-rating.

2.4   Representation Agencies or Information Offices in Romania

Offices set up by foreign companies to carry out promotional or preliminary activities for the main company, are not regarded as permanent residences for activities subject to VAT and therefore are not taxable subjects.

2.5   Importers

Importers of goods and services are taxable persons if such goods and services are licensed to enter Romanian territory and are not specifically exempt from VAT.

2.6   Reverse Charge

The VAT legislation stipulates that the tax is imposed on the beneficiaries (ie it is a 'reverse' charge) where goods are imported on a lease basis, and where services involve such activities as advertising, consultancy, study and research, cession or concession of copyrights, patents, licences, trademarks or other similar royalties carried on by an entrepreneur with a headquarters or residence abroad and used by beneficiaries whose headquarters or residence is in Romania. This regulation also applies to foreign investors.

3   WHAT IS TAXABLE?

3.1   General

The supply of goods or services which are independently conducted by private or legal persons is taxable. These goods and services include:

- asset (goods) deliveries and services performed while carrying out a professional activity
- transfer of property rights over assets between taxable persons, and between taxable persons and public institutions or private persons

- imports of goods and services.

The above operations can be divided into two categories:

- operations resulting in the transfer of property rights over goods, irrespective of the legal form of transfer, such as: sale or exchange of goods, and contribution in kind to the capital of a commercial company
- operations that represent services.

3.2   Supply of Goods (Delivery of Assets)

A supply of goods means the transfer of property rights in the goods from the owner to the beneficiary, either directly or through an agent acting on his behalf.

The most frequent form of transfer is a sale in which the goods are assimilated, for example:

- the sale or lease (with payment by instalments) of goods under a contract which stipulates that the transfer of ownership will take place after the payment of the last instalment or on an agreed upon date
- the taking over by the taxable person of goods or services in any form for his private use or to be provided free of charge to individuals or to a legal person. An exception is made for goods and services provided free of charge, within the limits and for the purposes stipulated by the law
- use by the taxable person for his own activity of items manufactured in his own business, with the exception of those items directly incorporated in taxable goods.

At the same time, goods exchange operations (ie barter) are taxable, since they have the effect of two distinct and separate sales, even where direct delivery is made to the final consumer on the distributor's instructions.

3.3   Transfer of Property Rights in Goods

The term 'transfer' is defined as the passing of all property rights between taxable persons, and between taxable persons and companies, organisations or private persons, regardless of the form of the transfer.

Taxable assets include all construction work, irrespective of its nature (civil, industrial, commercial, agricultural, etc), building sites located within city limits, and construction work that cannot be detached without being damaged or without damaging the building itself (such as power units, pipes or boilers set in the ground).

Transfers achieved through several transactions (ie chain transactions) are also taxable.

3.4   Services

The main taxable services are as follows:

- construction-erection work
- goods transport and related services
- goods and real estate leases
- intermediary or commission operations
- repairs of any type
- advertising, consultancy, study, research or specialist activities
- banking, financial, insurance or re-insurance activities

- sales related to the 'on the spot' consumption of food and beverages, eg restaurants
- patents, licences, trademarks and commercial marks
- any binding obligation on a person to carry out manual labour or intellectual work with a view to obtaining profit, other than goods delivery.

3.5   Self-Supply of Goods and Services

The use by the taxable person, during the process of carrying out his own activity, of goods manufactured by him is deemed to be a supply of goods and is taxable. Nevertheless, taxable persons may deduct the applicable VAT if they can justify that the goods are intended for their taxable activity and that they are their property.

3.6   Import of Goods and Services

The import of goods or services is subject to VAT whether or not the legal person who imports them is a taxable person, unless the goods or services are specifically exempted from VAT (see section 7.2).

4   PLACE OF SUPPLY

4.1   Supply of Goods

Only the transfer of property rights of goods located in Romania is subject to VAT. Therefore, the import of goods becomes taxable (unless specifically exempt) at the time when they enter Romania and are entered on the customs declaration.

4.2   Supply of Services

Services are taxable when provided in Romania, irrespective of the location of the provider's headquarters or residence (unless they are specifically exempt).

4.3   Reverse Charge

See 2.6 above.

5   BASIS OF TAXATION

5.1   Taxable Amount

VAT is imposed on the value received or receivable by the supplier. It includes all the amounts, values or services received or to be received by the supplier in exchange for the goods delivered or the services provided, such as:

- the price negotiated between the buyer and the seller plus other expenses owed by the buyer for the goods which are not covered by the price
- the price negotiated for the services provided
- amounts related to commissions for intermediary operations
- the market price or, when not available, the costs related to the services provided by the taxable person for his own use or free of charge for other private or legal persons
- the price of the sale directly out of the customs house or through auctions.

The following are not included in the taxable amount:

- the amount assigned by the State Budget to finance investments, to cover losses and balances between the cost and the price of goods, and to finance inventories used by the State in special cases like wars, calamities, etc
- rebates and other discounts granted directly by the supplier to the customer
- penalties for the total or partial non-fulfilment of the contract obligations
- interest received for delayed payments.

Where the quantity, price or other elements listed in the invoices or similar documents are partially or totally rejected, the taxable amount is reduced accordingly. Returned packages are treated as rejected goods.

Price discounts can be omitted from the taxable amount if the amount is specific to the buyer's benefit and it does not represent payment for a service.

5.2   Self-Supplies
The taxable amount is determined according to the market price or, if not available, according to the total cost of the goods provided by the taxable person.

5.3   Imports
The taxable amount includes:

- the value for customs purposes expressed in 'lei' (the Romanian currency), at the exchange rate established by the Romanian national bank for customs operations as published on the previous Friday
- transport costs incurred outside Romanian territory
- loading, unloading and handling costs paid for outside the country
- insurance costs and any other related expenses incurred outside Romania
- any other levy or excise duty.

The customs value should be documented on invoices or other documents issued by the exporter and deposited with the customs authorities.

5.4   Other Taxes and Excises
The taxable amount for both domestic and imported supplies includes all other taxes such as customs and excise duties payable by the buyer.

5.5   Chargeable Event

5.5.1   Internal Supplies
As a general rule, the chargeable event occurs at the time when:

- goods are supplied, real estate is transferred or services are provided
- goods are sold to the beneficiaries through intermediaries or consignment
- documents are issued, certifying the taking over of goods purchased or manufactured by an economic agent, to be used in any way or to be made available free of charge to private or legal persons
- the discount period expires or when the instalments are due, for goods and services to be paid for in instalments as well as for successive payments or returns

- returned goods which are previously exported goods are sold by the domestic beneficiaries
- documents are certified that an economic agent provided services free of charge to private or legal persons
- coins or tokens are collected for goods sold through automated vending machines.

5.5.2 Imports

The chargeable event occurs when goods are declared for customs purposes or when beneficiaries receive/take over imported services.

In the case of imported goods which are in transit or in a warehouse or under a temporary admission regime in Romania, the chargeable event occurs at the time when the goods are removed from the warehouse, are no longer in transit or under a temporary admission regime and the customs formalities are drawn up according to their new destination.

5.6   Time of Payment

As a general rule, the VAT is due when the chargeable event occurs. VAT is payable within a period of time which runs from the date on which the goods were delivered or the services were provided.

Exceptions to the general rule are as follows:

- When an invoice is issued before the goods are delivered or the services provided, the tax is payable on issue of the invoice
- Tax is payable when payments on account are received for services provided (including real estate activities) or, if authorised by the fiscal authority, on the date the taxable person becomes entitled to receive payment on the basis of invoices or other substituting document issued
- Real estates entrepreneurs can choose to pay the VAT when the works are completed, subject to agreement with the authorities.

6   TAX RATES

6.1   Rules

Currently there are three VAT rates:

0%: – export of goods, and services provided directly in connection with the export of goods, that are carried out by taxable persons domiciled in Romania
   – services provided by taxable persons domiciled in Romania and contracted with foreign beneficiaries
   – international transport of persons to and from countries, performed by authorised taxable persons domiciled in Romania
   – international transport of exported goods
   – goods and services destined for the use of diplomatic missions, consulates and international intergovernmental representations accredited in Romania, as well as for their staff, under terms and conditions determined by the Ministry of Finance, on a reciprocal basis
   – goods purchased at exhibitions organised in Romania or, in ordinary commercial

activity, mailed or carried abroad by a purchaser whose domicile or head-office is outside Romania, under the terms and conditions established by the Ministry of Finance
- goods and services used in the carrying out of any activities on Romanian territory which are directly financed by non-refundable subsidies and loans granted by foreign governments, international bodies and non-profit charity organisations, under terms and conditions established by the Ministry of Finance
- bread manufacturing and trading

9%:
- meat (animal or poultry) sold as such (including canned products)
- fish and fish products, natural or processed (including canned) except for roe
- milk, condensed milk and other dairy products
- edible oils and fats
- medicines for human or veterinary use, pharmaceutical products, medicinal plants, medical equipment, and other goods meant exclusively for medical purposes

18%:
all other goods and services which are not specifically exempt or taxable at the 0%, or 9% rates including domestic goods transport.

7   EXEMPTIONS

7.1   *Exemptions with Credit for Input Tax*
The zero rate works as an exemption with entitlement to recover input VAT.

7.2   *Exemptions without Credit for Input Tax*
The following are VAT-exempted and do not confer any right to recover input tax:

- health and social services units
- scientific, teaching, cultural and sports institutions, scientific research and technological development centres related to national programmes for research and development, fundamental research in the technical field including geological surveys and oil exploration, financed through public funds
- individuals working at home
- authorised freelancers who work individually
- individual farms and privately-owned farming associations
- sight impaired (ie blind persons) and handicapped individuals' organisations
- public institution cafeterias, except for those that function as public restaurants or cafes
- banking, financial insurance and re-insurance institutions, the national lottery and the State Mint when manufacturing medals, badges or coins
- goods and services which represent contributions in kind to the capital of a commercial company
- activities related to shows, asset sales, cab driving and gambling (because these are liable to other specific taxes)
- the public guardian body, organised as a public institution, whose activities are not meant for profit but to protect goods and to defend the public order
- activities carried out by taxable persons whose total turnover from the main activity and other ancillary activities, does not exceed 10 million lei per annum

- certain specified imported goods and services that, by law or Government regulations, are free from customs duties
- imported machines, tools, installations, equipment and means of transport required for investment which are contributions in kind or which are purchased from the contributions in cash made by the foreign investors to the capital of an enterprise
- imported goods that are marketed in a duty-free regime, as well as through those shops that are exclusive to diplomats and their staff
- goods that are imported without paying customs duties, in keeping with the customs regime applicable to individuals
- goods and services resulted from or financed directly from assistance or non-refundable loans granted by foreign Governments, international organisations as well as non-profit and charity organisations, under the terms stipulated by the Ministry of Finance
- gold imports of the National Bank of Romania
- repairs and alterations to Romanian aircraft and ships performed outside Romania
- civil aircraft and items listed by the Romanian customs regulations for Imports and manufactured in those countries that signed the Agreement for Civil Aircraft Trade
- imported goods similar to tax-exempt domestic goods, such as: publishing, printing and selling of newspapers (the VAT on domestic and imported papers being deductible), except for advertising and publicity activities: publishing, printing and selling of books, magazines, radio and television services, except for advertising and publicity activities or pornographic and violence-inciting publications; products and services imported for the population consumption.

8   CREDIT/REFUND FOR INPUT VAT

8.1   *General Rule*
In principle the VAT charged on goods and services may be reduced by the amount of VAT paid on those purchases and imports which are applicable to the taxable activities.

No deduction is permitted in respect of the VAT paid on:

- goods and services destined for the fulfilment of exempt activities
- goods and services destined for private use or for the use, free of charge, of other private or legal persons
- goods and services purchased by the supplier or entrepreneur on behalf of the customer and subsequently invoiced to that customer
- services in respect of transport, hotel accommodation, restaurant-related and other services carried out in the course of the intermediary activity for the use or consumption of tourists
- other expenses that are not directly and exclusively related to the activity carried out by the company, such as: entertainment, leisure, rental and maintenance of cars used for non-profit activities.

8.2   *Partial Exemption*
Where a taxable person carries out both taxable and exempt activities, the amount of VAT deductible is determined by the ratio of taxable activities to total activities.

8.3   Time of Recovery

The amount of VAT payable (output VAT) on each monthly return is reduced by the amount of VAT recoverable (input VAT). If input VAT exceeds output VAT the excess may be recovered at the end of a quarter by filing a 'recovery request' with the tax authorities. It will be refunded within 30 days of filing the return.

Where a taxable person carries out export activities exclusively and the output tax in the return form is less than the input VAT, the maximum amount to be recovered shall be determined through a formula.

Where an economic person is partially exempt (ie he carries on both taxable and exempt activities) any excess of input tax over output tax in a period shall be carried forward and set against the tax liability arising in subsequent periods.

9   ADMINISTRATION OBLIGATIONS

9.1   Registration

All taxable persons are required to register with the local tax authority by submitting a registration form within 15 days from the date on which they started to carry out their taxable activity or the date on which the nature of such activity changes.

Taxable persons must request cancellation of their registration when their activities cease.

9.2   Books and Records

Taxable persons are required to keep adequate records, as follows:

■   adequate accounting books to allow the assessment of VAT due for the goods and services provided and input VAT for goods and services purchased or manufactured in their own businesses and destined for taxable activities
■   daily records of the factors which are taken into account when determining the output VAT in respect of goods and services supplied and in respect of input VAT.

9.3   Invoices

Taxable persons are required to issue invoices which contain the following information:

■   the serial number
■   the date of the invoice
■   the supplier's name, address and registration number
■   recipient's name and address
■   description and quantity of the goods or services rendered
■   price per item and total value without VAT
■   the amount of VAT charged.

Purchasers are required to obtain from the suppliers' invoices or substitute documents for the goods and services purchased and to check that such documents contain all the information required.

Importers are required to draw up the customs declaration forms for imports and to determine the amount of custom duty and VAT payable.

9.4   VAT Returns

Taxable persons must make monthly returns by the twenty-fifth day of the following month.

In addition, by 15 August of each year, they must provide to the local tax authorities information regarding their possible taxable activities for the following year for control purposes.

9.5   Power of the Authorities

If VAT is incorrectly calculated or paid, the tax authorities may issue an assessment for the estimated underpaid amount. The taxable person must pay the estimated amount within seven days from the date of the assessment. Such assessments are binding and the tax will be paid over by the commercial banks in which the taxable persons have their accounts even if the taxable person does not accept the assessment. However, see section 9.8 below.

9.6   Statute of Limitation

The period of limitation for the issue of assessments is five years from the date on which the liability was incurred.

9.7   Penalties

Various penalties apply as follows:

- delay in filing tax returns eg. a fine ranging from 600,000 lei to 2 million lei
- inaccurate keeping of records, with the obvious purpose of reducing the amount of tax payable or inaccurate filing of tax returns; a fine equal to the unpaid tax plus a fee equal to the same unpaid tax plus interest
- failure to pay in due time; a surcharge of 0.3% for each delayed day.

9.8   Appeals

A taxable person may appeal to the local tax authorities against a VAT assessment issued to him within 30 days from the date of the notification of the assessment. A further appeal may be made to the Ministry of Finance within 30 days of an unfavourable decision by the local tax authorities. The decision of the Ministry is final.

Appeals are subject to a stamp tax of 2% of the amount in dispute but, in any case, will not be less than 1,000 lei.

10   SPECIAL VAT REGIMES

10.1   Agricultural Activities

Activities carried out by agricultural enterprises while they are working on land belonging to individuals whose right to the land is constituted or re-constituted, are liable to VAT as follows:

- agricultural produce delivered to the individuals mentioned above do not represent a transfer of property and are not VAT-taxable
- agricultural produce kept by the agricultural enterprises as reward for the agricultural work they have carried out are VAT-taxable when they are subsequently sold to individuals or legal persons
- agricultural produce belonging to the individuals mentioned above which are

marketed to third parties through the agricultural enterprises which carried out the agricultural work, are not VAT-taxable and should not be listed in the VAT documents of the agricultural enterprise.

Agricultural work carried out by commercial companies which provide services for agriculture (ie AGROMEC, etc) are liable to VAT in different ways, depending on the beneficiary and the payment method, as follows:

- agricultural activities paid for in cash are liable to VAT
- agricultural activities paid for in kind are taxable and must be listed as distinct activities in the accounting documents of both the provider and beneficiary, as follows:

  - the commercial company (the provider) must produce an invoice to cover the fee for the work carried out on behalf of the agricultural enterprise at the time when the latter takes over the products, and should charge VAT at 18% on the fee. Part invoicing is not permitted
  - the agricultural enterprise should produce an invoice for the produce delivered to the commercial company. The taxable amount is the fee for the work done and is charged at 18%

- work paid for in kind and carried out on behalf of individual farmers or farmers' associations is regarded as expenses made on account of the agricultural products to be withheld after the harvest and is not taxable.

Advances given to individual farmers and farmers' associations by taxable persons especially authorised by the State are liable to VAT as follows:

- advances given directly to farmers as cash or raw materials, financed through credits obtained by taxable persons, are not liable to VAT because they represent expenses paid on account of the agricultural produce to be received after harvest
- advances given to farmers by taxable persons especially authorised by the State through commercial companies are not liable to VAT
- the commercial companies which provide agricultural services are liable to VAT in respect of their work.

Activities arising out of the Land Leasing Law are liable to VAT as follows:

- the lessee, as an individual and in his capacity as a farmer, is exempt from VAT
- the lessee as a legal person is liable to VAT if his total turnover from economic activity (including operating the rented commercial goods) is more than 10 million lei
- neither the lessee nor the owner, usufructuary nor any other legal owner of agricultural goods is liable to VAT in respect of rent paid
- the rent paid in cash is VAT exempt.

The rights of individuals whose status as shareholders has been established on the basis of item 36 of Law 18/1991 and which have been determined by the law either as a percentage of the profit the enterprise per hectare or as a counter-value for agricultural produce are not liable to VAT.

When the payment is in kind using products that are not those stipulated by the law, the provider of the activity is liable to VAT.

11   BIBLIOGRAPHY

VAT Legislation, Ministry of Finance
Financial Law, Ioan Condor

Contributor: Adriana Gheorghiu
                    Ernst & Young Romania
                    B-dul Maresal Averescu 8-10
                    Sector 1, Cod 71316
                    Bucharest
                    Romania
                    Tel: +40-1-6552540
                    Fax: +40-1-3128703

RUSSIA

1   GENERAL BACKGROUND

Value added tax (VAT) was introduced in Russia on 1 January 1992 by the Law of the Russian Federation of 6 December 1991 'Concerning Value Added Tax' and the supporting Instruction No.1 of the State Tax service of the RSFSR of 9 December 1991 'Concerning the Procedure for the Calculation and Payment of Value Added Tax'.

The VAT law has been amended seven times since 1 January 1992, two of the most important amendments being:

■   Law No. 2813-1 of 22 May 1992 which introduced further exemptions from VAT including exemptions for medical services and equipment
■   Law No. 4178-1 of 22 December 1992 which introduced VAT on the import of goods as from 1 February 1993. The rate of VAT was also reduced from 28% to 20% as from 1 January 1993.

2   WHO IS TAXABLE?

Under current legislation, payers of VAT include the following:

■   enterprises and organisations which, in accordance with legislation of the Russian Federation, have the status of legal entities (including enterprises with foreign investments) and which carry out production and other commercial activities
■   full partnerships which sell goods (work and services) in their own name
■   individual (family) private enterprises which carry out production and other commercial activities
■   branches, departments and other economically autonomous subdivisions of enterprises, which are located in the territory of the Russian Federation and independently sell goods (work and services)
■   international associations and foreign legal entities which carry out production and other commercial activities in the territory of the Russian Federation.

The requirement to charge VAT on taxable goods and services applies to both Russian legal entities and foreign legal entities which carry on commercial activities within Russia. A foreign legal entity does not need to have a permanent representation (permanent establishment) for it to be subject to VAT.

There is no concept of registration for VAT purposes. Foreign legal entities are either payers of VAT or they are not. Therefore if the representative office is making taxable supplies, VAT will be payable on those supplies.

This chapter reflects the law on VAT in Russia as at 31 December 1994.

3   WHAT IS TAXABLE?

3.1   Goods and Services Supplied in Russia

VAT liability arises on the taxable supply of goods or services in Russia and on the importation of goods into Russia.

The legislation provides that the taxable base for VAT purposes should include turnover from the sale of goods, work performed and services rendered in the Russian Federation. In addition, VAT should be charged on the customs value of goods and equipment imported into Russia.

A taxable supply of goods includes:

- turnover from sales of goods and services within an enterprise for its own consumption, expenditure for which is not treated as production and distribution expenses, and from sales to an enterprise's own workers
- turnover from the sale of goods (work and services) without payment in return, in exchange for other goods (work and services)
- turnover from the transfer free-of-charge or partly-paid transfer of goods (work and services) to other enterprises or citizens
- turnover from the sale of mortgaged objects, including the transfer of such objects to the mortgagee in the event of the failure to fulfil the obligation which is secured by the mortgage.

Although not all exempt goods and services carry a credit, such credit is available for VAT suffered on expenditure relating to exports of goods of own manufacture. Exported goods of own manufacture are exempt from VAT, although recoverability of input VAT is restricted to expenses associated with the sale of goods (eg storage handling costs). VAT on goods purchased for export is not recoverable. This means that any VAT suffered on expenditure relating to the export of goods and services is recoverable. In the case of goods and services which are not exported, VAT suffered on related expenditure will be offset (recovered) against the VAT payable in respect of taxable supplies.

VAT suffered on expenditure relating to taxable goods and services can be offset immediately. However, in the case of VAT paid on capital expenditure, the tax is offset over six months in equal amounts from the time the assets are put into use.

3.2   Import of Fixed Assets

The general rule is that equipment imported into Russia will be subject to VAT unless the equipment is treated as a temporary import or as a contribution to the charter fund of a Russian company.

VAT is payable on the import of fixed assets into Russia with the following exceptions:

- goods which are imported into Russia as a contribution to the authorised capital of an enterprise with foreign investment during the year following the initial State registration of the enterprise registration are exempt from VAT
- Order 49 of 30 January 1993 'Concerning the Application of VAT and Excise Duty on the Import of Goods into the Russian Federation and on the export of goods from its territory' supported by Instruction No.01-20/741 describes how VAT should be calculated on the import of goods and sets out the available exemptions.

3.3   *Import of Services*

Imported services are not currently subject to VAT in Russia, although services provided within Russia are subject to VAT. Many foreign companies supplying services to Russian enterprises are likely to find themselves having to provide part of their services in Russia and these services would strictly be subject to VAT, notwithstanding that the supplier may have no presence whatsoever in Russia. The issue of how VAT is to be collected in these circumstances has not been addressed by the legislature. It is probable that some form of reverse charge mechanism will be introduced in the future.

4   PLACE OF SUPPLY

4.1   *Supply of Goods*

Russian VAT will be applied where goods are sold in the customs territory of the Russian Federation. VAT is also payable on the customs value of goods physically imported into the Russian Federation. This VAT is payable at customs. Goods imported into a bonded warehouse are not considered to be in the customs territory of the Russian Federation and therefore no VAT is assessable until the goods are released.

4.2   *Supply of Services*

4.2.1 *Exports of Services*

On 17 December 1994, Joint Letter No.VZ-6-05/433 of the State Tax Service of the Russian Federation of 15 November 1994 and No.154 of the Ministry of Finance of the Russian Federation of 14 November 1994 Concerning the Classification of Services (Work) as Exported in Value Added Tax Settlements was published.

This letter is significant in that it provides long-awaited guidance as to the nature of services which qualify for exemption from Russian VAT and Special Tax under Article 5 of the VAT Law. Article 5 provides that exported goods are exempt from VAT.

In general the letter adopts the so-called 'place of services' test in determining whether or not services are exported. Although specialised industries are addressed separately, generally only services physically performed outside the CIS are considered exported. Previously many, if not most, taxpayers have treated services received outside the CIS as exported for VAT purposes.

The new procedures established by this letter are effective beginning with what the letter terms 'turnover from the sale of work and services for December 1994'. This phrase is not amplified in the letter in any way, which leaves it unclear as to whether services invoiced in December, or services for which payment is received in December, or services performed in December should be subject to VAT as provided in the new procedure. The reference to sales, however, is closer to 'invoiced' or 'received' than 'performed'. The effective date, therefore, may be controlled by the method of accounting.

The letter specifically provides that, in the event that taxpayers and tax authorities use another taxation procedure for such work and services, no resettlements with the budget shall be made for the period which has elapsed and no fines shall be imposed.

Additional clarification is needed as to the effective date but, in the absence of clarification, charging VAT on all services invoiced after November would appear prudent. We were, however, informed orally by sources at the Ministry of Finance that the intention was to apply the new procedure to services performed after November 1994.

For purposes of the export of services exemption, services must be exported beyond the Member States of the CIS. The letter specifically states:

> 'until international agreements have been concluded, settlements of Russian enterprises, institutions and organisations for goods (work and services) sold to economic entities of Member States of the CIS should be carried out at prices (tariffs) increased by the amount of value added tax'.'

Regarding exported services, the letter states:

> 'For taxation purposes, the following types of services and work are regarded as exported:
>
> 1 Services (work) provided outside the territory of Member States of the CIS by value added tax payers who have been registered in the Russian Federation in accordance with the established procedure in accordance with agreements (or other equated documents) concluded with foreign legal entities and physical persons:
>
> – services (work) related to the preparation and implementation of scientific, educational, sporting and cultural programs;
> – advisory, information and auditing services;
> – medical services;
> – services and work associated with immovable property, including construction and installation and maintenance work;
> – services involving freight transportation and the conveyance of passengers if the point of departure and the point of destination are located outside the territory of Member States of the CIS;
> – other types of services (work).
>
> 2 Services involving the transportation of exported freight (except for pipeline transport services), including across the territory of the Russian Federation, and services relating to the transit of foreign freights (via the territory of Member States of the CIS), provided that they are covered by standard transportation documents, which are provided by Russian value added tax payers in accordance with agreements (or other equated documents) concluded with foreign legal entities and physical persons.
>
> 3 Services involving the transportation of oil, oil products and gas by pipeline transport, including when provided in the territory of the Russian Federation, subject to the conclusion of direct contracts for such services between Russian value added tax payers and foreign legal entities and physical persons and provided that the fact that the goods have crossed the border of CIS countries is confirmed in accordance with the established procedure.
>
> 4 Services involving the forwarding, loading, unloading and reloading of exported goods, including when provided in the territory of the Russian

Federation, subject to the conclusion of direct contracts for those services between Russian value added tax payers and foreign legal entities and physical persons.

5   *If no direct contracts exist for the performance of the services envisaged in points 2, 3 and 4 involving the transportation, forwarding, loading, unloading and reloading of exported freights in the territory of the Russian Federation, invoices for the performance of such services shall be presented to the exporters of the goods inclusive of value added tax, which shall subsequently be refunded to exporters (taken into account) in accordance with the established procedure.*

6   *International passenger and baggage carriage services, including carriage across the territory of the Russian Federation, provided that they are covered by standard international transportation documents.*

7   *International communications services (postal, telephone, telegraph, space, etc) which are partly provided outside the borders of Member States of the CIS are exempt from value added tax only to the extent of turnover from their sale in the territory of foreign States. Value added tax is, therefore, levied on receipts from the performance of international communications services, reduced by the amount of payments:*

–   *to foreign communications administrations, international, communications organisations, companies, etc, which are recognised by private operators, associated with lease payments for international communications channels and international postal services;*

–   *in respect of contributions to international communications organisations of which the Russian Federation is a member;*

–   *to other communications enterprises in event that international communications services are provided in conjunction with them.*

The following services (work) shall also be regarded as exported irrespective of where they are provided by value added tax payers which have been registered in the Russian Federation in accordance with the established procedure under agreements (or other equated documents) which have been concluded with foreign legal entities and physical persons if those services are consumed outside the territory of Member States of the CIS:

–   *services involving the transfer or concession of copyrights, patents, licences and industrial property certificates (for inventions, industrial samples, trademarks, commercial models);*

–   *the leasing of movable property, including transport facilities, provided that they are exported beyond the boundaries of Member States of the CIS and the appropriate customs documents are drawn up;*

–   *scientific research and experimental design work if carried out in the territory of the Russian Federation, provided that the results of such work in the form of scientific and technical documentation are transferred, subject to preparation of the appropriate customs documents, for use outside the territory of Member States of the CIS;*

—   *services and work performed directly in space, provided that the results of such work (services) are used outside the territory of Member States of the CIS.*

In the event that records relating to the exported services which are envisaged in points 1 to 7 above are not maintained separately for sales in the territory of Member States of the CIS and sales in the territory of foreign States, value added tax shall be levied in full on turnover from services sold'.

4.2.2 Imported Services

Imported services are not assessable to VAT under the Russian legislation although the term 'imported services' is not defined in the law. In practice, the tax authorities take the view that any portion of an 'imported service' which is provided in the Russian Federation should be subject to VAT. Any such services should be apportioned at the discretion of the tax payer. There is no reverse charge mechanism in Russia.

5 BASIS OF TAXATION

5.1 Value of Supplies Made in Russia

VAT is charged at the rate of 20%, except in the case of food products and certain goods for children in which case the rate is 10%. The legislation also provides a list of goods and services (including exports) which are exempt from VAT.

The taxable turnover for VAT purposes is calculated by reference to the price of the goods or services sold. This applies where the price is calculated on the basis of free market prices and tariffs, or on the basis of State regulated prices and tariffs.

Where the transaction is not made at free market or State regulated prices, the VAT Law provides a specific procedure for the calculation of taxable turnover.

This procedure applies in the following situations:

- the transaction involves an exchange of goods or services (eg barter arrangement);
- a transfer free of charge or a partially-paid transfer;
- the sale of goods at prices which do not exceed the cost of production.

For the above transactions, the VAT law states that:

'Taxable turnover shall be determined on the bases of market prices prevailing at the time of exchange or transfer (including those prevailing at exchanges), but not lower than the prices which are determined on the basis of the actual cost of production of the goods (works and services), and profit, as calculated on the basis of the maximum profitability rate which is established by the Government of the Russian Federation for goods (works and services) for monopoly enterprises'

Article 4.1

Payment for labour made in kind with goods of the enterprise's own manufacture is subject to VAT. Taxable turnover is the cost of such goods as determined on the basis of free market or State regulated prices.

Where trade discounts are granted, the amount of the discounts are subtracted from taxable turnover.

5.2   Import of Goods

With effect from 1 February 1993, the import of taxable goods is subject to VAT. VAT is calculated on the customs value of the goods and is payable at customs. Any VAT paid on the import of goods can be offset against VAT collected if the entity concerned is making taxable supplies in Russia.

VAT on imported goods is regulated by Order 49 of 30 January 1993 'Concerning the application of Value Added Tax and Excise Duty on the Import of Goods into the Russian Federation and on the Export of Goods from its Territory'.

Certain goods are exempt from VAT on import:

- foodstuffs (except those which are excisable) and raw materials for their manufacture
- equipment and devices used for scientific research
- children's goods
- technological equipment and spare parts for such equipment
- medicines, medical products and medical information.

5.3   Time of Supply

The VAT law states that the primary time of supply point is when payment is made. Article 8.2 specifically states:

> 'A sale shall be considered to have been completed on the day that funds are received into accounts in banking institutions for goods (work and services) or, in the case of cash settlements, on the day that the cash is received'.

Article 8.2

However, for enterprises who are permitted to define the time of supply on an invoice basis, then this basis would apply. Consequently the VAT treatment should follow the accounting treatment.

Letter No.4-06/69H of the State Tax Service says, however, that where an enterprise invoices in hard currency and is subject to the compulsory sale, then the VAT shall be payable part in hard currency and part in roubles. In these circumstances, the VAT cannot be calculated until payment is received.

Ernst & Young has taken up this matter with the Ministry of Finance on an informal basis and we have been advised as follows:

- enterprises using the invoice basis of accounting should seek payment in advance from their customers so that, when the invoice is issued, the proportion of VAT which is payable in hard currency and the proportion which is payable in roubles can be calculated
- if it is not possible for such an enterprise to obtain advance payments, then it must change the basis of its accounting from an invoice basis to a cash basis.

Where goods or services are exchanged or transferred free of charge, the day that the sale is completed shall be the day when they are transferred (performed).

6   TAX RATES

The VAT rates are currently as follows:

3%:   applies where there is no full exemption from the payment of VAT and excise duty (see section 7.2), or where there is a temporary import of other goods. For each complete or incomplete month 3% shall be paid of the whole amount which would be payable if the goods were released for free circulation

10%:   food products (with the exception of those subject to excise duty), and certain children's goods as approved by the Government of the Russian Federation, including toys, certain clothing items, drawing pads and albums

20%:   all other goods (works and services) which are not exempt or liable at the 3% or 10% rates.

Imports of goods are taxed at the 20% rate except for goods temporarily imported (see above) or goods which are subject to the 10% rate when supplied internally in Russia (which are exempt – see section 7.1).

7   EXEMPTIONS

The VAT law provides exemptions from VAT for a number of goods and services, divided into two categories: those exempt with credit and those exempt without credit.

7.1   Exemption with Credit for Input Tax

If goods and services are 'exempt with credit' from VAT it means that, while VAT is not chargeable on the supply, the input VAT suffered with respect to those goods and services can be reclaimed from the Budget. In practice however, there are problems in obtaining VAT refunds on a timely basis. In addition, the refunds are made in roubles and there is potential for exchange rate losses. Article 5.1 (a-e) lists goods and services that are exempt from VAT with credit:

- exported goods and services (see section 4.2.1 for exported services)
- goods and services intended for official use by foreign diplomatic and similar representations
- rent payments for apartments.

7.2   Exemption without Credit for Input Tax

Input VAT suffered with respect to goods and services that are exempt without credit cannot be reclaimed. Therefore, the VAT thereon which has been paid to suppliers should be included in production and distribution costs.

Article 5.1 (f-y) lists the goods and services that are exempt from VAT without credit:

- operations connected with insurance and re-insurance, and the issue and transfer of loans
- operations connected with the circulation of hard currency, money and bank notes
- turnover from casinos, gaming machines, winnings from race course stakes
- sales of certain minerals and metals for further treatment and turnover from sales to

the State Fund of Precious Metals and Precious Stones

■ certain goods which are imported, including foodstuffs (except for those subject to excise duty) and raw materials for their manufacture

■ charter fund contributions

■ temporary imports viz:

- transport facilities which are used for the international conveyance of goods and passengers, including containers and other reusable tare

- professional equipment and implements belonging to foreign legal entities and physical persons which are needed by them to perform services or work in the territory of the Russian Federation

- goods for display at exhibitions, fairs, symposia and other similar events, and auxiliary equipment and materials intended for use in displaying goods

- equipment and materials for scientific research and educational purposes, provided that such equipment and materials remain in the ownership of the foreign legal entity or physical persons and provided that they are not of a commercial nature

- materials for the rectification of natural calamities, accidents and disasters which are transferred free-of-charge to State bodies and institutions

- packaging

- samples of goods, provided that they remain in the ownership of the foreign legal entity or physical person and provided that they are not of a commercial nature

- other temporarily imported goods as determined by the State Customs Committee of the Russian Federation.

In addition to the above, Letter No.4-06/76H of 19 November 1992 provides exemptions from VAT for the leasing of office accommodation to foreign trade and other representations of certain countries. This letter lists the countries whose representations are exempted from VAT on leasing of office accommodation and includes the USA and the majority of European countries. It should be stressed that this exemption only applies in the case of accredited representative offices.

8 CREDIT/REFUND FOR INPUT VAT

Input VAT is the tax paid on the purchase of goods and services in Russia. In cases where a company is making vatable supplies the input tax can be offset against the tax collected from customers. In this case, the input tax available for offset is limited to the tax suffered on expenditure included in the cost of production. Where a company makes supplies which are exempt with credit (eg exports) the related input tax can be reclaimed.

The framework for accounting for VAT is given by the Russian Charter of Accounts for Book-keeping. The mechanism of accounting for VAT is governed by the VAT Instruction and the Cost of Production statute.

Article VIII (21) of the Instruction states that :

> 'the amount of value added tax payable to the budget shall be determined as the difference between the amounts of tax received from customers for goods (work, services) sold to them and the amounts of tax on material resources, fuel, work and

services whose cost has actually been taken (written off) to production and distribution costs during the reporting period'.

The treatment of costs in determining taxable profit for Income and Corporate Profit Tax purposes will determine the treatment of the VAT paid on those costs. Where certain types of expenditure are not included in the cost of production (eg food for staff), no amount of VAT paid on these costs can be reclaimed or offset against output VAT. Similarly, where there are limits on the deductibility of certain costs (eg training and representational costs), the amount of VAT paid on such costs which can be reclaimed or offset is limited to that paid on the amount of the cost which is included in the cost of production.

Irrecoverable VAT should normally be included in the cost of production and is therefore deductible for Corporate Profits Tax purposes.

Where the amount of VAT paid (with respect to the purchase of goods and materials whose cost has been taken into the cost of production), exceed the amount of VAT collected on the sale of goods and services, the excess payments will be recoverable against future payments of tax, or reimbursed within ten days of the receipt of the relevant computation by the taxing authorities.

In theory, reimbursements of tax by authorities should be made on a timely basis and in the currency in which the tax was originally remitted. However, in practice, obtaining repayment of VAT generally requires numerous reminders and such repayments are normally made in roubles. In addition to being detrimental to cash flow, the declining value of the rouble means there is considerable exposure to exchange losses.

One practical solution is to seek offset of VAT against payments of other taxes, both federal and local. Although there is no provision in the legislation for such offsets, it does happen in practice. However, there may be difficulties in obtaining an offset against local taxes since VAT is a federal tax with amounts paid being disbursed to the federal budget while proceeds of local tax payments go to the local budget.

9   ADMINISTRATIVE OBLIGATIONS

9.1   Registration
There is no concept of separate VAT registration procedure in Russia. Entities are either payers of VAT or they are not.

9.2   Books and Records
The amount of VAT on goods (work and services) sold should be shown in cheque registers and in registers showing the receipt of funds from letters of credit. Where VAT is not chargeable the registers should also state that the amounts are '(VAT) Tax Free'.

In journal orders, ledgers, perforated papers and other bookkeeping registers relating to the procurement of material valuables and sales of goods (work and services) and other assets, the amount of tax should be shown in a separate column on the basis of settlement documents.

9.3   Invoices/Settlement Documents
The VAT Instruction states that the amount of VAT paid when purchasing goods and services must be clearly shown as separate entries on settlement documents. When

documents are produced for goods and services which are exempt from VAT then these should be annotated '(VAT) Tax Free'.

In settlement documents for goods (work and services) sold, the amount of VAT should be shown in a separate line. When goods are despatched, services rendered, and work performed which are not taxable, settlement documents should be inscribed '(VAT) Tax Free'. Settlement documents where the amount of tax is not shown should not be accepted for execution by banking institutions.

9.4   VAT Returns

The procedures and deadlines for payment of VAT depend on the monthly amounts of VAT payable to the budget and on the size of the entity.

The following deadlines apply:

Average Monthly VAT (payable in Roubles)	*Deadline*
Up to 1 million	Quarterly
Between 1 million and 3 million	Monthly
More than 3 million	Three times monthly

For payments in excess of 3 million roubles per month, tax should be paid three times a month in equal instalments not later than the fifth, fifteenth and twenty-fifth days of the month. In practice, many tax offices are not able to cope with receiving VAT three times a month and accept monthly payments instead.

As from 1 July 1993, the procedure for VAT payments has been changed for 'small' enterprises. These enterprises must pay VAT quarterly regardless of the amounts due monthly. Under current regulations, enterprises are considered to be 'small' where the average number of employees does not exceed the following levels:

- up to 15 persons in non-production and retail trade sectors
- up to 50 persons in other sectors related to production
- up to 100 persons in science and scientific services
- up to 200 persons in industry and construction.

In all other cases, tax returns should be presented to the tax inspectorate not later than the twentieth day of the month following the reporting period.

9.5   Correction of Returns

Where a return requires amendment this must be done without unreasonable delay. If the amendments are made before the tax authorities discover the error or omission, the taxpayer is required to pay a penalty of 0.7% of the unpaid amount of tax for each day of the delay in payment, starting from the day when the tax was due.

9.6   Powers of the Authorities

Tax authorities have extensive rights in regard to inspection and seizure of records. Officers of the tax authorities have the right to audit all documents associated with calculation and payment of VAT and to investigate any premises of taxpayers which are used for deriving income.

419

The right of the tax authorities extends to the possible liquidation of the enterprise, the annulment of the registration and the declaration of transactions as invalid. The taxpayer can appeal the decisions of the tax authorities and the actions of their officers.

A tax inspector can suspend the taxpayer's bank accounts in the event of the failure to submit documents to the tax authorities associated with the calculation or payment of taxes. If the bank fails to comply with the instructions of the tax authorities, it can be fined.

The tax police have more detailed and extensive rights than the tax inspectors. They may be armed and have the right to use weapons in order to fulfil their duties. Tax police officers operate independently but should execute their tasks in co-operation with the tax authorities and other State bodies. The main objectives of the tax police include discovering tax crimes and delinquency, providing for the security of tax inspectors and preventing corruption within the tax authorities.

9.7   Penalties

Fines and penalties for VAT offences are governed by Article 13.1 of Law No.2118-1 of the Russian Federation of 27 December 1991 'Concerning the Fundamental Principles of the Taxation System in the Russian Federation'. In line with this law, the primary penalties applicable to VAT are as follows:

Violation	Penalty
Failure to submit or late submission of tax returns	10% of amounts of tax payable at the next filing deadline
Late payment of tax	0.7% of the unpaid tax for each day of delay beginning with the original deadline established for payment
Concealment or under-declaration	Fine equal to the amount of the tax.

Additional penalties may apply where, for example, input tax has been overstated.

9.8   Appeals

Every taxpayer has the right to lodge complaints against the decisions of tax authorities and the actions of their officers. If the taxpayer is dissatisfied with a decision of his local tax inspectorate, he should complain in the first instance to the regional tax inspectorate. The complaint must be examined and a decision issued not later than one month after the complaint is submitted to the tax authority.

In the event that the taxpayer does not agree with a decision of the State Tax Service, he can appeal to the Arbitration Court of the Russian Federation. The court procedure is held in accordance with the rules applied to all ordinary cases examined by the Arbitration Court.

10   SPECIAL VAT REGIMES

10.1   Retail Trade and Public Catering Enterprises

Where goods (including imported goods) are sold at free retail prices VAT should be charged on the sales margin of the goods. VAT should be calculated at the rate of 16.67% and 9.09% of the taxable turnover.

10.2   Transportation

The following are taxable persons:

- railway authorities, rail transport production associations and the Belgorod Department of the Southern Railway
- air companies, airports, air squadrons, technical aviation bases and other civil aviation enterprises
- steamship lines, ports, accident and rescue teams, authorities of shipping routes and other naval and river transport enterprises
- motor transport production enterprises and associations.

Receipts earned from the conveyance of freight, passengers, luggage, freight luggage and mail within the limits of the CIS, irrespective of the final destination of the passenger or freight will be assessable to VAT. In addition, all types of paid services rendered to passengers at stations, in trains, at ports and airports will be assessable to VAT.

When railway tickets are sold for international destinations, the proportion of the cost of the ticket in respect of the conveyance of the passengers and goods over the territory of the CIS will be assessable to VAT.

10.3   Intermediary Activities

Stock-piling enterprises, wholesalers, supply and marketing enterprises and other enterprises which perform intermediary services (both delivery of goods to consumers and other types of services), and which earn income in the form of mark-ups (discounts), commissions and other levies should calculate tax from the amount of income at the rate of 16.67% and 9.09% as appropriate.

10.4   Sale of Fixed and Intangible Assets

The amount of VAT paid on fixed and intangible assets should be deducted from the amounts of VAT payable to the budget in equal instalments over a six-month period beginning at the time when the asset was first put into use. Where assets are purchased for non-production requirements or cars and minibuses are purchased the VAT paid cannot be recovered.

In the case of the sale of fixed and intangible assets which were acquired in 1992 at prices which exceed the purchase price, VAT is calculated as the difference between the amount of tax paid to the supplier and the amount received from customers.

Where the assets were acquired in 1993, VAT should be calculated by taking the difference between the tax on the selling price and the amount of tax which had not yet been recovered/offset prior to the sale of the assets.

10.5   Enterprises in the Far North

Because of weather conditions in the Far North regions of Russia it is not possible to ship goods at all times of the year and consequently goods which will not be required for some time are shipped early, ie in the summer. Enterprises located in the Far North and certain other specified areas which carry out the early delivery of goods and materials may offset against VAT on the sales of goods (work and services) any VAT paid to suppliers for goods and materials purchased (rather than the amount of VAT in respect of goods and materials utilised, ie written off to production cost).

11 SPECIAL TAX

In December 1993, President Yeltsin introduced a new federal tax of 3% called 'Special Tax'.

This tax is levied specifically to raise funds for financial support to major sectors of the economy and has been levied in the same way as VAT since 1 January 1994. Basically, it is therefore just an increase in the rate of VAT to 23%, the only discernible difference between the taxes at this stage being the budget to which they are payable. Special tax only applies to goods despatched and work and services performed on or after 1 January 1994. Invoices should show Special Tax in a separate line in the same manner as VAT.

There remain some unanswered questions relating to Special Tax but the general answer is that if VAT applies, then Special Tax applies.

Contributor: Bill Henry
                Ernst & Young
                Podsosensky Pereulok 20/12
                103062 Moscow
                Russia
                Ph: 7 095 927 0569
                Fax: 7 095 917 3607

SLOVAK REPUBLIC

1   GENERAL BACKGROUND

Value added tax (VAT) was introduced into the Slovak Republic on 1 January 1993 replacing the single-stage turnover tax inherited from the previous planned economy, and which had consisted of 1,506 different tax rates on manufactured and imported goods.

Slovak VAT is a two-rate structure, with most goods liable to VAT at 25% and most services liable to VAT at 6%.

Control of VAT is vested in the Financial Authority.

2   WHO IS TAXABLE?

2.1   *General*

Basically, 'taxable persons' making 'taxable supplies' will be required to charge VAT.

'Taxable persons' are essentially individuals or legal entities who carry on a commercial activity and are registered for VAT. Consequently, a private individual is not usually a 'taxable person' and so has to pay VAT on his purchases without being able to claim a refund of the tax.

From 1 January 1994 registration is mandatory where Slovak turnover exceeds Sk750,000 (approximately US$25,000) in the previous three months or, for new businesses when the turnover is expected to exceed Sk1,500,000 (approximately US$50,000) for the next three months. Once this threshold is reached, it is necessary to inform the financial authorities of this fact and register for VAT purposes. Failure to do so on time could lead to penalties relating to both late payment of tax and late filing of returns.

A 'taxable supply' includes the delivery of goods and the transfer of real estate property (excluding the transfer of land) involving a change of ownership, the provision of services, and the transfer or exploitation of rights ensuing from industrial or other intellectual property, within the framework of a business enterprise.

'Taxable supplies' also include the provision of goods, services, buildings and structures, and the transfer and exploitation of rights:

- by a taxpayer for his own personal consumption if he is a natural person; for purposes not connected with business activities, if they are supplies which, in the event of business activities, are not subject to tax
- for purposes not connected with business activities in the case of received taxable supplies to which a tax deduction has been applied.

This chapter reflects the law on VAT in the Slovak Republic as at 31 December 1994.

The use of passenger cars and returnable glass containers which have been manufactured by a taxpayer, who is not entitled to claim a tax deduction is also considered to be a taxable supply within the framework of the legislation.

2.2   Government Bodies

To be considered a 'taxable supply', a supply must be made within the framework of 'business activities' which, for this purpose, are defined as systematic activities which are independently conducted for the purpose of making a profit by a natural person or an entity.

As the activities of government bodies fall outside this definition of business activities, supplies made by government bodies are outside the scope of the Act.

2.3   Group Taxation

The Slovak Act contains no provisions to enable businesses under common control to be grouped under the same VAT registration. Thus, transactions between such entities are liable to VAT in the same way as those with unconnected parties, irrespective of how closely they are connected in terms of common management.

2.4   Foreign Firms

Foreign firms which are commercially registered in Slovakia and which supply goods and services in the Slovak Republic are obliged to register and account for VAT if their Slovak turnover is over the specified limits.

Foreign firms which do not supply taxable goods and services in the Slovak Republic are not permitted to register for VAT.

2.5   Branch Offices

The Act requires a representative office of a foreign entity which makes taxable supplies in the Slovak Republic and whose Slovak turnover exceeds certain limits to register and account for VAT on the supplies which it makes.

In practice, however, the Financial Authorities will not register a branch or representative office of a foreign entity unless the representative office is registered in the Companies Register, as the principle of a VAT agent does not exist within the jurisdiction of the Authority.

2.6   Importers

VAT is due on both the permanent and temporary importation of goods into the Slovak Republic and is payable at the point of entry. Generally, imported goods are liable to VAT at the same rate as those supplied within the Slovak Republic, the taxable amount being the sum of the base for customs duty assessment, the customs duty payable on the goods, plus any consumption tax payable on the goods. For the determination of the VAT tax base any import duties are notionally increased to remove the effect of any treaties or other concessions reducing duty payable.

If the person importing the goods is an agent of an overseas supplier, the import agent is obliged to charge tax to the buyer and has no right to a deduction.

Goods that are only imported temporarily are subject to taxation at the rate of 3% per month or part of a month of the tax which would have been payable on the goods if they were to be released into free circulation. This tax is payable when the goods are imported permanently or re-exported.

3 WHAT IS TAXABLE?

VAT liability arises on all taxable supplies, including supplies in kind, made in the Slovak Republic, whether or not for consideration.

3.1 Supply of Goods
A taxable supply of goods means the delivery of goods and the transfer of real property, including the delivery of buildings, structures and building works (even in the form of a lease contract with a subsequent purchase of the leased goods), involving a change of ownership of title. The transfer of land is not considered to be a supply of goods.

The term 'goods' is defined as tangible movable assets, including thermal and electric energy, gas and water.

3.2 Supply of Services
The supply of services is the provision of activities or materially tangible results of activities which are not goods.

3.3 Self-Supply of Goods and Services
The following self-supplies are also taxable supplies:

- the provision of goods, services, buildings and structures, and transfer and exploitation of rights by taxpayers for private use if the taxpayer is a private person
- the provision of goods, services, buildings and structures, transfer and exploitation of rights for purposes not connected with business activities, in the case of supplies which, in the event of business activities, are not subject to tax
- the provision of goods, services, buildings and structures, transfer and exploitation of rights for purposes not connected with business activities, if a tax deduction has been received for those goods.

The self-supply of passenger cars and returnable glass containers which were manufactured by the taxpayer is considered to also be a taxable supply in circumstances where the taxpayer is not entitled to claim a tax deduction on these goods.

3.4 Importation of Goods
The mere importation of most goods gives rise to a taxable supply. Imported goods which are exempt from duty, such as software, are exempt from VAT, subject to certain exceptions.

Imported goods are defined as:

- goods cleared for free circulation in the Slovak Republic
- goods cleared and registered for temporary circulation in the Slovak Republic, to enable further processing, modification or repair before being returned abroad
- re-exported goods cleared and registered for temporary circulation in the Slovak Republic for the purpose of temporary use
- goods cleared for temporary use.

4   PLACE OF SUPPLY

4.1   Supply of Goods

For the purposes of the VAT Act, the place where goods are supplied shall be:

- the place where the goods are located at the time when the process of their transport or despatch begins, provided that the delivery of the goods is connected with their transport or despatch, regardless of who is effecting the transport or despatch
- the place where the goods are installed or assembled, if the delivery of the goods includes such installation or assembly
- the place where the goods are located at the time of their delivery, if the delivery is effected without their transport or despatch.

If real estate is transferred, or a building or structure is delivered, the place of the taxable supply is the place where the real estate or the structure concerned is located.

4.2   Supply of Services and Transfer of Rights

In the case of the provision of services and the transfer and exploitation of rights, the place of taxable supply is generally the place where the person providing the service or effecting the transfer and exploitation of rights has its seat or its permanent establishment where it provides the services. If the provider has no seat or permanent establishment, it shall be the place of the person's residence or the place where the person is usually staying.

4.2.1   Exceptions

The exceptions to this general rule are as follows:

- for services relating to real property or structures, including services provided by real estate agencies, assessors, architects and construction inspectors, the place of supply is the place where the real property or structure is located
- if transport services are being provided, the place of supply is the place where the transport originates
- for services associated with cultural, artistic, sporting, scientific, educational, entertainment or similar events, including agency, organisational and auxiliary services relating to such activities, the place of supply is the place where the services are actually rendered.

5   BASIS OF TAXATION/CHARGEABLE EVENT

5.1   Supplies within the Slovak Republic

Where the consideration takes the form of money the amount on which tax is chargeable is normally the total sum paid or payable to the person supplying the goods or services, including all taxes, commission, costs and charges whatsoever but not including the VAT chargeable in respect of the transaction. VAT must, therefore, be returned on the VAT-exclusive price.

Where goods or services are supplied and the consideration does not consist or does not consist wholly of an amount of money, and where certain goods are supplied free of charge, the amount on which tax is chargeable is the open market or arms length value of the goods or services supplied.

5.2 Imports

The value for VAT purposes of imports is the value used for customs duty purposes plus the customs duty and any Consumption Tax payable on the goods.

For the calculation of VAT paid on imported goods, if customs duty payable is reduced by virtue of International treaties and other decrees in force in Slovakia, the tax base should be notionally increased as if that reduction did not apply. Of particular relevance for this purpose are any customs reductions resulting from the application of GATT arrangements, goods receiving preferential customs treatment either by virtue of customs union with the Czech Republic or under the Central Europe Free Trade Agreement (CEFTA), and goods imported from developing countries.

5.3 Chargeable Event

A tax liability is established on the day the taxable supply is realised. A taxable supply is considered as having been realised at the following times:

- in the case of a sale of goods under a sales contract, the date specified in the contract; if no date is specified, it is the day the goods are delivered or paid for, whichever is the earlier
- in the case of the transfer of real estate, the day when ownership of the property is assumed or the right of management is transferred
- for the provision of services, the day when the services are rendered or paid for, whichever is the earlier
- in the case of the transfer and exploitation of rights, the date on which the contract becomes effective
- in the case of a taxable supply provided without consideration, the date specified in the contract, or the day when delivery of the taxable supply without consideration is effected or such a supply is provided, depending on which occurs earlier
- in the case of taxable supplies made for personal consumption by a taxpayer who is a natural person and for purposes not related to business activities, the day of the receipt of the goods or services
- in cases not listed above, on the day of payment.

Where taxable supplies realised through vending machines, or where payments for taxable supplies are made with credit cards and other means of payment replacing money, the supply will be considered as having being realised on the day the taxable person removes the money or tokens from the relevant machines or equipment, or ascertains in a different manner the amount of sales.

In the case of lease contracts, and contracts for work where the taxable supply is carried out in the form of a partial supply or a recurrent supply, every partial or recurrent supply shall be considered to be a separate taxable supply. For this purpose, the taxable supply shall be deemed to be realised on the last day of the taxable period in which it is provided.

The payment of an advancement is not a realisation of a taxable supply.

Tax is normally payable on imported goods at the time of importation.

6   TAX RATES

Currently there are two tax rates:

6%:   most foodstuffs (excluding confectionery), fuels, and pharmaceuticals.

25%:   restaurant and public catering, repairs and maintenance, tourist travel services, accommodation services, commercial and agency services, and various works of a manufacturing nature.

7   EXEMPTIONS

7.1   *Exemption with Input Credit*

The following supplies are exempt from tax liability, however the taxpayer providing the supplies is entitled to claim a tax deduction on the inputs for that supply:

- international transport of goods and scheduled international transport of passengers, and services related to international transport. International transport is understood to mean transport:

  - from a place abroad to another place abroad via the Slovak Republic
  - from a place abroad to a place in the Slovak Republic
  - from a place in the Slovak Republic to a place abroad
  - between two places in the Slovak Republic as part of international air and river transport

- export of goods: goods cleared in accordance with the export regime whose final delivery abroad is certified on the respective tax document by the customs authority
- export of services. The provision of services to foreign countries is exempt from VAT provided they are not used in the Slovak Republic. Final use, consumption or exploitation of the service rendered and its exclusive provision in relation to activities abroad, is decisive for the exemption.

7.2   *Exemption without Input Credit*

The supply of certain goods and services is exempt from VAT and the suppliers are not permitted to charge VAT or to claim an input credit where it is attributable to the purchase or importation of such goods or services. They include:

- postal services
- radio and television broadcasting
- financial operations
- insurance business
- transfer and lease of land and building sites (although an option to tax does exist)
- training and education
- health services and goods
- social welfare
- lotteries and similar games
- the sale of an enterprise.

There is often a practical difficulty with these provisions in determining exactly what transactions fall within their scope, particularly in the financial sector.

7.3   Exempt Imports

Imported goods are tax exempt provided that they are subject to exemption from customs duty. However, regardless of any exemption from customs duty, VAT will apply to:

- the import of goods intended for educational, scientific and cultural purposes, as well as the import of scientific apparatus and instruments
- the import of religious objects
- goods imported for the benefit of handicapped persons, unless they were donated
- goods exempt from customs duty provided within the framework of the general system of preferential tariffs or under international agreements of customs union or free trade zones.

7.4   Lease of Land and Constructions

Most property transactions are exempt from VAT (including the transfer of buildings acquired longer than two years prior to transfer), and the vendor or landlord cannot recover VAT on costs, although there is an option for taxation in the case of commercial property.

The option to tax is not permanent, however. Once a business has opted to tax a building or site, it must inform the fiscal authorities and is obliged to keep to the decision at least until the end of the year following the year in which the decision was delivered to the fiscal authority.

7.5   Sale of Passenger Cars

If a taxable person sells a passenger car in the course of his taxable activity which he bought without claiming a tax deduction, the sale is exempt from liability to pay VAT.

8   CREDITS/REFUNDS FOR INPUT VAT

8.1   General Rule

Taxable persons are entitled to deduct the tax if the purchased goods, structures, transferred real property, accepted service or transferred and exploited rights will be used to obtain turnover from taxable supplies. No deduction may be claimed unless the taxpayer has a proper VAT invoice to prove the claim.

A taxable person whose business activity is that of purchasing second-hand passenger cars for resale shall be entitled to a tax deduction of the input tax.

VAT incurred on the purchase of passenger cars (unless the purchaser's business consists of buying and selling cars) and returnable glass bottles is specifically not deductible.

8.2   Partial Exemption

Persons who make taxable supplies and other supplies such as exempt supplies are entitled to recover VAT on the taxable supplies only. In such cases, only a proportion of the businesses total input VAT may be recovered. The amount of allowable input tax for the period is determined by multiplying the total input tax by the following coefficient:

$$\frac{\text{Total taxable supplies for the period (exclusive of VAT)}}{\text{Total of all supplies for the period (exclusive of VAT)}}$$

The calculated coefficient must be rounded upwards to two decimal places.

Further, there are de minimus limits so that, if the coefficient calculated exceeds 0.95, then the entire amount of the input tax for the period may be deducted by the taxpayer. However, if the calculated coefficient amounts to less than 0.05, none of the input tax incurred for the period may be deducted.

No alternative calculations are proposed.

Proceeds from the sale of an enterprise, rent and taxable activities carried out abroad under certain legislation are not included in the total income in the denominator.

The ratio should be calculated separately for each tax period. At the end of the calendar year the calculation is repeated to compute the overall recovery rate for the whole year. Any difference between the calculation for the whole year and the calculation for each month is accounted for in the tax return for the last tax period of the year.

8.3   Excess Deductions
Refund of an excess tax deduction is payable within 30 days from when the return on which it is claimed is lodged. This is dependent on whether the taxpayer claiming the refund has any tax liabilities outstanding. In this case, the refund will be applied to that other liability.

8.4   Bad Debts
In many cases, VAT charged to customers must be paid to the financial authorities before payment is received. VAT cannot be recovered in the event of non-payment; therefore, this will result in a cost to the supplier, as credit notes may not be issued in such circumstances.

9   ADMINISTRATIVE OBLIGATIONS

9.1   Registration
Registration for VAT is mandatory where turnover exceeds Sk750,000 (approximately US$25,000) in the three previous months, or for new businesses, when expected turnover for the next three months exceeds Sk1,500,000 (approximately US$50,000).

Persons who exceed these thresholds are obliged to apply for registration not later than 20 days after the end of the month in which they exceeded the turnover limit.

Taxpayers may apply for cancellation of their registration one year after the effective date shown on their certificate of registration in cases where their turnover for the preceeding three consecutive months did not exceed Sk750,000 (approximately US$25,000) and, at the same time, their turnover for the preceding 12 consecutive months did not exceed Sk3 million (approximately US$100,000).

No provisions exist to enable businesses under common control to be grouped under the same VAT registration.

Individuals are also required to register if they make taxable supplies on the basis of an association agreement or similar contract with other individuals and the total of all the supplies made under the association exceeds Sk750,000 in the previous three months. A taxable person, who is not a taxpayer, who concludes a contract of association with a taxpayer will be considered to be a taxpayer from the date of conclusion of the contract. This person is required to lodge his own return and fulfil his own tax duty.

A person who is obliged to register and does not do so may be fined up to Sk1 million (approximately US$33,000).

9.2 Books and Records

Taxpayers are required to keep all documents relevant to the assessment of tax for five years from the end of the calendar year in which the tax liability arose.

Records must be kept of all received and issued tax documents and debit and credit notes. For received taxable supplies, records must list separately supplies from abroad and from the Slovak Republic split between the individual tax rates. In the case of taxable supplies made, taxpayers are obliged to keep records listing separately supplies exempt from taxation, supplies designed for exportation and domestic supplies divided according to the individual tax rates, and also non-taxable supplies.

9.3 Invoices

Where a taxpayer makes a taxable supply, he is required to supply a 'tax document' within 15 days after the day of making the taxable supply. The tax document is required to show the following:

- commercial name, seat or permanent residence, place of enterprise and tax identification number of the taxpayer
- commercial name, seat or permanent residence, place of enterprise and tax identification number of the taxpayer for whose benefit the taxable supply is made
- serial number of the document
- designation and quantity of the respective goods, or the scope of the taxable supply
- date of issue of the document
- date of realisation of the taxable supply
- total amount of the price before tax
- rate of the tax
- total amount of the tax rounded up to the next ten hellers or, as the case may be, stated also in hellers.

Where a tax document refers to a number of supplies with different rates, or a mixture of exempt and taxable supplies, the total amount of each category and the tax applicable to each category must be listed separately.

9.4 VAT Returns

Taxpayers are required to submit a tax return within 25 days from the end of the tax period, even if the return is negative. Payment of any tax due must also be made at that time. The basic taxable period is a calendar month.

If the taxable person's turnover for the proceeding calendar year or the assumed annual turnover is less than Sk10 million (approximately US$330,000), the taxable period is a calendar quarter.

Quarterly taxpayers may opt for a monthly tax period at the beginning of the next calendar year.

9.5 Correction of Returns

Provisions exist to enable a taxpayer who has incorrectly calculated a tax liability or a refund to lodge an additional return to the Financial Authorities. The return must be lodged within six months of the tax payment date in situations where a taxpayer's liability is to be decreased or an excess deduction is to be increased.

The additional return need only specify the differences against the tax return submitted originally.

9.6 Powers of the Authorities

The Tax Administrator monitors the accuracy and completeness of tax returns.

In general, taxpayers are required to calculate the tax in the tax return. However, the Tax Administrator may determine the tax base and the tax due by using any available method if any of the following apply:

- the tax return is not filed on time
- the tax return is not corrected within the time limit specified by the Tax Administrator
- the tax return includes incorrect or incomplete information with respect to matters that are crucial for the determination of tax.

If the Tax Administrator makes a determination concerning the tax base and the amount of tax, he will inform the taxpayer of the determination through a request for payment. This document also explains the grounds for his determination.

9.7 Appeals

A taxpayer may appeal against the tax base and the tax determined by the Tax Administrator, and against any other decisions not excluded by law. An appeal against a decision by the Tax Administrator may be filed within 30 days from the day after the date on which the decision is delivered.

Tax may not be assessed and a refund may not be claimed more than three years after the end of the applicable tax year. If the tax assessment is under review, however, the authorities may renew the three-year period by notifying the taxpayer of such action before the end of the period. However, tax may not be assessed more than ten years after the end of the applicable tax year.

VAT is a preferential debt in bankruptcy or liquidation.

9.8 Penalties

If a taxpayer fails to register correctly or on time, or to file a tax return, the Financial Authority shall impose a fine of up to Sk1 million (approximately US$33,000). Late filing of returns are subject to a penalty equal to 10% of the liability for the period.

In the case of errors in computing the amount of VAT payable, the penalty is 100% of the error if this is discovered by the Financial Authorities, and 20% of the error if it is corrected by the taxpayer himself and included in an additional tax return. Late payment penalties are imposed at the rate of 0.3% per day.

10   ACKNOWLEDGEMENT

The authors wish to thank Dirk Kroonen and Greg Hill of Ernst & Young CS Consulting, Prague, Czech Republic for their invaluable assistance in the preparation of this chapter.

Contributors: Glen Lonie and Zuzana Lachova
                  Ernst & Young CS Consulting
                  Ernst & Young Audit
                  PO Box 136
                  Riecna 1
                  81499 Bratislava
                  Slovak Republic
                  Tel: +42 7 330793
                  Fax: +42 901 700258

SWITZERLAND

1   GENERAL BACKGROUND

The Ordinance regarding value added tax (VAT) came into effect on 1 January 1995. For approximately 50 years prior to that, goods in Switzerland were subject to a turnover tax.

The Swiss Federal Taxation Authorities, VAT Department, in Bern is responsible for the administration of VAT. Import taxes are levied by the federal customs and duties department.

2   WHO IS TAXABLE?

2.1   General

'Taxable person' means any person who independently and regularly carries out commercial or professional activity in Switzerland, whatever the purpose or results of that activity. Turnover of goods, services and self-supplies must, in total, exceed SFr750,000 per annum. There is no liability to VAT if total annual turnover does not exceed SFr250,000 and the net tax payable after the deduction of the input tax regularly does not exceed SFr4,000 per annum.

The following persons are not subject to tax:

- farmers, foresters and gardeners, who exclusively deliver goods extracted from their own farms, forests and nurseries
- cattle dealers in respect of their turnover from sales of cattle
- painters and sculptors in respect of sales of their own artistic creations
- holding and management companies with a privileged Cantonal tax status.

2.2   Transactions with Branch/Subsidiary

A subsidiary is treated as a separate entity for VAT purposes unless it belongs to a VAT group. As transactions between branches of an enterprise take place within the same legal entity they are not subject to VAT. However, it is the current position of the Swiss tax authorities that cross-border supplies of services between the head office and the branch are subject to VAT according to the rules on cross-border supplies.

2.3   Government Bodies

State, regional and local government authorities and other bodies governed by public law are not considered taxable persons in respect of the activities or transactions in which they engage as public authorities or services provided solely to each other.

2.4   Fiscal Unity/Group Taxation

Legal entities with a place of business or fixed establishments in Switzerland that are closely related to each other may be subject to tax as a single entity. 'Closely related to each other'

This chapter reflects the law on VAT in Switzerland as at 31 October 1994.

is defined as a situation when two or more taxpayers are controlled by the same individual or legal entity through voting power or other means of control. The effect of group taxation is limited to the internal turnover between the domestic members of the group.

It is possible to include holding and management companies (exempted under section 2.1) in a VAT group thus making recovery of input VAT possible for these exempted companies also.

An application for group taxation must be filed with the taxation authorities. The taxation authorities have the power to compulsorily form a VAT group.

2.5   Foreign Entrepreneurs

Companies not resident in Switzerland are subject to VAT if their supply of goods and services in Switzerland in a calendar year exceeds SFr75,000.

2.6   VAT Representatives

A taxable entity or individual who does not reside in Switzerland must appoint a tax representative. The taxation authorities can demand that security for expected tax liabilities be provided.

2.7   Reverse Charge Mechanism

A kind of reverse charge mechanism exists in Swiss VAT regulations.

The place of supply for services is the place of business or fixed establishment of the organisation providing the service. For exceptions to this rule, see section 4.2.

The regulations stipulate that the import of services from abroad are subject to Swiss VAT if the recipient of the services is domiciled or has a fixed establishment in Switzerland and the services are used domestically. In this case the recipient of the service is responsible for the charging and administration of VAT. This tax liability exists for everyone (ie for both non-taxable persons and individuals) in so far as the imported services exceed SFr10,000 per annum. Companies subject to VAT may recover the input tax.

2.8   Importers

The importation of goods into Switzerland and the Principality of Liechtenstein is subject to VAT. The VAT is levied concurrently with the custom duties. Taxable persons who have provided security are allowed to pay VAT to the customs authorities within 60 days of the invoice. Persons who have not provided security must pay VAT immediately upon importation. Taxable persons are the importer, his agent and others in whose name the goods have been imported.

3   WHAT IS TAXABLE?

The following are subject to VAT unless specifically exempted:

- the supply of goods or services effected for consideration within the territory of Switzerland by a taxable person acting as such
- self-supply
- import of goods and services from abroad.

3.1 Supply of Goods

'Supply of goods' means the transfer of the right to dispose of tangible property as owner. Electric current, gas, heat, refrigeration, etc are considered tangible property. The supply of goods also includes all work on goods, even if the goods are not changed through this work or if no material was used (eg examination, adjustment, etc). The supply of goods also includes the letting of goods for use (rent or leasing).

Commission transactions consist of two transactions, ie between the supplier and the commissionaire and between the commissionaire and the customer.

3.2 Supply of Services

'Supply of services' means any transaction which does not constitute a supply of goods. An obligation to tolerate or refrain from an action or situation, and permitting the use of intangible assets or rights are also considered to be the supply of services.

3.3 Self-Supply of Goods/Services

Self-supply is to be taxed when a taxable person removes goods for which he is entitled to a recovery of input tax from his business for:

- non-business purposes, in particular for his personal use or the use of his personnel
- a tax-exempt activity
- no consideration (an exception is made for gifts of up to SFr100 per recipient per annum and for samples).

A taxable person who undertakes or allows the undertaking of construction work on properties destined for sale or rental/leasing must tax his self-supply at the market value, except when he opts to tax the turnover thereon.

Similarly, someone who uses goods or services which were obtained in a non-taxable transfer of assets, for an exempt purpose, must report these as a self-supply.

Self-supply does not include services. However, the goods used and the temporary use of facilities and operating equipment are also to be reported as self-supply.

3.4 Imports of Goods

The importation of goods is generally taxable. However, there are certain exceptions, for example: goods of minor value; certain goods which are not subject to duty, such as household effects of immigrants; coins, marketable securities and bank notes which are used as such; human organs and human blood; goods imported temporarily (with a document called a 'free pass').

If the goods are then exported, the tax may be refunded under certain circumstances.

Duty free zones are considered to be abroad. VAT on imports is due when the goods are released for free circulation domestically.

4 PLACE OF SUPPLY

4.1 Supply of Goods

The place of supply of goods is deemed to be the place where the goods are at the time when the right to dispose thereof is transferred or when they are dispatched or permitted to be used. If the goods are transported or sent to the customer (or in his name to a third party), the place of the supply is where the transport begins.

4.2 Supply of Services

The place of supply for services is deemed to be the place where the supplier has established his business or has a fixed establishment from which the service is supplied or, in the absence of such a place of business or fixed establishment, the place where he resides or has his permanent address.

Special rules exist for:

■ services in connection with the preparation and co-ordination of construction services: the place of supply is the location of the construction
■ transportation services: the place of supply is the country in which the distance covered lies
■ incidental services for transportation: the place of supply is the place where the work is carried out.

5 BASIS OF TAXATION

5.1 Supplies within Switzerland

The tax is calculated on the consideration. This includes all costs that the recipient (or a third party in his place) has incurred, including the reimbursement of all costs. Charges from public authorities are also part of the consideration, with the exception of the VAT itself.

The reimbursement of costs paid on behalf of a customer and in his name are not part of the consideration as long as they are separately invoiced to the customer. Similarly, subsidies and other contributions from public sources are not included in the consideration (they do however reduce the amount of recoverable input tax).

In the case of goods or services to related parties, the consideration must be comparable with that charged to a third party.

5.2 Self-Supplies

For a self-supply, the tax is calculated as follows:

■ in the case of a permanent withdrawal:
 – the purchase price for new goods; or
 – the market value at the time of the withdrawal for used goods

■ in the case of a temporary withdrawal, the amount which would be charged as rent to an independent third party.

For a self-supply of work carried out on construction projects, tax is calculated on the price (without land) which a third party would be charged.

5.3 Imports

In cases of importation the tax is levied on the consideration charged by the importer so long as the goods are imported to fulfil a sales or commission transaction; otherwise, it is levied on the standard value (uncontrolled price). The basis for the calculation includes all domestic and foreign taxes incurred, duty and other charges and levies but not the VAT. All incidental costs such as packaging, transportation and insurance to the first domestic destination are also included.

5.4   Chargeable Event/Time of Payment

Returns must be filed on a quarterly basis, although the taxation authorities may allow longer or shorter filing periods on request. Generally taxable persons file their returns based on invoiced consideration. All turnover invoiced during the period is to be included in the return. Invoices must be raised within three months of the supply. For advance and partial payments, taxes are due when the payment is received (cash basis). The taxation authorities can allow or demand the filing of returns based on consideration received. In this case, the taxable person files his return based on the consideration received during the period. Taxable persons filing under this method may only recover input tax on payments made during the period. Both the tax and the return must be submitted within 60 days of the period end.

VAT on imports is levied at the time the goods are imported. Taxable persons, who have provided security can pay their taxes within 60 days from the date when the customs authorities issued its invoice.

5.5   Credit Notes/Bad Debts

If the amount received as consideration is less than the invoiced consideration, the taxable person may reduce his VAT liability accordingly. The recipient must also reduce his recoverable input tax accordingly. A correction must also be made when a supply is returned or a bad debt is incurred.

In these cases the adjustment in VAT liability or refund must be made in the return for the period in which the reduction of the consideration occurred.

6   TAX RATES

Currently there are two rates:

2%:   water in pipes, food and beverages (other than alcoholic beverages and food and beverages supplied as part of hotel and restaurant services), cattle, fowl, fish, grain, living plants, seeds, cut flowers, feed for animals, fertiliser, medication, newspapers, magazines and books, and services of radio and television companies (except for services of an advertising nature)

6.5%:   all other supplies of goods and services which are not exempt.

7   EXEMPTIONS

7.1   Exemptions with Credit for Input Tax

The following supplies are exempt from VAT but the supplier is entitled to recovery of input tax:

- the export of goods (except for the rental of means of transportation)
- the transportation of goods for export, import and transit, and related services
- telecommunications services, as long as they originate abroad
- air transportation, where only the place of arrival or departure lies in Switzerland
- delivery of aircraft to airlines which operate international flights, and services for these aircraft and their loads
- services of travel bureaux, in so far as these services use third parties and are provided abroad
- services which are provided specifically in the name of and for the account of others by agents, when the commissioned turnover is either genuinely exempted from VAT or is fully realised abroad
- other taxable services to recipients with business establishments or residency abroad, as long as they are used there.

7.2   Exemptions without Credit for Input Tax

Providers of supplies outside the scope of the tax may not charge VAT on those supplies and may not recover input tax. These supplies are largely covered by the following areas:

- transportation of goods by public postal services
- hospital and medical care (human medicine)
- supply of human organs and human blood
- supply of services and of goods closely linked to welfare and social security work
- supply of services and of goods closely linked to the protection of children and young persons
- training, teaching, further education, courses, speeches
- cultural services such as musical productions, theatres, cinemas, museums, galleries, zoos, botanical gardens and sports events
- services of authors and composers and their management companies
- insurance transactions
- transactions in the field of currency and capital business such as the granting or management of credit, operations concerning banking deposits, current accounts, payments and money transfers, securities (although safekeeping and administration of securities and debt recovery businesses are taxable)
- transfer of rights relating to land and services provided by associations of condominium owners to the condominium owners
- leasing or letting of immovable property (excluding hotels, camp sites, installed equipment and machinery, sports facilities, safety deposit boxes, short-term letting of parking spots)
- supply at face value of postage stamps and other fiscal stamps
- betting, lotteries and other forms of gambling
- supply of returnable containers together with the goods contained therein.

7.3   Non-Taxable Transactions

7.3.1 Transactions within the Same Legal Entity

Transactions within a company or by an entity within a VAT group are not subject to VAT.

7.3.2 Transfer of Business

If a taxable person transfers his entire assets or a portion thereof during an incorporation, restructuring or merger to another taxable person, then he can fulfil his tax obligation through a declaration to the tax authorities. The recipient must declare the transaction as self-supply in so far as the assets transferred are not used for a taxable purpose.

7.4 Subsidies/Penalty Payments/Compensation

Subsidies and other public contributions are not part of taxable consideration. They do however reduce the amount of recoverable input tax. Payments for damages are not taxable.

7.5 Election to be Subject to VAT

Farmers, foresters, gardeners and cattle dealers (who are tax exempt) can elect to be taxable. The same is true for entrepreneurs whose turnover does not exceed SFr75,000 or SFr250,000 (see section 2.1).

Exempt turnover such as the transfer of rights in land, leasing or letting of land and the turnover of associations of condominium owners to the condominium owners is taxable if the supplier has waived its tax exemption and opted for taxation. The supplier can waive its exemption only if the recipient of the supply is a taxable person.

8 CREDIT/REFUND FOR INPUT TAX

8.1 General Rule

A taxable person can deduct VAT paid as input tax as long as the goods and services acquired are used to provide taxable supplies. The condition is that the VAT paid can be traced to a correct invoice from the supplier or to a receipt for the VAT paid on importation.

No input tax can be deducted by domestic or foreign entrepreneurs whose supply is totally exempt. Exempt supplies with full credit for the input tax and supplies made abroad which would have been taxable had they been made domestically allow input tax recovery.

If a taxable person has acquired supplies from non-taxable farmers, foresters, gardeners or cattle dealers then he can deduct input tax of 2% on the amount invoiced to him.

No input tax can be recovered for entertainment and the acquisition and repair of motorcycles over 125 cubic centimetres, sailboats, motor boats and sports aircraft. The recovery of input tax is limited to 50% of VAT on the supply of accommodation, food and beverages, business trips and automobiles.

8.2 Adjustment of Entitlement to Credit

If goods which were entitled to an input tax recovery when initially purchased are used later for a tax exempt purpose, the market value is to be taxed as self-supply (for real estate without the land portion).

If, at the time of the purchase of goods, the conditions for the recovery of input tax are not met, a later recovery of the input tax can only be made if, at the point where the conditions are met, the goods have not yet been used.

8.3 Partial Exemption

If a taxable person uses goods for both taxable and exempt purposes, the input tax can only be recovered in the appropriate portions. If the acquired goods are used mainly for taxable purposes, then the entire input tax can be reclaimed and the difference must be taxed annually as self-supply.

8.4 Time of Recovery

The taxable person can deduct the input tax in the period in which:

- the supplier's invoice is received (calculation based on agreed consideration), or
- the supplier's invoice is paid (calculation based on consideration received).

VAT on the importation of goods can be reclaimed in the period in which the customs declaration was accepted and as long as the taxable person is in possession of the original importation documents.

If the input taxes exceed the taxes on turnover, the difference will be refunded to the taxable person.

8.5 Refund for Foreign Entrepreneurs

The Ordinance which governs VAT empowers the Federal Finance Department to set up a system for the refund of VAT by foreigners. The system has not yet been established.

9 ADMINISTRATIVE OBLIGATIONS

9.1 Registration

Every entrepreneur who has an annual domestic turnover in excess of SFr75,000 must register as a taxable person within 30 days from the beginning of the tax liability.

Persons who only become liable to tax due to their importation of services must register within 60 days from the end of the year in which they are liable to tax.

9.2 Book and Records

Every taxable person must maintain in an orderly manner his business records and set up his bookkeeping system in such a way that the calculation of taxes on turnover and input taxes can be reliably determined. Individual transactions must be easily and exactly traced to the supporting document and the accounting records and vice versa. At the end of the fiscal year, the following detailed schedules must be prepared:

- inventory
- accounts receivable and accounts payable
- work in progress and services not yet invoiced
- prepayments received and made.

The company records, vouchers, business documents and other schedules must be kept for six years or until such time as the statute of limitations for the relevant taxes has passed.

9.3 Invoices

Taxable persons must, upon request from a taxable customer, provide an invoice which discloses the following information:

- name, address and VAT number of the supplier
- name and address of the customer
- date or period that the goods were delivered or the services rendered
- nature, object and volume of the delivery or service
- the consideration
- the taxes due on the consideration; if the consideration includes the taxes, then the tax rate must be shown.

The supplying entrepreneur must keep a copy of the invoice.

9.4 Tax Returns

Taxable persons must submit a quarterly declaration on the official forms together with the tax due within 60 days after the end of each quarter. On request, the tax authorities may authorise a different reporting period.

9.5 Power of Authorities

If the information provided by the taxable person is incomplete or obviously does not agree with the true state of affairs, the tax authorities will make an estimate according to its best judgement.

The tax liability expires five years after the end of the calendar year in which it arises.

9.6 Penalties

A taxable person must pay interest on late payments. The interest is set by the federal finance department and the same percentage of interest is paid by the tax authorities on late refunds.

If the obligation to submit a tax return is not fulfilled, then a penalty of up to SFr50,000 can be charged.

Tax evasion may be penalised with fines of between three and five times the tax evaded.

9.7 Objection/Appeal

Decisions of the federal tax authorities can be appealed against within 30 days following their notification.

Decisions taken with regard to an appeal may be further appealed against within 30 days of notification to the Federal Commission for Tax Appeals.

Final authority lies with the Federal Supreme Court.

10 SPECIAL VAT REGIMES

10.1 Small Entrepreneurs

Entrepreneurs who have an annual turnover of up to SFr500,000 can choose a simplified calculation method. They charge taxes at a rate of 6.5% or 2% but pay VAT to the tax authorities at a lower net tax rate for their specific branch. The difference is effectively the input tax recovery which does not have to be separately recorded.

10.2   *Financial Institutions*

Most of this turnover is outside the scope of VAT. An election to become taxable is not possible.

10.3   *Supply of Real Property*

The sale, leasing or letting of real estate is tax exempt. An election to be taxed can be made if the consumer is a taxable person.

10.4   *Second-Hand Goods*

For the sale of used motor vehicles, the taxable person can tax the difference between the purchase price of the used automobile and the sales price of the new automobile rather than the normal method in so far as he could not or does not want to recover any input tax. He may not disclose VAT on the invoice when he sells the vehicle.

10.5   *Paintings and Sculptures*

Painters and sculptors are not taxed for their own artistic creations.

10.6   *Tax-Free Regions*

Tax-free zones and ports are considered to be abroad; turnover which is realised in a tax-free zone is non-taxable foreign turnover.

Although technically foreign zones, the Principality of Liechtenstein, the German enclave of Büsingen and Campione d'Italia, are considered to be domestic and are thus within the scope of VAT legislation.

Special regulations apply to the Samnaun and Sampuoir valleys.

Contributors: Patrick Imgrüth/Dénes Szabó
                   ATAG Ernst & Young
                   Bleicherweg 21
                   P.O. Box 21
                   CH-8022 Zurich
                   Switzerland
                   Tel: +41 1 286 3111
                   Fax: +41 1 286 3147

TURKEY

1   GENERAL BACKGROUND

The Value Added Tax law (Katma Deger Vergisi Kanunu) came into effect on 1 January 1985. Before this, Turkey had a production tax (Istihsal Vergisi) which applied to a selected number of items and focused on a very narrow tax base. There were also different taxes on certain types of transaction such as banking, insurance, postal services, transportation, advertising and betting. Value added tax (VAT) is known in Turkey as Katma Deger Vergisi (KDV) and EC legislation and practice were taken into consideration when preparing the code.

For VAT purposes, the territory of Turkey excludes the tax-free zones established in Mersin, Antalya, Adana, Izmir, Istanbul, Trabzon and Filyos.

VAT is administered by the tax office responsible for the tax affairs of the enterprise, which is normally the place where the enterprise is located. VAT on imports is dealt with by the customs authorities.

2   WHO IS TAXABLE?

2.1   General

VAT is levied when a taxable person delivers taxable goods and services and on the importation of goods and services. There is no equivalent in Turkish VAT law of the term 'entrepreneur' although the term 'taxable person' used in Turkey serves a similar purpose. A taxable person is any person, other than somebody acting as an employee, who carries on a commercial, industrial, agricultural or professional activity in an independent capacity. An activity is characterised as the exercise of a business or profession if it is pursued in a sustained manner and for the purpose of realising sales, although not necessarily for profit. Persons who only make certain exempt supplies are exempt from VAT and are not required to register. However, persons supplying exempt services may opt to become taxable and may register and account for VAT (see section 7.5 'Election to be subject to VAT').

The list of transactions which are liable to VAT when supplied by a taxable person as defined above is extensive and includes:

- supply of goods and services
- the importation of goods or services
- persons who fulfil the customs formalities in respect of the transit of goods through Turkey, ie persons who are engaged in international transportation and who are not domiciled or established in Turkey
- the provision of postal, telephone, telegram, telex and other similar services
- radio and television services

This chapter reflects the legislation on VAT in Turkey as at 15 May 1995.

- the organisation of all kinds of betting, gaming and lotteries
- the organisation of shows, concerts and sporting events with the participation of professional artistes and professional sportsmen
- leasing of goods and rights such as immovable property (land, buildings, mines and rights which have the nature of immovable property)
- motor vehicles, machines, equipment, ships
- literary, artistic and commercial copyrights
- commercial and industrial know-how
- patents, trade marks, licences and other intangible properties and rights.

The leasing of immovable property, rights with the nature of immovable property or movable goods is only taxable if it forms part of the business assets of an entrepreneur.

2.2 Transactions with Branch/Subsidiary
Subsidiaries of foreign firms which deliver taxable goods and services in Turkey are treated in the same manner as other taxable persons, even where the goods and services are supplied to the parent company situated outside the State. Generally, transactions between branches of the same legal entity are not subject to VAT. Thus, supplies between a branch and its head office or another branch are not taxable in a few cases even if one of the parties is situated outside Turkey.

2.3 Government Bodies
To avoid distortions of competition, government and government-owned entities are liable for VAT for their supplies of goods and services that are of a commercial, industrial, agricultural or professional nature. The following activities provided by national and local public institutions, universities, political parties, trade unions, non-profit making organisations, agricultural co-operative societies, social security institutions and other officially qualifying organisations, in performance of their regular activities are exempt from VAT:

- goods and services supplied at hospitals, clinics, dispensaries, human blood and organ banks, public parks, monuments, botanical and zoological gardens, veterinarian, bacteriological, serological and similar laboratories, school dormitories, orphanages and homes for the aged
- goods and services supplied at theatres, concert halls, libraries, sports facilities, reading rooms and conference halls
- goods and services supplied for the purpose of promoting and encouraging scientific, artistic and agricultural activities
- all kinds of supplies without any consideration to the above organisations.

Government bodies are liable to VAT at the point of importation in respect of all goods and services imported by them, with some exceptions.

2.4 Fiscal Unity/Group Registration
The Ministry is authorised to group-register taxable persons and to set starting dates for the taxable periods of these groups.

2.5 Representative Office
A representative office (as opposed to a permanent establishment supplying taxable goods and services) is not subject to VAT. Neither is it entitled to recover any VAT incurred in Turkey.

2.6   VAT Representatives

A foreign firm is not obliged to appoint a representative or responsible person to act on its behalf if it is making taxable supplies in Turkey.

However, in circumstances where a foreign entrepreneur is not domiciled or established in Turkey the revenue authorities are authorised to treat any of the parties involved in a taxable transaction as liable to pay the VAT.

2.7   Reverse Charge Mechanism

Where a service is rendered abroad by a non-resident entrepreneur, who is not domiciled or established in Turkey, it is deemed to have been rendered in Turkey if utilised or 'accounted for' in Turkey. For tax purposes, 'accounted for' means either that the service has been paid for in Turkey or, if the payment is made abroad, that such payment is included in the accounts of the payer in Turkey. In this case, the recipient entrepreneur is required to declare and pay the VAT as a withholding agent – in effect the recipient is treated as if he himself had supplied the service.

2.8   Importers

Liability to VAT on importation arises by virtue of the act of importation and, therefore, private persons, government, local authorities and non-resident entrepreneurs are liable to tax in the same way as other persons and at the same rate as applies to the sale of similar goods within Turkey.

The agent of a non-resident entrepreneur is deemed to be an independent entrepreneur and is liable to pay VAT on importation.

3   WHAT IS TAXABLE?

VAT liability arises on the taxable supply of goods or services in Turkey for consideration by a taxable person in the course or furtherance of any business carried on by him or on the importation of taxable goods or services into Turkey.

3.1   Supply of Goods

The Turkish VAT law employs the term 'delivery' rather than 'supply of goods'.

'Delivery' is defined as the transfer of the right to dispose of goods by the owner or by a third party acting on his behalf to the recipient or to a third party acting on behalf of the recipient. In order for goods to be delivered it is essential that the right to dispose of them is transferred. Therefore, the loan of goods or the supply of goods to agents and consignees does not constitute a delivery.

The transfer of goods to the place or persons indicated by the recipient or a third party acting on his behalf is deemed to be a delivery. Delivery takes place at the commencement of transportation of goods (or transfer of goods to the transporter or the driver in the case where goods are shipped to the recipient or to those acting on his behalf). Thus, for VAT purposes, it is not necessary that the goods dispatched reach the point of destination or that the recipient himself be informed of the shipment. An exchange of goods is deemed to be two separate deliveries which attach VAT liability to both parties, the taxable base of which is the market value of the goods. Similarly, donations or gifts are also subject to VAT at the market value.

Supply of goods also includes the distribution of water, electricity, gas, heat, cooling and similar supplies.

Goods handed over subject to a hire purchase contract (ie where payment of the sale price is made in several instalments) are deemed for VAT purposes to be supplies of goods.

3.2   Supply of Services
VAT is levied on all services apart from those specifically exempt. The term 'services' is defined in an extremely wide sense, ie the performance or omission of any act which can be the object of legal relations which is carried out for a consideration.

Where goods or services are exchanged in a barter transaction, ie a service is supplied in exchange for a service rendered, then each transaction will be taxed separately in accordance with the general rules.

3.3   Supply of Immovable Property
Immovable property is defined by civil law and includes land, buildings, their components and accessory property, mines and certain rights in the nature of immovable property such as usufruct or servitude. The supply or lease (a service) of immovable property is subject to tax only when it comes within the scope of commercial, industrial, agricultural, or professional activities.

3.4   Self-Supply
If a taxable person supplies himself or his employees with goods of his business for private needs, this is considered to be a supply of goods and VAT must be paid on the market value of the goods supplied.

The same rule applies to the use or consumption of self-produced goods by a taxable person in his own business. If the self-produced goods are incorporated into goods which are later sold subject to VAT then there is no self-supply.

A self-service of services is not a taxable event but the private use of taxable services which are rendered free of charge to the owner or employees of a business or to other parties is liable to VAT.

3.5   Importation of Goods and Services
Importation of taxable goods is the introduction of goods into free circulation in Turkey and is a taxable event in itself. However, goods may cross the border without incurring VAT by using the transit regime.

Goods may also stay in a bonded warehouse without VAT becoming due until they are withdrawn, and in certain cases goods may be imported free of VAT if they are being imported for the purpose of processing prior to re-exportation. The importation of taxable services to Turkey is also liable to VAT (see section 2.7 'Reverse Charge Mechanism').

4   PLACE OF SUPPLY

VAT only applies to supplies of taxable goods and services within Turkey (excluding the tax-free zones).

4.1   Place of Supply of Goods

There are no special provisions in Turkish VAT law regarding the place of supply of goods, and VAT is chargeable only if the supply of goods takes place in Turkey.

Where goods are to be transported:

- where the goods to be delivered are in Turkey before transportation – the supply is taxable in Turkey with the important exception of export sales which are exempt with entitlement to recover VAT
- where the goods to be delivered are abroad before transportation – the supply is subject to VAT in Turkey at the point of importation
- where the goods are not transported, the supply is taxable in Turkey if the goods are in Turkey at the time of delivery or transfer of ownership
- where goods have been assembled or installed in Turkey before they are delivered, they are taxable in Turkey.

4.2   Supply of Services

4.2.1 General Rule

The general rule is that services are deemed to be supplied within Turkey if the service is physically performed in Turkey, utilised in Turkey or accounted for in Turkey. Any one of the conditions alone will fulfil the requirement for VAT.

4.2.2 Exceptions

For a number of specified services the general rule is not applicable. These are as follows:

- 'Transport services' are those supplied over the route on which the transport takes place, such services are subject to VAT in accordance with the general rules imposed for the supply of services within Turkey.
- 'Transport in transit services' are services which start outside Turkey, follow a route within Turkey and end outside Turkey. The portion of the service which is supplied within Turkey is liable to VAT.
- International transportation, ie transport which begins inside Turkey and ends outside Turkey or vice versa is exempt from VAT under the reciprocity principles.
- There are no special provisions with regard to the leasing of means of transport and thus the general rule applies.
- There are no special provisions with regard to immovable property.

4.3   Reverse Charge Mechanism

Although article 9(2)(e) of the Sixth EC VAT Directive is not incorporated into Turkish VAT law, the place of supply rules with regard to services serve the same purpose. Thus where a service is rendered abroad by a non-resident entrepreneur, who is not domiciled or established in Turkey, the service is deemed to have been rendered in Turkey if it is utilised or accounted for in Turkey.

The recipient entrepreneur is required to declare and pay the VAT in Turkey.

5 BASIS OF TAXATION

5.1 Supplies within Turkey

VAT is assessed on the total price received, or to be received (whether in cash or in kind) as consideration for the supply of the goods or services. Ancillary expenses, additional payments, commissions, wrapping expenses, interest relating to the supply (as opposed to financial interest), insurance charged by the seller and customs duties are part of the taxable base. Although VAT is not included in the price, supplementary tax (see section 11 'Supplementary tax') must be included.

If cash discounts are granted on the invoice, it is the net amount which is subject to VAT. Where the elements of the taxable base are expressed in a foreign currency, they will be converted into Turkish lira (TL) using the rate of exchange effective on the date the taxable event occurs.

5.2 Self-Supplies

Where depreciable business assets are self-produced or constructed and are used for business purposes the taxable base is the cost to the supplier. Where taxable goods which are self-produced are to be used in manufacturing non-taxable goods within the same enterprise the basis of taxation of the self-produced goods is their market value.

5.3 Imports

VAT due on the importation of taxable goods is assessed on the value determined for customs purposes. Where the customs duty is not computed on the value basis, or where an exemption from customs duty applies, the basis of taxation is the CIF (cost, insurance, freight) value. If that value is not determinable the basis of taxation is the value assessed by the customs authorities. The taxable value for customs purposes is defined to be the normal price, ie the price agreed upon by both parties on the open market value basis, and it includes the cost of transport and packing, fees for insurance, commissions and brokerage paid at the frontier. It also includes all taxes, duties, levies and charges plus the supplementary tax imposed by the VAT law and paid at importation, together with all expenses incurred prior to importation, and differences paid due to price and exchange rate changes.

5.4 Chargeable Event/Time of Payment

Different rules apply to goods and to services. VAT on goods becomes due as soon as the goods have been delivered. This is the case even if the corresponding invoices have not been issued. The full VAT will be due even if the price has not been paid for the goods or if it is paid by instalments. If an invoice or a similar document is issued prior to the supply of goods or services, the time of supply is the time of issuing the documents, but the VAT payable is limited to the amount indicated on the invoice.

As a rule, VAT on services is due when the service is rendered.

5.5   Credit Notes/Bad Debts

There is no provision for relief in respect of bad debts in the Turkish VAT law. However, where goods are returned, the taxable base may be adjusted by the issue of a credit note.

5.6   Non-Resident Entrepreneurs

Non-resident entrepreneurs who have a permanent establishment or representative in Turkey are treated in the same way as resident entrepreneurs. A permanent establishment means a fixed place of business in which the business of the enterprise is wholly or partly carried on. The term includes a place of management, branch, office, factory, workshop, mine, oil or gas well, quarry or other place of extraction of natural resources.

6   TAX RATES

The following main rates currently apply (but see section 11.2 for certain supplementary rates).

1%:   – dried grapes, figs, apricots and hazelnuts, pistachios, pine nuts, sunflower seeds, walnut and pumpkin seeds (all 15% VAT at retail state)

– liquorice plant root extract, anise, bayleaf, thyme, sumac leaf, arbour vitae, mahalep, soapwort, cumin, sesame, poppy seed, hemp seed, wild apricot seed, apricot seed, gum tragacanth, rapeseeds, carob, carob seeds, garden sage, bitter almonds, morel, common fennel seeds and coriander, sugar beet and fig (all 15% VAT at retail stage), black heat (bell heather), fibre and seeds, linden tea

– cotton (raw and fibre), mohair (tops and natural) (all 15% VAT at retail stage), cotton waste, wool and wool fleece

– dried beans, vetch, horse beans, chickpea, lentil and bowels of cattle, sheep and goats, etc (all 8% VAT at retail stage), wheat, barley, corn, soya beans, oats, rye, millet, unhusked rice, cattle, sheep and goats (including poultry and bees)

– goods supplied under financial leases, within the scope of the financial leasing law 3236 to and from financial leasing companies. (Leasing and delivery of automobiles are subject to 23% VAT and other land transportation vehicles are subject to 8% VAT if the transactions are carried within the scope of the VAT financial leasing law)

– newspapers and periodicals (23% VAT if supplied in a special cover)

– second-hand motor cars

– hide and raw skins of the cattle and horses mentioned in Customs Tariff Heading 41.02, of sheep and lambs in Tariff Heading 41.02, and of goats and kids in Tariff Heading 41.03 (all 15% VAT at retail stage)

8%:   – meat of animals for butchery and poultry and fish (excluding meat products produced with additional materials)

– residue of crushed seeds, bran, fish flour, meat flour, bone flour and blood flour used for feeding animals, all kinds of scientific mixed animal feed

– milk and yoghurt (without fruit and artificial flavours) eggs, feta cheese, olives, packaged dry tea, powder produced from the operation of sugar beet,

sugar in powder or cubes
- pounded wheat, rice, wheat flour, bread, semolina, macaroni
- vegetable margarine and oil for human consumption, raw oil, butter, crushed-olive cake and cotton seed used in their production
- fresh vegetables and fruits, potatoes, dried onions and garlic (but not the products thereof)
- natural gas supplies
- certain cash registers which fall within the scope of Regulation no. 3100
- certain tacographs indicated in Regulation no. 2918 of 13 October 1983
- admission fees to the cinema, theatre, opera and ballet halls
- education and instruction services performed at universities, high schools, private schools and crèches to which special permission is granted by the relevant Ministry under Law 625
- deliveries of paper of newspapers contained in the Custom Duty Tariff Heading 48.01 and printing-writing papers in the same Tariff Heading 48.02

23%:   numerous luxury goods.

7   EXEMPTIONS

A transaction is considered as exempt when, although within the scope of VAT, it is excluded from being subject to tax by a special provision of the law. As a rule, exempt supplies prevent an entrepreneur from recovering the tax incurred on purchases made in connection with the exempt supplies. However, the law provides that a number of exempt supplies confer entitlement to input credit.

7.1   Exemptions with Credit For Input Tax
An entrepreneur is entitled to recover the input tax incurred in connection with the following exempt supplies:

- goods exported from Turkey
- deliveries of means of transport by sea, air and railroad and floating installations and equipment to be used by taxpayers in their enterprises and deliveries and services which come into existence as a result of the maintenance and repair of them
- supplies to persons engaged in petroleum exploration activities within the scope of Petroleum Law no. 6326
- services supplied at harbours and airports for vessels and aircraft
- international transportation and supplies of agency services incidental thereto
- supplies to embassies, consulates, diplomatic and consular agents, subject to the condition of reciprocity
- supplies to international institutions and foreign agents connected with such institutions to the extent that the tax exemption is granted by an international agreement.

7.2   Exemption without Credit for Previously Paid VAT
Transactions which are subject to exemption without credit for previously paid VAT are:

- the supply of goods and services for cultural, educational, recreational, scientific, social and military objectives

- the leasing of immovable property except for the immovables included in the business assets of the enterprise. The transfer of certain businesses, ie from a sole proprietorship to a corporation, from a general or limited commercial partnership to a corporation, in the merger and consolidation of corporations, and of a sole proprietorship by reason of death to the legal beneficiaries
- banking and insurance transactions carried out by banks and insurance companies. However, services rendered by banks, bankers and insurance companies are subject to a banking and insurance transactions tax
- the supply of unprocessed gold, foreign exchange money, stocks and bonds, tax and duty stamps, vehicle tax stamps, official stamps and papers
- supplies by public institutions where bank notes, coins and official stamps are produced
- transportation of foreign crude oil, gas and their products through pipelines
- goods and services supplied at public institutions owned by the State or local administrations, hospitals, clinics, dispensaries, human blood and organ banks, public parks, monuments, botanical and zoological gardens, veterinarian, bacteriological, serological and similar laboratories, school dormitories, orphanages and homes for the aged
- goods and services supplied at theatres, concert halls, libraries, sports facilities, reading rooms and conference halls which are owned by public institutions
- goods and services supplied by the same institutions for the purpose of promoting and encouraging scientific, artistic and agricultural activities
- all kinds of supplies including services to be rendered by the same institutions without any charge
- supply of water for agricultural purposes and land improvement services rendered by public institutions, agricultural co-operative societies and farmers' unions
- supplies of military factories, shipyards and workshops in accordance with their statutory objectives.

7.3   Exempt Imports
Certain importations are exempt from VAT:

- goods and services which are exempt from VAT if supplied in Turkey
- samples and models of no commercial value
- all kinds of military equipment for the Turkish army
- publications to be distributed free of charge for advertisement purposes
- goods required for official or personal use by diplomatic or consular officials and their families within certain restrictions, subject to the condition of reciprocity
- personal luggage of passengers
- goods imported for the personal use of the president or the presidential residence
- household articles of individuals moving back to Turkey after having been resident abroad for at least two years
- articles intended for display at exhibitions or fairs
- goods donated for social, cultural and health purposes
- goods and services to which transit, trans-shipment, bonded warehouse, temporary storage, customs area and free zone regimes are applied
- temporary importation of certain goods
- certain goods re-imported after temporary exportation.

7.4   Non-Taxable Transactions

7.4.1 Transactions within the Same Legal Entity
Supplies within the same legal entity are not taxable. Supplies of services made between the foreign head office and its branch in Turkey or vice versa are treated as internal non-taxable transactions in a few cases.

7.4.2 Transfer of Business
The transfer to the legal beneficiaries of a sole proprietorship by reason of death is exempt from VAT provided the beneficiaries carry on the same business. The transfer of certain reorganisations is also exempt from VAT, for instance, the transfer of a business from a sole proprietorship to a corporation, mergers, and corporate consolidations.

7.5   Election to be Subject to VAT/Waiver of Exemption
Subject to the exceptions noted below persons making exempt supplies may elect to be subject to VAT in which case they will benefit from credit and refund mechanisms. A written application must be submitted to the authorised tax office and the waiver is deemed to cover the person's entire exempt transactions and remains in operation for a period of at least three years.

The excluded activities are:

- exempt supplies for cultural and educational purposes
- exempt supplies for social objectives
- exemptions for military purposes
- transactions that fall within the scope of banking and insurance transactions.

As there are no turnover threshold limits for the supply of taxable goods and services all entrepreneurs are liable to VAT irrespective of the size of their turnover.

8   CREDIT/REFUND FOR INPUT TAX

8.1   General Rule
A taxable entrepreneur can deduct the following input tax:

- tax suffered on supplies of goods or services which are carried out for his taxable activities (not for private purposes) provided the input tax is shown separately on an invoice
- VAT paid in respect of goods imported for use in his taxable activities.

The right of deduction may be exercised in the period in which the documents concerned are entered in the books, but only during the calendar year in which the taxable event has taken place.

The following VAT is not recoverable:

- VAT incurred in the acquisition of goods or services which are used or included in the supply of goods or services which are not subject to or exempt from VAT
- VAT incurred on the purchase of cars
- VAT incurred on the purchase of goods which are lost

■ VAT incurred on expenditure which is not deductible in determining income for income and corporation tax laws.

8.2 Adjustment of Entitlement to Credit

There are no special rules with regard to the adjustment of credit apart from the timing of some credits (see section 8.4 'Time of Recovery').

8.3 Partial Exemption

Where a person carries out both taxable and non-taxable/exempt activities he will be entitled to recover only that portion of the VAT which relates to taxable activities.

The Ministry of Finance and Customs has indicated that the VAT should normally be apportioned in the same proportion as cost of goods sold bears to total amount of sales.

For Example:	TL
Total sales	1,000,000
Sales with entitlement to credit	800,000
Sales without entitlement to credit	200,000
Cost of goods sold (on which VAT was incurred)	600,000
VAT paid on inputs	40,000

Credit which may be claimed is 80% ie:

$$\frac{800,000}{1,000,000} \times \text{actual VAT incurred (TL40,000)} = \text{amount recoverable (TL32,000) (80\% of TL32,000))}.$$

An additional payment of VAT amounting to TL8,000 must be made in the last return of the year on the basis that TL40,000 was recovered during the year.

8.4 Time of Recovery

Input credit can be claimed in the period in which the supply was entered in his records if the entrepreneur is in possession of the appropriate invoice. If the input VAT exceeds the output VAT the excess amount is not refunded but is carried forward to the following periods. Refunds are only available in the following cases:

■ VAT related to basic foodstuffs that are subject to reduced rate
■ VAT related to goods and services exempted with credit for previously paid VAT
■ exported goods.

However, the amount of the refund may be credited against other taxes owed to the treasury.

VAT incurred on certain capital expenditure may only be recovered over a three-year period.

8.5 Refunds for Foreign Entrepreneurs

There are no provisions in Turkish VAT law for the recovery of VAT incurred in Turkey by foreign entrepreneurs which have no residence, place of business, registered head office or business centre in Turkey.

9 ADMINISTRATIVE OBLIGATIONS

9.1 Registration
Every entrepreneur who carries out taxable transactions in Turkey must register with the local tax office where the enterprise is located irrespective of the amount of turnover. After registration the entrepreneur will get a tax number under which all VAT returns must be filed. If a taxable person has more than one place of business, registration will be made at the tax office which deals with the trader's individual or corporate income tax.

9.2 Books and Records
The entrepreneur must keep accounts in sufficient detail to permit the proper application of VAT law and inspection by the tax authorities. The accounts must include:

- a description of the taxable transaction, the taxable base, VAT computed and VAT deductible
- exempt transactions, together with the amount of credit available
- descriptions of transactions which are not subject to an input credit and the related amount of VAT
- changes in the taxable base and in the amount of credit available, and the amount of VAT paid, cancelled or refunded.

Taxable persons engaged in supplying goods must make a distinction in their inventories at the end of the accounting period between goods which are taxable and those which are not.

Small entrepreneurs and small farmers are not obliged to keep any records. However, small entrepreneurs who are taxed under a special regime are required to preserve the documents relating to their purchases and business expenses.

All records must be kept for a period of five years. The tax authorities may carry out tax audits and inspect the accounts and the outgoing and incoming invoices for a period of five years after the end of the year in which the VAT return was filed.

9.3 Invoices
Every entrepreneur must issue an invoice in respect of all goods and services supplied by him to another entrepreneur and must keep a copy. The invoices must be numbered sequentially and must contain the following information:

- the date of supply of the goods or services
- the name, commercial title, business address and the tax registration number and tax office of the supplier
- the name, commercial title, address and tax registration number and tax office (if known) of the customer
- a description sufficient to identify the goods or services supplied, the quantity, the price charged and the total amount invoiced
- the date of delivery of the goods and the number of the transportation manifest.

9.4 VAT Returns
All taxpayers, including those only liable in respect of received international services (reverse charge) must submit monthly returns. Persons who keep their records in accordance with the rules of the simplified method of bookkeeping are required to account on an annual basis.

9.5   Powers of the Authorities

If the VAT returns are not filed by the due date the tax authorities may estimate the amount of additional tax due and issue an assessment for that amount.

9.6   Statute of Limitation

The period of limitation for assessment of taxes is five years from the end of the year during which the tax return was filed.

9.7   Penalties for Late Filing/Late Payment

VAT law contains no provisions relating to crimes and penalties. Penalties for failure by the taxpayer to comply with his obligations are prescribed by the Tax Procedure Law which defines various acts of non-compliance with the tax laws that result in tax loss, including evasion of tax, gross fraud and fraud. The penalties range from 50% to 300% of the tax due, with imprisonment available in cases involving falsification of documents.

Non-compliance which does not result in a tax loss is punished by fixed coercive fines.

9.8   Correction of Returns

If an incorrect return is submitted and a breach of law is committed consisting of a 'tax evasion' or 'gross fault' or 'fault', it can be corrected through a procedure called 'repentance' provided for in Tax Procedure Law. If the VAT due is paid during the 15 days after the repentance petition is filed, no penalty is assessed apart from interest for delayed payment.

9.9   Objections and Appeals

A taxpayer may lodge an appeal against an assessment or penalty within 30 days after notification of the tax or penalty. The case must be brought before tax courts within a prescribed time.

Where no appeal has been filed within the prescribed time, the assessment and/or the penalty becomes final.

10   SPECIAL VAT REGIMES

10.1   Agricultural, Forestry Enterprises and Fishermen

Small farmers who are either exempt from income tax or taxed under a special regime in the Individual Income Tax Law are exempt from VAT. Other persons engaged in agricultural activities are subject to VAT in accordance with the general rules. Agricultural activities are defined in a very broad sense in the Individual Income Tax Law.

10.2   Construction Activities

Construction activities are taxed in accordance with the general rules.

10.3   Lump Sum Income Tax

Those who are subject to lump sum income tax (small tradesmen and small professional service fee earners) are also subject to VAT through a simple method known as the 'Lump Sum Yearly Basis of VAT'.

10.4 Retail Export Scheme

VAT suffered by non-resident travellers may be recovered in certain circumstances. Only goods costing more than TL50,000 (excluding VAT) qualify. Special invoices must be obtained and these must be cleared through customs on leaving Turkey.

10.5 Second-Hand Goods

There are no special provisions with regard to second-hand goods.

10.6 Small Entrepreneurs

The Ministry may identify certain small retailers to whom a special regime called 'compensatory taxation' may be applied. This scheme is designed to eliminate complexities and to release small retailers from administrative burdens by exempting them from the requirement to register or account for VAT, ie they do not charge VAT on their sales or recover any VAT on their imports. Alternatively, the amount of VAT being charged to them is increased by 30% thus increasing the price of the goods purchased. If taxable persons purchase goods from such listed retailers they are not entitled to recover any input VAT.

This regime may stay in force for ten years from the date of introduction of the VAT law (1 January 1985). Taxable persons who operate under the compensatory taxation provisions may elect to be subject to the general rules.

At present, compensatory taxation is not implemented in Turkey.

10.7 Travel Agencies

There are no special provisions with regard to travel agencies. However, the Ministry of Finance and Customs has issued a VAT Communiqué exempting from VAT all ticket agency fees which are generated through international transport activities between Turkey and foreign countries.

11 SUPPLEMENTARY TAX

11.1 General

Supplementary tax is imposed to compensate for the difference between the application of the earlier production tax rates and the VAT rates on certain products (mainly tobacco products and drink). The tax is applied at the production and importation stages only and tax paid on inputs can only be credited against supplementary tax charged and not against VAT. The taxable base is the same as for VAT but, while VAT is excluded from the taxable base for supplementary tax, supplementary tax is included in the VAT base.

The same rules with regard to assessment, computation, collection and other issues apply to supplementary tax as to VAT and supplementary tax must be shown as a separate item on invoices and customs receipts.

11.2 Supplementary Tax Rates

The current rates are as follows:

10%: all kinds of non-alcoholic drink (excluding Gazos, a kind of sweetened and carbonated soft drink, and fruit juices)

15%:   certain wines and beers

50%:   tobacco products (20% at importation), all kinds of spirits and fuel oil

60%:   playing cards (excluding toy cards), X-ray films

100%:   all kinds alcoholic drink (0% at importation).

The supplementary tax rates for tobacco products and alcoholic drink are raised to 80% for domestic deliveries and reduced to 0% at importation.

Contributor: Cemal Türklglu
                 Ernst & Young AS
                 Yildiz Posta Caddesi 26/16
                 Yesil Apartmani B Blok
                 80280 Esentepe
                 Istanbul
                 Turkey
                 Tel: +90 212 274 9966
                 Fax: + 90 212 274 9293

AFRICA

ALGERIA

1   GENERAL BACKGROUND

Value added tax (VAT) was introduced in Algeria on 1 April 1992. It replaced two taxes on consumption:

- the unique global tax on production (TUGP)
- the unique global tax on services (TUGPS).

2   WHO IS TAXABLE?

2.1   *General*
The following persons are subject to VAT:

- any individual or entity who, principally or accessorily, extracts or manufactures products, or models or transforms them in order to give them their final form or the final commercial presentation
- any individual or entity who provides ancillary services to a manufacturer in order to carry out operations dealing with manufacture or final commercial presentation such as packing, shipping or consignment
- any person who imports goods to Algeria
- any person who provides taxable services in Algeria.

2.2   *Transactions with Branch/Subsidiary*
Supplies of services or goods between a branch and its foreign head office are subject to VAT.

Furthermore, any entity which carries out business for the benefit of one or several branches of another company, and which depends on or is managed by this company, is subject to VAT. The dependence is defined as 'direct power of decision or decision taken through an intermediary'. The management by the company is defined as the holding of the majority in the share capital or in voting rights.

3   WHAT IS TAXABLE ?

VAT is payable on:

- import operations
- any sale and real estate operations
- any service other than those activities of an industrial, commercial or crafts nature which are already taxed and performed in Algeria usually or occasionally.

This chapter reflects the legislation on VAT in Algeria as at 31 December 1994.

Some operations are compulsorily subject to VAT, some are exempted from VAT (section 7 below), while others may be taxable under election.

3.1 Operations Compulsorily Subject to VAT
Operations compulsorily subject to VAT are:

- sales and deliveries made by manufacturers
- real estate works
- sales and deliveries of imported goods and merchandise which are realised by tradesmen
- self-deliveries of tangible assets
- rental and services operations and any operation other than real estate work or real estate sale
- sale of buildings or goodwill, intermediary operations on these, dividing into plots operations and sales made by the land owner, construction operations
- trade of second-hand goods other than tools, made partly or wholly with platinum, gold, silver, natural gems, antiques and collection objects, original art
- studies and researches realised by companies or partnerships, when one or several shareholders/partners do not participate in the work and are not "art men"
- shows and games of any nature organised by any person
- services relating to telephone and telex rendered by the Post and Telecommunication Office
- sales operations made by supermarkets.

3.2 Self-Supplies
Goods and services in respect of which the person has received an input tax deduction and which are diverted to private or non-business use are taxable.

3.3 Taxation under Election
Certain individuals or entities may elect to be VAT taxable when they supply goods or services to:

- exportation
- oil companies (exploration and exploitation)
- other persons subject to VAT
- companies benefiting from VAT exemption on their sales.

This election may be done on part or all the supplies.

4 PLACE OF SUPPLY

The rules for determining the place of supply are different for goods and services.

4.1 Supply of Goods
A supply of goods is deemed to be taxable in Algeria when the sale is made according to conditions of delivery of the goods in Algeria.

4.2 Supply of Services

Any service rendered, right sold, goods rented out or study made which is used or exploited in Algeria is subject to VAT.

5 BASIS OF TAXATION

5.1 Supplies within Algeria

VAT is assessed on the price of goods, works or services including any expense, duty or tax but excluding the VAT itself. If no moneys are received, VAT must be assessed on the total value of the goods or services received in exchange for the supply.

If cash discounts are granted on the invoice, the net amount is subject to VAT.

Stamp duties, consignment and transport expenses are also excluded from the taxable amount.

5.2 Self-Supplies

VAT due on self-supplies is calculated as follows:

- for tangible assets, the taxable basis includes the selling price of similar products or the value of the raw materials, the value of the services used in the manufacture and/or the salary expenses if the goods are manufactured by an entity for its own business, together with the normal profit on the manufactured goods
- for intangible assets, the taxable basis includes the purchase price and any other expense, tax and duty paid in order to acquire this asset and excludes VAT.

5.3 Imports

VAT due on the importation of goods is assessed on the value determined for customs purposes, to which should be added any tax or duty paid on the importation, with the exception of the VAT itself.

5.4 Specific Cases

The taxable amount for building work provided for non-Algerian companies includes any amount paid in non-Algerian currency at the exchange rate valid at the time the agreement is made.

The taxable amount for customs brokers is the gross remuneration realised, excluding the transport expenses.

5.5 Credit Notes/Bad Debts

If VAT has been collected on cancelled or unpaid operations, it may be either offset against VAT due on future operations or reimbursed (if the person who paid it is not any longer subject to VAT).

The statute of limitation for offsetting or reimbursement is four years after the VAT collection.

6   TAX RATES

Currently there are four VAT rates:

7%:   sugar, water, flour, electricity, newspapers and the construction of housing

13%:   food, hygiene, clothes, building works, advertising operations, books and movies

21%:   all other supplies of goods and services which are not taxable at the 7%, 13% or 40% rate or are not exempt

40%:   luxury and beauty products and all kinds of fuels.

7   EXEMPTIONS

Generally, supplies which are exempt do not confer a right to recovery of input tax unless specifically provided for.

7.1   Exemptions with Input Credit

The following operations are exempt from VAT but carry with them the right to recovery of input tax:

- any sale of exported goods if the seller keeps registers in order to identify these exportations, the customs form is complete, and the exportations are not contrary to laws and regulations
- any sale of goods manufactured in Algeria and delivered to customs warehouses legally set up
- supplies to oil companies.

However, the export of jewelleries, antiques, paintings, drawings, and sculptures cannot be VAT exempt.

7.2   Exemptions without Credit to Input Tax

- sales of goods already subject to an indirect tax (eg tax on tobacco) on manufacture, transport or consumption with a specific duty and a tax according to the value of the goods
- supplies by persons whose turnover does not exceed AD50,000 for service suppliers and AD80,000 for others
- supplies in Algeria between establishments of the same company
- equipment directly connected to prospecting, research, exploitation, transport by pipe activities of liquid or gaseous hydrocarbons, when they are acquired by or on behalf of the Sonatrach Oil Company or partner oil companies, as well as works and services rendered to Sonatrach
- operations realised by the Bank of Algeria and directly connected to its function of issuing currencies as well as other specific missions
- supply of basis food products
- supply of certain agriculture equipment
- geological and mining research
- new cars or used cars less than three years old and under ten horsepower
- the importation of goods or equipment benefiting from a customs exemption or from

an exceptional customs admission regime
- the importation of certain vessels devoted to sea traffic, equipment and nets for maritime fishing, 'Air Algérie' planes
- import of gold
- goods imported for barter.

8   CREDIT/REFUND FOR INPUT TAX

8.1   General Rule

The principle is that the VAT mentioned on invoices and import documents is recoverable if the input tax was incurred with a view to achieving taxable transactions.

This important restriction prevents entrepreneurs from recovering input VAT on:

- goods, services and buildings not used for the needs of a business subject to VAT
- private cars and transport of persons which do not constitute the main tool used for the business of the enterprise
- goods, services and buildings delivered or acquired by persons subject to VAT according to a simplified procedure ('Forfait')
- goods or services offered free of charge
- services, spare parts and equipment used for the repair of goods for which input tax recovery is not allowed
- supplies of certain services which are taxable are not entitled to recover input VAT
- operations performed by foreign companies subject to VAT withheld at source, brokers, taxi holders, land agents – taxed at 7%
- sport meetings, shows, telex and telephone operations – taxed at 13%
- concerts – taxed at 21%.

8.2   Partial Exemption

Entrepreneurs making both taxable and exempt supplies are allowed to recover only the input VAT relating to taxable supplies.

If the goods or services purchased are used both for taxable and exempt supplies, the creditable input tax is calculated in the ratio of the operations subject to VAT or exempt deliveries to the total turnover.

In particular instances, the tax authorities may authorise or oblige tax payers to attribute specific percentage of deduction to various departments of activities within the enterprise.

8.3   Time of Recovery

Algeria allows immediate recovery only if the goods purchased qualify as depreciable assets. For all other goods and services, recovery is possible in the month following that of the invoicing or filing of the import document.

VAT paid on depreciable assets is recoverable if:

- the assets are new and acquired for operations subject to VAT or VAT exempt with credit
- the assets are recorded for accounts purposes at their purchase price less the VAT recovery

■ the assets are kept for at least five years. If not, VAT must be repaid based on an apportionment of the number of years left.

When recoverable input VAT is in excess of output VAT, the excess credit can be offset against the output VAT of following months.

Except for export operations or purchase of goods or services free of any tax, the excess input VAT cannot be reimbursed.

9   ADMINISTRATIVE OBLIGATIONS

9.1   Registration

Within 30 days of the beginning of operations subject to VAT, any individual or entity must file a declaration of existence. This declaration is filed with a certified copy of the Articles of Association.

Foreign entities or individuals which do not have a permanent establishment in Algeria and which carry out studies or technical assistance services for public administrations or companies must also file a declaration of existence with a copy of their contract.

9.2   Books and Records

Entities or individuals which are subject to VAT must keep adequate accounting books to justify all their transactions. When they are charging different VAT rates, their corresponding supplies must be accounted for separately.

9.3   VAT Returns

Every month, the individual or entity carrying out operations subject to VAT must file a VAT return in order to declare the supplies realised during the preceding month. The deadline for filing is the twenty-fifth day of each month.

This filing may be done on a quarterly basis if the average monthly VAT due during the preceding year was less than DA2,500 or if a specific request is forwarded to the tax authorities.

9.4   Payment of the VAT

VAT is payable when the return must be filed.

Tax payers who have been making supplies for more than six months and who have a permanent establishment in Algeria may be authorised to pay VAT by instalment. Each instalment corresponds to one-twelfth of the VAT due on the gross income realised during the 12 preceding months, after deduction of input VAT. A yearly return must be filed before 1 April of each year and the additional VAT due, if any, must be paid by 25 April. Authority to file returns and pay VAT accordingly must be requested before 1 February.

VAT due on services rendered by individuals or entities which do not have a permanent establishment in Algeria is withheld at source by the client and paid over to the authorities. It is a withholding tax mechanism since all foreign companies rendering a service must file a legal declaration of existence with the various tax and social authorities.

9.5   Powers of the Authorities

Late filing of a monthly return entails a penalty of between 15% and 25%.

When a tax return is inaccurate the penalty is:

10%:   if the amount of tax underpaid is less than DA100,000

15%:   if the amount of tax underpaid is between DA100,000 and DA200,000

25%:   if the amount of tax underpaid is over DA200,000.

Any fraud entails a 200% penalty.

Any late payment entails a 10% penalty when the payment is made within 30 days following the deadline and a 3% penalty per month of delay, with a maximum of 25%, when the payment is made more than 30 days following the deadline.

The statute of limitation is four years, and two years may be added in case of fraud.

10   SPECIAL VAT REGIMES

10.1 Small Businesses
VAT payers who carry out their activity as individuals or through partnerships may account for VAT according to a simplified procedure ('Forfait') during a two-year period if their annual gross income is:

■   between AD50,000 and AD800,000 for service providers
■   between AD80,000 and AD1,500,000 for other tax payers.

The amount of VAT due for the year is assessed on the value of the taxable transactions after deduction of input VAT. The taxable basis is negotiated with the tax authorities.

VAT is payable in quarterly instalments corresponding to one-fourth of the VAT due for the year. The payment must be made on the last day of each calendar quarter.

10.2 Free Operations
Some persons may obtain permission from the tax authorities in order to import or acquire free of any VAT a certain number of products.

This regime is provided for the following supplies:

■   goods and services acquired by oil companies' suppliers directly used in activities of prospecting, research, exploitation and transport by pipe of liquid and gaseous hydrocarbons
■   purchases or importation of goods realised by an exporter in order to be exported or re-exported in the same state, and goods used in the manufacture, conditioning or packing of products to be exported
■   purchases of raw materials and specific packing in order to manufacture VAT exempt products
■   purchases of equipment by newly-established companies carrying out an activity having priority on the national plan of development.

Such a purchase free of any VAT is authorised on an annual basis and according to the amount of goods purchased during the preceding year.

11   FURTHER READING

Memento Algérie, Editions Fiduciaires, France Afrique, 1994

Legal Gazette, 31 December 1990.

Contributor: Anne Ermel
                    HSD Ernst & Young
                    Societe d'Advocats
                    Tour Manhattan
                    Cedex 21
                    92095 Paris la défense 2
                    France
                    Tel: +33 1 46 93 65 70
                    Fax: + 33 1 47 67 01 06

EGYPT

1   GENERAL BACKGROUND

General Sales Tax (GST) was introduced in Egypt by Law no. 11 of 1991. The first stage of the tax was applied on 3 May 1991 by the General Sales Tax Law which abolished the previous Consumption Tax Law No. 133/1981 which previously applied to certain commodities. The Executive Regulations of Sales Tax Law, was issued in June 1991. GST is administered in respect of internal sales of goods and services by the General Sales Tax Authority and tax on imports is controlled by the Customs Department.

The tax is collected at three stages:

1   the producer, the importer (of some types of commodities) and the renderer of some services are assigned to collect the tax due and pay it to the Tax Department
2   wholesalers collect the tax and pay it to the Department
3   retailers collect the tax and pay it to the Department.

2   WHO IS TAXABLE?

The following persons are liable to pay GST:

- producers of goods and renderers of services whose gross sales in a financial year or part thereof exceed LE54,000
- importers irrespective of the level of sales
- producers of commodities listed under Schedule No.(1) of the General Sales Tax Law, irrespective of the level of sales
- registered distribution agents irrespective of the level of sales.

3   WHAT IS TAXABLE?

GST is levied on:

- the legal disposal of goods or services
- all imports of goods included in Schedule No.(1) unless such goods are specifically excluded from taxation
- locally produced commodities included in Schedule No.(1) except such goods which are specifically excluded from taxation
- services included in Schedule No.(2) of the General Sales Tax Law
- goods/services used by a taxpayer for a private/personal purpose
- goods and services exported abroad – taxed at a zero rate.

This chapter reflects the law on GST in Egypt as at 31 October 1994.

4   PLACE OF SUPPLY

Goods which are physically located in Egypt at the time of supply are liable to tax. Similarly services supplied in Egypt (and where such services come within the scope of tax) are liable to Egyptian GST. Importations of goods into Egypt are liable to GST with the exceptions of goods which are specifically excluded. Exports of goods or services from the Free Zones/Markets are taxed at the zero rate.

5   BASIS OF ASSESSMENT

5.1   Taxable Amount

The amount of tax due is based on the amount paid as recorded on the tax invoice. Normal commercial discounts and conditional cash discounts are not included in the taxable amount of goods or services.

The taxable amount of goods does not include the amount paid for repair, maintenance, installation or transportation.

5.2   Imports

In respect of goods imported from abroad, the taxable amount is the value agreed with the Customs Department plus the amount of customs duties on such goods.

5.3   Chargeable Event

The tax is due at the time of selling the commodity or rendering the service by the taxpayer.

With regard to the importation of goods, tax is due when the commodity is released by the Customs Department, ie when the customs duty is settled.

6   TAX RATES

The following rates apply:

0%:   – dairy products, or those produced from milk (ie cheese, yoghurt) by replacing one or more of its natural elements
      – subsidised oil produced from plants and used for food, whether the oil status is natural, liquid, frozen, or refined
      – products of grinders except luxury flour or exported flour
      – types of canned meats or meat products
      – types of canned fish and fish products except caviar or similar types and smoked fish
      – vegetables, fruits, serials, peons, salt, pepper whether canned, fresh, frozen, or conserved except where they are imported
      – Halwa Tehinia
      – food products sold directly to the final consumer by restaurants or non–tourism places
      – all types of bread with controlled/subsidised prices
      – natural gas and potagas if it is stored for sale in retail sale
      – waste or by-products of the food industry, poultry and cattle feed and food for

animals, birds and fish except that used for feeding cats, dogs and ornamental fish
- popular clothing products distributed by the Ministry of Supply
- paper used in newspapers or used for writing and printing
- books or university notes
- magazines and newspapers
- macaroni produced from normal flour
- exports of goods and services by persons operating in Free Zones and Free Markets
- imports of goods and services which are necessary for the authorised activities by persons operating in Free Zones and Free Markets, except private cars.

1.625%: imported medicines

5%:   - tourism hotels and restaurant services
- tourism transportation services
- air-conditioned transportation by buses between provinces
- services rendered by artists' agents in organising public or private festivals
- services consisting of the provision of sound & light festivals
- coffee
- all products made of flour and sweets except bread
- soap and cleaning materials and products for household usage
- fertilisers
- purifiers and poisons against insects and rats used for agricultural purposes
- gypsum
- wood – manufactured and non-manufactured
- local medicines
- iron bars (reinforcing irons) used for construction and waste steel and iron
- fax and telex services

10%:   - services used by sound and light utilities

- local telephone and telegraph services
- international communication services (wireless, satellite, etc), international telegrams, international phone calls, local or international transfer of information
- installation services, telephone (wireless and others)
- agency services
- security and cleaning services
- express international postal services
- express highway charges
- private car hire
- real estate agency services
- car sales agency

25%:   - coloured television sets larger than 16 inches, or sets attached with other appliances
- display refrigerators used in commercial stores, hotels and other places
- deep-freezers larger than 10 cubic feet
- records and broadcasting units
- air-conditioning units
- cameras and their spare parts
- perfumes and cosmetics used for hair and skin care
- chandeliers and their spare parts

- video tapes
- cars with cylinder capacity of more than 1600m, caimans, jeeps, buses and tractors used for tourism

32.5%:–imported aerated water

60%: – local aerated water.

Certain other products and services are taxed on a fixed amount basis. Many of these are specified in Schedule no. 1 of the General Sales Tax Law as follows:

Tea:	LE144.756 per net ton subsidised tea LE1166.662 (portion) for imported extra packed tea
Sugar:	LE43.60 (approximately) per net ton of subsidised sugars
	LE58.60 for triangle-shaped solid sugar
Tobacco:	Ranging from 200% at a minimum rate of LE50 for each kilogram produced to 50% (at a minimum rate of LE16 for each kilogram)
Petroleum products:	
Benzine	LE43.30 per ton for imported benzine LE280 per ton for super benzine LE250 per ton for local normal benzine
Local or imported white spirit	LE1.75 per litre
Kerosene	LE0.010 per litre
Solar	LE0.010 per litre
Diesel oil	LE0.008 per litre
Mazott	LE0.50 per ton
Lubrication oil	LE11 per ton
Lubrication products	LE9 per ton
Ethanol	LE7.5 per litre pure (changed/denatured)
	LE15 per litre liquid (non-changed/un-denatured)
Spirits:	Vermouth, other fermented liquors and other spirits 100% on the value amount (at a minimum rate of LE7.5 on each litre liquid)
Beer:	
Alcoholic	100% of value – minimum rate of LE200 per hecto litre (local and imported)

Non-alcoholic	60% (local and imported)
Plantation oil:	Non-subsided at a rate of LE37.40 per each net ton.
Animal lubrication oil:	LE40 per each net ton.
Water cement of all types:	Imported (at a rate of LE1.40 per each ton) Local (at a rate of LE2.50 per each ton)

Rates of VAT have been amended many times in the past and are likely to be so amended in the future.

7   EXEMPTION

7.1   *Exemption with Credit for Input Tax*
Goods which are zero-rated, including those set out at the 0% rate in section 6, and exported goods and services confer an entitlement to recovery of input tax for the supplier. The supplier of zero-rated goods and services has the right to recover the tax paid on all inputs used in their supplies. The zero rate for exports applies to the products listed in section 6.

7.2   *Exemption without Credit for Input Tax*
The supply of certain goods and services is exempt from tax. The suppliers of such goods and services are not permitted to charge tax nor are they entitled to recover any of the tax they have paid at previous stages if it is attributable to the supply of exempt goods and services. The following goods and services are exempt from tax:

- the transit of goods under the supervision of the Customs Department
- goods and services purchased or imported for the personal usage of diplomatic or foreign consulate members, their spouses and minor children
- goods and services bought or imported by embassies and consulates for official use except food, cigars, cigarettes and alcoholic syrup
- goods imported for the personal use of embassies and consulate staff, such as personal belongings, home furniture and one car for each employee
- samples used for analysis purposes by governmental laboratories
- non-commercial personal belongings, eg decorations, educational and sporting prizes
- goods imported without value in return for previous imports which were lost, destroyed or rejected in circumstances where the tax due was previously paid on them, subject to agreement with the Customs Department
- the accompanied personal belongings of passengers coming from abroad
- all re-importations of exported items on which the tax due on them has already been paid, subject to examination by the Customs Department
- gifts, donations and prizes offered to government bodies or local authorities with the approval of the competent minister
- items of a scientific, educational or cultural nature imported by concerned institutes with the approval of the competent minister
- all goods, equipment, appliances or services required for armaments and used for defence and national security purposes, together with all materials, spare parts, etc

used in the production of armaments so used
- electric wheel-chairs and their spare parts, and manufactured replacement parts for the human body whether they are portable, used or installed in the human body.

8   TAX CREDIT AND TAX REFUND

In the tax calculation, a registered taxpayer may deduct the tax previously charged on goods sold by the taxpayer.

The registered taxpayer has the right, within the monthly taxable period to deduct from the total tax due on his taxable sales the amount of tax previously levied on the following items:

- the amount already paid by the taxpayer on the purchase of the input goods or services if the goods are locally produced, provided he can produce invoices
- the amount paid on imported goods during the taxable period
- the amount of tax previously paid over to the authorities which is the subject of a credit note provided:
  - the maximum amount recoverable is the actual amount paid over;
  - the sales tax return was actually received by the tax authorities; and
  - the taxpayer issued a dated and numerated credit/debit note.

A taxpayer is not entitled to a tax credit or refund in respect of goods or services taxed at the 5% or 10% rates – scc section 6 above as such goods or services are either themselves subject to tax or are inputs used in the production of other taxable goods or services.

9   ADMINISTRATIVE OBLIGATIONS

Every taxpayer whose total sales amounts to or exceeds the registration limit (LE54,000) in any financial year or in a part of it, has to apply to the department in order to register his name. Accordingly he has to collect the tax and pay it to the administration within a fixed period.

9.1   Returns
Every taxpayer has to submit a monthly declaration to the department within two months from the end of the monthly accounting period even if he has not realised the minimum taxable amount of sales or services.

9.2   Records
Every registered taxpayer has to maintain proper records and books of account showing all his transactions and operations.

9.3   Invoices
For tax purposes every registered taxpayer must issue an invoice in respect of each sale of taxable goods and on each performance of any taxable service. Each invoice should bear the taxpayer's registration number.

10   SPECIAL REGIMES

According to the General Sales Tax Law and its executive regulations, the Chief of the Tax Department may issue special administrative rules which are considered necessary for the correct and efficient application of the Law, depending on the nature of the activities of some producers, importers and service renderers. These rules are issued following agreements concluded with different representative organisations and associations. Examples of the sectors in which regulations have been issued by the department:

- spinning and weaving products and ready-made clothes
- furniture and wooden products
- wood importers
- the construction industry
- candy produced from all types of farina
- dry candy production
- bakeries
- gold and silver products
- bamboo products.

Contributor: Taha Khalad
                 Zarrouk Khaled + Co
                 A member of Ernst & Young International
                 PO Box 110/12655
                 1 Wadi El Nil Street
                 Mohardessen, Giza
                 Cairo
                 Egypt
                 Tel: +20 2 3032229
                 Fax: +20 2 3032228

KENYA

1   GENERAL BACKGROUND

The value added tax (VAT) law is contained in the Value Added Tax Act, 1989 and came into operation on 1 January 1990. It has since been amended substantially through the 1990 to 1994 Finance Acts.

VAT is controlled by the Commissioner of VAT and his officers. The Commissioner is responsible for the control, collection of and accounting for tax under the direction of the Minister of Finance.

2   WHO IS TAXABLE?

2.1   *Taxable Persons*
Any person, including sole proprietors, partnerships and limited companies, who in the course of his business has manufactured and supplied, or expects to manufacture and supply taxable goods, or has supplied or expects to supply taxable services the value of which exceeds in any of the following periods the values shown below is a taxable person.

Period (Months)	*Services & General Designated Goods (Kshs)*	*Manufacturers (Kshs)*
12	1,800,000	900,000
9	1,350,000	675,000
6	900,000	450,000
3	450,000	225,000

2.2   *Fiscal Unity/Group taxation*
In certain circumstances, the Commissioner of VAT may allow a group of companies to be registered as one person.

3   WHAT IS TAXABLE?

Not all supplies of goods and services are taxable in Kenya. For instance, the coverage of VAT is restricted to the manufacturing level in respect of goods while, for certain specific taxable services, all entities supplying such services and with turnovers above the minimum levels are required to register.

VAT is chargeable on the supply of manufactured goods and specific services within Kenya in the course of furtherance of business. It is also chargeable on the importation of goods and services into Kenya. Exceptions to the tax are dealt with either by zero-rating or by exemption. Salaries and wages paid by an employer to his employees are not subject to VAT.

This chapter reflects the law on VAT in Kenya as at 31 December 1994.

3.1 Imports

Importers need to register and must pay any VAT due at importation. Goods sold by businesses operating in the Export Processing Zones to persons in other parts of Kenya are regarded as imports.

3.2 Self-Supplies

Where a manufacturer takes goods from stock for his own use he must pay VAT based on the amount he would charge third parties/customers for the same goods.

4 PLACE OF SUPPLY

Only the supply of goods physically located in Kenya at the time of supply, the supply of specified services in Kenya, and the importation of goods into Kenya are taxable.

5 BASIS OF TAXATION

Where taxable goods or services are supplied by a registered person to a person independent of him, the taxable value is the price for which the supply is provided. Where supplies are made in any other manner, the taxable value is the price at which the goods would have been sold in the ordinary course of business. Where such a price cannot be determined, the price is subject to regulations decided by the Commissioner of VAT.

'Taxable value' should include any charges made to the customer for packaging, advertising, financing, servicing, warranty or commission. The costs of transportation, erection, or returnable containers may normally be excluded from the taxable value under arrangements specified in the Regulations. Cash and other discounts actually allowed are relieved of tax.

5.1 Imports

Where taxable goods are imported into Kenya, the taxable value is the sum of the following amounts:

- the value of such taxable goods ascertained for the purpose of customs duty in accordance with the Customs and Excise Act, whether or not any customs duty is payable on the goods
- the amount of the customs duty, if any, payable on the goods.

6 TAX RATES

Currently there are four VAT rates:

0%: – exports of goods and services
– sales to businesses operating in Export Processing Zones
– exports of basic needs goods
– exports of fertilisers, pesticides, insecticides and farm implements

5%:   general goods

18%:
- accountancy, including auditing, bookkeeping and similar services
- management and related consultancy services
- computing and related services
- services supplied in the course of altering, processing, assembling, packing, packaging, bottling or manufacturing of goods owned by another person
- services supplied by land and building surveyors, quantity surveyors, insurance assessors, fire and marine surveyors, loss adjusters and similar services
- services supplied by security organisations
- mail and parcel courier services, excluding postal services supplied by KPTC
- advertising services
- legal and related services
- services supplied by architects (including landscape architects) and draughtsmen
- services supplied by consulting engineers
- services supplied by auctioneers, estate agents and valuers
- commission agency services, excluding insurance agency
- services provided by brokers, but excluding insurance brokers and tea and coffee brokers dealing exclusively in tea and coffee for export
- secretarial agencies (including typing and photocopying agencies)
- services provided in connection with designated goods by designated dealers
- telecommunication services
- leasing video tapes
- entertainment services
- accommodation provided by a hotel owner or operator
- restaurant and hotel services
- laundry and other cleaning services
- beauty parlours and health clubs
- hiring and leasing services
- repair and maintenance services
- goods transportation services
- conference services
- services supplied by contractors
- car park services
- balloon safari services
- photographic services
- industrial raw materials
- designated goods

30%:   luxury goods.

7   EXEMPTIONS

7.1   Exemptions with Credit for Input Tax

While exemption does not create the right to recover VAT, the zero rate operates in practice in a similar fashion. Strictly, a zero-rated supply is taxable, but at a nil rate of tax.

This means that a registered person who supplies zero-rated goods does not have to charge output tax to his customers, but can recover any input tax that has been charged by his own suppliers.

7.2 *Exemptions without Credit for Input Tax*

Exempt supplies are business transactions on which VAT is not chargeable at either the zero rate or other rates. Exempt supplies are not taxable supplies and do not form part of the taxable turnover. Exempt supplies include:

- valuations
- awards
- delivery orders
- acknowledgements of debt
- letters of allotment of shares or share certificates
- proxies, etc.

8 RECOVERABLE VAT

Output tax is the value of taxable supply multiplied by the VAT rate. Input tax is the value of taxable input multiplied by the VAT rate. When the output tax exceeds the input tax, a payment of the excess is made to the VAT office with the return form. When the input tax is greater than the output tax, the balance is carried forward to the next return. In certain circumstances, the Commissioner may pay any excess of input tax over output tax to the registered person if he is satisfied that such excess is a regular feature of the business. When a registered person provides both taxable and exempt supplies, the input tax that is not directly attributable to the former is apportioned. The preferred method of apportionment is set out in the regulations. However, different methods of attribution are allowed if approved by the Commissioner.

Tax on certain inputs is non-deductible. The list includes:

- all motor vehicle fuels and oils for use in such vehicles
- all motor vehicles, motor vehicle bodies, and all goods and services for repair and maintenance of such vehicles
- furniture, fittings and ornaments or decorative items in buildings, other than items permanently attached to buildings
- household or domestic electrical appliances, with some exceptions
- liqueurs and other spirits, alcoholic beverages and soft drinks
- entertainment services
- accommodation and other hotel services
- restaurant services.

The Minister for Finance may, by publishing an order in the Official Gazette, waive wholly or in part tax payable in respect of any taxable supplies if it is in the public interest to do so.

A repayment is made if any tax is paid in error or if, in the opinion of the Minister for Finance, it is in the public interest to do so. Relief may also be given because of doubt or difficulty in recovery of tax.

9   ADMINISTRATIVE OBLIGATIONS

9.1   Registration

Every taxable person is required to register with the VAT authorities by completing and submitting an application form (Form VAT 1). A designated dealer should register for VAT on receipt of designated goods for sale. No minimum amount is specified in the case of designated jewellers and sawmillers.

A person who is not obliged to register for VAT because he does not qualify under the income limits may volunteer to be a taxable person.

A difficulty could arise where service-supplying firms also trade in taxable goods for which the mere trading in the goods would not require VAT registration. For example, the sale of photocopying equipment or supplies by a non-manufacturer would neither be taxable nor require registration, but if the same firm also supplied photocopying services it would be required to be registered and would have to collect VAT on all its supplies of taxable goods. This could put it at a competitive disadvantage as compared to a firm merely trading in photocopying machines. To solve this problem a special provision has been introduced to allow for partial registration whereby a trader could apply to the Commissioner to be exempted from collecting VAT on sales of taxable goods but would still be required to collect VAT on the supply of taxable services.

9.2   Returns

A taxable person must make monthly returns in a prescribed form (Form VAT 3). The latter shows details of tax on goods and services charged to his customers during the preceding month (output tax) and tax suffered on goods and services charged by his suppliers (input tax).

VAT is payable to the Commissioner of VAT and is due by the twenty-seventh day of the month following that in which the tax became due. The tax is due and payable on the earliest of the following events:

- when the goods or services are supplied to the purchaser, or
- when an invoice is issued in respect of the supply, or
- when payment is received for all or part of the supply.

9.3   Invoices

A registered person who makes a taxable supply is required to furnish the purchaser with a tax invoice at the time of supply. A tax invoice includes:

- name, address and VAT number of supplier
- date of supply
- number of invoice
- name and address of person being supplied
- type of supply
- amount payable before VAT
- tax rate
- tax charged.

However, retailers are required to quote on their price tags or labels VAT-inclusive prices.

Where any taxable person sells taxable goods for cash, a tax invoice must be issued on the spot at the time of receiving cash and delivering the goods to the customer.

9.4 Record-Keeping for VAT

A registered person must keep records of all supplies made and received and a summary of VAT for the period covered by the return. The records must be in a form acceptable to the VAT authorities and be available for inspection.

9.5 Powers of the Authorities

Penalties are imposed for:

- failure to register
- failure to keep proper records
- fraudulent accounting
- failure to comply with a notice
- failure to give a VAT invoice
- charging VAT when not registered
- failure to pay tax and late payment.

Both financial and custodial penalties can be imposed.

A late payment penalty of 3% per month or part thereof is charged on unpaid tax.

9.6 Appeals

Appeals may be made to the Tribunal by an aggrieved party. The decision of the Tribunal is final.

Contributor: Geoffrey G. Karuu
Ernst & Young
Mamlaka Road
Nairobi
Kenya
Tel: +254 2 727640
Fax: +254 2 716271

SOUTH AFRICA

1   GENERAL BACKGROUND

Value added tax (VAT) was introduced in South Africa on 30 September 1991, replacing a retail sales tax system which had been in operation since 3 July 1978.

Legislation is contained in the Value-Added Tax Act 1991, as subsequently amended in 1991, 1992 and 1993. The Commissioner has issued 14 VAT Practice Notes to assist in the interpretation of certain provisions of the legislation, but they have no statutory recognition or effect.

Overall control of VAT is vested in the Commissioner for Inland Revenue. VAT on imports is administered by the Customs Department. VAT on internal transactions is administered by the local Receivers of Revenue.

2   WHO IS TAXABLE?

2.1   General
Any person other than somebody acting as an employee, who supplies goods or services in the course of an enterprise and whose annual turnover exceeds, or is likely to exceed, R150,000 from the supply of goods or services must account for VAT. A profit motive is not required; thus, certain non-profit-making organisations are subject to VAT in accordance with the general principles.

2.2   Transactions with Branch/Subsidiaries
Subsidiaries of foreign firms which supply taxable goods and services in South Africa are treated in the same manner as other taxable persons, even where the goods and services are supplied to the parent company situated outside the State. Transactions between branches of the same legal entity are not subject to VAT unless the branches are separately registered for VAT purposes.

2.3   Government Bodies
The State is not a taxable person in respect of any of its activities. However, supplies by a public authority, division or department of central government of goods or services which are of the same nature as those supplied by commercial enterprises may be deemed to be taxable by the Commissioner in consultation with the Treasury. Most supplies of goods and services by local authorities are subject to VAT.

2.4   Fiscal Unity/Group Taxation
The term 'fiscal unity' is not used in the South African legislation and there are no provisions for group registration or submission of group VAT returns.

This chapter reflects the law on VAT in South Africa as at 31 December 1994.

2.5 Foreign Firms

Foreign firms which carry on an enterprise in or partly within South Africa are subject to the same VAT requirements as local businesses.

2.6 Representative Office

The Act does not contain any special provisions for representative offices.

2.7 VAT Representatives

A foreign business making taxable supplies in South Africa and which is liable for VAT registration may appoint a South African agent to take responsibility for its VAT responsibilities. The Commissioner has the power to declare any person to be the VAT agent of any other person.

2.8 Reverse Charge Mechanism

Persons who receive certain services (such as copyrights, patents, advertising and consultancy services) from non-resident suppliers are obliged to account for VAT on the value of the services unless they would otherwise qualify for an input credit in respect of the VAT on the imported service, in which case the imported service is ignored.

Where the imported service would normally be exempt or zero-rated, the recipient is not required to account for any VAT.

2.9 Importers

Persons who import goods into South Africa are subject to VAT at the same rate as that applying to the sale of similar goods within South Africa.

3   WHAT IS TAXABLE?

VAT liability arises on the supply of goods or services for consideration by a vendor in the course or furtherance of any enterprise carried on by him and on the importation of goods or services into South Africa.

3.1 Supply of Goods

The term 'goods' includes tangible movables, land, buildings and other fixed structures or works, sectional title units, shares in shareblock schemes, time-sharing interests, gold coins and postage stamps. An intangible real right in any of the above (for example, a usufructuary interest or a registered long lease) also constitutes goods.

Excluded from the definition of goods are coins and other legal tender and South African revenue stamps, except when any of these items is disposed of as a collector's item, and rights under a mortgage bond or pledge.

The term 'supply' covers all forms of supply, so any sale, cession, lease, rental or other form of supply of goods will be taxable.

3.2 Supply of Services

Services means anything done or to be done which is not a supply of goods or money. It includes the granting, cession or assignment of any right and the making available of any facility or advantage.

3.3 Deemed Supplies

A number of supplies of goods or services are deemed to be made in certain circumstances. These include betting and gambling transactions, the receipt of an indemnity payment under a short-term insurance contract and a deemed supply of goods on deregistration of an enterprise.

3.4 Self-Supplies of Goods

There is a self-supply of goods when a person diverts to private or exempt use, goods which he has imported, purchased, manufactured or otherwise acquired and in respect of which he was entitled to a VAT input credit.

3.5 Importation of Goods

The importation of goods is a taxable event irrespective of the status of the importer or the nature of the importation. Goods imported into a bonded warehouse are not liable to VAT until removed from the warehouse.

4 PLACE OF SUPPLY

The Act does not set out any special provisions for the place of supply. A supply can be subject to VAT even if it is made outside South Africa provided it is made in the course of an enterprise carried on in or partly within South Africa. In many, but not necessarily all, cases a supply made outside South Africa will be zero-rated.

5 BASIS OF TAXATION

5.1 Supplies within South Africa

Where the consideration takes the form of money, the taxable value of the supply is normally the total sum paid or payable to the person supplying the goods or services including VAT and all other taxes, commissions, costs and charges whatsoever. The tax fraction (14/114) is applied to the total consideration to ascertain the VAT payable.

Special rules apply where the consideration is not in money, to supplies between connected persons, fringe benefits and certain other transactions.

5.2 Self-Supplies

Self-supplies of goods, ie the use of goods for which an input credit has been obtained by a vendor in respect of an exempt or non-business activity, are liable to VAT on the basis of their cost to the vendor.

5.3 Importations

The value of imported goods for the purposes of VAT is the value for customs purposes plus 10% of that value plus all import duties.

5.4 Chargeable Event/Time of Payment

A supply of goods or services is deemed to take place:

- at the earlier of the time an invoice is issued or any time any payment (other than a deposit) is received by the supplier
- in the case of supplies between connected persons, at the time the goods are removed by or made available to the purchaser, or the time the services are performed, unless an invoice is issued on or before the day on which the tax return should be submitted for the tax period during which the supply would otherwise be deemed to have been made
- in the case of a rental agreement or periodic service agreement, on the earlier of the date a payment becomes due or is received
- in the case of agreements for the progressive or periodic supply of goods or services, on the earliest of the date a payment becomes due or is received or a specific invoice is issued.

A number of special rules apply to certain specific types of transactions.

5.5 Cash/Invoice Basis

VAT due must normally be accounted for on the basis of the value of invoices issued in the appropriate VAT period. However, an alternative payments basis is allowed in the case of a vendor with a turnover of less than R2.5 million per annum, a public or local authority, and an association not for gain.

5.6 Credit Notes/Bad Debts

A registered person may adjust his liability for tax in respect of goods returned to him, discounts or other price adjustments allowed or bad debts written-off by him subsequent to his having accounted for the output tax. A credit note must be issued except in the case of a prompt payment discount if the terms of the discount were clearly stated on the original tax invoice.

6 TAX RATES

The standard rate of tax is 14%. It applies to all taxable supplies other than those subject to the zero-rate.

0%:
- movable goods consigned or delivered to an address outside South Africa
- movable goods delivered for conveyance to another country by a purchaser who is ordinarily resident or carries on business there if the sale concerned is in terms of an approved export incentive scheme
- movable goods (and related services) delivered to the owner or charterer of a foreign-going ship or aircraft for use or consumption in such ship or aircraft
- rental of goods used exclusively in another country or, if not exclusively so used, used in a commercial concern based in another country from where the rental payments are made
- fuel subject to the fuel levy under the Customs and Excise Act
- certain agricultural inputs, subject to various conditions
- certain basic foodstuffs (18 categories)
- the supply to a registered vendor of an enterprise as a going concern

- the transport and related insurance of passengers or goods to, from or wholly outside the Republic, including transit passage within the Republic, whether by air, sea, rail or other means
- services rendered in respect of land or movable property situated in another country even though the services themselves might be rendered within the Republic
- services rendered exclusively in another country
- repair, cleaning and processing services in respect of foreign-going ships and aircraft, trains operated by non-residents, and goods temporarily imported into the Republic for those purposes
- movable goods used in the repair or treatment of any goods temporarily imported to the Republic for that purpose
- services supplied to persons resident in another country at the time the services are rendered, provided they are not in relation to land or movable property situated within the Republic (except in the case of repair services referred to immediately above)
- services related to registration, acquisition or enforcement of intellectual property rights for use in another country.

14%: all other taxable goods and services.

7 EXEMPTIONS

7.1 Exemptions with Credit for Input Tax

The Act does not specifically provide for exemption with credit for input tax. However, financial services which are normally exempt supplies are defined as zero-rated supplies where the services:

■ comprise the insuring or the arrangement of the insurance of passengers on international transport services

■ are supplied directly in respect of exported goods or movable property in another country

■ are supplied to a person who is a resident of and present in another country at the time the services are rendered, provided the services are not connected with goods situated in South Africa.

7.2 Exemptions without Credit for Input Tax

The supply of certain goods and services is exempt from VAT. The suppliers of such goods or services are not permitted to charge VAT nor is an input credit allowed in respect of the purchase or importation of any goods or services attributable to the making of the exempt supply. The goods and services are as follows:

■ financial services: lending money or providing credit, any dealings in stocks, shares, debentures, futures, the operation of current, deposit or savings accounts, management of unit trusts, provision of life insurance and retirement benefits

■ education

■ local passenger transport services (other than by air)

■ rental of long-term residential accommodation

- assessment rates charged by local authorities
- certain supplies by non profit making organisations.

7.3   Exempt Imports

Certain importations are exempt from VAT, such as personal effects of travellers, personal goods imported on permanent transfer of private residence, temporary imports and goods re-imported. Certain restrictions and qualifications apply to some of these items.

7.4   Election to be Subject to VAT

Persons whose turnover from activities which are otherwise taxable does not exceed R150,000 per annum are not obliged to register for VAT, but may elect to do so.

8   CREDIT/REFUND FOR INPUT VAT

8.1   General Rule

In computing the amount of tax payable by him a vendor may deduct the tax relating to most goods and services purchased or imported by him which are used for the purposes of his taxable business. No deduction may be made for the tax paid on goods and services used for any other purpose. To be entitled to the deduction the registered person must have a proper tax invoice.

A credit is not permitted in respect of the tax suffered on any of the following:

- entertainment expenses as broadly defined
- purchase, lease or importation of passenger cars (except in the case of a motor dealer, car hire trader or taxi operator)
- club subscription and fees.

A vendor who purchases second-hand goods from a private individual, or a registered person who did not qualify for an input credit may take an imputed credit based on the tax fraction.

8.2   Partial Exemption

Persons who make taxable and non-taxable or exempt supplies are entitled to recover VAT incurred in making the taxable supplies only.

Where the purchases or imports are used in making both taxable and non-taxable or exempt supplies an apportionment of the input VAT is allowed. In determining the allowable input tax credit, the direct attribution method is first applied and thereafter the turnover method or any other appropriate method which has been negotiated with Revenue.

8.3   Time of Recovery

A taxable person is entitled to recovery of input tax, subject to the rules to entitlement outlined above, when he has a valid tax invoice. It is not necessary that he has paid for the goods (except in the case of a deemed input credit for second-hand goods) or that the supplier has paid the output tax to the authorities.

The claim to input tax credit should be made in the VAT return for the period in which the invoice is issued.

8.4   Refund to Foreign Businesses and Tourists

Special procedures have been laid down for the refund of VAT to persons resident in or conducting a business in another country who purchase and take delivery of goods in South Africa. The procedures differ between holders of passports issued by Botswana, Lesotho, Namibia and Swaziland ('BLNS' countries) and those issued by other countries.

In the case of non-BLNS residents and businesses, refunds of VAT are claimable from the VAT Refund Administrator at designated departure points from South Africa, subject to compliance with administrative procedures.

Refunds to BLNS residents and businesses are handled by the vendor and his customer on compliance with certain documentary procedures.

9   ADMINISTRATIVE OBLIGATIONS

9.1   Registration

Any person who supplies taxable goods or services in the course of his enterprise, or who elects to become taxable, must register with the local Receiver of Revenue. This includes persons who supply zero-rated goods and services but does not include persons who make exempt supplies only.

Branches of the same legal entity may in certain circumstances be permitted to register separately. This will not, however, interfere with the overall liability of the legal entity. Application in writing must be made to the local Receiver of Revenue.

Group registration is not permitted.

Persons whose turnover from activities which are otherwise taxable does not exceed R150,000 per annum are not obliged to register for VAT, but may elect to do so.

9.2   Books and Records

Registered persons must keep full records, for a period of five years, of all business transactions which may affect the liability to VAT. The records must be kept up to date and must be sufficiently detailed to enable a trader accurately to calculate his liability and the Receiver of Revenue to check the calculation if necessary. Failure to keep proper records could result in a fine of R4,000 or 12 months' imprisonment or both.

9.3   Invoices

An inadequate tax invoice will deprive the recipient of his right to deduct VAT. The tax invoice must contain:

- the words 'tax invoice' in a prominent place
- an individual serial number
- the name, address and VAT registration number of the supplier of the goods or services
- the name and address of the person to whom the goods or services are supplied
- the date of supply
- a full description of the goods or services supplied
- the quantity of goods supplied

- the consideration (exclusive of VAT)
- the amount of VAT
- the inclusive price.

In certain cases a modified tax invoice is permitted.

Debit and credit notes must contain:

- the words 'debit note' or 'credit note'
- the name, address and VAT registration number of the supplier
- the name and address of the person to whom the goods or services were supplied
- the date of issue of the debit or credit note
- information sufficient to identify the original transaction
- the reason for the issuing of the debit or credit note
- the amount of the debit or credit (excluding VAT), the attributable VAT and the inclusive debit or credit.

9.4   VAT Returns
Each vendor must by the twenty-fifth day of the month following the end of each tax period file a return with the Receiver of Revenue showing the amount of tax deductible and due by him for the period and must pay the tax due by the same date.

A tax period will generally be two months, but will be one month in the following cases:

- where the vendor's turnover exceeds R18 million per annum
- where the vendor so elects
- where the vendor repeatedly defaults on his obligations.

9.5   Correction of Returns
There are no specific provisions for the correction of VAT returns.

9.6   Powers of Authorities
Authorised Revenue officials have extensive powers in regard to the inspection and seizure of records and there are penalties if any authorised officer is impeded in his duty by the registered person or his employees. The statutory limit for inspection is five years except in the case of fraud or neglect where there is no limit.

Where a taxable person fails to make a VAT return, or where the Receiver is of the opinion that VAT has been underpaid, the authorities may issue an estimated assessment of the tax due. This can be displaced only by lodging a detailed objection within 30 days.

9.7   Penalties
The penalty for non-compliance with the provisions of the Act is a fine of R4,000 or 12 months' imprisonment or both.

The penalty for tax evasion activities is a fine of R4,000 or 24 months' imprisonment or both.

Penalty interest of 10% on unpaid tax plus a further 1.2% for each month the tax remains outstanding is leviable on late payments.

9.8   Appeals

Where a person is dissatisfied with any formal determination of the Receiver of Revenue, with any assessment of the payable amount made on him, or with any refusal or restriction of a repayment claim made by the Receiver, he may appeal to the Value Added Tax Board of Review in writing within 30 days of the notification of determination, assessment or refusal.

The Board of Review, which is independent from the Revenue Department, is the first Court of Appeal. If either person is dissatisfied with the Board's decision he may appeal to the ordinary Courts.

10   SPECIAL VAT REGIMES

10.1   Agents

Supplies made by an agent are deemed to be made by the principal and not the agent. For example, a company is deemed to make a supply if an independent agent makes the supply on the company's behalf. The principal must account for VAT in relation to the supply made.

Supplies made by a registered person to an agent are deemed to be received by the principal and not the agent. For example, the principal is deemed to receive a supply when an agent makes a taxable purchase of land. Here the principal, and not the agent, may deduct an input tax.

An agent may be treated as if he were the principal when receiving a supply directly connected with, or with the arranging of, the importation or exportation of goods, provided certain criteria are met. This arrangement enables the agent to deduct VAT paid on inputs relevant to the importation or exportation of the goods.

10.2   Auctioneers

Auctions, where goods are sold on behalf of clients, may proceed on the basis that all the goods being offered are charged with VAT. This is because an auctioneer may, with the consent of his principal, have a non-taxable supply which is made on behalf of his principal, treated as if it were a taxable supply and made by the auctioneer himself.

10.3   Accommodation Enterprises

Generally, long-term residential accommodation in a dwelling (house or flat) is exempt from VAT (see section 7.2). However, the supply of accommodation by hotels, boarding houses, hostels, residential hotels, holiday resorts, home owners, hospitals and similar establishments is a taxable supply. Special rules for the valuation of the taxable supply are laid down.

10.4   Catering and Canteens

Restaurants and similar establishments are subject to all the usual rules of VAT, except that they are not precluded from claiming an input tax credit on the acquisition of 'entertainment' goods (see section 8.1), provided that they make supplies of meals and refreshments for a charge at least equal to cost. The supply of free or low cost meals to staff does not affect the claiming of the input tax credit.

Subsidised staff canteens supplying below cost meals to employees are not entitled to claim input tax credits and do not charge VAT on the charge for the meals. When a charge to employees is at least equal to cost, input tax credits may be claimed and VAT must be charged to the employees.

Hostels, canteens and tuckshops operated by educational institutions are exempt from VAT and therefore do not qualify for input tax credits.

11   FURTHER READING

Ernst & Young VAT Handbook, Juta & Company
Value Added Tax Manual, Juta & Company
Value Added Tax, Butterworths

Contributor: Ian MacKenzie
Ernst & Young
PO Box 2322
Johannesburg, 2000
South Africa
Tel: +27 11 4981000
Fax: +27 11 4981110

TUNISIA

1   GENERAL BACKGROUND

Value added tax (VAT) was introduced in Tunisia by law No. 88-61 of 2 June 1988. It replaced three taxes: the Tax on Production, the Tax on Consumption and the Tax on Services.

2   WHO IS TAXABLE?

2.1   General
Any person who supplies taxable goods or services in the course of business, whether on a regular or occasional basis, is taxable (assujetti). The term 'business' applies to any operation carried out independently in Tunisia by producer, trader and service supplier.

The legal status of the person is irrelevant and VAT will thus apply to corporate bodies, individuals, liberal professions, residents and non-residents.

Persons may also elect to be taxable (see section 7.3 'Election to be Subject to VAT').

2.2   Transactions with Branch/Subsidiary
Supplies of services or goods between a branch and its foreign or Tunisian head office are subject to VAT.

An entity dependent on another taxable entity is also subject to VAT. Any entity is considered as being dependent on or managed by another entity when, directly or through intermediaries, this other entity has a power of decision or holds a blocking majority in the share capital of the dependent entity.

3   WHAT IS TAXABLE?

VAT is due on any business carried out in Tunisia which is of an industrial or craft nature as well as on any commercial transaction other than sales. This applies whatever the legal status of the person who supplies the taxable transactions and whether it is on a regular or occasional basis.

The following operations are also subject to VAT:

- imports
- resales in the same state of industrial or public works equipment
- resales in the same state by wholesalers
- commercial presentation of products not used in agriculture or fishing
- sales of plots by land owners
- real estate work

This chapter reflects the legislation on VAT in Tunisia as at 1 January 1995.

- sales of buildings or goodwill by persons who usually purchase these goods with a view to resale
- food consumed on the spot
- self-deliveries.

4   THE PLACE OF SUPPLY

VAT is chargeable in Tunisia only if the operations are conducted in Tunisia. The rules for determining if the operations are conducted in Tunisia are different for sales and other activities.

4.1   Sale

Any sale is subject to VAT when it has been effected under the conditions of delivery in Tunisia.

Any imported good is considered as delivered in Tunisia even when it is delivered to a person (buyer) other than the one who filed a customs clearance return (customs agent).

4.2   Other Operations

Any operation other than sale is subject to VAT when the service rendered, the right sold or the rented good is used or exploited in Tunisia.

5   BASIS OF TAXATION

5.1   Supplies within Tunisia

VAT is assessed on the total invoice price and includes any expense, tax or duty, as well as the value of the goods remitted for the payment, but excludes the VAT and any grant, subsidy or packing.

In the case of the sale of passenger transport vouchers, VAT is assessed on 6% of the gross amount of the transport voucher.

In the case of the sale of buildings and going concerns by persons who usually purchase these goods with a view to resale, VAT is assessed on the difference between the selling price and the purchase price, including any expense, duty and tax (but excluding the VAT itself).

5.2   Self-Supplies

VAT due on self-supplies is calculated on the basis of the selling price which would be applicable to a similar product or on the basis of the cost price.

5.3   Transactions with Branch/Subsidiary

When an entity is dependent on another entity whose head office is outside Tunisia, VAT is assessed as for domestic transactions on all transactions concerning goods and services.

When a selling entity and a purchasing entity are interdependent and the purchasing entity is not subject to VAT, the VAT will be due by the selling entity but assessed on the selling price of the purchasing entity and not on the value of the supply.

5.4   *Imports*

VAT due on the importation of goods is assessed on the value determined for customs purposes, to which should be added all taxes and duties paid (except for the VAT itself).

6   TAX RATES

Currently there are four rates in Tunisia:

6%:   electricity and gas, medicine, soap, hotels and restaurants, some fruits and vegetables

10%:   transport, software

17%:   all supplies of goods or services not exempt or subject to the 6%, 10% or 29% rate

29%:·   meat, fish, tea, coffee, imported fruits, butter, mineral water, drinks, tobacco products, perfume, clothes, jewellery, electronic and electric products, cars, boats, motorcycles and pencils.

7   EXEMPTIONS

A transaction is considered as exempt when, while being within the scope of VAT, it is not subject to tax by reason of a special provision of law. As a rule, exempt supplies prevent an entrepreneur from recovering the tax incurred on purchases made in connection with these exempt supplies. However, the law provides for a number of exempt supplies to be entitled to input credit.

7.1   *Exemptions with Credit for Input Tax*
The following exemptions are with credit for input tax:

■   any business carried out within the frame of exportation
■   delivery of goods to be placed under customs' specific regime of temporary admission.

7.2   *Exemptions without Credit for Input Tax*
These exemptions are listed in an appendix to the VAT Code and mainly apply to the following:

■   importation, manufacture and sale of flour, milk, olive and soya oil and sugar
■   social or cultural services of associations or foundations
■   educational services provided by schools and universities
■   importation of equipment and sale of water or equipment for agriculture
■   importation of equipment and sale of newspapers, tourism brochures
■   importation and sale of drilling equipment, exploration and exploitation of liquid and gaseous hydrocarbons
■   maritime and air transport
■   services linked to maritime transport
■   telecommunications.

7.3   Election to be Subject to VAT

Taxable persons making certain exempt supplies may elect to be subject to VAT on their entire activities.

This option may be exercised at any time of the year, by way of filing a specific return. The option covers a period expiring on 31 December of the fourth year following the election and is tacitly renewable.

8   CREDIT/REFUND FOR INPUT TAX

8.1   General Rule

The principle is that all the VAT paid on goods and services by a Tunisian entrepreneur is recoverable. However, this principle applies only if the input tax was incurred with a view to making a taxable supply.

This restriction prevents entrepreneurs from recovering input VAT on:

- goods and services obtained for exempt supplies. Exports and international trade transactions are allowed a full deduction although they are exempt from VAT
- goods and services used for private consumption
- cars, even when used in the course of a business
- services obtained in connection with private cars such as repairs, transport and renting.

8.2   Partial Exemption

Taxable persons who make both taxable and exempt supplies are allowed to recover only the input VAT relating to taxable supplies.

When the taxable person is partially subject to VAT, the input VAT paid on goods other than assets and on services is deductible according to the 'attribution method'. Indeed, if the goods or services purchased can be attributed to taxable supplies, the credit for input VAT will be fully allowed. In contrast, if attribution is made to exempt supplies, it will be totally disallowed.

If the goods or services purchased are used both for taxable and exempt supplies the creditable input tax is calculated according to the ratio of the turnover of supplies which are entitled to credit to the total turnover. This method is also applicable to assets and overheads.

The applicable ratio is calculated at the beginning of each calendar year, according to the ratio of the preceding year. The final ratio is determined at the end of the year and, if an additional portion of VAT can be recovered, it must be adjusted accordingly before the month of January of the following year. Any such additional credit can be offset on the VAT return but not refunded. No adjustment is allowed for input VAT on non-depreciable assets.

8.3   Time of Recovery

Input VAT cannot be recovered before it has actually been accounted for by the supplier.

When recoverable input VAT is in excess of output VAT for a month, the excess can be offset against output VAT of the following month.

The excess of input VAT may also be refunded by the Tunisian tax authorities up to a limit of 20% of the total input VAT paid in each calendar year. This limit does not apply to export operations or when a taxable activity ceases.

9   ADMINISTRATIVE OBLIGATIONS

9.1   Registration
Before commencing business, entrepreneurs must file a declaration of existence and a copy of their articles of association or legal agreement with the Tunisian tax authorities.

9.2   Books and Records
Taxable persons must keep adequate accounting books to justify all their transactions returns, records, etc.

9.3   Invoices
Invoices must contain the following information:

- date of the operation
- name, address and tax registration number of the supplier
- name and address of the purchaser
- price of the goods or services excluding tax
- rate of the tax and corresponding VAT due.

Suppliers must use sequentially numbered invoices.

9.4   VAT Returns
Every month, the taxable person must file a VAT return of his taxable supplies for the preceding month. This declaration must be filed by the twenty-eighth day of the following month for companies, and by the fifteenth day of the following month for individuals.

When the return shows a VAT credit, ie, an excess of input over output VAT, it can be carried forward and used until completely offset against output VAT.

9.5   Powers of the Authorities
The tax authorities have a period of three years to correct a VAT return. This period ends on 31 December of the third year following that in which the taxable supply took place.

Late payment of tax entails the payment of interest at the rate of 1.25 % per month plus a penalty amounting to:

- 10% for a late filing under two years
- 20% for a late filing of between two and three years, or fraud
- 30% for a late filing over three years, or repeated fraud.

Contributor: Anne Ermel
HSD Ernst & Young
Societe d'Advocats
Tour Manhattan
Cedex 21
92092 Paris la Defense 2
France
Tel: +33 1 46 936570
Fax: +33 1 47 670106

ZIMBABWE

1 SALES TAXES IN GENERAL

The Sales Tax Act, which imposes a tax on the sales value of certain goods and services, is administered by the Department of Taxes. Tax on imports, which is dealt with in the same Act is administered by the Director of Customs.

2 WHO IS TAXABLE?

The tax is levied on sales of goods by persons, companies, etc, ie registered operators, auctioneers and motor dealers in the normal course of business, on goods sold by private sale where the sale is discounted by a finance agent, on all services which are not specifically exempted, and on the importation of goods to Zimbabwe.

2.1 Government Bodies and Local Authorities
Supplies by government bodies or local authorities are not subject to Sales Tax. However, the provision of telecommunications services provided by the Post and Telecommunications Corporation is taxable as is the provision of air transport services by Air Zimbabwe (both statutory bodies).

3 WHAT IS TAXABLE?

'Sale' is defined as including barter, exchange and hire of goods and the supply of a service. For Sales Tax purposes the sales value of a contract of hire is the full amount receivable under the contract.

3.1 Goods
Where a taxable person disposes of goods acquired in the normal course of business, the transactions are deemed to be sales in the following circumstances:

- the goods are taken for his own use or donated to another person (unless such goods are otherwise unsaleable)
- the goods are attached to other goods the ownership of which changes hands (by sale or otherwise)
- where the purchaser and seller of a motor vehicle are introduced by and pay commission to a motor dealer, the vehicle is deemed to have been sold by the motor dealer.

3.2 Services
All services other than those which are specifically exempted and those for which payment is made outside Zimbabwe are liable to Sales Tax.

This chapter reflects the law on VAT in Zimbabwe as at 31 January 1995.

3.3   Imports

Three taxes are applicable to imports:

- customs duty is levied under the Customs and Excise Act at a variable rate on the import value of goods based on the GATT system
- Surtax is currently levied at 10% of the import value (net duty)
- Import Tax is levied on the import value (gross of duty) at the same rate applicable to the goods for Sales Tax purposes.

These taxes are levied on all imports unless the importer is a taxable person importing goods for resale in the normal course of business in which case Sales Tax is charged on the deemed value of the goods, which is determined by adding:

- the value of the goods for customs purposes (determined under the Customs Act)
- the amount of customs duty payable
- a prescribed amount which will not exceed 60% of the value of the goods plus customs duty payable. This does not apply to unsolicited gifts.

3.4   Temporary Importation

Goods may be imported free of tax for a period of 30 days or less. This allowance is at the discretion of the Director of Customs and requires monetary deposit or suitable guarantee sufficient to cover any customs duty, Surtax and Import Tax which might be payable. Where the period of temporary importation will exceed 30 days, written application must be made to the Department of Customs prior to the proposed date of entry. An import licence issued by the Ministry of Trade and Commerce is required in all cases.

4   PLACE OF SUPPLY

Sales tax is only applied to the supply of taxable goods which are physically located in Zimbabwe at the time of supply, to the importation of goods which are not exempt, and to the supply of taxable services by a person established or resident in Zimbabwe, irrespective of where the services are to be used.

5   BASIS OF TAXATION

5.1   Taxable Amount

The taxable amount is the total sum payable by the purchaser under the agreement of sale and includes the cost of delivery (unless this is by public carrier).

The following allowances by the seller should be deducted when calculating the value of sales:

- cash or settlement discount
- amounts allowed for defects
- container returns (unless these are exempt)
- the value of goods returned or sales subsequently cancelled.

In addition, sales values should not include the following payments by the purchaser:

- compensation for breach of the sales agreement
- licence or registration fees
- insurance premiums to insure the goods being sold
- certain prescribed costs such as stamp duty and interest and insurance while in transit.

6 RATES OF TAX

Currently there are three rates:

12.5%: most taxable goods and services, including consumables, specified services, agricultural plant and equipment, and specified vehicles such as ambulances and forklift trucks

15%: hotel accommodation, air conditioners and various household items

20%: motor vehicles, including substantially completed kits, motorcycles, accounting machines and a variety of office equipment (excluding cash and sales registers), and luxury items.

7 EXEMPTION

The following supplies are currently exempt from Sales Tax:

- exports by a registered operator
- the sale of unprocessed agricultural produce by a licensed farmer
- the sale of unprocessed agricultural produce from communal land
- the sale of minerals (including limestone) by registered mine operators
- certain sales between registered operators or their agents, eg goods intended for resale, raw materials intended for further processing, and items intended for use as packaging
- the sale of certain goods which are intended for use in the production of agricultural, mining, industrial and manufactured products
- the sale of prescribed goods (Note: the latest detailed schedule appears in Statutory Instrument 89 of 1992 published as a supplement to the Government Gazette, 6 November 1992)
- the provision of services as listed in SI 215 of 1994 (published as a supplement to the Government Gazette, 30 September 1994)
- foodstuffs such as raw, dried or smoked fish and meat, but excluding bacon, sausages and hams
- detergents for use in a dairy
- certain medical and orthopaedic appliances
- carbonated drinks, clear and opaque beer, spirits and various tobacco products
- goods temporarily imported for repair or other approved purposes
- the hire of books
- the hire of aircraft other than for the carriage of passengers
- the provision of air transport or tours (excluding accommodation and food) where payment is made outside Zimbabwe

- supplies by the State, local authorities or statutory corporations excluding telecommunications services performed by the Post and Telecommunications Corporation and air transport services provided by Air Zimbabwe
- financial transactions, services rendered by any banks or building societies, the exchange of bank notes or foreign currency, the provision of loans, securities and transfer of ownership of any shares, and services rendered by insurers, insurance agents, insurance brokers and actuaries (but not loss adjusters)
- health services rendered by a person registered under the Medical, Dental and Allied Professional Act, Psychological Practices Act and Chiropractor Practitioners Act. Also accommodation and treatment at a hospital, clinic or similar institution
- immovable property as it refers to construction, additions, improvements, sales and letting of buildings, bridges, roads, wells and other works of a permanent nature
- intellectual property, the creation, licensing, transfers or assignments of rights including trademarks, copyrights and similar rights
- transport of goods imported into or exported out of Zimbabwe or in transit in a continuous journey catering, maintenance and repair services in respect of the operation of any aircraft or train belonging to a person not ordinarily resident in Zimbabwe; transport for any person by public rail service or by road (on a stage carriage); transport of goods which are exempt from Sales Tax
- special services – a large number of agencies, institutions and organisations are listed. Examples are trusts of a public character, clubs and trade unions
- the supply of educational services at any permanent institution
- imports of certain raw materials to be used by a registered operator or factory in manufacturing or processing
- imports of prescribed goods intended for use in mining and agriculture, manufacturing or industry
- import of certain other prescribed goods.

Customs duty is suspended if the reserve Bank certifies that the importation is financed using remittable dividends and the Secretary for Industry and Technology or the Secretary for Trade and Commerce certifies that the importation is essential and approved.

8   CREDIT/REFUND FOR INPUT TAX

As tax is payable only on the value of sales made to persons who are not registered for Sales Tax there is no input tax to deduct.

8.1   General Rule
In calculating the amount of Sales Tax payable in a tax period a taxable person is entitled to deduct:

- the value of goods exported from Zimbabwe
- goods sold to other taxable persons after discounts and credits
- costs which do not attract any liability to Sales Tax such as the value of farm produce or the cost of transport.

8.2   Other Credits

Agriculturists, hoteliers, industrialists, manufacturers and miners operating in a designated growth area may claim refunds of Sales or Import Tax on purchases of capital goods to be used exclusively in those operations.

In addition, the purchase of capital goods (excluding road motor vehicles) or building materials used by persons exclusively in the operation of an approved new project may qualify for refunds of sales or Import Tax.

Under certain conditions the Director of Customs may refund or remit all or part of the tax paid in respect of:

- prescribed personal and household goods imported by a person who enters or has entered Zimbabwe for the purposes of taking up residence or employment
- the personal effects of any passenger in his possession, on his entry into Zimbabwe or which are imported within such period after entry as the Controller may allow
- certain goods imported after having been exported from Zimbabwe
- certain goods exported unused within two years from the date on which tax was paid
- certain other prescribed goods, eg for diplomatic or foreign aid purposes.

8.3   National Projects

There is a provision for a rebate of customs duty, Surtax and Import Tax on goods imported temporarily for certain national projects. Such projects must have the approval of the Ministry of Finance.

9   ADMINISTRATIVE OBLIGATIONS

9.1   Registration

Registration is mandatory for:

- auctioneers, motor dealers and finance agents
- traders who supply services where the aggregate sale value amounts to Z$60,000 or more
- any other trader who supplies or in the opinion of the Revenue office will supply goods with an aggregate annual (April to March) sales value of Z$250,000 or more.

Manufacturers who make annual supplies of between Z$50,000 and Z$250,000 may opt for registration should they so wish.

Auctioneers, motor dealers and finance agents must apply for registration within 30 days of commencing business.

Traders must apply within 30 days of their aggregate sales turnover reaching the Z$250,000 limit, and those traders who supply services must register within 30 days of their aggregate supplies reaching the Z$60,000 limit.

Where a trader has more than one place of business, details of all locations must be given. The Revenue officer will issue either one or several certificates depending upon the system of accounting used by the applicant.

9.2 Cancellation of Registration

When trading ceases, or when annual sales fall, or are anticipated to fall below the Z$250,000 or Z$60,000 limits, the registered operator must notify the local tax Revenue office who will withdraw his registration certificate. He must pay tax on the inventory held when his registration is cancelled.

The liability is the amount of tax which would have been paid on the goods had a registration certificate not been held.

9.3 Returns

Every taxable person is required to submit, on the prescribed form, on the last day of every month, a statement of all sales transacted during the preceding month.

The following is an example of a calculation of amount payable. A taxable person would show the following on his monthly return form in respect of sales and auction sales subject to tax at the lower rates:

Total cash and credit sales of goods (including Sales Tax charged)			25,000.00
Less credits passed and/or journalised			1,000.00
Subtotal			24,000.00
Deduct:			
Exemptions at sale value:			
(a)	goods exported from Zimbabwe	nil	
(b)	goods sold to registered operators after discounts and credits	3,000	
(c)	other – specify separately, eg		
	– transport	500	
	– farm produce	500	4,000.00
Net taxable sales during month (including tax)			20,000.00
Tax on net taxable sales at 12.5%			2,500.00
Less 1/9th thereof			278.00
			2,222.00
Add tax at 12.5% on goods applied to own use or use of another person, at cost 504			63.00
Total due for the month			$2,285.00

The deduction of one-ninth from the net taxable sales is an allowance for tax on tax at 12.5%. In the case of sales subject to tax of 20% the deduction will be one-sixth.

9.4 Invoices

Special invoices for the purposes of Sales Tax are not required in Zimbabwe.

9.5 Penalties

Any person liable for tax who fails to pay the amount due shall pay, in addition to the tax payable, an amount equal to the tax due. However, if the Revenue officer is satisfied that there was reasonable cause for the failure to pay, he may reduce the amount as he considers fit.

The wilful misuse of registration certificates is an offence subject to a fine of up to Z$10,000 or imprisonment of up to three years. Failure to register or to lodge returns and pay the relevant tax without reasonable cause is liable to a fine of Z$50 per day for each day the offence continues.

Any person who without reasonable cause contravenes any provision of the Act is liable to a fine not exceeding Z$2,000 or imprisonment for a period of not less than six months.

Contributors: Max S. Mangoro and Dave Robinson
                 Ernst & Young
                 PO Box 62
                 Harare
                 Zimbabwe
                 Tel: +263 4 751808
                 Fax: +263 4 791240

NORTH, CENTRAL AND SOUTH AMERICA

CANADA

1   GENERAL BACKGROUND

With effect from 1 January 1991, a Value Added Tax (VAT) was introduced into Canada at the federal level, replacing the former federal sales tax and known as the Goods and Services Tax (GST). The province of Quebec adopted a provincial VAT type tax on 1 July 1992. Eight of the remaining nine provinces of Canada currently impose a retail sales tax. Pursuant to an election promise in 1993 to replace the GST, the federal government has launched a review of the GST, and various alternatives are being considered. Although the government initially indicated that the GST would be repealed by 1 January 1996, it has since announced that it will not rush the reform process to meet this deadline. The federal government is currently examining the possible implementation of a national value added tax which would replace the existing GST and provincial retail sales taxes. Discussions between the federal government and the provinces are currently under way.

The GST is applicable to a broad range of supplies of property and services made in Canada. Unlike traditional value added taxes, the GST is designed as a tax on the purchaser and an obligation is imposed on the vendor to collect the GST as agent for the Crown.

The tax is contained in Part IX of the Excise Tax Act. Regulations are also enacted. The GST is administered by Revenue Canada (the Department of National Revenue). Various concepts in the GST parallel those in the Canadian federal Income Tax Act.

For the purposes of the GST the territory of Canada includes:

- the seabed and subsoil of the submarine areas adjacent to Canada's coast over which the government of Canada, or of a Province, may grant rights to explore for, or exploit, any minerals (ie including petroleum, natural gas, related hydrocarbons, and sand and gravel)
- the seas and airspace above those submarine areas with respect of any activities carried on in connection with the exploration for, or exploitation of, minerals.

2   WHO IS TAXABLE?

2.1   General
All persons engaged in commercial activities in Canada are required to register for the GST with the following exceptions:

- small suppliers (ie persons who provide less than C$30,000 of taxable supplies per annum)
- persons whose only commercial activity is selling real property otherwise than in the course of a business
- non-residents who do not carry on business in Canada.

This chapter reflects the law on GST in Canada as at 31 October 1994.

For GST purposes a 'person' means an individual, partnership, corporation, trust or estate or a body that is a society, club, union, association, commission, or other organisation of any kind.

'Commercial activity' means:

- a business carried on by a person
- any adventure or concern of a person in the nature of trade, except to the extent the adventure or concern involves the making of an exempt supply
- the making of a supply (other than an exempt supply) by a person of real property, including anything done by the person in the course of or in connection with the making of the supply.

Activities engaged in by an individual are not considered to be commercial activities unless there is a reasonable expectation of profit.

Persons registered under the legislation and persons who are required to be registered are referred to as 'registrants'.

2.2   Government
The federal government and related institutions pay GST on supplies in the same way as any other business. Canadian constitutional law provides that one level of government cannot tax another. In general, the provincial governments do not pay GST and supplies to provincial governments are treated as if they were zero-rated. Supplies by government are generally treated in the same way as those by other persons. However, a number of supplies made by governments are exempt.

2.3   Fiscal Unity/Group Transactions
Unlike some European VAT systems, under the GST there is no group registration facility, and each member of any closely related group is required to file separate returns (subject to status). Closely related groups of corporations can elect to deem supplies (other than certain exclusions such as real property) between members as being made for no consideration. This effectively zero-rates sales between members. For the purposes of determination, A is closely related to B if both are resident in Canada and registered for GST purposes, and at least 90% of the value and number of full voting right shares of B's capital stock are owned by:

- corporation A
- a qualifying subsidiary of A
- a corporation of which A is a qualifying subsidiary
- a qualifying subsidiary of a corporation of which A is a qualifying subsidiary
- any combination of the above or
- if B is a prescribed corporation in relation to A.

Special rules apply where the closely related group includes a financial institution. Relief may also be available to clubs or associations which operate as branches or members of a larger organisation, as the legislation provides that two unincorporated organisations may jointly apply to have one of the organisations deemed to be a branch of the other.

2.4   Foreign Businesses
Non-residents who carry on business in Canada and who make taxable supplies in Canada

or elsewhere which exceed the small supplier threshold limits are required to register:

■ if the non-resident solicits orders in Canada for supply by the non-resident of publications where the publications are delivered by mail or courier, or

■ where the non-resident makes supplies of admissions in respect of a place of amusement, a seminar, an activity or an event.

2.5 Representative Office

A non-resident with no permanent establishment in Canada who applies for or is required to be registered for GST must provide and maintain security in an amount and form satisfactory to the Minister of National Revenue.

'Permanent establishment' means:

■ a fixed place of business, such as a branch office, factory, workshop, mine, oil or gas well, quarry, etc, or

■ a fixed place of business of another person acting on behalf of the non-resident in Canada (other than a broker, general commission agent or other independent agent).

2.6 Reverse Charge Mechanism

The GST due on imported tangible personal property is generally collected by Canada Customs under the authority of the Customs Act at the time customs duties are collected. Tax is not payable on importations of certain goods listed in the non-taxable importations schedule and the zero-rated supplies schedule of the legislation.

Imported services and intangible property cannot practicably be taxed at the border by Canada Customs; instead they are subject to tax on a self-assessment basis. Consequently, the Canadian recipient must self-assess and remit the tax where these supplies are for use in Canada other than exclusively in a commercial activity.

3 WHAT IS TAXABLE?

The GST legislation provides that every recipient of a taxable supply shall pay tax in respect of the supply equal to 7% of the value of the consideration for the supply.

For GST purposes, a 'taxable supply' means a supply that is made in the course of a commercial activity, which by definition excludes an exempt supply.

'Supply' generally means the provision of property or a service in any manner, including sale, transfer, barter, exchange, licence, rental, lease, gift or disposition.

At present, there is a standard rate of 7% and a zero rate. The provision of both standard and zero-rated supplies qualify the supplier for input tax credits (see section 8 below).

GST is applied to a wide range of property and services supplied in Canada, and to imports.

3.1 Supply of Property

Property means any property, whether real or personal, movable or immovable, tangible or intangible, corporeal or incorporeal, and includes a right or interest of any kind, a share and a chose in action, but does not include money. Tangible property generally means goods.

3.2   Supply of Services
'Services' are deemed to mean anything other than property, money or anything that is supplied to an employer by a person who is or agrees to become an employee of the employer in the course of or in relation to the office or employment of that person.

3.3   Self-Supply of Goods and Services
Self-supply occurs (where an input tax credit has been claimed for the original supply) in the following circumstances:

■   business assets are appropriated for personal use
■   a builder of residential premises commences to use it as a rental property
■   capital property is applied to an exempt business use
■   where certain benefits are conferred on officers or employees.

3.4   Imports
With the exception of certain prescribed goods, tax is payable on all importations of goods (see section 2.6 above).

4   PLACE OF SUPPLY

4.1   Supply of Goods
A sale of goods is deemed to take place where the property is delivered to the purchaser. Any other supply of goods is deemed to be made where possession or use is given to the recipient. Real property is deemed to be supplied where the property is situated.

4.2   Supply of Services
A service is generally deemed to be supplied in Canada if it is performed in whole or in part in Canada. It is deemed to be supplied outside Canada if it is performed wholly outside Canada. As an exception, a supply of telecommunications services is deemed to be made at the place where the facility or instrument for the emission, transmission, or reception of the service is ordinarily situated.

4.3   Intangible Personal Property
A supply of intangible personal property is deemed to be made in Canada if the property may be used in Canada and the recipient is a Canadian resident or GST registrant, or the intangible personal property relates to Canadian real property or to a service to be performed in Canada.

4.4   Air Transportation
For the purposes of air transportation, the area of GST taxation is increased from Canada to include the United States (except Hawaii) and the islands of St Pierre and Miquelon. This has the effect of taxing flights terminating and originating within the taxation area where the tickets are purchased in Canada. These transborder flights may be zero-rated where the flights are part of a continuous international journey.

5   BASIS OF TAXATION

5.1   *Value of Consideration*
The value of the supply or any part of it is deemed to be:

- where the amount is expressed in money, the amount of money (converted to Canadian currency where necessary)
- where the amount is not expressed in money, the fair market value at the time of supply.

All federal taxes, duties and fees payable by the supplier or the purchaser, other than the GST, are included in the base on which GST is levied. However, provincial sales taxes and other prescribed taxes are not included.

Discounts are included in the value of the consideration where the invoice is for the full amount, even if the discount is subsequently taken. If the invoice is shown net of discount then the value of the discount is not included, even if the discount is not taken.

5.2   *Self-Supply*
The value of a self-supply is generally calculated as the fair market value of the supply.

5.3   *Imports*
The value of imports is the value for customs purposes. In addition, it includes customs duties and tariffs.

5.4   *Chargeable Event/Time of Payment*
Tax in respect of a supply is generally payable by the recipient on the earlier of the date of payment and the date on which the consideration becomes due.

6   TAX RATES

At present the following rates apply:

0%:   prescription drugs, medical devices, basic groceries, agricultural and fishing supplies, exports, certain travel services, certain transportation services, supplies for international organisations and officials, and certain financial services

7%:   all supplies of goods and services unless covered in the zero-rating or exempt schedules in the Excise Tax Act.

7   EXEMPTIONS

7.1   *Exemptions with Credit for Input Tax*
This category includes all supplies within the zero-rating schedule.

In addition, where supplies of all or substantially all of the assets of a business are sold and where supplies are made to provincial governments, zero-rating will, in effect, apply.

7.2 Exemptions without Credit for Input Tax

This category includes all the supplies within the exempt supplies schedule. The specific provisions must be reviewed to determine what aspects of the supply are exempt. The general headings are:

- real property
- health care services
- educational services
- child care and personal care services
- legal aid services
- public sector bodies (including government, municipalities, universities, school authorities, hospital authorities, non-profit organisations and charities)
- financial services (other than those in the zero-rating schedule)
- ferry, road and bridge tolls.

In addition, a closely related member of a group containing a financial institution may elect to exempt supplies between itself and the financial institution, subject to certain conditions.

7.3 Non-Taxable Transactions

The following types of supplies are considered non-taxable:

- supplies outside Canada
- donations and grants of money and most sponsorships
- discounts not included in the price of goods
- fincs, penalties and interest
- supplies where the supplier has a turnover of less than C$30,000 a year and has not registered
- prize-winnings in cash, such as lotteries, horse races, etc.

7.4 Election to Tax

In certain circumstances, registrants may elect to tax otherwise exempt supplies as follows:

- public service bodies may elect to tax, on a property-by-property basis, supplies that would otherwise be exempt supplies of real property (this option is also available to individuals or trusts where the beneficiaries are individuals)
- educational organisations may elect to have certain courses taxed
- professional associations and public sector bodies may elect to have certain memberships taxed.

8 CREDIT/REFUND FOR INPUT TAX

8.1 Full Input Tax Credits

Full input tax credits are generally available to registrants for all the tax paid or payable on all purchases that relate exclusively to a commercial activity. These credits are available on a period-by-period basis and on a tax-paid or tax-payable basis.

For GST purposes 'exclusively' is generally considered to mean 90% or more. In the case of capital personal property (other than automobiles), the limit is 'primarily' (more than 50%) rather than 'exclusively'.

8.2   No Input Tax Credits

For registrants other than financial institutions no input tax credits are available on acquired supplies where the commercial use is 10% or less.

In the case of capital personal property (other than automobiles), the limit is 50% or less.

8.3   Non-Deductible Statutory Provisions

In addition, input tax credits cannot be reclaimed for:

- membership fees or dues to any club the main purpose of which is to provide dining, recreational or sporting facilities
- any property supplied by lease, licence or similar arrangement, exclusively for the personal consumption, use or enjoyment of the registrant, an officer, shareholder, beneficiary of a trust or any other related individual
- any acquired supplies where no GST was paid (for example, exempt supplies, zero-rated supplies and wages)
- 50% of GST incurred on business-related meal and entertainment expenses.

8.4   Partial Input Tax Credits

Where commercial use exceeds 10% and is less than 90%, input tax credits must be apportioned to commercial and non-commercial use.

8.5   Public Sector Bodies

To the extent that any of these entities and supplies relate to real property, input tax credits can be claimed in full if a primary commercial use is involved.

8.6   Financial Institutions

Input tax may be recovered by a financial institution on a proportional basis to the extent that the supplies are used in commercial activities.

8.7   Nominal Input Tax Credits

In addition to the above input tax credits, refunds are available as rebates (see section 10.1 below).

8.8   Refund for Non-Residents

While a system of reciprocity exists between registered businesses in countries with a VAT system, the only refund mechanism in the GST is the tourist rebate. Refunds are available to non-residents for tax paid on short-term accommodation and certain goods supplied in Canada which are subsequently exported from Canada. Refunds are also available in respect of conventions held in Canada where at least 75% of the attendees are non-residents of Canada.

8.9   Time of Recovery

Where the registrant should receive a refund, the return will generally be filed within one month of the end of the reporting period.

9 ADMINISTRATIVE OBLIGATIONS

9.1 Registration
Every person required to be registered in Canada must apply to the Minister of National Revenue within 30 days after the date of the first taxable supply (see section 2 above).

9.2 Books and Records
Books and records must be kept in English or French in Canada, for six years and must be available for inspection on request. Books and records may be kept outside Canada where the registrant undertakes to make them available for audit in Canada or agrees to pay all reasonable travel expenses incurred by an auditor in going to the place where the records are kept.

9.3 Invoicing
The information required on invoices increases with the value of the invoice. Documentary requirements are:

- for invoices of less than C$30.00, the vendor's name, tax point and total consideration
- for invoices between C$30.00 and C$150.00, in addition to the above, the vendor's GST number and the GST charged
- for invoices over C$150.00, in addition to all of the above, the recipient's name, a description of each supply, and the terms of sale.

Sufficient documentary evidence is very broadly defined and includes statements, invoices and written contracts. With ministerial approval, in some cases, no supporting documents are needed and books of record will suffice.

9.4 GST Returns
Returns may be filed monthly, quarterly, or annually as follows:

- monthly: more than C$6 million of annual taxable plus zero-rated supplies
- quarterly: C$6 million or less of annual taxable plus zero-rated supplies
- annually: C$500,000 or less of annual taxable and zero-rated supplies (with quarterly instalments and annual adjustments).

Both quarterly and annual filers may elect to file monthly.

9.5 Power of Authorities
The Minister has the power to:

- authorise persons to carry out audit of books and records at any reasonable time
- authorise persons to carry out enquiries into the affairs of any person in order to obtain information relating to the administration and enforcement of the GST legislation
- assess:
    - any registrant for taxes remittable
    - any taxpayer for taxes payable otherwise than on an importation of goods
    - receivers, executors and other representatives of a taxpayer
    - any person for penalty and interest
    - directors of corporations for taxes payable or remittable by the corporation
    - officers, and in certain cases, members of unincorporated bodies for taxes

payable or remittable by the body
- non-arm's length transferees
- refunds and rebates payable to a person.

9.6 Penalties

Penalties and interest can be imposed in cases of evasion, fraud, failure to comply with various requirements, and late payments and remittance of returns.

A penalty can include fines and imprisonment.

9.7 Appeals and Objections

Appeals against decisions on assessments may be made first to the Minister, second to the Tax Court of Canada, third to the Federal Court of Appeal, and finally to the Supreme Court of Canada.

There is some facility for informal as well as formal appeals.

10 SPECIAL VAT REGIMES

10.1 GST Credit

To lessen the impact of the GST on low and modest income families, the government has established a tax credit refund programme. The credit is paid by cheque four times a year, in equal instalments, to eligible families and individuals. Payment amounts are indexed to the cost of living.

10.2 Rebates of GST Paid

Partial and full rebates of GST paid are available in a variety of circumstances.

Rebates are available:

- to employees and partners for business-related purchases
- in respect of new housing
- in respect of real property by a non-registrant who subsequently makes a taxable sale
- to non-residents
- for legal services under a provincial legal aid plan
- to public service bodies, including municipalities, universities, schools, hospitals, charities, and certain non-profit organisations
- for payments made in error.

10.3 Simplified Accounting

Certain small businesses may elect to use one of the simplified accounting methods designed to reduce paperwork and bookkeeping costs related to the collection and remittance process.

10.4 Supplies by Charities

Subject to certain limited exceptions, all supplies of personal property and services by charities are exempt from GST. Charities are eligible for a rebate of a portion of the tax paid on a supply, provided the supply in not attributable to a taxable activity undertaken by the charity and the particular supply is not denied the rebate through regulation.

11   FURTHER READING

Goods and Services Tax – GST Handbook for accounting professionals and financial executives, Ernst & Young/Canadian Institute of Chartered Accountants (CICA)

The Complete Guide to the Goods and Services Tax (3d ed), Ernst & Young/Canadian Institute of Chartered Accountants (CICA)

Goods and Services Tax Question and Answer Guides

-    *Health Care Sector,* Ernst & Young/Canadian Hospital Association

-    *Registered Charities and Registered Amateur Athletic Associations,* Ernst & Young/Canadian Society of Association Executives (CSAE)

-    *Trade, Professional and Other Non-Profit Associations,* Ernst & Young/Canadian Society of Association Executives (CSAE)

Contributor: Peter Wood
                    Ernst & Young
                    Ernst & Young Tower
                    222 Bay Street
                    Toronto
                    Canada
                    Tel: +1416 864 1234
                    Fax: +1416 864 1174

CHILE

1 GENERAL BACKGROUND

VAT was introduced in Chile by Decree-Law 825 of 1974, and since then has been modified on many occasions, the last amendment being in January 1994. Prior to VAT a sales and services tax was in effect.

Chilean VAT is inspired by the French model and is technically similar to those of other European and Latin American countries.

The VAT law is complemented by regulations, instructions, circulars and directives of the National Services of Internal Taxes ('the Service'). In the case of dispute with the Service, final settlement may be sought from the judicial courts. Control of VAT and other local taxes is in the hands of the Service. The control of imported goods is exercised by the Custom Houses.

2 WHO IS TAXABLE?

2.1 *General*
According to the VAT law, taxable persons are divided into two groups: sellers of goods and providers of services. Other operations may also be subject to tax irrespective of the status of the person, as in the case of importation of goods.

A 'seller of goods' is defined as any individual or juridical entity who habitually conducts operations which are considered to be sales. In some cases habituality is not a requisite, as in the case of import of goods. The tax, however, is charged to the buyer according to the normal VAT procedures.

'Sale' is defined as any agreement aimed at transferring, for a pecuniary consideration, movable goods or a quota or share in such goods, as well as any contract considered by the law to be a sale. The transfer by a building enterprise of real estate which was built entirely by the enterprise or partially by third parties on its behalf is also considered to be a sale.

'Service' is defined as an action or activity for the benefit of another and for which the supplier receives a remuneration, commission, interest or any other kind of compensation, provided such an action or activity is classified under certain items of the Income Tax Law (usually commercial and industrial activities).

Those persons liable for VAT include:

- any person who is habitually engaged in selling tangible movable goods
- producers and construction enterprises that for any reason sell raw materials
- any person making a contribution of tangible movable goods to a company or partnership
- construction enterprises that habitually engage in selling their own tangible immovable

---

This chapter reflects the VAT legislation in Chile at 31 January 1995.

property, provided that the property has been wholly or partially constructed by the enterprise; and contractors and subcontractors in respect of installation of fixtures and general construction contracts

- any person rendering services subject to VAT
- importers, whether or not habitual.

2.2   Government Bodies

The State, government bodies and enterprises are all liable to VAT in respect of sales, services and imports made by them.

2.3   Communities

Communities and de facto partnerships are also subject to VAT, since the co-owners and de facto partners are jointly responsible for the liabilities of the respective community or de facto partnership.

2.4   Substitution of Taxpayer

The normal taxable persons for VAT are sellers and recipients of remuneration for certain services. However, when the seller or the recipients of fees are not easily controlled by the Service, it may change the taxpayer by imposing the VAT liability on the buyers or payers of the fees instead. An example of this is the case of small farmers and minor sellers who may lack the information necessary for proper tax compliance, etc.

3   WHAT IS TAXABLE?

VAT liability arises on the taxable supply of goods (both movable and immovable), building contracts, the performance of certain services, and other actions or activities considered to be taxable as sales or services as mentioned in section 2.1 above.

Activities considered as sales or services for the purpose of assessing VAT include:

- imports, whether they are habitual or not
- capital contributions made to partnerships or corporations which are current assets from the point of view of the contributor
- assignment of movable goods forming part of the current business assets of a company or partnership executed during the liquidation of such corporation or partnership
- appropriation of the current business assets of an enterprise effected by a seller or by the owners, partners, directors, or employees of the enterprise for their own or their families' use or consumption. For these purposes, any inventory deficiency shall be deemed to be such an appropriation or withdrawal of merchandise, subject to tax
- free delivery of goods made by sellers for promotional or marketing purposes
- general building contracts, including one-off contracts and the installation of fixtures
- sale of a commercial enterprise which includes movable tangible goods
- lease of movable goods, and of real estate which includes movable goods and/or machinery, equipment, etc required for a commercial or industrial activity, and of all kinds of commercial tangible assets. The portion of the lease price which corresponds to the fiscal valuation of the real estate as such, is exempted from tax
- leasing/licensing of trade marks, licences and similar intangible property rights

- parking of cars and other vehicles in parking lots
- agreement to sell real estate owned by a building enterprise and leasing of real estate with option to purchase.

To be taxable, services must correspond to the activities contemplated in Nos. 3 and 4 of Article 20 of the Income Tax Law, namely:

- industry, commerce, mining, transportation, exploitation of maritime resources and other extractive operations, airline companies, insurance, commercial banking, savings and loan associations, administrators of mutual funds, financing and similar entities, building enterprises, radio, TV, journalism, publicity, data processing and telecommunication enterprises
- brokers; commission agents having a permanent establishment, auctioneers, customs agents, shippers and others engaged in maritime, port and customs activities, insurance agents (except individuals); schools, academies, private educational institutions, and similar institutions; clinics, hospitals, laboratories and similar operations, and entertainment enterprises.

4   PLACE OF SUPPLY

The sale of movable or immovable goods and the supply of services are subject to VAT if located in Chile, irrespective of the place where the agreement to sell is executed or the nationality or residence of the parties involved. Services utilised in Chile are also subject to VAT.

5   BASIS OF TAXATION

5.1   Taxable Amount

The basis for the assessment of VAT is the price of the corresponding operations, including the following items:

- readjustments, interest and financing expenses of deferred payments (including penal interest) that may accrue in the corresponding monthly period
- value of containers together with any deposits paid for guaranteeing their restitution (although the Service may permit the exclusion of such deposits)
- taxes, with the exception of the VAT itself.

5.2   Imports

In the case of imports, the tax basis is the cost, insurance, freight (CIF) value, or customs value if applicable under the Brussels Convention, including the customs duties payable in respect of the importation.

5.3   Chargeable Event

VAT on the sale of goods is due at the date of the invoice, and sales must be invoiced in the month that the goods are delivered. Delivery may be made by an actual transfer or by the fact of putting the goods at the disposal of the buyer.

Services are also taxed at the date of issue of the invoice. They must be invoiced when remunerations or fees are actually paid.

Payment of VAT to the Treasury must be made during the first 12 days of the calendar month following the date of the invoice.

6   TAX RATES

0.5%:   sales of second-hand cars and other motorised vehicles. This is strictly not a VAT rate and it does not give rise to any entitlement to recovery.

18%:   all taxable goods and services.

50%:   surcharge: on the first sale or import of certain goods such as articles of gold, silver, platinum, ivory, jewellery and others considered as luxury goods.Various special surcharges: alcoholic beverages at the level of first sale.

7   EXEMPTIONS

7.1   Exemption with Credit for Input Tax
The following are exempt from VAT but carry with them the right to recovery of input tax:

- exports
- raw materials produced in Chile if they are incorporated in goods to be exported and if approved by the Service
- contracts to let, sub-let, charter, sub-charter or use, or right to use, any ships under the Chilean flag, concluded with non-residents
- international goods transport by land, sea, rivers, lakes or air, and international air passenger transport
- income received from services rendered to persons not domiciled or resident in Chile, provided such services are qualified as exports by the customs authority.

7.2   Exemptions without Credit for Input Tax
The following actions/activities are exempt from VAT and the seller/supplier is not entitled to any input VAT recovery:

- passenger transportation effected by maritime and railroad enterprises, local public transport effected by buses, etc
- insurance premiums covering the freight risks of imports and exports, and those covering ships and goods located outside the country; insurance covering earthquake risks; readjustable life insurances; premiums and expenses related to reinsurances
- interest derived from any financing operation and/or negotiable instrument, and from any kind of credit with the exception of interest on deferred payments of sales
- professional services and those received by individuals rendering personal services without the employment of capital
- benefits which are not considered income for tax purposes; income subject to sole additional tax according to the Income Tax Law (for instance, payment of royalties and other remuneration to non-residents)
- income derived from journalist enterprises, TV and radio entities, but excluding commercial advertising

- activities of educational establishments with respect to income exclusively derived from educational activities
- medical services performed in State hospitals
- social security institutions
- imports made by certain public entities
- the importation to Chile by immigrants of personal effects, household goods, tools, labour equipment, a car and a sports boat, provided these goods are not subject to import registration
- foreign investors ruled by Decree Law No. 600, with respect to capital goods forming part of the corresponding investment project. National investors may also enjoy this exemption with respect to projects similar to those approved for foreign investors
- imports under the regime of temporary admission, customs deposit, free warehouse, or similar establishments.

8   CREDIT/REFUND FOR INPUT TAX

8.1   General
A taxable person may reduce the amount of VAT payable on his total sales and services by:

- discounts granted to clients after the sales or services have been invoiced
- reimbursements paid to customer, corresponding to the price of returned goods, provided the refund is made within three months of the date of delivery
- amounts returned to customers corresponding to guarantees for the return of containers
- VAT charged on inputs acquired in the same monthly period (fiscal credit).

The VAT payable must be increased by the VAT on discounts granted by suppliers after the goods or services supplied have been invoiced. It must also be increased by the VAT on the price of goods given back to suppliers provided that the goods have been returned within three months from the date of the original delivery.

In addition, to qualify for input credit, the following legal requirements must be complied with:

- the VAT must have been paid on the acquisition of current or fixed assets for use in the taxpayer's business, or for general expenses related to the same business
- the acquired goods must not be related to VAT exempted operations
- the acquired goods must not be expressly excluded by law from input tax recovery, such as the importation, acquisition and leasing of automobiles, station wagons and similar vehicles
- the VAT must be charged separately in the invoice issued by the supplier. In the case of imports, the VAT payment must be substantiated by the corresponding Treasury receipt
- invoices must be issued in accordance with the formal legal requirement (forms correlatively numerated and sealed by the Treasury) and duly recorded in the corresponding accounting records

8.2   Special Recovery of Input Tax
Taxable persons and exporters who are exempt in their export business and wno have

accumulated input tax for a period of six months without being able to set it off against output VAT may obtain a refund from the Treasury, provided the input tax relates to the acquisition of fixed assets, including real estate, or services related to these assets.

The refund is effected by either setting off the input tax against any other tax, or by requesting a direct reimbursement from the Treasury.

If the input tax relates partially to the acquisition of fixed assets and partially to current assets and/or general expenses, the input credit is calculated on a proportional basis.

8.3 Apportionment of Input Tax Credit

Where a person sells goods or performs services which are exempt from VAT, the VAT incurred on the acquisition of goods and services is not allowed as an input credit and it is a cost for the seller of goods or provider of services which are exempt.

If the input tax cannot be attributed specifically to taxable or exempt operations (as in the case of energy, telecommunications and other general expenses) the input tax credit will be allowed in a proportion corresponding to the taxable operations according to a specified formula.

8.4 Refund of Input Tax to Exporters

Exporters are entitled to recover the VAT incurred on the acquisition of goods and utilisation of services employed in their export trade. There are two methods of recovery:

- by deduction of the VAT from the VAT payable on taxable internal sales and performance of services
- by direct refund from the Treasury through a request made in the month following the export operation.

International transportation of cargo by land, sea or air, and of passengers by air, also qualifies for this refund of VAT. There is a special procedure whereby an exporter may obtain early payment of an anticipated refund when a future export is approved by the Treasury and a guarantee is given to the Service.

9   ADMINISTRATIVE OBLIGATIONS

9.1 Registration

All VAT payers must register with the Service before they commence business.

9.2 Invoices

Taxable persons are required to issue invoices for their transactions with other taxable persons for:

- all taxable sales or services supplied to other taxable persons
- sales of (or for promises to sell) immovable property
- contracts for the installation of fixtures
- general construction contracts.

When dealing with final consumers, ie non-taxable persons, they are required to issue Boletas (simplified invoices).

Standard or simplified invoices must also be issued for exempt transactions.

In the case of transfers of tangible movable goods the invoices must be issued on the actual or symbolic delivery of goods. In the case of supplies of services they must be issued in the same tax period in which the consideration is either collected or put at the disposal of the supplier. Invoices must be issued by the fifth day following the end of the relevant tax period.

9.3   Tax Returns

Each calendar month is a tax period and a VAT return must be filed within 12 days of the end of each tax period along with the payment of tax due. The return must be submitted even if the taxpayer has no taxable transactions or has only exempt transactions.

VAT on imports is payable prior to the clearance of the goods through customs. Persons not subject to corporate tax may pay the VAT due on imports by way of instalments.

9.4   Powers of the Authorities

When a taxable person fails to file a return, or when the return is not reliable or is incorrect, or when the documents or accounting records are not reliable or are not kept in accordance with the regulations, then the tax administration may make an assessment of the VAT due. The time limit for an assessment is three years for an incorrect return, and six years if a return is not filed or has been intentionally filed falsely.

9.5   Penalties

The penalty for failure to file a return on time is 10% of the tax due, plus a further penalty of 2% per month or part of a month thereafter. The total fine is restricted to 30% of the tax due.

Incomplete or incorrect returns which generate an assessment for additional tax are subject to a fine of between 5% and 20% of the additional tax due.

Failure to issue invoices and other documents will incur a fine ranging from 50% to 500% of the value of the transaction. The business may also be closed down for up to 20 days, and repeated infringements may result in imprisonment.

Fraud is punished by imprisonment and a fine of up to 300% of the tax evaded. A taxpayer who obtains a tax refund by means of fraudulent transactions is liable to a fine of up to 400% of the unlawful refund together with imprisonment.

9.6   Appeals

Taxpayers have 60 working days from the date of the relevant notice in which to object to an assessment and to decisions affecting the amount of VAT they have to pay. Such appeals will be decided in the first instance by the regional director of the tax administration. Any appeal against his decision must be made to a Court of Appeals within ten days of the date of the decision. Further appeals may be made to the Supreme Court.

Contributor: Juan de Dios Vergara
                 Ernst & Young
                 Casillas 50080 and 2186
                 Santiago
                 Chile
                 Tel: +56 2 6395 081
                 Fax: +56 2 6383 622

COLOMBIA

1 GENERAL ASPECTS

Value added tax (VAT), known in Colombia as 'sales tax', was introduced in 1965. The law has been amended substantially many times since then.

Internally, VAT is administered by the Tax and Customs Administration. VAT on imports is administered by the same authority.

2 WHO IS TAXABLE?

A taxable person is any corporation, partnership or private person who sells taxable goods or who renders taxable services as an independent entrepreneur. It does not include the action of employees.

VAT on goods brought into Colombia is payable by the importer at customs clearance. If the goods are sent directly by a foreign firm to a final customer in Colombia who appears as the actual importer, VAT due on imports will be payable by the Colombian customer.

2.1 Government Bodies
Government bodies are subject to VAT. Exemptions applicable to government bodies with respect to their income tax are not extended to VAT.

2.2 Foreign Entrepreneurs
Entrepreneurs without an establishment in Colombia but who supply services which are taxable in Colombia are subject to VAT. However, no mechanism has been established to collect this tax. A foreign entrepreneur is also taxable in Colombia when he acts as the importer of the goods.

3 WHAT IS TAXABLE?

VAT is applied:

- on the sale of tangible goods located in the country
- on services rendered within the country
- on the importation of goods.

Structurally, although known as 'sales tax', it operates as a value added tax since sales taxes paid by suppliers are offset against sales taxes collected from customers. The net amount is paid to the tax authorities bi-monthly.

This chapter reflects the law on VAT in Colombia as at 31 December 1994.

3.1 Goods

Sales of goods are defined as:

- operations involving the transfer of rights in tangible goods, either as gratuities (donations) or on an onerous basis
- the retirement of such goods made by the party responsible for its own use or to be included as part of the company's fixed assets
- the import of goods.

All goods sold for export purposes are exempt from VAT, with a right of reimbursement of the amount of tax paid on their acquisition or production.

3.2 Services

Services are defined as any activity or work rendered by individuals or legal entities without an employment relationship with the contracting party.

All services are taxable except those listed in section 7.2 below.

4   PLACE OF SUPPLY

VAT is chargeable in Colombia only if the supply of goods or services takes place in Colombia.

5   BASIS OF TAXATION

5.1 Supplies within Colombia

The taxable value of goods and services is their full value, including all added values such as financing, installation and insurance commissions.

The taxable value is specified by law, that is, the value may not be lower than the market value; exceptions to this rule are provided only for oil and gas derivatives, the price of which is fixed periodically by the Ministry of Mines and Energy.

5.2 Importers

In the case of imported goods, the value for VAT purposes is the cost insurance freight (CIF) value increased by customs duties. The VAT must be included in the VAT return based on the date of the importation return, which means that it has already been paid.

5.3 Chargeable Event/Time of Payment

In the case of the sale of goods, the chargeable event occurs at the time of issuing the invoice, and if no invoice is issued, it occurs at the time of delivery of the goods.

In the case of the provision of services, the chargeable event occurs at the time of issuing the invoice or at the completion of the service, whichever occurs first.

In the case of telephone services, the chargeable event occurs at the time the user pays for the service.

In the case of the international air and/or sea passenger service, the chargeable event occurs when the party responsible is informed that the ticket is issued.

5.4 Imports

In respect of imports, the chargeable event occurs when the goods are imported although, if importations are made under the long-term temporary importation licence system, the VAT is accrued and paid with the customs duties in semi-annual instalments.

6 TAX RATES

At present there are six different tax rates:

0%: exports, sales of books and magazines of a scientific or cultural nature and sales of goods to international marketing companies

14%: all other supplies of taxable goods and taxable services

15%: insurance purchased abroad

20%: certain types of motor vehicles and motorcycles

35%: wines, liquors and recreation vessels

45%: motor vehicles whose value exceeds US$35,000

7 EXEMPTIONS

7.1 Exemptions with Credit for Input Tax

The following operations are taxed at the rate of 0%:

- exportation of goods
- sales in Colombia to international marketing companies, provided that the goods are actually exported
- sales of books and magazines of a scientific or cultural nature.

7.2 Exemptions without Credit for Input Tax – Services

The following services are exempt from VAT:

- labour
- life insurance policies
- rental of real estate
- leasing and interest derived from loan transactions
- elementary, high school and university education rendered by institutions recognised by the government
- publicity, radio, press, TV, cinemas, security services, cleaning and temporary employees' companies
- utility companies (except the provision of telephone services)
- medical, dental and hospital services
- transportation services, including:

- – domestic and international freight, including port and airport services
- – domestic passenger services

■ engineering and architectural services relating to the construction of housing intended for poor people.

7.3   Exempt without Credit for Input Tax – Goods

The following goods are exempt from VAT:

■ goods expressly classified by the law as excluded from VAT in accordance with the NANDINA customs tariffs. In general, these are goods in their natural condition or goods that have not suffered any process of manufacture
■ raw materials used to manufacture medicines, insecticides or fertilisers
■ machinery used for the agricultural and livestock sector, together with heavy machinery intended for basic industries, provided it is not manufactured in the country
■ natural gas, natural gasoline, crude oil intended for refining.

7.4   Goods Outside the Scope of VAT

The following goods are not covered by the VAT system and, therefore, are not to be taken into account for VAT purposes:

■ real estate
■ goods classified as fixed assets for the seller.

8   CREDIT/REFUND FOR INPUT TAX

The principle is that all VAT paid on goods and services by a Colombian entrepreneur is recoverable. However, this principle applies only if the input tax was incurred with a view to achieving taxable or exempt transactions.

There are several requirements which must be fulfilled before input tax can be offset. For example:

■ VAT must be identified on the supplier's invoice unless it relates to a fuel purchase
■ the purchase or service operation must correspond to those recognised by income tax regulations as a cost or deduction
■ goods or services should be intended for taxable operations, unless the responsible party is an exporter or seller of exempt goods
■ if the party responsible for the VAT sells both goods subject to VAT and goods excluded/exempt from VAT and there are costs or expenses common to these operations, only that proportion attributable to taxable and exempt supplies may be offset
■ VAT paid for the acquisition of capital goods (eg machinery and equipment) is not recoverable on VAT returns (although it is in income tax returns), even if the goods are imported or purchased under a leasing agreement and an irrevocable purchase option for the lessee has been agreed. In general, VAT on the acquisition of fixed assets is not deductible on VAT returns.

9   ADMINISTRATIVE OBLIGATIONS

9.1   Registration
All persons liable to pay VAT, including exporters, must register with the national salesmen's register within two months of commencing their taxable activities.

Further, exporters must register with the national exporter's registry in order to obtain a refund of VAT paid on the purchase of goods and services or imports.

9.2   Books and Records
Taxable persons should keep a special account to record VAT on their purchases and that generated from their sales. The balance of this account at the end of each bi-monthly period should correspond to the figure in the VAT return.

9.3   Invoices
Invoices must contain specified information, including a pre-printed tax identification number.

9.4   VAT Return
VAT returns should be signed by the legal representative and the statutory auditor and filed bi-monthly together with any balance payable. Any refund due to the taxpayer may be:

- transferred to the following bi-monthly period
- used to compensate other unpaid national taxes due, including tax withholdings, penalties and interest
- requested as a refund, which will take the form of a cheque or a TIDIS (tax refund paper) to pay taxes. The Tax and Customs Administration will select the method of refund.

10   SPECIAL TAX REGIMES

10.1   Real Estate
In real estate construction contracts, the base for VAT is the constructor's own income (fees agreed or contract's estimated profit). The VAT deductible is limited to the proportion between the taxable base within the contract's total income.

10.2   Passenger Transport
In the case of international passenger services, 50% of the amount of round-trip tickets is subject to VAT, while one-way tickets are taxed on the full amount.

Contributor: Pedro Pablo Guardía
Ernst & Young
Transversal 22 No. 100–15
Bogotà
Colombia
Tel: +571 621 0411
Fax: +571 610 3060

EL SALVADOR

1 GENERAL BACKGROUND

Value added tax (VAT) was introduced in El Salvador on 1 September 1992 replacing the 5% Cumulative Stamp Tax levied on the sale of merchandise, goods and services.

2 WHO IS TAXABLE?

2.1 General
The following are subject to VAT:

- producers, wholesalers, retailers and any other persons effecting taxable sales or transfers, either habitually or in the course of their business or activity
- importers of taxable goods or services, whether or not habitual
- persons rendering services habitually.

The following may be treated as taxable persons:

- corporations and individuals
- estates
- de facto companies
- trusts
- co-operatives.

2.2 Foreign Businesses
When the supply is made by a person who does not have a domicile or residence in El Salvador, the recipient of goods or services is responsible for the payment of the VAT.

2.3 Government Bodies
State and local government bodies are liable to VAT.

Other government institutions, agencies and enterprises may also be considered to be taxable persons, even when they are exempt from all taxes under their statutes.

2.4 Fiscal Unity/Group Taxation
The term 'Fiscal Unity' and 'Group Taxation' are not used in El Salvador legislation.

3 WHAT IS TAXABLE?

VAT is levied on the transfer, importation and self-consumption of tangible movable goods, as well as on the supply and importation of services.

This chapter reflects the law on VAT in El Salvador as at 31 October 1994.

VAT liability arises on the taxable supply or importation of goods or services in El Salvador for consideration by taxable persons, corporations and individuals acting in the course of business.

3.1 Supply of Goods

The transfer of tangible movable goods includes not only a complete sale but also any agreements or contracts relating to the full or partial transfer of the title to such goods.

Taxable transfer includes:

- sale of tangible movable goods effected through public auctions and the assignment of goods made to pay debts
- barters
- payments in kind
- the lending of goods for consumption by the borrower
- contributions of tangible movable goods forming part of the stock-in-trade made to companies, legal entities or any other entity even if it has no legal existence
- transfer of tangible movable goods forming part of the stock-in-trade effected upon a business expansion, transformation, merger or other business reorganisation
- assignment of tangible movable goods forming part of the stock-in-trade effected upon the dissolution, liquidation or capital reduction of a company, legal entity, de facto company or any other entity even if it has no legal existence
- transfer of an establishment of business enterprise, only in respect of tangible movable goods forming part of stock-in-trade which are included in the transfer
- the establishment or transfer, for a consideration, of the use or usufruct of goods, or the right to exploit or to appropriate products extracted from quarries, mines, lakes, forests, plantations and the like
- the promise to sell followed by a transfer
- in general, any delivery of goods which grants to the recipient the power to dispose of the goods as an owner.

3.2 Supply of Services

Although the Law does not contain a definition of services it provides that, in order for services to be taxable, they must originate from an agreement or contract in which the recipient promises to pay a consideration for the services.

Taxable services include:

- technical assistance and elaboration of plans and projects
- letting of tangible movable goods, whether or not the letting includes a purchase option or a promise to sell
- letting, sub-letting and the transfer of the temporary use or benefit of commercial establishments or immovable property for commercial or industrial activities
- performance of engineering works on a cost plus basis
- construction works, whether for a fixed price or on a cost plus basis
- land, air or maritime transportation of cargo and air or maritime transportation of passengers
- independent personal services.

3.3   Self-Supply of Goods

Taxable transactions include the withdrawal from the enterprise of taxable goods forming part of the stock-in-trade by the taxpayer (or by the enterprise's partners, members of the board of directors, managers or personnel) for his personal use or consumption. Also, any unjustifiable shortage of goods from the enterprise's inventories, or the supply of goods made through raffles or gifts for advertising and similar purposes is taxable. However, gifts destined to be given to charities are not taxable.

3.4   Importation of Goods/Services

The importation of goods (including customs auctions) and the importation of services are taxable.

An importation of services is deemed to exist when the activity necessary to produce the service is carried out abroad and the service is supplied to and used by a recipient domiciled in El Salvador. The concept may apply to technical assistance, trade marks, patents, models, know-how, computer programs and the letting of tangible movable goods.

4   PLACE OF SUPPLY

4.1   Supply of Goods

Transfers are taxable when goods are located or registered in El Salvador (even if they are temporarily located abroad), independently from the place where the agreement or contract is concluded. Goods shipped from the country of origin to El Salvador are taxable when transferred to domiciled purchasers even if they are not VAT taxpayers.

4.2   Supply of Services

Services are taxable when they are supplied in El Salvador independently from the place where the agreement or contract was concluded and where the payment is made. The service is deemed to be supplied in El Salvador when the activity necessary to produce the service is carried out in El Salvador.

If services are supplied partially in El Salvador, only that part of the service supplied in the country is taxable. However, certain services supplied in El Salvador (eg services related to transportation or goods in transit through the country) are fully taxed even though they are not exclusively used therein.

5   BASIS OF TAXATION

5.1   General Rule

As a rule, the taxable amount is the price or consideration for the supply of goods or services or, in the case of imported goods or services, the customs value.

5.2   Value of Supply

The value of the transfer of tangible movable goods is the price of the transaction. In the case of auction sales, the price is increased by the amount of the commission and fees. In the case of transfers of commercial establishments, the taxable amount is the value of the tangible movable goods included in the transfer. In the case of barter and other exchanges, each party is treated as a seller and the taxable amount of each sale is the value of the goods involved.

5.3 Self-Supplies
In the case of self-supplies of goods, the basis is the value established by the taxpayer in his documents and records. This value cannot be lower than the current market price.

5.4 Importation
The taxable amount of imports is the cost insurance freight (CIF) value or customs value, plus customs duties.

5.5 Time of Supply

5.5.1 Transfer
The liability to VAT arises upon the issue of the document supporting the transaction. If the price is paid or the goods are delivered prior to the issue of the relevant document or, if no document is required, the liability for the VAT arises upon the payment of the price or delivery of the goods.

5.5.2 Services
The liability for VAT arises upon the issue of the document supporting the transaction, the conclusion of the service, the delivery of goods (in the case of letting, sub-letting and transfer of the temporary use or benefit of goods), the delivery of goods or work (in the case of services including the delivery or transfer of goods or the performance of work) or the full or partial payment of the consideration.

5.5.3 Self-Supply of Goods
In the case of self-supply of goods, the liability for VAT arises upon the withdrawal of goods from the enterprise.

5.5.4 Importation
The liability for VAT arises once the importation is carried out or upon compliance of the requirements for the use of the imported services.

6   TAX RATES

There are two tax rates:

0%:   exports

10%:   all other taxable supplies of goods and services.

7   EXCLUSIONS AND EXEMPTIONS

7.1 Exempt Persons
Persons with a turnover below 50,000 colones or total assets below 20,000 colones are not

treated as taxpayers for VAT purposes. This exemption is not applicable to companies or importers. In computing the limits referred to above, taxpayers who have more than one establishment must combine the figures from each establishment.

Exempt persons can elect to be treated as taxpayers for VAT purposes.

7.2 Exclusions

Compensation for damage, natural disaster or injury is not considered to be a service.

7.3 Exempt Transactions

The following goods and services are exempt from VAT:

- beans, white corn, rice, fruits and vegetables in their natural state
- liquid and powder milk
- medicines and pharmaceutical products for human use and raw materials for their production
- cash and foreign exchange, securities and financial documents are considered to be intangible movable property for VAT purposes and are therefore tax-free
- health services rendered by government institutions or by institutions of public interest approved by the tax administration
- letting, sub-letting or transfer of the temporary use or benefit of dwelling-houses
- dependent personal services
- cultural public events authorised by the tax administration
- educational and teaching services rendered by schools, universities and similar institutions
- interest on deposits with and on loans made by banks and financial institutions
- interest on bearer securities issued by the State, its autonomous agencies or by private institutions (in the latter case through a stock exchange)
- supply of electric power, water and drainage services supplied by State-owned enterprises
- premiums paid for personal insurance, as well as reinsurance in general.

The importation of the goods listed above is also exempt. Furthermore, an exemption may apply to imports made by diplomatic and consular corps, international organisations, passengers and crews, as well as to gifts donated from abroad to charities or under international conventions entered into by El Salvador. Imports made under ad honorem appointments for diplomatic or consular positions are liable to VAT.

8   CREDIT/REFUND OF INPUT TAX

As a rule, the tax is the difference between the liability originating from chargeable transactions and creditable taxes.

A taxpayer may credit against his VAT liability the tax charged to him on the acquisition of goods or use of services, or paid by him on imports.

In order to be creditable, the tax must originate from expenses necessary or useful for the taxpayer's business or activity, such as general expenses, acquisition of tangible movable goods destined to the stock-in-trade or to fixed assets and expenses incurred in respect of services relating to chargeable or zero-rated transactions.

A taxpayer who habitually acquires goods or uses services may credit against his VAT liabilities the tax which he has withheld on payment to small-sized taxpayers.

In the case of goods, services and imports attributable to both chargeable and exempt transactions, the credit is calculated on a proportional basis.

The excess of credits over liabilities may be carried forward and added to credits of subsequent tax periods without limit. The excess is normally not refunded, even in the case of termination of the taxpayer's businesses or activities. However, taxpayers who, after their first six tax periods (up to a maximum of 18 consecutive months from the beginning of their activities, show an excess of credits over liabilities originating from the acquisition of fixed assets, may credit the excess against any internal tax or customs duty or charge. Moreover, a refund may be obtained by exporters in respect of tax credits which cannot be used within six tax periods, provided that the exporters do not have any other outstanding tax debts. If the exporter additionally engages in internal sales or services, the refund is calculated according to the ratio of exports to total sales of the same tax period.

Enterprises operating within the free zones or fiscal areas with the approval of the Internal Revenue Service can be considered as exporters for VAT purposes.

9   ADMINISTRATIVE OBLIGATIONS

9.1   Registration and Records
Taxpayers (including persons habitually engaged in imports and exports) must register with the tax administration and are required to keep special books and records.

9.2   Invoices
Taxpayers are required to issue and deliver a special document known as a 'comprobante de crédito fiscal' (credit voucher) for each supply of goods or services made to other taxpayers, whether taxable or exempt and to keep copies for five years.

In the case of transactions with final customers, VAT taxpayers must issue and deliver a 'factura' (invoice) which may be replaced by other documents authorised by the tax administration.

9.3   Tax Period and Returns
The tax period is the calendar month and a VAT return must be filed within the first 10 working days of the month following the tax period together with the payment of any tax due. Head offices, branches and agencies are treated as a single taxpayer and must file a joint or consolidated return.

The VAT on imports is assessed by customs offices together with the assessment of import duties.

9.4   Powers of the Authorities
The tax administration may assess the VAT due where:

- the taxpayer does not file his return
- the return or supporting documents are not credible or they are incomplete
- the taxpayer does not keep or keeps untimely or improperly his accounting records, or the records are not credible or lack supporting documents or he refuses to display them, or does not provide the clarifications required by the tax administration.

The official assessment may be based on:

- actual and direct knowledge of the facts giving rise to the tax and its amount
- circumstantial evidence based on, for instance, invested capital, number and amount of the transactions made in previous periods, inventories, the level of purchases and sales, the value and rotation of inventories, the value of the fixed assets, salaries paid to employees, and expenses incurred in fuel and electric power
- a combination of both.

9.4.1 Limitation on Assessments and Collection

The time limit for issuing an official VAT assessment is three years when a return has been filed and five years when it has not been filed. These terms are computed from the end of the term allowed for filing.

The right of the Treasury to collect the VAT expires five years after maturity of the tax. Nevertheless, if no timely return is filed or there is a dispute regarding the existence and/or amount of the tax, the term is two years from the date on which the tax becomes final and collectable.

9.4.2 Penalties

Taxpayers who fail to file returns on time are subject to a fine equal to 10% of the tax due (1,000 colones minimum), while those who file a false or incomplete return are subject to a fine equal to 20% of the tax due (minimum 2,000 colones).

Taxpayers who fail to pay the tax within the relevant term are subject to a fine equal to 10% of the tax due and to an interest charge equal to 2% of the tax for each calendar month or fraction thereof elapsed from the month following the month in which the tax was due, while those who pay less than the tax due are subject to a fine equal to 10% of the unpaid tax and to an interest charge equal to 2% of the unpaid tax for each calendar month or fraction thereof elapsed from the month following the month in which the tax was due.

Tax fraud is subject to a fine between 100% and 500% of the evaded tax without prejudice to the penalty that may be applicable under the Criminal Code.

The VAT Law provides an additional schedule of penalties applicable to other violations.

9.5 Appeals

Taxpayers may appeal against assessments by the tax administration within 15 days from the day following that on which the notice of the assessment was served. The appeal is decided by the Court of Appeals, an administrative court whose members are appointed by the Executive Branch, which may review both the evidence and the application of the law.

Contributor: Guillermo Napoleon Guzman (deceased)
Formerly of Ernst & Young
San Salvador.

JAMAICA

1 GENERAL BACKGROUND

The value added tax system was introduced in Jamaica on 21 October 1991, and is known as the GCT (General Consumption Tax). In effect, it replaces several indirect taxes which had, over the period of time, become cumbersome and difficult to administer. The main indirect taxes it supersedes are as follows:

- Excise Duty and Consumption Duty
- Entertainment Duty
- Additional stamp duty with a few exceptions, ie some goods subject to Special Consumption Tax
- Caricom Duty
- Retail Sales Tax
- Telephone Service Tax
- Hotel Accommodation Tax.

The need for the introduction of a value added system to replace the very unwieldy and outdated tax system was highlighted in the Jamaican Tax Reform Programme which was commissioned in 1984 by the then Prime Minister, the Rt Hon Edward Seaga. The implementation of the tax was jointly funded by the United States Agency for International Development (USAID) and the Jamaican Government. The legislation of the GCT is contained in the General Consumption Tax Act, 1991 as amended. The operation of the Act is contained in the Jamaica Gazette Supplement proclamation, rules and regulations issued on 19 October 1991 and entitled The GCT Regulations 1991 as amended by various issues in Jamaica Gazette.

Since its introduction in 1991, there have been various changes; the most important one taking place on 21 June 1993, when the rate of tax changed from 10% to 12.5% and many items changed their tax status from zero-rated to exempt.

Contained within the GCT Act 1991 is a section identified as Special Consumption Tax. This Special Consumption Tax relates to the imposition of indirect tax on items such as alcoholic beverages, tobacco and petroleum products which, under the old law, were subject to excise and consumption duty.

2 WHO IS TAXABLE?

2.1 General
Any person, other than somebody acting as an employee, who supplies taxable goods or services within Jamaica in the course of carrying out a taxable activity and whose annual turnover (including exempt activities) exceeds JA$144,000 (October 1994 JA$33.40 = US $1)

This chapter reflects the legislation on General Consumption Tax in Jamaica as at 24 April 1995.

must register as registered persons and account for GCT. A person whose turnover is below the threshold may opt to be a taxpayer.

A taxable activity is defined as being an activity carried on in the form of a business, trade, profession, vocation, association or club, which is carried on continuously or regularly by any person whether or not for a pecuniary profit and involves or is intended to involve, in whole or in part, the supply of goods and services (including services imported into Jamaica) to any other person for a consideration.

A taxable activity includes anything done in connection with the commencement or termination of that activity. A taxable supply does not include a private recreational pursuit or hobby, employment under a service contract or any exempt activity.

2.2   Transactions with Branch/Subsidiary
Subsidiaries of foreign firms which supply taxable goods and services to Jamaica are treated in the same manner as other taxable persons, except where the goods and services are supplied to the parent company situated outside the country. Transactions between branches of the same legal entity are not subject to GCT.

2.3   Government Bodies
Where a government body carries out a taxable activity it is subject to tax in respect of that taxable activity. Goods purchased or imported or taken out of bond by or on behalf of, and services rendered to, government bodies can be obtained as zero-rated when otherwise the goods and services would be standard-rated.

2.4   Foreign Firms and Individuals
Whilst the Act is not specific in respect of the treatment of foreign firms or individuals who supply goods or services in Jamaica, if they maintain an establishment or have stock in Jamaica they are obliged to register and account for GCT if their annual turnover is in excess of the threshold. Foreign firms or individuals who do not supply taxable goods or services in Jamaica are not subject to registration.

2.5   Group Taxation
The GCT Act does not provide for special treatment for group transactions. Therefore, transactions between members of a group are subject to tax. This includes management fees and intercompany services.

2.6   GCT Representative
A foreign firm or individual is not obliged to appoint a representative or responsible person to act on its behalf if it is not making taxable supplies in Jamaica. However, the Commissioner has power, by notice in writing, to make the agent residing in Jamaica who acts as agent of the foreign firm or individual responsible for the obligations of the foreign firm.

2.7   Importers
Goods imported into Jamaica are subject to GCT at the same rate as that which applies to the sale of similar goods within Jamaica. The place of supply of services is deemed by the GCT Act to be in Jamaica if the services are performed or utilised in Jamaica, as the case may be.

3   WHAT IS TAXABLE?

GCT liability arises on a taxable supply for consideration by a registered taxpayer in the course or furtherance of any business carried on by him and on the importation of goods into Jamaica.

3.1   *Supply of Goods*
A supply of goods includes:

- the sale, transfer or other disposition of goods by a registered taxpayer so that goods sold, transferred or otherwise disposed of no longer form part of the assets of the taxable person
- the exercise of a power of sale by a person other than a registered taxpayer in satisfaction of a debt owed by a registered taxpayer
- the provision of services.

A taxable supply does not take place where the goods are supplied:

- as collateral for a loan
- on their transfer to a trustee pursuant to his appointment as such
- as gifts supplied free of charge in the course or furtherance of a taxable activity where the value of the gift is less than US$100
- as a sample of any goods to customers or intended customers in a form not ordinarily available for use as a taxable supply.

A taxable supply of goods includes:

- the transfer of ownership of goods by agreement
- the handing over of goods under a hire purchase contract
- the handing over by a contractor of goods made up from material and goods supplied by a taxable person to be used for private or exempt purposes (ie self-supply).

Where a registered taxpayer receives an amount by way of reimbursement, recovery or otherwise in respect of goods or services acquired by him for the purpose of making taxable supplies, the goods or services are deemed to be taxable supplies.

3.2   *Supply of Services*
A supply of services includes any supply by others that is not a supply of goods but is done for a consideration (including the granting, assignment or surrender of any right). General insurance contracts, commissions and fees in respect of financial services are taxable supplies.

3.3   *Self-Supplies of Goods and Services*
A self-supply takes place when a registered taxpayer diverts to private or exempt use goods which he has imported, purchased, or otherwise acquired and in respect of which he is entitled to a GCT deduction or has manufactured for use in an exempt activity or for his own use.

3.4   *Importation of Goods*
GCT is levied and collected at the time the goods are entered for home consumption under

the Customs Act. The person importing the goods is liable to pay GCT to customs on the same document which is used to pay the customs duty. Goods imported into a bonded warehouse are liable to GCT at the time that they are cleared for custom purposes.

4   PLACE OF SUPPLY

4.1   Supply of Goods
The place of supply of goods is deemed to be in Jamaica if:

- the supplier is resident in Jamaica, or
- the supplier is not resident in Jamaica but the goods are in Jamaica at the time of supply.

4.2   Supply of Services

4.2.1 General Rule
The general rule is that the place where services are supplied or deemed to be supplied is where the person supplying the service is resident (ie Jamaica).

4.2.2 Exception
A taxable supply is not deemed to take place in Jamaica if the supplier is not resident and the services are not performed or not utilised in Jamaica.

4.3   Supply of Exports
The circumstances in which goods or services exported are zero-rated are as follows:

- goods which have been entered by the supplier for export pursuant to the Customs Act and which have been exported and in respect of which a customs certificate of exportation has been issued
- services which are supplied to a person who is not resident in Jamaica and the benefit of the supply of which is not realised in Jamaica.

5   BASIS OF TAXATION

5.1   Supplies within Jamaica
GCT is chargeable on the supply in Jamaica of goods and services by a registered taxpayer in the course or furtherance of a taxable activity in Jamaica by that taxpayer by reference to value of goods and services. GCT is due and payable at the time of supply.

5.2   Imported Goods
GCT is levied and collected at the time the goods are entered for home consumption under the Customs Act. The person importing the goods is liable to pay GCT to customs on the same document which is used to pay the customs duty.

5.3   Chargeable Event/Timing Of Liability

5.3.1 Liability to GCT
Both liability to GCT and the right to an input tax credit arise:

- on the earlier of the day that:

    - an invoice for the supply is issued by the supplier, or
    - payment is made for the supply, or
    - the goods are made available or the services are rendered, as the case may be, to the recipient

- when the goods are made available to the recipient:

    - under an agreement for hire purchase, or
    - under an agreement whereby the recipient has an option to return the goods to the supplier

- in the case where the goods or services which are supplied progressively or periodically under an agreement, the earliest of the day:

    - when an invoice is given
    - when payment is made
    - when payment becomes due

- when payment becomes due or is made (whichever is earlier) where a contract provides for the retention by the recipient of part of the purchase price pending satisfactory completion of the contract or part thereof
- when a coin or token is removed from a machine, meter or other device where the supply is made from a machine, meter or other device operated by a coin or token
- when payment is made to a broker or insurer in the case of a contract of insurance other than a policy of life insurance, health insurance or re-insurance
- at the time of registration of a second sale of a motor vehicle.

5.4   Value of Supply on which GCT is to be Calculated

5.4.1 Supplies within Jamaica

The value of a taxable supply other than an imported taxable supply is determined in the following manner:

- if the consideration for the supply consists wholly of money, the value is the consideration (excluding GCT)
- if the supply is for consideration partly consisting of money, then the value of the supply is deemed to be its open market value
- if the supply is not the only matter to which the total consideration applies, the value of the supply is that part of the consideration applicable to the supply
- in the case of self-supply, the value of the supply is the cost incurred by the registered taxpayer in acquiring that supply
- if the consideration for the supply is payable by a connected person, the value of the supply is its open market value.

5.4.2 Imports

The value of a taxable supply imported into Jamaica is the aggregate of:

- the value of that taxable supply for customs duty purposes
- the amount of customs duty payable

- any additional stamp duty on inward customs warrants, and
- any special consumption tax payable in respect of that taxable supply.

5.4.3 Taxable Supplies Imported into Jamaica by a Non-Registered Taxpayer

The value of a taxable supply imported into Jamaica by any person who is not a registered taxpayer is the aggregate of:

- the value of that taxable supply for customs duty purposes
- the amount of customs duty payable
- any additional stamp duty on inward customs warrants
- any special consumption tax payable in respect of that taxable supply
- such percentage of the total value of the preceding costs as may be determined by the Commissioner, having regard to the price which the supply would fetch on a similar sale made by a retailer on the open market.

5.4.4 Self-Supply

The value of a taxable self-supply is equivalent to the cost of the goods and services.

5.5 Cash/Invoice Basis

GCT due and available for tax credit is normally accounted for on the basis of the tax point date on the invoice or date of payment, whichever is the earlier. The following taxpayers may be permitted to account for tax on a payment basis:

- registered taxpayers whose gross annual taxable supplies are less than JA$1 million
- registered taxpayers involved in the supply of insurance contracts and in the supply of telephone services
- registered taxpayers who render professional services.

For taxpayers whose turnover is less than JA$500,000 output tax can be accounted for on a cash basis using a simplified accounting method as described in section 10.1.

5.6 Bad Debts

Where a registered taxpayer, who is required to account for tax on an invoice basis and has accounted for a debt which has been written-off, in whole or in part, and has made reasonable effort to collect, he may, during the taxable period when the bad debt was written off, deduct from the output tax being accounted for the amount relevant to the bad debt.

The amount available for relief is:

- in respect of a supply not under a hire purchase contract: bad debt x 1/9
- in respect of a supply under a hire purchase contract: (bad debt - hire purchase charge) x 1/9.

6 TAX RATES

Taxable supplies are taxed at a rate depending on the nature of the supply. There are currently two general rates:

0%: – exports. All goods and services which are exported by a registered taxpayer are taxed at a zero-rate irrespective of their tax status within Jamaica. There is no mechanism to extend this privilege to non-registered taxpayers or non-residents other than by way of acquisition through a duty-free outlet such as a duty free shop located within the tourist areas or at the airports

– certain specified goods and services. The list of goods and services which are zero-rated is extensive. It includes the classical relief for export, diplomatic items and health. However, the list also includes a long list of qualifiers for receiving motor vehicles at zero-rate, energy-saving devices, farm equipment, fertiliser, sports equipment, items under various incentives legislation, books, newspapers, items used in schools, central government departments and other government agencies, and coverings and containers. Prior to 18 June 1993, the list of zero-rated items included most basic food items and agricultural activities, but on that date the status of nearly all the items affected was changed to exempt

12.5%: all other taxable goods and services except those chargeable at the zero rate or other specified rates.

Specified Rates: Special rates apply to specific items. For example, the tax on motor vehicles is based on the engine capacity, and the rate ranging between 14% for vehicles with an engine capacity not exceeding 1000cc and 157.3% for engine capacity exceeding 2000cc.

7 EXEMPTIONS

7.1 Exemption with Credit for Input Tax
Zero-rated goods and services do not carry a real charge of GCT but they confer a right to recovery of input tax credit. Generally there is no credit entitlement in respect of supplies of exempt goods or services.

7.2 Exemption without Credit for Input Tax
The list of goods and services which are exempt is extensive. The major items include construction operations, transportation of goods and people, postal services, basic foodstuffs, water and sewage, electricity, medical services, and financial services, but does not include general insurance and fees or commission charged in respect of financial services.

In addition, petroleum products (excluding lubricating oil and grease) are not subject to GCT but to Special Consumption Tax (SCT).

8 CREDIT/REFUND FOR INPUT TAX

8.1 General Rule
In computing the amount of tax payable, a registered taxpayer may deduct the tax relating to most goods and services purchased or imported by him which are used for his taxable businesses. No deduction may be made for tax paid on goods and services used for other purposes, such as those used in exempt activities or for personal use. To be entitled to the

deduction, the registered taxpayer must have a proper GCT invoice or a stamped copy of the customs entry.

8.2 Exceptions

8.2.1 Where a Registered Taxpayer Makes Both Taxable and Exempt Supplies
He is entitled to claim as a credit:

- in respect of the taxable supplies, all of the tax paid or payable in respect thereof
- in respect of the exempt supplies, all of the input tax paid or payable in respect thereof, if(and only if) the exempt supplies are not more than 5% of the value of the total supplies or JA$48,000, whichever is less
- where the taxpayer is unable to identify the input tax paid or payable in respect of the exempt and taxable supplies, such proportion of the tax paid or payable as is attributable to the total taxable supplies. There are no special rules with regard to the apportionment of input tax credits.

8.2.2 Where a Registered Taxpayer Incurs Capital Expenditure
All the input tax paid or payable by the registered taxpayer at the end of the taxable period can be claimed if:

- the consideration for the machinery and equipment (capital goods) is JA$20,000 or less
- the machinery or equipment is approved under the Modernisation of Industry Programme for his business or
- the value of the goods that he exports is at least 25% of the value of the goods he manufactures or an amount equivalent in Jamaican dollars to US$5 million, as the case may be.

In all other cases the registered taxpayer can claim over a period of twenty-four months the input tax paid or payable on machinery or equipment (capital goods) in equal monthly instalments.

8.2.3 Where a Registered Taxpayer is Charged for Taxable Supplies in the Course of Conducting his Business
He can claim as a tax credit 50% of the input taxes relating to the following:

- hotel accommodation or services rendered thereto (equivalent to 2.95% of the tax-inclusive amount)
- services rendered in a restaurant, club, or similar establishment or in catering services
- services incidental to the provision of entertainment
- expenses incurred in respect of motor vehicles
- the cost of leasing private motor cars.

8.2.4 Where a Motor Vehicle is Purchased and Used in the Taxable Activity
The registered taxpayer can claim as a tax credit over a twenty-four month period:

- 5/90 of the cost (not exceeding an amount in Jamaican dollars equivalent to US$35,000) of any private motor car

- all of the tax for any other motor vehicle, provided the rate does not exceed 10%
- 1/9 of the cost (including GCT) of any motor vehicle where the rate of tax exceeds 10%.

For motor vehicles used for leasing or U-drive car rental exceeding 45 days, all the GCT paid on the vehicle may be claimed subject to the maximum cost – the Jamaican dollar equivalent of US$35,000.

8.2.5 Materials Relating to Construction/Repair of Premises

Except for those carrying on a tourism activity, a registered taxpayer is not entitled to claim as a tax credit any tax paid or payable in respect of any materials used in the construction of or repairs to any premises in relation to his taxable business.

8.3 Refunds

Where in any taxable period a registered taxpayer is entitled to a tax credit which is in excess of the amount of tax chargeable on supplies made during the taxable period, he may apply to the Commissioner for a refund of the excess or he may carry forward the amount of excess as a credit to a subsequent taxable period.

8.4 Export of Exempt Goods

Where a registered taxpayer exports exempt goods he may claim as a tax credit any tax paid or payable in respect of such goods exported.

8.5 Tourist Activity

Where a registered taxpayer carries out a tourism activity licensed under the Tourist Board Act he may deduct two special tax credits (see section 10.2).

9 ADMINISTRATIVE OBLIGATIONS

9.1 Registration

All persons engaged in a taxable activity are required to apply for registration under the GCT Act. A person includes an individual, a corporation and a partnership (which is defined to include an unincorporated body, a joint venture and trustees of a trust). Persons engaged exclusively in an exempt activity are not required to register. Persons whose gross value of supplies for a 12-month period is less than JA$144,000 are registered as registered persons. Registered persons are exempt persons and as such do not collect tax nor are they entitled to input tax credits. Where a person exceeds the threshold he must notify the Commissioner within 21 days. A person whose gross value of supplies in the month of application and the 11 months immediately preceding the making of the application is not less than JA$144,000, or whose average monthly value in respect of a period less than 12 months, is JA$12,000 is registered as a registered taxpayer. As such he must collect and account for tax. A registered person may elect to become a registered taxpayer.

Every business is required to register for a Business Enterprise Number (BENO) if it is carrying on a business in Jamaica. The BENO assigned to a person becomes his GCT registration number.

Where the Commissioner is satisfied with the details on the application for registration, he will complete the registration and issue a Notice of Registration (in respect of persons operating below the threshold) or a Certificate of Registration (to persons above the threshold).

The certificate of registration issued to registered taxpayers shows the name of the taxpayer, the GCT registration number and the effective date of registration. A certificate of registration or an official copy of the certificate must be prominently displayed in each business outlet. A taxpayer data sheet is issued together with the certificate and contains all relevant information for filing the returns.

A registered taxpayer's obligations are to:

- issue tax invoices as required under the GCT Act and Regulations
- collect the appropriate tax in respect of the goods and services which he supplies
- file returns and remit by due date any tax payable
- maintain proper books and records.

9.2 Books and Records

A registered taxpayer must keep, at his principal place of business or, where applicable, at such branch or division in respect of which he is permitted to file separate returns, full records for a period of six years of all business transactions which may affect his liability to GCT. The records must be kept up-to-date and must be sufficiently detailed to enable the taxpayer to calculate his tax liability and, if necessary, for an authorised person to check the calculation.

A person who fails to keep proper records or other documents relating to any taxable supply or to produce such items to an authorised person commits an offence and is liable on summary conviction in a Magistrates' Court to a fine not exceeding JA$10,000 or to imprisonment for a term not exceeding 12 months or both.

9.3 Invoices

Registered taxpayers are required to issue a tax invoice to all other registered taxpayers to whom taxable goods or services are supplied. Tax invoices and credit/debit notes must contain the following information:

- the words 'Tax Invoice' stated at the top
- the name, address and registration number of the registered taxpayer issuing the tax invoice
- the serialised number of the tax invoice
- the date on which the supply is made
- the name and address of the registered taxpayer to whom the taxable supply is made
- the quantity and description of the taxable supply
- the total amount of the consideration for the taxable supply
- the rate of tax and the amount of tax payable
- the total amount of the consideration and the tax applicable to the taxable supply.

Only one tax invoice can be issued in respect of a supply and this must be issued within seven days of the supply. A tax invoice must be prepared for goods for own use and marked 'Own use'. A replacement invoice must be clearly marked 'copy' and signed by the registered taxpayer issuing it.

In the case of general insurance supplied by a broker or insurer the receipt for the premiums is deemed to be a tax invoice. The receipt must contain the particulars specified for a tax invoice.

Persons operating under the Tourism Scheme must invoice on a tax-included basis.

9.4   GCT Returns

Each registered taxpayer must furnish a return and pay to the Commissioner the amount of tax, if any, in respect of the taxable period to which the return relates by the end of the next succeeding month. A person accounting for tax on the cash basis must file returns and pay any tax due by the fifteenth day of the succeeding month.

The taxable periods are:

- one calendar month, where the taxpayer's gross annual value of taxable supplies is JA$1 million or more
- two calendar months, where the taxpayer's gross annual value is less than JA$1 million.

Persons who file bi-monthly returns are assigned specific filing periods by the Commissioner so that some taxpayers file at the end of even months and others at the end of odd months.

9.5   Amended Returns

Where a return requires to be amended, a supplementary return must be filed for the period during which the error or omission occurred and any additional tax that may be due must be remitted. Penalty and interest arises from the original due date. Where the supplementary return involves a repayment of tax, it will be repaid without additional interest if the repayment is made within 90 days of filing the amended return.

9.6   Powers of the Authorities

The Commissioner has the power to assess the GCT payable by a registered taxpayer when:

- a return appears to the Commissioner to be incomplete or incorrect
- if the taxpayer has failed to furnish a return
- goods no longer form part of the taxable supply of the registered taxpayer and no satisfactory account can be given by the taxpayer.

The Commissioner may also assess a registered person one who is not a taxpayer or a non-registered person where that person:

- is over the threshold but has not applied for registration as a registered taxpayer and has made taxable supplies, falsely represents that GCT is payable on that supply
- falsely represents the amount of GCT payable
- wrongfully receives or seeks to recover an amount of GCT.

Authorised persons may carry out an audit, examination or inspection of books, records, etc, or inspect any property or goods described in the inventory of the property and goods of a taxpayer.

Authorised persons may search premises, make copies of books, etc, and retain books for a period up to seven days where a search warrant has been granted by a Justice of the Peace. They may also take samples of any taxable goods.

The Commissioner may defer the payment of tax payable by a taxpayer who has made a return. He may also defer the payment by manufacturers of input tax on imported raw materials, intermediate goods and spare parts to the time of filing returns. As a result, an immediate tax credit is allowed and no tax is payable.

Where a registered taxpayer is in default of payment of tax, the Commissioner may recover the amount from a third party who owes money to the taxpayer. The recovery is effected at any time by issuing a notice in writing to the person who is required to make a payment in money to, or who keeps or retains money on behalf of, the registered taxpayer. The notice instructs the debtor to pay over to the Commissioner for the account of the registered taxpayer the amount stated in the notice within the time specified.

The Commissioner may make refunds of overpayment by taxpayers and tax paid by approved organisations (such as organisations concerned with the welfare of children, the aged or the disabled and charitable organisations), diplomats and non-registered exporters.

9.7   Minister May Remit
The Minister of Finance may, upon application in writing by a person liable to pay tax under the Act, waive, remit or refund in whole or in part any tax payable under the Act if in the circumstances of the case he considers it just so to do; and such waiver, remission or refund may be subject to such terms and conditions as the Minister thinks fit.

9.8   Penalties
Penalties can be imposed by the Commissioner under the following circumstances:

- a person liable to be registered who does not apply for registration is liable to a penalty of JA$200 for each month during which he is not registered
- a person liable to be registered as a registered taxpayer who does not apply for registration is liable to a penalty equal to 30% of the tax assessed
- a registered taxpayer who fails to make a return and pay tax by the due date is liable to a penalty of 30% of the tax which should have been paid
- a registered taxpayer who does not make a return or pay tax (by the due date) for two or more taxable periods within a 12-month period is liable to a surcharge in respect of the third period and each subsequent taxable period for which a return is not made or tax not paid, equal to 10% of the amount of tax due or payable
- interest is payable at 2.5% per month or part thereof on the amount of any tax, penalty, or surcharge from the date on which the tax, penalty or surcharge become due until the date it is paid.

Any penalty, surcharge or interest may be added to any tax due and be recovered as if it were tax.

9.9   Objections and Appeals

9.9.1 Objections
If a taxpayer or any other person is not satisfied with an assessment, amended assessment

or any decision by the Commissioner, he may object to that assessment or decision.

The objection must be made in writing within 30 days of the date of service of the assessment or decision, and state precisely the grounds for the objection. The Commissioner may extend the time for filing an appeal where a taxpayer or person has objected to an assessment made upon him. The Commissioner shall give notice in writing to the taxpayer or persons of his decision in respect of the objection.

If the Commissioner fails to hand down his decision within six months of the receipt by him of the objection, and the delay is not due to the taxpayer's or person's omission or default, the assessment shall be null and void.

If a taxpayer is dissatisfied with the decision of the Commissioner (other than a decision relating to an assessment made on the taxpayer or person) he may appeal to the Revenue Court within 30 days of the receipt of the decision (or a longer period if so specified by the Revenue Court) without filing an objection with the Commissioner.

9.10 Notification of Changes
Every person is required to inform the Commissioner in writing within 21 days of any change of business address or name, sale of the business or part thereof, giving all details.

9.11 Cancellation of Registration
The Commissioner may cancel the registration. However, he must notify the taxpayer, who may object and who must return the Certificate of Registration when the decision is finalised.

10   SPECIAL GCT REGIMES

10.1 Simplified Accounting Methods
In order to keep the GCT as simple as possible for small businesses (eg persons with annual sales, including GCT, not exceeding US$500,000), three simplified accounting methods are available.

The three methods eliminate the need to separately track exempted, zero-rated and other sales taxed at 12.5%. They provide a way to determine the net GCT to be remitted or refunded without keeping track of every GCT transaction.

For example under the 'quick method scheme' (the scheme used by many small taxpayers), the taxpayer would:

- charge GCT at the standard rate
- multiply total sales for a taxable period by a percentage specified for his particular business group (see below)
- deduct input tax credit for capital expenditure*, if any
- remit the resulting amount.

---

*It should be noted that while a person does not get an input tax credit for supplies and services, a tax credit is available in respect of capital assets.

10.2 Quick Method Percentages

GROUP NO.	BUSINESS GROUP	MAXIMUM ANNUAL SALES	PERCENTAGE (%)
1	Manufacturers – eg furniture, craft, clothing, sawmills	500,000	5.6
2	Services – eg body shops, electricians, barbers/hairstylists, repair shops	500,000	9.0
3	Retailers – eg clothing and shoe stores, hardware stores, stores selling less than 25% zero-rated goods	500,000	5.6
4	Retailers – eg grocery and convenience stores, specialty food outlets, etc, selling 25% to 50% zero-rated goods	500,000	4.5
5	Retailers – eg grocery and convenience stores, specialty food outlets, etc, selling 51% to 74% zero-rated goods	500,000	2.6
6	Retailers – eg grocery and convenience stores, green groceries, butchers, bakeries, etc, selling 75% or more zero-rated goods	500,000	1.9
	Accounting, auditing, land surveying, legal and quantity surveying	Not eligible	

10.3 Tourism Activities

Tourism in Jamaica is an area of business where much foreign exchange is generated, thus providing essential foreign income for the country. It is also a very competitive field, particularly within the Caribbean, and much effort is expended in attracting tourists to Jamaica in preference to other destinations. As a result, it was decided to provide a special incentive to businesses in this sector, including hotels, resort cottages, and other tourist accommodation, camp sites, water sports, tourism attractions and tour operators.

Registered taxpayers who carry out a tourism activity and invoice for services rendered on a tax-inclusive basis can calculate their net tax payable in accordance with a formula or scheme generally known as the 'tourism scheme'. The essence of the tourism scheme is that a tourism enterprise may account for net tax on the difference between output tax calculated on taxable sales and an enhanced tax credit system and thus account for tax at an effective rate approximately equal to 50% of the standard rate.

Contributor: Elizabeth Hartley
                Ernst & Young
                28 Beechwood Avenue
                PO Box 351
                Kingston 5
                Jamaica
                West Indies
                Tel: +1 809 9261616
                Fax: +1 809 9267580

APPENDIX

On 24 April 1995, the standard rate of GCT was revised to 15% from $12^{1}/2\%$ for all items except:

- major inputs to construction which remain at 121/2%
- education supplies for approved institutions which are available at zero-rate
- listed over-the-counter drugs for mainly widely used items
- certain basic grocery items have been reclassified as exempt.

The Special Scheme for Tourist Board operations still applies at the same rate. Certain relief has been given to taxation on motor vehicles used in tourism.

Special Consumption Tax has been increased for all categories resulting in an overall increase by approximately 5%.

The aggregate customs and GCT rates on the purchase of motor cars is increased by 5%.

On 23 May 1995, the Government announced that the penalty of 30% for non-filing of a return or non-payment of tax is revised to 15%, retroactive to 1 May 1995.

MEXICO

1   GENERAL BACKGROUND

Value added tax (VAT) was introduced in Mexico on 1 January 1980, replacing the commercial receipts tax generally known as the Sales Tax.

Since VAT is a federal tax, it is both regulated and collected by the Ministry of Finance and Public Credit, the highest federal tax authority in Mexico.

Since it took effect, VAT has become the second most important tax for the Mexican government, second only to Income Tax.

2   WHO IS TAXABLE?

2.1   General
All persons or corporations, whether Mexican or foreign, who carry out any of the four following activities in Mexico, are subject to VAT:

■   transfer of the ownership of assets
■   provision of independent services
■   leasing of any type of assets
■   import of goods or services.

2.2   Transactions with Branches or Subsidiaries
A branch or subsidiary of a foreign entity is also subject to VAT whenever it performs any of the activities mentioned in section 2.1, including those transactions carried out with the parent. Only when a Mexican entity has transactions with its own branches located in Mexico is VAT not payable.

2.3   Foreign Entities and Offices of Representation
A foreign entity has neither the right nor obligation to register as a federal taxpayer for VAT and Income Tax purposes unless it carried out the activities mentioned in section 2.1 above through a permanent establishment in Mexico. Representation offices of foreign entities are required to register with the federal taxpayer registry even though they are not engaged in business activities in Mexico.

3   WHAT IS TAXABLE?

3.1   Sales of Goods or Assets
All transfers of ownership, including those in which the seller maintains control over the

---

This chapter reflects the legislation on VAT in Mexico as at 15 April 1995.

goods transferred, will be considered as sales of assets. The following are also considered to be sales of assets:

- awards, even when made in favour of the creditor
- contributions to an entity or to an association
- the transfer of assets through financial leasing
- the transfer of assets through a trust
- the ceding of rights over assets held in trust
- the transfer of ownership of tangible assets or the right to acquire ownership through the transfer of credit instruments
- inventory shortages of business entities.

The term 'assets' or 'goods' is defined as tangible or intangible, new or used.

3.2 The Provision of Services

The following activities are considered to represent the provision of independent services:

- the obligation to carry out an activity performed by one party for the benefit of another
- the transportation of goods or persons
- insurance or reinsurance, bonding or re-bonding
- carrying out a mandate, commission, intermediation, agency, representation, brokerage, consignment, or distribution
- technical assistance and the transfer of technology
- all other obligations to do, not to do, or to permit, performed by one party for the benefit of another.

3.3 Temporary Use or Enjoyment of Assets

'The temporary use or enjoyment of assets' is defined as the leasing, use, or any other act permitting the temporary use or enjoyment of tangible assets in exchange for payment.

3.4 Importation of Goods or Services

The following are considered to be the importation of goods or services:

- the introduction of goods into Mexico
- the acquisition by residents in Mexico of tangible goods sold by non-residents
- the temporary use or enjoyment in Mexico of tangible goods actually delivered abroad
- the use of services in Mexico, whenever such services are provided by foreigners.

3.5 Non-Taxable Transactions

The transfer of ownership due to death is not considered as a sale, nor are donations made by companies which have the right to claim the deduction for income tax purposes.

Services rendered in a subordinate capacity in exchange for the payment of a salary are not considered the providing of independent services.

4 PLACE OF SUPPLY

4.1 Sales and Services Considered to be Carried Out in Mexico

Sales are considered to be made in Mexico whenever the assets are located in Mexico, shipped to the buyer or, if not shipped to the buyer, whenever the actual delivery is made in Mexico. The sale of intangible assets is considered to be made in Mexico whenever either the buyer or the seller resides in Mexico.

A service is considered to be provided in Mexico whenever it is totally or partially carried out by a resident in Mexico, including the subsidiaries or branches of foreign entities. In the case of international transportation, the service is considered to be provided in Mexico whenever the point of departure is located in Mexico. Only 25% of the service provided in connection with international air transportation is considered to be provided in Mexico.

The leasing of tangible assets is considered to have taken place whenever the assets to be delivered to the person who will make use of them are located in Mexico.

4.2 The Time of Importation
Goods or services are deemed to be imported and the tax is, therefore, payable in the following cases:

- at the time the importer files the respective customs declaration
- at the time temporary imports become permanent imports
- in the case of tangible assets acquired from foreigners to be used in Mexico, whenever partial or total payment of the price is paid, or whenever the document covering the transaction is issued.

5 BASIS OF TAXATION

5.1 Taxable Amount
Any amount charged or collected (either for taxes, interest, or any other concept) in addition to the contracted price, is the taxable amount.

In addition to the contracted price, any amount received in respect of taxes, travel allowances, expenses of all kinds, reimbursements, and any other concept will be considered to be the taxable amount for the provision of services.

5.2 Chargeable Event

5.2.1 Goods
The sale of assets is considered to be completed whenever one of the following occurs:

- the goods are shipped to the buyer. If the goods are not shipped, the sale occurs at the time they are actually delivered
- when the agreed price is partially or totally paid
- when the receipt covering the sale is issued.

5.2.2 Services
The tax must be paid at the time each payment is due to the provider, and must include any advance payment received. In the case of construction work contracted with the Mexican government, the tax is payable at the time payments for partial completion of work and advance payments are received.

VAT is payable at the time the payments (including advance payments) to the person granting the temporary use or enjoyment of assets are due.

5.3   *Temporary Use or Enjoyment of Assets*
As in section 4.2 above, the taxable amount includes the contracted price plus other amounts charged for taxes, maintenance expenses, structures and contract penalties.

5.4   *Imports*
The taxable amount for the importation of tangible assets is the value used for the payment of import duties plus any other amount connected with the imports.

6   TAX RATES

There are three tax rates:

0%:   – export of goods
- the sale of tangible or intangible assets by a resident in Mexico to a resident abroad
- payments made abroad for the use of intangible assets provided by residents in Mexico
- the use abroad of services provided by residents of Mexico in connection with:

  - technical services and technical assistance
  - maquilla operations for exports
  - advertising
  - commissions and intermediations
  - insurance and insurance-related services
  - personal independent services provided to residents abroad by residents of Mexico

- non-industrialised animal and vegetable products
- meat in its natural state
- milk and eggs and their derivative products *
- wheat and corn flour *
- bread and tortillas *
- edible vegetable oil *
- pasta for soups, except canned *
- coffee, salt and sugar *
- ice and natural water, except when packed or bottled in containers smaller than ten litres
- certain types of tractors for agriculture
- services provided to farmers
- services connected to the grinding or milling of wheat or corn
- services connected to the pasteurisation of milk
- the temporary use or enjoyment of tractors used for agricultural purposes
- patented medicines *
- foodstuffs*, with the exception of the following:

---

*These items are subject to the 15% rate when sold to business companies

  - beverages other than milk
  - syrups used to prepare soft drinks, concentrates, powders, or extracts from which soft drinks are obtained, when dissolved

- gold jewellery, gold or silver work and artistic pieces whose minimum gold content is 80% (except when it is sold to the general public)

10%:   all activities performed by residents in the Mexican border zone (as long as the actual delivery is done there) except for alienation of real property

15%: – the sale of foodstuffs prepared for consumption when sold
     – all other supplies of goods and services which are not exempt.
     – the sale of foodstuffs prepared for consumption where sold

Imports are taxed at the rate applicable to equivalent supplies made in Mexico.

7   EXEMPTIONS

7.1   Exemption with Credit for Input Tax
Generally, there is no credit entitlement in respect of supplies of exempt goods or services. However, the zero rate operates in a similar manner. Zero-rated goods and services do not carry a real charge to VAT but they confer a right to recovery of input VAT.

7.2   Exemption without Credit for Input Tax
VAT is not paid on the following:

- land
- constructions attached to land, for use as personal residences
- books, magazines and newspapers
- used property, except for that sold by companies
- tickets and other documents allowing participation in lotteries or any type of contest
- domestic and foreign currency, as well as gold and silver coins
- sales of shares, notes receivable, and credit instruments
- gold ingots whose minimum gold content is 90% sold to the general public
- services provided free of charge
- payments of school tuition, whenever the schools are accredited under the Federal Education Act
- public land transportation for humans, except for train transportation
- maritime transportation of goods by foreigners
- farming and life insurance
- interest in the following cases:
  - interest on transactions either subject to the 0% rate or exempt from payment of the tax
  - interest received or paid by credit institutions
  - interest on mortgage loans provided to home owners
  - interest on workers' savings funds
  - interest on Mexican government securities
  - interest of credit instruments traded on the Mexican Stock Exchange

- admission tickets for public performances
- professional health services whenever a medical degree is required to provide the service, and they are provided by individuals or by civil partnership
- the temporary use or enjoyment (leasing) of goods where the property is used exclusively as a personal residence or for farming purposes
- the temporary use or enjoyment (leasing) of tangible assets whose use or enjoyment is granted by foreigners who have no permanent establishment in Mexico, if the related import duties (including VAT) have been paid
- temporarily imported goods
- luggage, or household goods, in the case of changing residence from abroad to Mexico
- imported assets or goods donated by foreigners to the Mexican government
- works of art intended for permanent public display
- the import of goods or services which are either exempt or subject to the 0% tax rate.

8   Credit/Refund of Input VAT

Only residents of Mexico are entitled to recover the VAT paid to suppliers of goods or services, and even then only if the claimant's activities are subject to one of the three rates (0%, 10% or 15%). The VAT paid must refer to transactions that are deductible for Income Tax purposes. Whenever one part of an entity's activities is subject to taxation and another part is not, only the VAT paid on the part subject to taxation may be credited. A refund may be requested whenever a company has a favourable VAT balance.

9   ADMINISTRATIVE OBLIGATIONS

9.1   Registration

Mexican or foreign companies which have a permanent establishment in Mexico must register with the Ministry of Finance and Public Credit.

This registration is applicable for both Income Tax and VAT. Branches of foreign entities must also obtain authorisation from the Ministry of Commerce and notify the Ministry of Foreign Affairs that they will engage in business activities in Mexico.

9.2   Books and Accounting Records

Accounting records must be kept, with details of activities subject to the different tax rates recorded separately. Receipts must be issued which segregate the VAT passed on to buyers of goods, temporary users and recipients of services.

9.3   Tax Returns

Monthly tax returns must be filed, together with payment of the tax, no later than the seventeenth day of the month following the one for which the return is being filed. The annual tax return for the period January to December must be filed no later than 31 March of the following year.

9.4   Correction of Tax Returns

Previously filed tax returns may be amended on up to two occasions provided the company has a favourable balance. Whenever a company shows tax differences payable, interest is imposed from the month in which the payment was omitted through to the month in which the difference is paid, applying the inflation factor for such period. Whenever the company shows taxes payable, the two-amended-returns limit does not apply .

Contributor: Gabriel Amante
Ernst & Young
Mancera, S.C.
Plaza Polanco
Jaime Balmes No. 11
Torre 'D' Floors, 4, 5 & 6
Col. Los Morales Polanco11510,
Mexico City
Mexico
Tel: +52 5 557 5555
Fax: +52 5 255 0999

PANAMA

1 GENERAL BACKGROUND

Value added tax (Impuesto a la Transferencia de Bienes Corporales Muebles: ITBM or 'VAT') came into force on 1 March 1977.

In 1991 the rules were modified by Law No.31 which broadened the tax base and added a higher rate for certain classes of goods.

The General Directorate of Revenue is entitled to set the legal or doctrinal interpretation of the tax laws. Their decisions are complementary to the legislation.

2 WHO IS TAXABLE?

2.1 Persons Subject to VAT
The following persons are considered subject to VAT:

- businessmen and manufacturers carrying out taxable transactions, provided the yearly average of their total gross income during the fiscal year (including income derived from exempt transactions) is at least B/.18,000 (B/.1=US$1)
- importers of taxable goods, either through regular or temporary operations
- persons rendering services as non-employees whenever these services involve the transformation of raw material into finished goods and an industrial licence is required
- every individual or corporation, national or foreign.

2.2 Transactions with Branch/Subsidiary
No special regulation applies to transactions between a branch and its foreign head office. They are both considered to be independent taxpayers and therefore supplies between them are subject to VAT.

2.3 Government Bodies
The State and other public entities are taxable persons.

2.4 Fiscal Unity/Group Transactions
The concept of fiscal unity does not exist in Panamanian VAT law.

2.5 Foreign Entrepreneurs
Foreign undertakings are liable to Panamanian VAT when they make taxable supplies of goods and services within Panama or when they import goods into Panama.

This chapter reflects the law on VAT in Panama as at 31 October 1994.

2.6   Representative Office

A Representative Office of an overseas business is subject to Panamanian VAT if it makes supplies of taxable goods and services within Panama or if it imports goods into Panama.

2.7   VAT Representatives

This concept does not apply to Panama.

2.8   Reverse Charge Mechanism

There is no reverse charge mechanism in Panama.

2.9   Importers

Goods brought into Panama are subject to Panamanian VAT at customs clearance. The tax is due by the importers, although certain exemptions apply.

3   WHAT IS TAXABLE?

Taxable transactions include the transfer of tangible personal property within the territory through purchase and sale, exchange, payment in kind, contribution to a corporation, assignment or any other act, contract or agreement which may imply a transfer of, or whose purpose is to transfer ownership of tangible personal property.

3.1   Supply of Goods

The term 'supply' means the transfer of goods for consideration. The term 'goods' applies to tangible new or used movable properties. Utilities such as electricity, gas, heat and similar intangibles do not qualify as goods. Land and buildings are not subject to VAT.

3.2   Supply of Services

Taxable services means the rendering of services as non-employees in situations where an industrial licence is required because raw materials are being transformed into finished goods. Dress makers, tailors, hairdressers, shoe repairers, and similar non-industrial licence services do not pay VAT.

3.3   Self-Supply of Goods/Services

The transfer of goods or services within the enterprise itself is not subject to VAT, except for those transferred to partners, owners, dignitaries, legal representatives or shareholders.

3.4   Importation of Goods

The taxability of imported goods is based on the act of importation itself. The liability to any VAT is settled with customs at the time of importation. Authorised temporary imports are not subject to VAT.

4   PLACE OF SUPPLY

VAT only applies to supplies transferred within Panama.

4.1   Supply of Goods
A supply of goods takes place in Panama when at the time of transfer the goods are in Panama. Goods being exported from Panama are exempt from VAT.

4.2   Supply of Services
Services are deemed to be rendered in Panama if the supplier has his domicile or is established within the territory of the State.

4.3   Reverse Charge Mechanism
The reverse charge mechanism is not used in Panama.

5   BASIS OF TAXATION

5.1   Supplies within Panama
In the case of the sale of goods with incidental services (transportation, packing, installation, financing interests, etc), the tax base is the total amount billed including the incidental services less the discount and bonuses generally used in each business.

In the case of services rendered which include goods whose transfer is taxed, the tax base will only consist of the value of the goods.

In sales through promotional systems, the tax base will be the value of the goods.

In the case of services rendered by a person who is not an employee and who transforms raw material into finished goods utilising an industrial licence, the tax base will be the cost of such service.

5.2   Self-Supplies
In the case of goods which the taxpayers may utilise for personal use, the tax base will be the selling price of the goods.

5.3   Imports
Imports will take into account the carriage insurance freight (CIF) value plus any taxes, duties, fees, contributions or custom duties chargeable on the imported goods.

5.4   Chargeable Events/Time of Payment
Liability to VAT on sales of goods arises at the moment the invoice is issued by the seller even though the goods may be delivered later.

In the case of supermarkets and establishments with a large amount of retail sales, the liability to VAT arises at the moment goods are delivered, provided there is an authorisation from the General Directorate of Revenue that the document issued by the cash register may be treated as an invoice.

A taxable event on imports occurs at the moment of the declaration at customs, and before their introduction to the fiscal territory.

VAT should be paid monthly or quarterly according to the monthly average level of the business's gross income. Businesses whose monthly average gross income is higher than B/.5,000 are considered first class and should pay on a monthly basis. Second class businesses are those whose monthly average gross income is higher than B/.1,500 and less than B/.5,000, and they should pay on a quarterly basis.

Taxpayers who have a variable average income cannot change their classification during the calendar year.

Taxpayers just commencing operations are allowed to submit an estimate of their anticipated average monthly income and they are classified on the basis of that estimate under either Class One or Class Two. Taxpayers classified according to their own estimate may change their classification after the first six months of operation.

5.5 Credit Notes/Bad Debts
When a credit note is issued cancelling all or part of an invoice, the entrepreneur may deduct the VAT shown on the credit note from the output VAT when filling his VAT return.

VAT charged on invoices which remain unsettled, ie bad debts, cannot be recovered.

6 TAX RATES

There are three rates:

0%: exports of goods, transfers to the Panama Canal Commission and to the Armed Forces of the United States. Imports and local purchases of goods made by companies that export more than 90% of their production

10%: cigarettes and alcoholic beverages

5%: all other taxable supplies.

7 EXEMPTIONS

7.1 Exemptions with Credit for Input Tax
The zero rate is the equivalent of exemption with credit for input tax.

7.2 Exemptions without Credit for Input Tax
Exemptions without credit for input tax are as follows:

- sales of produce of agricultural, livestock and other producers in a native State and those subject to simple processes (excluding flower shops)
- sales made by fishermen, and hunters of products in a natural state or when they have undergone a simple process
- transfers of goods within free zones
- transactions affecting goods in customs areas and warehouses and whose ownership is transferred through the endorsement of documents
- the import and sale of foodstuffs, medicine and fuels specified by law
- the import and sale of agricultural input materials.

7.3 Non-Taxable Transactions
Non-taxable transactions include:

- supplies of goods and services by producers or businessmen whose average gross income is below B/.1,500 monthly or B/.18,000 annually, are exempt from taxation
- the transfer of negotiable documents and titles and values in general
- expropriations and sales by the State
- transfer of goods caused by marriage divisions
- transfer of goods caused by death, and donations subject to inheritance and donation tax
- any service rendered which does not include transfer of goods.

8   CREDIT REFUNDS FOR INPUT VAT

8.1   General Rule

If in a tax period the tax paid on imports and local purchases of goods exceeds the tax collected on sales, the balance will be credited to the following period. The tax credit is the amount of tax paid by the taxpayer on his imports, local purchases or taxable services received when they are related to non-exempt transactions. The taxpayer must have vouchers (invoices) which separately indicate the amount paid.

The tax paid on internal acquisitions and imports which are part of the cost of goods exported, re-exported or transferred to authorised agencies of the government of the United States of America located in the Panama Canal Zone will be repaid. Where taxpayers would be in a continuous repayment position because of their level of exports, etc they may obtain cancellation certificates from the General Directorate of Revenue.

The certificates issued and certified by the Ministry of Finance and Treasury bear the person's name, are transferable through endorsements, and have coupons attached which are equivalent to the face value.

8.2   Adjustment of Entitlement to Credit

No special rules apply to the review of apportioned input credits in respect of capital goods.

8.3   Partial Exemption

The tax charged on imports and local purchases directly intended for taxable transactions is considered as tax credit. However, when tax is charged on imports and local purchases intended for exempt taxation or those not subject to tax, such tax will not be deductible as tax credit, but will be acknowledged on the taxpayer's income tax return as a deductible expense.

Where the taxpayer carries out both taxable and tax-exempt transactions and, as a result, it cannot be determined whether the payment of tax on an acquisition is to be considered a tax credit or a deductible expense, the deduction as tax credit will be made in proportion to the amount of taxable transactions over total transactions for the period. The portion not recognised as tax credit will be considered as a deductible expense on the taxpayer's income tax return.

8.4   Time of Recovery

Input tax credit is applied to the period in which the tax is paid. Whenever there is a favourable balance such credit is recovered in the next period following the one in which the tax credit exceeds a tax debit. Taxpayers with a continuing favourable balance may obtain a cancellation certificate (see section 8.1) which is transferable.

8.5   *Refund for Foreign Entrepreneurs*

There are no provisions for refund of tax to a taxable person who is not located in Panama in respect of the VAT suffered on goods or services purchased in or imported into Panama.

9   ADMINISTRATIVE OBLIGATIONS

9.1   *Registration*

Every legal or natural person should register as a taxpayer at the General Directorate of Revenue. Commercial and Industrial licences cannot be issued unless a trader is registered.

Persons who make supplies which are subject to VAT are required to fill out a 'Taxpayer Master File' form issued by the administration. In this form they must estimate their main and secondary activities and the amount of their monthly transactions so that they can be classified as either Class One or Class Two taxpayers at the time of registration.

9.2   *Books and Records*

Commercial and industrial taxpayers must keep books of account which record all their transactions.

Taxpayers subject to VAT are required to maintain an account in their accounting records called 'National Treasury' (ITBM). In this account they credit the tax attributable to their taxable transactions and debit the amount of tax paid on their imports and local purchases. The tax charged on imports and local purchases directly intended for taxable transactions will be treated as a tax credit.

Whenever a tax is charged on imports and local purchases intended for exempt transactions or those not subject to tax, such tax will not be deducted as tax credit. In this case the tax paid should be debited in another account named 'Tax on transfer goods' and will be acknowledged on the taxpayer's income tax return as a deductible expense.

Taxpayers must issue invoices for all transfers related to the sale of goods and services rendered.

Records must be kept for inspection by the VAT authorities which may occur at any time within five years from the first day of the month on which the tax should have been paid. However, this period may be extended by any written action from the authority.

9.3   *Invoices*

VAT taxpayers should issue invoices or equivalent documents for every transaction related to the transfer of goods and services rendered.

Invoices must show:

- the name and tax identification number (RUC) of the issuer
- the date of the transaction
- the total tax applicable to the transaction, indicating tax separately
- the total amount charged.

There is a special system which treats printed cash register tapes as sales invoices. This can be used by those taxpayers who cannot issue invoices manually due to the volume of their transactions, and who request permission from the General Directorate of Revenue to utilise this procedure.

The documentation should use a consecutive numbering system and at least one copy must remain in the issuer's files.

9.4   VAT Returns
Importers should pay the tax before bringing the imported goods into the fiscal territory. Appropriate forms must be filed for the Customs declaration.

VAT should be paid monthly or quarterly according to the monthly average level of the business gross income. VAT declarations and tax payment should be made simultaneously within 15 days after the tax period.

9.5   Powers of the Authorities
The administration has the power to examine and audit a taxpayer's records to detect non-filing taxpayers, collect payments from delinquent taxpayers and make adjustments to incorrect tax returns.

9.6   Objections/Appeals
Appeals go first to the General Directorate of Revenue and in the second instance to a Commission for Appeals at the General Directorate of Revenue.

10   SPECIAL VAT REGIMES

The VAT law does not consider any special VAT regimes other than those mentioned in section 7 'Exemptions'.

11   FURTHER READING

Ramón E. Fábrega F., *Código Fiscal de Panamá*, Título XXII, Litografía e Imprenta LIL, S. A., San José, Costa Rica, 1991.

Dr. Arturo Hoyos y Lic. Victoria Romero de Hoyos, *El Impuesto Sobre Transferencias de Bienes Muebles (I.T.B.M.). Disposiciones legales reglamentarias y consultas absueltas por el Ministerio de Hacienda y Tesoro*, Segunda Edición, Panamá, 30 de Septiembre de 1981.

José Javier Rivera, *VAT in Panamá*, Rivera & Rivera, Abogados, Contadores.

Contributors: Jose A Mann and Cristobel Fasce H.
Ernst & Young
Calle 51 Bella Vista, No 26
Panama
Tel: +507 64 2633
Fax: +507 63 7719

PARAGUAY

1   GENERAL BACKGROUND

Value added tax (VAT), known in Paraguay as 'Impuesto al Valor Agregado', was introduced on 1 July 1992, as part of the Tax Reform. It is administered by the Under Secretary of Taxes. It taxes the transfer of goods or services inside the national territory, and the importation of goods. Imports are administered by Direccion General de Aduanas (Customs).

2   WHO IS TAXABLE?

2.1   *Persons Subject to VAT*
The following are subject to VAT:

- individuals who provide personal services
- single-owner companies established in the country when they carry out commercial, industrial and service activities
- companies with or without legal status, private companies in general as well as individuals or companies established abroad or their branches, agencies or establishments when they carry out commercial, industrial or service activities
- self-supported organisations, public companies, decentralised organisations and mixed-economy companies that carry out commercial, industrial or services activities
- those who introduce permanent goods into the country (importers).

2.2   *Transactions with Branch/Subsidiary*
No special regulation applies to transactions between a branch and its foreign head office. They are considered to be two independent taxpayers and therefore transfers between them are subject to VAT.

2.3   *Government Bodies*
The State and other public entities are taxable persons if they carry out commercial, industrial or service activities.

2.4   *Fiscal Unity/Group Taxation*
The concept of fiscal unity does not exist in the Paraguayan legislation.

2.5   *Foreign Entrepreneurs*
Foreign entrepreneurs with no establishment in Paraguay are subject to VAT.

2.6   *Representative Office*
Representative offices are also taxable entities.

This chapter reflects the law on VAT in Paraguay as at 12 January 1995.

2.7 Importers

Goods brought into Paraguay are subject to VAT at customs clearance. The tax is payable by the importer.

3   WHAT IS TAXABLE?

VAT is levied on:

- the transfer of property
- the provision of services, excluding personal services provided for dependants
- the import of goods.

3.1 Transfer of Goods

The transfer of property is any operation for which a payment is made or which is obtained free for the purpose of transferring property rights or for giving those who receive the goods the right to use them as if they were the owners.

The name given by the parties to the operation and the payment conditions are irrelevant.

The transfer concept includes the following operations:

- the use or personal consumption of company goods by the company's owner, partners and directors
- the use of goods with an option to buy or that which in some way foresees their transfer
- the transfer of companies, the cessation of part of a company with or without legal status, mergers, takeovers and transfers to company owners, partners and shareholders made by closure, total or partial dissolution, and final liquidations of commercial and industrial firms or services
- contracts with a promise to transfer possession
- goods handed over in consignment.

3.2 Provision of Services

The provision of services is any activity which is not regarded as a supply of goods which provides the other party with an advantage or benefit. It is irrelevant whether the service is supplied for payment or free. Examples of services are:

- loans and financing
- services on projects, excluding materials
- insurance and re-insurance
- brokers in general
- the cessation of the use of goods
- the practice of professions, arts or trades
- the transportation of goods and people
- the personal use of company services by the company's owner, partners and directors.

3.3 Importers

The importation of goods means the entry of goods into the VAT territory of Paraguay. The VAT is due at the time of customs clearance.

4   PLACE OF SUPPLY

4.1   Supply of Goods

A supply of goods (transfer of property) is taxable when the goods are inside national territory, regardless of the place where the contract was signed.

4.2   Supply of Services

The provision of services is taxable when it is supplied within Paraguayan territory. Technical assistance will be considered implemented on national territory when it is used in the country.

5   BASIS OF TAXATION

5.1   Supply within Paraguay

The taxable amount is the net price obtained at the delivery of the goods.

5.2   Self-Supply

When a supply is made for personal use or consumption, the taxable amount is the internal market's sale price for an equivalent supply.

5.3   Importation of Goods

For imports, the tax obligation begins at the moment the goods are registered as entered at the customs office, and the taxable amount is determined by the customs value at the normal tax rate (10%).

5.4   Time of Payment

VAT due is payable in the month following the taxable event.

5.5   Credit Notes/Bad Debts

Any credit note used to cancel all or part of an invoice can be used to reduce the VAT payment.

6   TAX RATES

There is a single VAT rate of 10% for all taxable supplies and services.

7   EXEMPTIONS

7.1   Exemption with Credit for Input Tax

Exports are exempted with a right to recover input VAT under a special fiscal credit arrangement explained below.

Exporters can receive a refund of the fiscal credit on the purchase of goods and services which are directly attributable to their exports. This will be credited against the fiscal debit in cases where the exporter also carries out taxable operations. If a surplus exists, it may be used to pay other taxes, or it may be refunded under conditions established by the administration which is empowered to adopt other procedures for the use of such credit. The deadline for repayment of an excess cannot exceed 60 days from the date of a request, on the condition that the request is accompanied by documents justifying the credit.

7.2 Exemption without Credit for Input Tax

The following supplies of goods and services are exempt (without a right to recover input VAT):

- unprocessed agriculture and livestock products
- foreign currency, public and private securities, certificates and shares
- gambling tickets and documents
- fuels that are oil by-products
- inherited goods
- the importation of:
  - crude oil
  - goods imported in travellers' personal baggage, in keeping with customs regulations
  - goods imported into the country by accredited members of the diplomatic and consular corps, and by members of international organisations
  - movable goods directly used for the industrial or farming productive cycle imported by investors

- payment of interest on public and private securities
- renting of real estate
- certain financial intermediary services including loans granted by foreign banks, with the following exceptions:
  - negotiating, on behalf of third parties, the purchase and sale of securities, and operating as an agent for the payment of dividends, amortisation, and interest
  - issuing credit cards, except by entities established abroad
  - mandates and commission whenever they are not related to authorised financial operations
  - managing certain security portfolios and rendering financial services
  - collection services and rendering of technical and managerial assistance
  - renting movable goods

- loans granted by:
  - savings and credit co-operatives
  - the Agricultural Development Fund (CAH)
  - the System of Savings and Credit for Housing
  - the National Development Bank
  - the National Livestock Fund

- services rendered by accredited permanent or temporary employees contracted by embassies, consulates and international organisations accredited by the national government according to the existing laws
- activities of political parties; organisations for social assistance, charitable action, and education; institutions for scientific, literary, artistic, union, physical education, and sports training; and associations, federations, foundations, corporations, and other

entities with legal recognition, provided they are non-profitable and their dividends or surpluses are not directly or indirectly distributed among their members but used exclusively for the purpose for which entities were created

■   the activities of recognised religious organisations which are linked exclusively with the exercise of cult and religious services.

8   CREDIT/REFUND FOR VAT

VAT must be calculated and remitted monthly. VAT payable is the difference between the 'fiscal debit' and the 'fiscal credit'.

Fiscal debit is the sum of the VAT accrued from taxable operations during the month. Deductible from the fiscal debit is the VAT on refunds, allowances, discounts and bad debts.

Fiscal credit is the sum of:

■   VAT included in purchase invoices for the month
■   VAT paid during the month on imported goods.

Fiscal credit can be deducted on the condition that it comes from goods or services that are directly or indirectly related to taxable operations.

When the fiscal credit is higher than the fiscal debit, the surplus can be recovered in the next VAT return as a surplus.

9   ADMINISTRATIVE OBLIGATIONS

9.1   Registration
Taxpayers must submit a declaration as soon as they begin their activity. All taxpayers must have a RUC (a taxpayer ID).

9.2   Books and Records
The administration requires taxpayers to keep special registers, bookkeeping arrangements, or other appropriate accounting records to comply with the VAT Regulation in accordance with the taxpayer's category.

9.3   Invoicing
Taxpayers are obligated to present invoices for each operation or service rendered and they must keep a copy of the invoice until that tax is paid. The tax rate must be listed separately in the invoice or document unless a regulation expressly authorises its inclusion in the price.

9.4   VAT Returns
VAT returns have to be filed on a monthly basis.

9.5   Violations and Fines
Tax violations are default payments, infringements of regulations, non-payment and fraud.

If VAT (or any other tax) is not paid in due time, this is considered default payment, and it will be sanctioned with a fine calculated on the amount of tax not paid. The fines are as follows:

Period of default	Penalty as % of unpaid tax
1 month	4%
2 months	6%
3 months	8%
4 months	10%
5 months	12%
6 months	14%

All the terms will be computed from the day after the deadline.

A default payment will also be sanctioned with a surcharge (or monthly interest) calculated on a daily basis to be established by the executive branch, which can be increased up to 50% until the obligation is paid. But the interest cannot be more than the regular market interest charged by the Central Bank on loans to commercial banks in force when the calculation was made.

10 SPECIAL VAT REGIMES

10.1 Purchase or Sale of Used Articles
Where used articles are bought or sold from or to individuals who are not taxpayers, the administration will establish percentages estimating the appropriate added value of the traded product.

10.2 Agriculture
Agricultural producers included in the income tax will be in the same bracket as exporters with regard to refunds (see section 7.1). They will be entitled to a refund of 50% of the VAT on goods and services bought on the local market and abroad that are linked to agricultural activities under the terms and conditions established in this article.

10.3 Temporary Imports
Goods brought into the country under the temporary admission regulation for transformation, manufacture, improvement, and export will receive the same fiscal treatment accorded to exporters.

Foreign goods which are brought in under the above regulation to be repaired or finished in the country will be considered in the same manner.

10.4 Simplification of Tax Collection System
When, as a result of practical reasons, trading characteristics, or supervision difficulties, it is advisable to simplify the tax collection system, the Executive Branch may establish that collections be made at various stages or at one particular stage of the economic cycle of a product, based on its retail market price. The Executive Branch will establish the procedure for establishing that price, except when it is officially fixed.

10.5 Tax Payment Deadlines

The administration is empowered to establish tax payment deadlines longer than 30 days for taxpayers whose VAT payments do not exceed a certain amount. The administration is also empowered to grant special payment prerogatives to taxpayers who, because of the characteristics of the activity, trading methods, or other justified reasons, encounter difficulties in meeting the general regulations.

Contributor: Antonio Britez
Ernst & Young
Casilla de Correos 2295
Asuncion
Paraguay
Tel: +595 21 495 581
Fax: +595 21 447 529

PERU

1   GENERAL BACKGROUND

Peru's sales tax (referred to as VAT in this chapter) came into effect on 1 November 1981 and replaced the tax on goods and services that had previously been in force. VAT is levied on the sale in Peru of taxable goods, the supply of taxable services rendered or used in Peru, the first sale of real estate made by its constructors, construction contracts, and on the importation of goods. The VAT is administered by the Tax Administration Superintendency (Superintendencia de Administracion Tributaria, SUNAT).

2   WHO IS TAXABLE?

2.1   General
VAT is levied on taxable transactions carried out in Peru by taxable persons and on imports. A taxable person is any person who carries on a business activity. Individuals who are engaged in an occasional transaction are not deemed to be taxable persons within the meaning of the VAT law. The legal status of a person is irrelevant. VAT thus applies indifferently to individuals, associations of individuals and juridical persons.

2.2   Transactions with Branch/Subsidiary
Subsidiaries and branches of foreign firms which carry on taxable transactions are treated in the same manner as any other taxable person, even if the taxable transactions are carried on with a parent company located outside of Peru.

2.3   Government Bodies
State and local authorities are not taxable persons; however, they are liable to VAT in respect of all goods imported by them.

2.4   Fiscal Unity/Group Taxation
This procedure is not contemplated in the Peruvian VAT legislation.

2.5   Foreign Firms
Foreign firms can only supply taxable services and perform construction work.

2.6   Representative Office
Representative and information offices of foreign firms are subject to VAT only if they make taxable transactions.

This chapter reflects the legislation on VAT in Peru as at 31 December 1994.

2.7   VAT Representatives

A foreign firm is not required to appoint a fiscal representative in Peru because the respon-sibility for VAT payment lies with the consumer.

2.8   Reverse Charge Mechanism

Persons who receive from abroad, for business use, certain services (such as copyrights, patents, consultancy, etc) are obliged to account for VAT on the value of the services (see section 4.3 'Reverse Charge Mechanism').

2.9   Importers

Persons who import goods into Peru are subject to VAT at the same rate as that applying to the sale of similar goods within Peru.

3   WHAT IS TAXABLE?

VAT is levied on the sale in Peru of taxable goods, the supply of taxable services rendered or used in Peru, the first sale of real estate made by its constructors, construction contracts and on the import of goods.

3.1   Supply of Goods

A taxable supply of goods means transfer of ownership, irrespective of the name given to the agreement. The term 'goods' includes movable property and its rights, ships and airships.

3.2   Mixed Transactions

As there is only a single rate, there are no specific rules applied to mixed transactions consisting of supplies of goods and services (see section 6 'Tax Rates').

3.3   Supply of Services

A supply of services can be defined as any action that an individual provides to another and for which he receives an income which is considered as derived from a business activity, and the rental or leasing of real estate, furniture and equipment by juridical persons.

3.4   Disposal of Goods

The disposal of goods by their owner or by a company is subject to VAT, with the exemption of the following:

- disposal of raw materials and consumer goods to be used in the manufacture of goods produced by the company
- disposal of goods delivered to third parties to be used in the manufacture of other goods for the company
- disposal of goods by a constructor to be used in the construction of a property
- loss, theft and destruction of goods
- disposal of goods that will be used by the company, provided that this is necessary for the performance of taxable transactions
- disposal of goods to be delivered to workers as a working condition, provided that these are indispensable for the delivery of their services.

3.5   Importations of Goods

With certain exemptions, the mere importation of taxable goods is a taxable event irrespective of the status of the importer or the nature of the importation (see section 7.3 'Exempt Imports').

3.6   Construction Contracts

Construction activities which are included in Division 45 of the Standard Industrial Uniform Classification of Economic Activities are subject to VAT.

3.7   First Sale of Real Estate by its Constructor

The first sale of real estate which is entirely built by a constructor or partially built by a third party at his request is taxable. A constructor is a person who is habitually dedicated to this activity.

4   PLACE OF SUPPLY

4.1   Supply of Goods

A sale of goods is taxable only if the goods are sold in Peru to local persons. If the goods are exported, they are not subject to the payment of VAT.

4.2   Supply of Services

Services are taxable if they are rendered or used in Peru. The export of some services is exempt from VAT (see section 7.1 'Exemption with Credit for Input Tax').

International air transport tickets issued overseas to be used in Peru are liable to VAT.

4.3   Reverse Charge Mechanism

The place of supply of services such as copyrights, patents, hiring of movable goods, advertising, consultancy and financial services, provision of staff, etc by a person established or resident outside Peru to a person resident or established in Peru is generally where the recipient of the services has his business. This gives rise to the 'reverse charge' concept in that the recipient is held to be liable to VAT on the value of the services he has received and will be entitled to the normal input VAT deduction if he is a taxable person. Thus a fully taxable person will ultimately not have to pay VAT, but an exempt person is obliged to register and is not entitled to input credit in respect of such services.

5   BASIS OF TAXATION

5.1   Supplies within Peru

Where the consideration takes the form of money, the amount on which tax is chargeable is normally the total sum paid or payable to the person supplying the taxable transaction including all taxes, commissions, costs, and charges whatsoever, but excluding the VAT chargeable in respect of the transaction.

Where goods or services are supplied and the consideration does not consist of or does not wholly consist of an amount of money, and where certain goods are supplied free of charge, the amount on which tax is chargeable is the open market (or arms-length) value of the goods or services supplied.

The following are excluded from this basis of taxation:

- deposits paid by buyers on returnable goods containers
- discounts recorded in invoices, provided that these are usual in business
- currency exchange differences generated between the time of the tax obligation and the total or partial payment of the price.

5.2   Goods Made up from Materials Supplied by Customers
Materials or components supplied by customers are not included in the basis of taxation.

5.3   Disposals of Goods
VAT due on disposals of goods is calculated on the basis of the fee-paid operations conducted by the taxable person with third parties, or otherwise the market value will be applied.

The VAT paid cannot be considered as a cost or expense by the company.

5.4   Imports
The basis of taxation of imports is the value of the imported goods according to the provisions of the customs law and includes transport cost, duties and other levies.

When the value is expressed in a foreign currency it must be converted to Peruvian currency at the exchange rate in force at the time of importation.

5.5   Construction Contracts
VAT is applied on the construction value.

5.6   The First Sale of Real Estate by its Constructor
The taxation basis is the total income received less the corresponding land value which is subject to a tax levied at a rate of 3% on the sale or transfer of real estate, payable by the buyer.

5.7   Chargeable Event/Time of Payment
VAT becomes due:

- in the case of a goods sale, at the date of billing or at the time the goods are handed over, whichever occurs first; in the case of ships or aircraft, at the date the sale agreement is signed
- in the case of disposals of goods, at the date of disposal or at the time of billing, whichever occurs first
- in the supply of services, when the invoice is issued or when the fees are received, whichever occurs first; in the case of the provision of electricity, water supply and telecommunication services, at the receipt of payment or at the maturity date of the service payment, whichever occurs first
- in the case of imports, at the time of clearance of the goods through customs
- in the case of construction contracts, at the date of billing or upon total/partial receipt of payment, whichever occurs first

■ in the first sale of real estate by its constructors, at the date of total/partial receipt of payment.

VAT due for each period is payable within the 12 working days of the month following the VAT period. There is a payment schedule which varies every month, and which goes from the ninth to the fifteenth working day of the month following the VAT period.

5.8 Credit Notes – Bad Debts

If a taxable person gives a credit and issues a credit note, he is allowed to reduce his VAT liability accordingly. The customer must correspondingly reduce his input tax deduction. VAT cannot be adjusted if the taxable person does not or only partially receives payment.

6 TAX RATE

The current rate is as follows:

18%: applicable to all taxable transactions.

7 EXEMPTIONS

7.1 Exemption with Credit for Input Tax

The following supplies are exempt from tax but suppliers are entitled to recover input tax incurred in respect of their purchase of goods and services (see section 10.1 'Exporters'):

■ exports of goods
■ export of the following services:
  – consultant and technical services
  – rentals of furniture and equipment
  – advertising, marketing research and public opinion polls
  – data processing, application software, etc
  – provision of staff
  – commissions on loan assets
  – financing operations
  – insurances and reinsurances
  – tour guide services provided by tour operators to travel agencies domiciled abroad
  – payments from overseas operators for input telecommunication services.

Services are considered as exported when they are rendered by a person domiciled in Peru in favour of a non-domiciled person, provided that these services are used abroad.

7.2 Exemption without Credit for Input Tax

Supplies of the following goods and services are exempt from output tax and do not qualify for credit of any related input VAT incurred:

■ goods – fish, vegetables, potatoes, fresh fruits, coffee, tea, cereal, seeds, fresh milk, cacao and cotton

- credit services rendered by banking, financial and credit institutions
- public inland transportation, except air transportation
- international freight transportation and complementary services
- cultural activities
- popular and university cafeterias
- certain activities performed in jungle regions (see section 10.2)
- construction and repair of vessels under a foreign flag
- interest from nominal bonuses issued by Peruvians. The supplier can waive his exemption in order to obtain input credit.

7.3   Exempt Imports

Certain importations are exempt from VAT such as:

- donations to the public sector
- religious institutions and foundations
- personal goods and household furniture exempt from customs duties, except vehicles
- goods for fire fighters
- goods acquired with foreign donations for the execution of public works under agreements
- special vehicles and prosthetic appliances for the exclusive use of handicapped people
- goods acquired by universities, higher education institutions and cultural centres
- temporary imports
- goods in transit and raw materials for the manufacture of goods which will be exported.

Certain restrictions and qualifications apply to some of these items.

7.4   Transactions Outside the Scope of VAT or Non-Taxable

7.4.1   Transfer of Business

Transfer of goods due to fusion, division, or transfer of business are not liable to VAT. The tax credit of the absorbed company is not lost.

7.4.2   Election to be Subject to VAT

An individual whose monthly turnover does not exceed 12,000 Peruvian soles (approximately US$5,454), can pay a single tax instead of VAT and income tax, based on a scale which could vary from 10 to 220 Peruvian soles (approximately US$5 and US$100, respectively).

8   CREDIT/REFUND FOR INPUT VAT

8.1   General Rule

In computing the amount of tax payable by him a taxable person may deduct the tax relating to goods and services purchased or imported by him which are used for the purposes of his taxable business. No deduction may be made for the tax paid on goods or services used for any other purposes.

To qualify for credit:

- the expense must be considered as a cost or expense for income tax purposes
- the expense must be related to taxable operations, except export operations
- the tax must be shown separately on the invoice, except when the invoice is issued by a non-domiciled supplier
- the invoice must be issued in accordance with local regulations, except when this is issued by a non-domiciled person
- the invoice and customs clearance document must be registered in the purchase book.

8.2   Adjustment of Entitlement to Credit
There are no special rules with regard to the review of apportioned input credits in respect of capital goods.

8.3   Partial Exemption
Persons who make taxable and other supplies such as exempt supplies and supplies which are outside the scope of VAT are entitled to recover VAT incurred in making the taxable supplies only.

When the purchases or imports are used in making both taxable and exempt/outside the scope supplies an apportionment of the input VAT is allowed. The allowable input tax credit is usually calculated in the ratio of the turnover of taxable supplies to the total turnover of all supplies. Alternatively, the input tax may be determined by identifying the purchases used for taxable supplies.

8.4   Time of Recovery
Input VAT may be claimed in the month in which a supply is made if the taxable person is in possession of the appropriate invoice which should not be more than two months old. The VAT on imports may be claimed in the month in which the import VAT is paid. If input VAT exceeds output VAT the balance is carried forward to the following months until it is totally applied.

8.5   Refund to Foreign Persons
Goods acquired by tourists to be carried abroad may qualify for a VAT refund. This refund system will be in force when the Ministry of Economy and Finance authorises it.

9   ADMINISTRATIVE OBLIGATIONS

9.1   Registration
There is only one registry 'Registro Unico de Contribuyentes' (RUC) for all tax purposes.

9.2   Books and Records
Taxable persons must keep up-to-date two registers which contain the detailed information requested by the tax authorities. Any delay in updating must not exceed ten days. In one register, taxable persons must record all taxable transactions performed, and in the other, all acquisitions of goods and services.

9.3 Invoices

Invoices must contain the following information:

- the supplier's name, address and tax registration number (RUC)
- the printed word 'invoice'
- correlative number of the invoice
- printing data
- the consignees of the original invoice and of the copies
- name of the recipient of the supply and RUC number
- description of the goods or services supplied
- unit price
- tax, shown separately
- total amount billed
- date of issue
- name, address and RUC of the printer of the invoice.

The amount of VAT paid does not need to be shown separately for sales to final consumers.

Failure to comply with any of these formal requirements may deprive the customer of recovery of input VAT (unless a correction is made by the issuer or a new invoice meeting the formalities is submitted).

9.4 VAT Returns

Taxable persons should file sworn monthly returns of the taxable and exempt transactions performed during the preceding month. Both the return and the payment must be filed together on the due date (see in section 5.7).

The VAT payable on taxable imports must be determined by the Peruvian customs authorities in the customs clearance document.

9.5 Correction of Returns

Where the tax payable on a return needs to be increased this will be valid at the presentation of an amended return. Otherwise it will be valid when the authorities make an assessment. In this way the taxpayer will not be liable to fines. Interest will arise from the original due date.

9.6 Powers of the Authorities

If VAT is not paid by its due date, the tax authorities will notify the taxable person and give him three days to make payment. If he does not comply, the tax authorities will issue an assessment for an estimated amount.

9.7 Penalties

A fine can be assessed for the late filing of a tax return, calculated on the basis of a percentage of the tax unit (UIT) which is currently 2,000 Peruvian soles (approximately US$909). In case of late payment, the default interest rate (tasa de interes moratoria – TIM) which is currently 2.5% per month, may be assessed. These interests are capitalised at the end of each year.

9.8   Appeals

A taxpayer may file an appeal with the tax authorities against a VAT assessment notice. The appeal must be filed within 20 days from the date when the assessment notice is received. An appeal may be filed after the 20-day limit provided the tax is paid first. If the tax authorities do not amend the tax assessment as requested, further appeals to the Tax Court or to the Supreme Court are possible.

9.9   Statute of Limitation

The general statute of limitations runs for five years. If a taxable person has not filed a return the period for assessment is extended to seven years, and in the case of a withholding agent it is extended to eleven years.

10   SPECIAL VAT REGIMES

10.1 Exporters

The tax paid by exporters on their purchases of goods and services may be recovered subject to the input VAT rules. This credit may be applied against VAT, income tax or any other tax considered as a public treasury income. If automatic compensation is not possible, the net credit balance could be refunded by way of negotiable credit notes.

10.2 Business Located in the Jungle Region

Services provided in the jungle region, the sales of goods produced and used in that region, raw materials used in the manufacturing of such goods, regional natural products, and the import and sale of goods specified in the 'Convenio de Cooperacion Aduanero Peruano Colombiano' of 1938 are exempt from VAT.

To qualify for these benefits, the taxable person must be domiciled and have its accounting and administrative offices located in the jungle, at least 75% of its operations must be carried out there and it must be registered at the Jungle Public Registry.

Contributor: Victor Vega
                   Partner
                   Ernst & Young
                   Alonso y Asociados
                   Apartado 3601
                   Lima 100
                   Peru
                   Tel: +51 14 631818
                   Fax: +51 14 634523

TRINIDAD AND TOBAGO

1   GENERAL BACKGROUND

With effect from 1 January 1990 a general indirect tax on consumption called the Value Added Tax (VAT) was introduced into Trinidad and Tobago. The Trinidad and Tobago VAT legislation is contained in the Value Added Tax Act 1989 and the subsequently enacted Regulations. The tax is administered by the VAT Administration Centre of the Board of Inland Revenue but VAT on imported goods is collected by the Customs and Excise Department.

The introduction of the broad-based VAT was accompanied by the elimination of the following taxes:

- Purchase Tax
- Excise taxes on edible oils and matches
- Consolidated Special Levy
- Wireless licences
- Electricity and telephone taxes
- Hotel Room Tax
- Airline Ticket Tax
- Domestic Stamp Duties (the Stamp Duty on imports was retained).

The major excise taxes on petroleum, alcohol and cigarettes and the special tax on motor vehicles were substantially retained, but in a slightly modified form to maintain, when combined with VAT, the same level of taxation on these commodities.

2   WHO IS TAXABLE?

2.1   General

VAT is a tax on consumer expenditure. It is payable on the importation of goods into Trinidad and Tobago and the supply of goods and prescribed services within Trinidad and Tobago. It is levied and collected at each stage of the production process by registered persons but is not a tax on business. Only a registered person may charge and collect VAT.

Any person (individual, company, partnership, etc) conducting a business activity in Trinidad and Tobago whose commercial supply of goods or services in any 12-month period exceeds or is likely to exceed TT$120,000 in value (excluding VAT) is required to register with the VAT Administration Centre of the Board of Inland Revenue.

The concept of 'business' is fundamental in considering whether or not a liability to VAT arises and the term is defined in the Act as including any trade, profession or vocation. The Act deems certain activities to be a business even though they may not normally fall within the above definition, for example, the activities of a club, association or organisation, and an activity involving the admission, for a consideration, of persons to any premises.

This chapter reflects the legislation on VAT in Trinidad and Tobago as at 31 December 1994.

Bodies having objects in the public domain that are of a political, religious, philanthropic, philosophical or patriotic nature are not regarded as carrying on a business. Employees and directors are also not considered to be carrying on a business.

2.2 Transactions with Branch/Subsidiary

Generally, transactions between the head office and a branch of the same company are considered to be internal transactions and therefore not vatable. By comparison, transactions between a company and its subsidiaries are vatable (see section 2.4 'Fiscal Unity/Group Registration').

2.3 Government Bodies

Government bodies are liable to comply with the VAT Act like any other person. However, where goods are imported or taken out of bond by or on behalf of central government, any municipality, county council or the Tobago House of Assembly for its own use and these goods are exempt from customs duty, then they will also be free from VAT.

2.4 Fiscal Unity/Group Registration

If a registered person consists of more than one unit, division or branch, then accounting for VAT as one single enterprise is generally required. However, if separate accounts are kept for the individual units, divisions or branches, and the units can be separately identified by virtue of the business activity it carries on and the location of the units, then they may, upon request, be registered and account for VAT separately. Liability to register is dependent on the gross commercial supplies of the entire organisation, rather than that of each branch or division. Also, the parent body remains liable for all the debts and obligations of each branch or division.

There is no group registration facility under the VAT system and so, where a company has one or more subsidiaries, each one is required to file separately.

2.5 Foreign Persons

Foreign persons are generally liable to account for VAT in relation to commercial supplies made in Trinidad and Tobago in excess of the registration limits if the goods are in Trinidad and Tobago at the time of supply or the service is performed in Trinidad and Tobago by the foreign person. If these commercial supplies exceed the threshold limit these persons are required to register for VAT.

Foreign persons with a fixed establishment in Trinidad and Tobago, including branches or agencies, are treated in the same manner as Trinidad and Tobago resident registered persons.

2.6 VAT Representatives

An agent or representative in Trinidad and Tobago that carries on a taxable activity on behalf of an absentee principal is liable to register, file VAT returns and account for VAT in respect of that activity.

2.7 Reverse Charge Mechanism

The concept of reverse charges in respect of services received from abroad is not used in Trinidad and Tobago.

2.8 Importers

Goods imported into Trinidad and Tobago, whether by a registered person or not, are subject to VAT at the applicable rate. Although an importer can place a bond as security for the

VAT and this will enable him to be able to enter the goods, no credit for this VAT can be claimed until the VAT is actually paid.

3   WHAT IS TAXABLE?

A registered person is liable for VAT on the commercial supplies of goods and prescribed services he makes within Trinidad and Tobago. Commercial supplies are taxable at one of two rates, depending on the nature of the supply. There is a standard rate of 15%, which is the rate applied to the vast majority of commercial supplies. However, some supplies are taxed at 0%, which is the rate applied to all supplies listed in Schedule 2 of the VAT Act. The advantage of zero-rating is that, although the supplies bear no tax, the registered person can claim a credit for VAT paid on any purchases he makes to enable him to make those supplies. In summary, all commercial supplies listed in Schedule 2 are taxable at 0%. Any other commercial supplies are taxable at the standard rate of 15%.

The term 'supply' is defined in the VAT Act as including 'all forms of supply and, in relation to services, includes the provision of any service'. The term 'supply' therefore is very wide and includes the transfer, sale, lease, or other disposition of a good or the provision of any service.

A 'commercial supply' is a supply of goods and prescribed services made in the course of, or furtherance of, any business. A prescribed service means any service not contained in the list of exempt services.

Therefore where a supply is not exempted under Schedule 1 (the list of Exempt Services) or Schedule 3 (supplies that are neither a supply of goods nor services) it will be a commercial supply.

3.1   Supply of Goods
The term 'goods' means all kinds of personal or real property, but does not include choses in action or money.

3.2   Supply of Services
In addition to the normal meaning of 'services' the legislation specifies that the following are supplies of services:

- the production of goods by applying a treatment or process to goods belonging to another person
- the supply of water other than in a container, the supply of natural gas, any form of power, refrigeration, or air conditioning
- the hiring, rental or leasing of goods
- the supply of anything for consideration which is not a supply of goods
- the lease or rental of an interest in land or a building or other structure attached to the land.

3.3   Self-Supply of Goods/Services
VAT is payable on the withdrawal by the owner of goods and services from his own business when such goods and services are for private use, for exempt use or for purposes which fall outside the scope of the Act.

3.4 Importation of Goods

VAT is charged on the entry of imported goods into Trinidad and Tobago. The goods are entered at the time that they are cleared and delivered out of customs control. The VAT is calculated by multiplying the value of the imported goods by the tax rate applicable. The value for this purpose is the sum of:

- the value for duty purposes
- insurance and freight
- stamp and import duties
- any other charges (eg excise duties/import surcharge).

3.5 Deemed Supplies

Certain transactions are deemed to be commercial supplies where:

- the stock in trade is being disposed of in the course of a business being transferred as a going concern
- goods of a business are used for non-business purposes
- goods of a business are seized and sold to satisfy a debt
- a person ceases to be registered but continues to carry on business; the stock in trade is deemed to have been supplied
- an indemnity payment is made under a contract of insurance in respect of a loss incurred in the course of business; the payee is deemed to have made a commercial supply.

4 PLACE OF SUPPLY/RESIDENCE

4.1 General

The place of supply is important because only supplies made in Trinidad and Tobago are chargeable to VAT. The rules regarding the place of supply are as follows:

4.1.1 Supplies for Residents

A supply is considered to take place within Trinidad and Tobago if the supplier is resident in Trinidad and Tobago.

4.1.2 Non-Residents

Generally, a supply is not regarded as taking place in Trinidad and Tobago if the supplier is not in Trinidad and Tobago. However, in the case of a supply made by a person not resident in Trinidad and Tobago, the supply would be regarded as taking place within Trinidad and Tobago if:

- the goods are in Trinidad and Tobago at the time of supply, or
- the service is performed in Trinidad and Tobago by a person present in Trinidad and Tobago at the time the service is performed.

This rule is subject to an exception that, where a non-resident makes supplies to a registered resident, the supply would be regarded as taking place outside Trinidad and Tobago unless both parties agree otherwise.

4.2 Reverse Charge Mechanism

Services are deemed to be supplied in Trinidad and Tobago and subject to VAT only if physically performed by a person in Trinidad and Tobago at the time of performance. The reverse charge mechanism in respect of the supply of non-performed services such as copyrights, patents and trademarks does not apply in Trinidad and Tobago.

5   BASIS OF TAXATION

5.1   Value of Supply

The VAT charged on a supply is calculated by multiplying the value of the supply by the rate of tax charged. Where the consideration for the supply is made wholly in money, the value of the supply is the consideration, excluding any tax and road improvement tax on motor vehicle fuel.

Where the consideration is not paid in money or partly paid in money, or where the transaction is between associated persons (not dealing with each other at arm's length) the value of the supply is the open market value.

5.2   Self-Supplies

Where a registered person ceases to carry on business (or ceases to be registered but continues to carry on business), any goods on hand that have not been supplied by him at the time when he ceases to carry on business (or ceases to be registered), are deemed to have been supplied by him at that time. The deemed supply is regarded as a commercial supply and he is regarded as both the supplier and the recipient.

The value placed on such deemed supply for VAT purposes is the lesser of the cost of the goods at the time of acquisition or the open market value of the goods.

5.3   Imports (Value of Supply)

For VAT purposes, the value of goods imported into Trinidad and Tobago is the total of the amount of the value of the goods determined in accordance with the Customs Act (whether or not duty is payable under the Act) plus any duties, taxes (other than VAT) and other charges due at the time of entry of the goods (see section 3.4).

5.4   Chargeable Event/Time of Supply

The time of supply identifies the tax period in which a transaction is to be taxed. The tax period is the period of two months for which a registered person is to account for VAT to the Board of Inland Revenue.

The general rule is that a supply takes place on the earliest of the following:

- the date the invoice is issued
- the date of payment
- the date when the goods are made available or, in the case of services, when the services are supplied.

A number of special rules cover particular circumstances, including:

- where supplies are made under an agreement for hire purchase, or with an option to purchase, or with an option to return, the supply is made when the goods are made available to the recipient
- where services are supplied continuously (as in the case of electricity), the time of

supply is the invoice date

- where services are supplied under an agreement that requires periodic payments, the time of supply is when an invoice is given or, where no invoice is given, the earlier of when payment is made or becomes due
- where goods are supplied periodically in a situation where payment becomes due at the time of the issue of an invoice, the time of supply is the earliest of:
  - the date an invoice is given
  - the date of payment
  - the date when payment is due

- with respect to construction projects, where the agreement states that payment will be made at various stages of construction, eg a deposit, a payment on completion of foundation, etc the supply at each stage takes place at the earliest of:
  - the date the invoice is given for that stage
  - the date payment for that stage becomes due
  - the date payment for that stage is made

- with respect to imports, the time of supply is when the customs entry is made.

5.5 Payments/Cash Basis

Registered persons are not allowed to account for VAT by reference to the date of cash payment.

5.6 Credit Notes/Bad Debts

A registered person's tax liability is evidenced by his tax invoices. If any of those invoices incorrectly reflect the terms of a supply made by him or to him, either because of an error or an adjustment of the terms after the issue of the invoice, the registered person may issue or accept a debit or credit note as evidence of the actual terms of the supply. He can then adjust his tax calculation for the period upward or downward to reflect amended terms of supply.

A registered person may be allowed to claim bad debt relief if he satisfies the following conditions:

- he must have already accounted for VAT on the supply in respect of which the amount is outstanding
- all or part of the consideration must be outstanding despite reasonable efforts having been made to collect it
- 12 months must have elapsed since the time that the amount in question became due and payable
- the amount must have been written off in his books as a bad debt.

He can claim relief for this bad debt in the first tax return immediately following the end of the 12 months mentioned above.

6   TAX RATES

The current rates are:

0%:   all supplies listed in Schedule 2 of the VAT Act, in summary:
  - unprocessed food of a kind used for human consumption, rice, flour, milk,

      margarine, bread, baby formulas and baby milk substitutes
- birds, fish, crustaceans or other animals of a kind generally used as (or yielding or producing food for) human consumption, and any draught animal
- animal feeding stuffs suitable for any animal referred to above
- seeds and other means of propagation of plants and plants that are used for providing food or feeding stuffs
- preparations formulated for agricultural use, including fertilisers, insecticides, herbicides and fungicides
- self-propelled agricultural equipment, agricultural tractors and agricultural implements for attachment to agricultural tractors, etc
- water and sewage services supplied by a public authority
- bus services supplied by the Public Transport Service Corporation under the Public Transport Service Act
- medicines and drugs of a kind available only by prescription as well as certain 'over the counter 'drugs
- aeroplanes and ships imported by or supplied to the State or State Corporations
- repair of aeroplanes and ships used in international commercial services
- goods supplied to a destination outside the territory of Trinidad and Tobago
- goods supplied to a destination within a free zone under the Trinidad and Tobago Free Zones Act
- natural gas and crude oil
- services supplied for a consideration that is payable in a currency other than that of Trinidad and Tobago to a recipient who is not within Trinidad and Tobago at the time when the services are performed
- veterinary services and pest control services
- international freight and ancillary services
- unconditional gifts of goods or services to an approved charitable, sporting or religious organisation
- domestic travel between Trinidad and Tobago
- goods and water for consumption or sale on board an aeroplane or ship in the course of providing international commercial services
- charter of ships or aircraft for use in international commercial services
- books, but excluding brochures, pamphlets and leaflets, newspapers, magazines, journals and periodicals, photograph and stamp albums.

15%:   supplies of goods and services which are not exempt or taxable at the zero rate.

7   EXEMPTIONS

Exempt supplies are those which are specifically listed in Schedule 1 of the VAT Act and are not liable to VAT.

7.1   *Exemptions with Credit for Input Tax (Zero Rate)*
Under the Trinidad and Tobago VAT Act certain goods and services are zero-rated. Although the phrase 'exemptions with credit' is not used in Trinidad and Tobago, in effect zero-rating is exemption with credit since it allows the attributable input tax to be recovered. For example, where goods and services are exported under certain conditions these are zero-

rated. Since the exporter is able to recover all the VAT on his inputs, this effectively makes such exports free of VAT.

7.2   Exemptions without Credit for Input Tax

All the services which are specifically listed in Schedule 1 of the VAT Act are exempt supplies and, accordingly, no credit for input tax incurred in respect of these supplies is allowed. They are as follows:

- medical, dental, hospital, optical and paramedical services, other than veterinary services
- bus and taxi services, other than bus services supplied by the Public Transport Service Corporation under the Public Transport Service Act
- school fees paid to an approved institution
- real estate brokerage
- rental of residential property
- accommodation in hotels, inns, guest houses for any period in excess of 30 days
- public postal services
- betting, gambling and lotteries
- financial services
- services supplied to a person not resident in Trinidad and Tobago to an approved enterprise under the Trinidad and Tobago Free Zones Act for the carrying on of an approved activity in a free zone
- services performed by a financial institution licensed under the Financial Institutions Act in respect of which Financial Services Tax is payable.

Certain imports are not subject to VAT, such as personal effects of travellers, trophies, goods imported or taken out of bond by or on behalf of the Central Government, Municipality, County Council or the Tobago House of Assembly for its own use, temporary imports, goods re-imported after being repaired abroad, goods for manufacture in bond under regulations, goods in transit and goods imported by a highly capital intensive enterprise.

7.3   Non-Taxable Transactions

The following transactions listed in Schedule 3 of the VAT Act are regarded as neither a supply of goods nor a supply of services and therefore are outside the scope of the VAT:

- the sale of an interest in land or a building or other structure attached to land
- the supply in the course of business of:
    - any gift, the value of which does not exceed TT$20, generally available to customers of the business
    - a trade sample
    - any securities, patent or other right to intellectual property, (such as copyrights) or any other chose in action (such as a licence or right granted with respect to land).

Other transactions which do not give rise to a liability to VAT as they are deemed not to be a taxable activity are:

- supply of an employee's services under a contract of employment
- supplies not made by a taxable person

- supplies made outside Trinidad and Tobago
- supplies not made in the course of business.

7.3.1 Transactions within the Same Legal Entity
Transactions between branches and divisions of the same corporate body do not attract VAT.

7.3.2 Transfer of a Business
Upon the sale, transfer or other disposition, whether for consideration or not, of a business as a going concern, the sale, transfer or other disposition of any stock in trade held for the purposes of the business shall be regarded as being a commercial supply.

7.3.3 Dividends
Dividends represent the distribution of profits, and are not the consideration for any supply.

7.4 Election to be Registered for VAT
A person who makes taxable supplies where the value of these supplies is less than the registration limits may nevertheless register for VAT at the discretion of the Board of Inland Revenue.

8 CREDIT/REFUND FOR INPUT VAT

8.1 General Rule
A registered business is entitled to claim credit in its return for input tax suffered on expenditure by way of offset against output tax. Where this results in a claim for a refund the Board of Inland Revenue is liable to pay interest of 6% if the VAT refund is not made within six months from the date of the claim. If the Board of Inland Revenue is carrying out reasonable inquiries, however, the six-month period does not begin until those inquiries have been completed.

9 ADMINISTRATIVE OBLIGATIONS

9.1 Registration
Any person who makes commercial supplies in excess of the registration limit of TT$120,000 must register for VAT.

9.2 Books and Records
Books and records of a business must be retained for a minimum period of six years and must be kept in sufficient detail to allow a registered person to calculate the tax liability correctly and in a manner that will enable the Board to verify the figures used in the VAT return. In 1992 the Board of Inland Revenue published the Value Added Tax (Books and Records) Regulations, 1992. These detail the books and records that are to be kept by a registered person for any tax period and require that a registered person keep a 'VAT Account' containing a summary of the totals of output tax and input tax in the specified manner.

9.3 Invoices
All businesses making supplies of goods or services at the standard rate are obligated to issue a detailed tax invoice if the customer requests one. A tax invoice must contain a

number of items of information. Where a customer does not require a tax invoice to claim input tax but the supply is for more than TT$20 the registered person is required by the Act to give him a simplified tax invoice. The details required on this type of invoice are less onerous than the tax invoice required for claiming input tax. Gas stations, cinemas and fast food outlets are exempt from the requirement to issue a tax invoice even if the supply is over TT$20, unless a customer specifically asks for one.

9.4   VAT Returns

As a general rule registered persons are required to file returns on a bi-monthly basis by the twenty-fifth day of the month following the end of the reporting period. To even out the cash flow to the government and to assist the administration in processing the returns, these periods have been staggered with registrants filing in alternative months so that every month the VAT Administration Centre receives approximately half of the total number of VAT returns. VAT returns must be filed with one of the VAT regional offices, together with a cheque in settlement of the liability (where appropriate), on or before the due date.

Upon request the Board may allow persons who are almost always in a refund position to file monthly returns, for example: exporters, energy-based companies, diplomats and regional organisations. With the approval of the Board, quarterly, semi-annual or annual returns can also be allowed.

9.5   Powers of the Authorities

Under the VAT Act the Board has been given similar powers to those under the Income Tax Act. Some of these powers are as follows:

■   If, upon demand made by the Board, a person neglects or refuses to pay any tax or any portion thereof, the Board by warrant under its hand may allow an 'authorised person' to distrain the person charged by his goods and chattels. For the purposes of levying any such distress, the authorised person may break open, in the day time, any house or premises, calling to his assistance any police officer. The distress has to be kept for seven days and, if the person still does not pay, the distress shall be sold by public auction and any surplus after deducting for costs shall be returned to the owner of the goods distrained.

■   Where disputes as to assessments arise, the Board may by notice in writing ask any person to furnish a schedule containing such particulars as it may require, or to attend before it and give evidence with respect to his income, and to produce all books or other documents under his control relating to his income.

9.6   Estimated Assessments

The Board of Inland Revenue has the power to make estimated assessments in certain circumstances. It may assess the amount of tax that should be payable or the refund that should be due to a person where:

■   a person fails to furnish a return in accordance with the VAT Act

■   a person requests the Board, in writing, to amend a return that the person has furnished under this Act, or

■   the Board is not satisfied with a return made by any person or as to any matter on the basis of which the return was prepared.

In addition, where a person who is liable to be registered for VAT but has not done so makes a commercial supply, the Board may assess the amount of tax that would have been payable if he had been registered. The Board may also assess a person as being liable to pay an amount if that person falsely represents that tax is charged on the supply, or falsely represents the amount of tax charged on the supply, or wrongfully recovers or seeks to recover an amount represented to be in respect of tax.

9.7 Periods of Limitation
Except in cases of fraud or wilful neglect the Board of Inland Revenue has a period of six years to correct or assess a VAT return.

9.8 Penalties
When the VAT Act was first enacted the majority of the offences under the Act had to be prosecuted in a Magistrate's Court and this was a very lengthy process.

The Act was amended in 1992 to allow the Board to be able to issue infringement notices with respect to certain offences and these carried a lower penalty than the maximum that could be imposed by a magistrate. They are as follows:

Offence	Maximum Administrative Fine
Failure to display a certificate of registration	TT$500
Failure to notify the Board of a change in status	TT$500
Failure to file a return by the due date	TT$100
Failure to issue a tax invoice	TT$500

The major offences under the VAT Act that are punishable on summary conviction are:

Offence	Penalty on Summary Conviction
Where a person who is required to be registered but is not registered, makes a commercial supply	TT$15,000 and imprisonment for one year
A non-registered person charging VAT	TT$30,000 and imprisonment for two years
Failure to display a Certificate of Registration	TT$3,000 and a further TT$100 for each day the offence continues
Failure to file a return by the due date	TT$500
Failure to issue a tax invoice, when requested, in the format stipulated	TT$3,000
Failure to keep proper books and records.	TT$15,000 and imprisonment for one year
Certain penalties imposed administratively, including failure to make payment of VAT to the Board by the due date	Penalty of 8% of the amount outstanding and interest at the rate of 2% per month or part of a month.

9.9 Objections and Appeals
Decisions on assessments may be appealed against in the first instance internally to the VAT Objection Section, secondly to the Tax Appeal Board, thirdly to the Court of Appeal and finally to the Privy Council in England.

10 SPECIAL VAT REGIMES

10.1 Free Zones and Bonded Warehouses

Bonded warehouses and free zones are designated enclosed areas in which goods may remain without liability for VAT arising at importation. The government has designated certain areas as free port areas and it has also recently designated the areas used by certain enterprises as a free zone.

10.2 Supplies to Fishermen

Where a person imports capital equipment such as marine engines, fishing nets and boats solely for the purpose of carrying on the business of commercial fishing, that person may apply to the Minister responsible for marine exploitation to have the VAT waived.

On approval by the Minister, the Customs and Excise Division will allow entry of the imported goods at 0%.

A person who intends to purchase capital equipment in Trinidad and Tobago for the purpose of commercial fishing must obtain a pro-forma invoice in duplicate from his supplier detailing the item to be purchased and the amount of VAT applicable. He can then submit this to the Minister responsible for marine exploitation, together with an application for waiver of VAT.

On obtaining a certificate of waiver from the Minister, the person can present this to the equipment supplier who then makes the supply as if no tax is payable on it, ie, the supply of the capital equipment is zero-rated and the commercial fisherman pays no tax on the purchase.

10.3 Second-Hand Goods

Current VAT legislation does not contain any special provisions for the treatment of second-hand goods.

However, where a person purchases a used motor vehicle from a person registered under the VAT Act the purchaser will be exempt from Transfer Tax on producing to the Licensing Authority a Tax Invoice showing that VAT was paid.

Contributor: Nigell Romano
Principal
Ernst & Young, Port of Spain
P.O. Box 158
Port-of-Spain
Trinidad
Tel: +1 809 623 1005/9
Fax: +1 809 623 1314

UNITED STATES OF AMERICA

1 GENERAL BACKGROUND

The United States system of government is a federalism with federal and state governments sharing responsibilities and authorities. Powers not delegated to the federal government under the United States Constitution are reserved for the states. To the extent state tax laws do not conflict with the United States Constitution and laws, the taxing rules of each state are supreme within the boundaries of that state's taxing jurisdiction. Most states authorise their political subdivisions, including counties and municipalities, to impose local taxes. The multiple levels of taxing authority in the United States distinguish taxes in the United States from taxes in most other countries and present challenging issues of co-ordination and harmonisation.

The United States federal government does not currently have a value added tax (VAT). However, many types of consumption tax are currently being considered, including a value added tax, personal expenditure tax and business transfer tax. For the purposes of this chapter, all consumption taxes will be referred to as value added taxes.

Although the federal government does not have a VAT, most state governments in the United States have a retail sales tax (RST) and two states have more traditional VATs. This chapter focuses on these existing VAT systems, while the attached appendix discusses in detail the background and current developments concerning congressional consideration of a federal VAT. If a federal VAT is enacted, supplements to the chapter will be available free of charge from your local Ernst & Young office.

1.1 Federal Government

The first significant VAT proposal was introduced in 1980 as a credit-method, destination-based VAT. Several VAT proposals are currently before Congress. One of them would adopt a 5% VAT with no exemptions. The revenues generated would be used to reduce the federal budget deficit and fund health care reform. A second proposal would replace the individual and corporate income taxes with two consumption taxes: a progressive-rate income tax on consumption for individuals and a flat-rate tax on cash flow for businesses. A third proposal would replace the corporate income tax, the payroll tax and most of the individual income tax with a subtraction method VAT. Finally, a fourth proposal would adopt a two-part, flat-rate consumption tax to replace the current corporate and personal income taxes.

The question is frequently asked: 'Why is the United States one of the only developed countries in the world without a (federal level) VAT?'. Unlike most tax systems in the European Union, there is no existing indirect taxing system in the United States that pyramids the effect of turnover taxes. Also, the need to create fiscal harmony among Member States of the European Union is not similarly perceived in the United States. Third, the United States operates under a federal system which would require reconciliation of

---

This chapter reflects the position on VAT in the United States of America as at 31 May 1995

federal and state taxing systems. Finally, there is the belief that a VAT would allow the federal government to increase taxes with less accountability to its citizens.

1.2   State and Local Governments

State VAT was first proposed in the United States, at least technically, by Hawaii when it was still a territory. The second VAT introduced was a subtraction-method VAT imposed by Michigan in 1953 and revoked in 1968. Michigan reimplemented the tax, now called a single-business tax (SBT), in 1975. The third VAT was imposed by Minnesota but was declared by the Minnesota judicial system to violate the Minnesota constitution. The fourth VAT is the New Hampshire Business Enterprise Tax (BET) adopted in 1970.

Several other states have considered introducing VAT, including California, Florida, Georgia, Indiana, Texas, and West Virginia. Meanwhile, Hawaii, Indiana, and Washington impose a gross receipts tax.

Forty-five of the fifty states and the District of Columbia impose a retail sales tax (RST). RST is typically imposed by states on the sale of tangible personal property to final users within the jurisdiction. However, it may also cover certain services. Municipalities and counties may sometimes levy RST with the consent of the state. In a number of states, including California, Michigan, Washington, and Minnesota, the legal liability for the tax is on the seller rather than the purchaser.

1.3   State RSTs

RSTs were first adopted by state and local governments during the economic depression of the 1930s. At that time, land values and income from real property fell far more rapidly than did property taxes. Foreclosures to pay property taxes were common and pressure was put on local governments to diversify their revenue sources. Several state and local governments adopted RSTs in order to meet the pressing revenue demands brought on by these depressed economic conditions.

The use tax is a complementary tax to RST. Initially, the use tax was enacted separately from the sales tax. It was developed to protect state sales tax revenues from reduction due to purchases of goods outside the state. It was also developed to protect state merchants from loss of business to neighbouring states that have either no sales tax or a lower sales tax. Sales and use taxes are not exactly equivalent in all states and credits are usually allowed against use taxes to avoid double taxation. Although this chapter will focus on RST, it should be noted that a complementary use tax exists.

1.4   Michigan Single Business Tax (SBT)

The Michigan SBT is a consumption-type VAT that was adopted in 1975 to replace seven business taxes. It marked a return to the VAT business concept that prevailed in Michigan from 1953-1967 in the form of a business activity tax. This modified VAT measures the use of labour and capital in the business activity. The base of the tax is essentially profits, compensation and interest paid, less the purchase of depreciable property during the tax year. Various credits and deductions are also provided for. The tax rate is 2.35% of the adjusted tax base.

1.5   New Hampshire Business Enterprise Tax (BET)

The New Hampshire BET is imposed on the compensation, interest, and dividends paid by taxpayers engaged in business activities in New Hampshire. It is applicable to returns, taxes, reports, and fees due on account of taxable periods ending on or after 1 July 1993.

2   WHO IS TAXABLE?

2.1   Retail Sales Tax

RSTs are designed primarily to tax consumers on purchases of tangible personal property and certain services. The tax applies to ultimate consumers of the final product in the economic process and also to consumers who purchase tangible personal property at an intermediate stage in the economic process whereby the property is consumed by the purchaser. A minority of the states impose the RST liability on the seller rather than the purchaser.

2.2   Michigan SBT

The Michigan SBT must be paid by every person who has business activity within Michigan which is allocated or apportioned to the state. The requirement to file an SBT return is not imposed on a taxpayer unless the taxpayer falls within the definition of a 'person' and has business activity within Michigan.

A 'person' under the Michigan SBT consists of: an individual; a firm; a bank or financial institution; a limited partnership, co-partnership or partnership; a joint venture; an association; a corporation; a receiver, estate, or trust; or any other group or combination acting as a unit.

2.3   New Hampshire BET

Business enterprises carrying on business activities in New Hampshire with gross business receipts in excess of $100,000 during the taxable year, or an enterprise value base greater than $50,000, are subject to BET. Partnerships and limited liability companies are deemed to be taxable business enterprises. Tax-exempt organisations – such as religious, scientific, charitable, and educational organisations – are not subject to BET.

3   WHAT IS TAXABLE?

3.1   Retail Sales Tax

RST generally applies to the sale or transfer of tangible personal property to final consumers within a jurisdiction. In addition, the provision of certain enumerated services (generally non-professional services) may also be subject to RST.

A typical RST statute may impose tax on the receipts from retail sales of tangible personal property, including pre-written computer software; sales of gas, utilities and telephone and telegraph services; telephone answering services; and sales of such services as:

- information services
- processing and printing services
- installation, repair and maintenance services performed upon tangible personal property
- storage
- real estate maintenance, service and repair

- motor vehicle parking and garaging services
- interior decorating and designing services
- protective and detective services
- telephonic and telegraphic entertainment and information services.

RST may also be imposed on:

- food and beverages sold by restaurants and caterers
- occupancy of hotel rooms
- admission charges
- social or athletic club dues
- roof garden or cabaret charges.

Sales or purchases are transactions that involve the transfer of title and/or possession, exchange or barter, rental, lease or licence to use or consume (including the right to reproduce computer software), conditional or otherwise, in any manner or by any means whatsoever for a consideration, including the rendering of any taxable service for a consideration.

3.2   Michigan SBT
Michigan SBT taxes 'the privilege of doing business', not income, although income is a major component in the tax base. The starting point for determining the Michigan SBT tax base is United States federal taxable income. Various statutory modifications are made to arrive at the Michigan tax base, including those required to reverse the effects of the Internal Revenue Code amendments made after the Michigan tie-in date. Additions include: income from obligations of other states; income and SBT taxes; net operating loss carrybacks/carryovers; compensation paid; dividends, interest, or royalties paid; losses attributable to another taxable entity; and special deductions. Subtractions include: dividends, interest or royalties received; capital losses not deducted in computing federal taxable income; and gains attributable to another taxable entity.

3.3   New Hampshire BET
BET is imposed on the sum of all compensation paid or accrued, interest paid or accrued, and dividends paid by a business enterprise engaged in business activities in New Hampshire.

4   PLACE OF SUPPLY

The place of supply is usually the place where the goods are delivered. A vendor is obliged to collect a state's RST where such vendor has business operations within the state and if the product is received, transferred, or delivered within the state.

5   BASIS OF TAXATION

5.1   Retail Sales Tax
In the most basic cases, the consideration for a supply is the value in money, namely cash passing, without any deduction for expenses or payment discounts, but including any charges by the vendor to the purchaser for shipping or delivery. Where barter trading is involved, the consideration is deemed to be the value of the goods or services tendered in

exchange. Where the consideration does not consist or does not wholly consist of money, the value of the supply shall be taken to be its open market value. Free supplies of goods or services (where there is genuinely no consideration in return) do not give rise to a tax liability, although where goods or a succession of goods are given away in the course of business, then that is deemed to be a supply of the goods. Further, sales transactions between related parties are generally taxable. Special anti-avoidance provisions apply to sales between related persons, allowing states to impose open market value when they believe the price has been artificially depressed.

5.2   Michigan SBT

The calculation of the tax base begins with United States federal taxable income. The following additions are then made:

- income from obligations of other states
- income and SBT taxes
- Net Operating Loss carrybacks or carryovers
- carryback or carryforward of capital losses
- certain depreciation or amortisation
- dividends, interest or royalties paid, except oil and gas royalty income, cable television franchise fees, and 50% of other franchise fees
- compensation paid
- capital gains deduction of individuals if related to business activity
- special deductions or exclusions
- loss attributable to another taxable entity.

The following subtractions are then made:

- dividends, interest or royalties received, except oil and gas royalty income and 50% of franchise fee
- capital losses not deducted in computing federal taxable income
- gains attributable to another taxable entity.

These additions and subtractions result in the Michigan tax base which, after allocation or apportionment and additional adjustments, equals the Michigan adjusted tax base. These additional adjustments include an addition for proceeds from sale or disposition of tangible assets and a subtraction for the cost of acquiring tangible assets, business loss, and specific exemptions. This Michigan adjusted tax base may be subject to further adjustment at the taxpayer's option.

5.3   New Hampshire BET

The BET base is determined by adding a taxpayer's interest, dividends and compensation paid during a taxable year. Taxpayers which operate both in New Hampshire and elsewhere determine the BET base by applying special apportionment factors to each of its components. Compensation is apportioned according to the payroll factor used for the purpose of business profits tax. Interest is apportioned by a fraction comparing New Hampshire real and tangible personal property to total real and tangible personal property. New Hampshire dividends are determined by applying a three-factor formula, two factors for compensation and interest, and a third factor based on sales.

The BET base is reduced by the amount of dividends received from an affiliated entity if such dividends have previously been included in the payer entity's BET base. For purposes of this deduction, affiliation is determined according to principles of the Internal Revenue Code.

6   TAX RATES

6.1   Retail Sales Tax

Rates of RST for sales, use, and rental tax rates vary according to which taxing jurisdiction is involved. Different rates may also apply to repair services, installation services and freight. When taxable, non-standard rates also frequently apply to production machinery, farm equipment, motor vehicles and building materials.

6.2   Michigan SBT

SBT is imposed at the rate of 2.35% on the adjusted tax base.

6.3   New Hampshire BET

BET is imposed at the rate of .25% on the adjusted tax base.

7   EXEMPTIONS

7.1   Retail Sales Tax

Since the goal of RST is to limit the tax to retail purchases by the final consumer, sales for resale are exempted. 'Sales for resale' are sales to wholesalers, retailers, or others who resell the goods they purchase. Items purchased for use in manufacturing, fabricating, or processing personal property for sale are also usually exempted where the item becomes an ingredient or component of the product to be sold. The theory behind these exemptions is to prevent burdening the final consumer with higher prices that reflect the additional tax on the producers in addition to the sales tax itself (ie the 'cascading' effect).

Exemptions are usually allowed for manufacturing equipment and supplies that do not become a component part or an ingredient of the goods produced for sale. For example, this usually applies to chemicals which are used in the process but which do not become part of the product. Where such property is taxed, it is based on the theory that it is consumed by the manufacturer. However, taxing such goods results in a 'pyramiding' of sales taxes and therefore many states either exclude or exempt from tax the purchase of machinery that is to be used directly in manufacturing or processing goods produced for sale to consumers.

Various exclusions also exist with respect to services subject to RST. These may include interstate and international telephone services; information services that are personal or individual in nature; information services used by newspapers and radio and television broadcasters in the collection and dissemination of news; and services rendered by advertising agents or other agents or persons acting in a representative capacity.

In addition to exclusions from RST for certain types of property and services, receipts from the following may be expressly exempted from the state's sales or use tax: food, other than that sold by restaurants and caterers; drugs, medicines and medical equipment, and health products; and installation, repair and maintenance services.

Further exemptions often exist in the following areas:

■ property used directly and predominantly in research and development, including related fuel and utilities
■ packaging materials such as cartons, containers, and wrapping for use in packaging tangible personal property for sale
■ farming and fishing
■ publications
■ telecommunications
■ customer computer software
■ transportation
■ interstate or foreign commerce.

Exemption policies may be guided by the nature of the buyer, such as sales to governmental bodies or exempt organisations (eg religious, scientific, charitable and educational organisations). They may also be guided by the nature of the transaction, which is determined by the state's interpretation of the predominant business activity. Further, they may be guided by the frequency of the sale, such as whether the sale is isolated, casual, or occasional.

7.2   Michigan SBT
The first $45,000 of the adjusted tax base of every person is exempt. This exemption is increased by $12,000 for each partner and shareholder of a flow through corporation ('S corporation') or a professional corporation, to a maximum of an additional $48,000.

7.2.1 Government
SBT is not imposed on sales made by the governments of the United States, Michigan and other states, or by their agencies, political subdivisions and enterprises.

7.2.2 Tax-exempt Entities
In general, organisations that are exempt from federal income tax under the Internal Revenue Code (religious, scientific, charitable, educational, etc) are exempt from SBT, except to the extent of unrelated business income. The following organisations, however, are not exempt:

■ certain local benevolent life insurance associations, mutual ditch or irrigation companies, and mutual or co-operative telephone companies
■ certain farmers' co-operatives
■ certain civic leagues, non-profit social welfare organisations, or local associations of employees.

If a taxpayer is exempt from federal taxation only as a result of a treaty between the United States and a foreign country, the taxpayer would not be exempt from SBT.

7.2.3 Non-profit Co-operative Housing Corporations
Non-profit co-operative housing corporations are exempt from SBT in regard to housing services provided to their stockholders and members.

7.2.4 Agricultural Production Activities
Agricultural production activities are also exempt to the extent that they are performed by a

person whose primary activity is farming. The determination of whether a person's 'primary activity' is the production of agricultural goods is based on the value added in the tax base computation for both farm and non-farm activity.

7.2.5 *Insurance Companies*

Insurance companies are exempt from SBT on the first $130 million post-apportionment disability insurance premiums written in Michigan. This exemption does not extend to credit insurance and disability income insurance premiums. Where the insurer's gross premiums from insurance carrier services exceed $180 million, this exemption is reduced by $2 for each $1 of the excess.

7.3 *New Hampshire BET*

Certain small businesses (with gross business receipts of less than $100,000 or a BET base of less than $50,000) are exempt.

8 CREDIT/REFUND

8.1 *Retail Sales Tax*

There is no credit/refund mechanism for RST similar to a credit-method VAT.

8.2 *Michigan SBT*

8.2.1 *Small Business Credit*

A corporation whose adjusted business income is less than 45% of tax base is entitled to a small business credit provided that the corporation's gross receipts do not exceed $7.5 million, adjusted business income does not exceed $475,000, and no shareholder or officer has allocated income in excess of $95,000. The gross receipts limit is measured on a consolidated basis for members of a controlled group. Members of controlled groups must calculate the small business credit on a consolidated basis and allocate such credit among the members of the group.

Adjusted business income is business income plus loss carryforwards and carrybacks and compensation and directors' fees of active shareholders and officers. An active shareholder is one who owns at least 5% of outstanding stock of the corporation and who receives at least $10,000 in compensation, director' fees or dividends from the corporation.

A shareholder's or officer's allocated income for taxable corporations ('C Corporation') is compensation and directors' fees, or compensation and directors' fees plus the shareholder's share of business income/loss. A shareholder's share of business income/loss is computed by multiplying the company's business income/loss by the shareholder's ownership percentage in the company. For S corporations, compensation of officers of an S Corporation is not considered. The allocated income of a shareholder of an S Corporation is his compensation, director' fees and share of business income/loss.

To compute the credit, adjusted business income is divided by 45% of the tax base. This amount is then subtracted from 100% to determine the allowable percentage. If adjusted business income exceeds 45% of the tax base, no credit is allowed. If adjusted business income is negative, the percentage is 100%. If gross receipts exceed $6 million, the percentage is multiplied by 100% minus the ratio of gross receipts in excess of $6.5 million to $1 million to determine the credit.

The small business credit may also be computed as the amount by which the small business tax before credits exceeds 4% of adjusted business income. Taxpayers are allowed to claim the greater amount of credit calculated under the two methods. If the calculation is based on 4% of adjusted business income, the adjustment to the credit for gross receipts in excess of $6.5 million does not apply.

8.2.2 Credit for Taxpayer Electing Subchapter S Provisions
A credit is allowed for S corporations against the SBT liability. The credit is a percentage of the single business tax liability after the small business credit. The credit ranges from 10% to 20% depending on business income. For S corporations with business income of $40,000 or more, the allowable credit is 10% of the single business tax liability after the small business credit.

8.2.3 Other Credits
Various other credits are also allowed against the SBT, including a credit for certain contributions and a public utility tax credit.

8.3 New Hampshire BET
Any BET liability may be credited against the taxpayer's business profits tax liability. Unused credit amounts may be carried forward for five years. Effectively, this credit mechanism ensures that profitable businesses which pay business profits tax will not experience any increase in overall tax liability as a result of the enactment of the BET.

9 ADMINISTRATIVE OBLIGATIONS

9.1 Retail Sales Tax
The burden of collection is placed on the seller, who is obligated to register with the particular state, file returns and pay taxes. This burden requires the seller to account for all taxes and exemptions, if any. Failure of the seller to meet this burden results in assessment against the seller.

This burden is met by having on file exemption certificates from customers showing the buyer's state registration number, a description and exempt purpose of the property purchased, and the buyer's signature. The seller must also exercise care to determine that the property being sold is of a type normally sold to that customer for that customer's exempt purpose.

It may be the buyer's responsibility to claim its exemption or else risk assessment of tax where none was required. The use of vendors as agents of the state for collection purposes facilitates administration of the tax and allows states to maintain control over businesses through the registration process.

A large portion of cost in administrating RST consists of audits conducted regularly by state enforcement agencies. These audits are designed to uncover deficiencies in a seller's operations that lead to failure to charge tax, or to examine the taxpayer's purchases to verify that the correct amount of tax was paid on property acquired for taxable use.

9.2   Michigan SBT

The requirement to file an SBT return is imposed on every person whose allocated or apportioned gross receipts plus the capital acquisition deduction recapture are at least $40,000 for pre-1991 tax years, $60,000 for post-1990 and pre-1992 tax years, and $100,000 for post-1991 tax years.

The due date for filing the return and for payment is on or before the last day of the fourth month after the end of the tax year. Extensions may be granted by the Commissioner of Revenue upon a taxpayer's application and for good cause shown.

Estimated tax returns must be filed by taxpayers reasonably expecting SBT liability in excess of $600 or special adjustments to the tax base in excess of $100,000.

9.3   New Hampshire BET

Generally, BET returns are due on the same day as federal income tax returns. No estimated returns or payments are required with respect to BET.

10   SPECIAL VAT REGIMES

A wide variety of special rules apply to services, financial institutions, manufacturing, insurance companies, and certain other groups and industries.

BIBLIOGRAPHY

Tax Executives Institute, *Value Added Taxes, A Comparative Analysis*, 1992.

Weinberger and Garrett, *A National Consumption Tax, Why, What, and When*, Working Outline, 1993

Tait, *Value Added Tax, International Practice and Problems,* 1988.

Ernst & Young Accelerated Multistate Tax Training Program Materials, 1994.

CCH State Tax Reporter, Michigan, Volume 1, Single Business Tax

CCH State Tax Reporter, New Hampshire, Business Enterprise Tax.

APPENDIX

BACKGROUND OF UNITED STATES VAT

1   INTRODUCTION

The United States is one of the few industrialised countries without a federal tax imposed on the value added at each stage of the production and distribution process. Several reasons have been proffered as to why this type of 'consumption tax' has never been enacted in the United States. First is the fear expressed by state and local governments that a federal VAT would limit their ability to collect sales tax revenue. Concern has also been raised over VAT regressivity. Another explanation focuses on the accountability of the United States Government. A fear exists that a VAT may create a new government 'money machine' that will lead to more spending and more tax rate increases.

Nevertheless, because the United States federal budget deficit has worsened in recent years and proposals to increase income taxes have become increasingly controversial, policy makers have once again begun to mention the possibility of the adoption of a federal VAT. The possible gains appear significant. For example, a recent Congressional Research Service study found that the imposition of a broad-based VAT would generate net revenue of $27.7 billion for every 1% levied (assuming it coincides with reductions in personal and corporate income and social security taxes that would offset 25% of new VAT revenues). In addition, the Congressional Budget Office's list of spending cut and tax increase options for 1994 suggests that a 5% VAT imposed on a broad consumption base would increase net revenues by about $96 million in the fiscal year 1996 and $608 billion through 1999.

In addition to the potential for reducing the federal deficit, the enactment of a federal VAT would encourage savings and investment. Compared with the United States income tax (which taxes the return to savings and investment) a federal VAT would probably encourage savings and investment and could improve the nation's economic health.

Furthermore, the adoption of a federal VAT may increase the United States' competitiveness abroad. In the last 25 years, more than 75 countries (including many major United States' trading partners) have adopted some form of a national, border-adjustable consumption tax (ie a consumption tax that is rebated on exports and levied on imports). Replacement of some or all of current United States taxes with a border-adjustable VAT would allow United States' businesses to avail themselves of the benefits available under GATT for their exports. Under existing GATT rules, indirect taxes (such as those imposed under a VAT) may be adjusted at the border, while direct taxes (such as the United States income tax and payroll tax) are not eligible for such adjustment. VAT proponents argue that, while imports from United States' trading partners have the VAT rebated and face little, if any, new taxes (other than tariffs), United States' exports do not receive any type of rebate for taxes paid and are subject to tax again upon arrival at the importing countries. Thus, two levels of tax are imposed on United States' exported goods, as opposed to the single level of tax imposed on the goods against which they compete. A change in the United States tax system to a border-adjustable VAT would increase the competitiveness of United States' firms in the international market and would level the playing field considerably.

A federal VAT in the United States would be unique from most currently existing VAT systems, since the United States system of government is a federalism with federal, state and local governments sharing responsibilities and authorities. Powers not delegated to the federal government under the United States Constitution are reserved for the states. Laws enacted by the various levels of government are not of equal weight. The United States Constitution prevails both over federal laws and treaties and over state and local laws, while federal laws prevail over state and local laws. Where state tax laws do not conflict with the federal constitution and laws, the taxing rules of the state are supreme within the boundaries of the state's taxing jurisdiction. The multiple levels of taxing authority in the United States (ie national, state and local levels) would distinguish any United States VAT from other VATs currently in existence in other countries and would present challenging issues of co-ordination and harmonisation.

2   UNITED STATES VAT PROPOSALS

The idea of a federal VAT or consumption tax is not new to the United States. In 1980, Congressman Al Ullman, Chairman of the House Committee on Ways and Means, introduced the Tax Restructuring Act of 1980. This Act included the first extensive VAT bill to be proposed in the United States. It suggested a credit-method, destination-based VAT levied at a 10% rate on the supply of goods and services within the United States and on the importation of goods. Ullman's proposal exempted persons with taxable transactions for the year that did not exceed $20,000 and contained special rules for insurance contracts and consumer goods. In addition, various goods would have been zero-rated.

In 1985, Senator William V. Roth introduced the Business Transfer Tax Act. This was essentially a subtraction-method VAT that would have been imposed at 5% on a taxpayer's net business receipts and would have allowed firms to credit their business transfer tax liability against their social security (FICA) liability. Under Roth's proposal, businesses with expenses in excess of receipts were not entitled to a refund. Instead, they were required to carry forward such amounts to future years.

Senator Hollings introduced a VAT bill in 1989 entitled The Deficit and Debt Reduction Act of 1989 and a VAT bill in 1991 entitled The Deficit and Debt Reduction Act of 1991. The 1989 bill was essentially the same as the 1980 Ullman proposal, but would have established a Deficit Reduction Trust Fund in the Treasury Department to which revenues raised by the VAT would be dedicated. The 1991 bill would have imposed a credit-method VAT at a 5% rate with no exemptions. Special rules were provided for the resale of second-hand consumer goods and the sale of property and services by governmental entities and certain non-profit organisations. Further, the 1991 bill would have taxed any non-business sale of property or services in the United States of more than $1,000, as well as any non-business leasing of property in the United States where the fair market value of the leased property exceeded $1,000.

Congressman Richard T. Schulze introduced two VAT bills: the Business Alternative Minimum Tax Act of 1986 and the Uniform Business Tax Act of 1991. The 1986 bill included a subtraction-method VAT that imposed a 7% tax on the sum of 'net business receipts' arising from the sale or rental of property used in the United States and the performance of services in the United States. Taxes paid on excess business expenses had to be carried forward as a business expense of the next taxable year. Various items were exempted, and various business expenses were allowed or exempted. Governmental entities, exempt organisations, and taxpayers whose gross receipts did not exceed $10 million were exempt from the tax. The 1991 bill would have imposed a subtraction-method VAT at a 9% rate on business receipts arising from the sale or rental of property, the performance of services, and the sale or use of intangibles in the United States. Various transactions and expenses were exempted. A special rule was provided for financial institutions and insurance companies. Both the 1986 and the 1991 VAT receipts would have been credited against the FICA tax.

In 1991, Congressman John D. Dingell introduced the 'National Health Insurance Act' which would have established a national health care programme funded by a 5% credit-method, invoice-based, destination-principle VAT on the sale of property or the performance of services in the United States. Dingell's bill would have zero-rated various items, including sales to governmental entities and sales of consumer goods. Small businesses with annual taxable transactions of not more than $20,000 could elect to be exempt, provided that they were not in the business of selling or leasing real property or importing property.

In 1992, the Business Activities Tax (BAT) was proposed by Senators Danforth and Boren. These senators organised a consumption-based tax working group to receive input from business leaders, scholars and government officials concerning the structure, economic effect and political viability of a consumption tax proposal. The goal was to propose a broad-based consumption tax on business activities to address the national deficit, unacceptably low consumer savings and investment, and United States economic isolationism. BAT revenues would have been used to eliminate the corporate income tax, reduce payroll taxes, and change the personal income tax system to address regressivity concerns.

Senator Hollings introduced another VAT bill in 1994 that proposed a broad-based, 5% VAT without exemptions and a cut in numerous programmes in order to reduce the deficit and finance various new reforms sought by the Clinton Administration and Congress. This VAT would be imposed on top of the current tax structure, and would not be used to lower any existing taxes.

Several other bills have recently been proposed which seek to replace existing tax policy with some form of consumption or value added tax. One proposal, made by Representative Gibbons, calls for the adoption of a subtraction-method VAT to replace the corporate income tax, payroll tax and a substantial part of the individual income tax.

Another proposal, introduced in 1994 by House majority leader Dick Armey, would replace the current individual and corporate income taxes with a single rate tax on both individuals and businesses. The tax base for individuals would consist of earned income reduced by a substantial standard deduction. The tax base for businesses would consist of gross income less the cost of business inputs and employee compensation. This reform proposal differs from a subtraction method VAT in two aspects. First, it permits businesses to deduct employee compensation. Second, it contains no deduction for export sales and no tax on imported business inputs.

A third proposal, introduced in 1995 by Senator Specter, would replace the current income taxes on individuals and businesses with a flat rate on individuals' earned income and businesses' taxable income. This proposal, entitled the Flat Tax Act of 1995, is very similar to the change proposed by House majority leader Arrney discussed above. However, there are two notable differences: it would impose a 20% flat rate tax on both individuals and businesses and would allow individuals a deduction for mortgage interest and charitable contributions.

Finally, a proposal by Senators Domenici and Nunn, titled the Unlimited Savings Account (USA) Tax, seeks the imposition of a progressive tax rate on consumed income for individuals with a tax similar to a subtraction method VAT for businesses. Although hearings on these and other tax reform proposals are expected later this year, no VAT or consumption tax is expected to be adopted in the immediate future.

3   COMPLEXITIES OF A UNITED STATES VAT

3.1   *Competing Interests*
One of the significant obstacles which a United States federal VAT faces is the competing interests between the federal government and state and local governments. Politically, the federal government must harmonise with the states and take into account the concerns of state and local governments.

An important issue with respect to any federal VAT in the United States is its relationship with retail sales taxes (RSTs) imposed by state and local governments. Because of the similarities between RST and VAT, state and local governments may view a federal-level VAT as limiting their ability to raise revenue through RST. State and local governments already have seen various factors affecting their revenues, such as reduced federal grant funds, lost federal revenue sharing, and growing public opposition to property tax increases.

States may also view any required conformance of their tax base with that of a federal-level VAT as a loss of their independence or sovereignty. They may also be concerned about possible taxpayer confusion that could occur as a result of state and federal level consumption taxes with different tax rates and bases.

On the other hand, there are possible benefits to state and local governments arising from a federal VAT. For example, the tax base of a federal VAT would be broader than that of a state or local retail sales tax, since it would probably include services in addition to tangible personal property. RST has traditionally extended only to tangible personal property with limited taxation of services. Thus, if this revenue is shared or the tax is harmonised with the states, it may provide additional revenues to state and local governments due to its broader tax base.

3.2   *Co-existing Tax Systems*
The implications of a federal VAT co-existing with state and local RSTs are significant. The existence of two separate tax systems and a resulting increase in compliance costs (eg multiple registration systems, different tax liability calculations, different inclusions and exclusions of goods) would add an additional layer of complexity to the application of RST to out-of-state purchases. This complexity could be reduced if exactly the same goods and services are zero-rated or exempted by both the states and the federal VAT, and the RST is 'piggybacked' onto the federal VAT. Here, the federal or state levels of government could act as administrator, collector, and distributor of the tax to the jurisdictions.

Co-ordination of a federal VAT with the state RST systems would probably be difficult, if not politically impossible. The base of any VAT is likely to be much broader than that of an RST. Also, state tax administrators and policy makers would be cautious in having their tax systems tied too closely with the federal system since little control could be exercised over federal level changes that eventually affect state and local levels. Some type of provision for a mutually agreeable sharing of consumption tax revenues among the jurisdictions among other things would probably be essential to mitigate state and local concerns regarding harmonisation.

3.3 Requests for Exemptions and Special Treatment
Any tax base for a federal VAT would undoubtedly be subject to requests for exemptions and special treatment from various political constituencies. Presumably, proponents of a federal VAT must balance the need for administrative simplicity with the need to recognise social policy issues and special interest groups.

3.4 Administrative Costs
An Internal Revenue Service (IRS) study on administrative issues in implementing a federal VAT found that an estimated 13.3 million entities would register for VAT and an estimated 53.5 million returns would be filed in the first year, assuming businesses with gross receipts under $100,000 were exempt. Further, an estimated 28,125 full-time employees would be required to administer the tax, and estimated administrative costs of $5.98 billion over the first four years of implementation would be incurred.

3.5 Current Interest in a United States VAT
There is significant current interest in a federal VAT in the United States. However, this is just a snapshot in time, as public views on the benefits of a United States VAT are constantly changing. Leading policy makers believe that the United States Congress is likely to at least debate a value added tax during the next few years. Indeed, many of the proposals discussed in this chapter have been introduced only to serve as the basis for a full discussion of a broad-based consumption tax and the issues that would be raised by such a change in the tax system. There is certainly no consensus on the type of VAT that should be considered or the purpose to which VAT revenues should be used.

Contributor: Philip Tatarowicz
Ernst & Young, LLP
Sears Tower
233 South Wacker Drive
Chicago, Illinois 60606
USA
Tel: +312 8792171
Fax: +312 8794025

URUGUAY

1   GENERAL BACKGROUND

The Value Added Tax Law (Law No 14.100) has been in force since 29 December 1972.

Value added tax (VAT) is levied on goods and services transferred or rendered in the territory of Uruguay and on the importation of goods to Uruguay. Exports and some specified services are exempted.

The tax is computed using the subtraction method, crediting taxes paid on purchases against tax liability arising from sales.

VAT is administered by the Tax Office.

2   WHO IS TAXABLE?

VAT is levied on taxable transactions carried out in Uruguay by the following persons:

- persons subject to income tax
- persons who perform independent personal services or professional activities
- government bodies performing industrial and/or commercial activities
- activities performed by municipalities which are in competition with the private sector except in the case of activities by municipalities in order to reduce the prices of basic goods
- activities of non-profit making organisations which are not related to their legal objectives.

3   WHAT IS TAXABLE?

VAT is levied on the supply of goods and services.

3.1   Supply of Goods
The supply or transfer of goods in Uruguay is taxable. Supply or transfer means the delivery of goods with the transfer of title of property or giving to the recipient the power to dispose of goods as if he was the owner. Sales, exchanges, expropriation, etc are included in this definition.

3.2   Supply of Services
The rendering of services within Uruguay is taxable. Rendering of services means any activity which is not a transfer of goods but which gives an advantage or profit to the provider.

This chapter reflects the legislation on VAT in Uruguay as at 31 December 1994.

3.3   Import of Goods

The final importation of goods is subject to VAT (importation under a temporary bond is exempt from tax).

3.4   Self-Supply of Goods/Services

A self-supply is the application by a taxable person of goods forming part of the business assets for his private use or that of his staff, or the supply of services carried out free of charge by the taxable person for his private use or that of his staff.

4   PLACE OF SUPPLY

Transactions are taxable if the goods are delivered or the services performed in Uruguay irrespective of the country where the contract is done or the domicile, residence or nationality of the persons involved.

5   BASIS OF TAXATION

VAT is payable on the amount invoiced including other taxes. An adjustment to the price originally invoiced is also considered to be part of the taxable basis.

If a discount is given or a bad debt occurs the VAT liability should be reduced accordingly.

In the case of imports, VAT is levied on the cost insurance freight (CIF) value plus any surcharges on importation.

6   TAX RATES

Currently there are two VAT rates:

12%: – white bread, fish, meat, edible oil, rice, salt, sugar, coffee, tea, common soap, medicines, etc
      – interest on loans granted to persons not liable to pay income tax
      – hotel services.

22%: all other supplies which are not taxed at the 12% rate or exempt.

7   EXEMPTIONS

7.1   Exempt with Credit for Input Tax

Exports of goods and certain services are exempt from tax but exporters are entitled to recover the input tax attributable to such supplies.

7.2   Exempt without Credit for Input Tax

Transfers and imports of certain goods are exempted from the tax including;

- fruits, vegetables and horticultural products in their natural state
- foreign currency, precious metals, documents and securities
- immovable property
- transfers of accounts receivable
- machinery for agriculture and property related thereto
- tobacco, cigars and cigarettes
- fuel produced from petroleum (excluding fuel oil)
- goods to be used in agricultural production and raw materials for the production of such goods. The Executive Branch lists the goods and raw materials covered by the exemption
- mutton and fish
- interest on securities and bank deposits
- transportation of passengers
- banking operations carried out by banks and similar institutions (excluding interest received from persons who are not liable to pay income tax)
- compensation for personal services related to the health of human beings
- supplies made by non-profitable cultural and similar institutions, financial investment companies and companies with revenues under Uruguayan pesos 92,000 (this amount is established annually by the Executive Branch).

8   CREDIT OR REFUND ON THE TAX

Taxable persons may reclaim input VAT through their monthly or bi-annual VAT returns. Where the amount of creditable input VAT exceeds the amount of output VAT payable the excess can only be set off against VAT and other taxes payable in the future. If the excess is caused because the rate of input tax is 22% and the rate of output tax is 12% then the excess is a cost and cannot be set off. In the case of exporters or persons engaged in prospecting and exploration for minerals, the excess may be set off against other taxes due or may be refunded on application to the authorities.

9   ADMINISTRATIVE OBLIGATIONS

9.1   Registration
Taxable persons must register with the tax authorities within 30 days of commencement of business.

9.2   Invoicing
Taxable persons are obliged to issue invoices with the following requirements:

- the number of the invoice
- the name and address and VAT registration number of the vendor
- the name, address and registration number of the buyer
- a description of the goods transferred or the services rendered
- the taxable amount of the transaction.

9.3 Tax Return

Tax returns must be filed within 25 days of the end of each tax period. A tax period is a calendar six months for most taxable persons but one month for those with a large turnover.

9.4 Records

Taxable persons must keep records which are sufficiently detailed for the correct amount of VAT payable to be readily quantified. Taxable persons must keep detailed records of all sales or services supplied and of all sales and services acquired (including copies of invoices issued and original invoices received) for a period of five years.

9.5 Powers of the Authorities

The authorities have extensive powers to examine the records of a taxable person's activities, make estimated assessments where they consider that tax has not been paid or insufficient tax has been paid, and impose penalties for late filing, late payment, failure to keep records, etc.

Generally, the authorities can impose assessments, penalties, etc for a period of up to five years after the transaction has occurred.

A taxable person may file an appeal with the tax authorities against a VAT Assessment Notice. The appeal must be filed within 30 days from the date of the Assessment Notice. If the tax authorities do not amend the tax assessment as requested, further appeals to the Tax Court or to the Supreme Court are possible.

Contributor: Luis Montone
Partner
Cr. R. Villarmarzo y Asoc.
A member of Ernst & Young International
Avda. 18 de Julio 984, 4th Floor
Palacio Brasil
P.O. Box 1303
11100 Montevideo
Uruguay
Tel: +598 2 923145
Fax: +598 2 921331

VENEZUELA

1   GENERAL BACKGROUND

Value added tax was introduced in Venezuela on 16 September 1993, and is the first sales tax ever imposed in Venezuela. This tax has rapidly become one of the most important sources of income for the government.

The current system works as a combination of a wholesale tax (IVM) and a surtax imposed on any luxury consumption and was enacted on 27 May 1994 by the President of the Republic, under the authority of the enabling law of 18 April 1994 which authorises the President to issue decree-laws on all necessary tax legislation.

Control of the IVM and luxury consumption taxes is vested in the Venezuelan Tax Administration (Ministerio de Hacienda) and includes administration, inspection, collection and enforcement of the above-mentioned law.

Decree 187 published in the Extraordinary Gazette No.4727 of 27 May 1994 is the principal legislation governing IVM.

On 28 December 1994, regulations relating to the IVM and the luxury consumption taxes were issued on the Extraordinary Gazette No.4827; such regulations define certain aspects that were not specified in the Decree 187, and also provide specific instructions and procedures with regards to registration, administrative procedures, calculations, etc.

2   WHO IS TAXABLE?

2.1   General
As stated in Article 4 of the Income Tax Law, the Venezuelan tax system is based on a territorial basis in the sense that any activity that is performed or considered to be based in Venezuela is subject to taxes in Venezuela.

All types of corporations in Venezuela except banks, insurance and re-insurance companies receive the same tax treatment. Partnerships are taxed indirectly through the partners.

The IVM law classifies those taxpayers required to pay this tax in two categories as follows:

Ordinary Taxpayers
The term 'ordinary' refers to those taxpayers who are subject to tax on a habitual basis, including:

- habitual importers of goods and services
- producers, industrialists, manufacturers, assemblers, packers, bottlers, and others that habitually perform activities involving transforming goods
- merchandisers making sales to juristic persons (corporations), producers, industrials,

---

This chapter reflects the legislation on VAT in Venezuela as at 31 December 1994.

612

constructors, suppliers, other merchandisers, and individuals who are independent suppliers of services or if their sales either exceed 12,000 Tax Units (TU) during the fiscal year prior to 1994 or if they estimate their sales over that limit in the nearest fiscal year to the beginning of activities.

■ those corporations and/or individuals that supply services to corporations and to individual merchandisers whose sales either exceed 12,000 Tax Units during the fiscal year prior to 1994 or whose sales are over that limit to the nearest fiscal year prior to 1994 or whose sales either exceed 12,000 Tax Units during the fiscal year prior to 1994 or whose sales are over that limit in the fiscal year following the beginning of activities. (Each tax unit is equal to Bs1,000, the rate being adjusted by the Tax Administration during the first 15 days of each year based on the Consumer Price Index provided by the Central Bank (Article 229 of the Organic Tax Code))

■ leasing companies and universal banks, for their leasing operations, but only over the amortising portion of the good's price or cost, excluding any interest involved. (Note: all kinds of financial institutions in Venezuela are ruled by the General Banking and other Financial Institutions Law)

■ bonded warehouses, for their storing services, excluding any issue of financial papers for the warranty of the goods stored.

Occasional Taxpayers
The term 'occasional' is defined as those importers of goods and services who are different from 'ordinary taxpayers' (see Article 3 numeral 2 and 3 of Decree 187 establishing the IVM and Luxury consumption taxes).

Election to Register
Persons who perform 'taxable' activities but who are not obliged to register and become taxable persons may elect to do so (see section 9.1).

2.2   Government Agencies and Companies
Any public (government) entity constituted under the form of mercantile societies, autonomous institutions and other entities decentralised from the Republic, State, and Municipalities, and any entity which could be created by such, are treated as ordinary or occasional taxpayers if they perform any of the activities described in section 3 below, even if such entities or agencies are exempt from other taxes or laws.

2.3   Transactions with Branch/Subsidiary
Subsidiaries of foreign or national firms which supply taxable goods and services in Venezuela enjoy special treatment as a result of IVM.

Transactions between branches of the same legal entity are not subject to IVM. Thus supplies of goods and services between a branch and its parent entity or another branch, regardless of their location, are not taxable events for IVM purposes.

3   WHAT IS TAXABLE?

The Venezuelan tax system defines the operations, transactions and activities subject to tax as 'taxable facts' and, in this sense, the 'taxable facts' that are considered subject to IVM are the sales and disposal of movable goods, final imports of movable goods, the supply of independent services within the country, and import of such services.

3.1   Sales of Movable Goods
The sale of movable goods involves:

- the transfer of ownership of tangible goods that can be transported or made in a definitive form, whatever classification given to the parts involved
- sales with reservation of rights
- the transfer of movable goods (excluding commodities) which gives rights similar to those of an owner
- any other transfer in a definitive form in which the higher value of the transaction identifies an obligation to provide movable goods.

3.2   Disposal of Movable Goods
The disposal of movable goods by an ordinary taxpayer is considered a 'taxable event' in the following circumstances:

- the taxpayer used the goods in the natural course of business
- the goods are destined to be used by the partners, directors, or any other personnel of the company
- a transfer to a third party
- the goods are missing from the inventory and their disappearance cannot be justified to the tax administration.

3.3   Imports of Goods
The import of any merchandise or goods destined to stay permanently in the country is a taxable event even if such goods are exempt from custom duties in Venezuela.

3.4   Supplies of Services
The following services are considered to be subject to IVM:

- repairs, maintenance and alterations to movable assets and real estate activities, even when the contractor supplies the materials, water, electricity, and garbage disposal services
- the leasing of movable goods and any other right to the use of such goods or rights with purpose of profit
- the leasing or allowing the use of goods destined to be used in a going concern located in the country
- the leasing or cession of intangible assets such as brands, copyrights, author rights, artistic and intellectual activities, scientific and technical projects, researches, manuals, computer programs, etc. Intangible assets regulated by the Industrial, Commercial, Intellectual, Property and Technological Transfers Law.

3.5   Imports of Services
The import of services is subject to IVM when any of the services mentioned in section 3.4 above are contracted abroad and are either performed or used (or at least considered to be used) in Venezuela (see section 4 below 'Place of Supply').

4 PLACE OF SUPPLY

4.1 Goods
The sale or disposal of movable goods will be taxable only if the goods are located within the country at that time.

The importation of goods will be considered territorial, and therefore taxable, as soon as the transaction becomes liable to taxes (see section 5.4).

4.2 Services
The supply of services will be considered territorial if they are performed within Venezuela even if they are either imported from abroad or contracted, improved, or paid for outside Venezuela.

In the case of international transportation, only part of the service is considered to be supplied in the country. Therefore, only 25% of the cost of airfare and freight invoices issued in the country for each trip departing from Venezuela will be subject to IVM.

4.3 Reverse Charge
Where the seller of goods or supplier of services is not domiciled in Venezuela, the purchaser of the goods or recipient of the services will be the one responsible for the payment of the IVM. In the same way, commission merchants, authorised representatives, consignees, auctioneers and other representatives will be the ones responsible for the payment of IVM.

5 BASIS OF TAXATION/CHARGEABLE EVENT

5.1 Supplies of Goods in Venezuela
The invoice price shall be the taxable basis for the application of the IVM and Luxury Consumption Tax. However, if it is lower than the market value, the taxable basis will be the market value.

The taxable basis for industrial producers of alcohol, liquor, cigarettes and other tobacco products is the sales price excluding the national taxes, ie excise duties specifically attributable to such industries.

5.2 Imports or Supplies of Services in Venezuela
The amount subject to tax in respect of imports or supplies of services into Venezuela is the total amount invoiced for the service, including any transfer or supply of movable goods or the incorporation of such into the fixed assets. The value of the movable goods shall be included in the taxable base in each case.

In the case of imported incorporeal goods included or attached to a material support, such goods shall be valued and taxed separately.

When the payment for transfer of goods or supply of services is not made in money, the taxable base is the value agreed between the parties so long as such price is not lower than the market value. In the latter case, the taxable base will be the market value.

5.3   Imports of Goods

The taxable base for imported goods is the value at customs, including other taxes and expenses caused by the importation, but excluding the taxes mentioned in section 5.1 such as excise duty.

5.4   Additions to and Deductions from the Taxable Base

In order to determine the final taxable base for each good or service traded, the following extra charges should be added to the agreed price:

- adjustments, indexations or fixings of prices or values agreed before or at the time of making the contract; any commissions, interests, expenses of all kind or reimbursements, with the exception of any payments made on behalf of the purchaser or receiver of the service (payments related to the service), and excluding also any indexations already taxed
- the value of ancillary services provided in direct connection with the supply of movable goods and services such as packing, freight, transport, cleaning, insurance, warranties, storing, and maintenance
- the value of returnable packages/containers, or guarantee deposits for their return
- taxes related to operations are subject to IVM, excluding IVM taxes prior to the excise tax imposed on alcohol and cigarettes.

The taxable base should be reduced by:

- reductions in price
- normal discounts of a general character given at the time of the transaction, without special conditions.

Deductions from the tax base must be shown on invoices issued by the seller.

5.5   Transaction in Foreign Currency

When the taxable base is expressed in a currency other than Venezuelan bolivars, it must be converted to bolivars using the exchange rate provided by the Central Bank for the day on which the transaction occurred or, if such day is not a business day for banking purposes, the following business day.

With regard to imports, the conversion is made according to the Organic Customs Law and its regulations.

5.6   Chargeable Event

5.6.1 Supplies in Venezuela

Liability to IVM arises in respect of sales of goods, when:

- an invoice or its equivalent is issued, or
- the goods are paid for, or
- the goods are delivered.

In the case of a supply of a technical service such as electricity, telecommunications, cable television, disposal of garbage, or any other service provided by any technological means, liability arises at the moment that the bill or its equivalent is issued.

In the case of all other taxable services the liability arises when:

■ the invoice or its equivalent is issued, or
■ the service is performed, or
■ the service is paid for, or
■ when the invoice is required to be paid, or
■ the goods on which the service was performed are delivered or made available to the owner.

5.6.2 Imports

Imports of goods in a permanent form are liable to tax at the moment of filing the appropriate customs return.

Liability arises in respect of the importation of services such as technological services, instructions, or any other service which is subject to be registered or ruled by special laws and not subject to customs procedures or taxes, at the moment that the service is performed or received by the customer.

6 TAX RATES

The rates to be applied for IVM are fixed every year in the National Budget Law, subject to a minimum of 5% and a maximum of 20%. Tax related to luxury consumption is also new in Venezuela, being introduced in Decree 187 as a surcharge to luxury items subject to IVM. The extra rates are 10% or 20%, depending on the nature of the goods. The following are the rates currently imposed for IVM and Luxury Consumption Taxes:

0%:   exports of movable goods and services

12.5%: all goods and services which are not exempt, taxed at the zero-rate or subject to Luxury Consumption Tax

12.5%: plus 10% Luxury Consumption Tax:
– all kinds of alcoholic beverages
– cigarettes and all other tobacco products
– passenger or terrain vehicles with capacity for nine persons or less, whose factory value in Venezuela, or value in customs plus importation expenses, is equal in bolivars to a range between US$22,000 and US$44,000
– items manufactured with fine or cultivated pearls, precious or semi-precious stones, watches, pocket watches and similar to boxes of precious metals or plated in gold or platinum, etc
– items made of gold and silver work, and items made or plated with precious metals

12.5%: plus 20% Luxury Consumption Tax:
– cable TV services and the sale of video and films
– passenger or terrain vehicles with capacity for nine persons or less, whose factory value in Venezuela, or value in customs plus importation expenses, is equal in bolivars to an amount exceeding US$44,000
– yachts and other boats used for recreation and sports purposes

- motorcycles with more than 500 horsepower (cc)
- games activated with coins or chips and all other gambling activities
- fine fur coats
- satellite dishes.

7 EXEMPTIONS

7.1 Exemptions with Credit for Input Tax
The zero-rate, which carries entitlement to recovery of input tax and operates in the same manner as an exemption with credit.

7.2 Exemptions without Credit for Input Tax
Persons who supply exempt goods or services do not charge IVM and are not entitled to recover any input IVM.

The following supplies are exempt from IVM:

- sales of intangible movable goods such as fiscal stamps, shares, bonds, mortgages, mercantile documents, accepted invoices, financial papers issued by corporations, and other securities in general, representing money or credit value, apart from property rights over tangible assets and loans in money value
- sales made within the duty free zones or areas under special regimes
- food and products destined for human consumption such as meat, ham, salami, sausage, vegetables in their natural state, rice, cereals, flour and semolina, bread, pastas, eggs, canned tuna and sardines, dairy products, salt, sugar, coffee, oil, bottled non-carbonated water
- livestock
- concentrated food for animals and the raw material for its production
- medicines, and the material utilised in their preparation
- fuels derived from hydrocarbons
- wheelchairs, pacemakers, catheters, valves, artificial organs, and prostheses
- books, newspapers, magazines, as well as the paper used in their production
- cars, ships, airplanes, trains and wagons used for public transportation
- transactions and services provided by financial institutions (ruled by the general banking and other financial institutions law), including leasing companies and funds relating to the monetary market such as pension funds, credit institutions, retirement funds, co-operatives, stock markets, and savings and loans entities.
- insurance and re-insurance transactions and other operations, according to the special law regulating the sector
- services rendered under employment-type relation, according to the labour law
- imports of services described in section 8.3
- ground, aquatic, and air transportation within the country
- educational services provided by institutions registered in the Education ministry
- lodging, food services and related services to students, senior citizens, and disabled persons when the services are performed in institutions specially established for this purpose

- any services supplied to government agencies, not including commercial transactions, and work including intellectual performance
- medical services performed by public or private institutions, including those performed by individual physicians
- tickets to national parks, zoos, museums, cultural institutions, and all other non profit institutions exempt from income tax, tickets to movie theatres, cultural and sport events
- electricity for residential use, up to 800 kilowatts/hour per month, and residential telephone services up to 500 impulses per month, as well as the service provided in using pay phones
- water supply and residential services of garbage disposal.

7.3 Imports

The following types of imports are exempt from IVM:

- temporary imports of goods in accordance with customs legislation
- imports under the duty-free areas regulations
- food and products destined for human consumption such as meat, ham, salami, sausage, vegetables in their natural state, rice, cereals, flour and semolina, bread, pastas, eggs, canned tuna and sardines, dairy products, salt, sugar, coffee, oil, bottled non-carbonated water
- livestock
- concentrated food for animals and the raw material for its production
- medicines, and the material utilised in their preparation
- fuels derived from hydrocarbons
- wheelchairs, pacemakers, catheters, valves, artificial organs, and prostheses
- books, newspapers, magazines, as well as the paper used in their production
- cars, ships, airplanes, trains and wagons to be used in public transportation
- imports made by diplomatic and consular personnel according to international agreements subject to reciprocity
- imports made by international institutions or organisations of which Venezuela is a member and by their personnel, where there is an existing exemption according to international agreements
- imports made by international institutions or organisations that are exempt from any taxes according to international treaties
- imports made by travellers, passengers and crew members of ships, airplanes, and other vehicles, under the luggage customs regime
- imports made by government personnel serving abroad, so as long as the goods are used for family and personal purposes
- imports made by immigrants according to the customs regulations
- goods donated to non-profit institutions and universities
- bills and coins imported by the Central Bank
- imports of services supplied to government services, including commercial transactions and work involving intellectual performances.

8 CREDIT/REFUND FOR INPUT TAX

8.1 General

Similarly to the VAT system in other countries, the Venezuelan IVM system works as a function of fiscal debits and credits. The 'fiscal debit' in this case will be the amount resulting from the application of the corresponding rates (see section 6 'Tax Rates') to the taxable base on transactions subject to IVM. These debits shall be transferred to the purchaser or receiver of the goods or services traded.

Therefore, the 'Fiscal Credit' will be the amount of IVM invoiced by the seller or supplier of goods or services and paid by the purchaser or receiver of the goods or services.

The tax liability for IVM is calculated at the end of each month (see section 10.4 ' IVM and Luxury Tax Payments'), the amount of fiscal credits paid by the taxpayer being deducted from the amount corresponding to fiscal debits invoiced in the month.

8.2 Refunds for Input IVM

Where the fiscal credit exceeds the fiscal debit in any periodic return the excess will not be refunded (except for exporters) but may be set off against IVM due for other periods. Exporters who also make taxable supplies in Venezuela will be entitled to a refund for the IVM paid when purchasing (including importing) goods and services related to the exporting activity. The IVM refund paid to exporters has to be authorised by the Tax Administration, and can be made by requesting:

■ a special certificate for the amount of recoverable fiscal credit. These certificates can be used to pay other taxes, interests and fines and can be traded among other taxpayers or

■ a refund according to the administrative procedures established in the Articles 177 to 184 of the Organic Tax Code. Such procedures include the filing of a request for the credits with the Tax Administration. A decision on such a request must be made within two months. The refunds are usually granted in the form of credits against tax liabilities of the taxpayer and can also be traded to among other taxpayers.

9 ADMINISTRATIVE OBLIGATIONS

9.1 Registration

Every person or entity who supplies goods or services or who performs any activity which is subject to IVM and Luxury Consumption Tax is required to register at the Regional Tax Administration office in the corresponding district.

Taxpayers who have branches in several locations where they perform business and activities subject to this tax will be required to register individually before each Regional Tax Administration Office in each district. Each parent entity will be responsible for the payments payable by all US branch locations.

Merchants and suppliers of services who are not obliged to register (see section 2.2 'Ordinary Taxpayers') may elect to register and become taxable persons.

Once registered for the purposes of this law, taxpayers cannot be de-registered from the register unless they cease activities.

9.2   Books and Records
The Venezuelan Commercial Code requires merchants and all kinds of entities to keep, legalise, and update the following accounting and legal books:

- general journal
- general ledger
- inventory transactions
- shareholders' records book
- minutes of shareholders' and board of directors' meetings.

In addition to the above-mentioned books, all registered persons and entities subject to IVM and the Luxury Consumption Tax are required to keep full and detailed records of all transactions subject to these taxes, specifically books for purchases and for sales.

Such books must show a summary of the transactions for each month specifying the following:

- taxable base including all the adjustments applicable
- amount of fiscal debits and credits for the month
- summary of the sales of goods and supply of services exempt from IVM
- amount of exports of goods and services.

The Venezuelan Organic Tax Code requires registered persons to keep such records for six years from 1 January of the year following that in which the transactions take place (Article 51 of the Organic Tax Code).

9.3   Invoices
An inadequate invoice will deprive the recipient of the right to fiscal credit. All invoices and documents used as such must basically contain the following information:

- the word 'Invoice'
- must have a consecutive numeration
- the name and address of the taxable person or entity supplying goods or services
- RIF (Tax registration number) number of the supplier
- IVM registration number of the supplier
- address and telephone number of the parent company and branch suppliers
- date of issue
- name, address, IVM and RIF numbers, and telephone number of the person or entity that printed the invoices
- the name and address of the taxable person or entity receiving the goods or services
- IVM registration number of the receiver
- number and date of the delivery order or dispatch guide
- terms of the transaction (credit or cash, part payments, etc)
- description of the goods or the services provided, including quantity, unit price, total value of the sale, and payments involved

- specification of all additions and deductions, benefits and discounts to the base price of the goods or service being traded
- specification of the sub-total corresponding to the net price taxed, the amount corresponding to the IVM charged, and the total amount of the sale
- in the case of sales to persons or entities not subject to IVM, the amount corresponding to IVM shall be included with no detail in the total price of the sale.

9.4   IVM and Luxury Tax Returns and Payments

Every taxable person or entity must file a monthly return and pay the tax due for the appropriate month not later than the fifteenth day following the end of each taxable period (Article 30 of the IVM and Luxury consumption Tax Law).

Such IVM returns must show the sum of the fiscal debits included in all the invoices in the reporting tax period, as well as the sum of all the taxes charged and transferred as fiscal credits in the invoices received in the same period, including all the debit and credit notes related to those invoices.

The returns must also show the amount of fiscal credits carried forward from the prior month, and the ones to be carried forward to the next month. The total amount of sales which are liable to the surtax for luxury consumption must also be shown.

In the case of exports, the total amount of exports made in the month which are subject to the zero-rate must be specified.

All taxpayers are required to file monthly IVM returns even if no tax is due because, for instance, the amount of fiscal credits is higher to the amount of fiscal debits, or if the amount of fiscal debits is zero (0).

9.5   Powers of the Authorities

Authorised inspectors have extensive powers in regard to the inspection and seizure of records and there are penalties if an authorised officer is impeded or not provided with the information he requires.

Where a taxable person or entity either fails to make an IVM return or pay the appropriate amounts related to such tax, the authorities may issue an estimated assessment based on the correct figure or an estimate. This assessment may be appealed against.

The basis for an assessment will be the returns filed plus inventory comparisons between books and physical existence, and estimates of daily revenues for sales of goods and services.

9.6   Penalties

The Organic Tax Code establishes penalties and fines for non-compliance of certain formal requirements (Articles 99 to 108). Some examples are as follows:

Offence	*Penalty*
Failure to pay tax due	10% to 200% of the amount not paid
Underpayment of tax due	10% of the amount not paid
Late payment (under three months)	50% to 300% of the amount not paid
Late payment (more than three months)	Imprisonment from six months to three years.
Late filing	10 to 200 UT
No registration	50 to 150 UT
Failure to keep or to update books.	50 to 200 UT

10   FURTHER READING

Venezuelan Income Tax Law, May 1994
Wholesale and Luxury consumption Tax Law, May 1994
Regulations to the Wholesale and Luxury Consumption Tax Law, December 1994
VAT in Europe, Ernst & Young
Taxation In Developing Countries, Richard Bird and Oliver Oldman, 1990
Venezuelan Value Added Tax Law, September 1993
Comments on the IVM and Luxury Tax, Pérez-Mena, Everts, Báez, & Asociados, 1994
En Contacto bulletin, – Pérez-Mena, Everts, Báez, & Asociados, July 1994

Contributor: Edgar Dasilva
                 Perez-Mena, Everts, Baez Morales & Asociados
                 Edificio Mene Grande Piso 6
                 Los Palos Grandes – Caracas 1060
                 Venezuela
                 Tel: +58 2 2094272
                 Fax: +58 2 2855378

ASIA AND AUSTRALASIA

AUSTRALIA

1   GENERAL BACKGROUND

Australia does not have a value added tax; instead there is a wholesale sales tax (WST) on certain Australian manufactured goods and certain imported goods.

The WST applies to taxable goods at one point only, generally at the last wholesale sale, before they go into use in Australia.

A wide range of goods are exempt from WST, and those which are taxable are subject to several different rates.

The WST commenced operation in 1930 and, even though the relevant legislation was recently rewritten, the major concepts of this tax remain the same as they were over 64 years ago.

Over the last ten years it has often been suggested by politicians and business leaders that the WST be replaced by a value added tax. However, it is unlikely that this will occur in the near future.

The WST is administered by the Commissioner of Taxation through his department, the Australian Taxation Office (ATO).

2   WHO IS TAXABLE?

2.1   General
As WST is a wholesale tax, it is generally paid by manufacturers and wholesalers when selling taxable goods to retailers. In these circumstances the WST is shown on the invoice to the retailer and becomes part of the invoice price of the goods. However, the retailer does not generally show the tax on retail invoices, though the tax is usually passed on to consumers as part of the retail price.

Manufacturers and wholesalers also incur a liability to account for WST when they sell taxable goods by retail or apply them to their own use. However, in these situations the WST is still collected on the wholesale value of the goods, and there is no requirement for the invoice to show the amount of WST payable on the goods.

Under the WST legislation, every time goods pass through a sale (before they are sold by a retailer) they pass through an 'assessable dealing' and could in theory be subject to WST. Therefore, to ensure that taxable goods only bear tax once between manufacture/importation and consumption, the WST legislation provides a system of registration for those who manufacture goods or sell goods by wholesale. Every business that registers receives a numbered WST certificate. Registration is administered by the ATO.

This chapter reflects the law on Australian sales taxes as at 31 October 1994.

A business which purchases goods for resale by wholesale can quote its WST number to the vendor; the vendor is then obliged to sell the goods tax free. Thus, the payment of WST is deferred until such time as a purchaser of goods (generally a retailer) does not possess, or cannot quote, a WST number. The vendor is then required to charge WST by adding it to the invoice price at the applicable rate. The sales tax collected by the vendor is then remitted to the ATO.

Manufacturers are also permitted to quote their WST numbers to obtain business inputs (such as raw materials and manufacturing equipment) tax free.

2.2   Manufacturers

In general terms, a manufacturer is a person who engages in the manufacture of goods. 'Manufacture' in this context has its ordinary meaning, but also includes the following processes:

- primary production
- mining
- the developing of exposed photographic film
- the reproduction of video tapes and computer programs (in certain circumstances).

When manufacturers sell taxable goods they have manufactured to customers who cannot quote a WST number, those manufacturers are obliged to charge WST on the transaction and remit to the ATO the tax thus collected.

2.3   Wholesalers

Under the WST legislation, a wholesale sale is a sale of goods to a customer who will resell those goods. A wholesaler is thus a person who engages in making wholesale sales.

As noted above, wholesalers incur a liability to account for sales tax when they sell taxable goods to customers who cannot quote a WST number.

2.4   Retailers

A person who is purely a retailer cannot obtain a WST number. Consequently, a pure retailer will be charged WST by suppliers of taxable goods, but has no liability to account for WST when the consumer subsequently purchases the goods.

However, a retailer who is also a manufacturer or wholesaler can obtain a WST number, and will thus be liable, in some circumstances, to account for sales tax when selling taxable goods by retail.

2.5   Indirect Marketers

Under the WST legislation a retail sale of goods by a person who is not the manufacturer but who is a retail agent is known as an 'indirect marketing sale'. Such retailers ('indirect marketers') can register and obtain a WST number which they can quote when purchasing or importing taxable goods for resale via an indirect marketing sale. When the indirect marketer resells the taxable goods via an indirect marketing sale, it will have a liability to account for sales tax on those goods at the applicable rate.

The major indirect marketers in Australia are organisations such as Amway or Avon, who are also known as 'pyramid sellers' or 'direct sellers'.

2.6   Importers

Under the WST legislation the importation of taxable goods into Australia is an assessable dealing. Thus, if the importer of those goods intends to use the goods or to sell them by retail, WST is payable when those goods are imported. If the importer intends to resell the imported goods by wholesale, then the goods can be imported tax free, on quotation of the importer's WST number. The imported goods, like Australian manufactured goods, will then be subject to sales tax when they are subsequently resold to a customer who cannot quote a WST number.

2.7   Small Taxpayers

The WST legislation allows businesses whose annual liability to WST would be less than $A10,000 to opt out of the WST system. This means that such business cannot quote a WST number and must, like pure retailers, purchase all taxable inputs at a WST inclusive price. However, any goods manufactured or wholesaled by such businesses are exempt from WST.

2.8   Grouping Provisions

There are no grouping provisions in the WST legislation. This means that each group entity that is entitled to its own individual WST number must obtain it individually.

2.9   Government Bodies

In general, government bodies which manufacture goods have the same WST obligations as other manufacturers.

However, goods purchased by government departments and certain government authorities for their own use are exempt from sales tax, although such exemption does not apply to trading enterprises such as Telecom and Australia Post.

3   WHAT IS TAXABLE?

All goods manufactured in Australia or imported are taxable unless specifically exempted. However, goods that have passed into consumption in Australia are not subject to WST if they are subsequently resold by the consumer. Thus, for example, second-hand motor vehicles are not subject to WST.

Services are not subject to tax under the WST. However, if the selling price of taxable goods includes the value of any services supplied in manufacturing or distributing the goods, then the value of those services will form part of the taxable value of those goods.

4   PLACE OF SUPPLY

Australia is deemed to be the place of supply for WST purposes in respect of both goods manufactured in Australia which are not exported and of imported goods.

5   BASIS OF TAXATION AND CHARGEABLE EVENT

5.1   General

The amount upon which WST is payable is called the taxable value. Generally, the taxable value of goods is determined by their wholesale value, even though the taxable transaction or assessable dealing may be a retail sale or an application of goods to a taxpayer's own use.

5.2   Wholesale Sales

The taxable value of goods sold by wholesale is equal to the price for which they were sold. Consequently, since trade discounts and volume rebates reduce the selling price of goods, the taxable value of goods is also reduced by the amount of such discounts and rebates.

5.3   Retail Sales by a Manufacturer

The taxable value of taxable goods sold by a manufacturer by retail is equal to the 'notional wholesale selling price' of those goods. This notional price is the price for which the manufacturer could reasonably have been expected to sell identical goods by wholesale in an arm's length transaction.

Where the manufacturer sells the same goods both by wholesale and by retail it is relatively simple to calculate this notional price. The greatest difficulty in this area arises when a manufacturer only sells the relevant goods by retail.

In these circumstances the ATO has provided some guidelines to help manufacturers determine the appropriate taxable value of goods sold by retail. However, these guidelines are optional (see section 8.9 below on the effect of ATO rulings).

As a general principle, the notional wholesale selling price of goods will be less than the retail selling price.

5.4   Retail Sales by a Wholesaler

Wholesalers only have a liability to account for sales tax on their retail sales of taxable goods when they have purchased those goods tax free under quotation of their WST numbers. The taxable value in these circumstances is equal to the notional wholesale selling price of the goods.

5.5   Goods Applied to Own Use

In general terms, goods are applied to a taxpayer's own use when they are consumed by the taxpayer or given away free of charge by the taxpayer. The taxable value of any goods so applied is equal to their notional wholesale selling price if manufactured by the taxpayer, or equal to the price for which they were purchased if they were purchased under quotation of a WST number.

5.6   Indirect Marketing Sales

The taxable value of goods sold via an indirect marketing sale is equal to the notional wholesale selling price of those goods. Under a ruling of the Commissioner that is generally followed by indirect marketers, the notional wholesale selling price of goods sold via an indirect marketing sale is equal to the cost into store of the goods plus 35%. However, the ATO has recently announced that this taxable value will be altered in the next 12 months.

5.7   Special Rules

In certain cases special rules either include or exclude certain costs from the taxable value of taxable goods. For example, any royalties payable in connection with the manufacture or sale of taxable goods are included in their taxable value.

However, where computer software is embodied in (or in part of) goods, then the value of that software will not form part of the taxable value of the goods so long as the software is not embodied in a permanent microchip (ie a microchip that is neither reprogrammable nor erasable).

5.8   Chargeable Event

A liability to WST arises whenever goods are sold by a taxable person to a person who does not quote a WST number.

The net WST due must be reported and paid to the authorities within 21 days after the end of the month (or quarter in the case of smaller taxpayers) in which the taxable transaction took place.

6   TAX RATES

6.1   General

The general rule of WST classification is that all goods that have not previously gone into use in Australia are taxable at the rate of 21%, unless they are specifically exempted or specifically listed in the legislation as being taxable at some other rate.

The other common rates of WST are 11% and 31%, with special rates applying to passenger motor vehicles and wine.

11%:   In general, the goods taxable at 11% are, with some exceptions, domestic in nature. Examples include: household furniture, crockery, cutlery, glassware, and household drapery and soft furnishings. Bathroom fittings are also taxable at 11%, as are fruit juices, confectionery and biscuits.

21%:   Because of the general rule, the majority of goods are taxable at 21%. Examples include: pens, stationery and office supplies, computers, non-passenger motor vehicles, compact discs, video tapes, telecommunications equipment, etc.

31%:   The goods taxable at 31% are often labelled as 'luxury goods', and include: jewellery, fur garments, television sets, and cameras.

6.1.1 Rate Increases

From 1 July 1995, all the rates of sales tax, with the exception of those applicable to wine and luxury motor vehicles, have been increased by 1%.

7   EXEMPTIONS

7.1   General

There are two kinds of exemption that may apply to goods: unconditional exemption and conditional exemption.

7.2   Unconditional Exemption

Certain goods are unconditionally exempt, no matter who uses them or for what purposes they are used. Examples of such unconditional exemptions include:

- basic foodstuffs
- building materials
- clothing and footwear
- drugs and medicines
- fuel
- books and magazines.

7.3   Conditional Exemptions

There are two types of conditional exemption: that depending on the identity of the user, and that depending upon the type of use to which the goods are put. These exemptions serve to render otherwise taxable goods free of tax if the relevant requirements are met.

7.3.1 Exemption Based on the User

Goods for the use of bodies such as schools, public hospitals, charities and government departments are exempt from WST.

7.3.2 Exemption Based on Use

Uses which qualify certain goods for exemption from WST include mining, agriculture and printing.

7.4   Exemption Declarations

The WST legislation gives effect to conditional exemptions by providing for a system of exemption declarations. Thus, any person who does not have a WST number can obtain conditionally exempt goods free of tax by supplying the supplier with an exemption declaration.

A person who has a WST number can quote that number to acquire conditionally exempt goods free of tax.

7.5   Statutory Use Period

A person wishing to claim conditional exemption on any goods must intend when acquiring those goods to use them for the exempt purpose for the period of their effective life or for two years, whichever is the shorter.

7.6   Exported Goods

Goods that are exported prior to being used in Australia are not subject to WST. However, if exported goods that have not been used in Australia are subsequently reimported they will be subject to WST unless specifically exempted.

8   CREDITS

8.1   General

To ensure that WST is only paid once, at the correct rate and on the correct taxable value, the WST legislation provides that credits (or refunds) of WST are available in certain situations.

8.2   *Credit for Tax Overpaid*

Where a taxpayer overpays tax through using the wrong rate or taxable value, or even through clerical error, a credit of the amount overpaid may be claimed. However, before such a credit is payable it must be shown that the claimant did not pass the overpaid tax on to another person, or has refunded the overpaid tax if it was passed on.

8.3   *To Prevent Double Taxation*

A credit would also be available where a taxpayer purchased goods at a price including WST and then incurs a liability to account for WST when reselling the goods by wholesale.

8.4   *To Prevent WST Being Levied on Inputs*

It is a general principle that manufacturing inputs should not bear WST, as it is only the value of the manufacturing outputs that is supposed to be taxed. Hence, any taxpayer, other than those taxpayers who have opted out of the WST system (see 2.6 above), can claim a credit for any WST included in the price of business inputs.

8.5   *To Give Effect to Conditional Exemptions*

Sometimes a retailer may not know when purchasing taxable goods that those goods will be resold to another person who will be able to quote an exemption declaration. In these circumstances a WST credit will be due to the retailer, to ensure the relevant exemption has effect.

9   ADMINISTRATIVE OBLIGATIONS

9.1   *Registration*

As noted above, manufacturers and those who sell goods by wholesale can register for WST and receive a WST number. Registration is not compulsory for those eligible: however, it is wise from an administrative point of view.

9.2   *Books and Records*

Books and records must be kept by WST taxpayers for at least five years.

9.3   *Invoices*

If taxable goods are sold by wholesale to a person who does not quote a WST number, then the amount of tax payable on the goods must be shown on the invoice. There is no such requirement in regard to retail invoices.

9.4   *Returns and Payment*

The WST legislation requires all those registered persons who have made taxable sales to lodge returns showing the amount of tax payable. A remittance for the sales tax payable must accompany these returns.

If a taxpayer's annual WST liability is estimated to be under a certain amount (adjusted annually for inflation) then a return can be lodged, and the WST paid, within 21 days of the close of the quarter in which the relevant taxable transaction took place.

However, in most cases WST returns and payment are due within 21 days of the close of the month in which the taxpayer engaged in any taxable acts or transactions.

9.5   Penalties

Penalties are imposed by the ATO for the late lodgement of WST returns and for late payment of WST. The late lodgement penalty is currently 2% of the tax payable on the late return. The penalty for late payment is calculated at 16% per annum.

9.6   Assessments

Where the ATO considers that a taxpayer has paid too little WST on any transaction, it can issue an assessment requiring the taxpayer to pay further tax.

This usually occurs when the ATO considers the taxpayer has used an incorrect rate of tax or an incorrect taxable value, or has contravened one of the anti-avoidance provisions.

9.7   Anti-Avoidance Provisions

The WST legislation contains a general anti-avoidance provision which allows the ATO to attack any scheme entered into with the dominant purpose of avoiding WST.

In addition, the WST legislation requires a taxpayer selling to a related entity to account for sales tax on a taxable value that is equal to an arm's length price.

9.8   Objections and Appeals

Taxpayers can object in writing to assessments, decisions by the ATO to deny credits, and some other ATO decisions. These objections are reviewed by a different taxation officer to the one who made the assessment or the decision, and can be disallowed, upheld in part or upheld in full.

If the taxpayer's objection is disallowed or upheld only in part, then the taxpayer may have the decision on the objection reviewed by the Administrative Appeals Tribunal or the Federal Court.

9.9   Period of Limitation

Any WST unpaid after three years is automatically remitted, unless the ATO has by written notice required the payment of the tax within that period or the tax was not paid because of fraud or evasion.

9.10   Rulings

The Commissioner of Taxation is empowered to make written rulings as to the way in which the ATO will interpret and administer the WST legislation. These may be public rulings or private rulings provided to one taxpayer. However, they only bind the ATO and are not binding on taxpayers.

Further, if a taxpayer follows a ruling, the ATO cannot seek a retrospective adjustment if the ruling is later altered and more tax becomes payable under the new ruling.

10   FURTHER READING

Even though the Australian WST has a long history, few reference works refer to it. The only work of real substance is: *The Australian Sales Tax Guide*, CCH Australia.

Contributor: Peter Laverick
                 Ernst & Young
                 The Ernst & Young Building
                 321 Kent Street
                 Sydney
                 New South Wales 2000
                 Australia
                 Tel: +61 2 248 5555
                 Fax: +61 2 248 5314

BANGLADESH

1 GENERAL BACKGROUND

Value added tax (VAT) was introduced in Bangladesh with effect from 1 July 1991 under the Value Added Tax Ordinance (Ordinance No. XXVI of 1991), promulgated on 1 June 1991. The Ordinance replaced the Excise and Salt Act 1944 with respect to most excisable goods, the Sales Tax Ordinance 1982 and the Business Turnover Tax Ordinance 1982. VAT Ordinance itself was later replaced by the Value-Added Tax Act 1991 which was signed by the Acting President on 10 July 1991.

VAT in Bangladesh is of the consumption type (as opposed to income or gross product type) and is charged on consumer goods only (thus excluding capital goods).

As far as international trade is concerned, the destination principle has been adopted in preference to the origin principle. This means that, in relation to goods destined for consumers in Bangladesh, all added value is taxed at home. As a result, exports are zero-rated and imports are taxed.

2 WHO IS TAXABLE?

All persons are taxable who supply or import non-capital goods, who import non-capital goods and/or who supply certain services deemed by the law to be liable to VAT.

3 WHAT IS TAXABLE?

VAT is levied on:

- all goods imported into the country (except those listed in the First Schedule to the VAT Act 1991)
- all domestic supplies of goods (except those listed in the said First Schedule)
- all services listed in the Second Schedule.

3.1 Supply of Goods
'Supply of goods' means the transfer of the right to dispose of tangible property as owner.

Capital goods, both imported and domestically produced together with domestically produced unprocessed agricultural products, tobacco products, natural gas, textiles and petroleum products are not treated as supplies of goods for VAT purposes. However, imports of a specified list of goods is a supply for VAT purposes. Some goods imported or produced domestically are also exempted.

This chapter reflects the law on VAT in Bangladesh as at 31 October 1994.

3.2 Supply of Services

The term 'services' applies to all transactions which are not treated as a supply of goods.

The only services which are taxable under the VAT law are those listed in the Second Schedule to the VAT Act.

3.3 Imports of Goods

Unless specifically exempted the importation of all goods into Bangladesh is liable to VAT.

4 PLACE OF SUPPLY

VAT is chargeable in Bangladesh only when goods and services are supplied or deemed to be supplied in Bangladesh.

4.1 Supply of Goods

Where the goods are to be transported:

- if the goods to be delivered are in Bangladesh before transportation, the supply is taxable in Bangladesh unless they are export sales
- if the goods to be delivered are abroad before transportation, the supply is not subject to VAT in Bangladesh. VAT is nevertheless due on importation at the point of importation and payable by the importer or by the final customer in Bangladesh.

Where the goods are not transported:

- the supply is taxable in Bangladesh if the goods are in Bangladesh at the time of delivery or transfer of ownership.

Assembly or installation of goods in Bangladesh before they are delivered is also taxable in Bangladesh.

4.2 Supply of Services

Services are normally considered to be supplied at the place where the entrepreneur supplying the services is established or has a fixed base from which the services are supplied. Only certain selected types of services have been brought under VAT. Services like those related to education, health, housing and public administration have remained outside the tax net.

5 BASIS OF TAXATION

5.1 Imports and Supplies within Bangladesh

VAT is calculated on the total price charged for the supply of the goods or services inclusive of charges and commissions and, if applicable, supplementary duty and taxes (excluding VAT). This total must be declared and approved under the VAT Rules 1991. In certain cases, the cost of materials is excluded from the valuation base and no rebate is admissible.

The bases for assessment of VAT are as follows:

Category	VAT imposed on	Base for taxation or valuation
Import	Importer	Value of goods imported inclusive of customs duty and, if applicable, supplementary duty.
Domestic supply	Manufacturer/supplier	Manufacturer's price inclusive of charges and commissions and, if applicable, supplementary duty and taxes (excluding VAT) to be declared and approved under VAT Rules 1991.
Service	Provider of service	In general, gross receipts, excluding VAT and supplementary duty. (In certain cases, cost of all materials is excluded from the valuation base and no rebate is admissible.)

In addition, a supplementary duty at varying rates is levied on certain items listed in the Third Schedule to the Act. Such items include luxuries, non-essentials and socially undesirable goods.

5.2   Method of Computation of Tax Liability

A firm may compute its tax liability by the tax credit method rather than the account-based method, the former method being preferred in view of its compatibility with the consumption-destination type of VAT.

The tax credit method avoids direct calculation of value added; instead, the tax rate is applied to a component of value added (output and inputs) and the resultant tax liabilities are subtracted to arrive at the final net tax payable. Its other advantages are that the tax liability is linked to the transaction, and the invoice becomes the crucial documentary evidence, and it creates a good audit trail. Further, any tax period (monthly or quarterly) can be used under this method, while the account-based VAT would have to focus on the annual profit and loss account.

5.3   Chargeable Event/Time of Payment

5.3.1 Supplies of Taxable Goods and Services

VAT liability for goods arises when the goods are delivered; liability for services arises when they are effected. The amount owed can be deposited in the government treasury at any time prior to the filing of the monthly tax return required of all VAT-registered suppliers.

5.3.2 Imports

VAT at the import stage is payable before clearance of the imported goods from the customs area. Although payment of VAT takes place at the time of delivery of goods from producers' premises, VAT liability may be assessed earlier. Imported capital machinery may be cleared from the customs area by the manufacturer or importer against an undertaking without paying the VAT first.

6   TAX RATES

0%:   exported goods and services. Supplies of food-stuffs and other goods sent outside Bangladesh by foreign-bound transport for consumption outside Bangladesh. The zero-rating does not, however, apply to goods reimported or intended to be reimported into Bangladesh nor to goods which have been kept ready for export but have not actually been exported within 30 days or within the time extended by the Collector of Customs.

15%:   taxable services, including:
   - hotels and restaurants
   - decorators and caterers
   - automobile garages and workshops, dockyards
   - construction firms
   - warehouses
   - cold storage
   - advertising firms
   - firms operating telephones, teleprinters, telexes and faxes
   - indenting firms
   - freight forwarders and clearing and forwarding firms
   - travel agencies
   - water treatment and distribution authorities
   - goldsmiths, silversmiths and gold and silver retailers
   - printing presses and book-binding firms
   - auctioneers, land development firms, video cassette rental and recording shops
   - mechanised laundries
   - marketing centres for furniture and fixtures
   - repairing and servicing organisations
   - insurance companies, courier service firms and medical institutions
   - beauty parlours
   - all taxable goods and imports (except those listed in the First Schedule of the VAT Act 1991).

7   EXEMPTIONS AND EXCLUSIONS

7.1   Exemption with Credit for Input Tax
The zero rate acts as an exemption with entitlement to recover input tax.

7.2   Exemption without Credit for Input Tax
All goods, whether produced domestically or imported, that are listed in the First Schedule to the VAT Act, are exempt from VAT. The same applies to the services not listed in the Second Schedule to the Act. Domestically produced unprocessed agricultural products, tobacco products, natural gas, textile and petroleum products are excluded from the provisions of the Act, except at import stage. Capital goods, both imported and domestically produced, and bank cheques are also outside the jurisdiction of VAT. In addition, exemptions are allowed to business enterprises whose turnover does not exceed Taka1,500,000 (US$37,500).

7.2.1 Examples of Imports and Domestic Supplies of Goods Exempted Under First Schedule to the VAT Act 1991

Imports:

- cars and microbuses imported by firms located in Export Processing Zones, subject to certain conditions
- chemical fertilisers
- insecticides and pesticides for agricultural use
- books, booklets, newspapers and magazines
- rice, wheat and lentil grinding services
- all imported human vaccines, insulin, antibiotics, sera, toxins and cardio-vascular drugs
- all imported medicaments for therapeutic or prophylactic uses
- all contraceptives
- cotton yarn and thread.

Domestic supplies:

- all livestock
- fresh, cold or frozen meat(*)
- live, dried and de-boned fish (*)
- honey (*)
- fresh or frozen vegetables (*)
- black pepper, unless in dust or lump form (*)
- paddy (*)
- wet skin of livestock (fresh or salted, dried, lime- or acid-cleaned or preserved otherwise but not ready for further use)
- fire wood.

8   CREDIT/REFUND

VAT-registered suppliers or service providers are eligible to take instant credit of VAT paid on inputs against VAT payable on outputs. Persons wishing to set the credit against VAT on domestic supplies or services, must hold the VAT-paid invoice in case of domestically produced intermediate inputs/raw materials and the bill of entry in case of imported inputs.

If the total deduction of input tax in any tax period exceeds the output tax during the same period, the excess amount can be carried forward to the subsequent tax period and adjusted against the output tax due for that period.

8.1   Exemptions and Zero Rating

Exemptions and zero-rating differ in that exemptions are granted to entities such as small firms or firms producing or rendering specific products or services. While exempt firms do not have to file tax returns or pay VAT on their output, their inputs may still be subject to VAT, for which they are unable to claim any credit without filing tax returns.

Zero-rating, on the other hand, is applicable to a specific product or service. It means not only that a taxpayer does not pay any VAT on the value of his exports, but he is also fully compensated for any VAT he pays on inputs and, therefore, is truly exempt from VAT.

(*) not in packets or tin containers

8.2 Returned Sales

When a supply is cancelled and the goods are returned, the registered person is entitled to reverse the VAT paid on the returned sale after observing prescribed formalities.

8.3 Disposal of Waste Products and By-Products

The VAT Rules 1991 incorporate procedures relating to disposal of waste and by-products generated during the production of any taxable good. In such cases, the input credits taken must be proportionately adjusted before disposal of the waste or by-products.

8.4 Exports

Since exports are zero-rated, the exporter will not remit any VAT. However, VAT paid on inputs used in their production is refunded under the duty-clawback system available to exporters.

9 ADMINISTRATIVE OBLIGATIONS

9.1 Registration Requirements

Unless specifically exempted by a general or special government order, all domestic producers of goods other than those specified in the First Schedule to the VAT Act, all providers of taxable services specified in the Second Schedule to the Act, and all importers and exporters are required to register with the VAT authorities.

Each registered person has only a single registration number valid for all taxable activities.

The straightforward and gratuitous registration procedure is voluntary for some taxpayers but compulsory for those:

- whose yearly turnover is at least Taka1,500,000 (US$37,500)
- who want to start a business in taxable goods or services whose turnover is expected to exceed Taka1,500,000 (US$37,500); (here the individual or organisation must apply before commencing the business)
- who are engaged in an import or export business.

Taxpayers who are not required to pay VAT on the basis of their turnover may voluntarily register to pay VAT on their production of goods or supply of services. The application must be filed within the 30 days prior to the tax period for which the registration is sought.

Suppliers of taxable goods or services have to submit the prescribed application form to the nearest VAT office for registration. The application form must be accompanied by a declaration, in prescribed form, listing the drawings, plants, capital equipment, fittings, goods manufactured and their inputs. Once it is satisfied with the formalities, the relevant VAT authority will issue a registration number. Separate registration is required for each business location. The registration may be cancelled if the business is discontinued or if the taxpayer's turnover falls below the statutory taxable limit.

9.2 Books and Records

All taxpayers must maintain the following books of account on a regular basis:

- Sales book: This must chronologically list all sales transactions in three sections; the first records information relating to the invoice and particulars of buyers; the second records information about sales, including internal taxable sales, exempted sales and zero-rated sales; the third records all returned sales.

■ Purchase book: This records all purchases and, like the sales book, is divided into three sections. The first records all information relating to the invoice and particulars of suppliers; the second records the purchase price and taxes and duties paid; the third records information on returned purchases.

■ Current book of accounts: This determines the amount of VAT due and VAT actually paid for both taxable goods and specific services provided. Tax payments can be made through adjustments in this account. The credit available for input tax can be used to settle the liability for output tax.

Service providers need not maintain the current book of accounts. Nevertheless, they may adjust their tax liabilities for services rendered against credit for input taxes by making an adjustment on the tax return. However, the net VAT payments for services should normally be deposited directly into the treasury before filing the tax return on the twentieth day of the month following the tax period.

9.3   Invoices

A VAT-registered supplier has to issue a tax invoice for each supply in triplicate. The original must accompany the goods sold against the invoice up to the destination indicated in the invoice.

A VAT-registered service provider is also required to issue an invoice against each case of service provision. Importers are also required to issue subsidiary invoices during their sale of taxable goods although they cannot charge any VAT on the sale. The invoice has to show, among other things, the amount of VAT paid by the purchaser.

9.4   Powers of the Authorities

A taxpayer is liable to be fined up to Taka25,000 (US$625) if he does any of the following acts:

■ fails to apply for registration where such registration is required
■ fails to file VAT returns when due
■ conceals information relevant to registration
■ fails to respond to any summons from the VAT authorities
■ violates any other provision of the VAT laws.

For certain acts, a taxpayer will be liable to be fined up to Taka100,000 (US$2,500) or pay double the amount of VAT due on the relevant goods supplied or services rendered, and in applicable cases pay supplementary duty, whichever is larger. In addition, he may be sentenced to a maximum of one year's imprisonment or fined up to Taka100,000 (US$2,500) or both if he is found guilty of violating any of the specified acts.

These sanctions apply if the taxpayer:

■ fails to issue tax invoices or provides erroneous information which are pertinent in the invoice
■ fails to pay VAT, and in applicable cases supplementary duty, or fails to file the VAT return within the specified period, despite receipt of two notices from the VAT authorities to do so

- provides erroneous information which is pertinent to the tax return
- evades tax or attempts to do so by providing erroneous or forged documents to the VAT authorities
- does not maintain the books and records required under VAT Act or alters, destroys, disfigures such records or falsifies them
- knowingly provides false information or declarations
- prevents or tries to prevent the VAT authorities from entering his business premises to inspect or impound any relevant books or documents
- takes delivery or attempts to take delivery of goods for which he knows or has reason to know that the amount of VAT, and in applicable cases supplementary duty, was evaded
- takes credit for input tax by using false or forged invoices
- evades or attempts to evade the amount of VAT or supplementary duty
- issues any invoice, even though unregistered, showing the amount of VAT
- engages or helps to engage in any of the activities mentioned above.

If the registered service provider fails to file tax returns or pay VAT, and in applicable cases the supplementary duty, he will be required to pay the tax due together with a penalty of 2% per month.

Notwithstanding any other provision of the law, if a registered person fails to pay VAT, and in applicable cases supplementary duty, within three months after the tax period in spite of receiving two notices to this effect, or violates twice any provision listed above and any impounding provision of the law within a 12-month period, or fails to register despite being ordered to do so, his place of business will be placed under lock and key.

9.5 Impoundment

Taxable goods manufactured or produced by an individual prior to being registered are subject to being impounded. The impoundment provision is also applicable to taxable goods if they are removed, without invoices, by a registered individual from his business premises or the invoice does not accompany them to their point of destination. In case of such removals, the registered person or his representative or anyone connected with the removal, is subject to a fine of up to Taka100,000 (US$2,500) or double the amount of VAT and supplementary duty, if applicable, whichever is larger.

The impoundment will include all items found in the container along with relevant goods and also any transport used in their transportation. However, with guarantees from any scheduled bank that the said transport will be presented at the time and place specified by the Collector of VAT, it may be released subject to final adjudication of the impoundment. The adjudication of the impoundment will be determined under Customs Act in case of imports and by VAT Collector or another authorised person in case of domestic supplies and services. The relevant authority may impose fines in lieu of impoundment unless the good are illegally imported.

10   FURTHER READING

VAT Act 1991

VAT Rules 1991

Amendments to VAT Act and Rules to date

Zahid Hossain, First Secretary (Customs) at National Board of Revenue, *VAT in Bangladesh: Theory, Operation and Issues,* Bangladesh

VAT in Bangladesh : A Tax Payer's Manual, Dhaka Chamber of Commerce & Industry, Bangladesh.

Contributor: Mashtag Ahmed
S.F. Ahmed & Co.
128 New Eskaton Road
Dhaka 1000
Bangladesh
Tel: +880 2 419938
Fax: +880 2 836979

THE PEOPLE'S REPUBLIC OF CHINA

1 GENERAL BACKGROUND

In December 1993, the People's Republic of China introduced a new system of indirect taxation, effective from 1 January 1994.

The new system, comprising a new value added tax (VAT), consumption tax (CT) and business tax (BT), replaces the previous Consolidated Industrial and Commercial Tax (CICT) system. CICT was a commodities and turnover-type of excise and sales tax levied on certain taxable industrial and agricultural products and on imports, commercial retailing, communications, transportation, and service trades.

The principal legislation governing VAT is the VAT Regulations and the Detailed Implementing Rules promulgated by the PRC State Council in December 1993.

Control and collection of VAT is vested in the local office of the PRC State Taxation Bureau at the relevant municipal or county level. Internally, control of VAT is exercised by the tax officer in conjunction with the administration of corporate income tax and consumption tax. On imports, VAT is collected by the Customs authorities.

2 WHO IS TAXABLE?

2.1 General
All units and individuals (collectively referred to as 'taxable persons') who sell goods or provide processing, repairing and replacement services within, or import goods into, the PRC are obligated to pay VAT unless the relevant sales are less than the relevant taxable thresholds.

The term 'units' is defined to include state-owned enterprises, collectively-owned enterprises, private enterprises, foreign investment enterprises, foreign enterprises, joint stock companies, other enterprises and units, business units, military units, social organisations and other units.

A range of taxable thresholds has been stipulated by the State Council whereas the local taxation bureaux are vested with a discretionary power to determine the exact amounts dependent on the economic conditions of the relevant municipality and county. The statutory taxable thresholds are summarised as follows:

- for the sales of goods, a monthly turnover of RMB600 yuans to RMB2,000 yuans
- for services, a monthly turnover of RMB200 yuans to RMB800 yuans
- for daily transactions, a daily turnover of RMB50 yuans to RMB80 yuans.

This chapter reflects the legislation on VAT in the People's Republic of China (PRC) as at 31 December 1994.

A person who disposes of intangible assets or real properties is, however, not subject to VAT but rather to a BT of 5%.

2.2 Transactions with Branch/Subsidiary

Subsidiaries of foreign enterprises which sell goods or taxable services in the PRC are treated in the same manner as other taxable persons. Transactions between branches of an enterprise registered in the PRC are also subject to VAT except where the branches concerned are located in the same county (municipality).

2.3 Government Bodies

The State and local authorities (including administration units, business units, military units, social organisations and other units) are treated as taxable persons for the purpose of VAT.

2.4 Fiscal Unit/Group Taxation

The concept of 'fiscal unity' is not provided for in the VAT Regulations. Each individual member in a group is regarded as an independent VAT taxpayer.

2.5 Foreign Enterprises

Under the prevailing regulations, foreign enterprises are generally not allowed to sell goods or provide processing, repairing and replacement services directly in the PRC; therefore, the payment of VAT should not be an issue.

Foreign enterprises which do not sell goods or taxable services in the PRC are not permitted to register for VAT.

2.6 Representative Office

In accordance with the national measures of the PRC on the registration of representative offices of foreign enterprises, a representative office is only allowed to engage in liaison-type activities of a non-direct profit-making nature. Sales of goods by a representative office are prohibited. Therefore, no VAT issue arises. Instead, a representative office established by a foreign enterprise is chargeable to BT on the revenue derived in the PRC as computed in accordance with the relevant regulations.

2.7 Importers

Persons who import goods into the PRC are liable to pay VAT at the same rates as those applicable to the sale of similar goods in the PRC.

3 WHAT IS TAXABLE?

VAT liability arises on the supply of goods or taxable services in the PRC for consideration by a taxable person in the course or furtherance of any business carried on by him and on the importation of goods into the PRC.

Consideration includes cash, benefits-in-kind and other economic benefits.

3.1 Supply of Goods

'Supply' (sale) of goods means a transfer of ownership whether by delivery of the goods or otherwise. The term 'goods' includes electricity, heating, gas and other tangible assets but specifically excludes intangibles and real properties.

A supply (sale) of goods includes:

- sale by consignment through an agent
- sale of goods consigned by a principal
- the transfer of goods from one branch office to another branch office of the same taxable person for the purpose of furtherance of sale unless the branch offices are located in the same county (municipality)
- the application or appropriation of goods by a taxable person for the following purposes:

  – use in VAT-exempt activities
  – for capital investment
  – for appropriation to shareholders or investors
  – for the benefits of collectives or personal consumption
  – as gifts to other persons.

3.2 Provision of Taxable Services
'Provision of taxable services' means any provision in the course of business which is not a supply of goods. Taxable services are defined to include processing, repairing and replacement services only. Supply of other services is not chargeable to VAT. Non-taxable services include transportation, construction, banking and insurance, postage and telecommunications, cultural activities and sports, entertainment and servicing.

'Processing services' are the services performed by a contractor for the production of goods utilising raw materials and principal parts supplied by his customer and produced in accordance with the customer's specifications.

'Repairing and replacement services' is the repairing of damaged goods into its original state of condition.

3.3 Mixed Transactions
Special rules apply to mixed transactions consisting of the sale of goods and provision of non-taxable services. Mixed transactions carried on by enterprises and private enterprises engaged in production, wholesale and retailing of goods are considered as sale of goods and are chargeable to VAT. Other units and individuals conducting mixed transactions are regarded as providing non-taxable services and are not liable for VAT.

Food and drink provided in the course of operating such businesses as hotels, restaurants, cafes, public houses, catering businesses or businesses providing facilities for the consumption of food and drink are treated as provision of non-taxable services rather than supply of goods. They are therefore chargeable to BT rather than VAT.

3.4 Self-Supplies of Goods/Services
'Self-supply of goods' occurs when a person diverts to private or exempt use, goods which he has imported, purchased, manufactured or otherwise acquired and in respect of which he is entitled to an input VAT deduction.

3.5   Importations of Goods

The mere importation of goods is, with certain exemptions, a taxable event irrespective of the status of the importer or the nature of the importation. Goods imported into a bonded warehouse are not liable to VAT.

4   PLACE OF SALES

4.1   Sale of Goods

The place where goods are sold is deemed for the purposes of VAT to be:

- where the sale of goods requires their transportation, the place where the transportation begins
- in any other case, the place where the goods are located at the time of sale.

4.2   Provision of Services

The general rule is that the place where services are deemed to be provided for VAT purposes is the place where they are physically performed.

5   BASIS OF TAXATION

5.1   Sales within the PRC

Where the consideration takes the form of money, the amount on which VAT is chargeable is normally the total sum paid or payable to the person selling the goods or services including all taxes, commissions, costs and charges whatsoever but excluding the following:

- the VAT chargeable in respect of the transaction
- CT paid by the subcontractor on behalf of the seller on taxable consumer goods subcontracted for processing
- transportation expenses paid by the seller on behalf of the buyer provided that the relevant invoice is issued directly by the transportation company to and settled by the buyer.

VAT must, therefore, be returned on the VAT exclusive price.

A taxable person adopting the VAT inclusive price method in pricing its goods should use the following formula to compute the sales value of the transaction concerned:

$$\text{Sales value} = \frac{\text{VAT inclusive price}}{1 + \text{VAT}}$$

Where goods and taxable services are sold and the consideration does not consist of (or does not consist wholly of) an amount of money and where certain goods are supplied free of charge the amount on which tax is chargeable is the open market or arms-length value of the goods and taxable services as determined by the relevant local tax authorities.

5.2   Importations

The value of imported goods for the purposes of VAT is the value for customs purposes, plus any customs duty, CT and other charges levied either outside or, by reason of importation, inside the PRC (excluding VAT) on the goods and not already included in the import price of the goods.

Where the value is expressed in a foreign currency the amount must be converted to Renminbi (RNB) in accordance with the prevailing foreign exchange rate announced by the State Exchange Control Bureau.

5.3   Chargeable Event/Time of Payment
Liability to tax arises at the time when goods or taxable services are supplied.

The time when tax is due depends on the characteristics of the transaction and can be summarised as follows:

- If sales proceeds are received directly from the buyer, VAT is due at the date of receipt of the payment or the date of issue of the invoice, whichever is earlier, irrespective of whether the goods have been delivered.
- If sale proceeds are collected through a bank, the VAT is due at the date of despatch of the goods.
- If sale proceeds are collected by instalments in accordance with the relevant sale and purchase agreement, VAT is due on the payment date as stated in the agreement.
- If payment is made in advance, VAT is due on the date of despatch of goods.
- For consignment sales, VAT is due on the date of receipt of the sale confirmation list issued by the consignee.
- For the provision of taxable services, VAT is due on the date of payment or the date of issue of the invoice whichever is the earlier.
- For the importation of goods, VAT is due at the time of customs declaration.

5.4   Credit Notes/Bad Debts
A VAT taxpayer may adjust his liability for tax in respect of goods returned to him and discounts or other price adjustments allowed by him subsequent to his having paid the appropriate VAT. Adjustments will be used to reduce the VAT liability for the current VAT payment period.

6   TAX RATES

6.1   Rates
The current rates are as follows:

0%:   exported goods

6%:   taxable goods and taxable services provided by small-scale taxpayers

13%:   – food and edible plant oil
       – running water, air-conditioning, hot water, coal gas, liquefied petroleum gas, natural gas, biogas, coal products for civilian uses
       – books, newspapers, magazines
       – forage, fertiliser, agricultural chemicals, agricultural machinery, agricultural protection cover
       – other goods as specified by the State Council.

17%:   other taxable goods and taxable services.

A taxable person who supplies goods or taxable services with different VAT rates shall separately account for the sales value of such goods and taxable services. The highest VAT rate shall apply where the sales values have not been separately accounted for.

6.2   Small-Scale Taxpayers

Small-scale taxpayers are defined as:

- taxpayers engaged in production or the provision of processing/repairing services with an annual turnover of less than RMB1 million or
- taxpayers engaged in wholesale or retail businesses with an annual turnover of less than RMB18 million.

A small-scale taxpayer is chargeable to VAT at 6% on the taxable goods and taxable services he supplies. However, he is not entitled to claim any input VAT deduction in computing the net VAT payable.

A small-scale taxpayer who operates sound accounting systems, maintains proper accounting records and can also supply accurate information for VAT purposes may, upon approval by the local tax authorities, calculate the amount of VAT payable in accordance with the relevant provisions applicable to a general taxable person.

7   EXEMPTIONS

7.1   Exemption with Credit for Input VAT

The export of goods is zero-rated. The zero-rate works as an exemption with credit because the suppliers of zero-rated goods (ie exported goods) are entitled to input VAT credit notwithstanding that no output VAT has been paid.

Where the supply of exported goods accounts for a substantial portion of a supplier's total sales, the supplier may, upon approval from the local tax authorities, be entitled to recover the VAT previously paid. The claim for refund of VAT is to be applied on a monthly basis following completion of the export procedures with the customs authorities and production of the export declaration and other relevant documents.

If the exported goods are returned by the buyer or the customs authorities subsequent to the VAT refund, the taxable person must repay the VAT refunded.

However, the refund is not applicable to foreign investment enterprises established before 1994 to the extent of input VAT paid on goods and taxable services purchased domestically in the PRC.

7.2   Exemption without Credit for Input VAT

Supplies of certain goods are exempt from VAT. The suppliers of such goods are not permitted to charge VAT and no input VAT credit will be allowed where it is attributable to the purchase, production or importation of any of these goods.

These exempt goods include:

- agricultural products produced and sold by agricultural producers

- contraceptive medicines and appliances
- antique books
- imported equipment and apparatus used directly for scientific education and in scientific research, development and experiments
- imported products and equipment as free economic assistance from foreign governments and international organisations
- imported equipment required for processing and assembly operations and compensation trade
- products imported by organisations for the handicapped for their exclusive use
- sale of products which have been used by the seller.

Taxable persons who supply items eligible for tax exemption or tax reduction must account for the sales value of each such item separately. No tax exemption or reduction shall be given where the sales values have not been separately accounted for.

7.3 Exempt Imports
Generally, the importation of goods into the PRC in the form of capital contributed by the foreign investor of a foreign investment enterprise into that enterprise is exempt from VAT and customs duties. Such exempted imported goods include:

- machinery and equipment, spare parts and other materials (such as materials required for constructing plant (sites) and for installing and reinforcing machinery) stipulated as investment by the foreign investor
- machinery and equipment, spare parts and other materials imported with capital from within the total investment amount
- machinery and equipment, spare parts and other materials imported with additional capital due to their production and supply being unable to be guaranteed domestically.

7.4 Exemption for the Transitional Period
- Foreign Investment Enterprises (FIEs) which registered with the State Administration of Industry and Commerce before 1 January 1994 will be entitled to claim back the VAT, CT and BT paid over the hypothetical CICT and hypothetical Special Product Tax (applicable to motor vehicles only) calculated as follows:

  - Excess BT paid = actual BT paid minus hypothetical CICT
  - Excess VAT and CT paid = actual VAT and CT paid minus hypothetical CICT and Special Product Tax

- The concession only covers a defined period which is the shorter of:

  - 1 January 1994 to 31 December 1998 (ie five years) or
  - 1 January 1994 to the date of expiration of an FIE's operation period as approved before 1994.

- Tax refund is only applicable to excess VAT, CT or BT paid at the stage when goods are sold or services are provided in the PRC
- No tax refund for excess VAT and CT paid on the importation of goods is permitted without the approval of the State Tax Bureau
- No tax refund is permitted for excess VAT and CT paid on the sale of goods to Import

and Export Corporations in the PRC and

■ An annual tax refund of not more than RMB1 million may be approved by the Provincial or Municipal Tax Bureaux; otherwise, it must be endorsed by the State Tax Bureau.

The refund is to be processed on an annual basis and application must be submitted by the VAT taxpayer within 30 days after the end of the relevant year. However, in order to improve his liquidity, a taxpayer is allowed to apply to the local tax authority for monthly or quarterly provisional refunds with a final tax reconciliation made after the relevant year.

8   CREDIT/REFUND FOR INPUT VAT

8.1   General Rule

In computing the amount of VAT payable, a taxable person may deduct the VAT relating to most goods and taxable services purchased or imported by him which are used for the purposes of his taxable transactions. No deduction may be made for the tax paid on taxable goods and services used for any other purposes. To be entitled to the deduction, the taxable person must:

■ register with the tax authorities as a VAT taxpayer
■ maintain a reliable accounting system and be able to provide correct information for assessing the VAT liabilities
■ have a proper VAT invoice obtained from the vendor or a tax certification issued by the customs authorities.

8.2   Amount of Input VAT Deduction

The amount of input VAT deductible from output VAT is limited to the amount of VAT stated in the following VAT withholding statements:

■ the amount of VAT as stated on the VAT invoice obtained from the vendor
■ the amount of VAT as stated on the tax certification obtained from the customs authorities
■ the amount of deductible input VAT attributable to the purchase of tax-exempt agricultural products is 10% of the actual purchase value.

8.3   Non-Deduction

Input VAT on the following items is not deductible from output VAT:

■ purchase of fixed assets
■ purchase of taxable goods or services used in non-taxable activities
■ purchase of taxable goods or services used in tax-exempt activities
■ purchase of taxable goods or services for collective welfare or personal consumption
■ abnormal loss of purchased taxable goods
■ abnormal wastage of purchased taxable goods or services consumed in the production of merchandise or finished products.

8.4   Partial Exemption

Persons who make taxable and other supplies such as exempt supplies and supplies which are outside the scope of VAT are entitled to deduct input VAT incurred in making the taxable supplies only.

Where the purchases or imports are used in making both taxable and exempt/outside the scope supplies, an apportionment of input VAT is allowed. The allowable input VAT deduction is usually calculated in the ratio of the turnover of taxable supplies to the total turnover of all supplies. The relevant formula is:

$$\text{Total input VAT for the month} \times \frac{\text{Turnover derived from the sale in the PRC of taxable goods and taxable services for the month}}{\text{Total turnover for the month}}$$

8.5   Time of Recovery

Subject to the rules to entitlement outlined above, a taxable person is entitled to recovery of input VAT, when he has a valid VAT invoice or a tax certification issued by the Customs authorities. It is not necessary for him to have paid for the goods or for the supplier to have paid the output VAT to the tax authorities.

The claim to input VAT should be made in the VAT return for the period in which the invoice or import documents are issued.

9   ADMINISTRATIVE OBLIGATIONS

9.1   Registration

Any unit or individual who supplies taxable goods or provides taxable services within the PRC in the course of his business or who elects to become a VAT taxpayer (for instance, a small-scale taxpayer) must register with the local tax bureau in the county (municipality) in which the place of business is situated. This includes persons who supply zero-rated goods but excludes persons who produce exempt goods only.

When registration has been completed, a VAT number will be allocated by the relevant local taxation bureau. This will normally be the same number as that allocated to the taxable person for income tax purposes.

Branches of the same enterprise are required to register separately unless the head office and the branch(es) are located in the same county (municipality). However, subject to the approval of the tax authorities, the head office may be allowed to submit combined VAT returns for branches located in different counties (municipalities).

If a taxable person with a fixed business place intends to sell goods outside that fixed business place, he or it must apply to the local tax bureau in the county (municipality) in which the fixed business place is located for a 'certificate of VAT collection and management' in respect of business activities conducted outside his or its own location.

9.2   Place for Payment of VAT

Generally, VAT returns and payments must be submitted to the relevant local tax bureau with which the taxable person has registered. The exceptions are as follows:

- in the absence of the certificate of VAT collection and management, a taxable person which supplies taxable goods or services outside his or its own county (or municipality) must make VAT returns and payments to the local tax authorities of the place where the relevant goods or services are supplied
- a taxable person without a fixed business place which supplies taxable goods or services must make VAT returns and payments to the local tax authorities of the place where the relevant goods or services are supplied
- VAT returns and payments on imported goods must be made by the importer or its agent to the customs authorities to which the imported goods are declared.

9.3   Books and Records
Registered persons must keep full records of all business transactions which may affect his liability to VAT for a period of 15 years. The records must be kept up to date and must be sufficiently detailed to enable a VAT taxpayer accurately to calculate his liability and the tax authorities to check the calculation, if necessary.

9.4   Invoices
An inadequate invoice will deprive the recipient of his right to deduct input VAT. An invoice must contain:

- VAT registration numbers for the supplier and the buyer
- the date of issue of the invoice
- the name, address and telephone number of the taxable person supplying the taxable goods or services
- the name, address and telephone number of the taxable person to whom the taxable goods and services are supplied
- the bank account numbers of the supplier and the buyer
- a full description of the taxable goods or services supplied
- the quantity or volume of goods supplied
- the consideration (exclusive of VAT)
- the rate(s) of VAT and the amount of tax at each rate chargeable.

Where an invoice is required to be issued under one of the following circumstances, an ordinary invoice must be issued and the issuance of a VAT invoice is not permitted:

- the supply of taxable goods or services to non-taxable persons who do not have a VAT registration number
- the sale of VAT-exempt goods
- the supply of taxable goods or services by small-scale taxpayers.

9.5   VAT Returns

9.5.1 Payment Period
Different payment periods are provided for the assessment of VAT. A payment period may be one day, three days, five days, ten days, fifteen days or one month. The applicable payment period will be determined by the local tax authorities based on the amount of VAT payable by the taxpayer. If VAT payments cannot be made on a fixed period basis, they can be made on a transaction basis.

9.5.2 VAT Submission

A taxable person with a VAT payment period of one month is required to file a VAT return and pay the VAT for the period within ten days from the end of the period concerned. A taxpayer with a VAT payment period of one day, three days, five days, ten days or fifteen days shall make a provisional payment of VAT within five days from the end of the period, and shall, within ten days from the first day of the following month, file a VAT return and settle the VAT payable for the previous month.

VAT on imported goods shall be paid by the taxable persons within seven days from the day following the date of the statement of customs duty issued by the customs authorities.

9.6   Powers of the Authorities

Authorised tax officers have extensive powers in regard to the inspection and seizure of records. Where the tax officer is of the opinion that a taxable person has underpaid the VAT properly due he may issue an assessment based on the correct figures or an estimate of the tax due.

No local government or government department (including the tax authorities) is allowed to grant any exemption or reduction of VAT. The State Council of the PRC is the only authorised body which may formally determine whether or not a particular activity is a VAT-exempt activity and the rate at which tax is chargeable in relation to the supply of goods or the provision of taxable services.

Contributors: Alfred Y Shum and Ivan Chan
Ernst & Young
Hong Kong Macau Centre
10/F Office Building
Deng si Shi Tiao Li Jiao Shiao
Beijing, PRC 100027
Tel: +1 5011 520
Fax: +1 5011 519

INDIA

1   GENERAL BACKGROUND

There is no value added tax in India. There is, however, a turnover tax (known as 'Sales Tax') which is levied both by the central government and by each State government. Central government only has power to levy Sales Tax on inter-State transactions and the states only have power to levy Sales Tax on sales within the State. However, the States also collect tax on inter-State sales on behalf of the central government. Exports and import transactions are exempt from both Central and State Sales Tax.

2   WHO IS TAXABLE?

2.1   General

The basis of levy of tax varies from State to State. In general five systems have been in operation, namely:

- single point last stage tax
- multipoint tax
- two point tax
- composite tax
- single point first stage tax.

However, most States now use the last system in one form or another.

Under this system, tax is collected at the first point at which the sale takes place and no tax is collected thereafter. For example, when a manufacturer effects a 'sale' of his manufactured goods, the sale attracts Sales Tax and all subsequent sales of the product are considered as 'resales' which attract no liability to tax provided the goods so sold do not undergo any change in their form.

2.2   Taxable Person

The levy of tax is on the 'dealer'. The dealer means any person who carries on the business of buying or selling goods in the State, and includes the central or State government, when it carries on such business and also societies, clubs and other association of persons. Certain categories of persons are not considered as dealers. These include:

- those persons whose annual turnover is below the specified limit. For this purpose, dealers are classified into manufacturers, importers (ie persons who bring goods into the State either from abroad or from other states) and traders (ie resellers). The specified limits for each class differs from State to State
- an agriculturalist who sells exclusively agricultural produce grown on land cultivated by him personally

---

This chapter reflects the legislation on Sales Tax in India as at 31 December 1994.

■ an educational institution carrying on business in the performance of its function for achieving its objectives.

3 WHAT IS TAXABLE?

3.1 Supply of Goods

'Goods' means every kind of movable property (excluding newspapers, actionable claims, money, stock, shares and securities) and all other things attached to or forming part of the land which are agreed to be severed before sale or under the contract of sale. Some States also tax goods which are of intangible character, for example, import licences, trademarks, patents, etc.

The definition of a 'sale' for the purposes of Sales Tax levy is not confined to the definition of 'sale' under the Indian Sale of Goods Act, but includes transactions which are not regarded as sales under that Act but are 'deemed' sales under the Sales Tax Acts.

The category of 'deemed' sales now includes:

■ receipts from works contracts (eg construction contracts)
■ hire charges (eg lease rentals)
■ receipts from the supply of food and drink in restaurants
■ receipts from the supply of food and drink to members in social clubs.

Inter-State transfers not involving a sale, for example, a transfer of goods from the manufacturing location to a branch office or to a consignment agent, are not deemed to be sales.

In some States, separate enactments have been introduced to tax 'deemed' sales. For example, in Maharashtra, receipts from works contracts are taxed under the Maharashtra Sales Tax on the Transfer of Property involved in the Execution of Works Contract Act 1985 and lease rentals are taxed under the Maharashtra Sales Tax on Transfer of Right to use any Goods for any Purpose Act 1985.

3.2 Supply of Services

Sales Tax is not levied on services.

4 PLACE OF SUPPLY

4.1 Within India

The place of supply is the place where the goods are physically located in India at the time the sale is made.

4.2 Imports and Exports

All sales in the course of exports and imports are exempt from tax. A sale is deemed to take place in the course of export of the goods out of the territory of India only if the sale either occasions such export or is affected by a transfer of documents of title to the goods after the goods have crossed the customs frontiers of India.

Even a sale made preceding the sale occasioning the export of goods out of the territory of India is deemed to be in the course of export, if such sale was for the purpose of complying with the agreement or order or in relation to such export.

A sale is deemed to take place in the course of import of the goods into the territory of India only if the sale either occasions such import or is effected by a transfer of documents of title to the goods before the goods have crossed the customs frontiers of India.

5   BASIS OF TAXATION

The tax is levied on the gross value of turnover which for this purpose is defined as the aggregate of the amounts of sale price received and receivable by a dealer.

6   TAX RATES

6.1   General Rules
The rate of tax varies from State to State and as between different commodities within the same State. In general, articles of consumption produced for the more affluent sections of society, such as automobiles, air-conditioners, refrigerators, entertainment electronics, etc, carry higher rates of Sales Tax.

The rates of tax on raw materials and components are generally lower than the rates of tax on finished products and capital goods.

The current illustrative rates for the State of Maharashtra are as follows:

2% – 4%:   raw materials and items of common consumption

6% – 15%:   other items, apart from exceptional items

20%:   exceptional items such as large refrigerators, electronic systems, etc

25% – 40%: essential items such as food or drink in specified hotels or restaurants

25% – 50%: exceptional items such as liquor.

6.2   Central Sales Tax
There are two rates of Central Sales Tax:

4%:   sales for resales or for use in manufacture for sale, sales to State or central government

10%:   other sales.

6.3   Additional Levies
In some States there is a further levy in addition to Sales Tax. For example, in Maharashtra every dealer is liable to a levy of additional Sales Tax if his annual turnover exceeds Rs1 million and to a levy of turnover tax if his annual taxable turnover exceeds Rs1,200,000. The rate of additional Sales Tax is currently 15% of the Sales Tax; the rate of turnover tax is 1.25% of turnover if annual sales do not exceed Rs10 million and 1.5% of turnover if annual sales exceed that amount. The distinguishing feature between these additional levies and the

Sales Tax is that, while Sales Tax can be recovered from the customer, these additional levies have to be borne by the dealer.

7 EXEMPTIONS

The list of items which are exempt from Sales Tax varies from State to State but generally includes the following:

- articles of common consumption by the poor, for example, water, vegetables, certain categories of cloth, pulses, cereals, etc
- articles consumed by organisations of social value, for example, charitable institutions, hospitals, defence organisations, etc.

8 RECOVERY OF TAX

There are provisions for set-off, drawback and refund to avoid double taxation. For example, in those cases where Sales Tax is paid on the purchase of goods, exemption from Sales Tax is provided on subsequent sales of the goods or of other goods manufactured from such goods. Similarly if Sales Tax is paid in the State on purchases and thereafter the same goods are sold on an inter-State basis, the State Sales Tax paid is set-off against the Central Sales Tax payable. Equally, if the goods are exported, the Sales Tax paid on purchases is refunded.

9 ADMINISTRATIVE OBLIGATIONS

9.1 Registration

Every dealer is required to register and to obtain a registration certificate. On registration the dealer is allotted a registration number. A separate application has to be made for each place of business and a separate registration number is allotted for each such place.

The holding of a registration certificate entitles the holder to collect Sales Tax. Conversely, a person who does not hold a registration certificate cannot collect Sales Tax. It is, therefore, essential that a person who is liable to be considered as a 'dealer' obtain the registration certificate before he commences business or as soon as possible thereafter.

In addition to the registration certificate, dealers having a turnover in excess of certain specified amounts may, if they wish apply for the grant of special documents such as authorisation recognition permits, which give certain privileges. For example, the holder of such a document can effect purchases without paying any taxes at the time of purchase on declaration that the holder is entitled to a set-off on subsequent sale of the goods or other goods manufactured out of such goods. The grant of these additional certificates is restricted to certain States only.

9.2 Returns

All dealers are required to file periodic returns of Sales Tax. Depending upon the volume of turnover and the amount of Sales Tax payable, the returns are required to be filed either at the end of every month or at the end of every quarter. The return has to be filed normally within 30 days after the close of the period for which the return is prepared and the tax due has to be paid along with the filing of the return.

9.3   Records
Every registered dealer is required to maintain proper books of account in support of his business activity. The Sales Tax enactment in each State specifies the details of the books and records to be maintained, particularly regarding proper records of purchases and sales and of relevant forms, declarations, etc, to support claims for exemption.

9.4   Powers of the Authorities
Assessments are made by the Sales Tax Authorities for each assessment year (1 April to 31 March) on the basis of the returns filed. For the purposes of the assessment the assessing officer has the power to call for inspection of the dealer's books of account and other records.

9.5   Appeals
Every dealer has a right to appeal against the assessment made on him. The first appeal is made to the Assistant Commissioner of Sales Tax who is a departmental officer; a second appeal can be made to the Commissioner of Sales Tax (who is also a departmental officer) or to the Sales Tax Tribunal. The Tribunal is a quasi-judicial body independent of the Sales Tax Department. On all matters of fact, the decision of the Tribunal is final and binding but, on matters of law, a further appeal can be made to the High Court of the State in which the assessment is made and thereafter to the Supreme Court of India.

10   SPECIAL REGIMES

10.1   Industrial Enterprises
Most State governments offer incentives for the establishment of industrial enterprises in the State, and one form of incentive offered is special benefits under the Sales Tax Act.

While the actual incentives vary from State to State, normally they fall into three broad classes:

- exemption from the levy of tax
- deferral of Sales Tax collections
- interest-free unsecured loans.

The incentives which are currently offered in the State of Maharashtra are as follows:

- exemption from payment of Purchase Tax or Sales Tax on purchase of raw materials
- exemption from payment of State Sales Tax on sales of finished products
- exemption from payment of Central Sales Tax on sales of finished products in the course of inter-State trade and commerce
- deferment of collection of Sales Tax for ten years subject to such limits (varying between aggregate Sales Tax collection for 5 to 12 years with ceilings) as are specified
- an unsecured interest-free loan for a period of ten years of such amount as is specified (being the limits specified for deferment).

The above incentives, together with the different rates of tax in different States, are an important factor in influencing the location of industry.

11   VALUE ADDED TAX

There is no value added tax (VAT) in India at present but the matter is under active consideration. The need for a value added tax is felt in view of the following perceived deficiencies of the present Sales Tax system:

- under the 'single point first stage' levy, the tax is collected on the price at which the first sale is made under the distribution system, and the difference between this price and the ultimate price to the consumer escapes taxation
- where raw materials and components are used in manufacture, even after set-off, there remains a residual burden (usually 4%) at each stage of input. The cumulative effect of this burden is difficult to quantify. For the same reason adequate relief for drawback cannot be given on goods exported
- since different States levy different rates of tax, location of industries may be influenced by consideration of Sales Tax incidence, and other valid considerations may be ignored
- Sales Tax is generally levied on the sale of goods; services escape taxation
- through the process of stock transfers from one State to another, the benefit of Sales Tax may be denied to the State where the goods are manufactured and may accrue only to the State where the goods are sold.

Contributor: Yezdi H. Malegam
                 Partner
                 Ernst & Young
                 S.B. Billimoria & Co
                 Meher Chambers
                 R. Kamani Road
                 Ballard Estate
                 Bombay 400 038
                 India
                 Tel: +91 22 2621947
                 Fax: +91 22 2613361

ISRAEL

1   GENERAL BACKGROUND

Value Added Tax (VAT) was introduced into Israel on 1 July 1976 pursuant to the Value Added Tax Law 1975 (the VAT Law). The VAT Law applies the same general principles as VAT systems in other countries, with modifications for financial institutions and not-for-profit organisations.

The VAT Law covers the State of Israel, and there are reciprocal arrangements with the Autonomous Areas administered by the Palestinian Authority. Special VAT arrangements apply in Israel's free trade/free processing zones. The VAT Law is administered by the VAT authorities through its head office in Jerusalem and 15 local offices.

2   WHO IS TAXABLE?

2.1   General

Businesses in Israel are obliged to register for Israeli VAT purposes immediately upon commencement of operations, and must thereafter administer the VAT system of rules. A 'business' or 'dealer' is anyone who sells or renders services in the course of his business, and anyone who conducts a one-time transaction. A separate tax regime applies to financial institutions and to not-for-profit organisations (see section 10 below). Certain Exempt dealers whose turnover does not exceed NIS36,000 (approximately US$12,000) in the 1994 calendar year are exempt from the obligation to register for VAT purposes. The VAT Law also allows reduced bookkeeping and invoicing compliance by 'Petty dealers' in certain occupations whose turnover does not exceed NIS150,000 (approximately US$50,000) and who employ no more than two persons, including the proprietors. Petty dealers record input VAT and output VAT but may not issue VAT invoices to their business clientele nor may they request cash refunds of VAT where input VAT exceeds output VAT. Business dealers who do not qualify or choose not to be Exempt dealers or Petty dealers must register as 'Authorised dealers' and comply with the normal VAT rules.

2.2   Transactions with Branch/Subsidiary

Transactions between a company abroad and a subsidiary company in Israel are treated like any other import or export transaction. Certain export transactions are zero-rated (see section 7.1). A foreign company that has a branch in Israel must register for Israeli VAT purposes and account for VAT on its transactions. In practice, the VAT authorities generally aim to ensure that VAT is accounted for on billings to third parties, thereby effectively bringing intermediate head/office branch transactions into the Israeli VAT net. With regard to joint VAT files, see section 2.4.

This chapter reflects the legislation on VAT in Israel as at 31 December 1994.

2.3 Government Bodies

The VAT Law is also applicable to the State of Israel (Section 144B). Consequently, State bodies will typically be treated as not-for-profit institutions (see section 10.2) or as business dealers, as applicable.

2.4 Fiscal Unity/Group Transactions

Registered dealers may request to be registered as a single reporting unit (a 'joint file') for VAT purposes, similar to a partnership. One of the dealers who is permanently resident in Israel must be nominated to report and sign the VAT returns on behalf of the unit. Joint accounting records should also be maintained unless one of the dealers owns either 50% or more of the shares of the other dealer(s), or a partnership interest of 50% or more. Where the joint file conditions are satisfied, transactions between the dealers concerned are excluded from the scope of VAT.

2.5 Foreign Businesses

Foreign persons or entities that conduct any part of their business or activities in Israel are required to register and report thereafter for Israeli VAT purposes. These requirements cover, among others, foreign businesses that:

- render services in Israel, whether directly or through an agent or branch
- render services to an Israeli resident, or relating to assets in Israel. (See section 4 below for further details of business operations and activities deemed to be conducted in Israel.)

The foreign business must also appoint a local VAT representative within 30 days who will be responsible for all Israeli VAT matters.

2.6 Representative Office

The VAT Law does not recognise the income tax treaty concept of a permanent establishment. Consequently a representative office of a business concern will almost invariably be deemed to be a registerable business entity for VAT purposes, as outlined in section 2.5 above.

2.7 VAT Representatives

See section 2.5.

2.8 Reverse Charge Mechanism

Where a transaction is deemed to be rendered in Israel (see sections 2.5 and 4), but the vendor or service supplier is a non-resident who does not issue a valid Israeli VAT invoice (perhaps because he is not registered), the purchaser is obliged to account for the VAT concerned on behalf of the vendor (a reverse charge mechanism).

If the purchaser is an authorised VAT dealer, he may then recover the VAT as input VAT in the usual way . In principle, the reverse charge mechanism does not absolve the foreign resident of his VAT responsibilities.

Dealers, not-for-profit bodies and financial institutions may also apply a reverse charge mechanism if they receive certain services that are not supported by a valid VAT invoice from persons who derive most of their income from salary, pension or other allowance.

2.9   Importers

An importer of goods must be registered as an 'authorised dealer' for Israeli VAT purposes and must comply with the relevant import licensing requirements. VAT must be settled upon clearance of imported goods from the Israeli Customs. A bonded warehouse may be used to defer the payment of VAT and import taxes until such time as the imported goods are needed.

3   WHAT IS TAXABLE?

VAT is generally imposed at a rate of 17% on transactions deemed to be conducted in Israel and on imported goods.

A 'transaction' is essentially a sale of an asset or provision of a service by a dealer in the course of his business, including a sale of capital equipment and a one-time transaction (see below).

The term 'sale' is broadly defined. In relation to assets, a sale includes: rental, hire purchase, granting a licence to use for consideration, granting rights in an asset, appropriation for own use, expropriation, foreclosure, confiscation for consideration, gifts to employees and others. A 'sale' does not include any act relating to publicly traded securities, except for the sale or registration on a stock exchange of an interest in a 'real estate entity' whose principal assets are Israeli real estate.

A 'one-time transaction' is a one-off sale of goods or supply of a service where the transaction has a commercial character, as well as the sale of real estate to or by a dealer who is not in the business of selling real estate (except for a home sold to a financial institution or not-for-profit body).

3.1   Supply of Goods

A sale of goods (including rental and other transactions (see above) is liable to VAT. Most assets other than real estate are classified as 'goods'. Even intangible assets and rights of enjoyment (such as know-how) are treated as goods for VAT purposes, but not real estate rights, securities, traded instruments, nor options in them. Securities, traded instruments and options in them are, therefore, generally considered outside the scope of VAT except for the sale or registration on a stock exchange of an untraded interest in a 'real estate entity' (see section 3.3).

3.2   Supply of Services

A service transaction is liable to VAT. A 'service' is defined as any act done for personal gain which is not a 'sale' (see above), including credit transactions and deposits of money. In the case of an entity, a service also encompasses acts performed for the entity's members for nil consideration or in consideration for membership fees. Nevertheless, work performed by an employee for his employer is not classified as a service for VAT purposes. Accordingly, employees are not subject to VAT on their remuneration.

3.3   Real Estate

Transactions relating to real estate are generally subject to VAT, although an exemption applies to certain rental income (see section 7.2).

For these purposes, the term 'real estate' includes real estate rights (eg a leasehold interest) and rights in an entity whose principal assets comprise Israeli real estate (a 'real estate entity'). As indicated in 3.1, a sale transaction relating to real estate includes a sale, or registration on a stock exchange, of an untraded interest in a real estate entity.

3.4   Self-Supply
A self-supply of goods is regarded specifically as a 'sale' transaction that is liable to VAT. With regard to a self-supply of services where no consideration or gain is derived, it appears that no VAT liability arises unless the services are supplied to members of an entity.

3.5   Import of Goods
Imported goods are as stated in the VAT Law to be subject to Israeli VAT upon importation. In principle, this VAT liability extends to the importation of most intangible assets (other than securities) where these are classified as 'goods' (see section 3.1 above).

4   PLACE OF SUPPLY

4.1   Supply of Goods
Goods and other assets are regarded as sold in Israel if they are delivered to the purchaser in Israel. Exports and intangible assets are regarded as sold in Israel if the vendor is an Israeli resident.

4.2   Supply of Services
Services are regarded as rendered in Israel in the following cases:

- the services are rendered by a person or entity whose business is in Israel; a person who has an agent or branch in Israel shall be regarded as a person whose business is in Israel
- the services are rendered to a resident of Israel, to a partnership most of the rights in which belong to partners resident in Israel, or to a company which, for the purposes of the Income Tax Ordinance, is regarded as resident in Israel
- the services are rendered in relation to an asset situated in Israel.

An activity is regarded as conducted in Israel in the following cases:

- the activity is wholly or mainly conducted in Israel
- the activity is related to an activity conducted by someone mainly in Israel
- the activity is conducted in Israel but forms part of an activity conducted mainly abroad.

4.3   Reverse Charge Mechanism
A reverse charge mechanism exists where, inter alia, foreign residents do not issue Israeli VAT invoices to Israeli recipients of assets or services (see section 2.8).

5 BASIS OF TAXATION

5.1 Supplies within Israel

5.1.1 Price

The price at which transactions are deemed to be conducted is the agreed consideration, including:

- any tax, levy, fee or other compulsory payment imposed on the transaction (except under the VAT Law, Income Tax Ordinance or Land Appreciation Law) unless such payments are imposed by law on the purchaser
- any other costs incurred in carrying out the transaction which the purchaser has agreed to reimburse, including commission or interest on instalment payments, any other interest or payment relating to arrears, compensation for any breach of contract if the underlying transaction is not revoked, and packing costs.

5.1.2 Related Parties

Transactions between related parties should be conducted at an arm's-length price. If this is not determinable, the price should be taken as the cost plus a reasonable profit for that sector.

5.1.3 Excluded Items

Certain donations, support and other forms of aid are deemed to have no price for VAT purposes (see section 7.3).

5.1.4 Net Margin Basis

Dealers in certain spheres are permitted to account periodically for VAT at the usual rate (17%) of the net margin between sales and related purchases or expenditure. This net margin basis is generally applicable to dealers who trade in postage stamps, telephone tokens, revenue stamps, stamped debt instruments and the like, currencies, homes (unless purchased from a financial institution or a not-for-profit body), used cars (unless input VAT was claimable, for instance, by a driving school or car rental firm), and gold coins, medals or bars, subject to certain conditions. The net margin basis is also specified for trade in securities and other traded instruments, but this is considered an anomaly as such assets are excluded from the scope of VAT (see section 3.1).

5.2 Self-Supplies

Self-supplies should be valued on an arm's-length basis for VAT purposes (see section 5.1.2).

5.3 Imports

In the case of imported goods, VAT is generally imposed on their value for Israeli customs purposes, including any applicable import taxes thereon. The customs value will generally be based on the landed cost insurance freight (CIF) wholesale price as assessed by the Customs Authority. The import taxes (but not VAT) may be considerably reduced or eliminated in the case of goods originating in the United States of America, the European Union or the European Free Trade Association, pursuant to Israel's Free Trade Agreements with these areas. If goods are sent abroad for repair, renewal or improvement and then re-imported, only the value of the repair, renewal or improvement will be assessable to VAT.

5.4   Chargeable Event/Time of Payment

5.4.1 Supply of Goods
A sale of goods is liable to VAT upon delivery to the purchaser. If goods are delivered in stages, VAT arises at each stage.

Where goods are delivered to an intermediary party on a consignment basis against payment on account not exceeding 10% of the goods consideration, the VAT liability may be deferred until the goods are sold onwards by the intermediary.

Notwithstanding the foregoing, the VAT liability will crystallise on a cash-received basis in certain cases, including: dealers who keep books on a cash basis in accordance with the tax regulations (eg the liberal professions), asset rental transactions, reverse charge transactions with persons whose primary income is salary or pension or other allowance, and subscriptions to publications, concerts or shows.

Imported goods are subject to VAT upon clearance from the customs. Storing goods in a bonded warehouse will serve to defer payment of the VAT until the goods are released. In the case of imported intangible assets, newspapers and other printed matter, the VAT liability arises when buying or transferring foreign currency, or otherwise making payment, whichever is earliest.

5.4.2 Supply of Services
A service is liable to VAT when rendered. If a service is rendered in stages, VAT arises at each stage. Where a service is rendered continuously and cannot be divided into stages, the VAT liability arises upon completion of the service in certain cases and on a cash received basis in other cases. The cash received basis applies, among others, to: dealers who keep books on a cash basis in accordance with the tax regulations, the provision of credit (except by a financial institution) and reverse charge transactions with persons whose primary income is salary, pension or other allowance.

5.4.3 Real Estate
In general, the liability to VAT on a real estate transaction arises upon the earlier of handover of the property to the purchaser or registration of the purchaser's title in the Land Registry. In the case of building works, the VAT liability arises upon the earlier of completion of the work or handover of the relevant property. If the handover occurs in stages, the VAT liability will apply accordingly.

Building works include digging, demolition, drainage and sewerage, pipe-laying, road and path laying, land preparation, etc.

Notwithstanding the foregoing, a cash received basis of VAT liability applies to cash prepayments to dealers whose books are kept on a cash basis in accordance with the tax regulations, and to sales of air conditioning or central heating systems, prefabricated buildings, acoustic ceilings and elevators.

5.4.4 Self-Supply of Goods/Services
A VAT liability arises on the market value of self-supplied items as follows:

- Goods: when applied to own use

- Real estate: upon taking possession, commencement of own use or registration in the Land Registry, whichever is earliest.

Services not performed for consideration on a bona fide basis are outside the scope of VAT, unless the services are supplied to members of an entity.

According to Israeli Supreme Court decisions, the direct and indirect cost of providing meals to employees at a work place is liable to VAT. Alternatively, the VAT authorities may allow an employer to disclaim input VAT on the meal costs.

Assets left in a dormant business become liable to VAT two years after business has ceased as if a self-supply had occurred (Section 137A).

5.5 Credit Notes/Bad Debts

Credit notes (and debit notes) may be issued if a transaction was wholly or partly cancelled, or the terms or amounts were amended, or if an invoicing error occurred. A bad debt adjustment may only be made to the output VAT of a dealer that keeps books on an accrual basis if there is conclusive evidence that the debt is irrecoverable due, for example, to customer bankruptcy.

Where a credit note (or debit note) is permissible, then:

- if the relevant invoice has not yet been issued to the customer, it should be cancelled and retained
- if the relevant invoice has been issued to the customer, a subsequent invoice in the same period may be adjusted accordingly, or else a credit (or debit) note may be issued. It should be sent by registered mail, or receipt should be confirmed by the customer.

6 TAX RATES

Israel has a single standard rate of VAT, currently 17%. Certain transactions are exempt or zero-rated as outlined in section 7 below.

7 EXEMPTIONS

7.1 Exemptions with Credit for Input Tax (Zero Rate)

Where a sales output transaction is zero-rated, input VAT on related purchases may be credited in the usual way. Summarised below are the principal zero-rated transactions. Detailed rules apply in various cases:

(1) export of goods as evidenced by Israeli Customs documentation (except for a re-export of unset diamonds and precious stones that were exempt from customs duty and VAT on import)

(2) sale of an intangible asset to a foreign resident situated abroad or to a foreign-registered entity that conducts no business or activity in Israel requiring a VAT registration

(3)   sale of goods to a duty-free store

(4)   sale of goods by a duty-free store or by a ship or aircraft on international journeys *

(5)   rendering a service to a foreign resident except for:

-   services relating to tangible or intangible assets in Israel
-   services effectively rendered to Israeli residents in Israel
-   services effectively rendered to other foreign residents in Israel (but not the tourism services listed in (8) below, nor inland sailing trips and related meals provided) *

The foregoing three exceptions do not apply (ie zero-rating is possible) if the services were included in the price of imported goods for customs and VAT purposes.

The District Court has ruled in the Securitas Case that an overseas service recipient that is registered for any purpose in Israel (eg as a recognised foreign insurer) shall be deemed to be an Israeli resident. Hence, services to that recipient would not be zero-rated and VAT registration may be necessary.

(6)   ground services for ships and aircraft in Israel by a port authority or relating to goods handling

(7)   rendering a service abroad by a dealer, whose principal place of business is in Israel *

(8)   various tourism services for foreign residents, including hotel accommodation and related hotel services, car rental, excursions, internal flights in Israel, and hospitalisation *

(9)   sales of goods to new immigrants, returning residents, non-residents and any others who are exempt from purchase tax when importing possessions

(10)   air and sea travel tickets to and from Israel or between abroad and any other transport to and from a neighbouring country

(11)   air or sea cargo transport to and from Israel or between two places abroad and any other cargo transport to a neighbouring country

(12)   sale, lease or import of passenger aircraft and ships

(13)   unprocessed fruit and vegetable sales

(14)   the sale of assets, including equipment of a dealer or dealers, to a company solely in consideration for shares in that company provided that the dealer(s) holds at least 90% of the voting power in the company immediately after the sale. A subsequent sale of those assets will be liable to VAT even if the company ceased to be a dealer under the VAT Law

(15)   sale without consideration of all the assets of an entity in liquidation to the holders of rights in that entity proportionately to their holdings. A subsequent sale of such assets will be liable to VAT

(16)   sales of real estate between financial institutions or not-for-profit bodies, pursuant to tax-deferred reorganisation provisions (Sections 103-105 of the Income Tax Ordinance)

(17)   certain sales of goods to the Eilat Free Trade Area, and transactions between recognised enterprises within the planned Free Processing Zone(s) .

7.2   *Exemptions without Credit for Input Tax*

Certain sales output transactions are exempt from VAT, so that input VAT on related

---

*Detailed rules apply in various cases. For example, consideration should be received in foreign currency in instances 1,4,5,7 and 8 as a condition for zero-rating.

purchases may not be claimed as a VAT credit. Summarised below are the principal exempt transactions. Detailed rules apply in certain cases:

■ rental of residential accommodation for less than ten years, except in a hotel
■ transfer of real estate for key money, according to the terms of a protected tenancy, or rental of a protected tenancy property under the Protected Tenants Law
■ transactions of an exempt dealer (see section 2.1 above)
■ sale of any asset in respect of which input VAT was not claimable by law at the time of purchase or import. A pro rata sale exemption applies if part of the input VAT was not claimable
■ deposit of funds or granting of a loan by a dealer to a financial institution
■ sale of an approved rental building, as defined in the Law for the Encouragement of Capital Investments, after being rented out for at least five years, provided relevant conditions were satisfied
■ the import and export of unset non-synthetic diamonds, precious stones and semi-precious stones if exempt from customs duty, and transactions involving those items by a dealer whose sole business relates to such items
■ various other imports, including the following:

  – imports by new immigrants, returning residents and non-residents if they are exempt from customs duty upon entry to Israel
  – goods exported and re-imported unchanged or after repair, renovation or improvement free of charge
  – gift parcels exempt from customs duty
  – original works of art if they are exempt from customs duty and imported for a museum, educational institution, municipality or other approved public body
  – goods exempted under various international conventions
  – books and manuscripts imported by an educational or cultural institution
  – goods imported by representatives of foreign countries
  – goods imported into the Eilat Free Trade Area (except for vehicles and certain consumer appliances) and other planned Free Processing Zone(s), and most transactions within the Eilat Free Trade Area
  – miscellaneous items.

7.3 Non-Taxable Transactions

Certain transactions are effectively outside the scope of Israeli VAT, including the following:

■ transactions between members or partners who have elected a joint VAT file
■ wages and salaries derived by employees
■ transactions in securities (except for untraded rights in 'real estate entities' (see section 3.3)
■ dividends
■ certain donations, support or aid (see section 7.3.3).

7.3.1 Transactions within the Same Legal Entity

In principle, transactions within the same legal entity will not be considered to be transactions as such. Nevertheless, a dealer with more than one business or business unit may elect to treat each of these as a separate entity for VAT purposes (Section 55). In the case of a branch of a foreign company, the VAT authorities may seek to ensure that VAT on transactions with third parties is not effectively circumvented.

7.3.2 Transfer of Business
In principle, the transfer of business assets or liabilities is liable to VAT. By contrast, the transfer of shares in a company that owns a business is generally considered outside the scope of VAT, except for shares in an untraded 'real estate entity' (see section 3.3).

Certain asset/share exchanges and liquidation disposals are zero-rated, as are real estate sales involving financial institutions or not-for-profit bodies (see section 7.1, items marked (14) to (16).

7.3.3 Subsidies/Penalty Payments/Compensation
In general, each particular payment must be treated on its own merits.

Certain items need not be included in the 'price' of the transaction and are thereby excluded from the scope of VAT.

Such excluded items consist primarily of 'donations, support or aid' directly from the State Budget, including subsidies for basic foodstuffs, kindergarten teachers' salaries, public transportation, grants under the Law for the Encouragement of Capital Investments and supplementary grants for Jerusalem high-tech plants, government research and development grants, electricity supply grants, war and property fund compensation, overseas marketing promotion fund grants, approved export company fund grants, various employment and training subsidies, agricultural investment grants, and water and gasoline equalisation payments.

Also excluded are certain bilateral research and development fund grants (including the US-Israel fund, known as BIRD-F), and grants from the Jewish Agency for the Land of Israel, the World Zionist Labour Federation and the Injured Children's Fund.

7.4 Election to be Registered for VAT
The VAT authorities will only accept applications to register from persons or entities that produce evidence that business is (or will be) conducted in Israel, such as a lease or purchase agreement for premises or a customer agreement. Registering for VAT purposes in Israel can also have Income Tax implications. It is, however, possible to register as a business in the course of formation, with a view to recovering input VAT on purchases.

8   CREDIT/REFUND FOR INPUT TAX

8.1   General Rule
A dealer is generally entitled to claim a credit for input VAT based on a lawfully issued VAT invoice or a customs import document (or other approved document) bearing the dealer's name as the owner of the goods.

The input VAT credit must be claimed within six months after the issuance of the invoice or, in the case of an import, of the customs or other document . A business in the course of formation may be granted, upon application, a credit for input tax on purchases, including purchases incurred prior to registration for VAT purposes.

8.2   Adjustment of Entitlement to Credit

Input VAT is not claimable in certain instances. These include:

- purchases relating to exempt or non-taxable output transactions
- purchase of a sedan car (except in the case of car dealers, driving schools and car rental firms)
- purchases of assets or services with a dual business/private element, to the extent of the private element. Where the business/private split is uncertain, it is generally permissible to credit two-thirds of the input VAT if usage is mainly for business purposes, or one-quarter of the input VAT if usage is mainly for private purposes. The VAT authorities may, on occasion, consider the reasonableness of the split proposed
- purchase of a home, or improvements thereto, used by a dealer as his place of business
- entertaining expenses, unless related to foreign resident guests
- purchases from a Petty dealer (see section 2.1)
- employee meals at a place of work (unless the employees are invoiced with VAT).

8.3   Partial Exemption

Input VAT is not claimable on purchases which relate to exempt (or non-taxable) sales output transactions. Where some of a dealer's overall sales are exempt and some are liable to VAT, the input VAT on purchases relating to exempt sales must be disclaimed on a specific (not formula) basis. In practice, only relatively few types of transactions are exempt from VAT in Israel, so separate ledger accounts may be used to track exempt sales, related purchases, and disallowable input VAT thereon.

8.4   Time of Recovery

If a periodic VAT return shows a balance of input tax in excess of output tax, a refund is claimable. A refund may be requested by depositing a VAT refund application at an Israeli branch of a bank or post office (in lieu of making payment) provided the amount involved does not exceed NIS4,630 (approximately US$1,500). Refund applications above this limit must be submitted to the dealer's local tax office for consideration. By law, refunds should be effected within 30 days after the application is received, unless the VAT authorities decide to review matters.

8.5   Refund for Foreign Business

Foreign enterprises who incur Israeli VAT on their purchases may only recover the VAT by opening a VAT file, which implies the existence of a business presence in Israel (see section 7.4). Unlike some other countries, there is no procedure for claiming a VAT refund on the grounds that no business was done in Israel.

9   ADMINISTRATIVE OBLIGATIONS

9.1   Registration

A dealer must register with the VAT authorities no later than the date of commencing business in Israel. While most dealers are registered as authorised dealers, certain small businesses may be registered as Petty dealers or Exempt dealers with reduced compliance requirements (see section 2.1). A foreign resident that commences to conduct part of its business or activity in Israel must appoint a local VAT representative within 30 days and notify the VAT authorities accordingly.

9.2   Books and Records

Businesses in Israel must keep books and records that comply with comprehensive rules set out in the tax regulations. Payments received must be recorded immediately. With regard to VAT, separate ledger accounts must be maintained with regard to: sales output VAT, purchase input VAT, and the balance due to or from the VAT authorities. Books, records, underlying documents and invoices must be retained for at least seven years after the last book entry or invoice, whichever is latest (VAT Law Section 75).

9.3   Invoices

A dealer must issue an invoice within 14 days after the chargeable event generally, or within seven days where the chargeable event is the receipt of cash (see section 5.4 above). In principle, a short form 'transaction invoice' is sufficient unless the customer requests a more detailed VAT invoice.

In practice, VAT invoices are normally issued as a matter of course, since purchasers who are dealers are obliged to request VAT invoices for all transactions above a minimal amount (approximately US$40) or to pay by cheque crossed to the payee only.

Details that must appear on the VAT invoice include:

- printed sequential number
- the word 'original' printed on the original copy
- date
- despatch note number and date
- customer name
- customer address (if not already known to the dealer)
- description of the goods or service
- the units of measurement
- quantity
- price before VAT
- invoice total before VAT
- VAT rate and amount (marked 'Value Added Tax')
- invoice total including VAT
- signature of the dealer or invoice preparer on his behalf.

With regard to credit or debit notes see section 5.5.

9.4   VAT Returns

In general, Authorised and Petty dealers must file monthly VAT returns, accompanied by any payment due, within 15 days after each month-end. Bi-monthly returns are sufficient for dealers whose annual turnover is less than NIS365,000 (approximately US$120,000). The VAT returns and payments are submitted at a local bank or post office and transmitted to the VAT authorities. VAT arrears bear real (inflation adjusted) interest of 4% per annum.

9.5   Powers of the Authorities

The Israeli VAT authorities have broad powers of enforcement covering, inter alia, information demands, the imposition of penalties and attachment proceedings. In particular, a dealer's books and records may be disqualified if it is found that the dealer failed without good cause to record the receipt of money or the issue of goods from inventory in the prescribed manner, or failed to operate a till when so required, or otherwise failed to keep adequate books and records in accordance with the tax regulations. If the books are disqualified, or if VAT returns appear to be incomplete or inaccurate, the VAT authorities are empowered to issue best-judgement assessments. There may also be severe income tax implications.

9.6   Objection/Appeal

Objections to book disqualifications may be made to a Books Acceptability Committee or the District Court within 15 days after rejection of VAT returns based on such books (Section 74) or to the District Court within 60 days after the disqualification (Section 79).

Objections to a best-judgement assessment may be lodged with the Director of VAT within 30 days after delivery thereof. Tax not in dispute must be paid. A different VAT official will then consider the objection. If the outcome is adverse, the dealer may appeal to the District Court.

10   SPECIAL REGIMES

10.1   Financial Institutions

Financial institutions in Israel, primarily banks and insurance companies, pay a 17% Wage and Profit Tax in lieu of VAT. This tax is deductible for company tax purposes. Input VAT on purchases cannot be recovered by a financial institution under the normal VAT mechanism. Instead, input VAT is added to the related expenditures and will be deductible for Company Tax purposes to the extent that those expenditures are deductible revenue (not capital) items.

10.2   Not-For-Profit Institutions

Not-for-profit institutions whose annual payroll costs exceed NIS46,413 (approximately US$15,000) are liable to an 8.5% Wages Tax. In addition, not-for-profit institutions pay a separate Employers Tax of 4% of their wage costs.

10.3   Autonomous Areas

Under Israel's agreements with the Palestine Liberation Organisation, the Autonomous Areas are to impose their own VAT at a rate of 15% to 16% compared with 17% in Israel. These agreements also prescribe mutual VAT recognition and settling-up procedures to facilitate trade between Israeli dealers and businesses from the Autonomous Areas.

Contributors: Doron Kochavi and Leon Harris
                  Kost, Levary & Forer
                  A member of Ernst & Young International
                  88 Igal Allow Street
                  Tel-Aviv
                  Israel
                  Tel: +972 3 5164 561
                  Fax: +972 3 5164 565

JAPAN

1 GENERAL BACKGROUND

Consumption Tax (Shohizei), hereafter referred to as 'the tax', was introduced in Japan on 1 April 1989. The tax system was based on the European Union model but it has some significant differences, one of which is the use of a book basis rather than an invoice basis. On 1 October 1991 the tax laws were amended to some extent in such areas as the enlargement of the list of tax exempt items.

The tax is administered by either the Corporate or the Individual Affairs Department of the Tax Office, depending upon the fiscal status of the entity subject to taxation, with the exception of Consumption Tax on imports which is administered by Customs.

2 WHO IS TAXABLE?

Entrepreneurs, whether corporate or individual, resident or non-resident, who engage in selling and/or leasing goods or in providing services within Japan are subject to the tax.

Those entrepreneurs with an annual revenue of ¥30 million or less for the base year (the second year prior to the current fiscal year) are not subject to the Tax Regulations, but may elect to be so in order to be eligible to recover previously paid Consumption Tax. The annual revenue figure used to determine qualification for this exemption does not include tax exempt revenue.

A simplified tax system may be applicable for small entrepreneurs whose revenue is ¥400 million or less for the base year.

A marginal exemption can be applied for the current fiscal year during which taxable revenue is under ¥50 million (see section 10 'Special Consumption Tax Regimes').

2.1 Government Bodies
Government bodies are subject to the tax under the same rules as apply to the private sector.

2.2 Fiscal Unity/Group Taxation
No group taxation system exists in Japan and, therefore, each legal entity must file a tax return.

2.3 Foreign Entrepreneurs
The Consumption Tax Act does not contain any special provisions for foreign entrepreneurs. However, those foreign entrepreneurs having sales subject to Consumption Tax of ¥30 million or more for the base year should file a Consumption Tax return for the current year.

This chapter is updated to reflect the law on Consumption Tax in Japan as at 31 October 1994.

Even if the above case does not apply, a Consumption Tax return can be filed to recover input tax on goods or services purchased in Japan, as long as an application for selecting taxable status under the Consumption Tax law is filed by the end of the previous year.

2.4   Tax Representative
A foreign entrepreneur without an office or employees in Japan has to assign a resident tax representative to handle all matters regarding Consumption Tax.

2.5   Importers
Under normal circumstances, the tax is only applicable when consideration is paid for goods or services. Goods imported into Japan are an exception. Any goods imported into Japan, whether for consideration or free of charge, are subject to the tax. However, services provided from outside Japan are not subject to the tax since the place where the service is rendered is abroad.

3   WHAT IS TAXABLE?

The tax is levied on the supply of goods for consideration whether by sale or lease within Japan and on the provision of services for consideration provided within Japan. Additionally, the tax is levied on any goods imported into Japan, whether or not consideration is involved.

3.1   Supply of Goods
The term 'goods' applies to tangible assets such as property and inventory as well as intangible assets and includes such things as:

- transfer of assets by gift with or without consideration
- contribution in kind
- succession to a loan receivable.

The transfer of land is not subject to the tax.

3.2   Leasing
Leasing might well be included in the area of 'services'. However, since the Consumption Tax Act has classified it separately, it will be classified separately here. The term 'leasing of goods' applies to all operations which involve allowing the use of goods for consideration. It additionally includes allowing the rights to goods for consideration. This includes such things as:

- leasing of machines, automobiles and office equipment
- rent for warehouses or safe deposit boxes
- rent for intangible assets such as royalties on patents or copyrights.

The leasing of land and interest paid on loans are not subject to the tax.

3.3   Supply of Services
The following types of services are subject to the tax:

- construction work, repair, transportation and storage
- printing, advertising and intermediation

- performances, technical assistance and information supply
- supply of facilities, dramatic productions and supply of literary works
- professional services provided by entities such as attorneys, certified public accountants and tax advisers.

3.4 Self-Supply of Goods

The term 'self-supply of goods' is defined as any transaction in which:

- an individual entrepreneur consumes or uses, for his or her own use, inventoried or non-inventoried goods which have been provided for business purposes
- a company makes a gift of its assets to its directors.

3.5 Importation of Goods

Any goods delivered from a bonded zone are subject to the tax. Goods consumed or used within a bonded zone are considered delivered and are thus subject to the tax.

Any person or enterprise who imports goods, whether or not for business purposes, must pay the tax at the time of customs clearance.

The only exception is importation of items via the postal service with a value of ¥10,000 or less.

4 PLACE OF SUPPLY

The tax is levied on all goods and services supplied in Japan. Any supply of goods taking place outside of Japan does not fall within the scope of the Consumption Tax Act.

4.1 Supply of Goods

Principally, goods which were physically in Japan prior to the supply or lease of those goods are subject to the tax.

Goods for exportation are exempt from this definition.

The following is a partial list of goods subject to the tax, together with their respective places of supply:

Goods:	Place of supply:
registered ships	the registration office
non-registered ships	the supplier's office
aircraft	the registration or supplier's office
mining rights	the mining site
patents, utility model rights, design rights, trademarks	the registration office (if the registration is in two or more countries, the place of supply is considered to be the supplier's domicile)
copyrights, know-how or similar rights	the supplier's domicile

Goods:	Place of supply:
goodwill, fishing rights	the supplier's domicile
securities (except golf memberships)	existing place of securities
registered governmental bonds	registrar's office
investments in partnerships	domicile of the head office
mortgage bonds	existing place of mortgage bond
goods supplied in circumstances where the location of the goods is uncertain	office of the entrepreneur supplying the goods

4.2 Supply of Services

Services provided in Japan are subject to the tax. The following is a list of some of these, together with their respective places of supply:

Service:	Place of supply:
international transportation	the departure, delivery or arrival location of passengers and cargo
international communication or post	the place of sender or destination of message
insurance	office of the insurance company
information or design supply	office of the supplier
services rendered in connection with surveying, planning or projects which require knowledge of specific scientific or construction techniques (such as mining or building construction)	place from which the majority of the supplies and services are provided
services supplied if the location of services is uncertain	office of the supplier of the services

5   BASIS OF TAXATION

5.1 Supplies in Japan
The basis used for calculating the tax is the revenue from the sale or lease of the goods or services. This revenue includes any liquor, gasoline or other commodity tax applicable to the goods or services.

5.2 Self-Supplies
In the case of self-supply, when any individual entrepreneur consumes or uses goods for his or her own use, or when a company makes a gift of its assets to its directors, the fair market value of the goods becomes the basis for calculation of the tax.

5.3 Imports

For imported goods, the basis used for the calculation of the tax is the value of the goods for customs duty purposes (ie CIF value) plus any applicable commodity taxes and customs duty.

5.4 Chargeable Event/Time of Payment

The tax becomes due and payable at the time of supply or lease of goods or at the time of provision of services.

This time is determined by:

- the date of delivery of the inventory or property
- the effective date of the contract for transfer of patents or execution rights
- the final date (completion date) of the delivery of goods or services for lump-sum contracts
- the final date (completion date) of services provided for other than lump-sum contracts
- the contracted payment date or the date on which the supplier customarily receives consideration for the leased assets.

Special rules apply under circumstances such as trial sales, instalment payments, or construction contracts.

5.5 Cash Basis

Small businesses supplying goods at less than ¥3 million annually have the option of accounting on a cash basis.

5.6 Credit Notes/Bad Debts

The basis used for the calculation of the tax is after any credit notes or net of returned goods, discounts and rebates.

Relief for tax on bad debts is limited under the same regulations described in the Corporate Tax Act. Usually this is the result of insolvency, but also includes a cessation of transactions due to customer financial difficulties which continue for a year or longer.

6 TAX RATE

Under normal circumstances, the tax rate is 3%.

7 EXEMPTIONS

Goods and services exempt from taxation are those which are specifically defined as not being subject to the tax.

7.1 Exemption with Credit for Input Tax

Goods and services which are exempt from the tax and are allowed credit for input tax include:

- exports
- international transportation

- international communication
- sales, lease and repair of ships or aircraft used for international transportation
- interest on loans or cash deposits from non-residents (these are considered quasi-export operations).

7.2   Non-Taxable without Credit for Input Tax

Non-taxable goods and services which do not carry a right to recovery of tax include:

- capital, financial and insurance transactions (including the sale or lease of land, sale of securities, interest on loans, guarantee fees and insurance premiums)
- postal and revenue stamp sales by the government and certain government handling charges which are not in competition with the private sector
- merchandise coupons and pre-paid cards
- foreign exchange transactions
- subsidies, penalty payments and consideration
- dividends.

For political reasons, the following additional items are also non-taxable:

- public medical insurance services
- certain social welfare services, including services for the elderly and children
- school tuition fees, entrance examination fees, text books and the costs of developing and expanding school facilities
- rental payments for private residences
- childbirth and funeral expenses.

8   CREDIT/REFUND OF INPUT TAX

8.1   General Rules

In principle, all Consumption Tax paid on goods and services by an entrepreneur who is using those goods and services to make other taxable goods or services is recoverable by credit or refund. On the other hand the tax paid on goods and services by an entrepreneur who is using those goods and services to make other tax-exempt goods or services cannot be recovered by credit or refund.

If, during a given fiscal year, the taxable items' revenue ratio is 95% or greater, the taxpayer may obtain a credit or refund for the full amount of the tax which was included in the purchase price of the taxable items. If the taxable items' revenue ratio is less than 95%, the taxpayer may be eligible for a partial credit or refund of tax paid.

The taxable items' revenue ratio is calculated as A/B where:

A = total amount of transfer of taxable assets in Japan during the period
B = total value of transfer of all assets in Japan during the period.

For the purposes of this calculation, taxable assets includes items with tax exemption. For the calculation of the denominator, the following transfers are not included:

- transfer of means of payment, such as money, checks, etc
- transfer of monetary assets acquired in consideration of transfer of assets, etc

- transfer of government bonds, local government bonds, negotiable certificates of deposit with repurchase agreement.

Where an enterprise transfers securities, commercial papers or negotiable certificates of deposit, etc other than those items mentioned above, 5% of the amount of consideration must be included in the denominator for the above calculation.

Supplies from exempt entrepreneurs and second-hand goods from consumers are considered as having input tax. Tax exempt transactions are not considered as having input tax.

If the Consumption Tax on purchases has not been recorded as a separate line item, the tax is considered to be included as part of the purchase price. The amount of tax is thus calculated by dividing the purchase price by 1.03 for a resulting tax percentage of 3%.

8.2   Partial Credit or Refund

If the taxable items' revenue ratio is less than 95%, the maximum tax credit is limited to this percentage. There are two methods which may be used to determine the amount of tax credit or refund. These are described below.

8.2.1   Method 1 – Split and Prorate

The tax included in the purchase price of goods and services during the fiscal year is separated into three groups to which different tax treatments are applied:

- tax paid on the purchase of goods and services which were purchased for resale or export as taxable items or exempt with credit is fully creditable. A recapture of this tax credit may occur if the usage of fixed assets changes from a taxable to a non-taxable status within a three-year period
- tax paid on the purchase of goods and services which were purchased for a non-taxable use is not creditable. If the usage of those goods or services changes from a non-taxable to a taxable status, a partial tax credit may be claimed
- tax paid on purchases which are not identified as either taxable or non-taxable is creditable to the extent of the taxable items' revenue ratio. To calculate the amount of tax credit, the amount of tax included in the purchase price is multiplied by the taxable items' revenue ratio. The resulting amount is the amount of creditable tax. With advance approval from the Tax Authorities, the taxable items' revenue ratio may be replaced by a ratio of the number of employees, floor space or other reasonable factor reflecting an approximation of revenue from taxable versus non-taxable items.

8.2.2 Method 2 – Straight Proration

Using the straight proration method, the amount of tax credit is calculated by multiplying the amount of tax included in the purchase price by the taxable items' revenue ratio. The resulting amount is the amount of creditable tax.

8.3   Adjustment of Prior Tax Credit

When a taxpayer purchases a fixed asset, the tax included in the purchase price is creditable. An adjustment of this tax credit is required only when the item cost is ¥1 million or more and the taxable items' revenue ratio for the year in which the asset was purchased deviates by more than 50% from the average taxable items' revenue ratio for the current year and the two years following the purchase.

The adjustment should be made on the fixed assets held at the end of the third year after the purchase and requires a recomputation of the tax credit originally allowed by substituting the three year average taxable items' revenue ratio in the calculation.

8.4 Time of Recovery

The excess of input tax over output tax is refunded by means of filing a tax return.

If the taxpayer files on time, interest is added for the period between the day following the date on which the tax return is due to be filed and the day of the refund decision . If the return is filed after the due date, interest is added from the first day of the month following the month in which the return was filed to the day of the refund decision.

9   ADMINISTRATIVE OBLIGATIONS

9.1 Registration

There are no registration requirements and no registration number is assigned to taxpayers. Those who have been considered exempt due to an annual revenue of ¥30 million or less must file a declaration if their revenue status exceeds this amount.

9.2 Books and Records

Books and records must be kept for a seven-year period. The business accounting books will satisfy this requirement as long as supplementary information entries are made for tax purposes.

9.3 Tax Invoices

The Consumption Tax Act does not require the use of a tax invoice. Input and output tax is calculated based on the descriptions contained in the books of the business. These books/records must include the following details:

- the name and address of the recipient
- the transaction date
- the nature of the goods or services supplied
- the consideration (including tax).

The same information is required for sales or purchases, returns or discounts, goods eligible for tax refund and bad debt losses.

9.4 Consumption Tax Return

9.4.1 Interim and Final Returns

Entrepreneurs must file a tax return and pay any tax due within two months following the end of the fiscal year. The fiscal year for individual taxpayers is always the calendar year.

An interim tax return for the first half-year is required if the estimated tax due based on the prior year will exceed ¥600,000. If the estimated tax due exceeds ¥5 million, interim payments are required in May, August and November (in the case of fiscal years ending on 31 December). Each payment should be one-quarter of the prior year's tax or the taxpayer may elect to calculate tax due quarterly based upon the current year data.

9.4.2 Returns for Foreign Goods Removed from a Bonded Area
For imported goods, a tax return must be filed with the customs office and the tax is due on customs clearance.

9.5 Power of the Tax Authority
If interim tax returns are not filed by the due date, the estimated tax payable is determined by the prior year figures.

Officials of the National Tax Administration, Regional Tax Bureau, National Tax Office and Customs houses have rights to interrogate taxpayers and examine accounting records.

9.6 Penalties
A penalty of up to 15% of the tax liability can be imposed if the tax returns are not filed by the due date, including extensions granted. The penalty for late payment is 14.6% per annum of the balance payable, reduced to 7.3% per annum for the first two months.

10 SPECIAL REGIMES

10.1 Small Businesses

10.1.1 Marginal Exemption
Small entrepreneurs whose taxable revenue was ¥30 million or less for the two prior fiscal years are exempt from taxation. In order to avoid a sudden increase in tax burden, a marginal exemption is allowed for small businesses whose revenue is less than ¥50 million.

The marginal exemption is calculated as follows:

$$\frac{A \times (¥50m - B)}{¥20m}$$

Where
  A = tax payable before applying marginal exemption
  B = taxable sales for the current fiscal year.

¥30M is used for taxable sales for the above calculation if the actual taxable sales amount is ¥30M or less.

10.1.2 Simplified Tax System
Small entrepreneurs whose revenue is ¥400 million or less for the base year may, instead of basing the amount of input tax on actual tax paid, determine the amount of input tax by applying the following percentage to output tax paid:

  90% for wholesalers
  80% for retailers
  70% for manufacturing, construction and mining entities and the agriculture and fisheries industries
  60% for transportation, communications, real estate and service industries.

11   FURTHER READING

Showa Ota & Co, *Shin-shohizei no Jitsumu*, 1989, Chuokeizai-sha
Ministry of Finance, Tax Bureau, Second Taxation Division, 1989, *Shohizei no Kaisetsu,*
Ministry of Finance, Printing Bureau
Ernst & Young International Tax News, March 1989
Ernst & Young International Tax News, June 1991
Kokuzeisokuno No. 4371, June 24, 1991

Contributor: Shigeru Nomura and Kiyoe Ishida
Showa Ota Ernst & Young
Hitotsubashi Building
2-6-3 Hitotsubashi I
Chiyoda – Ku
Tokyo
Japan
Tel: +81 3 3288 2811
Fax: +81 3 3288 2259

KAZAKHSTAN

1 GENERAL BACKGROUND

Value added tax (VAT – known in Kazakhstan as NDS) was introduced by the Law Concerning Value Added Tax of 24 December 1991. This law was subsequently amended on 30 June 1992, 22 December 1992 and 1 April 1993. On 17 January 1992 the VAT legislation was revised by the Main Tax Inspectorate's Instruction which was subsequently amended on 17 August 1992 and 28 January 1993. Legislation concerning the distribution of VAT between Republican and local budgets is contained in the Law of the Republic of Kazakhstan Concerning the Revised Republican Budget for 1994 of 15 July 1994.

VAT is administered by the tax inspectorate responsible for the tax affairs of the enterprise, ie normally the tax inspectorate in the place where the enterprise is located. Tax inspectors also administer direct taxes.

Imports are not subject to VAT.

Future changes to VAT are likely to be introduced by a draft new tax code which is currently being debated by Parliament.

2 WHO IS TAXABLE?

2.1 *General*
VAT applies to all enterprises, associations, institutions and organisations which have the status of legal entities in the Republic of Kazakhstan, including the following:

- enterprises with foreign participation, international associations and foreign legal entities which engage in production and/or other commercial activity on the territory of Kazakhstan
- business partnerships selling goods, work or services in their own names
- individual (family) private enterprises, including peasant (farm) holdings, which carry out production and other commercial activities
- branches, divisions and other economically autonomous subdivisions of enterprises located in Kazakhstan and which independently sell goods, work or services (see section 2.2)
- individuals engaged in entrepreneurial activity without forming a legal entity, if their turnover exceeds 200 tenge a year (approximately US$4, as at December 1994).

2.2 *Transactions with Branch/Subsidiary*
Branches and other economically autonomous subdivisions of enterprises which are located in the territory of the Republic of Kazakhstan and which have settlement accounts at

---

This chapter reflects the law on VAT in Kazakhstan as at 31 December 1994.

banking institutions and independently sell goods, work or services are subject to VAT in their own right.

Transactions between head office and its foreign branches are considered to be export–import transactions and are not subject to VAT.

2.3 Government Bodies
Special provisions exempt non-profit making organisations (including governmental bodies such as municipalities) from VAT.

2.4 Fiscal Unity/Group Taxation
A branch, subdivision, subsidiary or similar entity and the controlling parent company can be regarded as a fiscal entity for VAT purposes, so long as both are located in Kazakhstan, and the branch is not recognised as a separate legal entity. Consolidation will be disallowed if separate bank accounts or accounting records are kept for the individual units, divisions or branches.

2.5 Foreign Business
Under the Kazakh VAT legislation payers of VAT are all foreign enterprises, associations, institutions and organisations which have the status of legal entities in the Republic of Kazakhstan, including enterprises with foreign investment, international associations and foreign legal persons which carry on productive or any commercial activity in the territory of the Republic of Kazakhstan and which independently sell their goods.

Persons engaged in entrepreneurial activity without forming a legal entity are taxable if their receipts from sales exceed 200 tenge (US$4) a year.

2.6 VAT Representatives
The fiscal representative for VAT is usually the same person as for profit tax declaration.

2.7 Importers
At present, VAT is not levied on imports although it is levied on the resale of goods which are imported.

3 WHAT IS TAXABLE?

The supply of goods, work and services by enterprises or entrepreneurs from Kazakhstan which are not exported outside the Commonwealth of Independent States (CIS) for a consideration is subject to VAT.

3.1 Supply of Goods
For the purposes of taxation, 'goods' are defined as all objects, manufactured articles, all production (including production of a technical nature), immovable property (including buildings and installations), electric and thermal power and gas.

The following are also considered as taxable:

- the sales value of goods exchanged in barter deals
- internal sales of goods within an enterprise for its own purposes, where such expendi-

ture can not be treated as a tax-deductible cost of production, and sales to an enterprise's own employees

- the turnover from free or partly paid transfers of a business to other enterprises or citizens, except when such transfers are to budget-financed institutions or to other institutions for charitable purposes
- the turnover from sales for foreign currency in the territory of the Republic of Kazakhstan.

The cost of returnable packaging is not included in taxable turnover unless this packaging is resold by the manufacturers.

3.2 Supply of Services
The provision of services is subject to VAT, including but not limited to:

- passenger and freight transport services, including the transportation of gas, oil, oil products, electrical and thermal power; services associated with the loading, unloading and reloading of goods, and with storage
- communications services, consumer services, housing and utility services (within State prices)
- advertising services.

3.3 Supply of Work
The taxable base for the sale of work is the value of construction, installation, repairs, scientific research, experimental design, technical, project investigation and other work which is performed.

3.4 Self-Supply of Goods/Services
The taxable amount of a self-supply of goods and services (where the expenditure cannot be treated as a cost of production – roughly equivalent to tax-deductible expenses in Kazakhstan accounting), is determined on the basis of prices for similar goods. Where these do not exist the taxable amount is based on the actual cost of production. For the manufacture of goods from raw materials, the taxable turnover is the cost of processing of the materials.

4   PLACE OF SUPPLY

VAT applies to supplies of goods and services taking place in Kazakhstan.

5   BASIS OF TAXATION

The taxable base is the turnover from the sale of goods, work and services performed in Kazakhstan. Turnover is defined as the cost of goods, work and services sold, using established prices. VAT is excluded from the calculation but excise and customs duties are included.

For barter transactions and free partly-paid transfers, turnover is determined on the basis of prevailing market price at the time of the barter/transfer. The market prices may not be lower than actual production cost.

Currently, VAT is not levied on imports, although it is levied on the resale of imported goods.

5.1   Intermediary Services

For intermediary services, the taxable turnover is the receipt from commissions, mark-ups and other levies.

5.2   Retail Enterprises

For retail enterprises, taxable turnover is the difference between the sales price of goods and the price at which settlement is made with suppliers, both including VAT (a special rate of 16.67% is used, giving an effective rate of 20%).

5.3   Other

For other types of enterprise, the taxable turnover is determined in the same way as for auction sale, wholesale transaction or other resale organisations.

5.4   Chargeable Event/Time of Payment

Sales are considered to have been completed on the day of receipt of cash/bank transfer. For enterprises which are permitted to recognise sales on a despatch date basis (ie joint ventures and other enterprises with foreign investment), sales are recognised for VAT purposes also on the date of transfer of goods or provision of services.

6   TAX RATES

Currently there are three rates:

10%:   essential goods as defined by the Cabinet of Ministers such as vegetables, milk and fish products, eggs, vegetable oil, sugar, tea, margarine, etc

13%:   public catering enterprises, ie cafeteria style restaurants as compared to restaurants or cafes

20%:   all other goods and services which are not taxed at the 10%, 13% or a higher rate or exempt

Higher rates: exports to CIS member states in which the VAT rate exceeds 20%.

7   EXEMPTIONS

The most significant exemptions from VAT are divided into the two categories given below:

7.1   Exemptions with Credit for Input Tax

The supply of certain goods and services is exempt from VAT but the supplier may reclaim the VAT paid on purchases which are attributable to such suppliers. Such goods include:

■   exports outside the CIS
■   goods and services intended for official and personal use by foreign diplomatic or similar representations

- services connected with the transport, loading, unloading and re-loading of export goods, including the transit of foreign freight across the territory of Kazakhstan
- municipal passenger transport services (excluding taxis), and suburban passenger transport services
- the construction of living accommodation
- property of State enterprises acquired through privatisation, and lease payments related to the leasing of enterprises formed on the basis of State enterprises.

7.2 Exemptions without Credit for Input Tax

Suppliers of the following goods and services are not obliged to charge or account for VAT but they are not entitled to recover any input VAT relating to these activities:

- operations connected with the issue, insurance, re-insurance and transfer of loans and operations relating to deposits, current, settlement and other accounts
- the issue, receipt and concession of patents, copyrights and licences
- public education services related to industrial training
- payment for teaching children, adolescents, art schools, sports clubs, pre-schools and boarding institutions for children, family-type children's homes and services for the care of the sick and elderly
- services of cultural and art institutions, tourist organisations, theatrical, sporting, cultural and educational events
- scientific research, project survey, geological prospecting, research and design, technical, and forest management work which is carried out using the State's budget resources or the non-budget resources of enterprises and associations, and work and services involving the prevention and rectification of natural disasters
- operations associated with the circulation of legal tender and securities
- the sale of postage stamps (excluding stamps sold for collection purposes) and lottery tickets
- activities performed by specially authorised bodies, for which a State duty is levied
- goods sold by State and Collective Farms for domestic State requirements and to school cafeterias, kindergartens, homes for the disabled, village hospitals and boarding homes
- agricultural products produced and sold by peasant farms.

7.3 Non-Reclaimable Items

VAT related to fixed and intangible assets is capitalised and written off to the cost of production via depreciation.

Goods, work and services used for non-production requirements are also not allowed to be taken as a reduction to output tax.

Goods and services used in connection with exempt supplies where no tax is reclaimable on inputs or chargeable on outputs cannot be recovered.

8   CREDIT/REFUND FOR INPUT TAX

VAT paid on raw and other materials, fuel, components and other articles which have been purchased and used for production purposes are taken as a reduction to the VAT collected from customers for the sale of goods, work and services.

Overpayments of VAT may be applied to future VAT obligations or reimbursed. The reimbursements should be made on a monthly basis, but not later than the fifteenth day of the month following the reporting month, so long as computations are presented before the tenth day of the month.

If the computations are presented after the tenth day, the refund must be made within five days of presentment. Refunds will not be made for computations presented one year after the month in which the last computations were presented to the tax authorities.

Exporters may reclaim tax on presentation of a customs declaration stamped 'export permitted'. This documentation confirms that the goods have left the territory of Kazakhstan (see section 3). Payment documents verifying the purchase and tax paid should also be presented. Goods must be exported within one year of purchase.

9   ADMINISTRATIVE OBLIGATIONS

9.1   Registration
There is no registration process for VAT in the Republic of Kazakhstan and no special bodies have yet been set up to administer it; the new tax is at present administered by the local and Republican tax inspectorates.

9.2   Books and Records
Books and records must be kept for three years and must be available for inspection on request.

9.3   Invoices
In settlement documents (payment orders, payment request orders, payment requests) for goods, work and services sold, the amount of VAT must be shown on a separate line and must be paid first and foremost. The amount of tax shall also be shown separately in cheque registers and in registers of the receipt of letter-of-credit resources.

Each VAT document should include the following information:

- the name, address and registered number of the enterprise
- the names of banks where the enterprise has settlement and other accounts
- a description of the supplied goods or the type and volume of services
- the rate of VAT
- the tax amount relating to the consideration.

9.4   VAT Returns
VAT returns should be submitted and tax paid at specified intervals which depend on the turnover level of the enterprises as detailed below:

9.4.1 Monthly VAT Returns
Enterprises with average monthly VAT payments in excess of 5,000 tenge (approximately US$100) must file a monthly VAT return. The VAT must be paid on the basis of the actual

turnover from the sale of goods, work or services for the calendar month which has elapsed, but not later than the twentieth day of the following month.

For enterprises with average monthly VAT payments in excess of 15,000 tenge (approximately US$300), the enterprise must make advance payments on the thirteenth, twenty-third and thirtieth day of the following month of one-third of the VAT paid for the previous month.

9.4.2 Annual VAT Returns
Enterprises with average monthly VAT payments under 1,000 tenge (approximately US$20), must file a VAT return and pay VAT on an annual basis, but not later than 20 January of the following year. However, approval of the Tax Inspectorate must be granted.

9.5 Powers of Authorities
The Main Tax Inspectorate has the right to establish any tax return period and payment deadlines it thinks fit.

9.6 Penalties for Late Filing/Payment
A penalty of 1.5% of the unpaid tax liability will be assessed for each day the return is overdue. The same penalty applies to each day the VAT payment is late.

9.7 Objections/Appeals
Taxpayers have the right to review the audit reports prepared for the Tax Inspectorate, appeal against the tax authorities' decisions, and present documentation supporting and explaining their tax calculations, tax payments, audit findings and their entitlement to specific tax deductions or exclusions.

Contributor: Aigul Begdullaeva
Ernst & Young Kazakhstan
Almaty 480051
Prospect Lenina 212a
Kazakhstan
Tel: +7 3272 541520
Fax: +7 3272 542385

KOREA

1   GENERAL BACKGROUND

Value added tax (VAT) in Korea was enacted on 22 December 1976 and became effective on 1 July 1977. VAT replaced the earlier indirect tax which had complex tax rates and tax payment procedures. The legislation, which has been partially revised on five occasions, is supported by presidential decrees which provide specific regulations concerning the details of assessment and collection of the tax. Internally, VAT is administered by the Office of National Tax Administration. VAT on imports is administered by the Office of Customs Administration.

2   WHO IS TAXABLE?

2.1   General
A person who engages in the supply of taxable goods or services independently in the course of business, whether or not for profit, is liable to VAT. Taxpayers include individuals, corporations (including the State, local authorities and associations of local authorities) and any bodies of persons, foundations, or any other organisations, which are not incorporated.

2.2   Transactions with Branch/Subsidiary
Since each place of business is subject to tax liability, VAT is imposed even on transactions within the same legal entity; thus supplies of services between a branch and its foreign head office are subject to VAT.

2.3   Government Bodies
Government bodies are not subject to VAT in respect of their activities of an administrative, social, or cultural nature. However, they are liable to VAT in respect of their commercial activities or activities which are deemed to be in competition with commercial concerns.

2.4   Fiscal Unity/Group Taxation
The head offices of corporations or headquarters of private companies may account for VAT on a combined basis after obtaining prior approval from the relevant tax office, if there are more than two places of business.

2.5   Foreign Entrepreneurs
Entrepreneurs who have no establishment in Korea but who supply taxable goods or services in Korea are subject to VAT. A foreign entrepreneur is taxable in Korea when he acts as the importer of goods.

Generally, a non-resident entrepreneur is considered to have an establishment for VAT purposes if he keeps in Korea a regular place of activity such as an office, shop, factory or

This chapter reflects the law on VAT in Korea as at 31 December 1994.

even just a fixed domicile from which the activity is exercised. A non-resident entrepreneur with an establishment in Korea is treated as a local company and should comply with all the rules applicable to Korean entrepreneurs.

2.6 Representative Office
Representative offices of foreign entrepreneurs are not regarded as taxable persons when they only carry out activities of a preparatory or auxiliary nature.

2.7 VAT Representatives
The concept of VAT representative does not exist in Korean VAT law.

2.8 Reverse Charge Mechanism
The liability for the payment of VAT due by a non-resident entrepreneur who does not maintain a fixed establishment in Korea is shifted to the recipient of the goods or services.

2.9 Importers
Goods brought into Korea are liable to VAT at customs clearance. The tax is payable by the importer. If the goods are sent directly by the foreign firm to the final customer in Korea who appears as the actual importer, the VAT due on the imports will be payable by the Korean customer.

3 WHAT IS TAXABLE?

3.1 Supply of Goods
The term 'supply' usually refers to the actual transfer of ownership of the goods from one person to another against payment. A supply of goods refers to the delivery or transfer of goods by any contractual or legal action. Specific types of delivery or transfer are as follows:

- cash sales, credit sales, instalment sales, deferred payment sales, conditional sales, time-fixed sales, consignment sales, etc
- delivery of goods under an exchange contract
- delivery or transfer of goods by such contractual or legal causes as public sale, auction, condemnation, investment in kind, etc.

Goods include tangible and intangible objects which have the value of property. Tangible goods include inventory assets such as commodities, products, raw materials and fixed assets such as machinery or buildings, etc. Intangible objects include motive power, heat, and other controllable forces of nature. 'Having the value of property' means having the use of objects and being able to market them. In practice there is some difficulty in deciding whether or not an intangible object has the value of property.

3.2 Supply of Services
The supply of services refers to the rendering of services or giving to a person the right to use goods, facilities or rights under any contractual or legal contract. Services include all services and other actions which have the value of property, other than goods, and are related to the following businesses:

- construction
- food and lodging
- transportation, warehouse, communications
- financing, insurance, real estate service. However, the leasing of farmlands, orchards, ranch sites and saltfields are excluded. Real estate transactions are regarded as providing goods
- social and individual service business
- allowing the use of commodities such as machinery, or facilities such as a wedding hall
- allowing the use of patent or trademark rights.

3.3   Self-Supplies of Goods/Services

The following cases are deemed to be supplies of goods/services and are, therefore, liable to VAT.

- *Self-supply:* where a trader directly uses or consumes, for his own business, goods that are acquired or produced in connection with his business. The applicable goods include goods produced or acquired from a taxable business and used or consumed for a VAT-exempt business, and goods produced or acquired from a taxable business and used as small passenger cars for non-business purposes or used or consumed for maintenance of such cars.

- *Supply for personal purposes:* where a trader uses or consumes, for personal purposes or that of his employees and with no direct relation to his taxable business, goods which he has produced or acquired. However, goods which are used:

  - as materials in the trader's taxable business
  - in an experiment for technical development
  - as a substitution for repair expense
  - for exchange of poor quality goods
  - in an exhibition for PR/advertising
  - for rendering of free after-sales services

  are excluded from this rule.

- *Donation:* where a trader donates goods produced or acquired in connection with his taxable business to his customers or to an unspecified large number of persons. However, free samples distributed for business purposes or goods subject to non-deductible input tax are excluded.

- *Inventory goods at the time of business closure:* where inventory goods at the time of cessation of a trader's business or where a registered trader does not actually commence business, are considered as being supplied to the trader himself.

- *Services:* in the case of self-supply of services, where a trader renders services directly for his own business, taxes are, in principle not levied. However, if the non-taxing of self-supplied services has a negative effect on competition with fellow traders who provide the same kind of services, the self-supply is taxed by order of the government. Also, supplies of services without consideration or supplies of labour under an employment agreement are not considered to be a supply of services.

3.4 Importation of Goods

Importation of goods means bringing the following commodities to Korea:

■ goods arriving in Korea from a foreign country
■ reimporting to Korea goods which had been exported under licence. However, bringing goods back to Korea which had been licensed for export but which had not been shipped from the bonded area is not considered an importation.

4 PLACE OF SUPPLY

VAT is chargeable in Korea only if the supply of goods or services takes place in Korea. The rules for determining the place of supply are different for goods and services.

4.1 Supply of Goods

The place of supply of goods is one of the following:

■ where goods require to be moved, the place of supply is where the movement of the goods starts
■ where the goods do not require to be moved, the place of supply is the place where the goods are located.

4.2 Supply of Services

The place of supply of services is one of the following:

■ the place where services are rendered or goods, facilities or rights are used
■ in the case of international transportation carried on by a non-resident person or foreign corporation in which the services are supplied both inside and outside Korea the place of supply is where passengers embark or freight is loaded.

4.3 Reverse Charge Mechanism

Where a non-resident entrepreneur who does not maintain a fixed establishment in Korea provides certain specified services to a Korean entrepreneur, the VAT liability will normally fall on the purchaser because the liability shifts to the recipient of the services but, where these services are used for VAT taxable businesses, the recipient is exempt from paying the VAT. These services are:

■ the letting of real estate, transfer of mining, illumination and quarrying rights, hire of automobiles and machinery, transfer of copyright in scientific works, patents, trademarks, formula and processing methods, the provision of films and tapes for radio, television and broadcasting
■ ship and aircraft chartering
■ the provision of information on technology and marketing
■ the provision of technology and the transfer of rights in technology
■ the repair of machinery
■ the transmission of information
■ the provision of films, records and tapes required for publishing books.

5   BASIS FOR TAXATION

5.1   Supplies within Korea

VAT is assessed on the total price received, or to be received, as consideration for the supply of the goods or services. On that basis, ancillary expenses, additional payments, commissions, wrapping expenses, interest relating to the supply (as opposed to financial interest), insurance charged by the seller and customs duties are part of the taxable basis. If no moneys are received, VAT must be assessed on the total value of the goods or services received in exchange for the supply.

5.2   Self-Supplies

VAT due on self-supplies is calculated on the basis of the purchase price of the goods or otherwise on the cost to the supplier.

5.3   Imports

VAT due on the importation of goods is assessed on the value determined for customs purposes, to which should be added taxes or duties paid on the importation.

5.4   Chargeable Event/Time of Payment

In the case of goods, VAT is due at the time of delivery when transportation is required, otherwise at the time when the goods are ready for use; in the case of services VAT is due at the time of rendering the services, or exercising rights, or utilising goods and facilities. In the case of importation, the VAT is payable at the time of customs clearance.

5.5   Credit Notes/Bad Debts

When an entrepreneur sells his goods on credit, he is required to pay VAT on the goods sold to the concerned tax authority even before he collects the payment. However, if the buyer goes into bankruptcy within three years from the date he sells the goods on credit, he can claim the refund of output VAT paid on the uncollected account receivables.

6   TAX RATES

0%:   exports and certain other categories of supplies (see section 7.1)

10%:   all other supplies of goods and services which are not taxable at 0% or exempt

7   EXEMPTIONS

7.1   Exemption with Credit for Input Tax

The following supplies are liable to VAT at the zero rate and qualify for recovery of input tax:

- exports
- goods supplied by designated suppliers which are purchased by foreign tourists and which are taken out of the country
- goods transferred by local letter of credit or a letter of purchasing approval under the External Trade Law which will be exported ultimately

- services rendered outside Korea
- international transportation (goods and passengers) services by ship or aircraft
- other goods or services supplied for earning foreign currency: the supply of goods or services to residents or unspecified persons (including domestic corporations), which are paid for either in a foreign currency or in the Korea Won but which indirectly contribute to earning foreign currency
- prescribed military materials supplied by designated military supply enterprises
- petroleum, etc supplied to groups and organisations established by the National Military Organisation Act
- subway construction services supplied directly to the State, a local government, or a subway corporation
- certain machines and material for agriculture such as manure, chemicals, etc
- certain machines and materials for fishery such as fishing gear, etc.

7.2   *Exemption without Credit for Input Tax*

The following supplies are exempt from input tax and do not qualify for input credit:

- basic unprocessed foodstuffs (including agricultural, livestock, marine and forest products)
- piped water
- briquettes and anthracite coal
- passenger transport services, except for passenger transportation services by aircraft, express (special or chartered) bus or special automobiles
- medical and health services including the services of veterinarians, nurses, midwives, pharmacists' medicine dispensing services and human blood
- certain educational services
- books, newspapers, magazines, official gazettes, communication and broadcasting, but excluding advertisements
- artistic works, cultural and non-professional sports events
- admission to libraries, science museums, museums, art galleries, zoos or botanical gardens
- personal services rendered in the course of business carried on by lawyers and accountants
- finance and insurance services
- other personal services rendered by actors, singers, radio performers, composers, writers, designers, professional sportsmen, dancers, waitresses, insurance salesmen, translators, shorthand writers, harbour pilots, etc
- academic and technical research services
- systems analysis and programming services
- monopoly goods and manufactured cigars and cigarettes
- letting of houses or the land pertaining to the house (of an area which is not larger than five to ten times the floor space of the house)
- postage stamps (excluding stamps for collection), revenue and certificate stamps, lottery tickets and public telephones
- such goods or services rendered by religious, charitable, scientific or other organisations which promote the public interest
- goods or services supplied by the government, local authorities, associations of local authorities or organisations which carry on business for the government

- goods or services supplied, without consideration, to the government, local authorities, associations of local authorities or public benefit organisations
- specified national houses and services relating to constructing such houses
- specified petroleum, etc used for farming or fishery
- petroleum, etc supplied directly to the Korea Shipping Association for the use of passenger vessels navigating along the coast
- petroleum, etc supplied directly to the Central Association of the Fisheries Co-operative Associations for the generation of power to be used on specified islands
- food supply service (confined to meals) supplied by a person operating a school, factory, mine or construction site or similar business place or by a person directly running a student welfare refectory
- supplementary equipment for handicapped persons
- agricultural management and farming services.

Importation of the following customs duty-exempt goods under the Customs Law are exempted from VAT:

- non-processed foodstuffs, including agricultural, livestock, marine and forest products which are used for food
- books, newspapers and magazines
- goods imported for scientific, educational or cultural use by a scientific research institute, educational institute or cultural organisation
- goods donated from a foreign country to a religious, charitable, relief or any other public benefit organisation
- goods donated by a foreign country to the State, local authorities or associations of local authorities
- duty-exempt goods of a small amount which are donated by a Korean resident and are recognised to be used directly by the donee
- goods imported through house-moving, immigration or inheritance
- personal effects of travellers, goods arriving by separate post and mailed goods that are exempted from customs duties or chargeable at the simplified tariff rates
- samples of commodities or goods for advertisement that are imported and exempted from customs duties
- other duty-exempt goods imported, without any consideration, for the purposes of exhibition, public display, prize shows, film festivals or similar events
- goods which are exempted from customs duties under the provisions of treaties, international law or practices
- duty-exempt or duty-reduced goods which are reimported after exportation of the goods provided that, in the case of the reduction of duty exemption of VAT is restricted to the duty-reduced portion
- duty-exempt or duty-reduced goods which are temporarily imported on the condition of re-exportation provided that, in the case of the restriction of customs duties, exemption of VAT is restricted to the duty-reduced portion
- other duty-free, duty-exempt or duty-reduced goods provided that, in the case of the reduction of customs duties, exemption of VAT is restricted to the duty-reduced portion
- stone coal
- goods for subway construction which are difficult to produce in Korea

- vessels to be used for taxable business
- bonded construction goods pursuant to the Customs Act to be used for taxable business
- articles to be used by the Exposition Organising Committee for the International Trade and Industry Exposition, and which are difficult to manufacture in the country.

7.3 Non-Taxable Transactions

7.3.1 Transactions within the Same Legal Entity

Goods taken out of warehouses which have facilities only for simple custody and administration are not taxable transactions. However, removals of goods from tax warehouses in order to sell them directly to purchasers are taxable supplies.

7.3.2 Transfer of Business

The transfer of a business or of a complete and independent branch of activity is not subject to VAT.

7.3.3 Subsidies/Penalties/Payments/Compensation

Subsidies from the government and other public agencies are not included in the VAT base.

Reserves for bad debts are not subject to VAT.

7.4 Election to be Subject to VAT

Traders may elect to become taxable persons in respect of their supplies of exempt goods/services for a period of three years from the first day of the first calendar year in which the waiver is intended to be applied.

8 CREDIT/REFUND FOR INPUT TAX

8.1 General Rule

The principle is that all the VAT paid on goods and services by a taxable person is recoverable.

No credit is available for input tax:

- where a tax invoice has not been received, or the tax invoice has not been submitted to the tax office, or the required information on the tax invoice is missing or is incorrect
- in respect of expenses not directly related to the business
- for small passenger car purchase and maintenance expenses which are unrelated to business operations
- in respect of supplies of entertainment expenses or equivalents
- in respect of tax-exempt goods or services
- in respect of input tax liability incurred before registration of the business.

8.2 Partial Exemption

Entrepreneurs making both taxable and exempt supplies are allowed to recover only the input VAT relating to taxable supplies.

If the goods or services purchased are used both for taxable and exempt supplies, the creditable input tax is calculated in the ratio of the turnover of supplies which are entitled to credit to the total turnover.

8.3   Time of Recovery

When recoverable input VAT is in excess of output VAT an application can be made to the tax authorities to obtain a refund of the excess. The refund is payable within 30 days after the filing of the claim.

9   ADMINISTRATIVE OBLIGATIONS

9.1   Registration

A person must register the required particulars of each place of business within 20 days from the business commencement date. However, the particulars may be registered even before the business commencement date if preferred. The competent tax office will issue a trader's registration certificate to the trader concerned.

9.2   Books and Records

A trader is required to enter details of all transactions into the account books of the business and to keep them at each place of business.

Where a trader supplies exempt goods or services together with taxable goods or services, he should record the necessary details separately in the books. He must keep the books in which trading details are recorded, together with every tax invoice or simplified tax invoice issued or received, for a period of five years from the date of the final return for the taxable period in which the transactions are made.

9.3   Invoices

When a registered trader supplies goods or services, he must issue an invoice to the other party. The contents of the invoice should contain:

- the registration number and the name and address of the taxable person
- the name, address and registration number of the purchaser
- a description of the goods/services supplied
- the value of the supply and VAT thereon
- the date of issue of the tax invoice
- other particulars as prescribed by the Presidential Decree.

Taxable persons who carry on certain businesses such as retail outlets, restaurants, hotels, passenger transport, etc may issue simplified VAT invoices in which the name of the purchaser and the amount of VAT need not be recorded separately.

All invoices must be issued in the month immediately following that in which the supply takes place.

9.4   VAT Returns

Taxable persons must file a VAT return and pay the tax due to the District Tax Office within 25 days (50 days in case of a foreign corporation) after the end of each VAT quarterly, ie 31 March, 30 June, etc.

9.5   Power of the Authorities

The tax authorities may amend the tax base, issue tax assessments or alter a tax refund for each tax period for any of the following reasons:

- failure to file the final tax return
- errors, or omissions found in the final return
- not submitting tax invoices wholly or partly in filing the final return
- concerns about tax evasion resulting from:
    - frequent movement of the place of business
    - establishing the place of business in the area in which the frequent movement takes place
    - suspension of business or closure of business

9.6 Objections/Appeals

An entrepreneur may request a reduction or a repayment of VAT if it was wrongly assessed/paid.

The claim must be filed to the director of the district tax office or to the chief of the National Tax Office through the director of the district tax office within 60 days from the date on which the taxpayer's rights or the profits thereof are violated by receiving unfair treatment, or failing to receive necessary treatment.

10   SPECIAL VAT REGIMES

10.1 Small Businesses

There is a special simplified regime for certain individual traders who supply goods or services in respect of which the VAT inclusive consideration during a calendar year falls under the following limits:

- VAT-inclusive consideration of less than 36 million Won (except for an individual trader who carries on a manufacturing, mining, or retail business, and an entertainment business applicable to a special consumption tax), or a trader who newly-establishes a business that falls under the guidelines of ineligibility for special taxation set by the Commissioner of National Tax Administration or
- VAT-inclusive consideration of less than 9 million Won – in the case of a transaction through a proxy, agent, intermediary, consignee or contractor where a trader carries on a business in which transactions are made through a proxy, agent, intermediary, consignee or contractor and other kinds of business at the same time
- where the VAT-inclusive consideration calculated by multiplying the aggregate consideration for supplies through a proxy, agent, intermediary, consignee or contractor and adding it to the aggregate consideration for other kinds of supplies is less than 36 million Won.

Where a taxable person qualifies for the special regime for small businesses, VAT payable is calculated by reference to the annual turnover. The output tax is deemed to be 2% of the gross annual turnover or 3.5% in the case of any transaction through a proxy, agent, intermediary, consignee or contractor. Such persons are entitled to input tax recovery amounting to 5% of the input tax shown on tax invoices submitted to the government. However, where the amount of input tax recoverable exceeds the amount of output tax payable, there is no refund of the excess.

A person eligible for this VAT treatment should issue simplified tax invoices.

A person entitled to this treatment must, with his preliminary tax return, pay an amount equal to one-half of the net VAT payable for the immediately previous taxable period. However, where the value of supplies for the preliminary return period are less than one-quarter of that for the immediately previous taxable period due to the closure or suspension of the business, the taxable person is obliged to pay VAT on his true taxable base.

A person eligible for this special treatment may elect to be taxed in the normal way.

11   FURTHER READING

Lee Sung Shik, *VAT Law Explanation*, Daehan Tax Association, 1990

Kim Du Chun, *The Theory and practical uses of VAT Law: history of taxation*, 1987

Lee Sang Won, Kim Bong Gun, *Comparison of transaction time under VAT Law and appliance of Zero-Rating*, Korea Tax Association, 1989

Contributors: Ken Cook and Yun Taik Auo
                Ernst & Young
                Dae Yu Building
                11-14th floor
                25-15, Yeoido- Dong
                Yungdeungpo-Ku
                Seoul
                Korea
                Telephone: 82 2 783 1000
                           82 2 783 5261
                           82 2 784 6991
                Fax: 82 2 783 5890
                           82 2 785 6991
                           82 2 786 6956

NEW ZEALAND

1   GENERAL BACKGROUND

The value added tax which New Zealand introduced on 1 October 1986 is referred to as Goods and Services Tax (GST). The New Zealand legislation is contained in the Goods and Services Tax Act 1985 and is substantially administered by the Inland Revenue Department. GST on imported goods and those subject to excise is administered by the Customs Department.

2   WHO IS TAXABLE?

2.1   General
A 'registered person' is required to charge GST on taxable supplies made and to account for this tax to the Revenue. A registered person is any person (including an individual, company, partnership, public/local authority) that conducts or intends to conduct a taxable activity.

A 'taxable activity' is the continuous or regular supply of goods or services for consideration, whether or not for profit. This includes ordinary business, trades, professions, public authorities, clubs, societies and charities.

'Taxable supplies' includes all supplies made (other than exempt supplies) by a registered person in the course of their taxable activity.

A number of activities are not taxable activities. These include employment income, hobby activities, and that part of any taxable activity that involves the making of exempt supplies, eg domestic dwelling rents.

Any person conducting a taxable activity in New Zealand whose supply of goods or services in any 12-month period exceeds or is likely to exceed NZ$30,000 in value (excluding GST) is required to register with the Inland Revenue Department as a registered person. Any person required by law to register but who fails to do so is deemed to be registered.

Persons are entitled to register for GST voluntarily when supplies are below the registration limits, and such registrations are commonplace. Registration enables a business to reclaim as input tax GST arising on expenditure which is attributable to its own taxable supplies of goods and services. Input tax cannot be recovered where it relates to exempt supplies.

2.2   Transactions with Branch/Subsidiary
Generally, transactions between the head office and a branch of the same company are considered to be internal transactions and therefore not taxable, even where the head office and the branch are in different countries. In contrast, transactions between a company and its subsidiaries will generally be a taxable supply (see section 2.4 'Fiscal Unity/Group Registration').

This chapter reflects the law on GST tax in New Zealand as at 31 December 1994.

2.3   Government Bodies
Government bodies are liable to GST like any other person.

2.4   Fiscal Unity/Group Registration
If a registered person consists of more than one unit, division or branch, then accounting for GST as one single enterprise is generally required. However, if separate accounts are kept for the individual units, divisions or branches, they may, upon request, be registered and account for GST separately.

A company with one or more subsidiaries is not automatically regarded as one entity. However, companies (and other business entities) may, upon request, be registered as one single enterprise, provided all the companies are themselves registered and there is a sufficient degree of common ownership and control.

Where registered persons are able to be grouped, then one must be nominated as the representative member and any taxable activity carried on by a member of the group is deemed to be carried on by that member and that member is required to account for all GST relating to the group. All members are jointly and severally liable for tax payable by the representative member.

2.5   Representative Office
A representative office of a foreign business will be required to register for GST where it makes taxable supplies in New Zealand. For example, a New Zealand sales and booking office of an international airline that does not operate out of New Zealand would be required to register, as the representative office would make the airline 'resident' for GST purposes and it would then be deemed to be making a taxable supply in New Zealand.

A foreign business distributing goods via an agent or representative in New Zealand is not required to register for GST purposes unless the supply is made in New Zealand.

2.6   GST Representatives
An agent or representative in New Zealand that carries on a taxable activity on behalf of an absentee principal is liable to file GST returns and account for GST in respect of that activity.

2.7   Reverse Charge Mechanism
The concept of reverse charges in respect of services received from abroad is not used in New Zealand.

2.8   Foreign Persons
Foreign persons are generally liable to account for GST in relation to supplies made in New Zealand if the goods or services are in New Zealand at the time of supply. Foreign persons are liable to GST when importing goods into New Zealand, whether registered or not.

Foreign persons with a fixed establishment in New Zealand, including branches or agencies, are treated in the same manner as New Zealand resident registered persons.

2.9   Importers
A foreign person is not obliged to register for GST if title to the imported goods passes outside New Zealand, and the customer himself imports the goods.

3   WHAT IS TAXABLE?

Taxable supplies are all supplies (other than exempt supplies) made in New Zealand in the course or furtherance of a taxable activity. GST is applied at either a standard rate (currently 12.5%) or a zero-rate. The zero-rate is, in effect, 'exemption with refund' (although this term is not used in New Zealand) and, where it applies, a nil rate of GST is charged on outputs, but full recovery can be made of GST on inputs.

3.1   Supply of Goods

The GST Act does not give an exhaustive definition of 'supply' but states that 'supply includes all forms of supply'.

This is intended to cover almost all types of transactions. The making available to another party of an identifiable commodity forms the central element of 'supply'. Leases and loans are all 'supplies'.

The term 'goods' means all kinds of personal or real property, but does not include choses in action or money. Personal possessions (other than choses in action or money) and real estate are therefore goods. A chose in action is a right to recover a thing (if withheld by action) of which a person does not have immediate enjoyment and possession. Debts, insurance contracts, shares and copyrights are examples of choses in action.

3.2   Supply of Services

The term 'services' is defined to mean anything which is not goods or money. Therefore, all commodities are services unless they are 'goods' or 'money'. For example, choses in action will usually be services as they are not 'goods' nor are they usually 'money'. Professional advice and repairs (other than the supply of materials) are other examples of services. Hence, all commodities other than money may be subject to GST.

3.3   Self-Supply Goods and Services

Special rules apply if goods and services have been initially acquired for the principal purpose of making taxable supplies but are later applied for either a non-taxable or an exempt purpose. An adjustment must be made when those goods and services are utilised for the non-taxable purpose. The registered person is deemed to have made a taxable supply of those goods and services and is required to account for output in respect of them. For example, a taxable supply is deemed to have been made where goods are applied for personal use by company personnel.

Conversely, an input deduction can be claimed for GST paid on goods and services acquired for a non-taxable purpose, but which are subsequently applied for the purpose of making taxable supplies. The deduction is allowed to the extent that the goods or services are applied for the making of a taxable supply.

3.4   Imports

The importation of goods (with the exception of fine metal) into New Zealand triggers liability for GST. GST is also levied on the excise duty in respect of goods manufactured in New Zealand (which are liable to excise duty). Motor vehicles, motor spirits, alcoholic beverages and tobacco products are the main goods affected. The collection of GST in these circumstances is administered by the Customs Department.

3.5   Deemed Supplies

A number of transactions which might not normally be considered to constitute a supply are specifically deemed to be a supply for GST purposes. This confirms the legislative intent to subject virtually all types of transactions to GST principles. Examples of transactions deemed to be supplies are:

- games of chance, lotteries and prize competitions
- activities of local authorities
- activities of public authorities
- placing of race bets and the supply of gambling chips.

4   PLACE OF SUPPLY

Whether or not a supply is deemed to be made in New Zealand is generally determined not by the place of supply but by the residence of the supplier. Thus a supply is deemed to be made in New Zealand if the supplier is resident in New Zealand. Where the supplier is not resident in New Zealand a supply is deemed to be made in New Zealand only if:

- the goods are in New Zealand at the time of supply, or
- the services are physically performed in New Zealand. For example, an overseas consultant makes a supply in New Zealand when compiling a report in New Zealand for a New Zealand company.

The non-New Zealand resident rule is subject to an exception. If the supply is made to a registered person for use in a taxable activity, it will be deemed to be supplied outside New Zealand unless the supplier and the recipient agree otherwise. So in the above example, the consultant's report is deemed to be supplied outside New Zealand if the recipient company is registered for GST purposes and the report is for use in a taxable activity, unless the consultant and the recipient company agree otherwise.

4.1   Chain Transactions

Where there is a series of agreements for the sale of the same goods from vendor to purchaser to sub-purchaser, etc, and all parties to the agreements agree that the goods should be delivered directly by the vendor to the last sub-purchaser, each seller in this chain is deemed to have made a supply of goods to the next sub-purchaser and is accordingly liable for GST. The net effect will be that if all sub-purchasers sell in the course of their taxable activity, all will be entitled to an input tax credit exactly equal to the amount of their liability on the sale. If one of them, however, is not selling in the course of his taxable activity, his sub-purchaser will not be liable to pay GST on such purchase. On the other hand, if this sub-purchaser sells in the course of his taxable activity, he will nevertheless have to charge his customer GST and account for same to the Revenue.

4.2   Reverse Charge Mechanism

Services are deemed to be supplied in New Zealand and subject to GST only if physically performed by a person in New Zealand at the time of performance. The reverse charge mechanism in respect of the supply of non-performed services such as copyrights, patents and trademarks does not apply in New Zealand.

5   BASIS OF TAXATION

5.1   Value of Supply

The general rule (and the rule that governs all arm's length sales which are solely for consideration in money) is that the value of a supply of goods or services will be the sum of the aggregate of the sum of money for the supply and the tax charged thereon. In other words, the tax inclusive basis of valuation is used. For example, if the sum of money for the supply is NZ$100, the GST will be NZ$12.50 and the value of the supply will be NZ$112.50, the total consideration in money provided. The GST payable may also be determined by the application of the 'tax fraction' to the total consideration. The tax fraction is:

$$\frac{(a)}{100 + (a)}$$ where (a) is the rate of GST.

Using the above example:

$$GST = \frac{12.5}{100 + 12.5} = 1/9th \times \$112.50 = NZ\$12.50$$

Where a supply is not for monetary consideration, or not wholly for monetary consideration, the value of that supply will be the 'open market value' of that consideration.

Although the value of most forms of supply will be determined by the general rules, certain classes of supply have special rules for determining the monetary consideration of the supply. Examples of these include:

- goods and services supplied pursuant to a credit contract (for example hire purchase agreements)
- the provision of accommodation for individuals in a 'commercial dwelling', for example, hotel, motel, camping ground, etc
- supplies made to an associated person
- tokens, stamps and vouchers.

5.2   Self-Supplies – Mixed Use Goods and Services

Goods and services initially acquired for the principal purpose of making taxable supplies but later applied to a non-taxable use are deemed to have been supplied in the course of a taxable activity, and the registered person is required to account for GST in respect of that deemed supply.

The value placed on such a deemed supply for GST purposes is the lesser of the cost of the goods and services to the supplier, or the open market value of the deemed supply made.

5.3   Imports

GST on imports is assessed on the value of the goods as determined for customs' purposes, to which should be added freight and insurance costs in the first place of destination in the country, as well as the taxes or duties paid on the importation, excluding GST.

5.4   Chargeable Event/Time of Supply

The general rule is that the time of supply of goods or services is the earlier of:

- the time an invoice is issued by the supplier to the recipient, or
- the time any payment is received by the suppliers.

A supply is deemed to be made, for example, at the time:

- a supplier issues an invoice for goods sold on credit, or
- a person pays a deposit on ordered goods for which no invoice will be issued until a later delivery date.

A number of special rules cover particular circumstances including:

- supply of goods to associated persons
- progressive supplies of goods and services
- supplies in the construction industry, etc.

5.5   Payments/Cash Basis

Certain registered persons may opt to account for tax by reference to the date of cash payment, rather than by reference to the date of issue of invoices.

Eligibility to adopt the payments basis is limited to:

- local authorities, public authorities and non-profit bodies
- persons whose total value of taxable supplies has not exceeded or is not likely to exceed NZ$1 million
- persons who satisfy the Commissioner of Inland Revenue that it is appropriate for them to use the payments basis because of the nature, volume and value of the taxable supplies and the nature of the accounting system.

The payments basis is particularly useful to those small businesses whose customers take extended credit for settling their debts. This scheme is also effective in providing automatic GST bad debt relief.

5.6   Credit Notes/Bad Debts

A refund of GST can be obtained by a registered person who issues a credit note to his customer. GST on uncollected debts can be recovered by the supplier.

6   TAX RATES

The various rates presently applicable are as follows:

0%:   –   exported goods
        –   exported services
        –   taxable activities disposed of as going concerns.

7.5%:   of 60% of the value of the supply (ie a real rate of 4.5%): this applies to the provision of long-term accommodation for individuals in a 'commercial dwelling' (for example, hotel, motel, boarding house, etc).

12.5%: –   all other supplies of taxable goods and services.

7   EXEMPTIONS

Exempt supplies are those which are specifically defined as not being subject to GST.

7.1   Exemptions with Credit for Input Tax

A transaction which is charged at 0% is in effect an 'exemption with credit', but this phrase is unknown in New Zealand. Zero-rating applies only if the supply would otherwise have been taxable at the standard rate. Note that the supply is still a taxable supply, albeit taxed at 0%.

Supplies which are exempt with a credit for input tax available include:

- goods exported or to be exported (subject to time constraints) pursuant to the Customs Act 1966
- goods which are not situated in New Zealand at the time of supply and which will not be imported into New Zealand
- a taxable activity supplied to another registered person as a going concern or part of a taxable activity which is capable of separate operations supplied as a going concern (for example, the sale of a complete business or part of a business)
- the supply of fine metal following its refining by the refiner to a dealer in fine metal where the fine metal is to be used as an investment item
- overseas transportation and arrangement of transportation of passengers and goods. Ancillary services such as loading, unloading, or handling overseas aircraft and ships are able to be zero-rated where these services are provided by the person supplying the international transport
- services supplied in connection with land and improvements to land situated outside New Zealand
- services supplied directly in connection with movable personal property (excluding debts) situated outside New Zealand when the services are supplied, or directly in connection with goods temporarily held in New Zealand
- services physically performed outside New Zealand
- services supplied for and to non-residents who are not in New Zealand when such services are performed, so long as the services are not performed in connection with land or land improvements within New Zealand or other personal property within New Zealand at the time
- the transfer or assignment of copyrights, patents, licences, trademarks or similar rights, where these rights are for use outside New Zealand
- services consisting of an obligation to refrain from carrying on a taxable activity outside New Zealand.

Limited exemptions apply to goods introduced in New Zealand by travellers. Personal and household belongings are not taxed when someone is establishing their main residence in New Zealand. GST relief is also available under certain conditions for goods which are temporarily taken out of and brought back into New Zealand. Examples include works of art, tools of trade, scientific specimens and racehorses.

7.2   Exemptions without Credit for Input Tax

The majority classes of activity which are exempt (and accordingly unable to obtain credit for input tax incurred) are:

- the supply of 'financial services', including lending, securities, equities, life assurance, superannuation and almost all other services provided by financial institutions apart from consulting services
- the supply by a non-profit body of any donated goods and services
- the supply of domestic rental accommodation
- the supply of any fine metal. 'Fine metal' is defined as gold, silver, or platinum that is of a required fineness.

7.3   Non-Taxable Activities

The following transactions do not give rise to a liability to GST as they are not deemed to be a taxable activity:

- private recreational pursuits or hobbies, if they are not carried on for commercial purposes
- occupation as an employee, and company directorships (other than employment and directorships accepted in the course of the person's own taxable activity)
- activities to the extent that they involve the making of exempt supplies (ie exemption without credit).

7.4   Transactions within the Same Legal Entity

These are outside the scope of GST, including transactions between branches, divisions of the same corporate body, irrespective of geographical location worldwide. Transactions between corporate bodies which are members of the same New Zealand GST group are also outside the scope of GST.

7.5   Transfer of a Business

Transfer of business (or part of a business which is viable in its own right) as a going concern is subject to GST at 0%. Therefore, input tax incurred in connection with the purchase or sale of a business can be reclaimed.

7.6   Dividend

The payment of a dividend is a financial service, and is therefore an exempt supply not subject to GST.

7.7   Election to be Registered for GST

A person who makes taxable supplies where the value of these supplies is less than the registration limits may voluntarily register for GST in order to reclaim input tax on expenditure. The person must, however, be making taxable supplies in the course or furtherance of a taxable activity.

8   CREDIT/REFUND FOR INPUT TAX

8.1   General Rule

In principle, all GST paid on goods and services by a registered person is recoverable. However, this applies only if the input tax was incurred with a view to making taxable supplies. Therefore, registered persons are prevented from recovering input GST on goods and services obtained for making exempt supplies.

8.2 Partial Exemption

If the goods or services purchased are used for both taxable and non-taxable supplies, only the input tax incurred on that portion attributable to the taxable supplies will be available for tax credit. The Commissioner of Inland Revenue allows a choice of three methods for registered persons to determine their portion of taxable and non-taxable use of any goods or services.

8.2.1 Direct Attribution Method

This method involves allocating a portion of the use of goods or services to the taxable and non-taxable activities. The goods and services that cannot be directly attributed to either activity are apportioned on the turnover method.

8.2.2 Turnover Method

The creditable input tax is calculated on the ratio of the turnover of supplies which are entitled to credit to the total turnover.

8.2.3 Special Method

Where the above methods are not appropriate an alternative method may be used with the consent of the Inland Revenue Department.

Where the input tax attributable to exempt activities for the next 12 months will not exceed the lesser of NZ$48,000 or 5% of the total taxable and exempt supplies, the business can treat itself as fully taxable.

8.3 Time of Recovery

A registered person is entitled to recovery of input tax, subject to the exempt supply restriction set out above, where they hold a valid tax invoice for the input tax incurred. It is generally not necessary to have paid for the goods or for the supplier to have accounted for the tax on the supply. The input tax claim need not be made in the period in which the tax invoice is issued.

A person who accounts for VAT on the payments received basis is entitled to reclaim input VAT on the basis of invoices actually paid.

The Commissioner is required to make refunds arising from an excess of input credits over output tax within 15 working days of the day following receipt by the Commissioner of the relevant GST return.

8.4 Refund for Foreign Registered Persons

A foreign business that is not a registered person is not able to recover GST incurred on importation of goods to New Zealand or on goods or services purchased in New Zealand.

9 ADMINISTRATIVE OBLIGATIONS

9.1 Registration

Any person who makes or intends to make taxable supplies in excess of NZ$30,000 per annum must register for GST with their local income tax office.

9.2   Books and Records

Books and records of a registered person must be retained for a minimum of seven years to enable ready ascertainment of that person's GST liability by the Commissioner of Inland Revenue.

9.3   Invoices

Generally, the supplier issues the tax invoice. A registered person making a supply must issue a tax invoice whenever the recipient of the supply (who is registered) requests one. The supplier must do so within 28 days of the request. However, a tax invoice is not required to be issued if the GST-inclusive cost of a supply is NZ$50 or less. A tax invoice must contain certain specified information, although the requirements are less onerous in the case of supplies costing between NZ$50 and NZ$200. A registered person cannot claim an input credit unless they hold a tax invoice.

A tax invoice must contain the following details:

- the words 'tax invoice' in a prominent place
- the name, address and registration number of the supplier
- the name and address of the recipient
- the date upon which the tax invoice was issued
- a description of the goods and services supplied together with the quantity or volume
- either:

  - the total amount of tax charged, the consideration excluding tax and the consideration inclusive of tax, or
  - where the tax is the tax fraction of the consideration, the total consideration for the supply and a statement that it includes a charge in respect of the tax.

9.4   GST Returns

Returns must be filed on a regular basis. The amount of tax payable by the registered person (or refundable by the Commissioner) in respect of a specific period must be set out in the return. The period covered by the return is called the 'taxable period'.

Taxable periods adopted by registered persons may be monthly (if the annual value of supplies exceeds or is likely to exceed NZ$24 million), bi-monthly or (if the value of supplies does not exceed NZ$250,000), six-monthly. Returns for the taxable periods must be filed by the last working day of the month following the end of the taxable period. Tax payable to the Commissioner must be paid at the same time, with additional tax being charged for late payment.

9.5   Correction of Returns

Where a return previously filed requires amendment, a replacement return should be filed promptly. In the absence of fraud, the Commissioner cannot amend a return to increase a GST liability after four years from the taxable period in which the return was furnished. A refund of an excess of GST paid may be obtained up to eight years after the taxable period in which the return was filed.

9.6 Powers of the Inland Revenue Department

The Inland Revenue Department may estimate the tax to be paid if a registered person has failed to file GST returns. The Inland Revenue Department has a period of four years to correct or assess a GST return.

9.7 Penalties

A fine of up to NZ$500 is payable in respect of the first failure to file a GST return and increases to NZ$1,000 for the third and subsequent convictions. Late payment of GST incurs an immediate additional tax of 10% of the sum unpaid. A further 2% additional tax compounding applies for each month that the GST remains unpaid.

There are a range of offences under the legislation, including failing to register, making false returns, falsifying records, obstruction of the Inland Revenue Department and failing to keep records. Although rarely imposed, fines of up to NZ$25,000 may be imposed in respect of some of these offences. Prison sentences have been imposed under the Crimes Act 1968 on people involved in GST fraud.

9.8 Objections/Appeals

A registered person may object to an assessment made by the Commissioner. A person has two months after receipt of an assessment to deliver or post to the Commissioner a written notice of objection.

A person may, by a written notice, request that an objection not wholly allowed by the Commissioner be heard by a Taxation Review Authority. Alternatively, the objection may be directed to the High Court as of right by either the objector or the Commissioner.

10   SPECIAL GST REGIMES

10.1 Agents

The GST Act provides for supplies made to and by an agent on behalf of a principal.

Supplies made by an agent are deemed to be made by the principal and not the agent. For example, a company is deemed to make a supply if an independent agent makes the supply on the company's behalf. The principal must account for GST in relation to the supply made.

Supplies made by a registered person to an agent are deemed to be received by the principal and not the agent. For example, the principal is deemed to receive a supply when his agent makes a taxable purchase of land. Here the principal, and not the agent, may deduct an input tax.

An agent may be treated as if he were the principal when receiving a supply directly connected with, or with the arranging of, the importation or exportation of goods, provided certain criteria are met. This arrangement enables the agent to deduct GST paid on inputs relevant to the importation or exportation of the goods.

10.1.1 Agents of Absentee Principals

Persons who carry on a taxable activity for and on behalf of absentee principals are deemed to be agents of the principal in respect of the taxable activity. They are required to make returns and are liable for any tax charged or levied in respect of the taxable activity.

10.2 Auctioneers

Auctions, where goods are sold on behalf of clients, can proceed on the basis that all the goods being offered are charged with GST. This is because an auctioneer may, with the consent of his principal, have any non-taxable supply made on behalf of his principal treated as if it were a taxable supply and made by the auctioneer himself.

10.3 Second-Hand Goods Deduction

The term 'second-hand goods' in the context of GST in New Zealand should not be confused with the term as used in other countries.

A registered person who purchases second-hand goods in the course of a taxable activity may be able to deduct the tax fraction of the purchase price as input tax. A deduction may only be made:

- if the goods are purchased for the principal purpose of making taxable supplies
- if the supply is a non-taxable supply by way of sale, and then only to the extent that payment in respect of the supply had been made during the relevant taxable period.

Where the supplier and the recipient are associated persons, the purchase price is deemed to be the lesser of the actual purchase price and the open market value of the supply.

For example, where a dealer purchases second-hand furniture from an unregistered person for NZ$1,000, the dealer is able to claim input tax on the furniture of NZ$111 (being one-ninth of NZ$1,000) even though no GST has been charged by the vendor.

The definition of second-hand goods is an exclusive one. The term 'second-hand goods' does not include livestock or second-hand goods consisting of or made from any 'fine metal'.

10.4 Real Property

Real property is treated in the same way as any other goods for GST purposes in New Zealand, and is not subject to any special regime. It should be remembered that the provision of domestic accommodation by way of rental is an exempt supply and is not subject to GST.

11   FURTHER READING

Garth Harris and Wayne Mapp, *Goods and Services Tax – The Application of the Act,* Butterworths, Wellington, 1986 - IV

Claudia Scott and Howard Davis, *The Gist of GST - A briefing on the goods and services tax,* Victoria University Press for the Institute of Policy Studies, Victoria University of Wellington, 1985 - IV

Carl Bakker and Phil Chronican, *Financial Services and the GST,* Wellington, Wellington University Press for the Institute of Policy Studies, Victoria University of Wellington, 1985 - IV

Contributor: Rodger Muir
      Partner
      Ernst & Young
      National Mutual Centre
      37-41 Shortland Street
      Auckland
      New Zealand
      Tel: +64 9 3774790
      Fax: +64 9 3098137

PAKISTAN

1 GENERAL BACKGROUND

Pakistan does not have a value added tax as such. However, there is a levy of Sales Tax which is to a great degree similar to the levy of VAT in various countries. Sales tax in Pakistan is, however, levied on the supply of goods only and does not extend to services.

Sales tax in its present form was introduced by the Sales Tax Act 1990. It replaced the Sales Tax Act 1951 and substantially modified the principles and methodology of taxation to bring it in conformity with the principles of a VAT system of taxation.

2 WHO IS TAXABLE?

Sales tax is intended to be imposed centrally on the supply of goods at the manufacturing, wholesale and retail stages as well as at the time of import. However, at present the levy of Sales Tax is applicable only to the imports and supplies of goods by manufacturers.

3 WHAT IS TAXABLE?

3.1 Supply of Goods
Supply means sale, transfer, lease or other disposition of goods in the course or furtherance of business carried out for consideration and includes:

- putting to private, business or non-business use any goods acquired, produced or manufactured in the course of business
- auction or disposal of goods to satisfy a debt owed by a person
- possession of taxable goods held immediately before a person ceases to be a registered person
- removal of goods from the manufacturing premises to the sale point or place of storage owned or operated by the manufacturer or his agent
- such other transactions as the Federal Government may specify by a notification in the Official Gazette.

Goods referred to above mean every kind of movable property other than actionable claims, money, stocks, shares and securities.

3.2 Supply of Services
Sales tax does not apply to any supplies of services.

This chapter reflects the law on Sales Tax in Pakistan as at 31 December 1994.

4 PLACE OF SUPPLY

The place of supply of goods manufactured in and imported into Pakistan is Pakistan.

5 BASIS OF TAXATION

5.1 Value of Supply

In respect of a taxable supply the value of the supply means the consideration in money, including the excise duty, if any, which the supplier receives from the recipient for that supply but excluding the amount of Sales Tax. Where the consideration for a supply is in kind, or partly in kind and partly in money, the value of the supply is the open market price of the supply excluding the amount of Sales Tax.

If the supplier and recipient are associated persons and the supply is made for no consideration or for a consideration which is lower than the open market price, the value of the supply is the open market price of the supply excluding the amount of the Sales Tax. In the case of trade discounts the value of the supply is the discounted price excluding the amount of Sales Tax provided that the invoice shows the discounted price and the related tax and the discount allowed is in conformity with the normal business practices.

If the transaction is of a special nature and it is difficult to ascertain the value of the supply, the value is the open market price.

5.2 Chargeable Event

A supply made in Pakistan shall be deemed to take place at the earlier of the time of delivery of goods and the time when any payment is received by the supplier provided that:

- where any goods are supplied by a registered person to an associated person and the goods are not to be removed, the time of supply shall be the time at which these goods are made available to the recipient
- where the goods are supplied under a hire purchase agreement, the time of supply shall be the time at which the agreement is entered into
- where the goods are removed from the manufacturing premises to the sale point by the manufacturer or his agent, the time of supply shall be the time of removal of goods from the manufacturing premises.

5.3 Imports

The value for imports is the value determined under Section 25 or 25B of the Customs Act 1969, including the amount of customs duties levied thereon.

5.4 Methods of Taxation

Essentially there are the following two methods of taxation:

5.4.1 General Sales Tax

Under this method the difference between the output tax and input tax is payable on a monthly basis (see section 8 for cases where the input tax in a particular period exceeds the output tax and a refund situation arises).

5.4.2 Fixed Sales Tax

The Central Board of Revenue with the prior approval of the Federal Government by notification in the Official Gazette may, in lieu of General Sales Tax, levy and collect such fixed amount of tax on any goods or class of goods payable by any establishment or undertaking producing or manufacturing such goods.

6 RATES

There are currently two rates of Sales Tax:

0%: – goods exported or deemed to have been exported out of Pakistan
– supplies of stores and provisions for consumption aboard a conveyance proceeding to a destination outside Pakistan
– such other goods that may be specified by the Federal Government through a Gazette Notification

15%: – all other goods. However, the Federal Government may by notification in the Official Gazette specify a special rate in respect of goods imported or produced in Pakistan or on any taxable supplies made by the registered persons. Moreover it may also specify as to whether the tax shall be charged on the wholesale or retail price. In addition to the above the Central Board of Revenue may specify a fixed amount of Sales Tax as discussed in 5.4.2 above.

7 EXEMPTIONS

7.1 Exemptions with Credit for Input Tax

Generally there is no credit entitlement in respect of supplies of exempt goods. However, the zero rate operates in a manner similar to exemption with credit.

When a zero-rated supply is made by a registered person, he is not required to charge Sales Tax on the goods as the rate of tax is 0%. However, he is entitled to recover the input tax he has paid.

7.2 Exemptions without Credit for Input Tax

Exempt supply means a supply which has been exempted by the Federal Government through a notification in the Official Gazette. The exemption may apply to any supplies made by a registered person in Pakistan or to any goods or class of goods. Further, the Central Board of Revenue may, by special order in each case stating the reasons, exempt any supply from payment of the whole or any part of the tax chargeable. Moreover, the Federal Government may, with reference to the nature of business activity, annual turnover or capital employed in business, exempt any person from the requirement to register under the Sales Tax Act 1990.

When an exempt supply is made, no Sales Tax is charged on the supply and the input tax cannot be recovered as the goods are exempted from Sales Tax.

8   CREDIT/REFUND FOR INPUT TAX

Input tax in relation to a registered person means:

- the tax levied on supplies of goods received
- the tax levied on imports of goods
- in cases of purchase from a non-registered person of second-hand goods or such other goods as the Federal Government may specify by notification in the Official Gazette, an amount equal to the tax fraction of the value of that supply.

Output tax means the tax charged by a registered person in respect of supply of goods made by that person.

In the event of input tax exceeding output tax in a period, the excess amount may be carried forward to the next period and may be treated as input tax for that tax period. If such excess is not recovered within six months following the tax period in which the credit first arose, the balance outstanding at the end of that period shall be refunded. However, please note that the recovery of input tax on acquisition of plant and machinery, spare parts of plant and machinery and machine tools may only be claimed in 25 equal instalments (ie over 25 tax periods).

9   ADMINISTRATIVE OBLIGATIONS

9.1   Registration
Every person who makes a taxable supply in Pakistan (including a zero-rated supply) is required to register for Sales Tax purposes.

9.2   Returns
There are three types of Sales Tax return:

- monthly returns: every registered person is required to file a monthly return in the prescribed form to the local Sales Tax Officer by the twentieth day of the following month
- special returns: the Collector of Sales Tax may require any person whether registered or not to furnish a return in the prescribed form not later than the date specified
- final returns: if a person ceases to be a registered person, he must furnish a final return in the prescribed form for the period since the last return has been filed to the date of cessation. This must be done within one month of the cessation.

9.3   Tax Invoices
A registered person is required to issue a serially numbered tax invoice when he makes a supply of goods. The invoice should contain the following particulars:

- the name, address and registration number of the supplier
- the name and address of the recipient
- the date of issue of the invoice
- the description and quantity of goods
- the value exclusive of tax
- the amount of Sales Tax
- the value inclusive of tax.

9.4   Records

A registered person is required to maintain and keep at his business premises the following records in either English or Urdu:

- records of supplies made indicating the description, quantity and value of goods, name and address of the person to whom supplies were made and the amount of tax charged
- records of goods purchased, showing the description, quantity and value of the goods, name, address and registration number of the supplier and the amount of tax on purchases
- records of zero-rated and exempt supplies
- invoices, credit notes, debit notes, bank statements, inventory records and such other records as may be specified by the Central Board of Revenue.

All records must be retained for five years.

9.5   Powers of the Authorities

When a registered person does not file a return or the amount of tax shown in the return is not correct, an officer of the Sales Tax Department may make an assessment of tax. The amount so assessed has to be paid within 14 days of the communication of the assessment order. If he is not satisfied with such assessment, the registered person may, within 14 days of the communication of the assessment order, file an appeal with the Sales Tax Department.

Moreover, the assessed person has also a right to be heard prior to framing of such assessment.

9.6   Penalties

Any person who:

- is required but fails to apply for registration under the Act
- fails to furnish a return within the due date
- fails to notify any change in the particulars of registration
- contravenes any other provision of this Act

is liable to a penalty of between 500 rupees (minimum) and 1,000 rupees (maximum) per day.

Any person who:

- does not issue a tax invoice or issues a tax invoice which is incorrect in its material particulars
- furnishes a return which is incorrect in its material particulars
- submits a false or forged document to any Sales Tax Office and thereby evades or attempts to evade payment of tax
- does not maintain records required under the Act or the rules made thereunder, or destroys, alters, mutilates or falsifies any such records or does not retain the records as required under the Act
- knowingly makes a false statement or false declaration, or gives false information
- attempts to commit or abets the commission of any of the acts specified above
- is not a registered person and issues an invoice in which an amount of tax is specified

shall be liable to a penalty of 25,000 rupees or the amount of tax due in the immediately preceding month, whichever is greater.

Where any of the acts specified above is committed by a corporate body or an association of persons (whether incorporated or not) the Chief Executive of that body shall be liable to a penalty of ten thousand rupees.

9.7 Additional Tax
Failure to pay tax within the specified time results in a liability to pay additional tax and surcharge at the following rates:

- 5% of the tax due during the first month or part thereof
- 10% of the tax due for the next month or part thereof
- 100% of tax due for the succeeding period
- surcharge at the rate of 1% for every month or part thereof on the total accumulated amount that remains unpaid after the expiry of three months.

Contributor: Mustafa Khandwala
Ford, Rhodes, Robson, Morrow
PO Box 4719
Karachi
Pakistan
Tel: + 92 21 2415582
Fax: + 92 21 2419592

THE PHILIPPINES

1   GENERAL BACKGROUND

Value added tax (VAT) was introduced in the Philippines by Executive Order No. 273 which took effect on 1 January 1988. A new law, Republic Act No. 7716, otherwise known as the Expanded VAT Law, broadened the coverage of VAT by:

■   including sale of properties (ie intangible personal properties and real property) among the transactions subject to VAT
■   substituting VAT for certain taxes on services
■   removing certain transactions from the list of exempt transactions.

However, the new law, which was supposed to have taken effect on 28 May 1994 was questioned on constitutional grounds. The Supreme Court has recently declared the law as constitutional, but a timely motion for reconsideration has now been filed before it. Since no resolution on the motion has yet been reached, the law remains suspended. Because the law has already been declared as constitutional and it would be difficult for the court to reverse itself, the discussions below are based on the Expanded VAT Law.

VAT is an indirect tax which may be shifted to the buyer, transferee or lessee of the goods, properties or services. The Philippines adopts a consumption type of VAT imposed on all levels of manufacture, production, and distribution and follows the destination type of VAT by taxing imports of goods and zero-rating exports.

2   WHO IS TAXABLE?

2.1   General
Any person who, in the course of his trade or business, sells, barters or exchanges goods and properties, or renders services, or engages in similar transactions, shall be subject to VAT provided that the transaction is not exempt under Section 103 of the Tax Code.

Any person who imports goods, regardless of whether or not they are imported in connection with his trade or business, shall also be subject to VAT, unless the importation is exempt under Section 103 of the Tax Code.

2.2   Transactions with Branch/Subsidiary
Subsidiaries of foreign firms are treated as domestic corporations that have separate juridical personality from their foreign parent companies. Thus, any sale of goods or services by the subsidiary to its foreign parent company is subject to VAT. The rule of fiscal unity or group taxation adopted by certain foreign tax jurisdictions does not apply in the Philippines.

In principle, a branch is only an extension of its head office and, ordinarily, transactions between the head office and its branches are merely considered as transfers of goods without

This chapter reflects the law on VAT in the Philippines as at 31 December 1994.

consideration and are therefore not subject to VAT. However, where the head office is located in a foreign country, any goods received by the Philippine branch from abroad, including those from its head office, will be subject to VAT at 10%. Conversely, any goods shipped by the branch to its head office abroad shall be considered as exported and are thus zero-rated.

2.3 Government Bodies

The national government and the various local government units are exempt from VAT because they do not sell goods or services in the course of trade or business. They are, however, subject to VAT when they import goods. Certain corporations which are owned or controlled by the government perform proprietary functions, are engaged in trade or business and are subject to VAT just like any other private firm.

2.4 Foreign Firms

Foreign firms which are engaged in trade or business in the Philippines by habitually selling goods or services therein are subject to VAT. They are, therefore, obliged to register as VAT persons and to account for VAT if their annual gross sales or receipts exceed the appropriate threshold.

2.5 Representative Office

The activities of a representative office of a foreign business in the Philippines are limited to information dissemination, promotion of products and facilitating the orders of the customers of its head office. They are not supposed to earn any income from sources within the Philippines. They are, therefore, required to register as representatives but not as VAT persons. If by providing certain information, the representative office receives a fee or compensation therefor, such amount will be subject to VAT if the appropriate threshold has been exceeded.

2.6 Reverse Charge Mechanism

A seller of goods and properties or seller of services is subject to VAT. But where the seller of an intangible, such as copyright or patent, is located outside the Philippines, the buyer in the Philippines must withhold the 10% VAT on the royalty payment. In some foreign taxing jurisdictions, this is referred to as the reverse charge mechanism.

2.7 Importers

'Importer' refers to any person who brings goods into the Philippines, whether or not the importation is made in the course of his trade or business. It includes non-exempt persons or entities who acquire tax-free imported goods from exempt persons, entities or agencies. If the importer consigns or transfers his right over the imported goods before or at the time the goods are released from customs custody, the consignee or transferee will be deemed to be the importer.

3   WHAT IS TAXABLE?

VAT liability arises on the taxable sale, barter or exchange of goods and properties, or taxable sale of services, for a consideration by a taxable person in the course of his trade or business, and on the importation of goods into the Philippines.

3.1   Sale of Goods and Properties

'Goods' means any movable, tangible object which is appropriable or transferable, while 'capital goods' refers to goods with an estimated useful life greater than one year and which are treated as depreciable assets, used directly or indirectly in the production or sale of taxable goods, properties, or services. The term 'goods or properties' means all tangible and intangible objects which are capable of pecuniary estimation. It includes real property held primarily for sale to customers or held for lease in the ordinary course of trade or business and the right or privilege to use patents, copyright, equipment, motion picture films, tapes and discs, radio, television, satellite transmission and cable television time.

'Sale of goods and properties' may refer to a sale, barter or exchange. 'Sale' is a contract between two parties called the seller and the buyer, by which the former, in consideration of the payment or promise of payment of a price certain in money, transfers to the latter the title and possession of the property. 'Barter' means the exchange of goods without using money, while 'exchange' is a contract in which specific property or service is given in consideration for the receipt of property other than money.

3.2   Sale of Services

'Sale or exchange of services' means the performance of all kinds of services for others for a fee, remuneration or consideration, including:

- services performed or rendered by construction and service contractors
- stock, real estate
- commercial, customs and immigration brokers
- lessors of personal and real property
- warehousing services
- lessors or distributors of cinematographic films
- persons engaged in milling, processing, manufacturing or repackaging goods for others
- proprietors, operators or keepers of hotels, motels, rest houses, pension houses, inns, resorts
- proprietors or operators of restaurants, refreshment parlours, cafes and other eating places, including clubs and caterers
- dealers in securities; lending investors
- operators of taxicabs; utility cars for rent or hire driven by the lessees (rent-a-car companies), tourist buses and other common carriers by land, air, and sea relative to their transport of goods or cargoes
- services of franchise grantees of telephone and telegraph, radio and television broadcasting and all other franchise grantees except in electric utilities, city gas and water supplies
- services of banks, non-bank financial intermediaries and finance companies
- non-life insurance companies (except crop insurance) including surety, fidelity, indemnity and bonding companies, and similar services, regardless of whether or not the performance thereof calls for the exercise or use of physical or mental faculties.

3.3   Mixed Transactions

A single transaction may involve the sale of both goods and services as, for instance, when the seller of an air-conditioning unit also undertakes its installation. Where the sale involves both goods and services, the charges for the sale of goods must be separately indicated from the sale of services. This is because the tax base for the sale of goods is the gross selling price while the tax base for sale of services is gross receipts. Also, sellers of goods are liable to pay the output tax on sales made during the taxable period, even if still unpaid, while output tax on sale of services is due only if the compensation or fee is received during the period. Where such charges are not separately indicated, the whole consideration will be treated as gross sales pursuant to a sale of goods.

3.4 Deemed Sale

The term 'sale' covers actual sales and transactions deemed sales. There is 'deemed sale' of goods when there is:

- transfer, use, or consumption not in the course of business of goods originally intended for sale or for use in the course of business
- distribution or transfer to shareholders or investors as share in the profits of the VAT-registered person or creditors in payment of debt
- consignment of goods if actual sale is not made within 60 days following the date on which such goods were consigned
- retirement from or cessation of business with respect to inventories of taxable goods existing at the time of such retirement or cessation.

3.5 Importation of Goods

Importation of goods is a taxable event regardless of the status of the importer or the nature of the importation, except for some exempt importations. The law at the time the goods are released from customs custody determines the kind of tax and the tax rate applicable on the imported goods. If, for example, the goods reached a Philippine port in December 1987 (ie prior to the introduction of VAT) but customs duty was paid and the goods were released from customs custody in January 1988 (after the tax was introduced), the goods will be subject to the 10% VAT rate.

4 PLACE OF SALE

4.1 Sale of Goods and Properties

VAT becomes due when there is a sale, barter, exchange, transfer or similar transaction intended to transfer ownership of, or title to, goods in the Philippines. In the case of imported goods, the place of sale is deemed to be the Philippines and the VAT is paid by the importer. In the case of export sale of goods, the place of sale is not material because, irrespective of any shipping arrangement that may be agreed upon which may influence or determine the transfer of ownership of the goods, the sale is considered as export sale. The tax location of a sale of real property situated in the Philippines is in the Philippines.

4.2 Chain Transactions

Where there is a series of transactions for the sale of the same goods from vendor to purchaser to sub-purchaser, etc and all parties to the agreements agree that the goods should be delivered directly by the vendor to the last purchaser, each seller in the chain is deemed to have made a sale of goods to the next purchaser or sub-purchaser and is accordingly liable for VAT. If one of the purchasers or sub-purchasers is not selling in the course of his trade or business and is not registered as a VAT person, his sub-purchaser will not be liable to pay VAT on such purchase. If this sub-purchaser sells in the course of business, he will nevertheless have to charge his purchaser VAT and account for the same.

4.3   Sale of Services
The sale of a service occurs at the place where the service is rendered. However, lease of properties is subject to VAT irrespective of the place where the contract of lease was executed if the property is leased or used in the Philippines.

5   BASIS OF TAXATION

5.1   Sale of Goods and Properties
The basis of taxation is the gross value in money or 'gross selling price' which means the total amount of money or its equivalent which the purchaser pays or is obligated to pay to the seller in consideration of the sale, barter or exchange of the goods or properties, excluding the VAT, sales returns and allowances, and sales discounts which are granted and determined at the time of sale which are expressly indicated in the invoice. The excise tax, if any, on such goods forms part of the gross selling price. Where the consideration is not paid for in money, the prevailing fair market value at the time of sale, barter or exchange will be applied although, where the gross selling price is unreasonably lower than the actual market value, the Commissioner of Internal Revenue is authorised to determine the appropriate tax base.

5.2   Deemed Sale
A registered person must account for VAT both on the market value of certain transfers or dispositions of property made for other considerations (such as gifts and goods taken out of the business for personal use or consumption), and on the value of any self-supplies or deemed sales. The output tax based on the market value of the goods deemed sold will be imposed as of the time of the occurrence of the transaction. However, in the case of retirement from or cessation of business, the tax base will be the acquisition cost or the current market price of the goods, whichever is lower.

5.3   Importation of Goods
The tax basis will be the total value used by the Bureau of Customs in determining tariff and customs duties, plus customs duties, excise taxes, if any, and other charges. Where the customs duties are determined on the basis of the quantity or volume of the goods, the VAT will be based on the landed cost plus excise taxes, if any.

5.4   Chargeable Event/Time of Payment
In the case of sale of goods and property, the VAT accrues at the time of sale and issue of the VAT sales invoice. Regardless of whether the sale is a cash sale or a sale on credit, the VAT accrues upon the issue of the sales invoice. Bad debts arising from credit sales are not deductible from the gross sales for the period.

In the case of sale of services, the VAT accrues upon receipt (actual or constructive) of the amount of consideration or fee from the buyer of service. Even if no service has yet been performed, any deposit or advance payment is already subject to VAT. On the other hand, even if the service has been completely performed by the seller or contractor, no VAT will accrue until payment has been made.

6   TAX RATES

Currently there are two rates:

0%: – the sale and actual shipment of goods from the Philippines to a foreign country, irrespective of any shipping arrangement which may influence or determine the transfer of ownership of the goods so exported, and paid for in acceptable foreign currency or its equivalent in goods or services and accounted for in accordance with the rules and regulations of the Central Bank of the Philippines (CBP)
  – sale of raw materials or packaging materials to a non-resident buyer for delivery to a resident local export-orientated enterprise to be used in manufacturing, processing, packing or repackaging in the Philippines the buyer's goods, and paid for in acceptable foreign currency and accounted for in accordance with the rules and regulations of the CBP
  – sale of raw materials or packaging materials to an export-orientated enterprise whose export sales exceed 70% of total annual production
  – sale of gold to the CBP
  – export sales and sales falling under the Omnibus Investment Code of 1987 and other special laws
  – processing, manufacturing or repackaging goods for other persons doing business outside the Philippines where the goods are subsequently exported and the services are paid for in acceptable foreign currency, inwardly remitted to the Philippines and accounted for in accordance with the rules and regulations of the Central Bank of the Philippines
  – services other than those mentioned in the preceding sub-section, the consideration for which is paid for in acceptable foreign currency which is remitted inwardly to the Philippines and accounted for in accordance with the rules and regulations of the Central Bank of the Philippines
  – services rendered to persons or entities whose exemption under special laws or international agreements to which the Philippines is a signatory effectively subjects the supply of such services to zero-rate
  – services rendered to vessels engaged exclusively in international shipping
  – services performed by subcontractors and/or contractors in processing, converting, or manufacturing goods for an enterprise whose export sales exceed 70% of total annual production.

Effectively 'zero-rated sales' refers to sales of goods or services to persons or entities whose exemption under special laws or international agreements to which the Philippines is a signatory effectively subjects such sales to the zero-rate.

10%: on supplies and services which are not exempt or taxable at the zero rate.

7   EXEMPTIONS

A transaction is exempt from VAT when it is specifically exempted or outside the scope of VAT. The suppliers of such exempt goods, properties and services are not permitted to charge VAT and no input tax credit will be allowed where it is attributable to the purchase or importation of any of these exempt goods, properties and services.

7.1   *Exempt with Input Credit*
This concept is unknown in Philippine VAT law but the effective zero-rating operates in a similar manner.

7.2   *Exempt without Input Credit*
The following sales of goods and supply of services are exempt without input credit:

- sale of non-food agricultural, marine and forest products in their original state by the primary producer or the owner of the land where they are produced
- sale of cotton and cotton seeds in their original state, and copra
- sale or importation of agricultural and marine food products in their original state (except importation of meat), livestock and poultry of a kind generally used as (or yielding or producing) food for human consumption; breeding stock and genetic materials therefor
- sale or importation of fertilisers, seeds, seedlings and fingerlings, fish, prawn, livestock and poultry feed, including ingredients, whether locally produced or imported, used in the manufacture of finished feeds (except special feed for racehorses, fighting cocks, aquarium fish, zoo animals and other animals generally considered as pets)
- sale or importation of petroleum products (except lubricating oil, processed gas, grease, wax and petrolatum) subject to excise tax
- sale or importation of raw materials to be used by the buyer or importer himself in the manufacture of petroleum products subject to excise tax, excluding lubricating oil, processed gas, grease, wax and petrolatum
- importation of passenger and/or cargo vessels over 5,000 tons, whether coastal or ocean-going, including engines and spare parts to be used by the importer himself as operator thereof
- importation of personal and household effects belonging to residents of the Philippines returning from abroad and non-resident citizens coming to settle in the Philippines, provided that such goods are exempt from customs duty under the Tariff and Customs Code of the Philippines
- importation of professional instruments and implements, clothing, domestic animals, and personal household effects (except any vehicle, vessel, aircraft, machinery or other goods for use in the manufacture and merchandise of any kind in commercial quantity) belonging to persons coming to settle in the Philippines, for their own use and not for sale, barter or exchange, accompanying such persons, or arriving within 90 days before or after their arrival, upon the production of evidence satisfactory to the Commissioner of Internal Revenue that such persons are actually coming to settle in the Philippines and that the change of residence is bona fide
- sale by the artist himself of his works of art, literary works, musical compositions and similar creations, or his services performed for the production of such works

- export sales by persons who are not VAT-registered
- sale of real property not primarily held for sale to customers or held for lease in the ordinary course of trade or business or real property utilised for low-cost and social housing as defined by Republic Act No.7279, otherwise known as the Urban Development and Housing Act of 1992 and other related laws
- sale or lease of goods or property or the performance of services other than the transactions mentioned in the preceding sections, the gross annual sales and/or receipts of which do not exceed the prescribed amount and are subject to the 3% tax
- sales which are exempt under special laws or international agreements to which the Philippines is a signatory, except those granted by Presidential Decree Nos.66 (Export Processing Zone), 529 (Petroleum Act), 972 (Coal Mines Act), 1491 (Phividec Industrial Areas) and 1590 (Philippine Airlines), and non-electric co-operatives under Republic Act No.6938.
- services subject to other percentage tax
- services by agricultural contract growers, and milling for others of palay into rice, corn into grits, and sugar cane into raw sugar
- medical, dental, hospital and veterinary services except those rendered by professionals
- educational services rendered by private educational institutions duly accredited by the Department of Education, Culture and Sports, and those rendered by government educational institutions
- services rendered by individuals pursuant to an employer-employee relationship
- services rendered by regional or area headquarters established in the Philippines by multinational corporations which act as supervisory, communications and co-ordinating centres for their affiliates, subsidiaries or branches in the Asia-Pacific Region and do not earn or derive income from the Philippines.

7.3   Election to be Subject to VAT

Although persons who make taxable sales with an annual value of less than P500,000 (excluding VAT) are not required to become registered, a provision exists for them to apply to the Commissioner for voluntary registration. This is because persons who export goods or carry on small businesses would be placed at a disadvantage by not being registered if their customers are predominantly registered for VAT. Their customers would be unable to claim a credit for VAT included in their costs and as a result their prices might well be higher (and possibly uncompetitive) compared with registered suppliers. Similarly, new businesses with low levels of turnover could encounter problems if they were not allowed to register. Such businesses may want to register at the outset in order to claim credits for VAT paid on input, even though their annual sales will be less than P500,000.

The following exempt persons may, at their option, apply for registration as VAT-registered persons with respect to their export sales only:

- primary producers or the owners of the land engaged in the sale of non-food agricultural, marine and forest products
- those engaged in the sale of cotton and cotton seeds in their original state, and copra
- those engaged in the sale or importation in their original state of agricultural and marine food products; livestock and poultry of a kind generally used as (or yielding or producing) food for human consumption; breeding stock and genetic materials therefor

- those engaged in the sale or importation of fertilisers, seeds, seedlings and fingerlings, fish, prawn, livestock and poultry feed, including ingredients, whether locally produced or imported, used in the manufacture of finished feeds (except specialty feed for racehorses, fighting cocks, aquarium fish, zoo animals and other animals generally considered as pets)
- those engaged in the sale or lease of goods or property or the performance of services whose gross annual sales and/or receipts do not exceed the prescribed amount and are subject to the 3% tax.

8   CREDIT/REFUND FOR INPUT TAX

8.1   General Rule

A person who makes taxable sales can recover in full the VAT he has suffered on his business expenditure (input VAT) by claiming it either as a credit or, under certain conditions, as a refund.

Any registered person claiming a deduction for input tax in a VAT return must be able to support that claim with a VAT invoice or receipt.

A registered person making a taxable sale to another who is also a registered person, must provide him with a VAT invoice or receipt.

Refund of input VAT is allowed on export sales, zero-rated or effectively zero-rated sales, and capital goods.

Input tax on all expenditures may be credited against output tax for current or future taxable quarters.

On application by a VAT-registered person, the Commissioner of Internal Revenue must refund any input tax within 60 days from the date on which the application for refund was filed. The refund is made by warrants drawn by the Commissioner or by his duly authorised representative.

8.2   Export Sale

An exporter who is a VAT-registered person may, within two years from the date of exportation, apply for a tax credit certificate or refund of the input tax attributable to the goods exported, to the extent that such input tax has not been applied to output tax and upon presentation of proof that the foreign exchange proceeds have been accounted for in accordance with the regulations of the Central Bank of the Philippines.

8.3   Zero-Rated or Effectively Zero-Rated Sales

Any person, other than exporters, whose sales are zero-rated or are effectively zero-rated may within two years after the close of the quarter when such sales were made, apply for a tax credit certificate or refund of the input taxes attributable to such sales to the extent that such input tax has not been applied against output tax.

8.4   Capital Goods

A VAT-registered person may apply for a tax credit certificate or refund of input taxes paid on capital goods imported or locally purchased to the extent that such input tax has not been applied against output taxes. The application must be made only within two years after the close of the taxable quarter when the importation or purchase was made.

8.5   *Retirement from or Cessation of Business*

A person whose registration has been cancelled due to retirement from or cessation of business, or due to changes in status may, within two years from the date of cancellation, apply for a tax credit certificate for any unused input tax which he may use in payment of his other internal revenue taxes. Changes in or cessation of status from vatable to exempt may be caused by a change in business activity, or a reversion to exempt status for failure to go beyond the prescribed amount for two consecutive taxable years, or a reversion to exempt status by an exempt person who voluntarily registered.

9   ADMINISTRATIVE COMPLIANCE

9.1   *Registration*

Any person subject to VAT must register with the appropriate Revenue District Officer. A person who maintains a head or main office and branches in different places must register with the revenue district office which has jurisdiction over the place where the main or head office is located.

Any person whose transactions are exempt from VAT as discussed above may apply for registration as a VAT-registered person.

Any person who ceases to be liable for VAT, or an exempt person who voluntarily registered, can cancel his registration by filing an application for cancellation of registration.

9.2   *Invoices and Receipts*

Where a VAT-registered person sells goods or services to another person who is also VAT registered, he must issue a VAT invoice or receipt bearing his Taxpayer Identification Number (TIN) and the word 'VAT' so that the purchaser can credit the VAT due to him if such purchases are related to his business.

For 'deemed sale' transactions, an invoice must be prepared at the time of the occurrence of the transaction and, in the case of retirement from or cessation of business, an invoice must be prepared for the entire inventory. The invoice need not enumerate the specific items appearing in the inventory but need only make a reference to the description of the goods.

If the taxable person is also engaged in exempt operations, he should issue separate invoices or receipts for the taxable and exempt operations.

The VAT invoice or receipt must be prepared at least in duplicate, the original to be given to the buyer and the duplicate to be retained by the seller as part of his accounting records.

9.3   *Books and Records*

VAT-registered persons are required to maintain a subsidiary sales journal and subsidiary purchase journal on which their daily sales and purchases are recorded. They must also make a memorandum entry in the subsidiary sales journal to record withdrawal of goods for personal use.

9.4   VAT Declarations and Returns

Any person subject to VAT must file a monthly VAT declaration and pay the tax covering his gross sales or receipts for the first two months of every calendar quarter within 25 days after the end of each month, and file the quarterly VAT return and pay the tax within 20 days following the end of the calendar quarter, with any duly accredited bank located within the revenue district office where the principal place of business of the taxpayer is situated.

Only one consolidated return need be filed by the taxpayer for all the branches and lines of business subject to VAT.

For tax identification purposes, any person required to file a return will be supplied with a TIN which must be indicated on any return he makes.

9.5   Powers of the Authorities

The Commissioner or his authorised representative is empowered to suspend the business operations and temporarily close the business establishment of any person who violates a requirement of the VAT law. The temporary closure of the establishment will be for at least five days and will be lifted only upon compliance with the requirements prescribed by the Commissioner in the closure order.

9.6   Penalties

In addition to the amount of tax payable, a penalty equivalent to 25% of the amount due will be imposed in the following cases:

- failure to file any return on the date prescribed
- filing a return with an internal revenue officer other than those with whom the return is required to be filed
- failure to pay the tax within the time prescribed
- failure to pay the full amount of tax shown on any return required to be filed, or the full amount of tax due for which no return is required to be filed, on or before the date prescribed.

In the case of wilful neglect to file the return within the period prescribed by the Tax Code or regulations, the penalty is 50% of the total amount of tax due. If a false or fraudulent return is wilfully made, the penalty is 50% of the tax or of the underpayment.

The penalties form part of the tax and the entire amount is subject to interest at the rate of at least 20% per annum from the date prescribed for payment until the amount is fully paid.

Interest will also be assessed and collected on the unpaid amount of tax at the rate of 20% until the amount is fully paid; again, the interest forms part of the tax.

A person who fails to file a return without reasonable cause must pay P1,000 for each failure but the aggregate amount to be imposed for all such failures during a calendar year cannot exceed P25,000.

Any person convicted of criminal violations shall be subject to imprisonment in addition to being liable for payment of the tax. Payment of the tax due after such apprehension shall not constitute a valid defence in any prosecution for such violation or in any action for forfeiture of untaxed articles.

9.7 Appeals

A taxpayer can protest against an assessment by filing a request for reconsideration or re-investigation within 30 days from receipt of the assessment; otherwise, the assessment becomes final and unappealable. If the protest is rejected in whole or in part, an appeal may be made to the Court of Tax Appeals within 30 days from receipt of the rejection.

Contributor: Vic Mamalateo
                Ernst & Young
                Sixth Floor, Vernida IV Bldg.
                Alfaro Street
                Salcedo Village
                1200 Makati, Metro Manila
                Philippines
                Tel: +63 2 8109741
                Fax: +63 2 8109748

SINGAPORE

1   GENERAL BACKGROUND

On 9 February 1993 the Singapore Government issued a White Paper outlining proposals for a broad-based goods and services tax (GST), with an effective start date of 1 April 1994. This was followed by the Goods and Services Tax Act 1993 (GST Act 1993) which was given assent on 20 October 1993.

GST in Singapore is largely based on the New Zealand system, but draws heavily on the UK Value Added Tax Act 1983 in terms of detailed legislative drafting. Like the New Zealand system, the Singapore GST has a very broad base, with only a small number of exclusions. As a result only a modest rate of tax, 3%, will be imposed for the first five years at least. The GST imposed is traded off to a large extent against reductions in corporate and personal income taxes. In addition, very carefully considered rebates and subsidies are given to lower income groups.

GST is administered by the Controller of Goods and Services Tax as head of the GST Division of the Inland Revenue Authority of Singapore (IRAS). Certain aspects of the administration of GST on the importation of goods will, however, be the responsibility of Customs and Excise.

The analysis which follows provides a basic introduction to the tax. The analysis is based on the provisions of the GST Act 1993. A variety of matters of practical significance are not in fact covered in the Act itself but are addressed in regulations.

2   WHO IS TAXABLE?

2.1   *General*
The legal form in which a business is established – as a sole trader, company, partnership, club, statutory board, etc – is basically irrelevant. All are potentially taxable persons. Employees are not taxable persons, at least in their capacity as employees.

To be a taxable person, the entity concerned must be engaged in a trade, business, profession or vocation. Most categories of clubs, associations and societies are deemed to be carrying on business for GST purposes, and charging for admission to premises is also deemed to be a business activity.

An entity's position for income tax purposes is not determinative of its GST position. Whilst borderline situations plainly need to be looked at on the basis of their own particular facts and circumstances, an activity (such as the letting of property) which is treated as a passive investment activity for income tax purposes may well represent a business for GST purposes.

This chapter reflects the legislation on GST in Singapore as at 31 December 1994.

2.2 Transactions with Branch/Subsidiary

If a branch of an overseas business (as opposed to a subsidiary company of an overseas business) is registered for GST purposes, then any supplies of services between branch and head office or other branches of the same entity will be outside the scope of the tax. The Act nevertheless allows registration of such entities to enable recovery of input taxes.

2.3 Government Bodies

Statutory boards are liable for registration. Any taxable person who supplies goods and services to government ministries, departments and statutory boards will need to collect and account for GST from their customer in the normal way.

2.4 Fiscal Unity/Group Transactions

Provision for group registration is made in the Act. Inter-company transactions within a group of companies are thus outside the scope of the tax where group registration has been opted for. Separate divisional registration is also available for a company which carries on a number of separate businesses within a single corporate entity.

2.5 Foreign Businesses

Foreign businesses who supply goods or services within Singapore to a value in excess of the S$1 million registration limit will need to notify the IRAS of their liability to register. Provision is also made for registration to be effected through agents who act on behalf of the business locally.

2.6 Representative Offices

Representative offices of foreign businesses are capable of registration for GST, thus enabling them to reclaim input tax suffered even though, technically, they are not making supplies.

2.7 Reverse Charge Mechanism

Where a registered trader imports services into Singapore the original draft legislation required him to account for GST as if he had made the supply to himself. This was known as the 'reverse charge'. For the time being at least, this reverse charge has been de-activated and will therefore not be brought into effect.

2.8 Importers

A foreign business will have no GST registration requirement in Singapore if title to the goods passes before importation into Singapore, and the customer himself imports the goods. The customer will then be subject to GST on importation in his own right which he can recover, if registered, against his own outputs.

However, where the foreign business maintains a stock of goods in Singapore, these can be imported under the GST registration number of an import agent who will then charge GST as appropriate to the customer. The only remaining complication is that the local agent will have to charge GST on his commission in respect of those goods which are not then re-exported. The foreign business has no means of recovering the GST so charged. This problem can be avoided if the foreign business is separately registered through the import agent, but in its own name.

As an alternative, the agent can be treated as principal in the process and charge and recover the GST as if it were his own. However, the GST charged on the agent's commission can seemingly still not be recovered using this alternative.

3   WHAT IS TAXABLE?

3.1   *General*
There are two main categories of transaction that attract tax.

Firstly, the importation of goods into Singapore by anyone, not just a taxable person.

Secondly, taxable supplies made in Singapore by a taxable person in the course or furtherance of any business carried on by him; a taxable supply being any supply of goods or services made in Singapore, other than an exempt supply.

3.2   *Supply of Goods*
The transfer of the whole property in goods is a supply of goods for GST purposes. The distinction between a supply of goods and a supply of services is sometimes not entirely clear, however. The legislation specifies that the following (inter alia) are supplies of goods:

■   the supply of any form of power, electricity, gas, water, light, heat, refrigeration, air-conditioning or ventilation
■   the grant, assignment or surrender of any interest in or right over land, or of any licence to occupy land
■   where goods are produced by one person applying a treatment or process to another person's goods, the treatment or process is treated as a supply of goods.

3.3   *Supply of Services*
Anything which is not a supply of goods, but is done for a consideration (including the granting, assignment or surrender of any right) is a supply of services.

3.4   *Self-Supplies of Goods/Services*
Other than the reverse charge mechanism described above, there are presently no specific goods or services produced 'in house' which are targeted as being 'self-supplies' for GST purposes, although the legislation is structured so as to accommodate any that may be introduced.

3.5   *Importation*
GST is payable to Customs and Excise at the time when the goods are imported into Singapore. Where goods are kept in a Free Trade Zone or bonded warehouse, no GST is payable until such time as they are released for sale in Singapore. Where the goods are exported direct from the Free Trade Zone or bonded warehouse, no GST is payable at all. Similar arrangements apply under a 'major exporter' scheme to approved importers who re-export more than 50% of their imports so that no GST is paid on goods imported by this category of business.

Reasonable quantities of personal effects brought into Singapore by individual travellers are tax-free on importation. A S$400 limit applies for new articles brought into Singapore, although no exemption exists for holders of employment, dependent or student passes or work permits.

4   PLACE OF SUPPLY

4.1   Supply of Goods

In relation to a supply of goods, the place of supply is the place where the goods are physically located immediately before their supply to the customer. Thus, if the goods are at that moment in Singapore, the place of supply is in Singapore whether the customer is local or overseas. If the goods are overseas, the place of supply is overseas even if the customer is in Singapore (but in this case there will be GST payable on the subsequent importation of the goods into Singapore).

4.2   Supply of Services

The position with regard to services is a good deal more complex. The concept envisaged in the legislation is the United Kingdom concept for the place of supply being the place where the supplier 'belongs'. Very broadly, a supplier belongs in a particular country if he has a business establishment there. If he has establishments in more than one country, he 'belongs' where the establishment physically making the supply is located.

5   BASIS OF TAXATION/CHARGEABLE EVENT

5.1   Supplies within Singapore

The basic rule is that GST is charged on the (GST exclusive) selling price of the goods or services supplied. Where the selling price includes entertainment duty, excise duty, betting and sweepstake duties, lotteries duties or tax imposed under the Statutory Boards (Taxable Services) Act these amounts are included in the taxable value on which GST is charged; but where it includes stamp duties, these are excluded from the GST taxable value base.

One point of considerable practical importance relates to prompt payment discounts allowed to customers. Except where payment is due by instalments, these are deducted from the invoice price for the purpose of computing output GST, irrespective of whether the customer in fact 'earns' the discount by paying within the allowed time limit.

5.2   Imports of Goods

In respect of goods imported into Singapore, the Singapore-based importer will be required to account for GST on the purchase price inclusive of any import duty and the costs of commissions, packing, transportation, insurance and the like, up to the point of importation. An important feature of the charging of GST on imported goods is that it will be chargeable whether or not the importer is registered for GST.

5.3   Goods and Services Provided Free of Charge

The basic rule is that anything done free of charge is not a (taxable) supply.

The main exceptions to this rule are:

- goods (other than trade samples or low value business gifts) supplied by a taxable person free of charge are deemed to have a taxable value equal to their cost. Business gifts costing up to S$200 are disregarded for this purpose, as are trade and commercial samples of any amount

■ goods or services supplied free of charge or at an under-value between connected parties may be treated as supplied at their open market value.

It is a question of fact whether, and how much, consideration is given for a supply. Where non-monetary consideration is given, the value of the supply is the open-market value of that consideration unless the second exemption above applies.

5.4 Time of Supply/Chargeable Event

The time of supply determines when a supply of goods or services is treated as taking place. The taxable person must account for GST in the accounting period in which the supply occurs. The general rule is that the time of supply will be the earlier of:

■ the time the goods are removed or otherwise made available to the customer or, in the case of services, the time when the services are performed, which is generally taken as being the time when the work is completed, or

■ the time of payment, or

■ the time of issue of the tax invoice.

However, if an invoice is issued within 14 days of the removal (or the making available) of the goods or the performance of the service, the date when the invoice is issued becomes the time of supply. Special rules apply for certain cases, for example, involving services supplied continuously over a period of time. Goods physically supplied but on sale or return terms will be deemed supplied either when it becomes clear that the sale will be completed or 12 months after physical supply, whichever comes earlier.

Provision is made for the taxable person to request a direction from the Comptroller as to the time of supply in certain cases, or for regulations to determine the time of supply in other special situations.

5.5 Cash Basis of Accounting

Provision is made for certain traders to account for GST on a cash basis rather than on the more normal accruals basis.

5.6 Bad Debts

Relief for bad debts is given for irrecoverable debts which have been written off in the books of account, and where one year has elapsed or the Comptroller of GST is satisfied that the debtor is insolvent, and that proper attempts at recovery have been made.

6 TAX RATES

The present rates are as follows:

0%: goods exported from Singapore and international services.

3%: all supplies of goods or services which are not zero-rated or exempt. This rate will remain unchanged for the first five years from the introduction of the tax (ie 1 April 1994 to 31 March 1999). The Government then reserves the right to review the position.

7   EXEMPTIONS

7.1   *Exemptions with Right to Recover Input Tax*
There is no special exemption with right to recovery but the zero rate effectively operates in a similar manner.

7.2   *Exemption without the Right to Recovery of Input Tax*
The following supplies are exempt and input tax attributable cannot be recovered:

- rental and sale of residential land and buildings
- specified financial services
- unregistered businesses.

7.3   *Non-Taxable Transactions*
For a variety of reasons, certain transactions do not give rise to a liability to GST, but the justification for this varies according to the circumstances. The following non-taxable transactions are worthy of note:

- supply of an employee's services under a contract of employment
- supplies of services for no consideration
- supplies made outside of Singapore
- supplies otherwise than in the course of business
- supplies not made by a taxable person
- transfer of a business as a going concern is neither a supply of goods nor a supply of services. For the purposes of registration, the transferee is treated as having carried on the business before as well as after transfer. The transferee must keep all records relating to the post-transfer period
- dividends represent the distribution of profits, and are thus not considered as being the consideration for any supply.

7.4   *Election to be Registered for GST*
A person who makes taxable supplies which fall below the S$1 million registration limit may nevertheless apply to be registered voluntarily. Registration is at the discretion of the Comptroller of GST, and once registered, the business must remain so for at least two years.

8   CREDIT/REFUND FOR INPUT TAX

8.1   *General*
Supplies made at the zero or standard rate are known as taxable supplies. Input tax attributable to taxable supplies, including zero-rated supplies, is fully creditable. A registered business is entitled to claim credit in its quarterly GST return for input tax suffered on its expenditure by way of offset against output tax. Where input tax regularly exceeds output tax, the business is entitled to submit returns monthly.

8.2   *Partial Exemption*
This is the position applicable to a business which provides a mixture of both taxable (standard or zero-rated) and exempt supplies.

Given the limited categories of exemption envisaged, the main categories of businesses in this class are banks, insurance companies and similar financial institutions, together with property businesses dealing in both residential and commercial/industrial land. Given also, however, that interest income will be exempt for both banks and non-banks, many non-financial businesses may also be partially exempt to some degree.

The main issue with partial exemption is the apportionment of input tax. The tax which relates exclusively to the exempt outputs is not creditable. The tax which relates exclusively to the taxable outputs is fully creditable. The remaining balance input tax which does not directly correlate exclusively with either taxable or exempt outputs is termed 'unattributable' input GST.

Regulations set out the manner in which 'unattributable' input GST will be apportioned to taxable supplies. The basic method is by reference to the comparative turnover of taxable and exempt supplies; provision is made, however, for agreement with the Comptroller of any other method which appears fair in the particular circumstances. Banks and certain companies in the reinsurance industry have negotiated special fixed recovery rates for the first year and first five years respectively.

Certain de minimis provisions apply to disregard exempt transactions where these fall below a certain level (currently the lower of S$20,000 per month on average or 5% of all supplies), and certain categories of otherwise exempt supplies are treated as if they were taxable, when made by non-financial institutions.

9   ADMINISTRATIVE OBLIGATIONS

9.1   *Registration*

An entity with an annual level of taxable supplies in excess of S$1 million is obliged to register. An entity with a lower level of turnover can choose to register. The registration of these smaller scale enterprises will be discretionary rather than automatic, although quite what registration criteria the IRAS will apply is not yet precisely known. Clearly the enterprise will have to be carrying on or intending to carry on a taxable activity. As noted above, voluntary registration will be conditional on the entity committing to stay registered for a minimum period.

The value of all taxable supplies, whether standard or zero-rated, must be included in determining annual turnover for registration purposes:

Items to be excluded for turnover registration purposes are:

- any output GST potentially payable on taxable supplies
- the value of exempt supplies
- the value of supplies which consist of the capital assets of the business.

Registration is obligatory in two main circumstances:

- when turnover retrospectively exceeds S$1 million in a 12-month period. In this case the business must notify the Comptroller within 30 days of the end of the quarter in which the cumulative limit is exceeded, and registration is normally effected as from the end of the month in which the notification is due

■	as soon as there are reasonable grounds for believing that turnover for the following 12-months will exceed S$1 Million. In this case notification is required within 30 days of the start of the 12-month period and registration is normally effected from the end of the 30 days.

Special rules are provided for the transfer of businesses as going concerns and to preclude artificial splitting of a single business between separate legal entities with a view to each entity remaining below the S$1 million registration limit.

9.2 *Books and Records*
Books and records must be kept for a minimum of seven years. The records to be kept include copies of all tax invoices and receipts issued; tax invoices received; and documents relating to imports and exports, as well as more generally described business and accounting records.

9.3 *Invoices*
All businesses making supplies of goods and services at the standard rate are obliged to issue a tax invoice where the customer is a taxable person.

A tax invoice must contain a number of specified points of information, although the requirements are less onerous in the case of supplies with a value of less than S$1,000.

9.4 *GST Returns*
The normal basis will be three-monthly accounting periods, ie four quarterly GST tax returns each calendar year, although exporters who will regularly be in a GST refund position can request monthly returns. Present indications are that businesses will be able to request GST accounting periods that tie in with their own financial accounting year-ends. Small traders can opt for a six-monthly return period.

The return periods and the question of the time of supply are closely interlinked, since the return is made in respect of all supplies made in that period, irrespective of whether the GST which the business has to pay over has yet been received from the customer. On the other hand, the business will normally require a tax invoice in order to support its claim for input tax in that return period; mere payment to the supplier will not be sufficient.

The GST return, together with the payment due, have to be lodged within one month of the end of the return period. The system is based on self-assessment, except that the IRAS will raise assessments in the case of default, including failure to submit the return within the prescribed period.

In the case of repayment, the Comptroller does not have to make the refund until three months after the date on which the return was submitted (in the case of quarterly returns), or one month thereafter (in the case of monthly submissions).

9.5 *Periods of Limitation*
Except in cases of fraud or wilful neglect, time limits are set within which assessments covering mistakes can be raised. Assessments cannot generally be raised after the later of:

■	two years after the end of the return period, or
■	one year after evidence of facts, sufficient in the opinion of the Comptroller to justify the making of the assessment, comes to his knowledge.

9.6   Correction of Returns

Provision is made for a repayment of tax in cases where any money was overpaid as tax or erroneously paid as tax or penalty, except to the extent that the refund would 'unjustly enrich the claimant' (where for example he had recovered GST from his customers but would not be refunding it to them on receiving the refund due to him).

9.7   Penalties

Offences under the GST legislation include:

- making an incorrect return
- late payment
- failure to register
- wilful default or falsifying of records
- fraudulently obtaining refunds.

In serious offences, the offender will be liable on conviction to a penalty of three times the tax evaded, a fine not exceeding S$10,000, seven years' imprisonment, or both monetary penalties and imprisonment. For lesser offences, the maximum penalty is a fine of S$5,000, or six months' imprisonment if the fine is not paid. There are a number of other graduated penalties for a variety of specified offences.

9.8   Interest on Late Payments of GST

Penalties for late payment of tax are relatively severe. Essentially the penalties will be:

- 5% of the GST payable if late at all but not more than 60 days late, plus
- after the first 60 days, an additional penalty of 2% of the tax for each completed month thereafter up to a maximum of 50%

giving an overall maximum of 55% of the GST payable. As this is a penalty, it will not be deductible for income tax purposes.

Interest on refunds made late by the Comptroller is also paid (currently 2.13% per annum as representing the commercial rate). On the basis of present law, this will be subject to income tax in the hands of the trader.

9.9   Appeals

Provision is made for an appeals process. Any person may write to the Comptroller, by way of a notice of objection, for review and revision of any decision made by the Comptroller with respect to, broadly, the imposition and administration of the GST. Application for review and revision must normally be made within 30 days of the date of notification of the Comptroller's decision. A right of appeal to a Board of Review, and thereafter to the High Court (on points of law) is given where the person is not satisfied with the Comptroller's decision on his application for review and revision. A similar 30-day period is given in which to lodge this appeal to the Board of Review.

10   SPECIAL GST REGIMES

10.1 Retail Export Schemes

A retail export scheme has been put in place whereby visitors to Singapore can reclaim

GST paid on their purchases in Singapore. The scheme operates only in respect of departures from Changi Airport and is subject to minimum purchases of S$500. It does not apply to Singapore citizens, permanent residents, employment pass/work permit holders or people who have spent more than 365 days in Singapore in the two years prior to the date of purchase.

10.2 Second-Hand Goods Scheme

Where a taxable person has acquired any used goods on which no tax was chargeable on the purchase, or was itself a purchase from a trader operating the scheme, GST is charged only on the margin between buying and selling price. Approval has to be obtained to operate such schemes.

Contributor: Steven Timms
                 Partner
                 Ernst & Young
                 10 Collyer Quay # 21-01
                 Ocean Building
                 Singapore 0104
                 Tel: +65 535777
                 Fax: +65 5327662

TAIWAN

1   GENERAL BACKGROUND

In 1969 the Commission on Tax Reform of the Executive Yuan proposed a new tax. This was to be known as 'Business Tax' but, for the purposes of this chapter, it will be referred to as value added tax (VAT). The purpose of the proposal was to replace the multiple-stage gross receipts tax which had been in force since 1928.

On 1 April 1986 the revised Business Tax Law came into force and was subsequently amended in May 1988 to take into account the relaxation of foreign exchange rules.

2   WHO IS TAXABLE?

2.1   *General*

Under the Business Tax Law, two classes of business entities are distinguished: 'VAT entities' which compute their tax liabilities by offsetting input tax against output tax, and 'non-VAT entities' which compute their liability by multiplying their gross receipts by the prescribed tax rates. The taxation on 'non-VAT entities' is summarised in section 10.

According to the Business Tax Law, a taxpayer is defined as:

- a business entity which supplies goods or services
- a consignee or holder of imported goods
- a recipient of services supplied by a foreign enterprise, organisation, institute or association which has no permanent establishment within Taiwan. However, if an international transport enterprise which has no permanent establishment within the territory of Taiwan appoints a local agent, the agent will have the status of a taxpayer.

2.2   *Transactions with Branch/Subsidiary*

Subsidiaries of foreign companies which supply goods and services within the territory of Taiwan are treated in the same manner as other taxable persons, even where the goods and services are supplied to their parent company outside Taiwan.

Transactions between branches of the same legal entity within the territory of Taiwan are not subject to VAT. However, supplies between a branch and its head office or another branch are taxable if the parties are located outside Taiwan.

2.3   *Government Bodies*

VAT is not applicable to the activities of a government body unless it performs profit-related activities in Taiwan. The provincial and local authorities are not taxable persons in respect of their non-profit seeking activities.

This chapter reflects the legislation on VAT in Taiwan as at 31 December 1994.

2.4 Fiscal Unity/Group Taxation

The term 'fiscal unity/group' is not used in the Business Tax Law.

2.5 Foreign Firms

Foreign firms which supply goods or perform construction services within the territory of Taiwan must register at the tax office.

Foreign firms which have set up a branch office in Taiwan and which render services to Taiwan customers must also register.

Foreign companies which do not supply taxable goods or services within the territory of Taiwan are not required to register for VAT.

2.6 Representative Office

A representative office of a foreign company which only performs communication or quotation services for its head office, and is not involved in selling activities such as signing contracts or storing inventories for its head office, is not obliged to register for VAT.

However, if the foreign head office delivers inventories to Taiwan and their representative office distributes goods in Taiwan, the representative office must register and account for VAT. The services performed by the representative office to the foreign head office are subject to VAT.

2.7 VAT Representatives

Any foreign firm involved in sales activities in Taiwan is required to register for VAT. The foreign firm may choose to either set up a legal entity in Taiwan or appoint an agent to conclude sales in Taiwan.

International transport enterprises which conduct international transportation activities in Taiwan are required to appoint a VAT agent in Taiwan.

2.8 Imports

Any person who imports goods into Taiwan is subject to VAT at the same rates as apply to the sale of similar goods within Taiwan.

Goods and services (other than passenger cars) imported for business operation purposes by VAT-registered persons may be imported VAT-free. The VAT due upon import by persons engaged in the supply of both taxable and exempt goods or services will be computed proportionally as prescribed by the tax law.

3 WHAT IS TAXABLE?

The supply of goods and services within the territory of Taiwan and the import of goods are taxable. Professional services rendered by practitioners and services rendered by individuals in employment are excluded from liability for VAT.

3.1 Supply of Goods

The supply of goods is defined as the transfer of the ownership of goods to others in return for a consideration. The consideration is not limited to money. The term 'goods' includes new and second-hand goods, land and buildings.

The following are regarded as supplies of goods:

- goods produced, imported or purchased by an enterprise for sale but in fact transferred to itself or transferred to others for no consideration
- where an enterprise purchases goods under its own name on behalf of a third party and delivers the goods to the third party
- where an enterprise requests a third party to sell goods on its behalf
- where an enterprise sells consigned goods
- the exchange of goods for other goods.

Goods used to redeem debt or distributed to shareholders or investors are deemed to be samples of goods when an enterprise is dissolved or shutdown.

3.2 Mixed Transactions
When a business person sells land together with any construction on it, unless the prices for the land and construction are stated separately, the sale price of the construction will be calculated on the basis of the proportion of the assessed standard price of the building to the aggregate of the official value of the land as assessed by the government and the assessed standard price of the building.

3.3 Supply of Services
A supply of services is defined as the rendering of services or the provision of goods for the use of others for a consideration.

4 PLACE OF SUPPLY

4.1 Supply of Goods
VAT is only chargeable on imports and transactions which occur within the territory of Taiwan, so determination of the place of transaction is particularly important. According to the Business Tax Law, the place of supply of goods will be in Taiwan where:

- transport is required to effect the supply of goods, and the origin or destination of transport is within the territory of the Republic of China;
- transport is not required to effect the supply of goods, and the goods are located within the territory of the Republic of China.

4.1.1 Chain transactions
Where there is a series of agreements for the sale of the same goods from the vendor to the purchaser to sub-purchaser, etc each seller in the chain is deemed to have supplied the goods and is liable for VAT.

In certain cases, where one business person purchases goods on behalf of another business person, he might not be regarded as making taxable supplies. For instance, if the sales invoice is issued to the final buyer and there is no difference between the purchase payment and the reimbursement, the purchaser is not liable for VAT.

4.2 Supply of Services

4.2.1 General Rules
Where services are provided or utilised within the territory of Taiwan, the consideration for such services is taxable.

Branch offices or representative offices of foreign companies conducting sales-related activities in Taiwan for their head office are subject to VAT.

4.2.2 Exceptions
The place where the services are rendered is a factor in deciding VAT liability. There are exceptions as follows:

- the lease of an airplane to a foreign company for use outside Taiwan is deemed to be a taxable service in Taiwan
- international transportation services are deemed to be supplied within the territory of the Republic of China if the transport departs from the Republic.

4.2.3 Reverse Charge Mechanism
Where any non-resident person provides patent, copyright, trademark, or other secret methods or information to their customers in Taiwan, the purchaser shall pay the tax due on such services as if he had supplied them to himself. If the purchaser is a VAT entity, he may offset the VAT against his output tax because there is actually no VAT liability in connection with the services he has purchased. This is the so-called 'reverse charge mechanism'. The tax incurred in connection with the receipt of such rights is not recoverable if the customer is a non-VAT entity.

5 BASIS OF TAXATION

5.1 General
The tax basis of VAT is the sales amount, ie the total amount of consideration derived from the sales of goods or services, including all charges but excluding the VAT on such sales.

If the goods are subject to commodity tax, the sales amount should include the amount of commodity tax.

5.2 Goods made up from Materials Supplied by Customers
There is no special rule for goods made up from materials supplied by customers. However, if the selling price is unreasonably lower than the market price, the local tax office may determine the sales amount based on the market price.

5.3 Self-Supplies
VAT must be paid on the current market price for self-supplies of goods and services.

5.4 Importations
The taxable base of imported goods is the sum of the customs value, custom duties, harbour construction fees levied on importation and commodity tax, if any.

5.5   Chargeable Event/Time of Payment

Liability to VAT arises at the time when the seller collects payment from the customer or at the time when an account is recognised as receivable.

For transactions consisting of the exchange of goods, the VAT is due at the time when the goods are exchanged.

For general services performed, VAT is due at the time when such services are performed.

5.6   Cash/Invoices Basis

Any VAT due must normally be accounted for on the basis of the value of invoices issued during the VAT period.

5.7   Credit Notes/Bad Debts

Any VAT refundable in respect of sales returns or discounts, or recovered from purchase returns or discounts, shall be accounted for in the current tax period.

A refund of VAT which has already been paid will not be allowed in respect of bad debts.

6   TAX RATES

6.1   Rates

The following tax rates apply:

0%:   – export of goods
- export-related services, or services supplied domestically but utilised abroad
- goods supplied to departing passengers or passengers in transit by duly organised duty-free shops
- machinery equipment, raw materials, supplies, fuel or semi-finished products supplied to exported enterprises located in tax-exempt export zones, industrial parks, bonded factories or warehouses
- international transportation
- ships and aircraft used in international transportation
- goods or repair services supplied to ships or aircraft used in international transportation.

5%:   – all other goods sold or services performed in Taiwan which are not exempt

Various rates ranging from 0.1% to 25% apply to certain special VAT regimes and these are discussed in detail in section 10.

7   EXEMPTIONS

7.1   Exemptions with Credit for Input Tax

Zero-rating is defined as an exemption with credit for input tax previously paid.

7.2   Exemptions without Credit for VAT

The supply of certain goods and services is exempt for VAT. Suppliers of such goods and services are not permitted to claim credit for business tax previously paid. Currently, there are 30 items of goods exempt from VAT. The range of non-credit exemptions can be summarised as follows:

- land sold
- monopoly goods sold by government operated enterprises
- water supplied to farm land for irrigation
- agricultural pesticides, livestock, medicines, farm machinery and equipment, farm trucks (including gasoline) and electricity supplied to farmers for their use
- agricultural, forest, fishing or pastoral products or by-products sold by farmers
- fishing boats, nets, machinery, equipment and gasoline sold to fishermen for their own use in coastal fishing
- educational services rendered by schools and other cultural institutions
- textbooks which are approved by the educational administration for use by all school levels and important specialised academic writings encouraged by the government in accordance with the law
- goods or services supplied by student-run shops in professional schools which do not sell to outsiders
- newspapers, publications, news drafts, advertisements or programmes produced and supplied by legally registered publishers
- research services supplied by academic or science and technology institutes which are approved by the authorities concerned
- medical services, medicine, lodging and meals supplied by hospitals, clinics and sanitaria
- armaments, combat ships, military aircraft, tanks, reconnaissance and communication equipment related to warfare supplied to the defence authority for their own use
- services rendered by postal or telecommunication agencies
- stamp tax tickets and postage stamps
- fixed assets, which are not held in the course of regular business by a non-VAT entity
- bonds issued by the government
- gold bars, gold nuggets, gold leaf and gold coins.

7.3 Exempt Importation
The importation of any one of the following items is exempt from VAT:

- vessels and aircraft used in international transportation and deep sea fishing boats
- goods which are exempt from customs duties
- national ancient curios or remains.

7.4 Transactions Outside the Scope of VAT or Non-Taxable

7.4.1 Transactions within the Same Legal Entities
Transactions incurred within a legal entity with multiple branches and other fixed places of business within the territory of Taiwan are not liable for VAT.

7.4.2 Transfer of Business
The share transfer of a business or part thereof and the transfer of the goodwill or other intangible assets of a business in connection with the transfer of ownership, is not recognised as a supply of goods and thus is not liable for VAT.

7.4.3 Subsidies/Penalty Payments/Compensation/Waiver Of Debts

Subsidies, penalty payments, compensation, or waiver of debts which do not relate to sales activities are regarded as outside the scope of VAT and thus not taxable.

If the subsidies, compensation, etc are made in exchange for certain services performed by a business person, then such subsidy or compensation is liable for VAT.

7.4.4 Intergroup Lending and Rental Deposit Interest

Interest incurred in connection with intercompany lending transactions is not liable to VAT if the companies are not investment financing companies, banks or other financial services companies. Similarly, interest earned on bank deposits is also not subject to VAT. However, any deposit collected for leasing property is taxable.

8   CREDIT/REFUND FOR VAT

8.1   General Rules

The input tax paid by business persons on their purchase of goods or services is allowed as a deduction against output tax. In certain circumstances, input tax may be refunded.

8.2   Refunds of Input Tax

Excess input tax may be refunded in the following circumstances:

- the overpaid tax results from the sales of goods or services qualifying for zero-rating
- the overpaid tax results from the acquisition of fixed assets
- the overpaid tax results from the cancellation of registration because of amalgamation of ownership, or transfer, dissolution or closure of a business.

The input tax paid during the pre-registration period by a taxable person may be reclaimed after the taxable person has completed the registration. The taxable person should file an application with the local tax authority for this refund.

8.3   Exceptions

Input tax cannot be deducted from output tax in any of the following events:

- where supporting documents with respect to purchase are not obtained or kept
- the input tax was incurred on the purchase of goods or services for a use other than for the normal operation of the enterprise or its branch
- goods or services are for entertainment purpose
- goods or services are in reward for individual employees
- passenger cars are for private use.

8.3.1 Partial Exemption

Where a taxable person conducts both taxable and non-taxable activities, the input tax deductible is restricted only to the proportion of the enterprise's taxable operation.

8.4   Time of Recovery

A taxable person can deduct the input tax or claim a refund in each VAT return period.

9   ADMINISTRATIVE OBLIGATIONS

9.1   Registration

Each fixed place of business must file an individual application for business registration with the local tax authority before it commences business.

9.2   Books and Records

Every taxable person in Taiwan is required to set up and maintain account books consisting of a general journal and ledger for the timely recording of every transaction. If necessary, the taxable person can apply for permission to keep their accounting records on computer.

9.3   Invoices

Taxable persons who sell goods or services must issue unified invoices to the buyer at the time stipulated in the official time limit for issuing sale documental evidence. Business persons subject to a special VAT regime (see section 10.1) and small-scale enterprises may issue ordinary receipts to buyers instead of unified invoices.

Printed unified invoices can be bought from the government, or the enterprise may be authorised to print its own invoices. The forms, items to be recorded and the use of invoices are prescribed by the Ministry of Finance.

9.4   VAT Returns

All registered taxable persons must file bi-monthly returns on a prescribed form showing their sales and purchases and tax payable or refundable. The return and other appropriate documents must be filed with the tax office (whether or not there has been any sale) prior to the fifteenth day of the following month. Any tax payable must be paid to the government treasury in advance. The receipt for tax paid is enclosed with the return.

A taxable person who makes zero-rated supplies (ie foreign sales) may apply to the tax office for permission to file its return monthly.

9.5   Correction of Returns

Where the tax return needs to be amended, a specific application is required. If there is any error or omission, the taxpayer should voluntarily pay the tax amount plus the additional tax due plus the interest and then file a special return with the tax authority. Otherwise, he will be subject to a fine for underpayment. Similarly, if the tax has been overpaid, the taxable person can make a refund application to the tax authority.

9.6   Power of Authorities

Although the Constitution gives the tax authorities the power to levy taxes their right to collect the tax is limited.

In certain cases, the tax authorities have the power to investigate and check a taxpayer's liability. They also have the power to determine a business person's tax liability, and to refer it to a court of law for enforcement when and only when payment is not made in time.

The taxpayer must pay the following payments to the tax authorities in preference to his other creditors:

751

- all tax due
- surcharges for late filing, non-filing, or late payment
- interest
- tax collectible but not collected at the time of amalgamation, transfer of ownership, dissolution or closure
- tax payable before the time limit for paying tax expires.

9.7 Penalties

Taxable persons who fail to file the sales amount or the detailed list of unified invoices within the time limit shall be liable to a surcharge for belated filing of 1% of the tax payable for every two days overdue, provided that the filing is overdue for less than 30 days. If the filing is overdue in excess of 30 days, the business shall be liable to a surcharge for non-filing of 30% of the tax payable as determined by the tax authority.

The taxpayer is liable to additional assessment and will be fined between five and twenty times the amount of tax evaded and his business may be suspended in the following circumstances:

- transacting business without applying for business registration
- failing to file the sales amount or detailed list of unified invoices used thirty days beyond the prescribed time limit or to pay the business tax payable
- understating or omitting of the sales amount
- continuing to conduct business after applying for a cancellation of registration or after suspension of business by the tax office
- overstating input tax
- failing to pay tax 30 days beyond the prescribed time limit
- evading tax in any other way.

9.8 Appeals

Taxpayers have the right to appeal if they find that their tax liability was not determined according to the tax law. They may request rechecks by filing a petition with the tax authority that originally handled their case within 30 days after the expiration of the payment period. The request must be in a prescribed form and must indicate the reason(s) for recheck.

If they do not agree with the result of the recheck, they can file appeals and administration lawsuits.

10   SPECIAL VAT REGIMES

Under the current Business Tax Law, certain business entities are liable to VAT on their sales. However, where input tax in connection with the purchase of goods or services is not allowed as a credit against output tax, these business entities are known as 'non-VAT entities'.

10.1 Banks, Insurance Companies and Other Financial Services Companies

The VAT rate for enterprises engaged in banking, insurance, trust and investment, securities, short-term commercial papers and pawnshops is 5%. The VAT liability of these entities is calculated by multiplying the gross sales value by the tax rate, and input tax is not allowed for offset against the output tax. For enterprises engaged in reinsurance activities, the tax rate applicable is 1% on the income from reinsurance premiums. Again, the input tax incurred by such enterprises is not permitted to be deducted.

Banking enterprises which provide non-banking services such as storing, safe box leasing, etc, are allowed to apply for approval from the tax authorities to have such non-banking activities taxed in the normal manner.

10.2 Special Foods, Beverages and Services

Business enterprises engaged in the supply of special foods, beverages and services must also calculate their output tax by multiplying their gross sales by a VAT rate. Input tax suffered is not recoverable. The tax rates applicable are:

15%: night clubs and restaurants providing entertainment

25%: saloons and tea rooms, coffee shops and bars providing hostesses to entertain customers.

10.3 Small-Scale Business Persons

Small-scale business persons are allowed the choice of being taxed like the general VAT entities at the 5% rate or to be taxed on the gross sales method by applying the following tax rates:

0.1%: wholesale supplies of agricultural produce and small scale business persons supplying agricultural products

1%: small business entities which adopted the assessment method to report its sales.

For those small-scale business persons who choose to be taxed by the assessment method, 10% of the input tax on their purchase of goods or services for business operations may be deducted from the tax amount determined by the tax authority.

Small-scale business persons who choose to be taxed as general VAT entities should file an application for tax office approval in advance. Such approval lasts for at least three years.

11   FURTHER READING

Taxation in the Republic of China, Ministry of Finance, 1993 edition.

Contributor: Bell Cheng, Partner
Diwan Ernst & Young
9th Floor, Tapei World Trade Centre
International Trade Building
332, Keeling Road, Sec. 1, Taipei
Taiwan
Republic of China 10548
Tel: +886 2 7576050
Fax: +886 2 7204000

THAILAND

1   GENERAL BACKGROUND

VAT was introduced in Thailand in January 1992, replacing the Business Tax (sales tax) system, which had been operational for more than fifty years. The introduction of VAT is regarded as one of the most significant tax reforms undertaken by the government and has a far reaching effect on nearly all economic sectors of the country. The complexity of the Business Tax system and pervasive tax evasion in the past were the principal reasons for the tax reforms.

The administration of the VAT system is vested in the Revenue Department, which is also responsible for the collection of individual income tax, corporate income tax, specific business tax and stamp duty. In the case of importation of goods, the Customs Department collects VAT on the imports on behalf of the Revenue Department.

2   WHO IS TAXABLE?

Unless exempted by law (see section 7), taxable persons (ie persons subject to VAT) include the following:

- importers of goods or services
- sellers of goods in the course of their business or profession in Thailand
- providers of services in the course of their business or profession in Thailand
- persons deemed by the law to be traders, eg a local agent of an overseas corporation selling goods or providing services in Thailand.

Taxable persons may be natural persons or juristic bodies.

Companies engaged in oil and gas exploration, development or production in Thailand also come within the VAT system.

3   WHAT IS TAXABLE?

VAT is imposed on a sale of goods or a rendering of services by a trader in Thailand, on importation of goods into Thailand by an importer and on imported services (ie services that are performed overseas but used in Thailand) by any person.

The law defines the term 'sale' as to include the following:

- hire-purchase or instalment sale
- goods falling short of the underlying records ie inventory shortfalls
- having stock-in-trade or any other property remaining at the date of cessation of

---

This chapter reflects the legislation on VAT in Thailand as at 31 December 1994.

754

business (other than as the result of amalgamation or transfer of business to another VAT trader).

The term 'goods' is defined to include both tangible and intangible property likely to have value.

4 PLACE OF SUPPLY

4.1 Supply of Goods
The sale or transfer of goods is taxable if the goods are situated in Thailand at the time of sale or transfer.

4.2 Supply of Services
The general rule is that the place where services are deemed to be supplied is the place where the supplier has his place of business, his fixed establishment or his usual place of residence from which the services are supplied.

4.3 Reverse Charge Mechanism
In the case of services which are provided outside Thailand but which are used in Thailand, the recipient of the services must treat the services as if he had supplied them to himself, and he must charge himself VAT on the value of such services. If the recipient is entitled to full VAT recovery he can ignore the reverse charge.

5 BASIS OF TAXATION/CHARGEABLE EVENT

5.1 Basis of Taxation
The basis of taxation is as follows:

- Sales of goods and rendering of services: the tax base (taxable amount) is the value of goods and services supplied excluding:
  - prompt discount as clearly stated on a related tax invoice
  - output tax
  - compensation of subsidies as prescribed by the Director-General.

- Export sales: the tax base is the free on board (FOB) price of goods plus excise tax (if any) plus other taxes and certain prescribed fees (other than customs duty).
- Imported goods: the tax base is the cost insurance freight (CIF) value of goods plus excise tax (if any) plus customs duties plus other taxes and fees as prescribed in the Royal Decree.
- International transport: for the carriage of passengers, the tax base is the value of fares, fees and other benefits collectible in Thailand. For the carriage of goods, the tax base is the value of freight, fees and other benefits in respect of transport of goods out of Thailand, irrespective of the place of collection.

5.2 Chargeable Event
The point of time at which a trading transaction becomes liable to VAT depends on the nature of the transaction as follows:

- Sales of goods: the VAT is deemed to crystallise at the time the goods are delivered, or sales are collected, or a related tax invoice is issued, whichever comes first. However, the liability to VAT on sales of electricity, water, natural gas and goods of a similar nature is deemed to crystallise when consideration for the goods is received.
- Hire-purchase/instalment sales: the liability to VAT crystallises when an instalment falls due or a related tax invoice is issued, whichever comes first.
- Consignment sales: VAT crystallises when the agent delivers the consigned goods to the buyer, or sales are collected, or a related tax invoice is issued, whichever comes first. To qualify as a consignment sale, there must be a written agency agreement between the trader and the agent; otherwise, delivery of goods to the agent will be regarded as normal sales and subject to VAT immediately.
- Export sales: the VAT crystallises upon payment of export duties or upon placement of a guarantee for export duties, as the case may be. If the export is exempted from customs duties, the liability to VAT crystallises upon issue of an export entry form.
- Imported goods: the liability to VAT arises upon payment of import duties or placement of a guarantee for the duties as the case may be. If the import is exempted from customs duties, the VAT liability arises at the time the import entry form is issued.
- Supplies of services: VAT crystallises when consideration for the service is received or when a related tax invoice is issued, whichever comes first.
- Imported services: for imported services, ie services that are performed overseas and used in Thailand, the VAT liability is deemed to arise upon remittance of the service fee by the payer. Examples are management fees, technical assistance fees, and royalties. It is the duty of the recipient of the imported service to pay VAT on such service fees.

6   TAX RATE

Currently there are three VAT rates:

0%:   – export of goods
- rendering of services that are used abroad
- sales of goods or services to the United Nations, UN specialised agencies, embassies and consulates
- sales of goods or rendering of services to government agencies or state enterprises under the project funded by a foreign loan or aid
- service of international airlines or vessels of the country which imposes 0% VAT on airlines or vessels

1.5%:   small-scale traders with annual revenue of between Baht600,000 and Baht1,200,000. They are not, however, entitled to a credit for input tax on purchases of goods or services

7%:   imports of goods and all other supplies of goods or services which are not taxed at the 0% or 1.5% rate or exempt.

7   EXEMPTIONS

7.1   *Exempt with Input Credit*
The term 'exempt with input credit' is not used in Thai VAT law but the zero rate effectively operates in a similar manner.

7.2   *Exempt without Input Credit*
The following activities are exempt from VAT. Accordingly, suppliers are not entitled to a credit for any input tax paid on purchases of goods or services used in the provision of these activities.

- sales of agricultural produce and animals (except canned foods)
- sales of fertilisers, drugs or chemicals for the care of plants or animals, and insecticides or pesticides for plants or animals
- sales of ground fishmeal and animal feeds
- sales of newspapers, periodicals and textbooks
- rendering of services in the field of modern medicine, auditing, litigation and other independent professions as prescribed by the Director-General
- hospital services
- domestic transport of all types. However, providers of air transport services may elect to come within the scope of VAT
- international transport carried on by carriers in countries which do not impose VAT or similar tax on Thai carriers
- leasing of immovable property
- small-time traders with annual sales not exceeding Baht600,000.
- core business activities of commercial banks, finance, securities and credit financier companies, life and non-life insurance companies and real estate business. However, they are subject to the specific business tax at the rate of 3.3% of taxable revenue (but 2.75% for life insurance).

8   CREDIT/REFUND FOR INPUT TAX

8.1   *General*
VAT payable to the Revenue represents the excess of output tax over input tax in a tax period, ie a calendar month.

If input tax exceeds output tax, the taxpayer may opt for a tax refund or to carry forward the excess to the following month.

8.2   *Bad Debts*
In the case of bad debts written off in accordance with the criteria and procedures as may be prescribed by the Director-General, the VAT trader is allowed to deduct the output tax included in the bad debts against the output tax of the month when the write-off occurs.

9   ADMINISTRATIVE OBLIGATIONS

9.1   VAT Registration

A person who supplies goods or services in the course of business must register for VAT within 30 days after his taxable revenue exceeds Baht600,000. He is, however, also allowed to register before commencing business.

The registration must be made for each and every place of business (including factory and warehouse) by filing a relevant application with a local Revenue office. If he has more than one place of business, the VAT trader must submit an application for VAT registration with the local Revenue office in the district where his main office is situated.

9.2   Tax Invoices, Debit Notes and Credit Notes

9.2.1   Tax Invoices

A VAT trader must issue a tax invoice to the buyers of goods or recipients of services as soon as the liability to VAT on such sales or services crystallises. A tax invoice must contain the particulars as required by law, including:

- the words 'Tax Invoice'
- the date of the tax invoice
- the name, address and tax identification number of the seller
- the name and address of the buyer.

Copies of the tax invoices issued must be kept by the VAT trader for inspection by the tax authorities.

To facilitate the issue of tax invoices, the law allows retail sales businesses or service businesses involving a large number of customers such as department stores, supermarkets and restaurants, to issue a 'condensed' tax invoice in lieu of standard tax invoices as mentioned above. A condensed tax invoice requires fewer particulars than the standard one and may be issued by a cash register provided that prior approval is obtained from the Director-General.

9.2.2   Debit Notes and Credit Notes

In the case where a VAT trader needs to increase the value of goods or services previously sold for such reasons as incorrect pricing or wrong calculation, the trader must issue a debit note to the buyer, to whom any additional VAT resulting from the adjustment will be charged. A debit note is regarded as a tax invoice and must contain the particulars required by the law.

Conversely, a VAT trader may issue a credit note against previous sales of goods or provision of services under certain circumstances as prescribed by the law such as wrong pricing or wrong calculation, short delivery and goods defects. The reversed output tax on the credit note may be used as a credit by the seller. A credit note must contain particulars as required by law.

9.3   Books and Records

A VAT trader must maintain the following books and records in accordance with the format as prescribed by the law for a period of not less than five years after the return filing dates:

- output tax register
- input tax register
- stock and raw materials report (ie stock cards) applicable only to a VAT trader engaging in sales of goods.

If there is more than one place of business, a separate set of books and records must be maintained by each place of business.

9.4 Cash Register
A VAT trader engaging in a retail sales business may use a cash register for the purpose of issuing condensed tax invoices provided that approval has been obtained from the Director-General.

9.5 VAT Return Filing and Payment
A registered trader must file a monthly VAT return (Form Por Por 30) to the Revenue office together with the related VAT payment within 15 days of the end of the reporting month. If the VAT trader has more than one place of business, a separate VAT return and payment must be sent by each place of business to the respective Revenue office. A combined (joint) filing is possible only if permitted by the Director-General upon the trader's request.

In the case of imported goods, an import entry form is regarded as a VAT return and must be filed with the Customs Office before clearing goods from the ports.

For imported services, a special VAT return (Form Por Por 36) must be submitted to the Revenue office together with the related tax payment within seven days after the end of the month in which service fees are remitted.

VAT, if any, is due on the filing date. If input tax exceeds output tax, a VAT trader may either claim a tax refund or opt to set off the excess input tax in the following months by indicating his preference in the tax return.

9.6 Powers of the Authorities
The Revenue authorities have extensive powers in regard to the enforcement of tax compliance. Basically, they are empowered to enter a place of business of a trader during day time or during business hours to determine whether the trader complies with VAT law, and are empowered to order the trader to do any act necessary for the examination and to seize pertinent documents for examination.

The Revenue authorities have the right to assess VAT and impose surcharges and penalties on a trader within a period of two years as from the last day of the time limit for return filing or, in the case of late filing, within two years after date on which a tax return is filed (but not exceeding ten years as from the last day of the time limit for return filing). The statutory period is extended to ten years if no return has been filed.

If a trader is dissatisfied with an assessment to VAT imposed by the Revenue authorities he may appeal against the assessment by lodging an appeal within 30 days of the notification of the assessment.

9.7 Penalties and Surcharges
Penalties at various rates may be imposed by the Revenue authorities against traders for non-

compliance depending on the nature of such non-compliance. For example, a penalty of 200% of the tax may be imposed if the trader fails to file a tax return and pay the related tax to the Revenue Department. The penalty is 100% of the tax shortfall if the trader files an inaccurate or erroneous tax return. Such penalty may be reduced in accordance with the related regulation.

A tax surcharge at the rate of 1.5% per month can be applied to the tax that the trader has failed to pay or remit to the Revenue within the specified time. However, the surcharge shall not exceed 100% of the amount of delayed tax. Unlike the tax penalty, the surcharge may not be reduced.

9.8   Penalties

Punishments imposed under the VAT law may range from a fine to imprisonment of varying degrees depending on the nature of the offences. Those found guilty of wilfully evading tax by falsehood or fraud could be subject to a term of imprisonment of as long as seven years and a fine of as high as Baht200,000.

Contributor: Songdej Praditsmanont
                 Managing Partner
                 Ernst & Young
                 33rd Floor
                 Lake Rajada Office Complex
                 193/136-137 New Rajada-pisek Road
                 Bangkok 10110
                 Thailand
                 Tel: +66 2 264 0777
                 Fax: +66 2 2640790

GLOSSARY

Acquisition – intra-Community goods transaction within the European Union
Acquisition of the right to dispose as owner of movable tangible property dispatched or transported to the person acquiring the goods by or on behalf of the vendor or the person acquiring the goods to a Member State other than that from which the goods are dispatched or transported.

Appeals
A taxable person may appeal to the courts to arbitrate in certain disputes between the person and Revenue authorities, for example, additional tax imposed by the authorities, refusal by the authorities to repay tax which has been overpaid and formal interpretation by the authorities, etc. In some countries an appeal must first be heard by an independent arbitrator before going to court.

Normally there is a very short time limit within which the aggrieved person may lodge written notice of appeal.

Assujetti
French term referring to any person (individual or corporate body) carrying out, independently, transactions of an economic nature.

When a person qualifies as an 'assujetti' it means that this activity or the transactions he carries out are within the scope of VAT, although he might not have to pay VAT if part or all of the transactions are specifically exempt.

Chain Transactions
Several entrepreneurs/taxable persons may enter into subsequent transactions, involving the same goods. Each person within the chain is then deemed to have made a supply, even if the actual ownership is transferred directly from the first to the last recipient in the chain.

In some countries special rules apply to determine the place of supply of the goods involved in chain transactions.

Consideration
That which is given in exchange for the supply and on which the charge to tax is based. It may take the form of money, barter, or the performance of some service, the release from an obligation, etc.

Where goods or services are supplied for a consideration which does not wholly consist of money, the amount on which tax is chargeable is usually the open market value of the goods or services supplied.

When there is no consideration in any form there is no liability to VAT for services, (but supplies of goods may be deemed to be taxable supplies whether or not made for a consideration) and generally there is no entitlement to a credit for related input tax.

Even if there is no consideration in any form, goods and services used for the entrepreneur's non-taxable activities may be liable to VAT in certain circumstances.

Deferred accounting system
Under the deferred accounting system VAT is due at the time of removal of the goods from the port, or is payable by direct debit to the importer's bank account after the removal (ie on the fifteenth day of the month following the removal). The importer needs an appropriate guarantee.

Delivery
Delivery means the time at which the transfer of ownership of the goods occurs, thus triggering the liability to VAT. Transfer of ownership generally coincides with the handing over of the goods.

Distance sales
A distance sale (within the European Union) is one in which goods are sold to an unregistered person in a different Member State to that of the seller and the goods are transported by or on behalf of the seller to the customer's country.

Domicile
The term 'domicile' is used in civil law. It is the place from which a person (individual or corporate entity) conducts his business on a regular basis. It has the same meaning as 'registered office' where companies are concerned.

Election to be subject to VAT
In some countries persons supplying certain exempt services and goods may elect to become liable persons. (This will generally entitle them to a credit for input tax.)

Entrepreneur
Anyone, other than employees, independently conducting a trade, business or liberal profession will generally qualify as an entrepreneur.

One can be an entrepreneur whatever the form of trade or business. It therefore includes individuals, companies, trustees, partnerships, public corporations, local authorities, etc. An entrepreneur will be considered a taxable person if he makes taxable supplies.

Exempt
This term normally denotes supplies which are not liable to VAT. However, in some countries certain supplies may be exempt with credit or exempt without credit for input tax.

Exemption with credit for input tax
This applies to supplies, such as exports, international transport, etc where output tax is not chargeable but the supplier is entitled to recover input tax subject to local regulations. This is similar to zero-rating in other countries.

Exemption without credit for input tax
This applies to supplies which are specifically excluded from the charge to tax by local

legislation. Persons making such supplies are not entitled to recover any related input tax. They are, in effect, regarded as the end users.

Imported services

Services received from outside a country are sometimes referred to as imported services. Their liability to VAT depends on the place of supply as defined and they may sometimes give rise to the reverse charge mechanism.

Interest – commercial

Interest charged by suppliers is regarded as taxable when it is related to the late payment of taxable supplies.

Interest – financial

Interest charged for loans granted by banks or financial institutions, or by suppliers independently from the supply of goods or services, is not taxable.

Input tax

Input tax is VAT incurred by a person on the importation, acquisition or purchase of goods and services. It can be offset against output tax or refunded if in excess of output tax when it is attributable to the provision of taxable goods and services. The recovery of VAT is limited in the case of partial exemption and in respect of certain specific items.

Objections/claims

In order to obtain a reduction or a repayment of VAT wrongly assessed, an entrepreneur must file a formal request to the local tax authorities. Objections have to be submitted within certain time limits which differ from country to country. It is only after the tax authorities have made their decision that it can be appealed before the courts (see also 'Appeals').

Partial exemption

A taxable person who supplies goods and services some of which are taxable and some exempt is regarded as 'partially exempt'. In such circumstances input tax is generally only recoverable where it was paid on the purchase, acquisition or importation of goods or services which are attributable to the taxable business. Where tax was suffered on goods or importations which were used for both taxable and non-taxable purposes only a proportion of such input VAT may be recovered.

Postponed accounting system

Under the postponed accounting system, entrepreneurs/taxable persons in some countries may import goods without payment of VAT at the point of entry, but may defer payment until the next periodic VAT return.

Provided the importer is not exempt or partially exempt (ie he is fully taxable and thus entitled to a credit for input tax), no VAT will actually become payable.

Special application must be made to the tax authorities for permission to use the postponed accounting system and there are certain conditions which must be met. Normally only resident entrepreneurs qualify for the system.

Real estate/real property/immovable properties
These terms apply to land and buildings.

Registered person
A taxable person who has complied with the obligation to register with the tax authorities is a registered person. Not every taxable person is obliged to register for VAT because of de minimus limits or special regimes (for example, for farmers and fishermen).

Some taxable persons who are not required to register may do so voluntarily and in some countries persons supplying certain exempt services or goods may also register voluntarily.

Normally a taxable person is registered only once in respect of all his business activities, but in some countries it is possible to register separate parts or divisions of the same business.

Reverse charge mechanism
In certain cases liability to the tax shifts from the supplier to the recipient. This is achieved by deeming the recipient to be the supplier as if he had supplied the service to himself. He is also entitled to treat the deemed supply as a purchase. If the recipient is fully taxable there will normally not be any additional tax payable, but if he is exempt or partially exempt some of the VAT payable may not be recoverable.

This mechanism is applied differently in many countries. In the Netherlands, it also concerns goods and services provided in the Netherlands by foreign non-resident entrepreneurs. In Ireland, the United Kingdom and France it only concerns the supply of specified services imported by resident entrepreneurs.

Taxable person
Any person who supplies or intends to supply taxable goods or services in the course or furtherance of business is a taxable person. In some circumstances there are de minimus limits and taxable persons are only those persons making (or intending to make) supplies above these limits.

As in other fields of taxation, the word 'person' does not refer simply to individuals but also to trustees, partnerships, companies and public corporations. In some countries it also applies to local authorities in certain circumstances.

Taxable supply
The definition of 'taxable supply' is very wide. In respect of goods it includes the voluntary or involuntary transfer of ownership whether by delivery or otherwise. In respect of services it includes the performance, omission or toleration of any act which is not a supply of goods and where it is provided for a consideration.

Certain supplies of goods and services are specifically excluded from a charge to tax, ie they are exempt.

The distinction between supplies of goods and services is very important because different rules apply with regard to time and place of supply.

Trader
A registered person is often referred to as a trader.

Transfer of business

The sale of the assets and liabilities of a business by one taxable person to another is not regarded as a taxable supply in most countries. Normally input tax suffered in connection with such a transfer is recoverable.

In some countries all of the business must be sold as a going concern; in others the sale of part of a business which is not a going concern may also qualify as a non-taxable supply.

Waiver of exemption

In some countries, persons supplying certain exempt services and goods may elect to charge VAT on the supply and thus become taxable persons in respect of that supply. Such action will generally entitle them to a credit for input tax.

Zero rate

In some countries the rate of tax applicable to some taxable supplies, such as exports, foods, etc, is zero. Because the supply is liable to VAT, the supplier is entitled to recovery of input tax subject to local regulations. It is similar to the term 'exemption with credit' used in some other countries.